SUPPRESSED INTELLIGENCE REPORTS

We denounce censorship and
support freedom of speech.

CJ

Conspiracy Journal
PRODUCTIONS

SUPPRESSED INTELLIGENCE REPORTS

Compiled by Commander X and The Committee Of Twelve To Save The Earth

Revised Updated Expanded Edition

Published by Global Communications/Conspiracy Journal
Box 753 · New Brunswick, NJ 08903

Staff Members
Timothy G. Beckley, Publisher
Carol Ann Rodriguez, Assistant to the Publisher
Sean Casteel, General Associate Editor
Tim R. Swartz, Graphics and Editorial Consultant
William Kern, Editorial and Art Consultant

Sign Up On The Web For Our Free Weekly Newsletter
and Mail Order Version of Conspiracy Journal
and Bizarre Bazaar
www.ConspiracyJournal.com

Credit Card Order Hot Line: 1-732-602-3407
PayPal: MrUFO8@hotmail.com

THERE ARE FORCES AT WORK ALL AROUND US
By Commander X - For the Committee of 12

There are forces all around us who would like to do us in.

They are invisible. They are silent. They are cunning and they have no regard for you or your wellbeing despite what they might tell you.

We live in a great country...but there are utterly cruel beings at the center of our destruction who wish us to be slaves to their sinister thoughts and deeds. They want us to be part of their nefarious undertakings -- to take responsibility for that over which we have no control.

Here in this comprehensive book we take on the task of revealing much and exposing all.

Be at peace for there is still hope. Pray that the outcome will be in our favor.

COMMANDER X

CONTENTS

SUPPRESSED INTELLIGENCE REPORTS

PART ONE

The Greatest Conspiracy

Understanding the following essays may result in further understanding that your social environment is comprised mainly of individuals whose written and spoken words evidence a pronounced mental detachment from reality. These individuals, thinking, speaking and believing only in floating abstractions constitute a ludicrous spectacle of childlike machinations and monitions unfortunately nurtured by superior physical force and willingness to use violence to impose their ill conceived notions and values upon each other and innocent bystanders.

****

I am a conspiracy researcher, but not a raving fundamentalist, a statist, a theorist, a theist, a theosophist, an egoist, fascist (Republican), communist (Democrat), humanist, apologist for political or religious groups, or any other "ist" which you may be tempted to hang on me if you continue to read the information which is presented here. I am neither Democrat nor Republican; neither Anarchist nor Libertarian. I display no banners. I do not salute banners. I do not pledge allegiance. I do not stand for passing parades. I do not vote. I do not contribute time or money to candidates for public offices. I reject all authority outside of myself. I am my own temple. I am a member of no fraternal organization. I do not attend sporting events.

I watch very little television and only documentaries at that. I have not watched a sitcom for perhaps 17 years. I have been to only five motion pictures in the same period of time. I do not know the names of movie stars or sound recording artists because I believe they are not worth my time. I don't know the name of the Representative for this district, either State or Federal and for the same reason.

I believe Americans should grow as much food as they can for their own use and for sharing with neighbors. I think for myself but I am willing to read and hear the expressions of others and to use them in forming my personal goals if they make sense. I believe if every American owned at least one handgun or one long gun and was properly educated in its use and care, and was adamantly determined to use it defensively when required, we would have considerably less criminal activity, especially from members of the so-called federal government.

SUPPRESSED INTELLIGENCE REPORTS

My father was my only true hero.

I recognize and acknowledge that there were (and perhaps still are) many historic heroic figures. None of them ever were or ever will be lawyers, attorneys, counsellors, judges, presidents or politicians. Such professions are the anti-thesis of heroics. They are, all of them, male and female alike, liars and cowards of the first degree.

The closest you might come—if you wish to categorize me— is to say that I am a nonpartisan iconoclast, but only in the narrowest confine of each word.

nonpartisan (non-pär'-te-sun) ad.

l. impartial, nonaligned, neutral. A non-voter. iconoclast (h-kÄn-õ-klast) n. l. One who attacks traditional or popular ideas, institutions or misconceptions. I say in the narrowest confine of each word because Charles Fort has written, and I concur:

Honest Opinion (p. 92)

"Our own acceptance is that justice cannot be in an intermediate existence, in which there can be approximation only to justice or to injustice; that to be fair is to have no opinion at all; that to be honest is to be uninterested; that to investigate is to admit prejudice; that nobody has ever really investigated anything, but has always sought positively to prove or disprove something that was conceived of, or suspected, in advance."

No mortal is ever completely fair and no mortal can ever be completely disinterested, particularly if one's pleasure is attacking popular social, political or religious misconceptions.

If you feel compelled to comment on these reports, please be kind enough to leave all acrimonious phillipic out of your notes. I will trash them straightaway for I have no time to entertain hate mail. The worst will be forwarded to the postmaster for action. If it contains anything close to a death threat, the message, complete with your name and address, goes to the local FBI. Period.

Because I am reasonably well read and have a desire for questioning the authority of propaganda from any source, left, right or center; social, political or religious, I have spent the better part of my 65 years digging for "the truth."

During ten of my twenty years in the naval service I was assigned to duties within the intelligence community, including a tour at NRTSC in Suitland, Maryland, and a tour at DIA in Arlington, Virginia. In the middle years of that service I read as many as 300 books per year during a period of about six years (more than most people will read in a lifetime) trying to inch my way closer to the truth. Let me assure you that the truth is only rarely accessible. Too many times I've discovered to my everlasting dismay, after months of research, that truth is cloaked in misdirection and outright disinformation. And as you will soon discover in the following essays, your own city, county, state and federal governments would prefer that you never know the whole real truth about most of the activities in which they are engaged. But not knowing at least some of the truth could cost you your life. It has most certainly cost you your freedom.

It was once observed that nobody ever changed anything unless someone or something was pricking at their psyche. That is my mission—to prick holes in your psyche. Still, some of you will simply adopt a position of outright denial—like the ostrich with its head in the sand; perhaps if you refuse to see then it cannot harm you! Sadly, that is not the case for ostriches or for humans. Those who refuse to accept any of the information here are like the lost explorer feeding his tucker to the alligators, hoping they will get full before they reach him or, at the least, eat him last, which is nothing more than delaying the inevitable.

Unlike the secular media, which endeavors to present only one side of any issue; that is, the side which represents the ideas and concepts which they wish most to implant in your mind as being the only valid ideas, I will, at times, present ideas which may appear to be contrary to the current "patriot" viewpoint. I do so because I believe it is important to understand counterpoint to vital issues. Such essays may change your views about certain things or they may serve to strengthen your strongly-held convictions. The point is that by presenting more than one boring side of the world, you may be induced to think more introspectively about what you feel you believe. We cannot again be a free people as long as we cling miserably to old lies and misconceptions.

At the beginning of the Vietnam conflict, while serving a tour of duty at DIA, I was soundly chastised by a tradition-shod officer for reading the works of Chairman Mao. He accused me of being a communist. "But, sir," I replied, "how can we expect to defeat our enemies if we do not understand his political agenda and philosophical concepts?" He had no answer, but confiscated my book nonetheless. I hope he had the good common sense to read it but I suspect, since America lost that conflict*, neither he nor most of his colleagues read Chairman Mao (or Jefferson, Henry, Spooner, Marx, Engels or Trotsky, for that matter).

*(UDT/Navy Seal ops and Special Forces excepted).

****

THE "LAW OF THE LAND"

("The Land" is legally defined as the 10-mile square area known as Washington, D. C.)

There is a simple way to view this story by realizing we have two constitutions: (a) The dissolved Constitution of the united states of America and (b) The United States Constitution.

The second came about as a result of the incorporation of 1871/1878 which created the United States Government, which is a government for the District of Columbia. Of course, the Constitution provided for a government of the District of Columbia, but the politicians wanted to organize it differently, and the Constitution gave them the power to do as they please within the 10 mile square allotted to D.C.

The (original) Constitution of the United States of America, permanently and forever dissolved in 1861, actually has the 13th, 14th and 15th amendments (and possibly the 16th amendment) prior to 1871. After the incorporation of the United States, a new Constitution was created as by laws of the corporation, which dropped the 13th amendment (Titles of Nobility and Honor).

The 13th Amendment was in 1864, and the 14th in 1868.

They renamed the original 14th, 15th, & 16th amendments to the new 13th, new 14th and new 15th amendments. Then a new 16th amendment was added. One example of this is the Constitution of Colorado, which plainly shows the new 13th amendment abolishing slavery as the 14th amendment prior to 1871.

SUPPRESSED INTELLIGENCE REPORTS

This new Constitution applies to the Federal Zone only and hence it is lawful, but only there. It simply does not apply to the republic: it applies only to the UNITED STATES, a corporation having its seat of power in a 10-mile square area known as Washington, D. C. The incorporation created a democracy and gave them more flexibility to expand and enforce Roman Civil Law which was implemented during the war between the states. No amendment has been added to the original Constitution since 1871 (because the original Constitution was negated and dissolved in 1861), and the corporate amendments 16 to 27 of the corporate constitution are not applicable to the American republic. Got it?

I believe their intent is to one day make this new Constitution generally applicable to the entire Republic, by consent of the people (no dissent is consent, according to law). Cliff Hume

But how did this happen?

ROMAN CIVIL LAW ESTABLISHED:

NO PROTECTION IN ANY EVENT!

Eighty-five years after the so-called "independence" of the united states, seven Southern states of America walked out of the Second Session of the Thirty-Sixth Congress on March 27, 1861. In so doing, the Constitutional quorum necessary for Congress to vote was lost, and Congress was adjourned sine die, or "without day." This meant that there was no quorum to set a specific day and time to reconvene which, according to Robert's Rules of Order, dissolved Congress since there were no provisions within the Constitution allowing the passage of any Congressional vote without a quorum of the States. Since there was no longer a Congress, there was no longer any by-laws. Since there were no by-laws, there was no Presidency. Lincoln's second Executive Order unlawfully called Congress back into session days later, but not under the authority of the Constitution. As Commander-in-Chief, Congress was called into session under the Martial Law and rule of Lincoln. Congress has never reconvened under the provisions of the Constitution of the united states since that day. The corporate United States has been without a valid ratified Constitution (by-laws) since March, 1861 and America has been under Martial Law, in a constant state of "emergency" ever since. Lincoln, quite literally, became a dictator. His executive orders established a system of Roman Civil Law in America and that system has prevailed uninterrupted since April 1861.

America's Caesar: The Decline and Fall of Republican Government in the United States of America.

It was during this period that the original lawfully ratified 13th Amendment, "Titles of Nobility and Honor" was covertly removed from the original by-laws, to be replaced later by the present 13th Amendment known as the "Emancipation Proclamation," into a new set of by-laws which has never been ratified by anyone! Everyone just pretended that the original constitution was still valid. The so-called Constitution which exists today is a complete fraud. The first was dissolved and nullified in 1861, and the replacement has never been ratified. In short, the entire so-called federal government of the corporate United States is a legal, but not a lawful organization. It has no jurisdiction over any American outside the beltway—and actually never did—except at the point of a gun! The "laws" and statutes that unlawful "government" enacts apply only to the 10-mile square area known as Washington, D. C. and to some islands and military bases, forts, shipyards, docks and buildings which have been established by lease, confiscation and/or usurpation in the several states. It is fascism in the extreme.

The Complete Overthrow of the Public Liberties

The New York World, August 1863

This is the darkest hour since the outbreak of the rebellion. Congress, by the act passed yesterday authorizing the President to suspend the writ of habeas corpus throughout the whole extent of the country, has consummated the series of measures for laying the country prostrate and helpless at the feet of one man. It was not enough that Mr. Lincoln has been entrusted with the purse and the sword; that, with an immense power to raise or manufacture money he has unrestricted command of the services of every able-bodied man of the country, Congress has thought it necessary to give the finishing stroke to its establishment of a military despotism, by removing all checks on the abuse of the enormous monetary and military power with which they have clothed the President. What assurance has the country that we shall ever have another Presidential election? None whatever, except what may be found in the confidence, reasonable or unreasonable, reposed in the rectitude and patriotism of Mr. Lincoln.

If any person, in any part of the country, shall think it his duty to resist unconstitutional encroachments on the rights of citizens, Mr. Lincoln is authorized, by what purports to be a law, to snatch up that individual and immure him in one of the government bastiles as long as he shall see fit, and there is no power in the nation to call him to account. He can send one of his countless provost marshals into the house of a governor of a State, or any other citizen, in the dead of night, drag him from his bed, hustle him away under the cover of darkness, plunge him in a distant and unknown dungeon and allow his friends to know no more of the whereabouts of his body, than they would of the habitation of his soul, if, instead of imprisoning the provost marshal had murdered him.

With this tremendous power over the liberty of every citizen whom he may suspect, or whom he may choose to imprison without suspecting, the President is as absolute a despot as the Sultan of Turkey. All the guarantees of liberty are broken down; we all lie at the feet of one man, dependent on his caprice for every hour's exemption from a bastile. If he wills it, the State governments may continue in the discharge of their functions; but if he will it, every one of them that does not become his submissive and subservient tool can be at once suspended by the imprisonment of its officers. Considering the enormous power conferred on the President by the finance and conscription bills, a reasonable jealousy would have erected additional safeguards against its abuse. Instead of that, Congress has thrown down all the old barriers and left us absolutely without shelter in the greatest violence of the tempest.

So far as the detestable act passed yesterday is an act of indemnity to shield the President from the legal consequences of past exertions of arbitrary power, it is a confession that he, his secretaries, provost marshals, and other minions, have been acting in violation of law. It annuls all laws passed by the State legislatures for the protection of their citizens against kidnapping; it provides for taking all suits for damages out of the State courts and transferring them to the Federal tribunals, and before those tribunals the fact that the injury complained of was done under color of executive authority is declared to be a full and complete defense. It ever inflicts penalties on persons coming before the courts for redress of injuries, by declaring that if they are not successful, the defendant shall recover double costs. So that the aggrieved party must take the risk of this penalty for venturing to ascertain, in a court of justice, whether his oppressor was or was not acting under the authority of the President. To this alarming pass have matters come, that not only does every citizen hold his liberty at the mercy of one man, but he is liable to be punished for inquiring whether the man arresting him really possessed, or only falsely pretended to possess, that man's authority!

The attempt to disguise the odious character of this detestable act by a sham provision to its second section is an insult to the intelligence of the people. "The Secretary of State and the Secretary of War," so it reads, "are directed, as soon as it may be practicable," to furnish to the judges of the courts lists of the names of the persons arrested, that they may be presented to a grand jury for indictment. And who is to judge of this practicability? Why the secretaries themselves, or the President for them. They will furnish such lists whenever it suits their pleasure, and not before.

There is not only no penalty for neglecting to do this altogether, but the main purpose of the act is to protect these officers, and all persons acting under their directions, against all legal penalties for all arrests wherever made, and all detentions in prison however long protracted.

The ninety days during which Congress has now been in session are the last ninety days of American freedom. Our liberties had previously been curtailed and abridged by executive encroachments, but the courts remained open for redress of wrongs. But this Congress has rendered their overthrow complete, by first putting the purse and sword in the hands of the President and then assuring him of complete impunity in all abuses of this enormous, this dangerous, this tremendous power.

And, mind you, this power still rests with the President of the United States today in 2014 because we are still in a state of Declared Emergency and the federal government still functions as a military dictatorship under martial law, and all Americans are still considered to be "enemies of the State" with no voice in the military courts.

Waco. Ruby Ridge. Get it?

THE GREATEST LIE NEVER TOLD

"Contrary to what the news media, motion picture moguls, and government-controlled schools would have you believe, the Civil War was not fought to emancipate black Africans being used as slave labor in America. That was not even considered an issue at the time. Indeed, Lincoln had promised not to interfere in the slave trade!

"The Civil War was a conflict between proponents of States Rights and the Unionists. The Southern States, weary of being denied by the wealthy northern industrialists the rights to build a strong economy (because of excessive tariffs), and sickened by Unionist usurpation of States Rights, seceded from the Union (the states united) and formed the southern Confederate States of America. They elected their own President, Jeff Davis, wrote and ratified their own Constitution, and printed their own usury free, tax free money.

"This was definitely something the northern money-grubbers could not tolerate! Not only had they lost their grip on the whole of the South, they had lost control of their money, their economy, their industry, and the life energy of millions of people. The only thing to do was to declare the Confederate States evil because they condoned slavery (even if they did not) and go to war."

SUPPRESSED INTELLIGENCE REPORTS

CANNON FODDER

"The result was that the king's Central Bank gained control over the money, economy and energy of the people of both North and South (murdering Lincoln for good measure because he opposed a Central Bank); they wrested control of the government of the United States of America from the people and they (the bankers) managed to kill off thousands upon thousands of black and white free and indentured Americans on both sides, confiscated the property their widows and children could no longer support, and seated military tribunals as governors of every southern state, the governing power of which continues to this day in both the southern states and the northern.

"Proof of the military occupation of America can be seen by the gold-fringed "American" flag which hangs from a staff in every courtroom, school and most churches in this country. That is a military flag of occupation. Under the "Law of Flags" (Admiralty Law), all courts have been restructured as military courts (courts martial) and all suits at law are conducted as military tribunals presided over by the king's agents Esquires and Honors. As "enemies of the State," Americans have no voice in these courts.

"Lincoln, without a Congress for six weeks, had issued Greenbacks, unilaterally declared war and ruled the nation as a constitutional dictator with no limits to his power. The Constitution of the United States of America was negated during those six weeks and cannot be lawfully restored. The current President of the unlawful Windsor corporation, United States, today sits as a dictator with power that exceeds that of any tyrant known in the history of humankind.

"From the end of that war until this moment, our lives, fortunes and property have belonged to the wealthy foreign and domestic bankers who, sadly, control the very media which perpetrates and prolongs the great lie.

"Truth is: THE WRONG SIDE WON! Now we're going to have to do it again. But let's direct all our energies toward the real enemy this time." (name deleted) Historian, 1989

GENESIS OF THE "CIVIL WAR"

by Llewellyn H. Rockwell, Jr.

The historical event that looms largest in American public consciousness is the Civil War. One-hundred thirty-nine years after the first shot was fired, its genesis is still fiercely debated and its symbols heralded and protested. And no wonder: the event transformed the American regime from a federalist system based on freedom to a centralized state that circumscribed liberty in the name of public order. The cataclysmic event massacred a generation of young men, burned and looted the Southern states, set a precedent for executive dictatorship, and transformed the American military from a citizen-based defense corps into a global military power that can't resist intervention.

And yet, if you listen to the media on the subject, you might think that the entire issue of the Civil War comes down to race and slavery. If you favor Confederate symbols, it means you are a white person unsympathetic to the plight of blacks in America. If you favor abolishing Confederate History Month and taking down the flag, you are an enlightened thinker willing to bury the past so we can look forward to a bright future under *progressive* (communist) leadership. The debate rarely goes beyond these simplistic slogans.

SUPPRESSED INTELLIGENCE REPORTS

And yet this take on the event is wildly ahistorical. It takes Northern war propaganda at face value without considering that the South had solid legal, moral, and economic reasons for secession which had nothing to do with slavery. Even the name "Civil War" is misleading, since the war wasn't about two sides fighting to run the central government as in the English or Roman civil wars. The South attempted a peaceful secession from federal control, an ambition no different from the original American plea for independence from Britain.

But why would the South want to secede? If the original American ideal of federalism and constitutionalism had survived to 1860, the South would not have needed to. But one issue loomed larger than any other in that year as in the previous three decades: the Northern tariff. It was imposed to benefit Northern industrial interests by subsidizing their production through public works. But it had the effect of forcing the South to pay more for manufactured goods and disproportionately taxing it to support the central government. It also injured the South's trading relations with other parts of the world.

In effect, the South was being looted to pay for the North's early version of industrial policy. The battle over the tariff began in 1828, with the "tariff of abomination." Thirty year later, with the South paying 87 percent of federal tariff revenue while having their livelihoods threatened by protectionist legislation, it became impossible for the two regions to be governed under the same regime. The South as a region was being reduced to a slave status, with the federal government as its master.

But why 1860? Lincoln promised not to interfere with slavery, but he did pledge to "collect the duties and imposts": he was the leading advocate of the tariff and public works policy, which is why his election prompted the South to secede. In pro-Lincoln newspapers, the phrase "free trade" was invoked as the equivalent of industrial suicide. Why fire on Ft. Sumter? It was a customs house, and when the North attempted to strengthen it, the South knew that its purpose was to collect taxes, as newspapers and politicians said at the time.

To gain an understanding of the Southern mission, look no further than the Confederate Constitution. It is a duplicate of the original Constitution, with several improvements. It guarantees free trade, restricts legislative power in crucial ways, abolishes public works, and attempts to rein in the executive. No, it didn't abolish slavery but neither did the original Constitution (in fact, the original (Constitution of the united states) protected property rights to slave ownership).

NOTE: Petitions presented to Congress, including those by Ben Franklin, were debated for about four hours by the whole Congress. Their report, masterminded by Madison, made it UNCONSTITUTIONAL to manumit (set free) slaves at any time in the future, and this precedent was invoked many times in subsequent years.

Before the war, Lincoln himself had pledged to leave slavery intact, to enforce the fugitive slaves laws, and to support an amendment that would forever guarantee slavery where it then existed. Neither did he lift a finger to repeal the anti-Negro laws that besotted all Northern states, Illinois in particular. Recall that the underground railroad ended, not in New York or Boston-since dropping off blacks in those states would have been restricted-but in Canada! The Confederate Constitution did, however, make possible the gradual elimination of slavery, a process that would have been made easier had the North not so severely restricted the movements of former slaves.

SUPPRESSED INTELLIGENCE REPORTS

Now, you won't read this version of events in any conventional history text, particularly not those approved for use in public high schools. You are not likely to hear about it in the college classroom either, where the single issue of slavery overwhelms any critical thinking. Again and again we are told what Polybius called "an idle, unprofitable tale" instead of the truth, and we are expected to swallow it uncritically. So where can you go to discover that the conventional story is sheer nonsense?

The last ten years have brought us a flurry of great books that look beneath the surface. There is John Denson's The Costs of War (1998), Jeffrey Rodgers Hummel's Emancipating Slaves, Enslaving Free Men (1996), David Gordon's Secession, State, and Liberty (1998), Marshall de Rosa's The Confederate Constitution (1991), or, from a more popular standpoint, James and Walter Kennedy's Was Jefferson Davis Right? (1998).

But if we were to recommend one work-based on originality, brevity, depth, and sheer rhetorical power-it would be Charles Adams's time bomb of a book, When in the Course of Human Events: Arguing the Case for Southern Secession (Rowman & Littlefield, 2000). In a mere 242 pages, he shows that almost everything we thought we knew about the war between the states is wrong.

Adams believes that both Northern and Southern leaders were lying when they invoked slavery as a reason for secession and for the war. Northerners were seeking a moral pretext for an aggressive war, while Southern leaders were seeking a threat more concrete than the Northern tariff to justify a drive to political independence. This was rhetoric designed for mass consumption. Adams amasses an amazing amount of evidence-including remarkable editorial cartoons and political speeches-to support his thesis that the war was really about government revenue.

Consider this little tidbit from the pro-Lincoln New York Evening Post, March 2, 1861 edition:

"That either the revenue from duties must be collected in the ports of the rebel states, or the port must be closed to importations from abroad, is generally admitted. If neither of these things be done, our revenue laws are substantially repealed; the sources which supply our treasury will be dried up; we shall have no money to carry on the government; the nation will become bankrupt before the next crop of corn is ripe. There will be nothing to furnish means of subsistence to the army; nothing to keep our navy afloat; nothing to pay the salaries of public officers; the present order of things must come to a dead stop.

"What, then, is left for our government? Shall we let the seceding states repeal the revenue laws for the whole Union in this manner? Or will the government choose to consider all foreign commerce destined for those ports where we have no custom-houses and no collectors as contraband, and stop it, when offering to enter the collection districts from which our authorities have been expelled?"

This is not an isolated case. British newspapers, whether favoring the North or South, said the same thing: the feds invaded the South to collect revenue. Indeed, when Karl Marx said the following, he was merely stating what everyone who followed events closely knew: "The war between the North and the South is a tariff war. The war is further, not for any principle, does not touch the question of slavery, and in fact turns on the Northern lust for sovereignty."

Marx was only wrong on one point: the war was about principle at one level. It was about the principle of self-determination and the right not to be taxed to support an alien regime. Another way of putting this is that the war was about freedom, and the South was on the same side as the original American revolutionaries.

Interesting, isn't it, that today, those who favor banning Confederate symbols and continue to demonize an entire people's history also tend to be partisans of the federal government in all its present political struggles? Not much has changed in 139 years. Adams' book goes a long way toward telling the truth about this event, for anyone who cares to look at the facts.

May 11, 2000

Llewellyn H. Rockwell, Jr., is president of the Ludwig von Mises Institute in Auburn, Alabama. He also edits a daily news site, LewRockwell.com.

THE IDEA OF REPLACING ONE TYRANNY WITH ANOTHER,

OR REPLACING ONE FALLACY WITH AN EQUAL FALLACY:

The Constitution of the Confederate States of America

In 1861, after almost three-quarters of a century of use, an opportunity arose to analyze, delete, add to, and alter one of the greatest documents of all time; The Constitution of the united states. Given such test of time, such opportunity of reflection, how would some of the greatest legal minds change that document?

In answer to this question, the prospective forefathers met in Montgomery, Alabama, early in the year 1861, charged with this great task of surpassing the wisdom of James Madison, George Washington, Thomas Jefferson, Benjamin Franklin, John Adams and George Mason. The result of their 'reworking' is embodied in one of the most fascinating documents in history. The new Confederate Constitution would be patterned after the Constitution of the united states, changed only in those clauses where any hint of weakness or limitation was determined.

The first hint that the United States Constitution would stand as a model for the new Confederate States Constitution is evident in the first three words of that great new document, "We the People..."

As one reads through the draft of the new constitution, some of the most interesting points are evident: Originally, the right to vote was not limited to citizens! Upon reflection, however, such a restriction was included. The number of representatives to Congress for each State was determined by a count of the population of that State......except that slaves would count as 3/5 of a person...and most Indians as 0!

Of course, the "Bill of Rights" which established freedom of speech, of the press, to peaceably assemble and to petition the government, etc., were all included in the main body of the text.

No (ex post facto) law denying the right of property in negro slaves could be passed.

However, the importation of negroes of the African race, from any foreign country . . .

SUPPRESSED INTELLIGENCE REPORTS

was forbidden!

The most interesting article is that of eligibility for president. Anyone (even foreign born) who was a citizen of the Confederate States of America at the time of the adoption of the Constitution, was eligible. Also anyone who would become a citizen - but was born in the United States prior to December 20, 1860 was eligible. In either case the person must have had fourteen years residency in the Confederate States of America.

We the people of the Confederate States, each State acting (for itself, and) in its sovereign and independent character, in order to form a permanent federal government, establish justice, insure domestic tranquility, and secure the blessings of liberty to ourselves and our posterity - (to which ends we invoke) (invoking) The favor and guidance of Almighty God - do ordain and establish this Constitution for the Confederate States of America...

******

BUT ALL OF THAT NOTWITHSTANDING—

WAR AND EMERGENCY POWERS

Have you not heard of Roosevelt's "War and Emergency Powers Act" that officially and legally (but not lawfully) made every American an "enemy of the State" (the "State" being that 10-mile square area known as Washington, D. C.) with no rights in court? How can "enemies of the State" with no rights be "protected" under the State's by-laws, for crying-out-loud!? The State's "enemies" are specifically excluded! Don't you get it? All "laws" are nothing more than Executive Orders (dictats) because the so-called constitution and Congress have been non-issues since April 1861. The "State" is the corporation and the "courts" are their military tribunals, established as "governments" immediately following Lincoln's war, the common law courts having been forever abolished.

Does anyone imagine that the "enemies" of the Nazi State, regardless of who they were—and they were legion—could have been equally "protected" by the State's Constitution? Wake up! Open your eyes! Open your mind! Read all of these essays and you will understand.

And, by the way... if the lawfully dissolved Congress has reconvened covertly and unlawfully; that is to say, outside the limits of their own defunct constitution—so-called, which limits them to a jurisdiction within the 10-mile square area of Washington, D. C., does that not mean that all the "laws" they've foisted upon us since Lincoln's War are without meaning and invalid? Does it not mean that they are nothing more than a cartel of slick, well-organized criminals keeping us all as slaves to provide them with the manpower, resources and cannon fodder to help them enslave (democratize) the rest of the world?

We are paying the wages of a group of criminals (lawyers/agents Esquires) who do not have any right whatsoever (other than that they have an army at their disposal to kill any and all truculent citizens) to occupy or assemble at "Congress" under the guise of acting as the voice and conscience of the rest of us.

We can make a comparison between the cellular community and government. In theory, government exists as a representation of the will of the people, serving the best interests of the masses. Of course in practice it is usually quite the opposite, with the population subservient to a monolithic system of controls meant to primarily benefit a select few. Nevertheless, ideally a group of people were intended to respond to the needs of the whole, maintaining the best possible conditions for the community, while directing the actions of the various components of it in order to accomplish this. A government exists because the community is relatively healthy; for if there is no society to serve, there is nobody to govern.

Government is perceived as an entity unto itself, yet it is actually the sum of the portions of knowledge held by each of its components. Almost all systems have a specific leader, yet in most cases this is a symbolic position, and in situations where one person appears to wield authoritarian power, there are always thousands of people at lower levels who are making the system function; without their input, a ruler would be unable to hold such a position.

Political institutions reflect innate programming, and are a representation of our primate clan behaviour. We can compare it with cellular activity only in a perfunctory way, since the competitive nature of politics separates it from the purely logical order of the body.

SO WHO IS THE ENEMY HERE?

Native American Indians understood that the enemy "is a state of mind." Stockpiling guns to defend ourselves against the State or trying to get elected to some office may seem like powerful strategies, but, in fact, they are not. Both mimic the enemy, by attempting to fight the State on its own ground. Such strategies are doomed to failure because they only reinforce the attitudes that make it possible for the State to exist in the first place; i.e., that the "State" is a real thing with a life and existence outside of the human mind. If we want to deal voluntarily with other people, and have them deal with us likewise, then we need to practice freedom and liberty in our own lives. It may seem difficult to "resist not evil," but there are powerful reasons, both moral and utilitarian, for heeding that advice. "Those who fight evil necessarily take on the characteristics of the enemy and become evil themselves."

THE WORD GAME

"I pledge allegiance to the flag of the United States of America and to the Republic for which it stands, one nation, indivisible, with liberty and justice for all."

What exactly is taught by this pledge? Philosophically and psychologically, what does it mean for a person to pledge allegiance to a flag; not just any flag, but the symbolic representation of the United States? Why allegiance to this flag and this country? Why not Canada, England, Mexico, or all the others? Why swear allegiance at all? What's the purpose? There is no point to the pledge to a specific flag except to segregate. There is no point in segregating unless the U.S. is considered superior to the others. There is no preference in equal valuations. The lesson subliminally taught is that Americans are superior and more valuable than other "national beings." This conclusion is supported by the ever popular "proud to be an American." Completion of the statement is saying that one would be ashamed to be another nationality.

What core psychological relationship does the pledge express and imply? The denial of self and subservience to the "United States of America" is an open and clear declaration. Via logical inference, the pledger is positioned as property of the "United States." The essence of ownership is control. Ergo, control of the pledger by the "United States" is inherent in the pledge of allegiance. The oft heard phrase, "America's children" and similar utterances are not just a meaningless figure of speech. It states the condition of being regarded as property that nearly all accept with "pride".

SUPPRESSED INTELLIGENCE REPORTS

With real individuals left out of the thinking, "group identities" such as American, German, Russian, black, white, men, women, etc., presumes to "identify" on similarity providing unlimited latitude for judgmental purposes. Keep in mind as well that the decision as to enemy or friend is not made by the pledger, but by the "United States" to which the pledger is subservient. Since the United States is an abstract and not an entity, superior or otherwise, what happens to the pledged allegiance? Who receives it? How is it translated into action? What action?

The questions are answered by the underlying psychology and subliminal directives. Independent thinking and sense of individual responsibility are gone. The pledger lives only to serve. Serve whom? Roosevelt as he orders the round up and incarceration of "America's enemies" decided by physical features similar to the "Japanese enemy?" Hitler as he set his sights on conquering the world by the "supremacy of the Aryan nation?" Stalin and company in the endless bloody purges to save the purity of Communism? Or some present day "powerful leader" who seeks self value in domination? Or perhaps just follow the "leader" in blind obedience in a methodical destruction of the socio-economic system? In the final analysis, the whole thing comes down to unquestioning obedience, not to the "infinite entity," United states, but to a finite power-hungry human individual with the will to rule. While few if any individuals would openly and knowingly turn their life over to another individual without qualification, in the pledge and psychology of the pledge, this is precisely what they do. This is the ultimate destination of those who succumb to word games.

QUO VADIS? (Whither Bound?)

Nearly 40 years before the birth of Christ, the Roman orator Cicero offered this sage advice: *"The budget should be balanced; public debt reduced; the arrogance of officialdom tempered and controlled, the assistance to foreign lands curtailed, lest Rome fall."* The Romans ignored that advice. And guess what? The great Roman Empire crumbled and expired.

By 476 AD, the Roman Empire had vanished from Western Europe, "an event still felt by the nations of the earth." Now we'll paraphrase Shaw's quip: "Rome fell, Babylon fell. America's turn will come."

America's founders, essentially Anglo-Saxon, serious, honorable and God-fearing men, took the wonders of Western civilization to the New World; and in turn set in place a dynamic, amazingly innovative and inventive civilization of their own. American power peaked during and for a few decades after WW2. What have modern Americans done with their astounding inheritance?

Over the past 30 years, and particularly since 1990, they have allowed many of their deepest roots to wither, rot and die. US politicians, the media and many in the "liberal" churches have allowed and even promoted the casting adrift of the values, traditions and behavior that fostered America.

The signs pointing to US decline and cultural sickness have long been evident. America today, as James Reston once wrote, is "overpopulated, under-civilized, divided, corrupted and bewildered, destitute of faith and terrified of skepticism. War, crime, pollution, racial tensions, moral anarchy and political pessimism are the consequence."

Today, children are not required to achieve any degree of knowledge in school. No child is permitted to fail, none can be "left behind." They are cautioned not to cheat but, if they do and are caught, there is no punishment other than a low grade.

As a result, children grow to adulthood believing it is okay to cheat, to lie, to steal, to malign and to kill to get what they want. They grow to adulthood believing the world owes them a living. If they manage to survive college and secure a job, they expect to be able to stay at home and still receive a paycheck. They believe they can steal from the company, injure their colleagues or kill their boss if he or she chastizes them for anything. They are merely petulant little brats in adult clothing who expect someone to give them a six-figure job with no responsiblities, a five-figure automobile, a beautiful, obedient wife, a multi-million dollar house with a manicured lawn and they believe they have the right to kill anyone who can't or will not give it to them right now.

Somewhere along the line, a few of them begin to understand that life demands participation, work, committment, responsibility. But it is the wrong time to be learning such things. It should have been taught them in grade school.

Unfortunately for us, and for the nation and the future of humankind, any teacher who tries to instill in their wards honesty, truth, responsibility and dignity, is fired for his or her efforts because they are seen by school boards and the parents as being much too zealous, too rigid, too firm.

Entertainment, literature, films, TV and the like have become the domain of the degenerate. The rock culture, the very quintessence of decadence, the very negation of musical culture, has become one of America's greatest and most profitable export products. Listen, if you can bear it, to the popular music of the mindless zoids created by the modern education system. Witness, if you can bear it, the mindless reenactment of the sex act hourly on TV.

NOTE: The word, America, comes from the Peruvian/Mayan/Aztec word, Amaracu, meaning the feathered serpent. The "feathered serpent" is the symbol for Lucifer, the Devil, Satan. America, then, has a secret meaning: "The Land of Lucifer." All people living in this hemisphere are "Americans." North Americans; South Americans; Pan-Americans; Central Americans. And the symbols of those people include the eagle, representing the sun, and the serpent, representing Satan. The founders of this nation did not revere or worship the God of the Bible (as we have shown below), but revered and worshipped the sun as the symbol of Light, and Lucifer as the Bringer of Light. Lucifer means Lord of Light. Get it? See the brief essay, Amaracu.

FOUNDING FATHERS WERE NOT "CHRISTIANS"

To speak of unalienable Rights being endowed by a Creator certainly shows a sensitivity to our spiritual selves. What is surprising is when fundamentalist Christians think the Founding Fathers' faith had anything to do with the Bible. Without exception, the faith of our Founding Fathers was deist, not theist. It was best expressed earlier in the Declaration of Independence, when they spoke of "the Laws of Nature" and of "Nature's God."

In a sermon of October 1831, Episcopalian minister Bird Wilson said, "Among all of our Presidents, from Washington downward, not one was a professor of religion, at least not of more than Unitarianism."

The Bible? Here is what our Founding Fathers wrote about Bible-based Christianity:

Thomas Jefferson:

SUPPRESSED INTELLIGENCE REPORTS

"I have examined all the known superstitions of the word, and I do not find in our particular superstition of Christianity one redeeming feature. They are all alike founded on fables and mythology. Millions of innocent men, women and children, since the introduction of Christianity, have been burnt, tortured, fined and imprisoned. What has been the effect of this coercion? To make one half the world fools and the other half hypocrites; to support roguery and error all over the earth."

Jefferson again:

"Christianity...(has become) the most perverted system that ever shone on man. ...Rogueries, absurdities and untruths were perpetrated upon the teachings of Jesus by a large band of dupes and importers led by Paul, the first great corrupter of the teaching of Jesus."

More Jefferson:

"The clergy converted the simple teachings of Jesus into an engine for enslaving mankind and adulterated by artificial constructions into a contrivance to filch wealth and power to themselves...these clergy, in fact, constitute the real Anti-Christ.

Jefferson's word for the Bible? "Dunghill."

John Adams:

"Where do we find a precept in the Bible for Creeds, Confessions, Doctrines and Oaths, and whole carloads of other trumpery that we find religion encumbered with in these days?"

Also Adams:

"The doctrine of the divinity of Jesus is made a convenient cover for absurdity."

Adams signed the Treaty of Tripoli. Article 11 states:

"The Government of the United States is not in any sense founded on the Christian religion."

Here's Thomas Paine:

"I would not dare to so dishonor my Creator God by attaching His name to that book (the Bible)."

"Among the most detestable villains in history, you could not find one worse than Moses. Here is an order, attributed to 'God' to butcher the boys, to massacre the mothers and to debauch and rape the daughters. I would not dare so dishonor my Creator's name by (attaching) it to this filthy book (the Bible)."

"It is the duty of every true Deist to vindicate the moral justice of God against the evils of the Bible."

"Accustom a people to believe that priests and clergy can forgive sins...and you will have sins in abundance."

And; "The Christian church has set up a religion of pomp and revenue in pretended imitation of a person (Jesus) who lived a life of poverty."

Finally let's hear from James Madison:

SUPPRESSED INTELLIGENCE REPORTS

"What influence in fact have Christian ecclesiastical establishments had on civil society? In many instances they have been upholding the thrones of political tyranny. In no instance have they been seen as the guardians of the liberties of the people. Rulers who wished to subvert the public liberty have found in the clergy convenient auxiliaries. A just government, instituted to secure and perpetuate liberty, does not need the clergy."

Madison objected to state-supported chaplains in Congress and to the exemption of churches from taxation. He wrote:

"Religion and government will both exist in greater purity, the less they are mixed together."

These founding fathers were a reflection of the American population. Having escaped from the state-established religions of Europe, only 7% of the people in the 13 colonies belonged to a church when the Declaration of Independence was signed.

Among those who confuse Christianity with the founding of America, the rise of conservative Baptists is one of the more interesting developments. The Baptists believed God's authority came from the people, not the priesthood, and they had been persecuted for this belief. It was they - the Baptists - who were instrumental in securing the separation of church and state. They knew you can not have a "one-way wall" that lets religion into government but that does not let it out. They knew no religion is capable of handling political power without becoming corrupted by it. And, perhaps, they knew it was Christ himself who first proposed the separation of church and state: "Give unto Caesar that which is Caesar's and unto the Lord that which is the Lord's."

In the last five years the Baptists have been taken over by a fundamentalist faction that insists authority comes from the Bible and that the individual must accept the interpretation of the Bible from a higher authority. These usurpers of the Baptist faith are those who insist they should meddle in the affairs of the government and it is they who insist the government should meddle in the beliefs of individuals.

The price of Liberty is constant vigilance. Religious fundamentalism and zealous patriotism have always been the forces which require the greatest attention.

Editor's Note: We have received several requests asking for references to the quotes in this article. We are now able to include some of the references and links to other sites that relate to the beliefs of the founding fathers. While most of these politicians were diplomatic in their public expressions concerning religion, in their private conversations, voluminous writings and correspondences they expressed contrary beliefs.

Which beliefs are true? If a politician appears one way in public and another in private, which do you think better represents their true beliefs? How do you reconcile the inflamatory writings above with various pro-Christian statements that the same men made in the course of their careers? Could it be called politics, an attempt to appease Christians while ensuring a more rational government based on the separation of church and state? We can't be sure but it looks that way.

In addition, the Editor does not recognize the religious intentions of the so-called 'Founding Fathers' as relevant to discussions of political process today. As a descendent of Native Americans the editor feels there are a few things that these alien visitors must answer for before the imposition of their viral religion is discussed.

"The Christian right is trying to rewrite the history of the United States as part of its campaign to force its religion on others. They try to depict the founding fathers as pious Christians who wanted the United States to be a Christian nation, with laws that favored Christians and Christianity.

This is patently untrue. The early presidents and patriots were generally Deists or Unitarians, believing in some form of impersonal Providence but rejecting the divinity of Jesus and the absurdities of the Old and New testaments.

Thomas Paine was a pamphleteer whose manifestos encouraged the faltering spirits of the country and aided materially in winning the war of Independence: I do not believe in the creed professed by the Jewish church, by the Roman church, by the Greek church, by the Turkish church, by the Protestant church, nor by any church that I know of...Each of those churches accuse the other of unbelief; and for my own part, I disbelieve them all." From: The Age of Reason by Thomas Paine, pp. 8,9 (Republished 1984, Prometheus Books, Buffalo, NY)

George Washington, the first president of the United States, never declared himself a Christian according to contemporary reports or in any of his voluminous correspondence. Washington Championed the cause of freedom from religious intolerance and compulsion. When John Murray (a universalist who denied the existence of hell) was invited to become an army chaplain, the other chaplains petitioned Washington for his dismissal. Instead, Washington gave him the appointment. On his deathbed, Washinton uttered no words of a religious nature and did not call for a clergyman to be in attendance. From: George Washington and Religion by Paul F. Boller Jr., pp. 16, 87, 88, 108, 113, 121, 127 (1963, Southern Methodist University Press, Dallas, TX)

John Adams, the country's second president, was drawn to the study of law but faced pressure from his father to become a clergyman. He wrote that he found among the lawyers 'noble and gallant achievments" but among the clergy, the "pretended sanctity of some absolute dunces". Late in life he wrote: "Twenty times in the course of my late reading, have I been upon the point of breaking out, "This would be the best of all possible worlds, if there were no religion in it!"

It was during Adam's administration that the Senate ratified the Treaty of Peace and Friendship, which states in Article XI that "the government of the United States of America is not in any sense founded on the Christian Religion." From: The Character of John Adams by Peter Shaw, pp. 17 (1976, North Carolina Press, Chapel Hill, NC) Quoting a letter by JA to Charles Cushing Oct 19, 1756, and John Adams, A Biography in his Own Words, edited by James Peabody, p. 403 (1973, Newsweek, New York NY) Quoting letter by JA to Jefferson April 19, 1817, and in reference to the treaty, Thomas Jefferson, Passionate Pilgrim by Alf Mapp Jr., pp. 311 (1991, Madison Books, Lanham, MD) quoting letter by TJ to Dr. Benjamin Waterhouse, June, 1814.

Thomas Jefferson, third president and author of the Declaration of Independence, said:"I trust that there is not a young man now living in the United States who will not die a Unitarian." He referred to the Revelation of St. John as "the ravings of a maniac" and wrote: The Christian priesthood, finding the doctrines of Christ levelled to every understanding and too plain to need explanation, saw, in the mysticisms of Plato, materials with which they might build up an artificial system which might, from its indistinctness, admit everlasting controversy, give employment for their order, and introduce it to profit, power, and pre-eminence. The doctrines which flowed from the lips of Jesus himself are within the comprehension of a child; but thousands of volumes have not yet explained the Platonisms engrafted on them: and for this obvious reason that nonsense can never be explained." From: Thomas Jefferson, an Intimate History by Fawn M. Brodie, p. 453 (1974, W.W) Norton and Co. Inc. New York, NY) Quoting a letter by TJ to Alexander Smyth Jan 17, 1825, and Thomas Jefferson, Passionate Pilgrim by Alf Mapp Jr., pp. 246 (1991, Madison Books, Lanham, MD) quoting letter by TJ to John Adams, July 5, 1814.

James Madison, fourth president and father of the Constitution, was not religious in any conventional sense. "Religious bondage shackles and debilitates the mind and unfits it for every noble enterprise." "During almost fifteen centuries has the legal establishment of Christianity been on trial. What have been its fruits? More or less in all places, pride and indolence in the Clergy, ignorance and servility in the laity, in both, superstition, bigotry and persecution." From: The Madisons by Virginia Moore, P. 43 (1979, McGraw-Hill Co. New York, NY) quoting a letter by JM to William Bradford April 1, 1774, and James Madison, A Biography in his Own Words, edited by Joseph Gardner, p. 93, (1974, Newsweek, New York, NY) Quoting Memorial and Remonstrance against Religious Assessments by JM, June 1785.

Ethan Allen, whose capture of Fort Ticonderoga while commanding the Green Mountain Boys helped inspire Congress and the country to pursue the War of Independence, said, "That Jesus Christ was not God is evidence from his own words." In the same book, Allen noted that he was generally "denominated a Deist, the reality of which I never disputed, being conscious that I am no Christian." When Allen married Fanny Buchanan, he stopped his own wedding ceremony when the judge asked him if he promised "to live with Fanny Buchanan agreeable to the laws of God." Allen refused to answer until the judge agreed that the God referred to was the God of Nature, and the laws those "written in the great book of nature." From: *Religion of the American Enlightenment* by G. Adolph Koch, p. 40 (1968, Thomas Crowell Co., New York, NY.) quoting preface and p. 352 of Reason, the Only Oracle of Man and A Sense of History compiled by American Heritage Press Inc., p. 103 (1985, American Heritage Press, Inc., New York, NY.) Benjamin Franklin, delegate to the Continental Congress and the Constitutional Convention, said: As to Jesus of Nazareth, my Opinion of whom you particularly desire, I think the System of Morals and his Religion...has received various corrupting Changes, and I have, with most of the present dissenters in England, some doubts as to his Divinity; tho' it is a question I do not dogmatize upon, having never studied it, and think it needless to busy myself with it now, when I expect soon an opportunity of knowing the Truth with less trouble." He died a month later, and historians consider him, like so many great Americans of his time, to be a Deist, not a Christian. From: Benjamin Franklin, A Biography in his Own Words, edited by Thomas Fleming, p. 404, (1972, Newsweek, New York, NY) quoting letter by BF to Exra Stiles March 9, 1970.

The words "In God We Trust" were not consistently on all U.S. currency until 1956, during the McCarthy Hysteria.

Rejecting "revealed" religions (religions communicated to man by revelations) means that one might also reject the so-called prophets of those religions since the words, deeds and teachings of those prophets have come down to man by so-called "revelation." Those of you who have always believed the lie that America is a "Christian nation" are in for a rude awakening. Many of the so-called "founding fathers" and other famous influential American scholars and politicians were not Christians at all, but were Deists or Unitarians, and among them were Abigail Adams*, John Adams*, John Quincy Adams*, Ethan Allen, John C. Calhoun, William S. Cohen, Paul H. Douglas, Emily Taft Douglas, Millard Fillmore*, Benjamin Franklin*, Horace Greeley*, Hannibal Hamlin, Thomas Jefferson*, James Madison, Thomas Paine*, William J. Perry, Paul Revere*, Elliot L. Richardson, Francis George Shaw, Col. Robert Gould Shaw, Adlai Stevenson (1900-1965)*, William Howard Taft*, George Washington* and Daniel Webster* .

* People marked with an asterisk have appeared on postage stamps (in most cases, US stamps). *Deism is defined in Webster's Encyclopedic Dictionary, 1941, as: "[From Latin Deus; God, Deity] The doctrine or creed of a Deist." And Deist is defined in the same dictionary as: "One who believes in the existence of a God or supreme being but denies revealed religion,* basing his belief on the light of nature and reason."

Deists believe that a Prime Source created the cosmos and everything in it, including us, but does not intervene in human affairs, it (God) having gone on to other places to do other things. In other words, God created us but has no interest at all about what we do with or to ourselves or the planet. It is important to remember that the "founding fathers" read, admired and followed the precepts and formulas found in the "enlightened" literature of Europe. Those concepts are so closely related to Socialism and Communism that no intelligent person can wonder why America has evolved into a Socialist nation. I believe it was founded as such!

Unitarian-n.

1. An adherent of Unitarian Universalism. subscribes to the universal oneness (unity) of humankind. 2. A monotheist who is not a Christian. believes in one God but does not subscribe to the dogma of Christianity 3. A Christian who is not a Trinitarian. subscribes to the ideals of Jesus (Emmanuel) but not the dogma of the triune godhead. Colonel Ethan Allen's essay, Reason: The Only Oracle of Man, contains these words and I urge you to download and read it: Though "none by searching can find out God, or the Almighty to perfection," yet I am persuaded, that if mankind would dare to exercise their reason as freely on those divine topics as they do in the common concerns of life, they would, in a great measure, rid themselves of their blindness and superstition, gain more exalted ideas of God and their obligations to him and one another, and be proportionally delighted and blessed with the views of his moral government, make better members of society, and acquire, manly powerful incentives to the practice of morality, which is the last and greatest perfection that human nature is capable of.

****

The Unitarian ideal, embracing the concept of all humankind as equally the children of one Creator, is best summed up by the words of Thomas Jefferson:

"We hold these truths to be self-evident, that all men are created equal; that they are endowed by their Creator with inherent and inalienable rights; that among these, are life, liberty, and the pursuit of happiness; that to secure these rights, governments are instituted among men, deriving their just powers from the consent of the governed; that whenever any form of government becomes destructive of these ends, it is the right of the people to alter or abolish it, and to institute new government, laying its foundation on such principles, and organizing its powers in such form, as to them shall seem most likely to effect their safety and happiness."

—Declaration of Independence as originally written by Thomas Jefferson, 1776. ME 1:29, Papers 1:315

MORE WORD GAMES

(Editor's note): If the truths are self-evident and the rights (un)-inalienable, why did the "founding fathers" think they had to create a "government" to secure them to the people? If they are self-evident and (un)-inalienable, that means that everyone already knew it and none could take them away. The formation of the federal government under the so-called "constitution" was designed to take them away, not to protect them! And if you don't believe that, just try opting out of the "system" and see how quickly your "protector" comes skulking in the night to murder you and your family in your beds.

The final handwritten and signed Declaration of Independence contained the word, "unalienable," which means CANNOT be separated, surrendered, or taken away. The current Declaration of Independence now contains Jefferson's original word, "inalienable," which means SHOULD NOT be separated, surrendered, or taken away. "SHOULD NOT" implies, "but MAY BE," when someone feels it necessary to do so. If the two words have identical meaning, as some Constitutionalists contend, then why has the word been changed?

Common sense tells us the word has been changed because the words have different meanings, and politicians have selected the word which gives them the greatest amount of power and control.

****

Unitarians, like Deists, believe in a Prime Source but do not subscribe to the dogma of any church or "holy" book. Neither utters a creed of belief. Both embrace the humanitarian ideals of Jesus (Emmanuel), but not the bastardized messianic history of his life in the form in which it later appeared in the KJV of the Bible. In addition to introduction of a Bill concerning Freedom of Religion, Thomas Jefferson, using the text of the KJV Bible, wrote a chronology of the life, ministry and death of Jesus. The book has come to be improperly known as "The Jefferson Bible." SOME THINGS YOU PROBABLY DON'T WANT TO KNOW ABOUT THE KJV BIBLE

For the last three centuries Protestants have fancied themselves the heirs of the Reformation, the Puritans, the Calvinists, and the Pilgrims who landed at Plymouth Rock. This assumption is one of histories greatest ironies. Today, Protestants laboring under that assumption use the King James Bible. Most of the new Bibles such as the Revised Standard Version are simply updates of the King James.

The irony is that none of the groups named in the preceding paragraph used a King James Bible nor would they have used it if it had been given to them free. The Bible in use by those groups, until it went out of print in 1644, was the Geneva Bible. The first Geneva Bible, both Old and New Testaments, was first published in English in 1560 in what is now Geneva, Switzerland. William Shakespeare, John Bunyan, John Milton, the Pilgrims who landed on Plymouth Rock in 1620, and other luminaries of that era used the Geneva Bible exclusively.

Until he had his own version named after him, so did King James I of England. James I later tried to disclaim any knowledge of the Geneva Bible, though he quoted the Geneva Bible in his own writings. As a Professor Eadie reported it:

". . . his virtual disclaimer of all knowledge up to a late period of the Genevan notes and version was simply a bold, unblushing falsehood, a clumsy attempt to sever himself and his earlier Scottish beliefs and usages that he might win favor with his English churchmen."

The irony goes further. King James did not encourage a translation of the Bible in order to enlighten the common people: his sole intent was to deny them the marginal notes of the Geneva Bible. The marginal notes of the Geneva version were what made it so popular with the common people.

The King James Bible was, and is for all practical purposes, a government publication. There were several reasons for the King James Bible being a government publication. First, King James I of England was a devout believer in the "divine right of kings," a philosophy ingrained in him by his mother Mary Stuart.

A phrase one often hears is democracy and freedom. However, those uttering the phrase never stop to explain how two imposing their will upon the third constitutes freedom for the victim. Nevertheless, democracy is thought by many to be a "government of freedom and protector of individual rights." In addressing this popular illusion, perhaps it would be of some benefit to backtrack a bit and take a look at the psychological evolution that led up to the idea of "democracy and freedom."

In the days of the "divine right of a king" where a lone monarch's word was law and his every wish a command, no one spoke of freedom and individual rights. No one doubted that the concept, rule, was in practice. To the believers, this was the natural order of things and there could be nothing else. However, the ever present and ever-busy oppressive might of the "state" is proof enough that psychological subjugation was never quite complete. Although the concept, divinity, was never questioned, the monarch's connection to it more and more came under suspicion. Somewhere along the line, "earthly divinities" fell from grace and there began talk about freedom and rights that belonged to all. The old way was declared "immoral" and the new idea was heralded as the universal good. While the conscious mind desired and claimed the "morality" of freedom, the subconscious and emotions remained stuck in the old concept, rule. Subconscious was (and is) running the show. After the godhead, king, was banished, another was needed to accommodate the concept, rule, but invisible so as not to disturb self image by contradicting the claimed "morality" of freedom.

REAL DEFINITIONS TO PONDER:

Bill of Rights: Bill of Goods. The first ten amendments to the U.S. Constitution which proposes to summarize and guarantee fundamental rights AFTER the sine qua non of rights, the right of self ownership, is negated by the very Constitution of which the Bill of Rights is a part.

Constitution: (U.S.) A monstrous slave paper which assume ownership (by an abstract) of all persons and things in a particular geographical area. Said constitution presumes to guarantee "individual rights" while serving as the political and governmental base which automatically negates the concept of individual rights. (Inasmuch as said constitution is self contradictory, it is "unconstitutional" and "should" be abolished on these grounds.)

SUPPRESSED INTELLIGENCE REPORTS

Electorate (political): Individual who by voting elects to relinquish self determination in favor of "reciprocal slavery" while simultaneously assuming ownership of all those who dissent. Abandonment of self responsibility. (Electorate is made up of individuals who admit to be mentally incapable of running their own lives but do not explain by what rationale they are mentally capable of selecting someone to run it for them.)

Politician: A self-deluding illusionist who by his political participation admits that he is incapable of running his own life, yet presumes to run the lives of millions of others.

Senator: A political representative elected by those admitting mental incompetence to run their own affairs.

LEXICON OF DOUBLESPEAK

Eric Blair, aka George Orwell, popularized doublethink, doublespeak, newspeak ideas in his book **Nineteen Eighty-four**. More recently, William Lutz has reintroduced the ideas in Doublespeak and New Doublespeak. A casual observation of history and literature will indicate to any person of modest linguistic competence that the ideas of political and religious manipulation have relied heavily on doublethink and doublespeak for at least as long as any historical records have been kept. The intention here is to call attention to mass acceptance of currently popular doublespeak in news media, academia, and politics. This is what is meant here by doublethink and doublespeak:

DOUBLETHINK

The ability to hold at least two contradictory ideas in the mind without experiencing cognitive dissonance.

DOUBLESPEAK

The ability to speak or write two or more contradictory ideas without the speaker or writer being consciously aware of the contradiction. Doublespeak may be, and probably is, consciously used to deceive.

Belief: Denial of reality.

Competition: Creation of losers.

Congressional investigation: Cover-up by partisan polarization.

Constitution, U. S: A quaint, outdated document defining U. S. Government. It is subject to alteration by legislation, regulation, police misconduct and judicial (in)discretion.

Constitutional right: Privilege granted by Constitution as interpreted by judicial (in)discretion and journalistic misinformation.

Creditor: One of a tribe of savages dwelling beyond the Financial Straits and dreaded for their desolating incursions.

Crime: Any act or thought deemed by Statists to conflict with State interest. (See justice, State, and Statist.)

Debtor: One captured by the desolating incursion of a Creditor.

SUPPRESSED INTELLIGENCE REPORTS

Debt: Money.

Defense: Imperialistic aggression.

Democracy: American imperialism. Also, any form of government, preferably dictatorship established by controlled elections, that operates in the interest of international finance. Parliamentary forms of government composed of elected or appointed agents of finance are also included. Agents are commonly controlled by election campaign finance. A primary characteristic of democracies is that they consist of multitudinous, conflicting factions of powerless people who are impotent to challenge financial rulers.

Democrat Party: Left wing of political power monopoly in the U. S. A (communism).

Economics: Financial mythology. Arguably the best evidence of academic corruption.

Economist: Pathological doublethinker and doublespeaker.

Federal Reserve: Private, non-federal banking monopoly of the U. S. A.

Freedom: Voluntary compliance. Also, lack of restraint of international finance to exploit all resources including people by any means including mass murder.

Free Trade: Coerced and restrained trade operated exclusively through debt medium of exchange in the interest of international finance. (See freedom and trade.)

Gold standard: Financial trick that fools naive people into believing that gold actually backs money in such a way as to make the two synonymous and convertible.

History: Blend of both myth and selected facts alterable for political purposes. History is arguably second best to economics as evidence of academic corruption.

Journalist: Pathological doublethinker and doublespeaker. Media prostitute of misinformation and disinformation. (See news.)

Justice: Court verification of Statist beliefs expressed as law. Also, criminal or civil prosecution of any act or idea deemed by Statists to conflict with State interest.

Justice system: Injustice system. Enforcement of Statist belief by police power.

Law: Statutes, written by Statist thieves and murderers, defining acts and ideas as crimes. (See politician.)

Military: Any group of organized mercenaries who carry out mass murder and plunder on a large scale in the interest of international finance.

Money: Debt.

National interest: The interest of international finance which protects its self-interest by control of governments through political parties and Presidential appointments; leveraged ownership of press, entertainment, and industry; and military through government. (See democracy and freedom.)

News: Misinformation industry operated for the first purpose of commercial advertisement. Advertisement requires audience for revenue purposes which leads to sensationalism, prurience, and avoidance of truth. It often entertains as it misinforms. Secondary purposes include political and financial propaganda that support the political establishment that protects media and industrial owners who are financiers. The secondary purposes require complete subversion of journalistic ideology for the purpose of assisting official cover-up, making of false history, and distortion of truth by selectivity.

Politician: Pathological doublethinker and doublespeaker. Also, any combination of liar, thief, or murderer who uses doublethink and doublespeak to rationalize such activity as being in the public interest.

Reality: Reified mental constructs of journalists, politicians, and academics. (See reify, news, history, and economics.)

Reify: To believe that a belief is reality. Pathological ability of the human mind to substitute mentally created illusions for reality.

Republican Party: Right wing of political power monopoly in the U.S.A (fascism).

Revenue enhancement: Tax. (See tax.)

Right: When not a direction, a term used to express a mental figment, sometimes modified by other figments such as natural, legal, Constitutional, and civil, that implies a privilege of acting or believing in prescribed ways.

Sports: Industrial exploitation of competitive athletics.

State: A mythical entity that usually includes a geographical area bounded by mythical, arbitrary boundaries usually constructed and always protected by military force. States are normally believed to be larger than their constituent parts and transcendent over all else, including human life, within its territory.

Statist: One who believes The State is a real, transcendent thing. (See State.)

Sustainable development: Popular oxymoron.

Tax: Armed robbery by Statists.

Trade: Exchange of goods and services through exclusive medium of debt.

War: Mass murder and destruction performed by military organizations in the interest of international financial control of natural and human resources. Wars are variously reported by journalists as defense of national interest, defending or establishing democracy, or criminal terrorism depending on who hires them. (See military and journalist)

A professor of Anthropology for all of his adult life, Loren Eiseley tended to take the long view of most things. Eiseley presented humans as an evolving species with an uncertain future: uncertain in the sense that no one knows the form into which we may evolve, and, indeed, that we may even become extinct.

Eiseley makes an important point when he highlights the danger resulting from the fact that, for humans, culture has replaced instinct; and "just as instinct may fail an animal under some shift of environmental conditions, so man's cultural beliefs may prove inadequate to meet a new situation . . ." (92)

SUPPRESSED INTELLIGENCE REPORTS

THE INFLUENCE OF FREEMASONRY ON AMERICAN CULTURAL BELIEFS

Many signers of the Articles of Confederation, the Declaration of Independence and the original Constitution of the United States were Freemasons* and members of the Order Of The Quest, and, to my understanding, Freemasonry, being a nonsectarian organization, disavows "revealed" religions outright, while allowing each member to practice any revealed religion according to his own wishes, albeit not within the Lodge. "Revealed" religions include Christianity, Islam and Judaism. There are others, of course. Each supports its exclusive claim by a "holy" book, supposedly "revealed" to the mind of man by "God." But if there is but one supreme being, one "God," why so many religions, and why so many different revelations? Could it be that "God" is not wise enough to communicate the same message to all of humankind the same way at the same time? Or could it be, as I suspect, that humankind has erred in the interpretation of the so-called "revelation?"

*Is it true that all of George Washington's generals during the Revolutionary War were Masons? No. But 33 of the generals serving under Washington were Masons. A substantial number, but not "all." Is it true that all the signers of the Declaration of Independence were Masons? The Articles of Confederation? The Constitution? No. Masons constituted ten of the signers of the Articles of Confederation, nine were signers of the Declaration, and thirteen were signers of the Constitution.

(NOTE: It appears that the information here, taken from an official Freemasonry website, is in error. We have learned that 23 of the 39 signers of the constitution were either Freemasons or members of the Order of the Quest or Illuminati.

Additionally, Edmund Randolph, Grand Master of Virginia, was an active participant at the Constitutional Convention, though he didn't sign the document. It should also be noted that four Presidents of the Continental Congresses were Freemasons: Peyton Randolph of Virginia, John Hancock of Massachusetts, Henry Laurens of South Carolina, and Arthur St. Clair of Pennsylvania (Northern Light). Did George Washington turn down the title of "Grand Master of the United States." Yes, sort of. The American Union Lodge proposed that Washington become "General Grand Master of the United States," a title to be held in the "National Grand Lodge." However, there were many others who also disagreed with the idea, so it was never a serious proposal. Washington was Master of Alexandria Lodge No. 22 in Virginia, whose Grand Master was then Edmund Randolph. Washington was never Grand Master of Virginia (or any other jurisdiction).

I AM NOT A FREEMASON, BUT...

One of the most perplexing contradictions circulating within the so-called "patriot movement" in America is the claim that the Declaration of Independence and the federal Constitution, both of which were formulated, written and signed by so many Freemasons, are such sacred documents, but that Freemasons are somehow involved in a conspiracy to destroy the Republic they so laboriously and with so much blood have formed. No one has been able to explain this contradiction to my satisfaction.

If the so-called "patriots" believe the Masons are involved in this evil conspiracy, why do they (the "patriots") insist that the infamous documents originally created by Freemasonry be "restored?" It was, to my understanding, Freemasons who insisted on inclusion of the Bill of Rights as amendments to the federal Constitution. If patriots believe the Constitution is (or was) a valid document, can someone explain how this can be part of a conspiracy against Americans?

Either the Masons' documents creating a centralized federal government are valid and the Brotherhood is not the sinister organization envisioned by the so-called "patriot" community, or the Freemasons actually plotted to enslave an entire nation of free people when they drafted, ratified and enacted their so-called "constitution." One or the other; not a little part of each. If the Freemasons are evil, then so is their "constitution" which had to have been created to enslave all Americans if we are to believe the "patriots." If the Constitution is okay, then so are the Freemasons who created it.

Jefferson, A Mason, most certainly was influenced by them. But he clearly saw the "constitution" as nothing more than a set of by-laws for the proper (and secret) operation of the federal government, an opinion that is validated by Jefferson's statement that the constitutional by-laws delegate certain powers to the federal government and that those not delegated are reserved by the people or by the states. This separation of federal State, and states and people of those states cannot mean anything other than that the "Constitution" is NOT the by-laws of the republic at large.

"[The first step is] to concur in a declaration of rights, at least, so that the nation may be acknowledged to have some fundamental rights not alterable by their ordinary legislature, and that this may form a ground work for future improvements."

—Thomas Jefferson to John Jay, 1788. ME 7:18, Papers 13:190

"I consider the foundation of the [Federal] Constitution as laid on this ground: That "all powers not delegated to the United States, by the Constitution, nor prohibited to it by the States, are reserved to the States or to the people." [10th Amendment] To take a single step beyond the boundaries thus specifically drawn around the powers of Congress is to take possession of a boundless field of power, no longer susceptible of any definition."

—Thomas Jefferson: Opinion on National Bank, 1791. ME 3:146

"I was in Europe when the Constitution was planned, and never saw it till after it was established. On receiving it, I wrote strongly to Mr. Madison, urging the want of provision for... an express reservation to the States of all rights not specifically granted to the Union." — Thomas Jefferson to Joseph Priestley, 1802. ME 10:325 "Whensoever the General Government assumes undelegated powers, its acts are unauthoritative, void, and of no force." —Thomas Jefferson: Draft Kentucky Resolutions, 1798. ME 17:380 "[An] act of the Congress of the United States... which assumes powers... not delegated by the Constitution, is not law, but is altogether void and of no force." —Thomas Jefferson: Draft Kentucky Resolutions, 1798. ME 17:383

But Jefferson, ever the back-stabbing opportunist, had little good to say about the Constitution and the newly formed centralized federal government. In 1797, after John Adams was chosen President and Jefferson was chosen vice-President, Jefferson, far from supporting Adams, actually fed the opposition press disparaging stories about Adams and counseled the French to drag out treaty negotiations, acts which clearly cost Adams a second election to the Presidency.

After the Alien and Sedition Act was passed, Jefferson secretly wrote the Kentucky Resolutions,* which contended that the states had the right to nullify federal laws and actions. The

SUPPRESSED INTELLIGENCE REPORTS

Alien and Sedition Act, among other things, made it a crime to criticize the new federal government. What kind of freedom is that?

*[Resolutions passed in 1798 and 1799 by the Kentucky and Virginia legislatures in opposition to the Alien And Sedition Acts. The Kentucky Resolutions, written by Thomas Jefferson, stated that the federal government had no right to exercise powers not delegated to it by the Constitution. A further resolution declared that the states could nullify objectionable federal laws. The Virginia Resolutions, written by James Madison, were milder. Both were later considered the first notable statements of the STATES' RIGHTS doctrine.]

PLEASE RECALL that the argument over states' rights (not "slavery") is what led directly to the (un)civil war.

FREEDOM OF SPEECH

Article I, The Bill of Rights

Congress shall make no law respecting an establishment of religion, or prohibiting the free exercise thereof; or abridging the freedom of speech, or of the press; or the right of the people peaceably to assemble, and to petition the Government for a redress of grievances.

The first amendment to the Constitution of the United States was The Bill of Rights consisting of ten articles; however, it has become customary to refer to the Articles of The Bill of Rights as individual amendments. That custom will be followed here.

The 1st Amendment above relative to free speech seems clear and unequivocal. Does it mean what it says?

Apparently not.

In 1798, seven years after the adoption of The Bill of Rights, the Congress passed and President John Adams approved The Sedition Acts criminalizing certain speech, a clear abridgement or taking away of some freedom of speech. One would expect the Supreme Court to invalidate such a flagrant violation of the 1st Amendment, but one would be wrong. The Supreme Sophists invoked the common law doctrine of "no prior restraint" to uphold prosecutions under the Sedition Act.

It was ruled that the common law of the country remained the same as before the Revolution, that is, English common law. Under that scheme, one could not be restrained from speaking; but there was no protection from prosecution after the fact. [In English common law, truth is no defense, and it still remains that way, today; and the bigger the truth the bigger the libel.] The court ruled in favor of English common law in spite of the language of the second paragraph of ARTICLE VI, U. S. Constitution:

ARTICLE VI

This Constitution, and the Laws of the United States which shall be made in Pursuance thereof; and all Treaties made, or which shall be made, under the Authority of the United States, shall be the supreme Law of the Land; and the Judges in every State shall be bound thereby, any Thing in the Constitution or Laws of any State to the Contrary notwithstanding.

Did the Constitution stand for nothing in the eyes of the Supreme Sophists? If not, why not?

Jonathan Swift addressed the issue in satire approximately seventy years before:

In the tryal of persons accused for crimes against the State, the method is much more short and commendable: [compared to previously explained civil procedure] for if those in power, who know well how to choose instruments fit for their purpose, take care to recommend and promote out of this clan [lawyers] a proper person, his method of education and practice makes it easy for him, when his patron's disposition is understood, without difficulty or study either to condemn and [or] acquit the criminal, and at the same time strictly preserve all due forms of law. GULLIVER'S TRAVELS, Chapter V, "A Voyage to Houyhnhnms". c. 1726.

Jonathan Swift understood the labyrinthine, sophistic, doublespeak, "catch 22," nature of law and lawyers.

The decisions of the Supreme Court mentioned above reveal the political nature of judges. At the time, the Federalists, who had appointed the judges, were in power and under criticism. Some of the criticism had the tone of rhetoric of the French Revolution. The Federalists with their newly acquired power and recent memories of how they had overthrown the British government succumbed to their paranoia and tried to undo the First Amendment. The judges understood their "patron's disposition" and assisted.

Although many State Constitutions included freedom of speech provisions, arguments were put forward that the 1st Amendment did not prevent States from abridging freedom of speech. Even Thomas Jefferson, contrary to his reputed libertarian philosophy, resorted to doublethink and argued that the U. S. Constitution superseded the English law of seditious libel for the the federal government, but not for state governments.(1)

Under the plausible emergency conditions of the Civil War, The Bill of Rights was set aside almost entirely. Habeus corpus was suspended and persons were held without trial. Civilians were subjected to military courts. (Now, of course, we are ALL subjected to military courts).

Emergency conditions provide plausible justification for agents of government to use their power to deprive citizens of rights, privileges, and immunities. The United States government has resorted to that ploy more than once, as will be shown.

After the Civil War, The 14th Amendment ostensibly prevented states from violating The Bill of Rights, but the language of the The 14th Amendment does not include the word "rights." Instead, the words "privileges and immunities" are used.

ARTICLE XIV

Section 1. All persons born or naturalized in the United States, and subject to the jurisdiction thereof, are citizens of the United States and of the State wherein they reside. No State shall make or enforce any law which shall abridge the privileges and immunities of citizens of the United States; nor shall any State deprive any person of life, liberty, or property without due process of law; nor deny to any person within its jurisdiction the equal protection of the laws.

(If you have a Social Security number, you are a 14th Amendment citizen!)

In 1895, the Supreme Sophists struck again. They ruled that the 1st Amendment did not limit State's police power. Davis had been arrested in Boston, Mass. for speaking at the Boston Commons without a permit. Davis vs Mass, 167 US 43, 1895.

There was considerable resistance to the United States entering WWI. The Espionage Act was passed in 1917 with egregious violations of a sensible interpretation of the 1st Amendment to quell resistance to going to war. Hundreds of people were arrested and convicted for no other crime than speech.(2) Once again the Supreme Court proved to be no help for the citizen against government.

The Espionage Act was a classic example of legislative deception by labeling. While the act did contain some unnecessary espionage language because espionage was already a crime under other laws, the main language of the Act was directed against speech. And that's what almost all the prosecutions under the Act were about.

One of the rawest cases of prosecution under the Espionage Act was against the makers of a film called Spirit of '76. It was a film about the Revolutionary War and showed the British in a bad light. The Supreme Sophists upheld the prosecution because the British were now allies in World War I.(3)

For an interesting analysis of how emergency can be tortured into public economic and banking policy or any other abuse see War and Emergency Report.

World War II, of course, created another tension and instigated the Smith Act that practically duplicated the 1917 Espionage Act. Prosecutions under the Smith Act did not succeed as well as the earlier prosecutions pursuant to the Espionage Act.(4)

Following World War II there was the House Un-American Activities Committee with its abuses of alleged communists. What that Committee really abused was the Constitution.

There was a forced loyalty oath that cost people jobs and reputations; and, of course, Joe McCarthy.

After more than two hundred years of struggle, the need for which should have been obviated by the 1st Amendment, freedom of speech perhaps comes closer now to the ideology of the 1st Amendment than it did in 1798. It remains important to maintain vigilance because plausible emergency and powerful propaganda can easily create a climate of mob acceptance of, or even worse, demand for suppression. Apathy may be even more dangerous.

Notes:

1. Freedom of Speech and Press in Early American History: Legacy of Suppression, by Leonard W. Levy.

2. Freedom of Speech by Zechariah Chafee, Jr.

3. Declarations of Independence: Cross-examining American Ideology by Howard Zinn.

4. A Trial on Trial by Maximilian St.-George and Lawrence Dennis. ******* Lest my commentary on this issue lead someone to jump to the wrong conclusion, let me set the record straight from the outset. I am not in any way, shape, or form instigating, advocating, or even suggesting the "violent overthrow of government." Namely because it can't be done. Government is an idea and an idea can't be undone with a gun. If peace, harmony, and prosperity is the end desired, the idea, *government*, is a very bad idea. The purpose here is to displace the

fallacy-based idea, government, with the reality-based idea of individualism and freedom. Where the mind goes, the body will follow.

There is such a widely held belief in the absolute necessity of government that it seems that the only issue to be considered is what kind of government; meaning what form of implementation. It is as if government is an objective discovery rather than a subjective mental invention. The idea of government is no less enmeshed in absolutism than the idea of an omni god in formal religion. Indeed, that is how most emotionally regard it. This fact is daily evidenced in the language and attitude of millions as they call on "government" to fulfill their wants and needs. In this mental atmosphere, to raise and discuss the question of government vs non government is nearly impossible. Since the concept, government, is held in most minds as an absolute, they can hold no differentiating reference. If they can envision no alternative, they are without choice. They are mentally locked in and completely unable to grasp an idea that opposes what they hold as absolute. They may play with words and imagine that they grasp non-government, but they simply yield to the absolutism and delude themselves.

Rational logic condemns the initiation of force against peaceful people. Furthermore, rational logic holds that the State is inherently and necessarily an invasive institution, whose employees must eventually initiate aggression. A government whose employees were not prepared to use force would soon cease being a government because people would have the option of whether to support it or not. Faced with the loss of patronage and/or financial support, the State would have only two choices: either coerce people into paying up or restrict its services to those who voluntarily agreed to deal with it. Both history and theory tell us that this never has and probably never will occur. Government employees are the only group of people in society who regularly and routinely use physical force or its threat to collect funds to sustain themselves. To the conscientious rational thinker it makes no difference how government employees spend the money they coercively collect. What does matter is the invasive nature of the taxation process; that it relies on coercion. The very fact that government employees must resort to force proves that their services are unwanted.

****

THOSE WHO STILL BELIEVE AMERICA IS A "CHRISTIAN NATION"

SHOULD PAY PARTICULAR HEED:

The Treaty of Tripoli, passed by the U.S. Senate in 1797, reads in part: "The government of the United States is not in any sense founded on the Christian religion." The treaty was written during the Washington administration, and sent to the Senate during the Adams administration. It was read aloud to the Senate, and each Senator received a printed copy. This was the 339th time that a recorded vote was required by the Senate, but only the third time a vote was unanimous (the next time was to honor George Washington). There is no record of any debate or dissension on the treaty. It was reprinted in full in three newspapers - two in Philadelphia, one in New York City. There is no record of public outcry or complaint in subsequent editions of the papers.

****

SUPPRESSED INTELLIGENCE REPORTS

BELIEF

For the purposes of this discussion belief is defined as mental acceptance of a premise, image, or thought as being true or real without evidence, in spite of contrary evidence, or after repeated failure. Belief, in this limited definition, is purely a function of the human mind. It enables humans to know what is demonstrably false, not knowable, and what is not known by anyone else.

There is a large area between belief and knowing where a great deal is accepted on faith. It is not necessary for every human to re-prove that Newton's motion formulas are accurate in macro physics, that the earth is not the center of the solar system, or that the city of Tokyo exists. The truth and accuracy of those premises have been proven and established in the body of recorded human knowledge. While most humans do not know these things are true based on personal experience, these things are knowable and known by others. That is the slipperiest of slippery slopes. It leads to faith in experts, authorities, and gurus.

Faith in experts, authorities, and gurus that presumably know leaves humans vulnerable to manipulation and exploitation. Modest attention to the doublespeak of expert Alan Greenspan should be enough to reveal to any person of reasonable intelligence and linguistic competence that Greenspan is incompetent; self-deceived; or a willful, knowing liar. The economic exploitation that results from Greenspan's folly are equally obvious in statistical growth of debt published by the Federal Reserve System itself.

The quarreling exaggerations of environmental experts passing themselves off as scientists prevent accurate evaluation and making of rational policy on environmental issues.

Faith in authority has resulted in more mass murder and destruction of property over millennia than could be documented in a nominally sized encyclopaedia. Super murderers from Alexander and Qin Shihuangdi to Stalin, Hitler, Roosevelt, Truman, and Mao could not happen without participation in or acquiescence to their authoritarian madnesses. When authority is combined with the guru phenomena one gets Pharaohs, Popes, Jim Jones, and David Koresh, none of whom would have had any influence without the support of self-deceived believers.

Two sources of beliefs are environment and imagination.

The first and primary source of belief is environment with parents playing the preeminent role. There is a high statistical probability that children will acquire the beliefs of their parents and maintain them for a lifetime. Church is another source of belief. Education another. Dictionaries define educate as to persuade to feel, act, and believe in a desired way. Whose desired way? Perhaps, the greatest source of belief outside family is entertainment/information media, commercial institutions with nothing other than their own economic self-interest to guide actions.

Both truth and bullshit can arise from imaginative processes. With imagination you get science, mathematics, and technology. With imagination you also get religious, economic, and political bullshit. You get art and literature, too, which can represent either truth or bullshit; but often represents bullshit. Today, what is produced as art and literature is almost wholly commercial product.

The problem that confronts every human individual is to discriminate between what is real or true and imaginative bullshit.

Scientific processes provide ways of acquiring knowledge of the world in the venue of time, space, material, and energy. Once obtained, verified, and published, knowledge is available to everyone. Anyone and everyone can use accumulated knowledge to assemble functioning electrical circuits, for example, anytime and all the time. The circuits will work practically anywhere and everywhere. No amount of belief in magic or other form of imaginative non-knowledge can make an electrical circuit function or malfunction.

Scientific processes have no validity outside the venue of time, space, material, and energy because scientific processes are about measurement, prediction, and repeatability. No proof exists that there is any other venue except in human imagination, but uncounted venues exist in human imagination. What can be measured, predicted, and repeated in imagined venues? Nothing. How does one measure a dream?

Whether other venues exist is a matter of faith or belief. Other venues, so far, cannot be proven to exist or not to exist.

Money creation and resulting economic effects are matters to be considered in the time, space, energy and material venue even though money itself is an abstract or imaginary concept. By using scientific procedures of data collection and testing, the scientific ideal of measurement, prediction, and repeatability can become an attainable goal.

Consider the matter of inflation. Inflation has been a constant since the founding of the Federal Reserve as can be determined by data published by the Federal Reserve. The Federal Reserve Chairman of the Board of Governors, Alan Greenspan, continuously verbigerates anti-inflation rhetorical dogma. He pretends and appears to believe that he is fighting inflation by monetary policy. The result has been inflation, not only in his tenure; but also, during the tenure of every Chairman since the inception of the Federal Reserve. Alan Greenspan fits the definition of a true believer. He continues to believe in his monetary policy after 84 years of failed Fed inflation-fighting policy.

Greenspan mumbles a few words and the stock market shakes. Greenspan demonstrates the folly of believing in authoritarian gurus as surely as Jim Jones.

Thousands of gurus are spouting diverse imagined solutions to human problems in diverse imagined venues. Imagined venues are often called spiritual. If there are solutions to social problems exacerbated by monetary policy and resulting economic chaos, they can only be found in the proper venue. The only venue that matters is the here and now venue of time, space, matter, and energy where data can be collected, measured, and evaluated, informed policy instituted and revised as needed, and solutions obtained.

Brain scientists, medical doctors, psychiatrists, and psychologists cannot tell us how the brain works. They cannot tell us why humans believe what they believe without evidence, in spite of contrary evidence, and after repeated failure of beliefs to coincide with reality.

It may be that the brain makes physical connections that "wire" the brain so that to some extent it works like a computer and can only do what it is wired to do. New wiring occurs from life experience in the existing culture. If the culture is erroneous, the wiring will be erroneous.(1) If that attribute of the brain is true, it would help explain the difficulty of unlearning a belief. Whether true or not, there is no question about the ability of a human to learn contradictory new things when necessary conscious effort is made to do so.

When a human experiences something that contradicts previously established beliefs, a mental condition of cognitive dissonance arises that is uncomfortable. The discomfort apparently arises when brain chemistry is altered.

When some of the brain chemicals generally called endorphins were isolated and injected into rats, the chemicals were found to be many times more addictive than morphine. This raises the question whether the phenomenon of addiction plays a role in belief. If so, it would also help explain the difficulty of unlearning a belief. Observing an addict attempting to withdraw from addictive drugs suggests great difficulty both physically and psychologically for the addict. However difficult, many addicts have recovered from their addiction. It is also possible for a human to transcend cognitive dissonance and learn contradictory new things. Conscious effort is a way to learn new things.

Some beliefs appear to arise from wishful thinking. A reason research was conducted into brain chemicals was the anesthetic effect reported by victims of serious injury, especially involving terror. (A survivor of a mountain lion attack reported he could hear his bones breaking but did not feel it.) The possibility of an endogenous anesthetic chemical excited the research. The wishful thinking was that an endogenous drug would be non-addictive. Dreams of billions to be gotten by marketing a non-addictive pain reliever and Nobel-itis pushed scientists, and chemicals were found. Testing showed the chemicals to be extremely addictive when injected as an exogenous drug. Faced with contrary evidence, the scientists gave up their wishful thinking as good scientists must do when faced with contrary evidence. A Nobel Prize was awarded, but billions could not be gotten from a non-addictive pain reliever.

Economics is a field that is dominated by beliefs. Beliefs that do not lend themselves to the simple to state general procedure, find the chemicals and test them, used by scientists in the case of brain chemicals and their possible use as pain relievers. Economics is a field that contains so many variables that economists resort to generalized theories that cannot be proven scientifically. Economists have no control over real events. They cannot test their theories in the real world. Economics is pseudoscience.

The pseudoscience or nescience of economics is like religion. The foundation of economics rests on dogma, doctrine, and faith. Dogma and doctrine preached by guru economists to the faithful. Dogma and doctrines that are based on doublethink and contradiction. For intellectual corruption, economists have no peers.

Economists have rented themselves in service to ruling classes whose practice is confiscation of maximum wealth and property. This practice of ruling classes goes on in every society without regard to nominative labels. The practice does not change whether the label is socialist, communist, capitalist, mercantilist, monarchy, theocracy, junta, or democracy.

To maximize their profit and security, ruling classes must exercise social control. Social control is easiest when controllees subscribe to the same belief systems as their controllers. Controllees are less likely to notice being controlled and rebel against their controllers. They may even blame themselves when they recognize that they are disadvantaged. If the belief system fails, the ruling class is prepared to wield all necessary force through the mechanism of the state and its police and armies.

SUPPRESSED INTELLIGENCE REPORTS

CONTROL OF SOCIETIES AND ECONOMIES

A major mechanism that transfers unearned wealth and maintains social and political control in modern society is money; the power to issue money. This power is given to banks in nearly every country of the world. Banks issue money as interest bearing debt. They also determine how much money is issued.

Economists provide a major service to rulers by initiating economic theory that protects the interests of rulers. These theories are sometimes promoted as economic "laws." Journalists join economists in repeating the theories until they infect human minds like a virus or meme being passed from one mind to the other.(2) The theories become controlling beliefs and part of social culture. These theories keep the wealth flowing away from producers to non-producers.

1. A general theory among some brain scientists is that the structure of the brain is genetically determined, and learning is a process of using certain neural pathways to effect memory. But there are unproven arguments for all sorts of theories. No one, presently, knows how the brain works. 2. The brain is an energy intense organ. An extant theory is that due to its structure, there is a tendency for the brain to accept the most parsimonious route to interpretation of sensual inputs. Jumping to conclusions on little or no valid information or accepting the interpretations of experts, gurus, and authorities is to be expected. *******

To find out why America (and all other nations) will eventually be absorbed into a global government with no military or civil police forces at all, visit our website. This will make you gnash your teeth and tear your shirt! You military people and law enforcement agencies pay particular attention to this essay. But whence originated this incredible, insane idea to rid all nations of their armies and local police, and to place all military power and civil law enforcement into the hands of unelected foreign socialists and foreign mercenary soldiers at the United Nations? Right here:

I saw Trotsky again this summer (the summer of 1922) and asked him what he had done about reducing the army. Of course, because of the new economic policy, a Labor Army was out of the question. He told me that he had reduced the army from 5,300,000 to 800,000, including the navy. A greater reduction than that, he said, was impossible.

"We stand always ready to reduce our army," said Trotsky, "even to liquidating it fully, whenever our closest and our farthest neighbors accept a program of disarmament. In January we offered disarmament. Europe refused even the suggestion. Later we asked our close neighbors, with the same result. If America would only take the initiative in this respect," he shrugged and smiled, "well, we would support her with our whole heart."

Mirrors of Moscow: "Trotsky, Soviet War Lord;" 1923 Trotsky (a Jew) was born Lev Davydovich Bronstein, his father's name being Davyd "Lyova" Leontiyevich Bronstein. "Lyova" is one of the many similar diminutives of Lev, which literally means "Lion." His "Labor Army" was not to be used much for making war, but to build dams and bridges and roads and housing; i. e., to rebuild the crumbling infrastructure of Russia.

(Incidentally, Communism, Fascism and Capitalism are, all three, socialist economic experiments of Zionist).

AMERICA'S ENEMIES WATCH CAREFULLY

SUPPRESSED INTELLIGENCE REPORTS

I guarantee you that your enemies and mine will read these pages. They read them to get a sense of our determination, to get a handle on our agenda and philosophy, to see how far we are from finding proper solutions, and to revel in our failures and petty bickerings. And, occasionally, when they see something here that is truth, they begin writing foul-mouthed accusations and death-threats.

How To Recognize Infiltrators and Agents Provocateurs:

Here are some key "buzz words" and phrases to look for when trying to spot infiltrators or industry mouthpieces:

* saying "anecdote" is inferior to "solid scientific studies performed by experts" to discredit/invalidate victim's personal stories.

*"where's your proof?" or "can you prove that?"

* "who told you that!?" * correcting your grammar, spelling. Use "speak the King's English" insult.

* personal attacks/ sniper attacks to shut down talk on a specific topic in an open discussion. Sarcastic referral to mainstream media like "you've been watching Buffy The Vampire Slayer" and "reading too much Ladies Home Journal" or comments such as: "they border on the ruminations of tragic Shakespearean characters just short of the denouement. They are private thoughts that will neither help your cause nor the cause of other victims of medical negligence, political intrigue or globalist conspiracies."

* put-down comments about your presumed lack of "emotional," "spiritual," "mental," or educational" prowess.

* calling you a fascist or communist or labeling you as a "dangerous militant radical," or the same thing, a "Christian!"

* rewriting history. Insisting something is true when it clearly is not, and accusing you of rewriting history!

* Channeling direction in a conversation hitting too close to the truth to a more benign cause: "But to say that doctors are involved in a conspiracy of silence to protect their own is not to say that doctors are malevolent or malicious on average. The picture you and Dr. XXXXX paint is one that cannot be believed even if it is true"

* using the "painting with a broad brush" analogy. "This means that we must be careful not to paint with too broad a brush lest we turn potential allies into neutrals or even enemies."

* accusation words like "extremist," "radical," "idiot," "brain-dead," when an "unapproved" topic (the truth) has been presented.

* deliberate channeling of the "unapproved" topics to the "approved" list to halt further discussion.

* outright or veiled death threats to frighten away the more timid researchers.

On the surface, they claim to be conservatives, anarchists or libertarians dedicated to reforming oppressive governments; yet, with their death threats, prove they would be as ruthless or more so than the governments they claim they want to replace "when or if the revolution begins." The agents provocateurs claim to reserve the "right" to "eliminate with prejudice all idiots, radicals and brain-dead extremists" as soon as they seize power from the present government. In other words, to kill anyone who does not agree with them; rather like the Stalinist purges, the Nazi pogroms, or the actions of the present U. S. federal government, I'd say. This is what they are taught. It is that standardized Tavistock rote-response conditioning methodology. The formal name is Hegalian Trap or Hegalian Dialect. They are taught this....and that is why the trained lackeys say the same words and phrases over and over like broken records: they perform exactly as they have been trained...like a bunch of mindless, unfeeling robots: "When the researcher says so-and-so, you respond with this approved reply."

****

Throughout all of known history, literally every governmental system under any and every label has met the same fate: Failure. None produced and sustained the peace and prosperity promised. Indeed, the end result has been and is the exact opposite. Each and every one has either been taken over by an outside superior force or collapsed within due to declining economic conditions or increasing internal dissension and eventually violent revolution. Current systems, if not already in disarray, are in the same pattern of decline. Still, the ever-faithful pursue. They believe that this time things will be different. They will "control government." They will "limit government," and when these fail, they will "reduce government."

There are those who look upon the burgeoning bureaucracy and ever-increasing "welfare state" and pine for the good old days when the U.S. governmental system was in its infancy; when the rules and regulations were fewer in number and less offensive with more left to individual decision. They propose to wend their way back to that cherished bygone era by the same road that brought them here: Government and politics. I see no indication that they have studied the problem and understand how and why "minimal state" became maximum nightmare of rule. They mention neither a different psychology nor different means. They appear to assume that will and intent alone will bring fruition to their quest to "reduce government."

Just exactly what is it that they propose to control, limit, or reduce? What is government? This is the question that they perpetually refuse to definitively answer. Is government a thing of quantity that one may bind in chains to control it? Is it a growing physical something that one may enclose in a container to limit its growth? Is it a fat or some substance that one may render or compress to make it smaller? No, it is none of these things. Government is simply, unequivocally, and always initiation of force or coercion and nothing else.

****

"Why do some seek political office? Power. Nothing else."

former intelligence officer

****

ARE PATRIOTS READING THE WRONG LITERATURE FIRST? ARE PATRIOTS NOT READING IMPORTANT LITERATURE AT ALL? DO "PATRIOTS" EVEN UNDERSTAND WHAT THEY ARE TRYING TO ACHIEVE?

Hegel proposed that man was and should be free in a free society with a free economy. It was only those who came later who bastardized and used Hegel's philosophy to forge a nationalist/fascist state in Germany, the Soviet State in Russia and the Capitalist state in America. Click this link to read the Section entitled, Revealed Religions, of Hegel's Phenomenology of Mind, his first important work.

Here is a link to the entire book. It appears in about 50 sections. Quite large. And, incidentally, I am not suggesting that I either agree or disagree with anything or everything that Hegel or other writers propose. You will also find works by Marx, Engels, Trotsky and others at this link. It is amazing how the writings and rantings of so-called modern "patriots" often echoes and parrots completely or in part the writings of these proponents of global Socialism!

It is for that reason that I am not affiliated with any "patriot" organization. I feel that most of them haven't a clue about what they want to achieve or where they are leading their narrowly educated and barely literate herds of sheep.

Mind you, the New World Order agenda promises to rid humankind of both religion AND governments, and to give humankind a new freedom without the restraints of either, just as most Patriot/Militia organizations demand! Why, then, do "patriots" oppose the New World Order? Because most of them know that the New Order will simply replace the Old Order and tighten the chains with additional laws prohibiting dissension of any kind. Peace is defined as no opposition to Communism/Socialism/Capitalism.

You don't have to believe everything presented here. Indeed, I will be disappointed if you do believe these essays without first investigating on your own to verify the information. Those who claim their answers are the only answers and that everyone else is either uninformed or lying outright generally do not have your best interests at heart, particularly those who insist that Americans are somehow "protected" by the by-laws (constitution) of a bankrupt corporation known as the United States. The by-laws of a corporation are a legal contract affecting only members of the corporation who agreed to and signed the contract. Believe me, you aren't a member except, perhaps, by covert agreements! The "Constitution" was a legal contract binding only upon those who originally signed it. They are all dead. And when the last of them died, their legal contract died with them. It was not binding upon anyone who came after them and, indeed, was not even binding upon any of their contemporaries who had not signed it.

FEDERALISM AS A BASIS

Despite their common heritage, background, and homogeneity, the original states were 13 different and distinct political entities, each commanding considerable loyalty from its citizenry. However much the framers wanted a strong central government, they knew that they could establish one only by allowing the states to retain power or by making it appear that they did. They realized, or at least Hamilton did, that, as a practical matter, there could not be a double sovereignty; the framers persuaded the public to accept the Constitution by claiming that sovereignty was indeed divisible. Under the federal system they devised, the national government was given the authority to exercise only the enumerated powers granted it, but it had supreme authority in those areas.

State sovereignty was therefore largely a fiction; it was destined to have a stormy future, involving a bloody civil war.

SUPPRESSED INTELLIGENCE REPORTS

THE MOST REVEALING ESSAY YOU WILL EVER READ: THE UNITED STATES, BY CHARTER AND TREATY, IS A COLONY OF GREAT BRITAIN!

The corporation known as the United States is chartered by the royal family of England. The United States is legally—by charter and treaty—a colony of England! The "Constitution" was rewritten by King George's barristers and approved by the king himself to his advantage, not ours, before it was presented to the states for ratification.

No subject discussed within the so-called "patriot movement" in America arouses the anger and blood lust of those who believe they are protected by a constitution as does the mere mention that such belief is in complete error. The governmentalists, of course, want you to believe that the by-laws still exist and that you are protected by them. As long as you believe, you will always look in the wrong direction for answers and never find the solutions for the many violations to freedom that now exist in America. The first requisite in planning a covert operation is to create a diversion (the Restore the Constitution Movement, UTDC, CONSCON, etc.) so people cannot see the thieves running out the back door with the family silverware. The federalists and globalists understand that better than anyone else and have used it successfully to the disadvantage of the American patriot community.

Twelve states (all but Rhode Island) named 73 delegates to the Constitutional Convention. Of these, 55 came but only 39 signed the original Constitution on Sept. 17, 1787. The leaders of the convention were statesmen who in modern parlance would be called middle-of-the-road: George WASHINGTON, Alexander HAMILTON, James MADISON, John JAY, and Benjamin FRANKLIN.

Conspicuous by their absence were the firebrands of freedom, Patrick Henry and Sam Adams, and the author of the Declaration of Independence, Thomas Jefferson.

One of the greatest fears of the proponents of the constitution was the power of a free and diverse people, and they planned and organized their new government and its bylaws to prevent a free people from having much decision about it. In his keynote address at the Constitutional convention, Edmund RANDOLPH said: "Our chief danger arises from the democratic parts of our {state} constitutions. It is a maxim which I hold incontrovertible, that the powers of government exercised by the people swallow up the other branches."

****

"Allah does not destroy the men whom one hates."

African Proverb

****

If the environmentalists really believe the world is overpopulated, why don't they all volunteer to commit suicide?

****

WE ARE PROPERTY OF THE "STATE"

Amusing, though tragic, is the idea that the governmental system of the United States could do anything else but expand. The revered "founding fathers" did not set up a few protective rules and regulations and then go home. They set up a system where lawmaking was the occupation of hundreds, then thousands. In pursuit of this occupation, what else could happen except the continual increase in the number of laws and lawyers? Sure, now and then a law or two was repealed. This only temporarily shifted the favoritism from some to others. It did not deter them from their divinely appointed task to more and more bring all under the advisement and control of the "enlightened."

From the outset, the intent was made clear. Nothing was hidden. Official documents stipulated without equivocation that the "government" would regulate trade and commerce, coin and mint money, provide for the "common defense," etc., etc., etc. There is not a single line in the Declaration of Independence, the Constitution, or any governmental document that says that an individual will be left alone as long as he does not impose upon another or others. By commission and omission, all official decrees make clear that human individual is regarded as property of the god called "State." Do you think that the phrase, "America's children" and other such announcements are meaningless? An abstract, an "infinite entity" as a possessive noun? If this does not designate a god and ownership by the god, what does it mean?

So, is it any surprise that the manipulation and control of "State property" is an ongoing and forever escalating process? How did or does anyone conclude otherwise? Oh yes, the Constitution and "constitutional rights." To be quite blunt, the Constitution is a mish mosh of self-contradictory gibberish that says whatever anyone feels it says. Questions of "constitutional rights" are not settled by the conscious mind and intellect, but by emotions, and eventually by the gun. Since "constitutional rights" are a matter of feelings, by what does anyone propose to control and "delimit?"

'The State was organized in this country with power to do all kinds of things for the people, and the people in their short-sighted stupidity, have been adding to that power ever since. After 1789, John Adams said that, so far from being a democracy of a democratic republic, the political organization of the country was that of "a monarchical republic, or, if you will, a limited monarchy;" the powers of its President were far greater than those of "an avoyer, a consul, a podesta, a doge, a stadtholder; nay, than a king of Poland; nay, than a king of Sparta." If all that was true in 1789—and it was true—what is to be said of the American State at the present time, after a century and a half of steady centralization and continuous increments of power?'

A SCRAP OF PAPER

What, then, is a little matter like a treaty to the French or British State? Merely a scrap of paper—Bethmann-Hollweg described it exactly. Why be astonished when the German or Russian State murders its citizens? The American State would do the same thing under the same circumstances. In fact, eighty years ago it did murder a great many of them for no other crime in the world but that they did not wish to live under its rule any longer; and if that is a crime, then the colonists led by G. Washington were hardened criminals and the Fourth of July is nothing but a cutthroat's holiday.

The weaker the State is, the less power it has to commit crime. Where in Europe today does the State have the best criminal record? Where it is weakest: in Switzerland, Holland, Denmark, Norway, Luxembourg, Sweden, Monaco, Andorra. Yet when the Dutch State, for instance, was strong, its criminality was appalling; in Java it massacred 9000 persons in one morning which is considerably ahead of Hitler's record or Stalin's. It would not do the like today, for it could not; the Dutch people do not give it that much power, and would not stand for such conduct. When the Swedish State was a great empire, its record, say from 1660 to 1670, was fearful. What does all this mean but that if you do not want the State to act like a criminal, you must disarm it as you would a criminal; you must keep it weak.

The State will always be criminal in proportion to its strength; a weak State will always be as criminal as it can be, or dare be, but if it is kept down to the proper limit of weakness—which, by the way, is a vast deal lower limit than people are led to believe—its criminality may be safely got on with. So it strikes me that instead of sweating blood over the iniquity of foreign States, my fellow-citizens would do a great deal better by themselves to make sure that the American State is not strong enough to carry out the like iniquities here.

The stronger the American State is allowed to grow, the higher its record of criminality will grow, according to its opportunities and temptations. If, then, instead of devoting energy, time, and money to warding off wholly imaginary and fanciful dangers from criminals thousands of miles away, our people turn their patriotic fervor loose on the only source from which danger can proceed, they will be doing their full duty by their country. Two able and sensible American publicists—Isabel Paterson, of the New York Herald Tribune, and W. J. Cameron, of the Ford Motor Company—have lately called our public's attention to the great truth that if you give the State power to do something FOR you, you give it an exact equivalent of power to do something TO you.

FRAMEWORK OF FEDERAL GOVERNMENT

The framework of government established in the Constitution emphasizes four overriding concepts: popular control without majority rule; the limitation of governmental power; federalism; and a tripartite government.

Popular Control but NOT Majority Rule as Claimed!

The framers provided for ultimate control of the government by the people through the electoral process. Such control, however, was not to be exercised either easily or immediately, except perhaps over the House of Representatives. Originally, senators were to be chosen by the state legislatures and the president by the electors in the Electoral College. Since the state legislatures controlled the selection of senators, and presidential electors and seats in the state legislature were won in popular elections, it was assumed that the popular will would eventually have an effect on the choice of senators and presidents. It could also be argued that the people would have a voice in the choice of federal officials appointed by the president, with the advice and consent of the Senate, but this could be true of federal judges only in the long run, since they were given virtually lifetime tenure.

The framers, with their complex views on government, felt that the popular majority must be represented in the federal legislature. At the same time, they felt that they must not give over all legislative power to a popular majority. Consequently, they approved an arrangement by which one house of the legislature represented majority will and another house served as a negation of the first.

So it really isn't a "government of, by, and for the people," is it?

Article II

Section 1. The executive Power shall be vested in a President of the United States of America. He shall hold his Office during the Term of four Years, and, together with the Vice

SUPPRESSED INTELLIGENCE REPORTS

President, chosen for the same Term, be elected, as follows:

Each State shall appoint, in such Manner as the Legislature thereof may direct, a Number of Electors, equal to the whole Number of Senators and Representatives to which the State may be entitled in the Congress: but no Senator or Representative, or Person holding an Office of Trust or Profit under the United States, shall be appointed an Elector.

The Electors shall meet in their respective States, and vote by Ballot for two Persons, of whom one at least shall not be an Inhabitant of the same State with themselves. And they shall make a List of all the Persons voted for, and of the Number of Votes for each; which List they shall sign and certify, and transmit sealed to the Seat of the Government of the United States, directed to the President of the Senate. The President of the Senate shall, in the Presence of the Senate and House of Representatives, open all the Certificates, and the Votes shall then be counted. The Person having the greatest Number of Votes shall be the President, if such Number be a Majority of the whole Number of Electors appointed; and if there be more than one who have such Majority, and have an equal Number of Votes, then the House of Representatives shall immediately chuse by Ballot one of them for President; and if no Person have a Majority, then from the five highest on the List the said House shall in like Manner chuse the President. But in chusing the President, the Votes shall be taken by States, the Representation from each State having one Vote; A quorum for this Purpose shall consist of a Member or Members from two thirds of the States, and a Majority of all the States shall be necessary to a Choice. In every Case, after the Choice of the President, the Person having the greatest Number of Votes of the Electors shall be the Vice President. But if there should remain two or more who have equal Votes, the Senate shall chuse from them by Ballot the Vice President.

A perennial difficulty in the constitutional interpretation of presidential power is the meaning of the first sentence of Article II: "The executive Power shall be vested in a President of the United States of America." What is executive power? Presidents have held differing views of the powers inherent in their office. William Howard Taft took the view that the president had only the powers expressly given him in the other sections of Article II. In contrast, Theodore Roosevelt held that by virtue of the opening sentence of Article II the president, as steward of all the people, could do anything on behalf of the people that was not expressly denied him in the Constitution. On several momentous occasions Franklin D. Roosevelt asserted the power to do things expressly forbidden by the Constitution. For example, before the United States entered World War II, he traded some old destroyers to Britain in exchange for military bases, although Article IV, Section 3 of the Constitution gives Congress the exclusive power to dispose of property belonging to the United States. Abraham Lincoln also suggested that a president must occasionally suspend part of the Constitution to preserve the whole. And, of course, he did more than that; he suspended the entire original constitution.

Section 1 of Article II describes the electoral college system for electing the president. Paragraph 3 was superseded by another set of rules, the 12th Amendment.

How is it they believed they had either the right or the power to tell free people how and when they could or could not decide who their "leaders" would be, or even that there should be "leaders" at all? Everything they wrote only reinforces the false idea that free people should be ruled by an elitist class under direction of secret societies. Implanted false ideas! But what do you think about it? They didn't bother to ask your ancestors before they made the rules and they don't bother to ask you now. They claim to have the "law of the land" and that law makes you anything but free!

The State, not being a person, can be carried to any tyrannic action without any remorse. There is none to blush for it. It imprisons without inquiry. It punishes without trial, either by jury or solitary judge. It converts and perverts an anti-slavery constitution into pro-slavery conduct. It does things daily without shame, which no individual in it could do without soul-stirring contrition. It involves a system which absolutely shuts out the best men from public life, and selects only the mediocre, such as are capable of being used as tools and instruments. It pretends to defend person and property, and is the first to invade them, and that also in a more brutal manner than it allows to any of its individual members.

THE CONSTITUTION UNMASKED

It has been said that if a lie is big enough, told often enough and loud enough, it will be accepted by nearly all as absolute and unquestionable truth. I can think of no better illustration of this than the much revered, but a monstrous slave paper called "The Constitution Of The United States." Lysander Spooner called it "The Constitution Of No Authority." This gives too much credit. The very idea of intellectual or philosophical authority of one individual over another is necessarily based on the fallacy of superior being. Ergo, this eliminates the question as to whether the constitution is or is not authoritative. What remains is what will be examined.

I believe that we are in agreement that the constitution is words written upon a piece or pieces of material. I believe that we shall further agree that these words were written by a human person or persons and did not appear on the material by some mystical "divine measure." Where we may disagree is the "meaning" of the words, how they relate to you and me, and what else is said by logical inference, and logically implied by omission.

The constitution is believed by most to deal with the interpersonal relationships of human individuals. The first, foremost and ever present problem is that the writing and ideas in the constitution does not even recognize human individual as the real. If this seems a bit shocking and totally unbelievable to you, please tell me where is real individual in the concept of nation itself, or in "national interest," or "will of the people" and all other declarative expressions or logical inferences that volition and valuation exist independently of each individual?

Is it not clear that in the concept, "national interest," an individual is regarded not as an autonomous entity with individualistic values and personal goals, but is regarded only as property and means to an alleged universal goal of the "nation?" If I am mistaken, please show me. Show me real individual recognized as real individual, not as property of a mental invention called nation confusedly believed to be a corporeal thing holding interest.

Can anyone show me anywhere in the "constitution" or any law that it says that an individual will always be left alone if he does not impose upon another by offensive force or the threat of it? Can anyone show me anywhere in the "constitution" or any law that says that an individual will never be compelled by offensive force or threat of force to act against his non imposing wishes for the benefit of another or others, or be coercively compelled to act upon values not his own?

If not, pray tell by what rationale is it believed that the constitution has anything to do with individualism and freedom. Please do not tell me of the "protection," of laws against theft and murder. As a farmer does not allow some of his livestock to destroy other livestock, the "protective laws" are of the same ilk. Just try to opt out of the system, and although you impose upon none, you will quickly discover the quality and real oppressive nature of your "protector."

"Will of the people?" There is no such thing because there is no such entity as people. I am real. You are real. You have a will. I have a will. Sometimes we shall hold a common value. Sometimes we won't, but "will of the people?" The term, people, denotes a subjective category existing only in mind, not a physical "collective entity" with a "will."

If I list a hundred, a thousand, a million contradictions in and related to the constitution, will that make a difference? Will more induce you to reexamine your beliefs about the constitution? If not, perhaps, revealing a few of the gross absurdities will.

Suppose that I say that yesterday, I saw the nation, America, walking down the street. Everyone would think I was nuts, right? They would say that for the nation, America, to walk down a street, America would have to be a real physical thing with the capacity to walk, and this is not true. Yet, nearly all of these very same individuals speak of "national interest," or "for the good of the country" and find nothing wrong with it. How can there be "national interest" etc. unless nation is a real physical quantity, i.e, a thing that has the capacity to have interest. If it is insane to speak of America walking down the street, is it no less insane to speak of America holding interest.

Or how about "America's children?" Gee, I saw America at the mall last week and she didn't even look pregnant, and now she has millions of children?" Absurd? Of course, its absurd. That's the point, but keep in mind that I am only pointing out logical inference that is arbitrarily disregarded in the ever popular idea of attributing human characteristics to abstracts. Any arguments that can be lodged against "nation" walking down the street, or seeing "America" in the mall are also lodged against any idea that also depends on "nation" and "America" being physical quantities of volition and values.

Getting back to the revered constitution, it seems that from the outset and still ongoing is a bugaboo of conflict based on "interpretation" of what some word, phrase, sentence, paragraph, etc. in the constitution "means." Even as a child, I was somewhat puzzled about the constitution "written for all" yet could be "understood" only by nine persons elevated to "divine status" and called the "supreme court." So, what's all this "interpretation" stuff really all about?

Bringing it down to earth, "interpretation" means that the meaning of a word, phrase, etc. is whatever someone feels it to mean. Since subjective feelings are by nature individualistic and therefore, infinitely variable, what something in the constitution "means" is literally without limit. Since subjective feelings are not subject to proof or disproof, the "resolution" of conflicting differences as to "meaning" is eventually settled by the gun. (What is the "meaning" of the "supreme court" without the gun?)

In the scheme of things, i.e., programmed thinking, aka, "slavespeak," there is no distinction made between "interpretation" and defining; the former being subjective feelings and the latter being objective reality based. Since actual objective entity, real individual as an autonomous entity, is not recognized in the constitution, there is no common objective frame of reference by which to define the words, phrases, etc. in said constitution. Thus, there remains only "interpretation" of how and where the property, individual, fits into the concept of rule. This comes down to individual preference along with pretending that the preference has something to do with freedom. For sure, real individual is impossible to find in this mental mess.

As one classic example of confusion compounded by commotion, if memory serves, it is the 9th amendment that says something about the "rights retained by the people." There's certainly been a lot of "interpreting" done here. In fact, I remember an entire book on this although I can't presently recall the title.

Since there is no such objective thing as "people," we have a problem right away. Since there is no such thing as "objective rights" the problem gets out of hand real fast. The simple truth is that an individual can choose to act in any way within physical and mental capacity. Two (or any number) can choose to act like jungle animals in predatory fashion. One may choose this while the other does not. They can choose to settle their difference by reference to a mutually selected arbiter. They can choose to settle their differences by noodles at 20 paces, howitzers at 30 miles, or with Bowie knives with wrists strapped together. Or if each prefers a peaceful interpersonal relationship, they can agree to non initiation of force and non coercion, i.e., the concept of self-ownership.

If someone wishes to call the concept of self-ownership via agreement a "right," I have no objections as it fits the real condition. However, this is not the way the term, right, or rights, is usually used; which is why there is so much confusion and problem with "interpretation." By definition, the "right of self-ownership" is non restrictive of any action that does not utilize offensive force or the threat of it. The very instant that someone presume to enumerate "rights," reality goes out the window. "Enumerated rights" as in "constitutional rights" carry the inference of entitlement, of actions allowed. This in turn logically infers limited actions apart from the prohibition of initiation of force or coercion. To provide "entitlement of rights," i.e., to say what one can do is also to say what one can't do. So, here we are right back into the external ownership mess with enumerated "privileges at the point of a gun" foolishly believed to be individualism and freedom. Only from such thinking can one imagine that freedom can be qualified, i.e. increased or decreased.

To be sure, "The Constitution" and "The Law" are sometimes the "only game in town." If it suits my purpose, I will play the game, and quite well, I might add. But at no time do I imagine that the constitution and law is individualism and freedom oriented. If someone asks me what this statute or that law means, I answer, "What do you want it to mean?" I can do this by setting the context and playing it in a limited setting. While I prefer that things were much different, I am no martyr to some idealistic cause; and certainly not to one that is self contradictory and impossible to achieve. I refer to the ideas and efforts of those who imagine their "interpretations" of the constitution to be correct and all contrary ones incorrect. I refer to the folly of imagining that "interpretation" and "revision" can make of the constitution what it is not. I refer to the fact that the constitution is inherently anti individual and anti freedom and no amount of tinkering and personal imposition is going to make it otherwise.

THE "NEW NATION" IN THE TWENTIETH CENTURY

When plunder becomes a way of life for a group of men living together in society, they create for themselves in the course of time a legal system that authorizes it and a moral code that glorifies it. — Frederick Bastiat

SUPPRESSED INTELLIGENCE REPORTS

There is No Longer a Federal Government

In 1881, historian John A. Marshall described the spirit of encroachment and usurpation as follows:

When the arteries which convey the life-blood from the heart of the constitution to all parts of its body once become paralyzed, the most skilful treatment can never restore it to its original vigor and healthful condition. A partial recovery may be effected, but the disease remains.

Oppressive and illegal acts by one Administration may be adopted as established precedents for similar encroachments by succeeding ones; and who can gainsay the right? Surely, not the people, when they not only encourage, but are accessories in the wrong. Therefore, without a proper and conscientious regard for the majesty of the law, and the observance of personal rights, there is no security for permanence in free government (emphasis in original).(1)

Based on these principles, Republican Senator Charles Sumner predicted, "When Lincoln reinforced Fort Sumter and called for 75,000 men without the consent of Congress, it was the greatest breach ever made in the Constitution, and would hereafter give the President the liberty to declare war whenever he wishes without the consent of Congress."(2) Mr. Sumner was quite correct, but the background of his observation must be understood before we can make sense of American history from 1861 to the present.

In his book entitled Abraham Lincoln and the Second American Revolution, modern historian James M. McPherson wrote: [After the war] the old decentralized federal republic became a new national polity that taxed the people directly, created an internal revenue bureau to collect these taxes, expanded the jurisdiction of federal courts, established a national currency and a national banking structure.

The United States went to war in 1861 to preserve the Union; it emerged from war in 1865 having created a nation. Before 1861 the two words "United States" were generally used as a plural noun: "The United States are a republic." After 1865 the United States became a singular noun. The loose union of states became a nation (emphasis in original).(3) McPherson, who does not take sides with the South, perhaps admitted more than he intended in the above statement. The vast majority of Americans today are completely blind to the fact that there was no restoration of the "Union as it was" when the Southern States were subjugated in 1865, but rather the permanent establishment of a centralized military despotism which, although styled the "United States," bears no more relation to the Government of the United States of America under the Constitution than did that political body to the former Government under the Articles of Confederation. As Supreme Court Justice Story pointed out in 1833, "The Federal Government... as a creature of that compact [the Constitution], must be bound by its creators, the several States in the Union and the citizens thereof, having no existence but under the Constitution, nor any rights but as that instrument confers."(4) Prior to the 1860s, the Union was not a self-existent entity, but merely a condition arising from the common consent of the participating States. As such, the Union could neither create States — the new States were admitted to the Union after being created by the inhabitants of the Territory — nor compel their submission by force once admitted — a war between the States was only made possible by States acting in combination outside of the constitutionally-created Union against their sister States. The Government created by the Constitution was established to govern this voluntary compact of States and it was therefore their common agent, never their master.

It follows that, upon a dissolution of the Union, a destruction of the Constitution, and an overthrow of the sovereign States, the Government can no longer exist in organic law,(5) but must necessarily take on a "life" of its own under color of law(6) as a corporation with its own internal codes, rules, and regulations — all military terms. It has been judicially declared that "where congress creates a corporation merely by virtue of its authority to legislate for a particular territory, and not by a general act, the corporation is a foreign one in any state or territory other than that in which it was created."(7) Title 28, United States Code, Section 3002(15)(a) clearly defines the "United States" as "a Federal corporation" and elsewhere we are told that "the United States government is a foreign corporation with respect to a State."(8) Black's Law Dictionary defines a corporation as "an artificial person or legal entity."(9) Thus, the U.S. Government, with its permanent seat in the District of Columbia,(10) is a fiction comprised of other fictions ("U.S. citizens"), not the lawful government of real people (State Citizens) it was before the 1860s:

This self-formed corporate body has not merely an esprit de corps, but a oneness of will and purpose characteristic alike of a corporation, an oligarchy, or an autocrat; and the federal legislature, executive and judiciary, which were established as three absolutely independent institutions, to watch, and, if necessary, check one another, are now so unified as to act with one mind and will: thus practically changing them into a vast and chronic conspiracy against the people's liberty, as any gang of men, acting with one mind in the hiding places of the constitution and government, and constantly influenced by power and money, will gradually become.

Under the forms of a republican federation, then, we have a consolidated empire, and a corporate despot, just as the Romans had "an absolute monarchy disguised in the form of a commonwealth" (Gibbon). The parallelism will hereafter more fully appear.(11)

It is this corporate despot that has continued its subjugation of the people of both North and South through its municipal franchises, the fifty reconstructed "States of." That these are not the organic and sovereign States which comprised the original Union but are, by their very nature, foreign political entities which are only nominally republican, is evident from the fact that their elective franchises consist exclusively of U.S. citizens who, although they reside in the State, nevertheless have their legal domicile in Washington, D.C. and owe "unqualified allegiance" to the Government seated there.(12) Furthermore, the new State constitutions were all framed post-Reconstruction by these foreign residents and, at least in the South, contain provisions which openly repudiate State sovereignty and the right of the American people to self-determination:

With the shots "heard round the world," Americans rebelled against an oppressive foreign authority. Then, after a generation as semi-independent states, they entered into a compact as "the People" in order, as the Preamble to the Constitution reads, to "secure the Blessings of Liberty to ourselves and our Posterity." The purpose of the 1789 Constitution was to charter a government of limited powers that could never become a tyrannical overlord. To guard against government's tendency toward self-aggrandizement, the framers not only expressly delimited the powers of Congress but tried in the Bill of Rights to carve out certain areas of freedom — speech, press, assembly, religion, arms — that would remain beyond the federal government's reach. They would remain vested in "the People," who preceded and superseded the Constitution they established....

The recognition that the People are one group, an American nation, makes possible the sustained campaign to convert the elitist Constitution of 1789 into an egalitarian constitution of popular suffrage — that is, a constitution that bases democratic rule on the majority of all the people....

Nationhood, equality, and democracy — these are the ideas that forge a new Constitution. But Lincoln was a good lawyer, and lawyers always seek to camouflage conceptual transformations as the continuous outgrowth of language used in the past. That's why he invoked government "by the people" to capture the new principle of democratic rule. But the significance of the People had changed. They no longer exist as the guarantors of the Constitution, the bestowers of legitimacy. States and individuals can no longer set themselves apart from the nation. The people exist exclusively as voters, as office holders and as beneficiaries of legislation.

The relevant concept in the new Constitution, then, is not "We the People" but "We the citizens of the nation" —and this transformation is apparent in the post-Civil War amendments. The Fourteenth Amendment, for example, gives us our first concept of national citizenship. "All persons born or naturalized in the United States, and subject to the jurisdiction thereof" are henceforth citizens. Prior to the Civil War, we allowed each state to define for itself who could become a citizen of the state and, on that basis, a citizen of the country. The new definition of who belongs to the polity marks a new beginning (emphasis in original).(13)

Thus, according to this writer, the so-called "Civil War" somehow breathed life into the empty shell of the Story-Webster theory of the "people in the aggregate." It does not seem to bother such modern legal experts that the "campaign to convert the elitist Constitution of 1789 into an egalitarian constitution of popular suffrage" was, in reality, a lawless and bloody revolution which would have made Robespierre envious.

****

Tell you what: You write a constitution and send it to me with the claim that it is now the law of the land and that it makes me free and that I and my family must abide by it or face censure as traitors and enemies of your State. What do you suppose my reaction to your scrap of paper will be? An obscene gesture would be only the first outward sign of dismissal.

The "Constitution" does not make Americans free; it makes them complete and total slaves to a centralized federal government. Does any thinking person imagine that individuals (excluding those held as bondsmen or slaves), in this country were not free before the writing and enactment of the Constitution; that the writing of the Constitution suddenly made a whole nation of individuals "free?" How absurd! But even if Americans were, somehow, "protected" and made miraculously "free" under a corporation's by-laws, the 13th Amendment, the 14th Amendment, and the 16th Amendment, which have been found to be completely fraudulent, renders the entire contract invalid on its face, not only for Americans, but for all the members of the corporation. Do you see now why the President routinely legislates outside the restrictions of their constitution—so called? If any part of a contract is found to be fraudulent, the entire document is dishonored. And the so-called "Constitution" is not considered valid even by the politicians who purport to administer it!

SUPPRESSED INTELLIGENCE REPORTS

******

When King George's subjects known as the Colonies estimated that they had sufficient manpower and firepower, they concluded that George's rules and regulations were no longer tolerable. After dispatching "George and Company," they had a most excellent opportunity to set up a community of individualism and freedom. Unfortunately, this did not happen. Minds locked into the concept of rule talked much about individualism and freedom, but were incapable of envisioning and living it. After lopping off the branches of British grown tyranny, they proceeded to build upon the same root. They brought forth a governmental system of representative democracy with a Constitution, division of powers, and all sorts of checks and balances to "limit" their governmental system, to "control" it. A couple of hundred years later, we know just how successful this attempt was. What is not widely known is that the monstrous growth was inevitable, inherent in the system itself.

THE INMATES ARE IN CHARGE OF THE ASYLUM

A politician is a mentally incompetent person who is elected by the secret votes of other persons who admit, by voting, that they are mentally incompetent. In other words, the asylum is being run by the inmates!

If you vote, you compound the problem by validating the State's power over you! Casting a vote for a politician is akin to driving the getaway car for a gang of bank robbers and putting your stamp of approval on plunder of the "public" treasury. You become an accessory to an on-going monumental crime against all of America!

When a politician proposes to "get the country moving again," what does it mean? Nothing really, but it does have appeal to "patriotism and national pride" and emotionally connects the politician with those he is trying to convince. When a campaigning politician says that he will "create jobs," how is this promise to be translated into action? What do you suppose would happen if one required the politician to explain just exactly how he proposes to create the jobs? Suppose that in his explanation, he is not allowed to posit abstracts as beings. What then would be his answer? How is a job created? There are two ways: Free market or non-market.

Free market method: In addition to providing for his immediate needs, an individual works and produces something of value to another individual. The other individual does the same. A voluntary trade is made. Each, in effect, creates a job for the other on the basis of production and free market supply and demand. Isn't it amazing how rarely that one hears of voluntary trade and mutual exchange for mutual benefit?

Non-market, i.e., political method: A politician does not produce commodity goods or services, and has no production of his (her) own to trade. He (she) "creates jobs" by confiscation and allocation of what others produce. This may be done by distribution of tax dollars, subsidies, grants, regulatory legislation, etc. In all cases, it is the use of initiation of force or coercion favoring some at the expense of others. (If you stole a million dollars and spent it, wouldn't you be increasing demand and "creating jobs" in the area of your spending no less than the area chosen by a politician? Why is it illegal for you to do that which is the paid profession of a politician?)

The only things produced by politicians is misery, poverty and servitude. They survive is by leaching off of people who produce tangible goods.

48

SUPPRESSED INTELLIGENCE REPORTS

Trying to achieve liberty by way of political action is like allowing the government to print money in order to achieve prosperity. It won't work; and it's not right to try. Not only are the means not adapted to the end (in the practical sense) but the morality of such an undertaking is dubious, to say the least. Not only is democratic majority rule a myth that our political rulers wish to sustain, but it depends upon the implicit use of force to impose the policies of the winners on the losers.

.... Just as the way to lessen crime is not to join the ranks of criminals, so the way to lessen the harmful effects of politicians is not to swell their ranks by joining them.

SLAVES OF THE FASCIST STATE

The "slave analogy" illustrates the nature of the State. The condition of slaves relative to their master is more or less the same as that of subjects to the State. The master, by either directly or indirectly (through a foreman) exceeding his natural rights, denies his slaves' natural rights, just as the State, by its very existence, denies the natural rights of its subjects.

The condition of slaves is thus a given before the question of "voting rights" even arises. Their condition indicates that they have a ruler regardless of whether or not the slaves can vote and regardless of whether or not they even want a foreman. The same is true of the subjects of the State.

Suppose, then, that the slaves are granted a choice of, say, two foremen by the master. The slaves may cast ballots to decide which foreman will execute rule over the slaves. The foreman who receives the most votes will be the choice of all the slaves. Presumably, the slaves will each choose whomever he or she thinks is the lesser of the two evils. The situation of the slave thus becomes analogous to that of the subject who has been granted the "right to vote" for his ruler. In light of the slavery analogy the question arises: "What is immoral about choosing the lesser of two evils, if that is the only choice one has under the circumstances?"

First of all, the choice is one which affects the lives of others besides the chooser. Using the slave analogy, the vote of each slave isn't just a choice of which foreman will rule that slave, but is a choice of who will rule all of the slaves. Thus each slave who votes is acting in the capacity of the master respecting his slaves. To vote for a foreman is to take part in the process of other people's enslavement. It should be clear that, by voting, the slave in respect to his peers is going as far beyond his or her natural rights as the master (or the foreman) does respecting his or her slaves.

Moreover, the possibility certainly exists in the slavery analogy that not all the slaves may be in agreement as to which of the two foremen is the lesser of the two evils. Most importantly, some or all of the slaves may decide that the lesser of the two evils is still evil and on this basis refuse to vote. In either case, the immorality of voting is quite obvious.

It is also obvious that assuming one only has the choice of the lesser or greater of the two evils in the slavery analogy is begging the question. As Frank Chodorov once asked, in this regard: "Under what compulsion are we to make such a choice? Why not pass up both of them?"

Indeed there is nothing in the slavery analogy that says the slaves must choose one or the other of the two foremen. By making such a choice the slaves are merely doing yet another thing that the master wants them to do. Instead of choosing either foremen, one or more of the slaves may choose neither. This third choice, also open to the slaves, is a moral one for it doesn't affect coercion toward others, unlike voting, which does.

Furthermore, the refusal to vote is a first step toward restoring individual sovereignty. If the slave does what the master wants him or her to do he or she will forever remain a slave. The master, or the State, wouldn't give his or her slaves the "right to vote" if the slaves could thereby become free. By refusing to vote the slave is not doing what the master wants him or her to do. If most of the slaves refused to vote the master would have to choose the foreman for them. However, the master (and foreman) would then be up against a group that has refused to barter his or her individual sovereignty for the lesser of the two evils the master had originally offered; let alone give it up for nothing. And thus would it be for the State that failed to get barely any of its subjects to participate in the so-called electoral process.

****

STRIKE THE ROOT

There are a thousand hacking at the branches of evil to one who is striking at the root.
—Thoreau

THE ARRIVAL OF ORWELLIAN AMERICA

by Rick Gee

In George Orwell's classic novel 1984, Oceania is in a state of perpetual war with Eurasia. Even though the "Big Brother" state of Oceania insists that such has always been the case, the protagonist, Winston Smith, remembers that the states were in fact at one time aligned. The same is true of the United States and Osama bin Laden/Afghanistan. The CIA provided funding and arms to bin Laden during the decade-long proxy war with the Soviet Union. Now bin Laden, "The Evil One," has become the Goldstein character, who is held up as the "Enemy of the People." And our rulers readily admit that the War on Terrorism will last indefinitely.

To keep the masses in line and to suppress opposition, Oceania developed a language called Newspeak, which actually reduced the number and variety of words in use to render dissenting thought obsolete. Closely related to Newspeak is doublethink, in which someone is conditioned to either say the opposite of what he thinks or think the opposite of what is true.

The U.S. government has engaged in such obfuscations with the passage of the Uniting and Strengthening America Act by Providing Appropriate Tools Required to Intercept and Obstruct Terrorism. Yes, it's the USA PATRIOT Act. Clearly the name of the bill was concocted to fit the acronym. The purpose of this acronym is two-fold. One, it makes it politically dangerous for politicians to vote against it ("He voted against the Patriot Act? Who can we nominate to run opposite this traitor in the next election?"). Two, it stifles opposition among the American people. "You're either with us, or you're with the terrorists."

Since we are all in favor of stopping acts of terrorism, we should all be in favor of this legislation, right? But this legislation – which was not available for members of Congress to read before they had to vote on it – will do nothing to prevent future terrorism and much to increase the power of government over its subjects. The legislation, among other things:

SUPPRESSED INTELLIGENCE REPORTS

* Allows law enforcement agencies to search homes and offices without notifying the owner for days or weeks after, not only in terrorism cases, but in all cases - the so-called "sneak and peek" authority * Allows government agents to collect undefined new information about Web browsing and e-mail * Overrides existing state and federal privacy laws, allowing the FBI to compel disclosure of any kind of records upon the mere claim that they are connected with an intelligence investigation If you believe that the government could never use these unconstitutional powers against you because you're not a Middle Eastern "raghead," you are unfamiliar with history. J. Edgar Hoover's FBI became a de facto domestic political police force. Franklin Delano Roosevelt used the FBI to spy on his political enemies, especially antiwar groups.

The PATRIOT Act does not restrict its provisions to terrorism investigations. In fact, they may be used against anyone, whether or not he is a suspect related to terrorism. On the other hand, the act broadens the definition of terrorism to "an offense that is calculated to influence or affect the conduct of government by intimidation or coercion; or to retaliate against government conduct." While the PATRIOT Act ostensibly protects Americans against terrorism, in reality it protects the government against its own people.

With this new expanded, nebulous definition of terrorism now the law of the land, will I be considered a terrorist because I do not blindly follow everything George W. Bush and John Ashcroft decree; because I dare to write columns that question the actions of government? Do I "intimidate" government functionaries by exposing their duplicitous dealings? Will the editors of Strike-the-Root now be deemed terrorists for publishing my columns?

Earlier this month, John Ashcroft testified before Congress regarding President Bush's Executive Order that allows the president to try "terrorists" before military tribunals rather than in open court. Ashcroft's appearance was largely a dog-and-pony show, a political exercise designed to allow some Democrats on Capitol Hill to criticize the administration without disparaging President Bush directly, something they clearly cannot do in light of Dubya's 90% approval rating.

During the appearance, Ashcroft, who has recently engaged in an authoritarian power grab that would make Torquemada blush, uttered the following: "To those who pit Americans against immigrants, citizens against non-citizens, to those who scare peace-loving people with phantoms of lost liberty, my message is this: your tactics only aid terrorists for they erode our national unity and diminish our resolve. Our efforts have been crafted carefully to avoid infringing on constitutional rights, while saving American lives."

By now, the theme should be clear: you are either with us, or you are with the terrorists. Ashcroft attempts to manipulate "peace-loving people" into doublethink with some crafty doublespeak. It is Ashcroft and his minions who attempt to scare us with their alerts of impending terrorism, always based on "credible information," of course. And unfortunately, the loss of liberty is all too real.

As for his claim that constitutional rights will not be infringed upon and that American lives will be saved, this goes well beyond mere obfuscation; it is an outright lie. We already know that the government failed to save thousands of American lives on September 11, and the Constitution has taken a severe thrashing ever since.

Ashcroft concluded, "Charges of kangaroo courts and shredding the Constitution give new meaning to the term fog of war."

No, Mr. Ashcroft—it is not those who oppose your encroaching police state and global hegemony that perpetrate a "fog of war." It is you and your cohorts in government who wage the war – both the bombing campaigns abroad and the war on liberty at home – who are responsible for the "fog of war." And it is up to the lovers of freedom everywhere to lift the veil of euphemism in which we are assured, as were the people of Oceania, that "War is Peace. Freedom is Slavery. Ignorance is Strength." *******

A version of this column originally appeared in the December 2001 issue of The Valley News. December 28, 2001

Rick Gee resides in paradise, also known as Santa Fe, New Mexico. He writes about liberty, sports, film and other topics for The Valley News.

In addition to being a Root Striker, he is a columnist at anti-state.com and a commentator at LewRockwell.com.

****

We generally agree that the driver of a getaway car is liable for a bank robbery, even if he did not personally wield a gun or threaten force. Similarly, we hold legislators accountable for their unjust laws, political executives accountable for their unjust directives, and judges accountable for their unjust decisions. We do not exonerate these individuals just because they legitimize their actions under the "mask of law." Yet political and bureaucratic personnel rarely participate in law enforcement; they do not strap on guns and apprehend violators. This is left to the police.

Clearly, therefore, condemnation of the State as a criminal gang rests on the view that criminal liability can extend beyond the person who uses, or threatens to use, invasive force. Most of the individuals in government, though not directly involved in aggression, nevertheless "aid and abet" this process. Our theory would be irreparably crippled without this presumption. If criminal accountability is restricted only to direct aggressors, then the vast majority of individuals in the State apparatus, including those at the highest levels of decision-making, must be considered nonaggressors by our standards and hence totally innocent. We could not even regard Hitler or Stalin as aggressors, so long as they did not personally enforce their monstrous orders. The only condemnable persons would be in the police, military, and in other groups assigned to the enforcement of state decrees. All others would be legally innocent (though we might regard them as morally culpable).

Few are willing to accept this bizarre conclusion, but it automatically follows if we refuse to incorporate within our theory some idea of "vicarious liability" defined by Black's Law Dictionary as "indirect legal responsibility; for example, the liability of ... a principal for torts and contracts of agents."

HALF A TRUTH IS STILL A LIE

I am forever astonished at the ability of some people in the so-called "patriot movement" to proclaim the truth only half-way. I mean that whatever they have set in their minds as truth they pass on to others who accept it as gospel, but any other concept outside that envelope of understanding, although quite as valid as any other discovery, is condemned as the "subversive propaganda of communists." It is exactly this failure to accept any new discovery of truth (derived, as you can see, from existing documents which are easily obtainable) as having validity that prevents Americans from shedding the yoke of slavery. If you think you are not a slave as you labor under your chains, you will never seek the means for attaining liberty. Get this through your heads: Slavery was guaranteed and protected under both the original and the corporate Constitutions of the United States.

"Patriots" hold dear the words of the "founding fathers" almost as fervently as they do Bible text. If a founding father said something during the building of this nation, then it must be "the truth," particularly as it applies to the so-called "Constitution."

But Patrick Henry, who urged his fellow Americans to proclaim liberty by arming themselves for the coming battle with the king's armies, also said this about those who wrote and enacted the so-called Constitution:

"What right had they to say, We, the People? My political curiosity, exclusive of my anxious solicitude for the public welfare, leads me to ask: Who authorized them to speak the language of We, the People...? The people gave them no power to use their name. That they exceeded their power is perfectly clear."

Patrick Henry, Son of Thunder

They exceeded their power before they wrote it, they exceeded their power as they wrote it, and have they exceeded their power ever since. Common sense tells us that they did so and continue to do so to deceive the rest of America. But patriots, who find this suggestion contrary to all they think they know and understand, will condemn this statement as "communist propaganda" or some such, and they will discount it without ever investigating to see whether or not it is true. The reason "patriots" fear such statements is because they clearly show that the so-called "Constitution" was not and is not the "people's Constitution" but is a set of by-laws intended only as a set of rules regulating the actions of the newly-formed federal government, the truth of which is attested to not only by Henry's and Jefferson's statements, but by documents which are readily available in any library. In the context of the "Constitution" being a contract, then, "We, the people" meant only those who agreed to and signed the by-laws, nothing more, nothing less. During the framing of the so-called constitution, to be considered one of "the people" one had to own property as real property and a certain number of other human beings as slaves. If you held no property, you were not one of "We, the people."

Woman held no property and could not vote. Most men held no property and could not vote. Slaves, white or black or any other color, could not vote even after they were freed. Poor people could not vote. Only rich land holders/slave owners were considered to be "people." And this concept holds true today. Since we do not own property, we are not "people." We are chattel, the property of the elite rich. Before the introduction of the "Constitution," all eligible Americans were "electors." Now the criminals allow us to believe we are "voters" and that voting for an "elector" under the so-called constitution, is a "right." But if Americans are free and voting is a right, why must you register in order to cast your decision? If you must register, then it is a privilege, NOT a right and you are NOT free! If you don't register, then you don't vote. How can you call that freedom?

If you have to register your automobile or home, then they do not belong to you; they belong to the State in which they are "registered." If you register each of your children with a "birth certificate," then those children do NOT belong to you; they belong to those who purchase the certificates from the hospital, which, by the way, are legally known as "ports of entry"—as into a foreign country (you figure it out). Hint: it is 10 miles square.

The purchasers of your birth certificate and your child's birth certificate are the Federal Reserve Bank and the U. S. Department of Commerce. You become a negotiable commodity. They own you, your home, your consumable goods, your children and all your life energy until death as pay back in the form of taxation on the so-called "national debt" which they created out of thin air in the first place. Those "Federal Reserve Notes" you think are "money" are really nothing more than fancy IOUs! They are, quite literally, warehouse receipts for goods delivered! No matter what the politicians claim, we can't "pay down" a debt with paper IOUs. No matter what you think you believe, you cannot "buy" consumable goods with paper IOUs. No matter what the politicians try to implant in your head, the over-collection of "taxes" (the "surplus") they claim they will return to you are nothing more than IOUs. More DEBT for you! By offering you the money, they validate the IRS. By accepting the money you validate the oppressive taxing system they have established to enslave and rob you. No matter who keeps the money, THEY win! Get it?

One legal researcher stumbled onto the fact that a copy of every American's birth certificate is held by the Commerce Department of the federal government and was astonished to learn that a dozen foreign governments had actually endorsed his birth certificate in much the same way you would sign the back of a check for deposit.

These foreign nations, with which he had never had any contact, had endorsed the back of his birth certificate as though they were transferring ownership of the man, like his birth certificate was a negotiable security. This opened the door for discovery of what must be one of the most closely guarded secrets in the history of our corrupt secret government.

When the federal government became insolvent in 1933, it (under the communist, Franklin D. Roosevelt) pledged the life of every single man, woman and child in America as collateral for the so-called "national debt" through a series of secret financial manipulations.

To do this, they created a statutory, non-living artificial "person" on paper. This "person" is called a Strawman. When most Americans voluntarily accept the formal identity assigned by the government (social security and others), they actually assume the identity of the strawman which the federal government has created. The federal government then "sells" you to its money lenders and you are required by covert contract to work the rest of your life to pay for loans made by the criminals you call "politicians." They have assigned a value of one million dollars to each "person" they own and control through the strawman! They expect that each person will pay them $1,000,000 through some form of taxes during their entire life!

Is it all making sense now? Do you want to go out and purchase a firearm and a wheelbarrow full of ammunition? Well, don't! Instead, send $1.00 cash or a #10 self-addressed, stamped envelope (34¢) to: C-Media, Box 448, Jacksonville, Oregon 97530, and ask for information concerning "The Commerce Game Exposed." Learn how to get control of your strawman and how to use it to your advantage!!

****

To be born is to be born into servitude. As Stirner astutely observes: "Even at birth the children belong to the State, and to the parents only in the name of the State...." (The Ego And

His Own, pg-109) The significance of this observation is monumental. The ramifications and repercussions of the philosophical premise of all persons owned by an abstract (god) are all encompassing and affects thinking and life in ways and magnitudes you may never have considered.

The penchant and inclination toward the making of gods, placing real individual as property, appears to be deeply ingrained in the psyche of nearly all of mankind since the beginning. Though conscious mind frequently sees the folly of it, unconscious rules the day and few there be who ever dismiss these dominant anti individual fallacies that are passed from generation to generation to wreak havoc upon all areas of life. Minimal focus and brief inquiry reveals that "God," "Nation," "State," "Man," "Society" and the like are not things of substance, not corporeal stuff, not "superior beings," and not causal things, yet most minds are dominated by an emotional commitment to deeply seated feelings to the contrary. They think in abstracts, talk in abstracts and act in the name of abstracts, and are completely oblivious to the fact that they are merely reactively uttering programmed responses while imagining they are thinking independently.

If you were to ask a loving mother if she wished her son were dead, chances are she would be appalled at the question and adamantly make it known that she would find no value in such a situation. This is her conscious conclusion, but does it cover the entire situation? Suppose this son is killed in a war and the mother then says, "I'm proud that my son gave his life for his country." Does this not clearly indicate a value in the demise of her son? Is not "sacrifice" held in high value by many, if not most? Does not war serve as a viable means to fulfill this value in high form? Does it not logically follow that war is valued by many even as they consciously denounce it while unconsciously seeking it?

If we were to put the actual condition in words, the loving mother's answer to the question about valuing her son's death would be "yes AND no"- or "no AND yes." This seemingly extreme example points up not only the dual value system, but simultaneously demonstrates the dominant side of it as "country" is the revered "beneficiary" as the loving mother gains self value in her belief system by the "sacrifice."

I know of no word in the English language that gets more discussion time than the word freedom; nor any concept that seems to be more pursued with less accomplishment. Where the intelligence of some or many is more than sufficient to bring about a walk on the moon and technical innovations that stagger the imagination, the idea of freedom seems to be an ever-illusive something that is more a matter of subjective rhetoric than objective demonstration. What's wrong?

There are those who say we are all born free and all we need do is to believe and declare it. If this is the case, then all controversy over the concept, freedom, ceases with the declaration. However, it appears that such a declaration stands only as a declaration and the condition is no different than before the declaration; which points out that such a subjective declaration does not create objective circumstance.

There are those who contend that freedom is a valued and distant goal that requires many steps to reach; that there is a lengthy and complex procedure to follow and that departure from this delineated route means certain failure to achieve the valued end.

If freedom is simply a matter of subjective declaration, then each individual is master of his own situation. There is no controversy. There is nothing to complain about, and there is nothing more to say about it except to declare that freedom exists. Is this the actual condition? Or is the term and concept, freedom, necessarily referenced to an objective circumstance or merits no discussion at all? As for a long and multi-stepped route to freedom, this is contrary to objective circumstance which is recognized by the principle of "is or is not" without graduation between absolute conditions. As surely as an alleged existent either exists or does not exists, no relationship between existents can exist on a different plane independent of said existents upon which the relationship depends. Ergo, freedom either is, or is not.

It is human nature to seek and hold to what one values, and to discard that which one does not value. Are we to assume that for century after century non freedom and war prevails with few or none valuing it? We must either assume a gross incompetence to achieve a simple end, or consider that maybe there are circumstances here that have not be factored into the equation, thus cause goes unaddressed and resolution denied. Think for a moment of the "war hero." Does he not value his status, a value that he could not seek and achieve in freedom and harmony? What of the mother who is "proud that her son gave his life for his country?" Has she not achieved a value born of "great sacrifice" even as she mourns the loss?

What of the mother who sorely grieves the loss of a much loved son lost in battle? Did she try to dissuade him from volunteering? Did she hide him from the conscription officers? Or did she go along with it all because her highest value was not the life of her son to her or to himself, but lay in his value as "means" to the "goal" of the abstract "country?"

The extreme difficulty in conveying what I strive to convey is that understanding requires some fundamental understanding of the mind; and it is precisely the mind that is subordinated, and in effect, given to believe that it cannot understand itself, that it is to accept the programmed dictates without question and obey the "wisdom" of the "superior beings." Here, I am obliged to repeat for emphasis that I'm not talking about a conscious condition consciously known and openly available for direct examination and decision making.

Were this a conscious condition, it still would not immediately solve the problem, but it would be more available to remedy. However, it is not usually consciously known, and the subconscious domination is often most subtle and difficult to detect. It is not a condition of awareness of alternatives and making a conscious choice. It is an ingrained condition of philosophical absolutism that leaves the mind with the conclusion that there is no alternative, no choice, that the "way things are" (philosophically) is objective reality itself and one must yield to it. Personal modification of the prevailing philosophy of subservience is often regarded as an alternative while the base premise remains undisturbed.

Mind is prepared to be receptive to a list of obligations and values not expressed or implied to be of some individual's making, but explicitly or implicitly determined by "something" from outside of individual. These are regarded as "standards" of "morally right," "morally wrong," "success," and "failure," etc. Though one might on their own select some of the "standards" of behavior independently of external influence, the "ought condition" exists in a package form of dictates expressed or implied to be universal and objective values. It is this very mixture of individualistic elements psychologically combined with the anti individual elements that is most influential in "selling the package." Subordination is the main ingredient in the mix. It is from and within this "ought condition" that one judges others and self. And to measure one's self against the undefined goals and "universal values" is to find one's self always falling short and remaining in the role of subservience as taught from birth and reinforced by environment.

I am moved to recall a childhood incident which in retrospect, I see as a benchmark in my thinking, for it is recollection of my first very serious effort to understand by questioning. I was taught that "it is more blessed to give than to receive." It was "understood" that being "blessed" was a "good thing," and all those I knew, including self, wished to "do the good and be good." It occurred to me that for one to give and "do the good," there had to be someone to receive. If the giving was "good," does this not make the receiving "bad?" If giving meant that one was "blessed," doesn't it follow that receiving is not being "blessed;" that is, to give and be "good" is to rob the receiver of being "blessed" - which is "bad." Thus do we arrive at the premise of "good" AND "bad" that meld into one as a mental state of limbo without definition and without determination.

The "good AND bad" circumstance indicates allegiance to a "dual reality" wherein there is no clear and concise identification of real individual and real individual goals. This leaves the person forever attempting an impossible emotional balancing act between self and non self. All interest is self interest, but in the distortions of the "dual reality" this fact takes on disfavorable connotations and is denied with conflict and confusion reigning. The simple, but oft denied fact is all ends are individually chosen but are frequently attributed to something non individual and non real, i.e., a "superior being." Herein lies the internal and external division and psychological "justification" for oppression.

No matter what conscious mind might declare, a feeling of low self esteem and low self confidence is a judgment of self against imaginary "objective standards." Undefined and distorted language usage is a major part of this self-devaluing package. There is no escape from it with it. It must be dismissed and fall away or the mind remains held in a prison without walls. This is a choice we all must make - and default is a choice.

GOVERNMENT SCHOOLS AND CHURCHES ORGANIZED UNDER MILITARY TRIBUNALS CAN TEACH YOU NOTHING OF VALUE!

. . . Without a doubt, the most effective method by which the State creates a mystique is through control of education. The evolution of compulsory State-controlled schooling reads like a history of political maneuvering, in which the goal of teaching children literacy skills plays a minor role. Public education is by no means inept or disordered as it is made out to be. It is an ice-cold, superb machine designed to perform one very important job. The problem is not that public schools do not work well, but rather that they do. The first goal and primary function of schools is not to educate good people, but good citizens. It is the function which we normally label "State indoctrination."

"The simple step of a courageous individual is not to take part in the falsehood. One word of truth outweighs the world."

Alexander Solzhenitsyn

******

SUPPRESSED INTELLIGENCE REPORTS

If We Must Die

Claude McKay: (1919)

If we must die, let it not be like hogs

Hunted and penned in an inglorious spot,

While round us bark the mad and hungry dogs,

Making their mock at our accursed lot.

If we must die, O let us nobly die,

So that our precious blood may not be shed

In vain; then even the monsters we defy

Shall be constrained to honor us though dead!

O kinsmen we must meet the common foe!

Though far outnumbered let us show us brave,

And for their thousand blows deal one deathblow!

What though before us lies the open grave?

Like men we'll face the murderous, cowardly pack,

Pressed to the wall, dying, but fighting back!

*****

Ruby Ridge. Waco. Nothing more need be said.

Until all Americans unite with a single agenda, a single purpose, and are armed with truth, we will merely be confounded observers standing at the bottom of a dark, deep pit, fervently hoping to save the world, but really doing little more than breaking the fall of compatriots who are pushed in on top of us. Only by uniting in an especial effort devoid of conflicting paradigms and pretentious pedantic will we be able to form the human ladder upon which we may ascend to freedom. That is the real and true meaning of freedom: individuals united to defeat ignorance—created and perpetuated by federal militarized schools and churches—the eternal enemy of all humankind.

"Man is but a microbe lost in immensity. He peers about him and, by the uncertain light of his small intelligence, reads here a word, there a line in the great Book of Nature, and putting together these scattered fragments, makes a "Faith" which he defends with fanatical fervor. Dare to call in question its most inconsequential thesis and you are branded as an heretic; deny it in toto and you are denounced as an enemy of the Almighty! The curses of Brother Balaam no longer kill the body, but they are expected to play sad havoc with the soul! When the priest of Baal was en route to Moab's capital for cursing purposes an angel tried to withhold him, and even his burro rebuked him, but neither angels nor asses are exempt from the law of evolution. Now when a priest or preacher lets slip a curse at those who presume to question the supernal wisdom of his creed, the angels are supposed to flap their wings until Heaven is filled with flying feathers, while every blatant jackass who takes his spiritual fodder at that particular rick unbraids his ears and brays approvingly."

Last paragraph of Volume One; Brann the Iconoclast

SO YOU BELIEVE YOU ARE FREE? SO YOU BELIEVE YOU HAVE "RIGHTS?"

Edward Mandel House (a Jew) to Woodrow Wilson (a Jew): Chattel

Edward Mandell House had this to say in a private meeting with Woodrow Wilson (President) [1913-1921]

"[Very] soon, every American will be required to register their biological property in a national system designed to keep track of the people and that will operate under the ancient system of pledging. By such methodology, we can compel people to submit to our agenda, which will effect our security as a chargeback for our fiat paper currency.

"Every American will be forced to register or suffer being able to work and earn a living. They will be our chattel, and we will hold the security interest over them forever, by operation of the law merchant under the scheme of secured transactions. Americans, by unknowingly or unwittingly delivering the bills of lading to us will be rendered bankrupt and insolvent, secured by their pledges.

"They will be stripped of their rights and given a commercial value designed to make us a profit and they will be none the wiser, for not one man in a million could ever figure our plans and, if by accident one or two should figure it out, we have in our arsenal plausible deniability.

"After all, this is the only logical way to fund government, by floating liens and debt to the registrants in the form of benefits and privileges.

"This will inevitably reap to us huge profits beyond our wildest expectations and leave every American a contributor to this fraud which we will call "Social Insurance." Without realizing it, every American will unknowingly be our servant, however begrudgingly.

"The people will become helpless and without any hope for their redemption and we will employ the high office of the President of our dummy corporation to foment this plot against America."

Social Security is a State driven excise tax program. This state driven excise program collects the libel due by the State to the United States under the State Plan. This State plan, is the collection by devious means, of a perennial direct tax, imposed by the United States in Congress Assembled on August 14, 1935. This State driven Program is just another fiscal program implemented in the 1930's to support the bankrupted privately charted debenture center, better known as the Federal Reserve Banking System.

This Banking System had to close it's doors for On March 6th, for seven days, back in 1933. This banking system reopened it's doors for public business on March 14th, issuing notes of public indebtedness as currency. To pay the interest of these notes, the United States in Congress Assembled had to implement a perennial program for its fiscal social security. This program of social security is known as the Income Tax Act of August 14th, 1935. Whose social security was to be secured? Americans, or the General Fund of the United States in

SUPPRESSED INTELLIGENCE REPORTS

Congress Assembled?

Seventy-five years later, this promise of social security comes at a great cost to most Americans who participated in this program of funding the General Funds account of the United States in Congress Assembled. The United States, the third Party debt collector, takes the bacon and eggs, and leaves the government pensioner with nothing but debt.

Social Security is a lucrative Ponzi scheme. And I assure you that no politician will ever try to "undo" it. If it seems to you that this concept is self-destructive; that those who devised the plan to destroy Americans will also eventually destroy themselves when there is no more money to be stolen from the people, you are right. Why then, would anyone with any intelligence at all do such a thing? You may be interested, or amazed, or horrified, or even angered (if you are a Jew), to learn that Adolf Frankenberger Shicklegruber Hitler (himself a Jew) had it all figured out way back in 1923 when, obviously referring as much to his own destructive tendencies as to what he perceived to be the destructive behavior of Jews in general, he uttered these words:

"The truth," he said, "is, indeed, as you once wrote: one can only understand the Jew when one knows what his ultimate goal is. And that goal is, beyond world domination, the annihilation of the world. He must wear down all the rest of mankind, he persuades himself, in order to prepare a paradise on earth. He has made himself believe that only he is capable of this great task, and, considering his ideas of paradise, that is certainly so. But one sees, if only in the means which he employs, that he is secretly driven to something else. While he pretends to himself to be elevating mankind, he torments men to despair, to madness, to ruin. If a halt is not ordered, he will destroy all men. His nature compels him to that goal, even though he dimly realizes that he must thereby destroy himself. There is no other way for him; he must act thus. This realization of the unconditional dependence of his own existence upon that of his victims appears to me to be the main cause for his hatred. To be obliged to try and annihilate us with all his might, but at the same time to suspect that it must lead inevitably to his own ruin, therein lies, if you will, the tragedy of Lucifer."

FOR WHOM THE BELL TOLLS

The Bell doth toll for him that thinkes it doth; and though it intermit againe, yet from that minute, that that occasion wrought upon him, hee is united to God. Who casts not up his Eye to the Sunne when it rises? but who takes off his Eye from a Comet when that breakes out? Who bends not his eare to any bell, which upon any occasion rings? but who can remove it from that bell, which is passing a peece of himselfe out of this world?

No man is an Iland, intire of it selfe; every man is a peece of the Continent, a part of the maine; if a Clod bee washed away by the Sea, Europe is the lesse, as well as if a Promontorie were, as well as if a Mannor of thy friends or of thine owne were; any mans death diminishes me, because I am involved in Mankinde; And therefore never send to know for whom the bell tolls; It tolls for thee.

Neither can we call this a begging of Miserie or a borrowing of Miserie, as though we were not miserable enough of our selves, but must fetch in more from the next house, in taking upon us the Miserie of our Neighbours. Truly it were an excusable covetousnesse if wee did; for affliction is a treasure, and scarce any man hath enough of it. No man hath affliction enough that is not matured, and ripened by it, and made fit for God by that affliction. If a man carry treasure in bullion, or in a wedge of gold, and have none coined into currant Monies, his treasure will not defray him as he travells.

Tribulation is Treasure in the nature of it, but it is not currant money in the use of it, except wee get nearer and nearer our home, Heaven, by it. Another man may be sicke too, and sick to death, and this affliction may lie in his bowels, as gold in a Mine, and be of no use to him; but this bell, that tells me of his affliction, digs out, and applies that gold to mee: if by this consideration of anothers danger, I take mine owne into contemplation, and so secure my selfe, by making my recourse to my God, who is our onely securitie.

John Donne

****

We may never, in our lifetimes, discover the whole real truth concerning the evil agenda to strip humankind of all freedom but, sooner or later, if you read far enough, as I have done, you will discover a thread of both similarity and familiarity running through the reports; the same things repeated over and over by different people at different times in human history, and in different ways—what I call, "the inkling of truth," as we are able to perceive it. Whether you choose to act on the information or not is solely your business.

PART TWO

LOST CIVILIZATIONS

Nearly all of the 'lost civilization' theories have become associated with the legend of Plato's 'Atlantis', thus the concept and its study have been largely ignored by the serious academic community.

Yet ironically it is probably the legend of Atlantis itself, however fanciful, that has provided the foundation for the belief in the existence in a prehistoric civilization to account for the out-of-place knowledge and artifacts detailed in much of modern literature.

Atlantis was first mentioned by Plato in his work, the 'Timaeus', in which he detailed the mighty island of Atlantis and its proud peoples who, is the course of "a single day and night" were swept by earthquake and flood into the depths of the ocean.' Despite his pupil Aristotle's belief that the story was fantasy, invented to moralize on the nature and consequences of human ambition, Plato was adamant that the former existence of Atlantis was a matter of historical fact.

Whatever the truth, the legend certainly was considered factual for many centuries with even mediaeval sea-charts showing unknown 'Atlantis' islands.

Yet if there was a 'lost civilization' (regardless of its connection with or not to the Atlantis legend) it would have had to have had a home, and any identified location would have to provide supporting evidence that a civilization actually did live there, for, as Egyptologist Mark Lehner rightly points out, without evidence of remains, it would be safer to conclude that there was no former civilization, and the purported clues to its existence would have to be explained in some other way.

SUPPRESSED INTELLIGENCE REPORTS

Many locations for the lost civilization have been suggested with many of them centering on the Mediterranean area. A Dr. James Mavor set out one theory in his 1969 book, believing that the lost peoples were a Minoan civilization. This followed earlier claims first set out in the 1930s by Greek scientists Dr Angelos Galanopoulos and Professor Spyridon Marinatos .

There is certainly some evidence to support Thera, an island near Crete in the Mediterranean, being the location of an early civilization. Professor Marinatos, under the auspices of the Archaeological Society at Athens, began a systematic excavation of a town on the island, Akrotiri in 1967, after evidence of early habitation had been discovered there in the second half of the 19th century.

These excavations confirmed that Akrotiri had been one of the most important prehistoric settlements of the Aegean, and the various imported items discovered indicated a wide network of external relations. Not only as Akrotiri in contact with nearby Crete but it also communicated with mainland Greece, the Dodecanese, Cyprus, Syria and Egypt.

However, it appeared that the town's life came to an abrupt end in the last quarter of the 17th century BCE when the inhabitants were forced to abandon their homes as a result of severe earthquakes. An eruption of the island-volcano Thera followed, with volcanic materials covering the entire island and the town itself, preserving the buildings and their contents forming an intriguing time capsule just like as at Pompeii.

Despite evidence of early civilization, the evidence was not early enough, with the first signs of habitation being from the late Neolithic times (c. 4th millennium BCE.) Attention therefore turned to Crete itself, Thera's much larger neighbor, and a popular choice for the home of the 'missing' civilization.

A ceramic disc had been found at Phaistos on Crete which was around 3700 years old, however made from a clay not indigenous to the island, indicating that Crete had certainly been visited by that time. Indeed, other evidence suggests that the island was in fact occupied at least by 6000BCE; indicating the existence of a sea faring people who had boats that could be rowed out into open sea.

Whenever the civilization started, history records that by 1500BCE Crete had become the centre of a seafaring empire. However, within a very short time, this empire collapsed along with its infrastructure. In all probability this collapse was caused by the eruption of a volcano that destroyed the nearby island of Thera and also deposited layers of ash that would have destroyed harvests for decades. The eruption is also known to have triggered off a substantial tidal wave.

These events appear to fit the story handed down by Plato of the island paradise, Atlantis. Indeed the volcano at Thera erupted exactly 900 years before Solon received the original story of Atlantis from Egyptian priests leading to some concluding that Plato might have got his figures wrong; he should have referred to Atlantis being destroyed 900 years previously, not 9000 years. There were other indications that Crete could have been the legendary Atlantis. Crete was well known to the Egyptians as 'Keftui,' a land that was "the way to other islands and the continent beyond" exactly as Plato described Atlantis.

Not so, retorted Dr. Jurgen Spanuth, who was familiar with Plato's account of Atlantis. "Neither Thera nor Crete lies in the Atlantic … Neither island lies at the mouth of a great river, neither was swallowed up by the sea and vanished … in fact this great breakthrough in archaeology is a bubble that burst long ago."

Spanuth wasn't having any nonsense about some mythical lost continent lying somewhere in the Mediterranean. Absolutely not. No, as far as he was concerned, Atlantis was to be found on the sunken islands near Heligoland off the northwest German coast.

He attempted to prove his theory in his 1976 book 'Atlantis of the North' but, of course, could not.

History advises us of other submerged archaeological remains in the European area. Pliny the Elder and Strabo make reference to the Etruscan city of Spina in the Adriatic, which was once a thriving metropolis of trade and culture, but now completely submerged. Similarly, Dioscuria, an ancient Greek port of considerable size is now beneath the surface of the Black Sea. (1)

Other nominations for the location of 'Atlantis' within the Mediterranean have included a site off the coast of Morocco where scuba divers chasing fish discovered a well-built 9mile long under water wall traversing an underwater mountain. These ruins were investigated by Dr. J. Thorne who also noted the existence of roads going still further down the mountain into the inky depths of the sea.

However, T. C. Lethbridge, a Cambridge archaeologist and psychical researcher, believed that the missing civilization's home could have been located at Tartessos, which lay between two rivers in southern Spain, just outside the straits of Gibraltar (the Pillars of Hercules.) It is believed that the Carthaginians conquered this rich and civilized city before being destroyed by the 6th Century BCE, however it was reported to have written records that went back to 6000 year before its disappearance (2).

However, despite these romantic notions, there is no real evidence that Europe or its environs could have been the location of the missing civilization. Indeed Plato, who had suggested the idea of an Atlantis, had actually stated that the alleged colony lay beyond the 'Pillars of Hercules' at Gibraltar. And there appears to be some evidence that it may well have done.

The Azores are a group of islands lying 'beyond Gibraltar' that have frequently been proposed as a possible location of the lost civilization.

The first person to make such a proposal was Ignatius Donnelly (1831-1901). Donnelly was a respected statesman, who served in the US Congress from 1863 to 1869 and wrote several works, including a treatise on 'Atlantis, the Antediluvian World.' In that work he stated:

"Deep sea soundings have been made by ships of different nations; the United States ship Dolphin, the German frigate Gazelle, and the British ships Hydra, Porcupine and Challenger have mapped out the bottom of the Atlantic, and the result is the revelation of a great elevation, reaching from a point on the coast of the British Islands southwardly to the coast of South America, at Cape Orange, thence southeastwardly to the coast of Africa and thence southwardly to Tristan d'Acunha. ... The submerged land ... rises about 9000 feet above the great Atlantic depths around it, and in the Azores, St. Paul's Rocks, Ascension, and Tristan d'Acunha it reaches the surface of the ocean." (3).

"Evidence that this elevation was once dry land is found in the fact that the 'inequalities, the mountains and valley's of its surface, could never have been produced in accordance with any laws for the deposition of sediment, nor by submarine elevation; but, on the contrary, must have been carved by agencies acting above the water level." (4) Donnelly concluded that the area was the probable location of the missing Atlantis.

The then British Prime Minister, William Gladstone, was so impressed with Donnelly's finding's that he sent a letter of appreciation on publication of the book, and even went so far as to request that the British Parliament approve the use of the Royal Navy to search the area for evidence of the lost civilization. Unfortunately for Donnelly, the fleet was engaged elsewhere at the time and so the search never took place. (Unfortunately for Shakespeare, Donnelly also became famous for discovering a cipher in the bard's work suggesting that he had not written all that he was credited for, and that Francis Bacon was the true author of some of the texts.)

The Azores, themselves, are constantly subject to volcanic activity; pictures taken by the Space Shuttle and show volcanic smoke over Pico Island. Altogether there are five active volcanoes situated in the Azores area, and it may well be that such volcanic activity could account for the disappearance of an entire civilization just as it had in Crete.

Volcanic activity cannot just make living conditions untenable, but is also known to have a significant impact on the land and seascape. For example, in 1808 a volcano rose in San Jorge to a height of several thousand feet, and in 1811 a volcanic outpouring created a large island which was called Sambrina during its short above-water existence before it sank again beneath the sea. The Azore islands of Corvo and Flores have also constantly changed shape over the centuries, with large parts of Corvo presently under the sea (5).

More recently, on 14th November 1963, the skipper of a fishing boat off the south coast of Iceland radioed his base to report a large cloud of black smoke rising from the sea. He and his crew went on to watch as a huge explosion sent rocks hurtling into the sky, before a black land form emerged from the ocean depths. Within twenty-four hours the new island was higher than a house, and within a week its peak was 200ft above sea level.

Eruptions continued and, by 1967, the new island, named Surtsey (after the Norse fire god Surtur), had reached a height of 500 foot and was over a mile long. Today, colonized by birds and vascular plants, the island stands as proof that new land can emerge from the depths as quickly as an old one can sink into legend:- and there is evidence to suggest that some of the land now under water around the Azores was once above sea level, lending further support to the idea that these islands could have been the home of a lost civilization.

But for a civilization, there would not only have to be land but lost artifacts discovered on that land, and, again there is some evidence that such artifacts have been found. One such find was made by the crew of the SS Jesmond, a British merchant vessel of 1,495 tons that set off for New Orleans from Messina in Sicily at the end of the nineteenth century. In March 1882 the ship passed through the Straits of Gibraltar into the open sea. Some 200 miles west of Madeira, and a similar distance south of the Azores, the crew observed numerous dead fish and muddied waters. Later the same day smoke was observed, although it was assumed to be from another vessel. The following day, there were even thicker dead deposits of fish and the smoke was more visible, appearing to come from a land mass where charts and maps indicated there should be open waters.

The Captain of the Jesmond, David Robson, (Master's Certificate No 27911 in the Queen's

SUPPRESSED INTELLIGENCE REPORTS

Merchant Marine), cast anchor about 12 miles from the newly formed landmass, but far from sinking thousands of fathoms as the maps indicated, the anchor hit the sea floor after only seven fathoms.

Robson subsequently took a landing party ashore the new island to explore. When the ship ended its journey and docked in New Orleans and Robson gave an account of his findings to a reporter from the Times Picayune. He described how they had uncovered crumbling remains of massive walls and recovered artifacts including "bronze swords, rings, mallets, carvings of heads and figures of birds and animals, and two vases or jars with fragments of bone, and one cranium almost entire … [and] what appeared to be a mummy enclosed in a stone case… encrusted with volcanic deposit so as to be scarcely distinguished from the rock itself (6).

Robson advised the reporters who examined his finds that he intended to donate them to the British Museum, however at that point verification of these claims becomes difficult for the log of the SS Jesmond along with the offices of the ship's owners, 'Watts, Watts and Company' was destroyed during the London blitz of September 1940. The British Museum now has no record of any such donation from Robson (7).

Despite this lack of corroboration, there is other supporting evidence of Robson's discoveries. The unfortunately named Captain James Newdick of the steam ship Westbourne was sailing from Marseilles to New York during the same period when it reported sighting a large uncharted island in the area where Robson had landed. Other captains also reported floating fish which were eaten by the sailors, indicating that the fish's demise was sudden and not the result of some epidemic disaster (8).

History has also revealed that just as lands have emerged from the depths in that area, other land now under water was once above sea-level. One such piece of evidence was uncovered during the 1898 laying of a transatlantic cable . As during earlier attempts, the cable snapped and the workers were required to pull it to the surface for repairs. This incident occurred some 500 miles to the north of the Azores.

Whilst searching for the cable, the sea floor in the area was found to be composed of rough peaks, pinnacles and deep valleys, more reminiscent of land than the expected sea bottom. Grappling irons brought up rock specimens from a depth of 1700 fathoms. These rocks proved to be tachylyte – vitreous basaltic lava that cools above water under atmospheric pressure (9).

According to Pierre Termier, a French geologist who made a study of the incident, if the lava had solidified under water it would have been crystalline instead of vitreous (10).

Termier further surmised that the lava had been submerged under water soon after cooling, as evidenced by the relative sharpness of the material brought up. Although it cannot be ascertained exactly when this occurred, it was certainly within the last 15,000 years as lava decomposes in that time. Further evidence of more recent underwater activity comes from a discovery in 1923 when technicians from a Western Telegraph ship searching for a lost cable in the Atlantic detected that the rising ocean bed had thrown up the cable by 2.25 miles in only twenty-five years (11).

In 1949, Professor M. Ewing of Columbia University was exploring the mid-Atlantic ridge. At a depth of between two and three and a half miles, he discovered prehistoric beach sand.

65

This puzzled Ewing, as sand, being the product of erosion, should be nonexistent on the seabed. The conclusion reached was that either the land sank, or the ocean level was much lower in a past epoch (12).

There are other interesting finds. In the course of a submarine probe by the Geological Society of America in 1949, about a ton of limestone discs were lifted from the bed of the Atlantic, just south of the Azores Island chain. Their average size was about 6 inches with a thickness of 1.5 inches. The discs had a peculiar cavity in their centre. On the outside they were relatively smooth, but, in the cavities, they were rough. These 'seabiscuits' as they were called, did not appear to be a natural formation and could not be identified. According to the Lamont Geological Observatory (Columbia University) "the state of lithification of the limestone suggests that it may have been lithified under subaerial conditions and that the seamount may have been an island within the past 12,000 years." (13).

Other claims that the Azores may have been the location of a lost civilization were supported by alleged sightings in the area of underwater buildings and entire 'cities' made from aircraft as far back as 1942. These sightings first started when air ferry pilots flying from Brazil to Dakar glimpsed what appeared to be a submerged city on the western slope of mountains in the mid-Atlantic ridge.

However, despite all of this, there is no conclusive evidence that the Azores were ever home to a large technologically advanced civilization at any time in its past. There are, however, other possible locations for sightings of submerged architectural remains have been noted off Boa Vista Island in the Cape Verde Island chain. The Canaries have also been proposed as a possible location given that when the Spanish conquerors of those islands arrived they found remains of buildings and ancient cities, yet the Guanche's, who lived on them, were merely a stone age people who were no longer capable of constructing anything more than simple huts.

It would appear that the options for identifying a potential home for any lost civilization running out. Yet, as with the Azores, evidence of its remains could be hidden underwater.

That was certainly the vision of an American seer born into a small farming family in Kentucky, USA, in the last quarter of the nineteenth century. As a young boy, this seer, Edgar Cayce, would often tell his parents that he had been having strange visions, including talking to dead relatives. These events continued throughout his early years and later in his youth Edgar began entering self-induced trances. As a teenager he used these states to suggest cures for any ailments he may have been suffering from, and later he increased his activities to enter trance states to assist others who approached him for medical advice. By 1910, Edgar Cayce had become famous throughout America as a trance healer, psychic and Seer.

With a growing reputation, Cayce began individual 'life readings' for clients before making more prophetic visions affecting the whole of mankind. Such predictions included The Second World War, Californian earthquakes and the submersal of New York and Japan.

One of his more intriguing prophecies stated that Plato's legendary Atlantis would rise from the sea in 1968 or 1969 at a small Pacific atoll called Bimini. This prophecy led to great excitement and gave new impetus for the search for the legendary island.

The idea of Atlantis rising from the bottom of the ocean is not as ridiculous as it first sounds. As noted above, there is much evidence of land rising from the sea, however this has normally been associated with volcanic activity, which would surely destroy any traces of civilization and Cayce was clear that Atlantis itself would arise, not its remains spewed out by an angry volcano. However, there is evidence that land can rise and fall without associated volcanic activity.

Falcon (or Jack-In-The-Box Island) had been discovered in the South Pacific in 1780 by the Spanish explorer, Maurelle. The Government of Tonga planted over 2000 coconut palms on the island in 1892, however within two years, the trees, along with the island itself, had disappeared beneath the ocean (14). A similar fate befell the fortress of Caravan-Sarai in the Caspian Sea that had been erected in 1135AD only to slowly disappear into the sea. The fortress's very existence turned into legend, however it rose again from the sea floor in 1723 and is still visible (15). Similarly, the Temple of Jupiter-Serapis in the Bay of Naples had been built in 105BC but sank into the Mediterranean only to rise again in 1742AD (16).

The concept of ancient remains rising from the seas was therefore supported by documentary record, so, on hearing Cayce's words, those fascinated by the Atlantis mystery turned their attentions to the Bimini area. And sure enough, in 1968 as predicted, an American pilot, Robert Brush, spotted what appeared to be a strange square shape on the seabed in the very area where Cayce had stated Atlantis would reemerge. This shape had never been observed before, and appeared to support Cayce's vision of Atlantis arising from the ocean floor. Brush managed to photograph this apparent underground structure from the air and later showed the picture to the French born oceanographer, Dimitri Rebikoff.

Rebikoff, who had gained some twenty years experience of underwater exploration in the Mediterranean and was President of the Institute of Underwater Technology, decided to organize an expedition to the site to investigate. He approached Dr J. Manson Valentine, a paleontologist, geologist, underwater archaeologist and former Yale University professor to assist in this expedition.

In 1968 Rebikoff and Valentine discovered that the dark rectangle on the seabed was an ancient building, possibly a temple, but now covered in sea plants. The building itself measured approximately 100 by 75 feet in size and is located near the north end of Andros Island, the largest island in the Bahamas (17).

Rebikoff was well aware that some natural formations can be mistaken for man-made structures, however he commented "nature can make circular shapes and a lot of other shapes, but nature cannot make a square angle – that is always the work of man." Rebikoff was hopeful his discovery might lead to further discovery stating, "the archaeological rule is this – when you find a temple-like structure, there is a city or town around it (18)." Early indications appeared to suggest that this was finally the sunken remains of the missing civilization.

Valentine and Rebikoff donned diving gear and examined the submerged building. They stated they could make out chambers or rooms in the ruins on the seabed and they also noted that the building faced due east to west, resembling the Uxmal Temple of the Turtles in Yukatan.

Determined to prove their archaeological rule, Valentine and Rebikoff extended their underwater quest for other signs for an Atlantis emerging from the sea floor. They were not disappointed. Valentine takes up the story:

"The most exciting piece of evidence that on a grand scale [there] might indeed exist under the seas of our hemisphere [a lost city] came on the second day of September 1968, when the writer, diving in three fathoms off the north west coast of North Bimini, was amazed to discern an extensive pavement of rectangular and polygonal flat stones of varying size and thickness, obviously shaped and accurately aligned to form a convincing artifactual pattern.

"These stones had evidently lain submerged over a long span of time, for the edges of the biggest ones had been rounded off. Some were absolutely rectangular, sometimes approaching perfect squares. The larger pieces, at least 10 to 15 feet in length, often ran the width of parallel-sized avenues while the smaller ones formed mosaic like pavements covering broader sections. Where the sand had washed away between them, another deeper layer of stones appeared below." (19)

They named their discovery 'The Bimini Road' although it was not immediately obvious if it was a road, a sunken wall, foundation or even a dock. What was known was that it lay off the east coast of North Bimini and appeared to consist of blocks fitting together in a pattern, and according to researchers, supported by stone pillars placed underneath them.

Valentine and Rebikoff now had their underwater 'temple,' and road. What they needed were other ruins to complete their vision. They did not have to wait long, for their activities had generated growing interest in the area, and sure enough, further from Bimini, at a depth of about 100 feet, pilots of commercial and private planes began reporting sightings of vertical walls and even a great arch. This all gave further credence to the suggestions that the area may have been the remains of a city now lost under the sea.

D. G. Richards in an article in the Journal of Scientific Exploration gives an account of the investigations both amateur and professional of the Bimini waters. Richards concluded that there are indeed anomalies under the waters and he detailed three of these based on an aerial photograph taken at 6000 feet. Firstly he noted a 90-degree bend in the road which he considered was decidedly anomalous for a beach rock formation. Secondly he could identify a parallel row of stones and lastly a series of regularly spaced piles of stones which extended over 1.5 miles, cutting diagonally across ancient beach sites (20). Richards also employed a satellite image of the area from which he observed other 'regular' features, such as a triangle, a pentagon, and a sharp, right angle corner with mile long sides. However on actually inspecting these regularities from a small boat, Richards found no obvious structures of any kind, instead, he noted that sea grass and white sand had caused the patterns. Despite this, he concluded that these superficial patterns might reflect the presence of artificial structures under the sediments.

Valentine, himself, commented of the rocks that made up these supposed structures, "many of [them] are flint-shaped micrite, unlike soft beach rock. The lines of closely fitted stones are straight, mutually parallel, and terminate in cornerstones. The stone avenue does not follow the curving beach rock-line that follows the shape of the island, but is straight. The long avenue contains enormous flat stones propped up at their corners by pillar stones like the dolmens off the coast of Western Europe. Perfect rectangles, right angles, and rectilinear configurations are unaccountable in a natural formation. One end of the complex swings into a beautifully curved corner before vanishing under the sand. No-one has yet dug underneath it, so we don't know how far down the stones go." (21)

Dating tests have been applied to the rocks that comprise the Bimini Road, and although stones themselves cannot be dated, the fossilized mangrove roots growing over the stones of the Bimini Road, have given a date of 10-12,000 years old. This fitted in well with Plato's assertion that Atlantis had disappeared beneath the ocean in 9600BC, over 11,500 years ago. Could the ruins at Bimini actually be the lost Atlantis as Valentine et al had proposed, with added support from the vision of a respected psychic?

There was certainly supporting evidence. A dive made by the French submarine 'Archimede' off the northern coast of Puerto Rico, revealed flights of steps cut in the steep sides of the continental shelf off Andros. Whilst it has never been established where the steps lead to, it is clear that they were not cut underwater.

Furthermore, a submarine expedition of the Frenchman Jacques Cousteau explored a huge grotto off the same island, with stalagmites and stalactites under 165 feet of water . As these features can only be formed in the air, the grotto must once have been a cave well above sea level. From submarine sediments on the walls of the grotto, it has been ascertained that the cave went down into the sea some 12,000 years ago (22).

All this was very interesting, but not very scientific. Consequently, carbonate sedimentologists and other geologists decided to visit the Bimini islands to establish whether the claims being made had any validity. Detailed studies have been undertaken since that time by Ball and Gifford (1980), Gifford (1973) Harrison (1971), Shinn (1978) and McKusick and Shinn (1978). Other studies have been undertaken by Davaud and Strasser (1984), Strasser and Davaud (1986) and Supko and others (1970).

With grants from National Geographic, Gifford (1973) and later Ball and Gifford (1980) undertook a detailed study of the Road beginning with the assumption that it was indeed an archaeological site. For the study, they surveyed the three linear strips of slabs that make up the Road; completed photomosaics of the features composed of a linear concentration of slabs; described the orientation and physical characteristics of the slabs; surveyed in the position of the strips of slabs in relation to benchmarks on North Bimini; obtained core samples from individual slabs within the road; prepared petrographic thin sections from the cores and other samples from individual slabs and dated samples from the slabs by radiocarbon and uranium-thorium methods.

Their 1980 observations were that there was no evidence that the Bimini Road was anything other than a natural formation (23). (See Appendix I)

Their laboratory analysis found that the slabs that comprised the three linear features consisted merely of bedrock of local origin. Firstly, the shells and other grains that compose the slabs were found to be identical to the grains in the lose sediment underlying the slabs. Secondly, the carbonate cements that form the bedrock are typical of cements found in modern beachrock cements. Finally, the radiocarbon dates obtained from the slabs of beachrock ranged in age from 300 to 1200 BCE for the shoreward line of beachrock and a single date of about 4800 BCE for the seaward line of beachrock (24).

McKusick and Shinn (1980) obtained some oriented cores from one of the linear features. X-radiographs of seventeen oriented cores showed that the slope, particle size, dip direction, of the bedding is consistent from one block to another within two areas that they studied. If the blocks had been quarried from one site and then later laid out as a road, the original stratigraphy of the beachrock would not have been preserved. Clearly, these slabs represent beachrock that developed in situ along three shorelines. McKusick and Shinn also dated seven samples from the slabs and obtained dates ranging from about 750 to 1500 BCE The results of the scientific investigations onto the Road at Bimini conclude that the feature is not in fact man made, but beach rock that formed along the shore of North Bimini Island at three different shorelines during the Holocene era when the sea level was lower than present. Indeed, the lines themselves were not well founded or continuous enough to have served as any kind of road (25).

Despite this research, those wanting to find something mythical hung on, finally claiming that the formations must be man-made for they are unique. However, in fact, there are several places where rectangular slabs of bedrock are associated with carbonate beaches. These have been noted at Puerto Rico (26), Barbados (27) West shore of South Bimini (28) Joulter Cays, Bahamas (29) Heron Island, Australia (30) and Eastern Australia (31).

Greenland has also been suggested as the site of the lost continent. A north looking view of southwestern Greenland was taken on 14th November 1994 by the Space Shuttle Atlantis. The photograph shows numerous indentations, fjords, that were carved by the glaciers of the last ice age. Even today, the ice in the centre of Greenland is 11,000 feet thick, however, the geological records shows that once Greenland enjoyed a temperate climate; only not during a period when man walked on the surface of the Earth - effectively ruling the island out as a potential location of the lost race.

It appears that there is, in fact, no evidence for any large lost colony on Earth. Taking this to its logical conclusion, some have suggested that we are looking in the wrong place and rather than looking on the Earth, we should be looking inside the planet. Incredulous as it seems, such ideas did gain widespread support and will be mentioned here out of curiosity.

There is certainly some evidence of subterranean activity. Peter Kolosimo in 'Timeless Earth' writes of a tunnel system connecting Lima to Cuzco and from there on to the Bolivian border. "Apart from the lure of gain, these tunnels present a fascinating archeological problem. Scholars agree that they were not constructed by the Incas themselves, who had used them but were ignorant of their origins. They are in fact so imposing that it does not seem absurd to conjecture, as some scientists have done, that they are the handiwork of an unknown race..." (32)

Harold T. Wilkins, in his book 'Mysteries of Ancient South America' gives more details of this tunnel system. "One of the approaches to the great tunnels lay, and still lies, near old Cuzco, 'but it is masked beyond discovery'. This hidden approach leads directly into an immense 'subterranean', which runs from Cuzco to Lima, as the crow flies, a distance of 380 miles! Then turning southwards, the great tunnel extends into what, until about 1868, was modern Bolivia, around 900 miles! ..." (33)

Wilkins also advises of tunnels in the West Indies. "Similar strange tunnels of incredibly ancient date, and unknown origin, in the West Indies, were brought to the attention of Christopher Columbus when he visited Martinique." (34)

There is also apparently a huge complex of underground passages and halls beneath the South American continent at Ecuador. An Argentinian, Juan Moricz, claimed to be the legal owner of this strange underground world, however, convinced of the incalculable cultural value of his find, he asked the State of Ecuador to take control and set up a scientific commission to study the area (35). Erich Von Daniken describes this vast system of caves in his book 'The Gold of the Gods' and he details how Moricz guided him through the network, however Moricz claims this never happened. Indeed a report in the German Magazine Der Spiegel of March 1973 contains as admission from Von Daniken that he made this up (36).

However, the tunnels themselves are real, and similar underground passageways have also been found in Europe. Malcolm W. Browne in his article 'Underground Tunnels Threaten Town In Hungary's Wine Country' refers to over sixty miles of ancient tunnel systems of unknown origin and purpose which have been discovered beneath the town of Eger, Hungary, some of which have collapsed (37).

Amazing Stories magazine of October 1947 contained the following letter: "Sirs ... I don't know whether you are familiar with the Big Bend or not, but there is no more wild or desolate area in the country. Rugged mountains, cut by canyons, there are innumerable parts of it which have never known the foot of man.

... Finlay [a friend of the letter's author] spotted a mountain lion ... they managed to keep him in sight ... the lion, however, started up a faint trail up one side of the canyon to a small cave they could see about a hundred feet from the floor of the canyon. They followed him up this trail, but when they got to the cave – there was no lion! ... In the rear [of the cave] was a perfectly round hole ... they approached the hole and peered down into it. It was perfectly round – also it was about four or five feet in diameter. They couldn't see very far down it, but it appeared to descend rather sharply and at a steady gradient. The fellows gathered some dry grass from the canyon floor and made some torches. The incline of the bore was too steep for them to climb down so they tossed the torches down it. They just slid down further and further and disappeared into the gloom. They never did see or hear of the lion again.

"At first they thought they had stumbled into some old Spanish mine workings. But there was no sign anywhere of a dump that always goes with a mine. By all rights there should have been some sign of the earth and rock that had come out of that hole – but there wasn't.

"When they inspected the hole itself more closely, they were amazed at its symmetry and at the consistency of the section of the bore as far as they could see down into it. The fact that the bore was perfectly round puzzled them, too. If it was a mine shaft, it most certainly wouldn't have been round, but instead would have been flat on the bottom. The fact that the shaft extended straight and unwavering as a rigid pipe was cause for further amazement. Since the fellows had no rope with them, which would have been needed to descend the shaft, as well as lights, they scratched their heads awhile and then left.

"Finlay wanted to go back with equipment ... but ranchers are busy people and he never went back." (38)

A major advocate that the Earth is hollow, thus that these tunnels led to an 'inner world,' was Cyrus Teed.

Teed came to this conclusion shortly after the American civil war when he claimed to have had a vision, "the earth is a hollow sphere, and we live inside it. Everything in the universe is in here with us – planets, comets, stars – everything. What's outside the sphere? Nothing." (39)

Teed explored this idea in a book entitled 'The Cellular Cosmogony, or, the Earth a

SUPPRESSED INTELLIGENCE REPORTS

Conclave Sphere' which he wrote under the pseudonym 'Koresh'. According to Teed, the known world is on the concave, inner surface of a sphere, outside of which there is only a void. At the centre of the sphere, the rotating sun, half dark and half light, gives an illusion of rising and setting. The Moon is a reflection of the Earth's surface; the stars and planets reflect from metallic planes on the Earth's concave surface. The vast internal cavity is filled with a dense atmosphere that makes it impossible to see across the globe to the lands and peoples on the other side (40).

Teed also argued that there is no such thing as gravity; our feet are kept on the ground by centrifugal force. As bizarre as it sounds, Teed's proposal could not be refuted mathematically. Indeed he offered a $10,000 reward to anyone who could prove him wrong, but found no-one able to do so. (The trick is done by inversion, a mathematical transformation that lets a mathematician turn a shape inside out.)

Clearly, Teed's theories were hopelessly wrong. However the concept of a hollow earth continued to attract a following, with a 'photograph' taken by the ESSA-7 satelliteon 23rd November 1968 giving new impetus to the idea. This 'photograph' billed, as 'the most remarkable photograph ever taken' (41) was considered by the hollow earth theorists to be incontrovertible proof that the Earth is indeed hollow apparently showing a massive 'hole as the pole.'

However, the picture was not all it appeared, for the 'photograph' was actually a mosaic of television images taken during a twenty-four hour period at differing points along the satellite's orbit. The images were later processed by computer and reassembled to form a composite view of Earth as if seen from a single point directly over the North Pole. During this time the regions near the Pole were shrouded by the continuous darkness of the arctic winter, thus the unlighted area around the pole.

Yet the hollow Earth believers, and, yes, they still do exist, continue to present evidence which, in their view, supports the theory. Two photographs show a depressed area near the pole that is allegedly the opening to the hollow world.

Given that there is no obvious location for the missing civilization – either on the Earth or in it – some researchers have suggested that all evidence has been wiped out by a natural disaster than befell the world in prehistory. Indeed the great flood of the Bible is even cited as one of the consequences of this disaster and a find in the frozen wastelands of Siberia at the turn of the Twentieth Century provides tantalizing clues as to what may have happened.

References

(1) Tomas, A, 'Atlantis From Legend to Discovery' p.14 Sphere Aylesbury 1973

(2) Berlitz C, 'Mystery of Atlantis' p. 53 Souvenir Press London 1977

(3) Berlitz C, 'Mystery of Atlantis' pp. 57-8 Souvenir Press London 1977

(4) Scientific American 28th July 1877.

(5) Berlitz C, 'Mystery of Atlantis' pp. 66-7 Souvenir Press London 1977

(6) Hope, M 'Atlantis, 'Myth or Reality?' p. 80 Arkana, London 1991

(7) Hope, M 'Atlantis, 'Myth or Reality?' p. 81 Arkana, London 1991

(8) Hope, M 'Atlantis, 'Myth or Reality?' p. 81 Arkana, London 1991

SUPPRESSED INTELLIGENCE REPORTS

(9) Tomas, A, 'Atlantis From Legend to Discovery' pp. 15-16 Sphere Aylesbury 1973

(10) Termier, Pierre, 'L'Atlantide', Monaco 1913.

(11) Tomas, A, 'Atlantis From Legend to Discovery' p.15 Sphere Aylesbury 1973

(12) Tomas, A, 'Atlantis From Legend to Discovery' p.15 Sphere Aylesbury 1973

(13) Geographical Society of America Bulletins No. 60 (1949) and 65 (1954).

(14) Tomas, A, 'Atlantis From Legend to Discovery' p.14 Sphere Aylesbury 1973

(15) Tomas, A, 'Atlantis From Legend to Discovery' p.14 Sphere Aylesbury 1973

(16) Tomas, A, 'Atlantis From Legend to Discovery' p.14 Sphere Aylesbury 1973

(17) The Miami News 23rd August 1968, the Miami Herald 11th September 1968.

(18) Tomas, A, 'Atlantis From Legend to Discovery' p.14 Sphere Aylesbury 1973

(19) Ibid (20) Richards Douglas G, 'Archaeological Anomalies in the Bahamas', Journal of Scientific Exploration 2:181, 1988.

(21) Hope, M 'Atlantis, 'Myth or Reality?' p. 233 Arkana, London 1991

(22) Tomas, A, 'Atlantis From Legend to Discovery' p.122 Sphere Aylesbury 1973

(23) Ball, Mahlon M., and Gifford, John A., 1980, 'Investigation of Submerged Beachrock Deposits Off Bimini, Bahamas' Research Reports National Geographical Society, Vol. 12. 77 P21-38

(24) Gifford, John A, 1973, 'A Description of the Geology of the Bimini islands, Bahamas', University of Miami, Florida pp11-12

(25) McKusick, M., and Shinn, E.A., 1980 'Bahamian Atlantis Reconsidered', Nature, Vol. 287 No 5777 pp 11-12

(26) Kye, Charles A., 1959, 'Shoreline Features and Quaternary Shoreline Changes, Puerto Rico' US Geological Survey Professional paper No. 317-B, pp 49-140.

(27) McLean, Roger F., 1964, 'A Regional Study of the Distribution, Forms, Processes, and rates of Mechanical and Biological Erosion of a Carbonate Clastic Rock in the Littoral Zone.' Unpublished Ph.D. dissertation, McGill University.

(28) Ball, Mahlon M., and Gifford, John A., 1980, 'Investigation of Submerged Beachrock Deposits Off Bimini, Bahamas' Research Reports National Geographical Society, Vol. 12. P21-38

(29) Strasser, A., and Davaud, E., 1986, 'Formation of Holocene Limestone Sequences by Progradation, Cementation and Erosion; Two Examples from the Bahamas' Journal of Sedimentary Petrology, Vole 56 No 3 p 422-428

(30) McKusick, M., and Shinn, E.A., 1980 'Bahamian Atlantis Reconsidered', Nature, Vol. 287 No 5777 pp 11-12

(31) Randi, J., 'Atlantean Road: the Bimini Beach Rock' Skepical Inquirer Vol. 5 No. 3 pp 42-43 1981

(32) Kolosimo, Peter, 'Timeless Earth' p.40

(33) Wilkins, Harold T., 'Mysteries of Ancient South America' pp.169-170.

(34) Wilkins, Harold T., 'Mysteries of Ancient South America' p.175

(35) Stemman, R, 'Mysteries of the Universe' p. 162 Book Club Associates LOndon 1980

(36) Fate and Fortune Magazine p. 40 #2 1974.

(37) New York Times 8th November 1967 p. 2

(38) Amazing Stories pp 171-2 Oct 1947.

(39) Omni Magazine, October 1983.

(40) 'Mystic places' p. 147 Time Life Books,

(41) Trench, Brinsley, 'Secret of the Ages' p.116 Panther, 1976 Other References Quoted: Harrison, W., 1971, 'Atlantis Undiscovered; Bimini, Bahamas', Nature Vol. 230 No 5292 p.287-289

Davaud, Eric and Strasser, A., 1984, 'Progradation, Cimentation, Erosion; Evolution Sedimentaire et Diagenetique Recente d'un Littoral Carbonate (Bimini, Bahamas)'. (Translated title; 'Progradation, Cementation, Erosion; Recent Diagenetic and Sedimentary Evolution in a carbonate Coastal Environment, Bimini, Bahamas.) Ecologae Geologicae Helvetica, Vol. 77 No 3, pp 449-468

Shin, E. A., 1978, 'Untitled' Sea Frontiers, Vole 24, p130

Supko, P. R., Marszalek, D. S., and Bock, W. D., 1970 'Sedimentary Environments and Carbonate Rocks of Bimini, Bahamas' Miami Geographical Society Annual Field Trip, Guidebook No 4, p.30, Miami Geological Society, Miami, Florida.

Appendix I

1. The three features are unconnected at the southwest end; scattered blocks are present there but do not form a well-defined linear feature connecting the seaward, middle and shoreward features. No evidence exists anywhere over the three features of two courses of blocks, or even a single block set squarely atop another.

Not enough blocks lie in the vicinity of the three features to have formed a now-destroyed second course of blocks.

Bedrock closely underlies the entire area of the three features eliminating the possibility of excavations or channels between them.

Indications are that the blocks of the inner and middle features have always rested on a layer of loose sand. No evidence was found of the blocks being cut into or founded on the underlying bedrock surface.

In areas of the seaward feature where blocks rest directly on the bedrock surface, no evidence was found of regular or symmetrical supports beneath any of the rocks.

We saw no evidence on any of the blocks of regular or repeated patterns of grooves or depressions that might be interpreted as tool marks.

The inner and middle features are continuous only over a distance of about 50 meters. Though the seaward feature extends several hundred meters further to the north east, it too is not well founded or continuous enough to have served as some kind of thoroughfare. In fact, the only attributes of the three linear features that suggest a human origin are the regular shapes of some of the blocks. These are also attributes of natural bedrock deposits. (11)

THE LOST WORLD DISCOVERED?

The world as known to our ancient ancestors was made up of the Americas, Europe, Africa and Asia and then made complete with the 'discovery' by the west of Australasia. Yet the planet had a hidden continent, one that was only 'revealed' as recently as 1820. Indeed some maps before that time show no record of the continent even existing, merely leaving a space where the frozen landmass should have appeared.

According to legend, the Maori made the first sighting of the icebound southern ocean. However the first confirmed crossing of the Antarctic circle is credited to the British Captain, James Cook (1728-1779) in 1773 and it was to be a further forty-seven years before modern man first set eyes on mainland Antarctica during the Russian, British and United States expeditions of 1820.

These explorers 'discovered' a land that was bigger in area than either Europe or the United States and Mexico combined, but an inhospitable land, with an ice cap measuring 13,000ft thick in places and covering 96% of the continent's surface. It was to be a further seventy-five years before the first confirmed landing on Antarctic mainland on 24th January 1895, a landing that led to an argument over who was first ashore. Borchgrevink depicts himself as making the first landing, much to the apparent dismay of others in the boat.

Such bleak conditions, together with months of darkness make for a land where it is impossible for land mammals to survive, although whales and seals populate the surrounding seas, feeding off the masses of 'krill' there. Porpoises and dolphins are also attracted to the icy waters by the abundance of fish in the area, predominately Antarctic perches. This complete absence of predatory land mammals on Antarctica has proved to be a great attraction for birds, with Emperor penguins, Antarctic petrels and South Polar skuas breeding there and nowhere else.

Contrary to popular perception, snowfall is rare on the continent except at the coast, however blizzards are frequent, as loose snow is whipped up by winds at the margins of the ice cap. In all, these hostile conditions make for a barren, frozen wasteland where 'cold nightless summers, fade into colder sunless winters' (1).

Yet, as noted in the first chapter, it has been claimed that some people in our prehistory not only knew of this land but had even apparently mapped it before it became embedded in ice. These claims dominate many current 'alternative history' books such as Graham Hancock's, Fingerprints of the Gods, Colin Wilson's, From Atlantis to the Sphinx and Rand and Rose Flem-Ath's, When the Sky Fell, amongst others. These authors draw the conclusion that Antarctica could possibly be the location of the lost people and/or the location of the lost Atlantis.

Clearly, Antarctica as it appears today could not support any civilization; the cold and barren conditions would soon destroy any colony. Yet the popular conception of Antarctica as a continent that has been buried deep in ice for an eternity is flawed.

SUPPRESSED INTELLIGENCE REPORTS

Whilst certainly true that parts of Antarctica have been buried under ice for millennia, there is much evidence to suggest that before the Pleistocene era (c. 8,000-2m yrs BC), parts of the continent were once warm and ice free (2).

There is certainly evidence in the early years of this planet, during the Cambrian era, (480m – 590m years ago) of "a moderately warm sea stretching nearly or right across Antarctica, in the form of thick limestones very rich in reef building Archaeocyathide"

(3) and the Ohio Range Mountains in Antarctica contain rocks rich in fossils from 390 million years ago. Fossil bones of a land reptile, Lystrosaurus , which lived in Antarctica about 200 million years ago, have been found in sandstones that were deposited by ancient rivers (4) and fossilized remains of ancient ferns such as Dicroidium from the same period have also been discovered.

In March 1968 the National Science Foundation of the United States announced the discovery of a jawbone of a long extinct amphibian found in the mountainous central Antarctic region around 525km from the South Pole. This bone was part of the skeleton of a Labyrinthodont, a creature that lived in the river valleys of Gondwana and in the rift valley between Australia and Antarctica until it died out some 110 million years ago. This discovery was made by an expedition organized by Ohio University and led by geologist Peter J. Barrett who noted "it is clear that an amphibian of this type could only have survived in a hot climate, or at least a warm one and that therefore the Antarctic must once have been absolutely free of ice."(7)

Dr. Umbgrove, in his book 'The Pulse of the Earth', notes that the flora of Antarctica, England, North America and India had many plants in common during the Jurassic period (130m-180m years ago) (5) and there is also evidence that during this Jurassic period dinosaurs roamed the now ice-gripped continent.

This was discovered during an expedition to the Antarctic undertaken in 1990-1991 by Augustana Professor Dr. William R. Hammer and an accompanying field team. The team came across bones in the ice and on digging further, excavated Antarctica's first known dinosaur on Mt. Kirkpatrick, at an elevation of approximately 14,000 feet not far from the South Pole.

The bones indicated that they had discovered a crested therapod that the team named Cryolophosaurus ellioti, ('frozen crested reptile'). To date it is the only therapod to be found in Antarctica, although clearly there will be others of its kind buried under the ice cap. In addition to the dinosaur bones, the team also found bones from other creatures at the same site. These included a 'pterosaur' (flying reptile), a tritylodont, and most significantly, a plateosaurid prosauropod. (Significant as the animal's foot structure and size is nearly identical to two plateosaurid prosauropods found in Germany and China.) (6)

The evidence of a much warmer Antarctica in past times is supplemented by the British explorer, Sir Ernest Shackleton (1874-1922) who found coal beds within 200 miles of the South Pole (8), that could only have formed in the presence of extensive vegetation and, during the Byrd expedition of 1935, geologists discovered fossils on the sides of Mount Weaver, in latitude 86°, 58 minutes south, about the same distance from the pole and two miles above sea level.

These included leaf and stem impressions and fossilized wood. (9).

British geologists also discovered evidence of great fossil forests in Antarctica of the same type that grew on the pacific coast of the United States 20m years ago (10) and it would have been this ancient vegetation, later covered by warm seas and thick marine sediment, that produced the extensive coal seams that run through the Transantarctic Mountains (11). Admiral Byrd, one of Antarctica's most accomplished explorers, commented in 1949 that this coal seam was 'enough for the needs of the entire world' (12). Actually he was wrong, for the coal was of a poor quality, however, the thought itself was generous.

Other evidence of ancient landscapes and seaways near the South Pole has recently been found on these high peaks. Tree stems, roots, pollen, and tiny fossils of open water marine life, have been identified by Ohio State geologists Peter-Noel Webb, David M. Harwood and John H. Mercer as being 2-4 million years old from the Pliocene era. (13)

In 1952, Dr. Lyman H Dougherty of the Carnegie Institution of Washington, completing a study of these fossils, identified two species of a tree fern called 'glossopteris', once common in the southern continents of Africa, South America and Australia. He also found a giant tree fern of another species and identified a fossil footprint as that of a mammal-like reptile. Henry suggests that this may mean that Antarctica, during its period of intensive vegetation, played host to many different life forms. (14) Soviet Scientists have reported finding evidence of a tropical flora in Graham Land, another part of Antarctica, dating from the early Tertiary period. (15)

Shrub wood grew on the banks and shores of alpine streams and lakes during several interglacial periods, the researchers suggest. In relatively warm times, great open seaways may have reached deep into the Antarctic interior, and the great central ice caps may have retreated to much smaller ice caps and high alpine glaciers. (16)

Admiral Byrd, later of Operation High Jump fame, discovered the Edsel Ford Mountains in 1929. These mountains are of non-volcanic, folded, sedimentary rock, with the layers adding up to 15,000 feet in thickness. Thomas Henry, in his 1950 book 'The White Continent' suggests that they indicate long periods of temperate climate in Antarctica. "The greater part of the erosion probably took place when Antarctica was essentially free of ice, since the structure of the rocks indicates strongly that the original sediment from which they were formed was carried by water. Such accumulation calls for an immensely long period of tepid peace in the life of the rampaging planet." (17)

The evidence is plentiful, therefore, that the popular vision of a permanently frozen Antarctica is flawed and indeed, at some point in its past, the continent was sufficiently ice-free for it, or at least parts of it, to have been mapped. The question however is, was it ice-free at a time when mankind could have mapped it? If the Piri Reis map is accurate, then the answer must surely be yes.

This map, as discussed previously in 'Weird History' has strong credentials, however, there are clearly serious flaws in it suggesting that it should be treated with caution when cited as evidence of the existence of an early and lost civilization.

One such flaw is that of the island shown at 0° latitude and just east of longitude 47° W on the parchment. Hapgood refers to this island as "one of the major mysteries of the Piri Reis map" (18). He continues, "the details of the island are convincing. Some reproductions of the colored facsimile (but unfortunately not all of them) suggest by a deeper shade around the coasts that there were coastal highlands or mountains surrounding a great central plain. The harbours and islands off the coast are inviting. They are carefully drawn. There seems to have been an effort to achieve accuracy (19)." Hapgood notes that the island has now disappeared into the ocean, "submerged to a depth of a mile and a half." (20)

Hapgood was convinced that if he could only prove that this island had existed, then this would silence any doubters once and for all; for it was the degree of detail in the Piri Reis map that so convinced him of its accuracy (once realigned to modern scales). He therefore decided to approach the US Government for help and permission to search for underwater cities in the region of the St Peter and St Paul Rocks. By October 1963 Hapgood had presented a convincing enough argument to secure an interview with President Kennedy to discuss the matter further. However, as history records, fate intervened.

In actual fact, even if the interview had gone ahead, it would not have changed the fact that the island shown on the map is not presently submerged beneath the Atlantic nor did it ever exist.

We know this now because the US Navy has recently released satellite data gathered by the US Navy's Geostat spacecraft between the 31st March and 30th October 1986 that was used to prepare the first detailed topographic map of the entire ocean floor (21).

The Piri Reis 'missing' island should therefore have appeared on this map of the seabed, however the Geostat map shows no evidence of any such island nor any submerged mountains. Indeed the only topographic forms that can be seen in the area where the island 'should be' are numerous transform faults, ridges and trough topography that characterises normal oceanic crust.

If Piri Reis could 'invent' an entire island of considerable dimensions, then surely he could also make up the supposed outline of Antarctica?

Obviously the answer is yes, however, it should be remembered that Piri Reis readily admitted that he had merely complied his world map from twenty or more smaller maps, and these in turn were probably compiled from even smaller and older maps. Consequently, some areas of the overall map will be accurate whilst others inaccurate and without doubt the original source maps would have been the most accurate of all for these are the maps that would have actually been used by those who drew them. In essence, just because part of the map is erroneous, does not make it all so. Indeed, the map itself was a working tool used by mariners and others. It would hardly have enjoyed this status had it been so riddled with errors that it would have been safer to voyage blind.

Yet it is the outline of the Antarctic area we are interested, rather than that of South America, Africa or Spain. Clearly if there were other ancient maps of the area then this would lend credence to the idea that it really had been mapped before becoming entombed in ice. Hapgood himself realized this and searched for further supporting evidence. His search was to lead him to the Reference Room of the Library of Congress, Washington DC, America. Hapgood recalls:

"I found ... many fascinating things I had not expected to find, and a number of charts showing the southern continent. Then one day, I turned a page and sat transfixed. As my eyes fell upon the Southern Hemisphere of a world map drawn by Oronteus Fineaus in 1531, I had the instant conviction that I had found here a truly authentic map of the real Antarctica.

SUPPRESSED INTELLIGENCE REPORTS

"The general shape of the continent was startlingly like the outline of the continent on our modern maps. The position of the South Pole, nearly in the center of the continent, seemed about right. The mountain ranges that skirted the coasts suggested the numerous ranges that have been discovered in Antarctica in recent years. It was obvious, too, that this was no slapdash creation of somebody's imagination. The mountain ranges were individualized, some definitely coastal and some not. From most of them rivers were shown flowing into the sea, following in every case what looked like very natural and very convincing drainage patterns.

This suggested, of course, that the coasts might have been ice-free when the original map was drawn. The deep interior, however, was free entirely of rivers and mountains, suggesting that the ice may have been present there." (22)

The fact that this map shows the complete continent of Antarctica seems remarkable in itself, suggesting that far from mankind having made superficial contact with part of the continent, she or he was familiar with the entire area at least three hundred years before Antarctica was supposedly discovered.

Hapgood asked the Cartographic Section of the 8th Reconnaissance Technical Squadron, Massachusetts to evaluate both the Piri Reis and Oronteus Fineaus maps. In reply, he received the following letter from Captain Lorenzo W Burroughs, the chief of the section, who gave a summary of their findings:

"A) The solution of the portolano projection used by Admiral Piri Reis, developed by your class in Anthropology, must be very nearly accurate; for when known geographical locations are checked in relationship to the grid computed by Mr. Richard W. Strachan (MIT) there is remarkably close agreement. Piri Reis' use of the portolano projection (centered on Seyene, Egypt) was an excellent choice, for it is a developable surface that would permit the relative size and shape of the earth (at that latitude) to be retained. It is our opinion that those who compiled the original map had an excellent knowledge of the continents covered by this map.

As stated by Colonel Harold Z. Ohlmeyer in his letter (July 6, 1960) to you, the Princess Martha Coast of Queen Maud land, Antarctica appears to be truly represented on the southern sector of the Piri Reis Map. The agreement of the Piri Reis map with the seismic profile of this area made by the Norwegian-British-Swedish Expedition of 1949, supported by your solution of the grid, places beyond a reasonable doubt the conclusion that the original source maps must have been made before the present Antarctic ice cap covered the Queen Maud Land coasts.

It is our opinion that the accuracy of the cartographic features shown in the Oronteus Fineaus (sic) Map (1531) suggests, beyond reasonable doubt, that it was also compiled from accurate source maps of Antarctica, but in this case the entire continent. Close examination has proved the original source maps must have been compiled at a time when the landmass and inland waterways of the continent were relatively free of ice. The Cordiform Projection used by Oronteus Fineaus (sic) suggests the use of advanced mathematics. Further, the shape given to the Antarctic continent suggests the probability that the original source maps were compiled on a stereographic or gnomonic type of projection (involving the use of Spherical trigonometry.)

We are convinced that the findings made by you and your associates are valid, and that they raise extremely important questions affecting geology and ancient history, questions which certainly require further investigation." (23)

In order to explain these ice-free coastlines, Hapgood concluded that Antarctica must have been located a few thousand miles further north than its present location, and slipped to its current position in an 'Earth Crust Displacement'.

The idea behind Earth Crust Displacement is that ice builds up at the poles, and, on reaching a critical point, the outer crust of the planet slips under the weight of the ice, casting previously temperate areas into the polar positions. (This initially sounds impossible, however movement of the Earth's plates is now accepted, for example India drifting and crashing into Asia causing the rise of the Himalayas.)

It was this conclusion that led writers such as Graham Hancock, Rand and Rose Flem-Ath et al, to claim that Antarctica may, in fact, have been the location of the legendary Atlantis. Such a concept was certainly compatible with Plato's story; and would account for the destruction of the civilization as described by the author.

The continent was certainly big enough to be home for an entire civilization, and its location further north in the Atlantic would have made its position ideal as a central link between the 'old' and 'new' worlds, accounting for some of the connections discussed in this work.

However, the concept of Earth Crust Displacement is built upon a misunderstanding of plate tectonics. The crust of the Earth is not floating on a liquid nor even a semiliquid mantle. In fact, the crust is securely adhered to the mantle and connected by the asthenosphere, a layer more viscous than lava and certainly not fluid enough to allow for rapid movement.

In fairness to Hapgood, many of the studies that reached these conclusions were made after his theory was proposed, however more recent authors have been careless in continuing to propose this theory even after it has been unequivocally disproved. As noted earlier, Albert Einstein supported Hapgood's theory, however the conclusions he reached, like Hapgood's, were only as good as the data then available. Many years on, we now know the data to be obsolete.

The Crust Displacement theory also ignores some inherent evidence. If Antarctica had originally been located thousands of miles further north, or at least not covered in ice – it would reveal itself in its true form; split into East and West Antarctica, with a sea in-between its constituent parts. For Antarctica is only one huge continent when covered in ice and it has not been that free of ice for at least four million years.

It is inconceivable that the continent could have been situated away from the pole, but still under solid ice at its centre as the Oronteus Fineaus map inevitably suggests.

The only other way Antarctica could have been the home for a civilization is if it has been ice free in recent times – at least within the last twenty thousand years. Yet, the available evidence confirms that this is not the case.

Drilling was undertaken in 1967-8 at Byrd Station where a core drill went down 7,101 feet before it hit liquid water near the bedrock, then froze fast (24). In 1970 Soviet scientists began drilling at Vostock Station, high in the inland ice cap in east Antarctica. In 1981-2 French scientists reached more than 900m beneath a point called Dome C, near the centre of the huge ice cap. And since 1980 the Vostock ice drillers have bored through more than 2080m of the 3700m (12,140ft) of the ice under the station (25). "The Vostock core is the first to cover, completely and unambiguously, the entire last 150,000 years of the earth's ice-age cycle."

French Glaciologist, Claude Lorius, reported in 1985 after working with Soviet scientists on the ice-core (26). "It clearly goes back through earth's previous interglacial warm period, called the Eem or Sangamon, and well into the ice-age before that." Lorius continues, "That previous interglacial was similar but markedly warmer than our present warm spell, the Holocene. The beginning of the previous warming was as sharp and extensive as was the opening of the Holocene, between about 10,000 and 8000 years ago." (27)

A discovery made in 1996 also confirms that a least part of Antarctica has been under ice for millions of years. Space and ground based instruments identified a huge lake more than two miles below the continent, insulated by millions of years of ice that may still be a home to creatures that inhabited the planet more than 30 million years ago. Researchers know that there should be life in this underworld lake for Russian and American microbiologists have already examined microbes in samples of ice laid down a mere 400,000 years ago.

"We've found some really bizarre things – things that we have never seen before," noted Richard Hoover of NASA.

He and his Russian colleague have given the microscopic creatures temporary nicknames such as Klingon, Mickey Mouse, Porpoise and Sphere (28).

The discovery at such depths raises the hope that other stranger life forms will be found in the lake, particularly as volcanic heat deep in the rock may provide energy to sustain such forms of life. Antarctica is 58 times as big as Britain and there could be hundreds of lakes below the ice-sheet. "Every single one of them could be potentially of significance," said Dr Ellis-Evans of the British Antarctic Survey. "This is a whole new world opening up for us." (29)

It would appear that the maps are neither going to confirm Antarctica as the home of the missing civilization, nor as evidence of such a civilization. Indeed a closer scrutiny of the Oronteus Fineaus map in particular, reveals that it may be little more than a romantic pictorial of a southern continent. This map certainly does not resemble the subglacial bedrock topography of Antarctica, for example, Wilkes Land, which the Oronteus Fineaus map shows as solid land is occupied almost entirely by two large subsea basins and an archipelago of bedrock islands. (30) In a partially glaciated Antarctica this solid land shown on the map would also be under water.

The map also fails to show the Amery basin, which in either a partially or completely deglaciated Antarctica would be occupied by a 430 to 500 mile long bay lying perpendicular to the coast of Antarctica between Princess Elizabeth land and Mac Robertson land. (31)

The map has other faults. Because the bedrock surface underlying West Antarctica lies hundreds of meters below sea level, except for some bedrock islands, the coastline shown on the Oronteus Fineaus map would have had to have been to the edge of an ice sheet. Yet as noted above, Hapgood, claims the map shows rivers' mouths, fjords and other non-glaciated features on this glacial coastline. In essence, the map does not show an Antarctica free of ice, nor does it depict an accurate icebound Antarctica. Despite this, the map does exist and sufficiently resembles the continent to confirm that its makers had some knowledge of, or belief in, a southern continent.

However irrefutable proof of such a southern continent being mapped in prehistory could only be confirmed if an ancient map could be produced that accurately showed Antarctica in its separate landforms. It has been claimed that such a map does exist. It is called the 'Bauche Map' and was drawn in 1737 by Phillipe Bauche, an eighteenth-century French geographer. It has also been suggested that Bauche's source maps were older than those of Piri Reis or Oronteus Fineaus given that he appears to show Antarctica as it would have looked millions of years ago, in a partially glaciated state.

However, despite showing Antarctica as two landmasses, the map appears to have little else in common with the continent as we now know it to be. Critics argue that except for showing that there is a landmass there and a sea did flow through the middle, the map is of no academic value. Academically they are quite right, but how on Earth could an 18th Century cartographer possibly know that millions of years ago the hidden continent had an inland seaway running through its middle? The answer is simple, he could not, for the technology that revealed this has only been developed this century and man simply did not exist in any intellectual form when this knowledge was last known. And yet it appears that Bauche did know. Perhaps, however, there is another solution that fits the facts of these maps a little more comfortably and credibly.

History records that as early as the 6th Century BCE, Pythagoras was proposing that the Earth was round, and other academics, Parmenides (450BCE), Aristotle and Eratosthenes (276-194 BCE) agreed (32). By 150 CE the Egyptian geographer, Ptolemy, had concluded that the world was symmetrical and must therefore have a southern continent – Terra Australis Incognita, however he also believed that this southern continent was cut off from the known world by a 'Torrid Zone' of fire and fearful monsters (33). The concept then, of an undiscovered southern continent, has been held for over two millennia. Ptolemy's teachings, however, became lost in the Middle Ages, but were preserved by the Arabs. They reappeared in Europe from the 10th Century onwards as the Moors invaded Spain. Then in 1410, Ptolemy's works were translated into Latin and French and became accessible to a wider audience, stimulating curiosity to discover the unknown continent.

Later that century the fear of the Torrid Zone was finally overcome as Bartholomew Diaz reached the Cape of Good Hope in 1488 and was followed a decade later by Vasco de Gamma who went round it to reach India. The significance of these voyages being that it became known that Africa was merely an extension of the known world, the Torrid Zone was fictitious and the southern continent, if it existed, lay elsewhere and further south and was accessible. Then, in 1501 a Florentine seaman, Amerigo Vespucci, set off to explore the South American coastline. Exactly what areas Vespucci explored are unknown, but it appears that he charted the area, for when Magellan journeyed there in September 1519 he seemed to have knowledge of the coastline, noting: "This strait was a circular place surrounded by mountains, and to most of those in the ships it seemed that there was no way out from it to enter the said Pacific Sea. But the captain-general said that there was another strait which led out, saying that he knew it well and had seen it in a marine chart of the King of Portugal, which a great pilot and sailor named Martin of Bohemia had made (34)." Magellan also reported seeing land to the south, land that became known as Tierra del Fuego.

From information taken from Magellan's voyage, a map was later constructed in Antwerp in 1570. The map showed Terra Australis as extending south from Tierra del Fuego off the tip of South America. (It was not until 1577 when Drake charted the area that this mistake was rectified.)

The important point to note here is that early maps simply placed the southern continent, which had been 'known' about for centuries, somewhere outside known and charted areas. As a result of this, earlier maps appear to be more confident about the southern continent than slightly later maps which were based on actual data rather than accepted concepts. For example one 1620 Dutch map starts to show the outline of the southern coast of Australia and some tentative lines around Antarctica, from reports from ships that strayed south.

Now as far as the Piri Reis map is concerned it appears much more likely that its sources lay in slightly earlier cartography undertaken by peers such as Vespucci who had been in the area a mere 13 years previously than some 'lost civilization' who supposedly lived there – without trace – thousands of years before any civilization is known to have existed and in conditions that would have made living there an impossibility at that time.

It also appears suspicious that both the Piri Reis map and the map from Magellan's voyage both crush 'Antarctica' against Southern America, suggesting they are contemporaneous in origin rather than divided by thousands of years.

As far as the Oronteus Fineaus, Bauche and other ancient maps are concerned, they all date from no earlier than the beginning of the 16th Century – a time when we know voyages were taking place in the area and maps were tentatively being drawn, even if they were inaccurate.

Given that we also know that Antarctica had been in subzero temperatures for thousands of years, has had no plant life for millions of years, is bathed in darkness most of the year round and the so called ancient map 'evidence' of life there does not stand up to any real scrutiny, it is not hard to conclude that Antarctica was not the location of the lost people.

So how can the discovery of ferns, dinosaurs and other mammal life on a once warm Antarctica be explained? Here, at least Hapgood et al were treading on safer ground, for whilst Earth Crust Displacement may have been proved to be a fallacy, the theory of Continental Drift has is origins firmly rooted in science and fact.

This theory suggests that the Earth's crust is split into a number of 'plates' that support the continents. These plates are moved around the ocean spreading (the addition of new crustal rock along mid-oceanic ridges) and by convection currents in the rocks of the Earth's mantle, beneath the crust. This theory helps explain how fold and block mountains, volcanoes and earthquakes occur.

Antarctica then, was not always hiding in the sunless frozen wastelands of the planet, but many millions ago was located further north where it enjoyed a more temperate climate. When the Lystrosaurus roamed the continent, the Earth's land masses were much closer together, and by the time the Cryolophosaurus ellioti was making its mark on the planet, Antarctica had broken away to form its own continent.

Over millions of years the continents continued to drift away from each other, with India ploughing across the oceans to later collide with Asia and force up the Himalayan Mountains. Slowly the continent drifted into what is now called the Antarctic Circle, making conditions impossible for land mammals to survive.

So with Antarctica ruled out, it appears that the search for the location of any lost peoples

SUPPRESSED INTELLIGENCE REPORTS

has been exhausted. Yet despite this, there remain those intriguing puzzles that simply cannot be explained by conventional history. If no one on Earth can account for them, then perhaps we should be looking elsewhere.

References

1) Flem-Ath, Rand and Rose, 'When the Sky Fell' p.74, Orion, London 1995.

(2) Including Dr Jack Hough of Illinois University, supported by Carnegie Institution experts, Washington DC, and John G Weihaupt, a University of Colorado specialist in seismology, gravity and planetary geology, (Eos, the Proceedings of the American Geophysical Union, August, 1984.)

(3) Brooks, C E P., 'Climate Through the Ages' p245 McGraw-Hill, New York 1949.

(4) 'Antarctica, Great Stories From The Frozen Continent' p. 27 Readers Digest, 1985.

(5) Umbgrove, J H F, 'The Pulse of the Earth', p263 Second Edition, Martinus Nijhoff, The Hague, 1947.

(6) 'Science', 6th May 1994, Vol. 264.

(7)

(8) Chamberlain, R T., 'Origin and History of the Earth' in The World and Man as Science Sees Them' ed. F R Moulton, p80 Doubleday, Garden City 1937

(9) Hapgood, C H., 'Earth's Shifting Crust' pp59-60, Museum Press Ltd, London 1959.

(10) Henry, Thomas R, 'The White Continent' p113, 1950 New York William Sloane Associates.

(11) 'Ice On the World' Nat Geographic Jan 1987 P95.

(12) Kolosimo, Peter, 'Not of This World' p83, Sphere, 1971

(13) 'Ice On the World' Nat Geographic Jan 1987 P95.

(14) Henry, Thomas R 'Poles Wander; Earth Crust Falls Off' 27th January 1952 North American Newspaper Alliance.

(15) Saks, N V, Belov, N A, and Lapina, N N 'Our Present Concepts of the Geology of the Central Arctic. Translated by E R Hope from Priroda, Defence Scientific Information Service, Defence Research Board, Ottawa, Canada, 10th October 1955.

(16) 'Ice On the World' Nat Geographic Jan 1987 P95.

(17) Henry, Thomas R, 'The White Continent' p113, 1950 New York William Sloane Associates.

(18) Hapgood, Charles, 'Maps of the Ancient Sea Kings' p.55 rev ed., Turnstone Press, London 1979.

(19) Ibid

(20) Ibid

(21) Monasterky, R., Science News 13th December 1996, also Sandwell Dr D., Discov-

84

ery, 6th November 1995.

(22) Hapgood, Charles, 'Maps of the Ancient Sea Kings' p. 226 rev ed., Turnstone Press, London 1979.

(23) Ibid p.225

(24) 'Ice On the World' Nat Geographic Jan 1987 p.96.

(25) Ibid.

(26) Ibid.

(27) Ibid.

(28) The Guardian, 31st March 1998.

(29) Ibid.

(30) Drewry, D J (Ed) 'Antartica: Glaciological and Geophysical Folio' Scott Polar Research Institute, Cambridge.

(31) Ibid.

(32) 'Antarctica, Great Stories From The Frozen Continent' p. 68 Readers Digest, 1985.

(33) Ibi

(34) Ibid. 89

THE DOGON BELIEVE THEY CAME FROM THE STAR SYSTEM SIRIUS

In a remote, rocky, desolate and acrid region of Western Africa, a tribe called the Dogon scratch out a way of life that has changed little over the centuries. With traditions firmly rooted in agriculture, western technology has no place in their lives, although their philosophy and religion is both rich and complex.

The exact origin of the Dogon tribe is lost in history, however they are known to have settled in the Bandiagara Plateau, at the Southern edge of the Sahara desert (where they remain today) some time between the 13th and 16th centuries. They are originally believed to have been of Egyptian descent.

Today the tribe has a population of 600,000; 138,000 of whom live in Burkina Faso, with the majority of 462,000 living in Mali itself.

The Dogon way of life is steeped in astronomical tradition based on a knowledge kept by the tribe's priests that dates back to 3200 BCE. It is this knowledge that makes the tribe so remarkable, for they appear to know facts not supposedly known to man until the twentieth century.

The Dogon have long held that the star Sirius, some 8.7 light years away, has a companion star which is invisible to the human eye. They state that this companion star, which rotates on its axis, has a 50-year elliptical orbit around the visible Sirius and is extremely heavy. They also have knowledge of the rings of Saturn, Jupiter's satellites and other detailed astronomical data some of which, it has to be acknowledged, is inaccurate.

SUPPRESSED INTELLIGENCE REPORTS

This knowledge was first recorded by two French anthropologists, Marcel Griaule and Germain Dieterlen following discussions with four Dogon priests in the 1930s. Perhaps none of this seems remarkable, however Sirius B was only seen for the first time by telescope in 1970 when photographed by Irving Lindenblad of the US Naval Observatory. Yet the Dogon had apparently known about this second star for millennia.

The renowned astronomer, Carl Sagan concluded that the Dogon could not have acquired their knowledge without contact with an advanced technological civilization. He suggested, however, that the civilization was terrestrial rather than extraterrestrial in origin (1).

Sagan believed that the Dogon gained their knowledge from western travellers who visited the tribes during the 1920 and 1930s. His view is that these travellers would have discussed astronomy with the Dogon priests who would then have weaved this new information into older traditions, which in turn, mislead the anthropologists. However, this is purely conjecture, accurate though it may be.

It is true, however, that there have been French schools in that area teaching geography and natural history in their curriculum since 1907 (the Republic of Mali was formerly known as French Sudan). It has also been noted that there has been a nearby Muslim University at Timbuktu since the 16th century and evidence that some members of the Dogon fought side by side with the French during the First World War (2). Could these have been the sources of the Dogon knowledge?

Robert Temple, author of 'The Sirius Mystery' thinks not. "The two French anthropologists [Griaule and Dieterlen] started their work in 1931, and they are positive that the Dogon knew details about Sirius B when they arrived …Eddington revealed the superdensity of Sirius B around 1926 … so there is a narrow period …when one has to imagine some group of amateur Western astronomers rushing out to … Mali and implanting this knowledge in the presumably pliant minds of the Dogon."(3)

The Dogon account for their 'forbidden' knowledge, however, appears equally unlikely. They claim that a people from the Sirius system called the 'Nommo' or little blue people, visited Earth thousands of years ago.

The Nommos were described as ugly, amphibious creatures that resembled mermen and mermaids. (Incidently, it should be remembered that humans and other mammals originally evolved from amphibians.)

According to Dogon legend, the Nommos lived on a planet that orbits another star in the Sirius system. They landed on Earth in an 'ark' that made a spinning descent to the ground with great noise and wind. Temple gives the following account of this event. "The [Dogon] descriptions of the landing of the ark are extremely precise. The ark is said to have landed on the earth to the northeast of the Dogon country, which is where the Dogon claim to have come from originally.

"The Dogon describe the sound of the landing of the ark. They say the 'word' of the Nommo was cast down by him in the four directions as he descended, and it sounded like the echoing of the four large stone blocks being struck with stones by the children, according to special rhythms, in a very small cave near Lake Debo. Presumably a thunderous vibrating sound is what the Dogon are trying to convey. One can imagine standing in the cave and holding one's ears at the noise. The descent of the ark must have sounded like a jet runway at close range." (4)

The Dogon claim that not only did the Nommos give them knowledge about Sirius B, they also advised that Jupiter has four major moons, that Saturn has rings, and that the planets orbit the Sun. Much of this knowledge was not accepted or known until recent centuries.

These, then, are the two known accounts of how the Dogon received their knowledge of Sirius B (the tiny dot to the lower right of the large star Sirius.) Whilst Sagan's theory has more immediate appeal, it does not account for a 400 year old Dogon artifact that apparently depicts the Sirius configuration, nor the ceremonies held by the Dogon that can be traced back to at least the 13th Century to celebrate the cycle of Sirius A and B, nor how they knew about the super density of Sirius B, a fact only discovered a few years before the anthropologists recorded the Dogon story.

These facts are enshrined in ancient Dogon rituals, portrayed in sand drawings, built into their sacred architecture and can be seen in carvings and patterns dating back hundreds if not thousands of years.

So, how can this knowledge be accounted for? It certainly predates the modern 'discovery' of Sirius B by hundreds of years and therefore any talk of westerners contaminating the Dogon traditions becomes irrelevant.

Yet it is unlikely that if the Dogon had had early contact with an extraterrestrial race that this would have happened in isolation. We know that the Dogon originated elsewhere in Africa spreading out to Mali by the 13th to 16th centuries. There should therefore be evidence of this contact, if it did happen, in the traditions of other related cultures.

And there is, for the creatures described by the Dogon also feature in Babylonian, Greek and Sumerian mythology.

From Berossus, a Babylonian priest, there is a description of creatures known as the 'Annedoti', the 'Repulsive Ones'. These Annedoti were fishmen who introduced civilization. The first and most famous of these was called 'Oannes' or 'Oe', who instructed the Babylonians "in everything which could tend to soften manners and humanize mankind" (5).

THE REPTILIAN ALIENS

Fishbodied aliens are also featured in Greek mythology, notably in the island of Rhodes, with its culture-bearing gods, the 'Telchines'. (the hounds of Actaeon, according to legend, were the survivors of the Telchines.) Diodorus Siculus, the Greek historian, wrote that they were "the discoverers of certain arts and introduced other things which are useful for the life of mankind." (6). Other texts speak of them being "submarine magic spirits". They had "dog's heads and flippers for hands" (7). The Philistines also worshipped "Dagon and Atargis," two amphibian deities who had human bodies but the tails of fish.

There is also some evidence to tie the Dogon claims into Egyptian mythology. The Egyptian dog god Anubis is often identified with Osiris, companion of the goddess Isis. Temple concludes that as Isis herself was identified with Sirius, it is reasonable to suppose that her companion was identified with the companion of Sirius, suggesting that the Egyptians knew of the existence of Sirius B.

Temple realized the implications of his work: "When I started writing this book [The

Sirius Mystery] in earnest in 1967, the entire question was framed in terms of an African tribe called the Dogon … the result in 1974 is that I have been able to show that the information which the Dogon possess is really more than 5000 years old and was possessed by the Ancient Egyptians in the pre-dynastic times before 3200BC." (8)

It is this Egyptian connection that is so intriguing. We have already seen that from nowhere, the Egyptians suddenly formed a technologically proficient society with astronomical, mathematical and other knowledge that should have been unknown to them. Could the basis of Von Daniken's claims (as opposed to the evidence he draws on to support them) be accurate?

There is one piece of scientific fact that could prove or disprove the claims once and for all, for the Dogon speak of a third star, Sirius C, around which the Nommos' planet revolves. If the existence of this star is verified then the rest of the Dogon claims would have to be taken as probable fact. To date, however, there is no information on the existence of Sirius C. (It should be remembered that it was as late as 1930 that a planet was discovered in our own solar system, so Sirius C could well be undiscovered.)

Yet what we do have is a wealth of information regarding possible extraterrestrial contacts with the planet Earth, and when put together with the Dogon claims, the puzzles over forbidden knowledge, and pictorial evidence, a convincing case appears to emerge.

It is all too easy to assume that the extraterrestrial phenomenon is a product of a latter-day television age and gullibility. Yet sightings of mysterious objects in the sky go back into the depths of history.

Of course the further one goes back, the more fact, myth, culture and religious illustration become blurred, however there are some 'facts' that defy reasonable explanation.

One of the earliest possible 'records' of extraterrestrial contact was discovered by Tschi Pen Loa formerly of the University of Peking. He found drawings some 47,000 years old on a Hunan Mountain and on an island in Lake Tungting. These granite pictures showed people with large trunks and cylindrical objects in the sky on which similar figures are seen standing (9).

However, probably the earliest authenticated report of a UFO can be found in an ancient Indian text called the Samarangana-Sartradhara that dates back to at least 500BCE. In one passage of this text, there is a description of curious machines called 'vimanas', which can fly and be controlled by pilots. The same devices are described in the Hindu epics Mahabharata and Ramayana as military machines with the capability of carrying 'death' to anywhere in the world.

Roman writers make reference to strange sights in the sky. Livy (59 BCE-AD 17) described a 'sighting' in 214 BCE at Hadria in Italy that looked like an alter in the sky. Pliny the Elder (AD23-79) refers to 'gleaming beams in the sky' in his De Rerum Naturae, which describes how, in 66BCE, a 'spark' fell from a star to the Earth, became as large as the Moon, and then, shrinking in size returned to the sky.

Inevitably we can only speculate as to what was seen. Others who believe in ancient contact have presented cave and rock paintings in support of their arguments.

Such pictures have been quickly dismissed by others who claim that they are merely pictures of hunters wearing ceremonial headdresses or masks as a ritual part of their culture. Whilst this may be an acceptable explanation, it does not account for the similarity of pictures from cultures on opposite sides of the oceans thousands of years ago. For example, a picture from a prehistoric rock carving near Capo di Ponte in Italy, and a picture from the Toro Muerte Desert in Peru, on the other side of the Atlantic Ocean, show the headgear drawn is almost identical.

Of course, too much can be read into a couple of primitive pictures, if that's all that existed, but it in fact there are other strange representations noted in pictures and images throughout the world. For example, one ancient aboriginal cave drawing from 5000 years ago appears to show strange beings with nonhuman features.

In 1961, the Russian astronomer Alexander Kazantsev brought to the attention of the readers of the then Soviet magazine 'Smena' a discovery made by Henri Labote in the Tassili plateau in the Sahara desert. Labote had found sculpted rocks showing figures with strange rounded heads and other mysterious scenes. These sculptures have been dated to circa. 6000BCE (10).

These images are all the more remarkable because of their similarity to the costumes worn in rituals of the Kayapo Indians of Brazil, a tribe that has existed for at least 4000 years. This tribe's rituals commemorate Gods descending from the heavens bringing with them advanced knowledge and skills.

The ceremonial costume represents such a 'Teacher from Heaven.' Its resemblance to a modern day astronaut's suit is remarkable.

Similarly a 3000-year-old statue found on the Equador-Bolivian border also appears to represent a humanoid in a space suit.

Yet caution has to be advised when considering these ancient images for we can only cast modern day man's eyes over them and offer a modern interpretation of what our ancestors were attempting to record.

For some of the images, however, our knowledge of past cultures can offer a better insight into what the artists are trying to portray. For example, at first glance, the Egyptian mural appears to show in the upper left-hand area a helicopter, with the upper right image appearing to be a boat or even a submarine. The image below that resembles an airplane (or even a UFO) and the bottom image could be taken as a jet-plane.

Yet, in fact, the hieroglyphs are not a record of ancient knowledge of machines similar to modern technology, but merely a coincidental combination of quite common ancient Egyptian symbols.

Again, a Japanese Dogu sculpture has been proposed by some as the representation of a 'space-visitor'.

This 5000-year-old artifact shows a figure wearing what appears to be a helmet, and even goggles that should not have existed in that period of history.

However, although looking bizarre and out of place, the sculpture can hardly be deemed proof of extraterrestrial contact.

Nevertheless some of the ancient images are quite intriguing.

SUPPRESSED INTELLIGENCE REPORTS

Whilst one Neolithic cave painting from circa 3000BCE from southwest France seems to depict a landscape rich in wildlife but with strange circular discs dotted around the image, other ancient pictures appear to be much more explicit.

Take for example this cave painting from circa 2000BCE found on the Russian-Chinese border. It could of course be argued that our modern eyes can only interpret pictures in certain ways, however (and perhaps falling into this trap) it appears that the figure closest to the viewer is clutching some form of dial, the furthest away individual has a helmet on with antenna, and what appears to be a UFO under some form of propulsion hovering above them both. Few of the features in this picture appear compatible with images that should have formed the everyday world of ancient man.

One picture appears all the more convincing when compared with the plate which appears to show a type of alien known as a 'Grey' and a 'UFO'. This plate is thousands of years old, however the idea of 'Greys' is supposedly a totally modern concept, first featured in Hollywood blockbusters.

It will be remembered that other images of UFOs and alien type figures and astronauts also featured on the stones at Ica, whose origins are lost in the depths of time.

One of the earliest 'UFO' reports came from Ancient Egypt. Writer Brinsley Le Poer Trench quotes in his book 'Sky People' from a papyrus found amongst the papers of Professor Alberto Tulli, former director of the Egyptian museum at the Vatican. The papyrus was from the original annals of Pharaoh Thutmose III (d.1436BCE), the grandfather of the intrepid Thutmose IV who had investigated the pyramids. Unfortunately it was badly damaged with many of the hieroglyphics being unreadable. Despite this Prince Boris de Rachewiltz was still able to offer a translation:

"In the year 22, of the third month of winter, sixth hour of the day ... the scribes of the House of Life found it was a circle of fire that was coming in the sky ... it had no head, the breath of its mouth had a foul odor. Its body one rod long and one rod wide. It had no voice. Their hearts became confused through it; then they laid themselves on their bellies ... they went to the Pharaoh ... to report it.

"His majesty ordered ... has been examined ... as to all which is written in the papyrus rolls of the House of Life. His majesty was meditating on what had happened. Now after some days had passed, these things became more numerous in the sky than ever. They shone more in the sky than the brightness of the sun, and extended to the limits of the four supports of the heavens ... Powerful was the position of the fire circles. The army of the Pharaoh looked on him in their midst. It was after supper. Thereupon, these fire circles ascended higher in the sky towards the south..." (11)

There is also a written account of a 'contact' between humans and 'space' people that is said to have taken place during the reign of Charlemagne (742-814 AD). According to one account (12), a spacecraft took a group of humans into space and later returned them, only to find those left behind were convinced that the humans were members of the 'space race' who were viewed as sorcerers. The returning humans were seized, tortured and many put to death.

The contemporary account records, "one day, among other instances, it chanced at Lyons that three men and a woman were seen descending from these aerial ships. The entire city gathered about them, crying out that they were magicians and were sent by Grimaldus,

SUPPRESSED INTELLIGENCE REPORTS

Duke of Beneventum, Charlemagne's enemy, to destroy the French harvests.

"In vain, the four innocents sought to vindicate themselves by saying they were their own countryfolk, and had been carried away a short time by miraculous men who had shown them unheard of marvels, and had desired them to give an account of what they had seen."

It appears that even Christopher Columbus witnessed a anomalous aerial phenomena. He was on the deck of the Santa Maria at about 10pm on 11th October 1492 when he saw a "light glimmering at a great distance."

He summonsed another member of the crew who also watched as the light vanished and reappeared repeatedly.

The following century, on 4th April 1561, an aerial battle apparently took place over the city of Nuremberg. A contemporary account made reference to a "very frightful spectacle" in which luminous globes, crosses and tubes appeared to fight one another for about one hour in broad daylight.

All then fell to the ground 'as if on fire'. The citizens of Nuremberg believed they had been given a divine warning to improve their sinful ways.

Then just five years later, a similar event occurred in Basel, Switzerland and is represented in a 16th century woodcut. On this occasion, dark balls similar to those seen at Nuremberg filled the sky. "Many became red and fiery, ending by being consumed and vanishing" wrote one Samuel Coccius who reported the events of 7th August in the city's gazette. Such accounts are not limited to Europe.

Records of strange lights over Japan go back at least to the 10th century whilst in May 1606 residents of the (former) capital of Japan, Kyoto, saw a succession of fireballs in the sky. One of them hovered near the Nijo castle in front of a host of witnesses spinning like a wheel (13).

Of course we can never know exactly what was seen, it may well have been a little known phenomena called 'ball lightening'. One previously unpublished photograph shows this phenomena in the northeast of England in 1997. However it is difficult to conceive of any natural event that could lead to an observer detailing an event "in which luminous globes, crosses and tubes appeared to fight one another for about one hour in broad daylight."

SIGHTINGS AND MORE

Literature from medieval Europe also appears suggestive if not necessarily indicative of UFO sightings. One of the earliest references is in the works of St Gregory, 6th Century Bishop of Tours in France.

In his 'Historia Francorum' he related how, in 584AD "there appeared in the sky brilliant rays of light which seemed to cross and collide with one another," while in the following year "in the month of September, certain people saw signs, that is to say rays or domes such as are customarily seen ... to race across the sky." Elsewhere he describes 'golden globes' that on a number of occasions flashed across the French skies. However despite these descriptions, these 'lights' are in all probability natural phenomena. The 11th century painting also appears to show another natural phenomenon, a meteorite.

However there are accounts of objects sighted in the sky that seem to fall outside the 'natural' category. One such event took place at about 9.45pm on the evening of 18th August 1783 when four witnesses on the terrace of Windsor Castle observed a luminous object in the skies of the Home Counties of England. The sighting was recorded the following year in the Philosophical Transactions of the Royal Society.

According to this report, witnesses observed an "oblong cloud moving more or less parallel to the horizon. Under this cloud could be seen a luminous object which soon became spherical, brilliantly lit, which came to a halt ... This strange sphere seemed at first to be pale blue in color but then its luminosity increased and soon it set off again towards the east. Then the object changed direction and moved parallel to the horizon before disappearing to the southeast ... the light it gave out was prodigious; it lit us everything on the ground." The image was captured in an aquatint created by Thomas Sandby (a founder of the Royal Academy) and his brother Paul, both of whom witnessed the event. Tiberius Cavallo, one of the group who witnessed this event, concluded that all they had witnessed was a meteor, yet the movements and general descriptions of the object seen do not appear to support this idea.

In 1809 the Journal of Natural History and Philosophy and Chemistry published the experience of John Staveley, an observer at Hatton Garden, London. This observer was astonished by the sight of 'many meteors' darting round a black cloud during a thunderstorm. "They were like dazzling specks of light, dancing and traipsing thro' the clouds.

One increased in size till it became of the brilliancy and magnitude of Venus, on a clear evening. But I could see no body in the light. It moved with great rapidity and coasted the edge of the cloud. Then it became stationary, dimmed its splendor, and vanished."

(14) Historically, ocean sightings have been common. Since 1760 seamen have recounted sightings of unidentified flying objects in the form of a wheel. On 15th May 1879, a passenger aboard a ship, the 'Vultur' in the Persian Gulf watched as "two giant, luminous wheels" spun slowly towards the ocean. They were seen for thirty-five minutes and had an estimated diameter of forty meters and were about four meters apart. A similar phenomenon was reported to have taken place in the same area a year later in the same part of the ocean but from another ship, the 'Patna' (15).

In 1906 as a British steamer ploughed its way through the same gulf near Oman in 1906, an enormous wheel of light appeared. The vast 'wheel', apparently bigger than the ship itself, was revolving in the sky not far above the surface of the water at that point. Vivid shafts of light emitted from the huge wheel and passed right through the steamer, although these beams of light did not disrupt the functioning of the ship. This sighting of 1906 was one of eleven reports between 1848 and 1910 (16). Like most of the accounts, this one remarked on the eerie silence of the phenomenon. It could of course be argued that the sightings were merely visions of seamen too long at sea.

Yet a French token was minted in 1680 and appears to show such a wheel spinning in the sky over a hundred years before the first written account that remains available to us. Quite why the token was minted is now lost in history but it has been suggested that the design may be to commemorate a daytime UFO sighting.

In June 1881, the two sons of the Prince of Wales (one of whom was later to ascend to the throne as George V) were steaming off the coast of Australia when they noted an object in the sky that appeared to be an airborne, fully illuminous ship (17).

SUPPRESSED INTELLIGENCE REPORTS

Then on 12th August 1883 it appears that for the first time ever a 'UFO' was captured on camera. It happened at the observatory at Zacatecas, eleven thousand feet up a Mexican mountain.

The director, Jose Bonilla, had been observing 'formations' of circular objects that crossed the Sun on a west-east course. He counted 283 of the objects and was able to photograph one with a camera attached to a telescope.

Bonilla later reported in the astronomical press, "I was able to fix their trajectory across the solar disk ... some appeared round or spherical, but one notes in the photographs that the bodies are not spherical but irregular in form. Before crossing the solar disk these bodies threw out brilliant trains of light but in crossing the sun they seemed to become opaque and dark against its brighter background." (18)

One of the objects Bonilla photographed resembled a "five-pointed star with dark centre." It was suggested that he had only observed birds or insects crossing the path of his telescope, however Bonilla calculated that they appeared not as far out as the Moon.

Strange objects also are noted in paintings of biblical scenes. One 14th century fresco depicts the crucifixion and shows a man traversing the sky in an egg-shaped vehicle. The image is from a fresco in the Visoki Decani monastery and is called the 'Crucifixion'.

In the upper two sides of the fresco, which pictured the crucified Jesus, two objects are painted which could be interpreted as being ancient 'spacemen' in aerial crafts.

Another Russian fresco/icon has been interpreted as showing Jesus entering (or leaving) a vehicle which seems to emit rocketlike rays that throws (or protecting their eyes by throwing themselves) the near crowd to the ground.

One fresco is from the 15th Century and found near Kiev. However it is prudent to be cautious when considering such biblical images, for the Bible yields dozens of stories that later painters could interpret as space vehicles.

Yet the concept of extraterrestrial intervention in religion has strong roots and has been explored by many authors, using the Bible itself as a point of reference. Authors such as Mistaki, Le Poer Trench and Soviet astronomer Kazantsev suggest that angels could actually be 'spacemen'.

"According to Genesis 19:3 Lot took the two angels he met at the gate of Sodom to his house 'and made them a feast, and did bake unleavened bread, and they did eat.' But according to dictionary definitions angels are spiritual, ethereal beings. Angels who ate with Lot could not have been such beings ... Rev. H. Wipprecht of Cobalt, Canada, says that the Bible's description of angels fits 'intelligent beings' from other planets. In the Old Testament these 'mysterious messengers' were said to regularly visit the Earth from the sky, and on occasion actually intermarried with human beings. The angels who married earth women could not have been 'heavenly spirits.'" (19)

Le Poer Trench notes other references in Gen. 18:4-5,8: "Let me bring some water for you to wash your feet; you can rest here beneath this tree. I will also bring a bit of food; it will give you strength to continue your journey. You have honoured me by coming to my home, so let me serve you. They replied, "Thank-you; we accept ... He took some cream, some milk, and the meat, and set the food before the men. There under the tree he served them himself, and they ate."

Le Poer's belief in the extraterrestrial connection at times becomes tenuous, if not necessarily incorrect. He believes the following from Isaiah 13:3,5 is evidence that the 'armies of God' were an extraterrestrial expedition coming from space.

"The Lord has called out his proud and confident soldiers to fight a holy war and punish those he is angry with."

"They are coming from far-off countries at the ends of the earth. In his anger the Lord is coming to devastate the whole country."

However, other puzzling images appear in medieval paintings that cannot be so easily dismissed. For example, in a scene from a medieval tapestry portraying the life of the Virgin Mary, a black domed object can be seen in the background hovering above the skyline.

Equally intriguing is the object hovering in the background in a segment of a Renaissance painting of the Madonna and Child. The object appears to be radiating beams of light. It is difficult to account for such an image by any other means except to accept that it is indeed a UFO.

One such painting was executed for the Annunciation Church at Ascoli Piceno by Carlo Crivelli in 1486 (although some sources cite 1476).

Saint Emidius was the patron saint of the city and in his hands the model of the church can be seen. More intriguingly, however is what appears to be a flying disc in the sky, also emanating a beam of light.

This is perhaps the most remarkable of all the images for the 'UFO' can clearly be seen and is the same shape as commonly reported in the twentieth century, yet the painter Crivelli died in 1495! (The beam of light is also fascinating as many UFO encounters are associated with beams of white light coming from alien craft.)

Such strange phenomena continued to be observed throughout the centuries. On the 6th November 1896 the residents of Sacramento in California observed a light moving slowly across the night sky, apparently carried by a cigar shaped craft. Later in November a trolleyman named Charles Lusk made a further report that he had been standing outside his house and looking up at the sky when he saw a bright light cruising overhead. The craft was later spotted over San Francisco.

Speculation mounted that the craft had been launched by a wealthy but anonymous inventor, and sure enough, in the winter of 1896 a lawyer who became known as 'Airship Collins' announced that he represented a wealthy by anonymous inventor who had assembled the machine in the hills north of Sacramento.

So that was that, until a rival attorney claimed that it was in fact he who was the agent for the unknown inventor, and that two craft had been built, one in California and one in New Jersey. The purpose of the craft? To bomb Havana of course.

Reports of the phenomena continued throughout the month, then from March 1897 a stream of reports from across Texas and neighboring states flooded in, noting lights in the sky, some like "electric arc lights" others shaped like balls of wheels that were attached to huge craft shaped like a cigar.

SUPPRESSED INTELLIGENCE REPORTS

The Colony Free Press of Kansas had this explanation for its readers: "The Free Press ... is now of the opinion that the airship is not of this world, but is probably operated by a party of scientists from the planet Mars, who are out, either on a lark, or a tour of inspection of the solar system in the cause of science." (20). Of course, the editor may have been mistaken ...Then by May 1897 the reports ended as suddenly as they had begun.

Of course the reports could have been observations of airships, yet, it was not until 1900, that the development of rigid airships – 'dirigibles' -began, and not in America, but thousands of miles away in Germany. It may be, however, that this late 19th century phenomenon may have more Earthly origins, for it came a mere decade after Jules Verne published his 'Robur le Conquerant,' a book which included an illustration of 'The Clipper of the Clouds'

Yet there is other evidence of strange phenomena around the end of the 19th Century. The following letter was sent to the Editor of Scientific American Magazine by Warner Cowgill, US Consulate, Maracaibo and published on 18th December 1886:

"During the night of the 24th October last, which was rainy and tempestuous, a family of nine persons, sleeping in a hut a few leagues from Maracaibo, were awakened by a loud humming noise and a vivid, dazzling light which brilliantly illuminated the interior of the house.

"The occupants, completely terror stricken, and believing, as they relate, that the end of the world had come, threw themselves on their knees and commenced to pray, but their devotions were almost immediately interrupted by violent vomitings, and extensive swellings commenced to appear in the upper part of their bodies, this being particularly noticeable about the face and lips.

"It is to be noted that the brilliant lights was not accompanied by a sensation of heat, although there was a smoky appearance and a peculiar smell.

"The next morning, the swellings had subsided, leaving upon the face and body large black blotches. No special pain was felt until the ninth day, when the skin peeled off, and these blotches were transformed into virulent raw sores.

"The hair of the head fell off upon the side which happened to be underneath when the phenomenon occurred, the same side of the body being, in all nine cases, the more seriously injured.

"The remarkable part of the occurrence is that the house was uninjured, all doors and windows being closed at the time.

"No trace of lightening could afterward be observed in any part of the building, and all the sufferers unite in saying that there was no detonation, but only the loud humming already mentioned.

"Another curious attendant circumstance is that the trees around the house showed no signs of injury until the ninth day, when they suddenly withered, almost simultaneously with the development of the sores upon the bodies of the occupants of the house."

Eleven years later, then House of Representatives member, Alexander Hamilton reported the following:

"Last Monday night, about 10:30 we were awakened by a noise among the cattle. I arose, thinking that perhaps my bulldog was performing some of his pranks, but upon going to the door saw to my utter astonishment an airship slowly descending upon my cow lot, about forty rods from the house.

Calling my tenant, Gid Heslip, and my son Wall, we seized some axes and ran to the corral. Meanwhile, the ship had been gently descending until it was not more than thirty feet above the ground, and we came within fifty yards of it.

It consisted of a great cigar-shaped portion, possibly three hundred feet long, with a carriage underneath. The carriage was made of glass or some other transparent substance alternating with a narrow strip of some material. It was brilliantly lighted within and everything was plainly visible – it was occupied by six of the strangest beings I ever saw. They were jabbering together, but we could not understand a word they said.

Every part of the vessel which was not transparent was of a dark reddish color. We stood mute with wonder and fright, when some noise attracted their attention and they turned a light directly upon us. Immediately on catching sight of us they turned on some unknown power, and a great turbine wheel, about thirty feet in diameter, which was slowly revolving below the craft began to buzz and the vessel rose lightly as a bird. When about three hundred feet above us it seemed to pause and hover directly over a two-year-old heifer, which was bawling and jumping, apparently fast in the fence. Going to her, we found a cable about a half-inch in thickness made of some red material, fastened in a slip knot around her neck, one end passing up to the vessel, and the heifer tangled in the wire fence. We tried to get it off but could not, so we cut the wire lose and stood in amazement to see the ship, heifer and all, rise slowly, disappearing in the northwest.

We went home, but I was so frightened I could not sleep. Rising early Tuesday, I started out by horse, hoping to find some trace of my cow. This I failed to do, but coming back in the evening found that Link Thomas, about three or four miles west of Le Roy, had found the hide, legs and head in his field that day. He, thinking someone had butchered a stolen beast, had brought the hide to town for identification, but was greatly mystified in not being able to find any tracks in the soft ground. After identifying the hide by my brand, I went home. But every time I would drop to sleep I would see the cursed thing, with its big lights and hideous people. I don't know whether they are devils or angels or what; but we all saw them, and my whole family saw the ship, and I don't want any more to do with them.

Hamilton has long been a resident of Kansas and is known all over Woodson, Allen, Coffey and Anderson Counties. He was a member of the house of representatives. He staked his sacred honor on the truth of his story.

An affidavit follows:

As there are now, always have been and always will be skeptics and unbelievers whenever the truth of anything bordering the improbable is presented, and knowing that some ignorant or suspicious people will doubt the truthfulness of the above statement, now, therefore, we, the undersigned, do hereby make the following affidavit:

That we have known Alexander Hamilton for one to thirty years, and that for the truth and veracity we have never heard his word questioned, and that we do verily believe his statement to be true and correct.

Signed: E. W. Wharton, State Oil Inspector; M. E. Hunt, Sheriff; W. Lauber, Deputy Sher-

SUPPRESSED INTELLIGENCE REPORTS

iff; H. H. Winter, Banker; H. S. Johnson, Pharmacist; J. H. Stitcher, Attorney; Alexander Stewart, Justice of the Peace; F. W. Butler, Druggist; James W. Martin, Registrar of Deeds, And H. C. Collins, Postmaster.

Subscribed and sworn before me this 21st day of April 1897." (21)

In 1909 strange craft were reported in the skies over Massachusetts. These craft reportedly had powerful searchlights that lit up the ground as they passed overhead. By December of that year a wave of such sightings flooded in from across the New England States (22).

Then on the night of 30th August 1910 above New York City a long black cigar shaped object flew in low over Madison Square in full view of hundreds of people. According to the New York Tribune the object had red and green lights and made airplane engine noises. It circled once round the park then flew away. The following night it returned for a repeat performance (23).

Could this mystery object have been a plane? In 1910 there were only thirty-six licensed pilots in the whole of the United States and following a check by newsmen all planes were accounted for – only one was in the area. It was on Long Island and only had a range of 25 miles. The origin of the craft above New York has never been explained.

Other events have been similarly unaccounted for. One of the most famous of these took place at Edwards Air Force Base; the home of the Air Force Flight Test Center where for more than 50 years it has been at the leading edge of developments in the aerospace world. From America's first jet airplane to the landings of the Space Shuttle, Edwards AFB has seen more major milestones in flight than any other place on Earth mainly due to its ideal location. (Excellent all-year flying weather, relative isolation, varied topography as well as the vast expanse of Rogers Dry lake.)

Then on the night of 7th October 1965 Edwards become famous for another milestone, apparent contact with unidentified objects not from this Earth.

A transcript of the event follows:

Clark: Hello, this is Captain Clark, Alpha Lima.

Reed: Okay, Captain Clark. Lt. Reed.

Clark: Yeah.

Reed: We have some confirmed reports of some unidentified flying objects in your area.

Clark: Okay.

Reed: Approximately six or more from Edwards just south of Victorville. They are moving slowly and climbing slowly. They're red, white and green flashing lights.

Clark: Uh-ha.

Reed: And they have been confirmed on radar. We can't establish what these things are.

Observations of the objects continued with the following conversations being recorded:

SUPPRESSED INTELLIGENCE REPORTS

Voice 1: Three more of them. Well south and dim.

Voice 2: Okay.

Voice 1: I can still see a red light occasionally out of one of them.

Voice 2: Where are they from? That big bright one.

Voice 1: Beneath him and just a little bit south. And there's three of them almost in a straight line.

Voice 2: Uh-ha.

Voice 1: I don't like being the only one who's seeing these type of things. I still have a contact out there.

Voice 2: Oh, you do? Visual?

Voice 1: Yes.

Voice 2: What are all these objects? Do they look the same as the rest of them?

Voice 1: No, this one just appears to be flashing, nothing red or green involved.

Voice 2: Oh I see. Could be something else.

Voice 1: Alright, I have Alpha Lima in sight now.

Voice: Yeah, he says he's got a contact twelve o'clock, sixteen.

Voice: That's it.

The incident was investigated by former astronaut Dr Edgar Mitchell, who, on the 'Geraldo Rivera Show' stated "This is a real event. I have investigated it myself."

[On 8th July 1947 there were a series of sightings over Edwards AFB then known as Muroc AFB. In the morning of that day two spherical or disc-like UFOs were seen and then joined by a third object. The crew of technicians, all of whom were familiar with the latest aerial technology, observed a white-aluminium UFO with distinct oval outline descending, moving against wind.

Then in the afternoon a thin "metallic" UFO climbed, dove then oscillated over the field and was also seen by a test pilot in vicinity. This F-51 pilot watched a flat object "of light-reflecting nature" pass above his plane. No known aircraft were in the area. (These events were all made subject to sworn affidavits at the time. Astronaut Gordon Cooper also witnesses a UFO episode in 1957/58 at Edwards AFB detailed in 'Space Anomalies')]

There are also more explicit reports of unusual phenomena.

For example on 21st October 1978, a young, but experienced pilot, Frederick Valentich was flying his plane, 'Delta Sierra Juliet' to King Island, midway between Cape Otway, Australia to Tasmania.

At 7:06pm he contacted ground control at Melbourne Flight Service.

Parts of the Flight Service transcript of the ensuing conversation appeared in Australian newspapers including the Sun and the Australian on the morning of 23rd October.

SUPPRESSED INTELLIGENCE REPORTS

7:06pm

Pilot: MELBOURNE THIS IS DELTA SIERRA JULIET is there any known traffic below five thousand [feet]?

Flight Service Unit: DELTA SIERRA JULIET no known traffic.

Pilot: DELTA SIERRA JULIET I am seems [to] be a large aircraft below five thousand.

Flight Service Unit: DELTA SIERRA JULIET what type of aircraft is it?

Pilot: DELTA SIERRA JULIET I cannot affirm. It is four bright it seems to me like landing lights…

Flight Service Unit: DELTA SIERRA JULIET

Pilot: DELTA SIERRA JULIET the aircraft has just passed over me at least a thousand feet above.

Flight Service Unit: DELTA SIERRA JULIET roger and it it is a large aircraft confirm.

Pilot: … er unknown due to the speed it's travelling is there any airforce aircraft in the vicinity?

Flight Service Unit: DELTA SIERRA JULIET no known aircraft in the vicinity.

7:08pm

Pilot: MELBOURNE, it's approaching from due east toward me.

Flight Service Unit: DELTA SIERRA JULIET

Pilot: DELTA SIERRA JULIET it seems to me that he's playing some sort of game he's flying over me two three times at a time at speeds I could not identify.

7:09pm

Flight Service Unit: DELTA SIERRA JULIET roger what is your actual level?

Pilot: My level is four and a half thousand four five zero zero.

Flight Support Unit: DELTA SIERRA JULIET and confirm you cannot identify the aircraft?

Pilot: Affirmative.

Flight Service Unit: DELTA SIERRA JULIET roger standby.

Pilot: MELBOURNE DELTA SIERRA JULIET it's not an aircraft it is // open microphone for two seconds //

Flight Service Unit: DELTA SIERRA JULIET can you describe the er, aircraft?

Pilot: DELTA SIERRA JULIET as it's flying past it's a long shape // open microphone for three seconds // [cannot] identify more than [that it has such speed] // open microphone for three seconds // before me right now Melbourne.

7:10pm

Flight Service Unit: DELTA SIERRA JULIET roger and how large would the, er object be?

SUPPRESSED INTELLIGENCE REPORTS

Pilot: DELTA SIERRA JULIET MELBOURNE it seems like it's stationary what I'm doing right now is orbiting and the thing is just orbiting on top of me also it's got a green light and sort of metallic [like] it's all shiny [on] the outside.

Frederick Valentich in his Cessna 182 (left-type) then told ground control that the object had apparently just vanished and then asked whether he had seen a type of military aircraft.

7:11pm

Flight Service Unit: DELTA SIERRA JULIET is the aircraft still with you?

Pilot: DELTA SIERRA JULIET [it's ah nor] // open microphone 2 seconds // [now] approaching from the southwest.

Flight Service Unit: DELTA SIERRA JULIET

Pilot: DELTA SIERRA JULIET the engine is rough-idling I've got it set at twenty three twenty four and the thing is [coughing].

7:12pm

Flight Service Unit: DELTA SIERRA JULIET roger what are your intentions?

Pilot: My intentions are ah to go to King Island ah Melbourne that strange aircraft is hovering on top of me again // two seconds open microphone // it is hovering and it's not an aircraft.

Flight Service Unit: DELTA SIERRA JULIET.

Pilot: DELTA SIERRA JULIET MELBOURNE // 17 seconds open microphone //

Flight Service Unit: DELTA SIERRA JULIET MELBOURNE.

There then followed a long 'metallic' noise before all contact ceased. The plane never arrived at its destination, nor did a thorough visual and radio search discover what had actually happened. The plane was equipped with a standard radio survival beacon, thus the radio search, however no signal was ever received (24).

The following day an oil slick north of King Island was observed although no connection with Valentich's plane could be made (either way.)

Former NASA-contracted research scientist, Dr Richard Haines, concluded that this metallic noise which followed the last transmission contained "36 separate bursts with fairly constant start and stop pulses bounding each one; there are no discernible patterns in time or frequency." (25).

Objectors to the idea of UFOs not only claim that nearly all, if not all sightings are misidentified phenomena, but that any such sightings are merely figments of over active American minds.

Yet the reality is, sightings have been made across the world.

There is an image taken above Argentina in 1977.

This huge orb of light was seen by thousands of people and was photographed at

SUPPRESSED INTELLIGENCE REPORTS

Maspalomas on Gran Canaria in 1976. The was photographed at Maspalomas on Gran Canaria in 1976. The picture was released by the Spanish Air Force who could not explain the event.

Another image was photographed by a US Marine Air group pilot over the north-east China Sea during the Korean war.

Reproduced in Timothy Good's 'Beyond Top Secret' Good comments "While the sharply delineated straight line in the middle and the black lower half suggest photographic trickery, similar effects have been noted in other cases."

Of course visual sighting are always open to interpretation (and misinterpretation). Sometimes objects seen in the sky are very real, but also very secret and reports are unlikely to generate a candid response from the military.

One such secret military project was Project Mogul; a US top secret project to develop a means of detecting and monitoring Soviet nuclear weapons which conducted its operations from Alamogordo Army Air Field, New Mexico in June and July 1947 using high-altitude balloon arrays and attached instrument packages (26). It has been claimed that it was the wreckage from one of these Mogul flights that could account for the debris found at the infamous Roswell site, of which more later, and also at another crash at nearby Corona. This is certainly the view of Karl Pflock, a former CIA officer, whose career included a period as Deputy Assistant Secretary of Defence for Operational Test and Evaluation (27). The crash landing of a top-secret project in open territory would undoubtedly have led to the immediate sealing of the area and collection of all recoverable remains.

To demonstrate how easily balloons can be mistaken for UFOs, one photograph shows a high-level cosmic radiation balloon released by a British University and spotted over London, only to be reported as a 'flying saucer'.

Of course many of the reported sightings of UFOs are hoaxes. One picture shows farmer Richard Jennings examining a 'flying disk' that he found on his farm in Chippenham in Wiltshire, England on 4th September 1967 whilst a policeman looks on.

It was one of six found in a straight line from Somerset to Kent – all of which proved to be fakes.

In fact such hoaxes accounted for 33% of all sightings claimed to be UFOs in a formal United States Air Force investigation of the phenomenon in 1949. A further 32% could be accounted for astronomically, 12% were identified as weather balloons, however 23% remained unaccounted for (28).

It is this 23% that has long interested believers in extraterrestrial contact, a belief that has widespread support throughout the scientific community. As Carl Sagan stated "The earth may have been visited by various galactic civilizations many times (possibly in the order of 10,000) during geological times. It is not out of the question that artifacts of these visits still exist, or even that some kind of base is maintained (possibly automatically) within the solar system to provide continuity for successive expeditions." (29)

However, one of the main arguments against the likelihood of such alien contact is that the distances between us and our universal neighbors- even if they do exist - are so great that the possibility of physical contact can almost be ruled out.

SUPPRESSED INTELLIGENCE REPORTS

But can it be ruled in?

References

(1) Sagan Carl, 'Broca's Brain' Chapter 6, Random House, New York 1979.

(2) Story, R., 'Guardians of the Universe?' pp. 113-127, Book Club Associates, London 1980.

(3) Temple, R. 'The Sirius Mystery', Sidgwick and Jackson 1976.

(4) Temple, R. 'The Sirius Mystery', Sidgwick and Jackson 1976.

(5) The Unexplained . 297

(6) Ibid.

(7) Ibid.

(8) Temple, R. 'The Sirius Mystery', Sidgwick and Jackson 1976.

(9) Valee p. 1

(10) Valee p. 2

(11) Trench, Brinsley le Poer, 'The Sky People' Neville Spearman, London 1960.

(12) Trench, Brinsley le Poer, 'The Flying Saucer Story'. 105

(13) Alien Worlds, Ruben Stone p 10.

(14) The UFO Phenomenon p. 16

(15) 'Knowledge' p. 396, 28th December 1883.)

(16) Mysteries of the Universe p. 183

(17) Ibid p 18

(18) Randles, J 'UFOs & How to See Them' p.9.

(19) 'Angels Are Men From Space' Austr. FSR, Vol. I No. 3, September 1960. See also Toronto Daily Star, 5th January 1960.

(20) Mysteries of the Universe p. 181

(21) Hynek, J. A. H., Talk presented to the Hypervelocity Impact Conference, Elgin Air Force Base, Florida 27th April, 1960 as quoted in Valee, Jacques, 'Anatomy of a Phenomenon' pp. 16-17, Tandem, 1974.

(22) Blum, Ralph and Judy, 'Beyond Earth' p. 60 Corgi 1978.

(23) Keel, John A., 'UFOs: Operation Trojan Horse' p120, quoting the New York Tribune, G. P. Putnam's Sons, New York 1970.

(24) Chalker, W., 'The Missing Cessna and the UFO', pp. 3-5, Flying Saucer Review, Vol. 31, No. 5, 1986.

(25) Chalker, W., 'Vanished? – The Valentich Affair Re-Examined', pp 6-12, Flying Saucer Review, Vol. 30 No. 2 1984.

(26) Good,T 'Beyond Top Secret' p 462 Sidgewick & Jackson, London 1996

(27) 'Roswell in Perspective'

(28) Technical Report No. 102-AC-49/15-100 pp 94-95.

(29) Carl Sagan (1966 meeting of the American Astronautical Society, in Norman, Eric, 'Gods, Demons and Space Chariots' New York, Lancer Books 1970.

APPENDIX I:

A SELECTED CHRONOLOGY OF HISTORICAL 'SIGHTINGS'

This list is supplemental to episodes detailed in 'Towards the Sky', a gives a further selection of events from the many thousands reported over the past few centuries.

BCE 593 Ezekiel witnesses event which some writers have claimed sounds suspiciously like a UFO encounter. Josef Blumrich, former chief of the systems layout branch of NASA, set out to disprove such suggestions, however, from a careful analysis of the data available, he concluded that the vehicle described in the Bible actually was a UFO. His schematic is shown here.

BCE 218 In Julius Obsequen's book 'Prodigiorum Liber' there are reports of a shield flying through he sky, two moons seen at night, ghost ships in the sky and luminous lamps at Praeneste.

BCE 213 In Hadria, an 'altar' was seen in the sky, accompanied by a man in white clothing.

CE 60 A 'ship' was seen speeding across the sky at night in Scotland.

CE 763 While King Domnall Mac Murchada attended the fair at Teltown in Meath County, ships were seen in the air.

CE 776 A translation of 'Annales Laurissenses' reads: "Now when the Saxons perceived things were not going in their favor, they began to erect scaffolding from which they could bravely storm the castle itself. But God is good as well as just. He overcame their valor, and on the same day they prepared an assault against the Christians, who lived within the castle, the glory of God appeared in manifestation above the church within the fortress. Those watching outside in that place, of whom many still live to this very day, say they beheld the likeness of two large shields reddish in color in motion above the church ..." (1)

CE 919 In Hungary spherical objects shining like stars were reportedly traversing the sky.

CE 927 "In 927 the town of Verdun, like the whole eastern part of France, saw fiery armies appearing in the sky. Flodoard's chronicle reports that they flew over eastern Reims on a Sunday morning in March. Similar phenomena happened several times under King Pepin the Short, under Charlemagne, under Louis I, the Debonair. These sovereign's capitularia mention penalties against creatures that travel on aerial ships." (2)

SUPPRESSED INTELLIGENCE REPORTS

29.07.966 A luminous vertical cylinder was observed over the ocean. 23.08.1015 Two objects were seen 'giving birth' to smaller luminous spheres over Japan. 1034 A cigar-shaped object surrounded by flames flew over Europe following a straight path from south to east, before turning towards the setting sun. (3)

12.08.1133 A large silvery disk is reported to have come close to the ground in Japan.

01.01.1254 There "appeared in the sky a kind of large ship, elegantly shaped, well equipped and of a marvellous colour" over St. Alban's Abbey on a clear night according to Mathew of Paris' 'Historia Anglorum'. (4)

1290 A large silvery 'flying disk' was observed at Byland Abbey, Yorkshire.

01.11.1461 An object shaped like a ship passed over the town of Arras in France. Jacques Duclerc, a chronicler and counsellor to Duke Philip the Good, provided an account of this sighting in his 'Memoirs of a Freeman of Arras': "A fiery thing like an iron rod of good length and as large as one half of the moon was seen in the sky for a little less than quarter of an hour." (5)

1520 A round shape with a rotating light or beam, accompanied by 'two fiery suns' was described over the skies of Erfurt. (6)

1752 "Luminous sphere coming out of a bright cylinder" were noted in Augermanland, Sweden.

09.08.1762 An object was observed in front of the Sun by two different observatories in Switzerland.

30.08.1783 An object was observed over Greenwich that 'gave birth' to eight satellites which disappeared slowly towards the Southeast.

07.09.1820 Francois Arago wrote of this date in the 'Annales de chimie et de physique': "Numerous observers have seen, during an eclipse of the moon, strange objects moving in straight lines.

They were equally spaced and remained in line when they made turns. Their movements made a military precision." .07.1868 At Capiago in Chile and aerial construction was observed emitting light with an engine noise (7). 22.03.1870 An object was seen from the ship "Lady of the Lake" in the Atlantic Ocean that appeared to be a light-grey coloured disk that flew against the wind (8).

29.08.1871 Astronomer Trouvelot of the Meudon Observatory noted a number of objects that resembled those witnessed at Nuremberg and Basel. Among the objects he saw was a circle that first seemed about to fall, then descended "like a disk falling through water." (9)

24.04.1874 A Professor Schafarick saw above Prague "an object of such strange nature that I do not know what to say about it. It was of a blinding white and crossed slowly the face of the moon. It remained visible afterwards." (10)

23.03.1877 Reports of a "cloud cigar" at Vence, France where "fiery speres, extremely luminous, came out of a cloud of peculiar shape and went slowly toward the north for one hour." (11)

24.01.1878 John Martin, a Texas Farmer, observed a dark flying object, the shape of a disk, cruising high in the sky "at a wonderful speed." He used the word 'saucer' to describe what he saw. (12)

1883 The children and teacher at an elementary school at Segeberg reported seeing two fiery spheres in the sky with the apparent diameter of the full Moon. They were reportedly travelling side by side and not very fast, on a north-south course.

01.11.1885 The following report appeared in 'L'Astronomie': "M. Mavrogordato, of Constantinople , calls our attention to the following strange observations which have been communicated to him.

(i) On November 1, at 9:30pm, there was seen, west of Adrianople, an elongated object giving off a strong luminosity. It seemed to float in the air and its apparent disk was four or five times larger than the full moon. It traveled slowly and cast light on the whole camp behind the station with a brightness about ten times greater than a large electric bulb. (ii) In the morning of November 2, at dawn, a very luminous flame, first bluish, then greenish, and moving at a height of five to six meters, made a series of turns around the ferryboat pier at Scutari. Its blinding luminosity lighted the street and flooded the inside of the houses with light.". (13) 12.11.1887 L'Astronomie reported "On November 12, 1887, at midnight, near Cape Race, a huge ball of fire appeared, slowly emerging from the ocean to an altitude of sixteen to seventeen meters. This sphere started moving against the wind and stopped close to the ship from which it was observed. Then it rushed away in the sky and disappeared in the southeast. The whole observation had lasted five minutes."

08.01.1888 Luminous bodies were seen flying through the sky in lines for one hour, according to the 'Memoirs' of the Minor Brothers of Ragusa, Italy. 1893 Several observations of disks and wheels at sea were made mainly between Japan and China (14). 20.12.1893 A huge 'wheel' emanating noise appeared in the United States. It remained motionless for fifteen minutes before departing. 31.08.1895 At 8:00pm in Oxford England a disk was seen rising above some trees and disappearing into the east (15).

References

(1) Drake, W. R. 'Did UFOs Stop A War?' p. 13 FSR, IX, No 2 March-April 1963.

(2) 'Guide de la France Mysterieuse' Tchou, editeur a Paris, 1964. 108

(3) Valee p. 8

(4) Wilkins, H. T. 'Flying Saucers on the Attack' Citadel Press, New York, 1954.

(5) Wilkins, H. T. 'Flying Saucers on the Attack' Citadel Press, New York, 1954.

(6) Quincy, G., 'Catalogue of 1,027 UFO Observations' Valee p. 8.

(7) 'Zoologis' January 1868.

(8) Valee p. 8

(9) L'Anee Scientifique XXIX, 8.

(10) Astronomical Register XXIII, 205.

(11) 'L'Anee Scientifique', 1877 p. 45

SUPPRESSED INTELLIGENCE REPORTS

(12) 'Denison Daily News' 25th January 1878.

(13) 'L'Astronomie' 1885 and R Veillith, 'Lumieres dans la Nuit' Collection.

(14) Valee p. 15

(15) Times, 4th September 1895. 109

PART THREE

THE SCHOOL OF THE AMERICAN EMPIRE

Mumia Abu-Jamal

"... A society that becomes accustomed to using violence to solve its problems, both large and small, is a society in which the roots of human relations are diseased." - - Ignacio Martin-Baro, O. J.

It is virtually impossible for anyone to consider the horrific violence that has taken place in Central and Latin America, without accounting for the hideous roots of that violence, that grows and thrives in America.

For decades, the bloody flood from murders, massacres, rapes, torture and carnage, created a trail that could be traced to the very doorsteps of a U.S. military training institute known as the School of the Americas in Fort Benning, Georgia. Human rights activists have held increasingly swelling demonstrations at the SOA, and have dubbed it the "School of Assassins."

For years the Pentagon dismissed such criticism, and defended the SOA as an elite international training academy for "counter-insurgency", or, more obliquely, for "teaching democracy."

The graduates of SOA, however, constituted a kind of rogue's gallery of military despots and dictators, like Bolivia's Gen. Hugo Banzer Suarez, who brutally suppressed progressive church workers and striking tin miners; Like Guatemalan dictator Gen. Romeo Lucas Garcia (1978-82) whose rule saw over 5,000 political killings and about 25,000 civilians murdered by the Guatemalan army, and Gen. Juan Rafael Bustillo, of El Salvador, former air force chief, who, according to a 1993 U.N. report, both planned and covered up the massacre of six Jesuit priests, their housekeeper, and her daughter on Nov. 16, 1989, to name a few.

If you think of a massacre, the chances are great that the men who either ordered or committed the deed were SOA alumni. The El Mozote, El Junquillo, Las Hojas, La Cantuta, and San Sebastian Massacres were all the work of SOA-trained "death squads." Was it mere coincidence? When four U.S. churchwomen were raped and murdered, when Archbishop Oscar Romero was assassinated, when union members were killed, it was SOA grads who led in the carnage.

U.S.-trained and armed SOA people have been involved in so many military coups that Latin American locals refer to the school as the 'escuela de golpas' - - coup school.

Recently, the Defense Dept., stung by decades of negative publicity, officially "closed" SOA, only to immediately reopen it under the name, Western Hemisphere Institute for Security Cooperation (WHISC). Although not as catchy as SOA, WHISC promises to play the same game, by another name.

Shortly after the Jesuit murders, U.S.-trained Salvadoran troops surrounded the office of the Catholic archdiocese, and shouted, "Ignacio Ellacuria and Ignacio Martin-Baro have already fallen and we will continue murdering communists."

Ellacuria and Martin-Baro were Jesuit priests who worked with Christian-based communities, where the poor learned literacy, history and how to organize for human rights in the midst of monstrous military repression.

Martin-Baro was a brilliant liberation theologist and psychologist, who, like the revolutionary Franz Fanon, chose the side of the oppressed rather than the political, economic and military elite.

For this he was targeted by the U.S.-trained terrorists of the SOA, and it is for men and women such as he that imperial training camps, like SOA/WHISC exist.

Its name has changed, but the game remains the same.

Copyright MAJ '01

This article comes from THE FREEDOM JOURNAL

SCHOOL OF THE AMERICAS: SCHOOL OF ASSASSINS, USA

"We routinely had Latin American students at the School of the Americas (SOA) who were known human rights abusers, and it didn't make any difference to us."

Major Joseph Blair (retired), former SOA instructor

World War II was the "good war". After that conflict, most Americans believed that US intentions in the world were noble — the US was the punisher of aggression and a warrior for freedom. This image was for generations of Americans the measure by which they judged their country in world affairs. The war in Vietnam ended the illusion that America was always on the "right side". Today, America's image as a defender of democracy and justice has been further eroded by the School of the Americas (SOA), which trains Latin American and Caribbean military officers and soldiers to subvert democracy and kill hope in their own countries.

Founded by the United States in 1946, the SOA was initially located in Panama, but in 1984 it was kicked out under the terms of the Panama Canal Treaty and moved to the army base at Fort Benning, Georgia. Then-President of Panama Jorge Illueca called it "the biggest base for de-stabilization in Latin America," and a major Panamanian newspaper dubbed it " The School of Assassins."

Today, SOA instructors and students are recruited from the cream of the Latin American military establishment. The School trains 700-2,000 soldiers a year, and since its inception in 1946, more than 60,000 military personnel have graduated from the SOA.

If the SOA concentrated its training on protecting country borders from foreign aggression or safeguarding citizens from invasion by outside enemies, it would be considered an exemplary institution, worth the cost of American tax dollars and US prestige. But, the SOA has very different goals. Its curriculum includes courses in psychological warfare, counterinsurgency, interrogation techniques, and infantry and commando tactics. Presented with the most sophisticated and up-to-date techniques by the US Army's best instructors, these courses teach military officers and soldiers of Third World countries to subvert the truth, to muzzle union leaders, activist clergy, and journalists, and to make war on their own people. It prepares them to subdue the voices of dissent and to make protesters submit. It instructs them in techniques of marginalizing the poor, the hungry, and the dispossessed. It tells them how to stamp out freedom and terrorize their own citizens. It trains them to destroy the hope of democracy.

The School of the Americas (SOA) has been given other names — "School for Dictators", "School of Assassins", and "Nursery of Death Squads". And, countries with the worst human rights records send the most soldiers to the School.

Countries / Graduates (since 1946)

Argentina / 931 Bolivia / 4,049 Brazil / 355 Chile / 2,405 Colombia / 8,679 Costa Rica / 2,376 Dominican Republic / 2,330 Ecuador / 2,356 El Salvador / 6,776 Guatemala / 1,676 Honduras / 3,691 Nicaragua / 4,693 Panama / 4,235 Paraguay / 1,084 Peru / 3,997 Uruguay / 931 Venezuela / 3,250

When they return to their home countries, graduates of the SOA hold a rather unique and peculiar view of their countrymen. They look upon priests, social workers, journalists, and liberal intellectuals, not as assets to their societies, but as dangerous subversives, working to undermine the system that keeps these soldiers, army officers, and their sponsors in power.

Graduates of the SOA have been among the most repressive tyrants in Latin America, and their actions have been some of the most cruel and violent. In El Salvador, in 1989, a Salvadoran army patrol executed six Jesuit priests as they lay face-down on the ground at Central America University. According to the United Nation's Truth Commission Report on El Salvador in 1993, 19 of the 27 officers who took part in the executions were trained at the SOA.

In 1990, in El Salvador, populist Archbishop Oscar Romero was assassinated. Three-quarters of the Salvadoran officers implicated in the killing were trained at the SOA. Roberto D'Aubuison, the late leader of El Salvador's Death Squad, was implicated in the plot to assassinate Archbishop Romero. He also participated in numerous murders, including a massacre in the village of El Mazote, where more than 900 men, women, and children were killed. He graduated from SOA as well.

The U.N. Truth Commission's statistics reveal the extent of the School's murderous role in El Salvador .

Romero assassination 3 officers cited — 2 were SOA graduates. Murder of US nuns 5 officers cited — 3 were SOA graduates. Union leader murders 3 officers cited — 3 were SOA graduates. El Junquillo massacre 3 officers cited — 2 were SOA graduates. El Mazote massacre 12 officers cited — 10 were SOA graduates. Dutch journalist murders 1 officer cited — he was an SOA graduate. Las Hojas massacre 6 officers cited — 3 were SOA graduates. San Sebastian massacre 7 officers cited — 6 were SOA graduates. Jesuit massacre 26 officers cited — 19 were SOA graduates.

In other Latin American countries, graduates of the SOA have been equally prominent enemies of human rights. Former dictators Omar Torrijos of Panama, Guillermo Rodriguez of

SUPPRESSED INTELLIGENCE REPORTS

Ecuador, and Juan Velasco Alvarado of Peru, all overthrew constitutionally elected governments in their countries. Leopoldo Galtieri, the former head of the Argentina junta defeated in the Falklands War, was responsible for thousands of "disappeared" citizens who supported freedom and democracy in Argentina, and paid the ultimate price with their lives. He was an SOA graduate.

In Honduras, General Humberto Ragalado Hernandez, was trained at the SOA at the same time that he was linked to Columbian drug cartels, and the highest ranking officers in the Honduran Death Squad were trained at SOA as well.

In Peru, the most senior officers convicted of the February 1994 murder of nine university students and a professor, were graduates of the SOA. In Columbia, a 1992 human rights tribunal cited 246 officers for crimes against the people of Columbia. 105 of the officers were trained at the SOA. In Panama, ex-dictator Manuel Noriega, formerly on the CIA payroll, graduated from the SOA. He is now in a US prison, convicted of trafficking in drugs.

In Guatemala, a country of 10 million, the indigenous Mayan population of 6 million have endured the greatest suffering in Latin America. During more than 30 years of civil war, tens-of-thousands have been slaughtered, with the total killed estimated to exceed 200,000. Most of the ranking generals involved in the numerous coups and acts of terror and murder during this period were trained at the SOA.

In the 1970s and early 1980s, in Guatemala, thousands of political activists and opponents of government policies were assassinated. General Manuel Antonio Callejas y Callejas, Chief of Army Intelligence at the time, was cited by the UN as the individual responsible for most of those murders. He graduated from the SOA. One of the most vicious tyrants in recent Guatemalan history is Jose Efrain Rios Montt. General, dictator, and a former president from 1982-83, Rios Montt was proud of his political philosophy of "beans for the obedient; bullets for the rest". He was also a graduate of the SOA.

The impact of SOA graduates on Latin American freedom has been devastating. Armed with sophisticated training, modern weapons, and up-to-date techniques of control and surveillance, graduates of the SOA have terrorized their own countrymen for a generation.

In the name of its citizens and using American taxpayer dollars, the United States, the most-democratic of countries, has for decades been training some of the most anti-democratic leaders in the world. Administrations that have decried terrorism abroad, have encouraged terrorists right here at home —at the SOA.

Our country, for generations, a beacon of liberty and democracy to the world, should play no part in subverting democracy and killing hope in other countries. Americans who condemn world terror should condemn just as strongly America's training of Third World terrorists. It is time for all of us to demand that the School of the Americas be closed.

Call, fax, or write the President, and your Senators and Representative. Ask them to end funding for the SOA and stop training terrorists and murderers in America.

Ask them to support House of Representatives Bill — HR 2652 — introduced by Representative Joseph Kennedy (D-MA). This bill would close the School of the Americas and establish in its place an Academy for Democracy and Civil-Military Relations, to identify the proper role of the military in a democratic society and bring about civilian control over military matters in Latin America.

Father Roy Bourgeois founded SOA Watch to inform the American public about "the School of Assassins" and to close it down. But, he cannot do it alone. He needs the support of all Americans who abhor the training of terrorists and murderers in this country. Support SOA Watch and Father Roy Bourgeois at:

SOA Watch PO Box 3330 Columbus, GA 31903 706-682-5369

TEXTBOOK REPRESSION: US TRAINING MANUALS DECLASSIFIED

by Lisa Haugaard

Covert Action Quarterly magazine, September 1997

Several recently declassified US military training manuals show how US agents taught repressive techniques and promoted the violation of human rights throughout Latin America and around the globe. The manuals provide the paper trail that proves how the US trained Latin American and other militaries to infiltrate and spy upon civilians and groups, including unions, political parties, and student and charitable organizations; to treat legal political opposition like armed insurgencies; and to circumvent laws on due process, arrest, and detention. In these how-to guides, the US advocates tactics such as executing guerrillas, blackmail, false imprisonment, physical abuse, using truth serum to obtain information, and paying bounties for enemy dead. Counterintelligence agents are advised that one of their functions is "recommending targets for neutralization," a euphemism for execution or destruction.

On September 20, 1996, the Pentagon released seven training manuals prepared by the US military and used between 1987 and 1991 for intelligence training courses in Latin America and at the US Army School of the Americas (SOA), where the US trains Latin American militaries.

*****

The manuals' discovery has helped reinvigorate grassroots, religious, and congressional efforts to close the US Army School of the Americas. It proves on paper what so many have said for so long-that US training contributed to the devastating human rights violations in the region. Although Latin American militaries were perfectly capable of violating human rights and democratic principles without US sponsorship, the anti-democratic training methods advocated by the US provided -at the very least-a green light for repression. And for decades, the traffic was heavy. Techniques of control contained in the manuals were actively adopted by Latin American militaries, particularly in the 1970s and 1980s; in Chile's and Argentina's "dirty wars" in which thousands of dissidents disappeared; by military dictatorships in Brazil, Paraguay, and Uruguay; in the Central American wars, where tens of thousands of civilians were killed; and in the Andean countries, where human rights violations still abound. In most cases, the militaries being trained not only suppressed armed rebellion but also repressed democratic, civic opposition.

PAPER TRAIL

The paper trail begins with the mysterious "Project X." Like the Army manuals, the Project X materials "suggested militaries infiltrate and suppress even democratic political dissident movements and hunt down opponents in every segment of society in the name of fighting Communism," according to the Washington Post.

At least some of these teaching materials were pulled from circulation by the Carter administration, which was concerned they would contribute to human rights abuses in Latin America. In 1982, the Reagan administration asked the SOA to rush out a new counterintelligence course for Latin American militaries. The instructor asked to develop the course, Capt. Vic Tise, turned to Project X materials, stored at Fort Huachuca, Arizona, and updated them into lesson plans.

In 1987, the 470th Military Intelligence Brigade took the SOA lesson plans and turned them into textbooks: Handling of Sources, Guerrillas and Communist Ideology, Counterintelligence, Revolutionary War, Terrorism and the Urban Guerrilla, Interrogation, Combat Intelligence, and Analysis 1. These manuals were then used by US trainers in Latin America and distributed to Latin American intelligence schools in Colombia, Ecuador, El Salvador, and Peru. They came full circle back to the SOA in 1989 when they were reintroduced as reading materials in military intelligence courses attended by students from Bolivia, Colombia, Costa Rica, the Dominican Republic, Ecuador, Guatemala, Honduras, Mexico, Peru, and Venezuela. The US government estimates that as many as 1,000 copies may have been distributed at the SOA and throughout Latin America.

From start to finish, six of the seven Army manuals are how-to-guides on repressive techniques. Throughout their 1,100 plus pages, there are few mentions of democracy, human rights, or the rule of law. Instead, there are detailed techniques for infiltrating social movements, interrogating suspects, surveillance, maintaining military secrecy, recruiting and retaining spies, and controlling the population. While the excerpts released by the Pentagon to the press are a useful and not misleading selection of the most egregious passages-the ones most clearly advocating torture, execution, and blackmail-they do not reveal the manuals' highly objectionable framework. In the name of defending democracy, the manuals advocate profoundly undemocratic methods. Just as objectionable as the methods they advocate is the fundamental disregard for the differences between armed insurgencies and lawful political and civic opposition-an attitude that led to the deaths of hundreds of thousands of Latin American civilians.

OPPOSITION = REVOLUTION

The Counterintelligence manual, for example, defines as potential counterintelligence targets "local or national political party teams, or parties that have goals, beliefs or ideologies contrary or in opposition to the National Government", or "teams of hostile organizations whose objective is to create dissension or cause restlessness among the civilian population in the area of operations." This text recommends that the army create a "blacklist" of "persons whose capture and detention are of foremost importance to the armed forces." It should include not only "enemy agents" but also "subversive persons," "political leaders known or suspected as hostile toward the Armed Forces or the political interests of the National Government," and "collaborators and sympathizers of the enemy," known or suspect.

Throughout, the manuals highlight refugees and displaced persons as possible subversives to be monitored. They describe universities as breeding grounds for terrorists, and identify priests and nuns as terrorists. They advise militaries to infiltrate youth groups, student groups, labor unions, political parties, and community organizations.

SUPPRESSED INTELLIGENCE REPORTS

Even electoral activity is suspect: The insurgents "can resort to subverting the government by means of elections in which the insurgents cause the replacement of an unfriendly government official to one favorable to their cause"; "insurgent activity" can include funding campaigns and participating in political races as candidates.

One of the most pernicious passages, in "Combat Intelligence", lists ways to identify guerrilla presence. "Indicators of an imminent attack by guerrillas" include demonstrations by minority groups, reluctance by civilians-including children-to associate with US or their local troops, celebrations of national or religious festivals, or the presence of strangers. "Indicators of control by guerrillas" over a certain civilian population include the refusal to provide intelligence to government forces or the construction of new houses. Indications that insurgents are conducting psychological operations include accusations of government corruption, circulating petitions, attempts to discredit the government or armed forces, calling government leaders US puppets, urging youth to avoid the draft, demonstrations or strikes, or accusations of police or army brutality.

*****

A PURELY MILITARY RESPONSE

Civil society and government, too, are often viewed simply as impediments to military control. With no mention of the propriety of the practices, a number of the manuals advocate controlling information through censorship as well as by spying on and infiltrating civilian groups. In general, the population is a source of information at best, an enemy force at worst. The civilian government fares little better; it is one more entity to be reported on or pushed aside. Ways to impose curfews, military checkpoints, house-to-house searches, ID cards, and rationing are presented without reference to laws or the role of the legislature. Indeed, there is little discussion of the proper relationship between a civilian government and military authorities.

Much more effort is put into the role of the army in quashing revolutionary tendencies. Several of the manuals teach militaries and intelligence services how insurgencies develop and how to control them. The description of the former is generally simplistic and dated, with few references to the role official repression plays in fueling insurrection. The brief histories of El Salvador and Guatemala, for example, in "Terrorism and the Urban Guerrilla" skip over repression, human rights violations, or problems in democratic governance that contributed to the growth of revolutionary movements. Insurgents are reduced to manipulators of popular discontent, in thrall to Soviet style Marxism. While "Combat Intelligence" offers a more sophisticated explanation of the underlying reasons for revolutionary movements-such as the strains created by rapid modernization, the existence of corrupt elites and government repression-neither this manual nor any other suggests steps a civilian government might take as a political response to popular discontent. There is no limitation on when to use military and counterintelligence methods.

FROM BAD TO WORSE: THE CIA MANUALS

The two recently declassified CIA manuals make even more chilling reading. The CIA had written KUBARK Counterintelligence Interrogation in 1963 for use by US agents against perceived Soviet subversion. (KUBARK was the CIA's code name for itself.) While it was not intended to train foreign military services, its successor, Human Resource Exploitation Training Manual —1983, which drew heavily on material in KUBARK, was used in at least seven US training courses conducted in Latin American countries between 1982 and 1987, according to a June 1988 memo placed inside the manual. This 1983 manual originally surfaced in response to a June 1988 congressional hearing which was prompted by allegations by the New York Times that the US had taught Honduran military officers who used torture. The 1988 hearing was not the first time such manuals had surfaced. In 1984, a CIA manual for training the Nicaraguan Contras in psychological operations created a considerable scandal.

These two CIA textbooks deal exclusively with interrogation and devote an entire chapter each to "coercive techniques." Human Resource Exploitation recommends surprising suspects in the predawn hours, arresting, blindfolding, and stripping them naked. Suspects should be held incommunicado, it advises, and deprived of normal routines in eating and sleeping. Interrogation rooms should be windowless, sound proof, dark, and without toilets. The manuals do admonish that torture techniques can backfire and that the threat of pain is often more effective than pain itself. However, they then go on to describe coercive techniques "to induce psychological regression in the subject by bringing a superior outside force to bear on his will to resist." These techniques include prolonged constraint, prolonged exertion, extremes of heat, cold, or moisture, deprivation of food or sleep, disrupting routines, solitary confinement, threats of pain, deprivation of sensory stimuli, hypnosis, and use of drugs or placebos.

According to the Baltimore Sun, "the methods taught in the 1983 manual and those used by [the US-trained Honduran] Battalion 316 in the early 1980s show unmistakable similarities." The paper cites the case of Ines Murillo, a Honduran prisoner who claimed she was held in secret jails in 1983, given no food or water for days, and kept from sleeping by having water poured on her head every ten minutes.

Dismissive of the rule of law, Human Resource Exploitation Training Manual-1983 states the importance of knowing local laws on detention, but then notes, "Illegal detention always requires prior [headquarters] approval." The manual also refers to one or two weeks of "practical work" with prisoners as part of the course, suggesting that US trainers may have worked with Latin American militaries in interrogating actual detainees. This reference gives new support to the claims by Latin Americans held as prisoners and by US nun Dianna Ortiz, tortured by the Guatemalan army in 1989, that US personnel were present in interrogation and torture rooms.

In 1985, in a superficial attempt to correct the worst of the 1983 manual, a page advising against using coercive techniques was inserted and handwritten changes were haphazardly introduced into the text. For example, "While we do not stress the use of coercive techniques, we do want to make you aware of them and the proper way to use them," has been coyly altered to, "While we deplore the use of coercive techniques, we do want to make you aware of them so that you may avoid them." But the entire chapter on coercive techniques is still included, again with some items crossed out. Throughout, the reader can easily read the original underneath the "corrected" items. These corrections were made in response to the 1984 scandal when the CIA training manual for the Contras hit the headlines.

The second manual, KUBARK Counterintelligence Interrogation, is clearly the source of much of the 1983 manual; some passages are lifted verbatim. KUBARK has a similar section on coercive techniques, and includes some even more abhorrent elements, such as two references to the use of electric shock. For example, one passage requires US agents to obtain "prior Headquarters approval ... if bodily harm is to be inflicted," or "if medical, chemical, or electrical methods" are to be used. A third condition for obtaining prior approval is, ominously, whited out.

*****

IGNORANCE AS A DEFENSE

While none of the manuals was written or used on the Clinton administration's watch, the administration so far has failed to send a clear message repudiating such training methods and to take decisive action to ensure that such materials are never developed again. On February 21, 1997, the Department of Defense's inspector general completed another investigation. It admitted that in creating and using the seven army manuals "from 1982 through early 1991, many mistakes were made and repeated by numerous and continuously changing personnel in several organizations from Panama to Georgia to Washington, D.C." Without apparent irony, the report concludes that there is no "evidence that a deliberate and orchestrated attempt was made to violate DOD or U.S. Army policies.

The report claims that because these numerous US personnel did not know that it was against US policy to train Latin American militaries to use threats or force with prisoners, "neutralize" opponents, hold prisoners in clandestine jails, and infiltrate and spy upon civilian organizations and opposition political parties-all techniques described in the manuals-no disciplinary action was deemed necessary. The report, which Rep. Kennedy termed a "whitewash" and "hogwash," does not examine any systemic problem that might have led to "numerous and continuously changing personnel" over a ten-year period lacking a working knowledge of human rights. Thus, the report fails to assign either individual or collective responsibility for training Latin American militaries to violate human rights and use profoundly antidemocratic methods.

While the report concludes that the lesson plans and manuals somehow escaped oversight and could not be read because they were in Spanish, Rep. Kennedy's own investigation reveals these as mere dog-ate-my-homework excuses. Kennedy's report states that SOA instructors sent their lesson plans to Fort Huachuca and to at least two offices in Washington to be reviewed, al though the question of whether they were approved in Washington continues to be disputed. Moreover, the materials were approved for use in English before being translated into Spanish.

The report does demonstrate that little was done to implement the recommendations stemming from the 1991 investigation. In three agencies to which they were simply circulated as a memo, there was no record of it having even been received. In three others, it was received but did not result in any increase in oversight of foreign military and intelligence training. However, the report merely calls for the memo to be reissued as a "directive," rather than stimulating a serious discussion within the military and setting up workable oversight mechanisms.

All of the investigations into the various sets of manuals have been hampered by their basic premise: the disingenuous assumption that these manuals did not represent official US policy and somehow slipped through the cracks. But it was official US policy to train and arm repressive forces in Latin America, Vietnam, and other developing countries. The manuals fit squarely within that framework.

The slow, piecemeal surfacing of these manuals and the limited investigations at each point suggest that there may be many other inappropriate training materials still in circulation. Materials from the most intense days of the Cold War in the 1960s, which should never have been created in the first place, kept on being repackaged and reused despite a series of scandals and investigations that should have forced a full-scale review. That these manuals were used until recently in this hemisphere, however, is hardly shocking. They merely confirm what many long knew about US support for repressive militaries in Latin America. They prove that the United States not only provided the guns and the money for repression; the United States also supplied the textbooks.

TORTURE 101

IN THE US SCHOOL OF THE AMERICAS (SOA)

by Lisa Haugaard

The Pentagon revealed what activists opposed to the school have been alleging for years-that foreign military officers were taught to torture and murder to achieve their political objectives," says Rep. Joseph P. Kennedy Il (D-MA), who has waged a three-year campaign to close the U.S. Army School of the Americas (SOA). Hoping to elude media attention, the Pentagon waited until late on a Friday to release training manuals used at the school and distributed throughout Latin America that instructed officers on the use of torture, murder and blackmail in the fight against left-wing opponents.

The most egregious passages in the declassified manuals advocated such tactics as executions of guerrillas, extortion, physical abuse and paying bounties for enemy dead. One of the manuals offers the following techniques to recruit a guerrilla as an intelligence source: blackmail, false arrest, Imprlsonment of the potential recruit's parents and execution of all other members of his guerrilla cell. Another manual contains detailed instructions for making Molotov cocktails.

The Pentagon released the manuals after a sustained public pressure campaign focused on the role of the CIA in Guatemala, which was the subject of a June report by the President's Intelligence Oversight Board. Since the board's report mentioned the manuals, the Pentagon received requests to declassify them in their entirety.

The seven Spanish-language training manuals, totaling 1,100 pages, were prepared by the U.S. military and used between 1987 and 1991 for intelligence training courses in Latin America and at the School of the Americas. These manuals, with titles such as "Counterintelligence" and "Revolutionary War and Communist Ideology," were based on lesson plans used by SOA instructors since 1982. These lesson plans, in turn, were based in part on older material dating back to the '60s from "Project X," the U.S. Army's Foreign Intelligence Assistance Program. The U.S. government estimates that as many as a thousand copies of these manuals may have been distributed at the SOA and throughout Latin America.

In late 1991, after the Bush administration "discovered" the use of these manuals, the office of the assistant to the secretary of defense for intelligence oversight launched an investigation. The Pentagon provided the resulting report to congressional intelligence committees in 1992, but it remained sealed from the public until now. The investigation concluded that the manuals' authors and SOA instructors "erroneously assumed that the manuals, as well as the lesson plans, represented approved doctrine." When interviewed by the investigators, the manuals' authors stated that they believed intelligence oversight regulations applied only to U.S. personnel and not to the training of foreign personnel-in other words, that U.S. instructors could teach abusive techniques to foreign militaries that they could not legally perform themselves.

The response to this investigation was limited to damage control. The Bush administration ordered the retrieval and destruction of the manuals, and the U.S. Army Southern Command advised Latin American governments that the handbooks did not represent official U.S. policy. However, the whole episode was treated as an isolated incident. The individuals responsible for writing and teaching the lesson plans and manuals were not disciplined. SOA and other U.S. military instructors were not retrained. And military training programs were not rethought.

Along with the declassified manuals, the Pentagon released two dozen excerpts from the manuals that contain "objectionable and questionable material." Yet a preliminary examination of the manuals by Kennedy" office revealed other citations that describe techniques violating human rights. The "Interrogation" manual taught military officers to gag, bind and blindfold suspects, while the "Terrorism and Urban Guerilla" guide explains how to build mail bombs.

Analysts at the National Security Archive, a Washington-based research organization, point to sections of at least two of the manuals that equate democratic, non-violent and even strictly electoral campaigning with terrorist activity. "It is important to note that many terrorists are very well trained in subversion of the democratic process and use the system to advance their causes," one manual states. "This manipulation ends with the destruction of the democratic system. Discontent that can become political violence can have as its cause political, social, and economic activities of terrorists operating within the democratic system." Another manual warns that rebels are active in political organizations, legislative initiatives and political education, and that they can "resort to subverting the government by electoral means." This sort of analysis encourages military officers to perceive democratic challenges to a government as threatening and worthy of a military response.

One manual describes '60s activist Tom Hayden, currently a California state senator, as "one of the masters of terrorist planning." It is precisely this identification of activists for social change as terrorists that led death squads in Latin America to kill thousands of religious leaders, students. union members and human rights activists.

These manuals provide a paper trail to the counterinsurgency techniques taught at the School of the Americas. Since its inception in 1946 in Panama, the school has trained 57,000 Latin American officers and soldiers. (In 1984, under the terms of the Panama Canal treaty, the Pentagon moved the school to Fort Benning, Ga.) While the United States provides military training to soldiers from many other countries, only Latin Americans have a special school where they are trained in their own language. Despite its stated mission to promote human rights, the school has long had an unsavory reputation in Latin America, where it has been dubbed the "school of the assassins" and the "coup d'etat school" for the records of some of its notorious graduates. In the United States, Maryknoll priest Roy Bourgeois initiated a campaign in 1990 to close the school, opening an "SOA Watch" office right outside Fort Benning's gate. The effort to shut the school gathered steam following revelations that year that more than two-thirds of the Salvadoran officers cited for atrocities in the U.N. Truth Commission report were SOA graduates.

The school's opponents are not naive. They know that closing the school would not end U.S. training of Latin American militaries and intelligence services, since these activities can and do take place in other settings. Nonetheless, they believe that it would be an important symbolic victory.

In public relations efforts to counter the campaign, SOA officials emphasize the school's role in teaching human rights, democracy and civil-military relations. They point to recent changes in the curriculum that, they say, highlight these subjects. However, the main thrust of the school continues to be combat and intelligence training. The 1996 course catalogue lists courses in battle staff operations, commando operations, intelligence, border operations, artillery, psychological operations and helicopter operation and repair. Counterinsurgency techniques are listed as topics in several courses. Only one of the 32 courses taught at the school focuses on democracy. No separate course on human rights is offered, although a four-hour "mandatory human rights awareness training" session is included in several courses.

Even if human rights violations were not part of the curriculum, critics question the rationale for teaching combat and intelligence skills to Latin American militaries. During the Cold War, they point out, militaries used these skills to thwart democratic opponents of repressive regimes. Today, such skills are obsolete and in fact hinder the concerted struggle by Latin American citizens to assert civilian control over still powerful armies.

The revelations about the manuals give new impetus to efforts to close the school. Kennedy has twice tried to pass legislation that would have closed the school. Both attempts ended in defeat (with votes of 256-174 in October 1993 and 217-157 in May 1994). Supporters of the school maintain that the school's notorious graduates are "just a few bad apples," that it is premature "to throw the baby out with the bath water," and that the SOA exercises a positive influence upon Latin American militaries.

Last year, Kennedy tried a new approach. Seeking to gain the support of those in Congress who believe the United States can exercise a positive influence on Latin American military officers, Kennedy introduced legislation in November that would close the school but open a new U.S. Academy for Democracy and Civil-Military Relations. This school, to be run by the U.S. military with civilian oversight, would offer training solely in democracy, human rights, resource management and civil-military relations. The bill did not receive sufficient co-sponsors to be brought to the floor. In any case, religious and human rights activists who oppose the school were skeptical of this new strategy, doubting that the U.S. military could be trusted to teach democracy and human rights. The recent revelations about the manuals erode that trust even further.

The same month that Kennedy proposed the new academy, police arrested protesters at Fort Benning for trespassing as they re-enacted the 1989 massacre of six Jesuits in El Salvador. This April, 13 were sentenced to jail terms. Ten received two-month jail sentences. Father Bourgeois, who was sentenced to six months, and Vietnam vet Louis De Benedette and Jesuit priest Bill Bichsel, who each received four-month terms, are still behind bars, completing their jail time.

he school's opponents are planning another November vigil at Fort Benning this year. "The uncovering of the torture training manuals leaves no doubt that the instruction was an intentional and methodical part of the curriculum at the School of the Americas," says Carol Richardson, who is running the SOA Watch office while Father Bourgeois is in jail. "This should be the final nail in the coffin to bury the School of the Americas along with its despicable history and practice. Policy-makers should move quickly and decisively to cut SOA funding. Not one more dime of U.S. taxpayer money should go to support the training of terrorists, assassins and torturers."

Lisa Haugaard is legislative coordinator for the Latin America Working Group, a coalition of non-governmental organizations based in Washington, D.C. . This article was published in IN THESE TIMES magazine, October 14, 1996. IN THESE TIMES magazine 2040 N. Milwaukee Avenue, Chicago, IL 60647 e-mail itt@igc.apc.org

MEXICO PRACTICES WHAT SCHOOL OF THE AMERICAS TEACHES

by Darrin Wood

Covert Action Quarterly magazine, Winter 1996-97

Mexican generals implicated in serious human rights violations studied at the School of the Americas while the institution was routinely teaching torture techniques.

The US Army's School of the Americas (SOA) has never had much good press, but recently its reputation went into a tailspin. It all began with an item in the June 28, 1996 Intelligence Oversight Board's "Report on the Guatemala Review":

Congress was also notified of the 1991 discovery by DoD [Department of Defense] that the School of the Americas and Southern Command had used improper instruction materials in training Latin American officers, including Guatemalans, from 1982 to 1991. These materials never received proper DoD review, and certain passages appeared to condone (or could have been interpreted to condone) practices such as executions of guerrillas, extortion, physical abuse, coercion, and false imprisonment. On discovery of the error, DoD replaced and modified the materials, and instructed its representatives in the affected countries to retrieve all copies of the materials from their foreign counterparts and to explain that some of the contents violated US policy. I

Such practices in any case, the Pentagon assured, did not represent US government policy, and all instruction in torture, murder, and mayhem had been discontinued in 1991.

The government admission that the manuals did in fact exist and had condoned torture was made under pressure. Despite numerous first-hand sighting, no one had managed to hold onto a copy until one made its way to Congress member Joseph Kennedy. When the Pentagon learned that the Massachusetts Democrat had the hard evidence, it tried to beat him to the punch and release the excerpts. The seven manuals-nearly 1,200 pages in the original Spanish-recommended using "fear, payment of bounties for enemy dead, beatings, false imprisonment, executions, and truth serum." The chilling text forever disproved the School's claims that the Noriegas, Banzers, and D'Aubuissons who came out of SOA were just a few "bad apples." Rather, they were the bad seeds that SOA- acting as "Johnny Rotten-Appleseed"-had planted in the fertile ground of Latin American dictatorships.

SOA public affairs officer Maj. Gordon Martell was left hanging out to dry by the change in the official line. He had admitted that some SOA grads were guilty of abuses but had downplayed the impact. "Out of 59,000 students who have graduated from a variety of programs, less than 300 have been cited for human rights violations like torture and murder, and less than 50 have been convicted of anything." In fact, the low number had more to do with the level of impunity in Latin America than any failure of the students to master their lessons. And up until the end, the hapless Martell was denying that the manuals contained anything untoward. "All of the manuals used by the School of the Americas are approved by the Army, and the school has never done those things, ever, in its history."

TORTURE, LIES, AND VIDEOTAPE

Two people who had been on the trail of the manuals were Robert Richter, whose 1995 film, School of Assassins, was nominated for an Academy Award for Best Short Documentary, and Roy Bourgeois, a Maryknoll priest who had long opposed the school. After reading an article in CAQ that reported the existence of the manuals, they traveled to Paraguay. (The article had linked the manuals to serious human rights abuses performed under Operation Condor and documented that they taught torturers how to keep prisoners alive during sessions using electric shock).4 In Asuncion, Bourgeois and Richter met with Martin Almada, the activist and torture victim who had told CAQ of seeing the manuals and of having experienced their lessons first hand. Although the two did not find the instructional material, which had disappeared from the archive where it was catalogued, they ferreted out former SOA students who were now willing to talk. In Richter's updated version of the documentary, one of those former students revealed some of his "unconventional training":

Mr. X: "The difference between the conventional and the unconventional training is that we were trained to torture human beings. They would use people from the streets of Panama, because they would bring them into the base and the experts would train us on how to obtain that information through torture. And there were several ways of doing it. There was the psychological torture and there was of course the physical torture."

Bourgeois: "Are you saying that ordinary citizens were brought to the School of the Americas and used as human guinea pigs for torture?"

Mr. X: "Some of them were blindfolded and they were stripped and put in a certain situation, I mean setting, where they were tortured. At the time they had a medical physician, a US medical physician which I remember very well, who was dressed in green fatigues, who would teach the students in the nerve endings in the body, he would show them where to torture, where you wouldn't kill the individual. He would tell them how much the heart can tolerate, can hold up. And there were also times where they would revive the person with a powerful drug. When the person was [near death], the doctor will tell you this is enough, you can't go on anymore because this man will die. So it's very simple. If he hasn't talked yet, then you've got to stop because otherwise, he'll be dead."

Richter also talked with Jose Valle, an SOA graduate and ex-member of the US-backed Honduran death squad Battalion 3-16. "They told us we could respect human rights, that it was not necessary to beat the prisoners," he said. "But that was in the classroom. The problem was that in the actual situation the interrogators were told that they had to get the information out of the people in any way possible."

Based on interviews, Richter believes that the torture manuals-in use for seven years at Fort Benning- were used prior to 1982 and formed the basis for daily lesson plans at SOA.

THE SOA "REDEFINES" ITSELF

The increased public attention on the School of the Americas in the past few years has forced the School to scramble to justify its multi-million dollar budget and to fabricate a revisionist interpretation of its goals and curriculum. A recent article in the Spanish language edition of Military Review tries, without admitting past flaws, to "redefine" SOA's mission as the promotion of democratic principles and human rights in the hemisphere. "[...T]he School of the Americas has more possibilities than ever at this time to contribute to those causes that are so important for its adversaries, even though they might not be convinced of it without first abandoning the notion that any use of military force in Latin America is inevitably wrong.... " The article, according to its author, Army Lt. Col. Geoffrey B. Demarest, "is not directed to the enemies of the School nor does it offer any apology for what occurred in the past." An SOA graduate and an ex-assistant military attaché at the US Embassy in Guatemala, he has good reason to know what he is not apologizing for.

Demarest does acknowledge that SOA's makeover will not be easy because the concept of human rights "can be difficult for many Latin American officers, since many of them consider that that term has been employed in a propagandistic and damaging way for some legitimate uses of military force." And Demarest admits that the issue of human rights has been used for political expediency. "It is possible," he writes, "that the emphasis put on the subject of human rights has been a response to the School's critics, who have shown to be hardly convinced of its merit based on its role during the Cold War. With the end of said conflict, and in spite of the increased emphasis that the instruction in human rights receives, the School is still criticized because its fundamental concepts appear to be obsolete."

SOA vs. EZLN

Although the school is currently deep into a PR campaign to paint a smiley face on a death's head, those "fundamental concepts" still include the use of force to maintain the US "backyard" and to back the political and financial fortunes of those leaders who play ball in it. The role of SOA graduates in Mexico is a case in point. From 1953 to 1992, almost 500 Mexican military officers have received training at the SOA. Since the 1994 Zapatista uprising in Chiapas, Mexico has taken the lead in the number of Latin American military personnel receiving US military training. With millions of dollars in US military aid and training, Mexico has undergone a massive militarization in the past few years. To top it off, Bill Clinton and the Pentagon recently unveiled a plan to spend an additional $48 million on helicopters and training to shore up the Zedillo regime.

While it is impossible to know how many US-trained officers are participating in counterinsurgency operations, some evidence can be gleaned by checking SOA enrollment lists against press reports of military operations. The headquarters of the Mexican Army's 31st Military Zone, located at Rancho Nuevo near San Cristobal de Las Casas in Chiapas, had a kind of SOA class reunion feel to it when Zapatistas rose up in arms on December 31, 1993. Three of the army generals there -Gaston Menchaca Arias, commander of the Military Zone,

SUPPRESSED INTELLIGENCE REPORTS

Miguel Leyva Garcia, and Enrique Alonso Garrido- were all SOA alumni. Menchaca Arias and Leyva Garcia had been classmates at the SOA back in 1971.

However, Gen. Menchaca, who as a captain in 1971 when he studied "irregular warfare" at SOA, probably won't be the school's poster boy for military expertise. As the Zapatista Army was taking control of San Cristobal in the early morning hours of January 1, 1994, Concepcion Villafuerte of the San Cristobal newspaper El Tiempo, called the Commander at 1:45 am to ask him why there were so many armed people in the town. The US-trained specialist replied: "I don't know. Aren't they just people celebrating New Year's?"

As the fighting continued in early January of 1994, another SOA grad, Gen. Juan Lopez Ortiz, was sent into Chiapas with troops under his command from the states of Campeche and Tabasco. In a 1994 interview with the Mexican magazine Impacto, this SOA grad called the EZLN "very criminal people [who] dare to call themselves an army while they send people to their deaths, armed with wooden rifles; when they use innocent people as human shields and they cover their faces with ski masks." Lopez Ortiz had first made a name for himself in 1974 fighting the Partido de los Pobres (Party of the Poor) in the mountains of the Mexican state of Guerrero. That infamous campaign left hundreds of peasants "disappeared." In 1994, the troops he commanded in the town of Ocosingo massacred suspected Zapatistas in the town's market; the prisoners' hands were tied behind their backs before the soldiers shot them in the back of the head.

The February 1995 invasion by the Mexican army of territory controlled by the EZLN brought another SOA grad onto the scene. Gen. Manuel Garcia Ruiz (SOA Class of 1980the same year and course as Gen. Garrido), boasted to journalists of the army's "humanitarian" work in the aftermath of the invasion of the Lacandona jungle. According to the Mexican news weekly Proceso: "Brigadier Gen. Manuel Garcia Ruiz, with a diploma from the General Staff, was ordered to occupy Nuevo Momon, one of the Zapatista strongholds; on Friday, February 10, Lieut. Col. Hugo Manterola was killed in circumstances that still haven't been cleared up." Testimony compiled by the press states that there was an exchange of gunfire, which lasted approximately 10 minutes, between government and Zapatista soldiers. Gen. Garcia Ruiz's official version, however, denies that a confrontation occurred and claims that Manterola was the victim of a sniper.

Chiapas has also reportedly suffered the presence of a group of mercenaries from Argentina who were sent to the infamous 31st Military Zone in July of 1994 to help the Mexican Army perfect its counterinsurgency tactics. These same Argentines have worked for the CIA in the past in training US-backed death squads in Honduras led by SOA graduate Gen. Gustavo Alvarez Martinez.

SOA vs. EPR On June 28, a new guerrilla organization calling itself the EPR (Ejercito Popular Revolucionario-Popular Revolutionary Army) appeared in Guerrero during a memorial service for 17 peasants murdered by police in Aguas Blancas the previous year. In August, the EPR carried out coordinated attacks throughout Mexico. In their pursuit were SOA graduates in the states of Chihuahua, Guanajuato, Guerrero, Jalisco, Michoacan, Morelos, Oaxaca, Tamaulipas, and Yucatan. Some SOA grads who were stationed in Chiapas and are now involved in anti-EPR operations are generals Menchaca Arias, Garcia Ruiz, and Juan Lopez Orkiz.

With US-trained troops or weapons on the ground almost everywhere, US Ambassador to Mexico James Jones was coy about Washington's role. After the EPR's attacks in August, he said that although Mexico still hadn't directly asked for support from its friendly northern neighbor, the US would be more than willing to offer help and expertise in combating the new guerrillas. Mexico has yet to publicly accept that goodwill. But so far, military aid to Mexico, mostly under the guise of anti-drug campaigns, has led to many "gifts" of helicopters and airplanes.

Predictably, the militarization of Mexico, which was occurring before the appearance of the EPR, has been accompanied by an increase in the number of reported human rights abuses. Nowhere has that link been more prominent than in the long suffering state of Guerrero, whose 9th Military Region contains two military zones, the 27th, located in the tourist resort town of Acapulco, and the 35th, located in the town of Chilpancingo. From the June 1995 peasant massacre by police, to the recent allegations of the rape of 12 indigenous women by the army, Guerrero had more than its share of brutality-and of School of the Americas graduates.

In a report on the 1995 Aguas Blancas massacre, Proceso noted that five weeks after the atrocity, Gen. Adrian Maldonado Ramirez was relieved as the commander of the 35th Military Zone, which is in the same military region in which the atrocities took place. In 1978 and 1979, Maldonado Ramirez had studied "Joint Operations-Latin America" at SOA. So far, the scandal surrounding the government ambush of the unarmed civilians has resulted in the prosecution of the police officers who pulled the triggers and the resignation of Gov. Ruben Figueroa. With Maldonado Ramirez safely transferred, the possible role in the military in the ambush has remained unexamined. This omission is particularly troublesome in light of the statement by retired US Army Col. Rex Applegate that "[Mexican] army zone commanders generally work closely with state officials .. ".

The current commander of the 9th Military Region located in Acapulco is Gen. Edmundo Elpidio Leyva Galindo. During a search mission for the EPR in September, which he reportedly headed, one of his troops thought he saw some masked men running in an open field. Using a reporter's cellular phone the general ordered, "Shoot them, kill them." Leyva Galindo not only is a graduate of the School of the Americas, but was there for the same years and for courses as Maldonado Ramirez.

Leyva Galindo and Maldonado aren't the only former SOA classmates involved in the Mexican Army's pursuit of the EPR. Gen. Renato Garcia Gonzalez, the current commander of the 27th Military Zone in Acapulco, trained at the School of the Americas in 1980 along with Gen. Ruben Rivas Pena, the commander of the 28th Military Zone, located in the neighboring state of Oaxaca. Both coincided with the previously mentioned Gens. Enrique Garrido and Manuel Garcia Ruiz. Oddly enough, the states of Guerrero and Oaxaca were the sites of the EPR's strongest attacks on August 28, 1996.

COUNTERINSURGENCY WITH A HUMAN FACE

The latest disclosures about the School of the Americas have revived calls to shut it down-sort of. Activists have backed Rep. Joseph Kennedy's (D-Mass.) proposed house bill, HR 2652, which would "close the United States Army School of the Americas and establish a United States Academy for Democracy and Civil-Military Relations."

A closer look at HR 2652 doesn't leave much hope for Latin Americans. Under its new, blandly cheery name, the "Academy" would eliminate combat training with live ammunition and emphasize "human rights" and civilian control of the military. But, as a former SOA instructor wrote: "The military skills required to oppress indigenous populations were finely honed long before most Latin American faculty members and students were flown in at U.S. government expense for their vacations in Columbus [Georgia]." The Kennedy bill does not, however, ban such training at other institutions currently run by the US military.

The bill's supporters should probably also scrutinize the concept of "Civil-Military" relations. According to the US Army's Command and General Staff College Field Manual 100-20:

"Civil-military operations (CMO) include all military efforts to support host nation development, co-opt insurgent issues, gain support for the national government, and attain national objectives without combat. Successful CMOs reduce or eliminate the need for combat operations, especially when initiated early in the insurgency. They also help prepare the area of operations for combat forces, if they are required."

If HR 2652 passes, it runs the risk of converting SOA into a way for the Pentagon to continue business as usual while giving the appearance that the system works, human rights are a priority, and the bloodstains have been cleaned off the chalkboards.

In the "First Declaration of the Selva Lacandona" from Mexico's Zapatista Army, the General Command of the EZLN called for "summary trials against the soldiers of the Mexican Federal Army and the political police who have received courses and have been advised, trained, or paid by foreigners ... "

While that scenario may seem exaggerated, nonetheless, there should be a full investigation of those parts of the curriculum that have been connected to human rights abuses. Those found responsible for these and other abuses should be exposed, tried, and punished. Then the program should be ended and all US training of foreign militaries should cease. If that does not happen, the School of the Americas, or whatever name it goes by in the future, runs the danger of being, as Lt. Col. Demarest states in his article in Military Review "an even more useful organization in the post-Cold War world than it was during this conflict."

And that, given the role of the School of the Americas during those grim years, is a frightening concept.

Darrin Wood is a freelance journalist and film-maker based in Spain who has written for the Madrid Daily, El Mundo, and the Basque newspaper Egin.

ADMISSIONS AND OMISSIONS —THE CIA IN GUATEMALA

by Linda Haugaard

July 1996

"We at last have in writing what the U.S. government has denied for years-we have been fighting the dirty war in Guatemala," said Dianna Ortiz, a U.S. nun who was tortured by the Guatemalan military in 1989, and who has since sought to discover who was behind her torture. The president's advisory Intelligence Oversight Board (IOB) report on human rights cases and the CIA's role in Guatemala, released on June 28, shows that the CIA knowingly hired paid informants who were involved in assassinations, kidnappings and torture. The report also asserts that U.S. support was "vital" to the Guatemalan intelligence services.

SUPPRESSED INTELLIGENCE REPORTS

Buried on page 32 of the 67-page study is the revelation that from 1982-91, the School of the Americas and the U.S. Army's Southern Command used instruction materials in training Latin American officers, including Guatemalans, that "appeared to condone practices ... such as executions of guerrillas, extortion, physical abuse, coercion, and false imprisonment," The School of the Americas, under attack for the poor human rights record of its graduates, has long maintained that its instruction is above board and that notorious graduates are "a few bad apples."

According to the IOB, virtually the entire report was released to the public-an unusual occurrence due largely to intense public pressure on the Clinton administration. Some 400 CIA and Defense Department documents were declassified and released to the public at the same time, along with additional material from 450 of the 5,000 documents released by the State Department in May. American lawyer Jennifer Harbury's search for her husband, Guatemalan guerrilla leader Efrain Bamaca, who vanished March 12, 1992, after a skirmish with the Guatemalan army, led to last year's revelations of CIA involvement with human rights violators in that country. By means of repeated protests and hunger strikes, Harbury sought to force the U.S. and Guatemalan governments to release information relating to her husband's whereabouts. Finally, in March 1995, Rep. Robert Torricelli (D-NJ), a member of the House Select Committee on Intelligence, disclosed that the CIA had known for years that one of its paid assets, Col. Julio Roberto Alpirez, may have been involved in Bamaca's killing as well as in the 1990 assassination of Michael DeVine. The connection to the DeVine case was particularly startling, since the U.S. government had suspended military aid to Guatemala because of its failure to fully investigate and prosecute the case against the killers of DeVine, a U.S. citizen who owned an inn in the Guatemalan countryside.

After these allegations became widely publicized, the White House ordered the IOB in March 1995 to conduct a government-wide review of the DeVine and Bamaca cases, as well as any intelligence bearing on the torture, disappearance or death of U.S. citizens in Guatemala since 1984. These cases include the 1984 killing of Peace Corps volunteer Peter Wolfe, the 1985 killings of journalists Griffith Davis and Nicholas Blake, the 1989 stabbing of human rights worker Meredith Larson, the 1990 assault on social worker Josh Zinner, and the 1992 death of archaeologist Peter Tiscione. Many of these victims and family members had joined an informal network called "Coalition Missing" to demand an accounting on their cases.

As the months stretched into a year of waiting for the IOB's report, Sister Ortiz began a five-week vigil outside the White House in March. She was there all night as well as all but three hours of the day, sleeping fitfully in a sleeping bag, accompanied by members of religious and peace organizations. The vigil, which ended with a week's fast, attracted considerable congressional and public support. One hundred and one members of the House of Representatives signed a letter calling on President Clinton to declassify documents on Guatemala.

Human rights advocates are disappointed by how little the long-awaited report reveals about specific cases. Dianna Ortiz's case is barely touched upon, since the IOB decided to reserve judgement until the Justice Department's separate investigation into her case is concluded. The IOB said it had no information about her claim that a man with an American accent, called Alejandro by her torturers, was present at her torture. According to Ortiz, her torturers appeared to report to Alejandro.

SUPPRESSED INTELLIGENCE REPORTS

Citing conflicting information from intelligence sources, the report concludes that CIA paid asset Alpirez was not involved in the deaths of Bamaca and DeVine, although it asserts that he was involved in the interrogation of Bamaca and the cover-up of the DeVine case. Little new information is revealed in the cases of other U.S. citizens killed or wounded in Guatemala since 1984.

For Dianna Ortiz and other victims and relatives, the report provides little relief. "I know what few U.S. citizens know," she stated at a July 1 press conference. "I know what it is to be an innocent civilian, and to be accused, interrogated and tortured. I know what it is to have my own government eschew my claims for justice because they cause political problems for a close ally. I know what it is to wait in the dark for torture, and what it is to wait in the dark for the truth. I am still waiting."

The report, however, does provide a remarkable admission by the U.S. government of the extent of American involvement with the Guatemalan military and direct association with individuals implicated in serious misdeeds. While Alpirez is judged not to have participated in the DeVine and Bamaca killings-a judgment their widows still doubt-the report confirms that "several CIA assets were credibly alleged to have ordered, planned or participated in serious human rights violations such as assassination, extrajudicial execution, torture, or kidnapping while they were assets- and that the CIA's Directorate of Operations headquarters was aware at the time of the allegations." Moreover, "a number of the station's liaison contacts — Guatemalan officials with whom the station worked in an official capacity- were also alleged to have been involved in human rights abuses or in covering them up."

With the report, we now have the government's own admission that the United Statesfunded and supported the Guatemalan intelligence service as a partner in pursuit of mutual objectives as late as 1995. Publicly, the U.S. government had stressed a very different set of goals-U.S. support for democracy and human rights. "The funds the CIA provided to the Guatemalan liaison services were vital to the [Guatemalan intelligence services] D-2 and the [presidential guard] Archivos," the report says.. "This funding was seen as necessary to make these services more capable partners with the station, particularly in pursuing anti-communist and counternarcotics objectives. The CIA with the knowledge of ambassadors and other State Department and National Security Council officials, as well as Congress, continued this aid after the termination" of U.S. military assistance to Guatemala in 1990.

While the report asserts that CIA funds were not increased to compensate for the cut off of military aid, the $1 million to $3.5 mil lion per year that flowed from FY 1989 to FY 1995 represented a significant sum. Direct military aid in 1990 before the cutoff was only $9 million.

The report paints a picture of a CIA station that closely identified with its counterparts in the Guatemalan intelligence services and military. The end of the Cold War "had only a limited effect upon the mechanics of how the CIA carried out its business and upon the mindset of CIA officers dealing with Guatemala," the report says.

"Station officers continued to view the communist insurgents-who seemed to threaten a more democratic government-as the primary enemy. and they viewed the Guatemalan government and security services as partners in the fight against this common foe and against new threats such as narcotics and illegal alien smuggling."

Although U.S. Embassy officials were aware of CIA funding for the Guatemalan intelligence services, the station failed until the end of 1994 to inform them that its assets and contacts were involved in human rights abuses. In its reports to Congress on how CIA programs in Guatemala furthered respect for human rights, the station consistently put a positive spin on the actions of the Guatemalan intelligence services and withheld information concerning their involvement in human rights abuses.

The IOB report, rich in these kinds of revelations, comes to a set of disappointing conclusions and recommendations. It fails to challenge the propriety of the basic policy:

U.S. government association with the very forces most damaging to human rights in Guatemala. Instead, it says that occasional association with "unsavory" groups and individuals is necessary to further foreign policy goals. At a July 2 press conference, former CIA officer David MacMichael challenged the relative usefulness of such intelligence sources, and emphasized the damage this does to the United States. "If you lie down with dogs," he pointed out, "you get up with fleas." The IOB recommends that U.S. intelligence agencies establish clear "guidance" on the recruiting and maintaining of assets with human rights or criminal allegations against them. As the report notes approvingly, the CIA has recently issued such guidance in response to this scandal. But it includes a loophole allowing senior officials to approve use of such assets where national security interests warrant. Carlos Salinas of Amnesty International challenges such a loophole, given its implication that national security interests can outweigh human rights imperatives. "How can any one involved in human rights violations be considered an 'asset' to the U.S. government?" Salinas asks.

The IOB report itself judges the CIA leniently, since in most cases the agency broke no laws-there are only "guidelines" regarding reporting to Congress. This suggests the importance of establishing laws, not mere guidance, prohibiting the funding of individuals and institutions involved in gross human rights violations. Only the force of law would make lack of compliance a serious matter.

The IOB also admonished the State Department, the National Security Agency and other government agencies for failing to provide relevant information on cases to victims and relatives. In its recommendations, the IOB urges the State Department to provide information from intelligence reports where needed in briefings to such U.S. citizens.

Unfortunately, the report also comes down hard on administration officials and members of Congress who leak information to the public. This is a "backhanded slap" at Rep. Torricelli, says MacMichael. Without Torricelli's leak, none of this debacle might have come to light.

The IOB report on Guatemala offers an insider's peek at the shady underworld of CIA operatives. It shows that U.S. government support for foreign forces actively engaged in repressing their own people did not end with the Cold War. And as evidence about the U.S. role in Haiti and Honduras suggests, this practice is not limited to Guatemala.

REAGAN ADMINISTRATION'S LINKS

TO GUATEMALA'S TERRORIST GOVERNMENT

by Allan Nairn

Covert Action Quarterly magazine, Summer 1989

SUPPRESSED INTELLIGENCE REPORTS

Local businessmen and government officials involved with Guatemala's notorious death squads say they have struck a deal with Ronald Reagan which provides for restoration of U.S. weapon sales and training facilities to the Guatemalan military and police, curtailment of State Department criticism of the Guatemalan regime's massive human rights violations, and the ultimate prospect of U.S. military intervention to shore up that beleaguered Central American government.

Before his election, Reagan met personally with two leading spokesmen of the Guatemalan right and also through a series of visits to the country by aides and associates conveyed the details of what one U.S. businessman calls his promised "180 degree turn" in U.S. policy toward Guatemala. These visits include one at the time of the Republican Convention to offer Reagan's "salute" to Guatemalan president General Romero Lucas Garcia and inform him that "things were going to be changing."

High-level Guatemalan officials say that Reagan's assurances may already have led to an increase in the number of death squad assassinations and a senior leader of Guatemala's moderate Christian Democratic Party-already decimated by more than 34 assassinations of its top leadership in the last year-fears for his life.

THE CAMPAIGN CONNECTIONS

An ominous bargain has been struck by means of an extensive network of connections between the Reagan team and the Guatemalan extreme right, which include:

Junkets to Guatemala by a "who's-who" of the American New Right, sponsored by Guatemalan speculator and right-wing activist Roberto Alejos Arzu, who made his plantation available as a training site for participants in the CIA's Bay of Pigs invasion in 1961.

Those along on one trip in April 1980 included top executives of Young Americans for Freedom, the Heritage Foundation, Moral Majority, Young Republicans' National Federation, the American Conservative Union, Conservative Digest, and such right-wing activists as Howard Phillips of the Conservative Caucus and John Laxalt, president of Reagan's campaign organization Citizens for the Republic, and brother of the Reagan campaign chairperson, Senator Paul Laxalt.

A Spring 1980 meeting in California between Reagan and Guatemalan hotel magnate Eduardo Carrette-the man whom General Lucas [Garcia] has asked to be his new ambassador to the U.S. and a leading figure in Amigos del Pais, a pressure group comprised of businessmen and landowners which Guatemala's recently-resigned Vice President Dr. Francisco Villagran has compared to the John Birch Society.

The now extremely active Amigos paid a hefty $11,000 per month in retainer fees to Deaver and Hannaford, a Los Angeles-Washington, D.C. public relations firm headed by Reagan confidante Michael Deaver, which handled advertising for the Republican presidential campaign. Deaver is now White House Deputy Chief of Staff.

Pressure on Congress by Reagan associates to "lend a sympathetic ear" to the Amigos current lobbying campaign for the restoration of military aid and training for the Guatemalan military.

Several other Reagan advisors have visited Guatemala in the past year, including Roger Fontaine, National Security Council assistant for Latin American affairs and retired Lt. Gen.

SUPPRESSED INTELLIGENCE REPORTS

Daniel Graham, of his defense advisory committee, who also visited El Salvador for President Reagan. Fontaine, who is an established hard-liner in regional matters, is the former director of Latin American Studies at the Center for Strategic and International Studies, perhaps the nation's most conservative academic-activists center for Latin American affairs. He bolstered Guatemalan hopes in an interview published in the Miami Herald where he was quoted as saying, "It's pretty clear that Guatemalans will be given what aid they need in order to defend themselves against an armed minority which is aided and abetted by Cubans."

THE DEATH SQUADS

Guatemala's death squads with such names as "Secret Anti-Communist Army" and "Eye for an Eye" specialize in "disappearances" of their political opponents, routine torture, and high-noon machine-gun executions in downtown Guatemala City as well as the countries' outlying provinces.

Sources close to the Lucas Garcia regime report that the death squads are staffed and directed by the Guatemalan Army and Police under the command of President Lucas, Interior Minister Donald Alvarez Ruiz, and a group of top-ranking generals, with the assistance of Lucas's right-hand man, Colonel Hector Montalban, and national Chief of Police, Colonel German Chupina. Private businessmen provide the payrolls for the squads, and often assist in "compiling" the lists of troublesome labor, professional and political leaders as well as other suggested victims.

Cotton grower Raul Garcia Granados-a leader of the Guatemalan right who is the brother of Lucas's Chief of Staff and co-owner with Lucas of an estate in the northern Franja Transversal region-traces the lineage of the current death squads back four administrations to the late 1960s.

"Of course when they were organized, they were organized under the patronage and the approval of the government and the army," he said in a transcribed interview. "They have lists of people that are suspected to be communists of whatever kind, and they kill them. It's a war, you see, a war between the communists and the anti-communists. They [the death squads] have the sympathy of most of the Guatemalan people."

Elias Barahona, former press secretary to Interior Minister Alvarez Ruiz, who controls the national police, fled the country, declared he had become a member of the EGP (Ejercito Guerrillero del Pueblo) an anti-government guerrilla group, and in a Panama City press conference issued a 15 page statement detailing how Lucas and the generals run the death squad from the fourth floor of the National Palace Annex. He listed the address of houses used by the government for detention and torture of its kidnap victims.

Despite such mounting evidence, and the near-universal recognition that Guatemala is one of the worst human rights violators in the entire world; both Arano Osorlo, known as "the butcher of Zacape," and former Guatemalan vice-president Mario Sandoval Alarcon, generally considered high commander of the death squads, were invited to the Reagan inauguration.

GUATEMALA AND THE CARTER ADMINISTRATION

To the Lucas regime and the businessmen who support it, President Carter's human rights policy was an anathema. Lucas called Carter "Jimmy Castro." Feeling increasingly isolated and betrayed by Carter State Department policy in Guatemala, officials there chose to ignore Washington's urging that human rights violations be corrected.

Businessman Roberto Alejos complained: "Most of the elements in the State Department are probably pro-communist-they're using human rights as an argument to promote the socialization of these areas. We've gotten to the point now where we fear the State Department more than we fear communist infiltration. Either Mr. Carter is a totally incapable president or he is definitely a pro-communist element."

Milton Molina is a wealthy plantation owner who is reputed within Guatemala to have funded and ordered death squad attacks on dozens of peasants and workers. When asked about the squads in a transcribed interview, Molina replied, "Well, we have to do something, don't you think so?" Molina says he and his friends back Reagan "one hundred percent."

The death squads' defenders base their faith in Reagan on direct conversations with him and his top military and foreign policy advisors. According to a Reagan fundraiser, Reagan told ambassador-to-be Carrette, "Hang in 'til we get there. We'll get in and then we'll give you help. Don't give up. Stay there and fight. I'll help you as soon as I get in."

THE GUATEMALAN LOBBY

The Reagan camp's courtship of the Guatemalan right began in earnest with the December 1979 visit to Guatemala of a delegation from the American Security Council, a private ultra-hawk U.S. military lobby. One of the consultants on Guatemalan affairs for the ASC film "Attack on the Americas" was John C. Trotter, the notorious manager of Guatemala City's Coca-Cola bottling plant franchise. Trotter has been implicated in the death squad murders of a number of workers and union leaders at the bottling plant and was removed from management by Coca-Cola headquarters after an international union and church-led boycott of Coke protesting the situation at the plant in Guatemala.

Trotter is also a director of the Guatemala Freedom Foundation, a pro-Lucas international lobby group founded by Roberto Alejos, which is more extreme than the Amigos del Pais organization. Alejos hosted the ASC delegation and helped set up an itinerary which included visits with President Lucas and the Guatemalan military high command, helicopter tours to inspect rural counter-insurgency activities, and a cocktail party with Guatemalan businessmen at Alejos's estate. The delegation was headed by two Reagan associates- retired General John K. Singlaub who has served as ASC's Director of Education, and retired Lt. Gen. Daniel Graham, the former Defense Intelligence Agency head, who maintains an office at ASC's Washington, D.C. headquarters.

As an advisor to Reagan, Graham retains his position as co-chairperson for the Coalition for Peace Through Strength, a Washington lobby composed of retired military personnel, pushing for a larger defense budget, The Missouri branch of the Coalition met with Guatemalan and Salvadoran business and political leaders in St. Louis last May. Among the Guatemalan visitors were Manuel Ayau and Roberto Alejos. Ayau is a member of his nation's most ultra-conservative party, the National Liberation Movement, which is allegedly directly linked to paramilitary death squads freely operating in the country. He is considered to be the ideologue of the more extremist sector of the business community, and is also on the board of GFF.

SUPPRESSED INTELLIGENCE REPORTS

Alejos and Ayau are now well-known figures in Washington. With extensive help from their PR people, they have met with Congressional staff and State Department officials in the hopes of enlisting support for their political position.

PUBLIC RELATIONS

Their publicity is handled primarily by MacKenzie, McCheyne, Inc. of Washington, D.C. In the past, this firm received hundreds of thousands of dollars from the Somoza government of Nicaragua. It also promotes the El Salvador Freedom Foundation, which purports to be to the right of the Salvadoran junta, and it openly arranged the April 1980 Washington press conference given by Roberto D'Aubuisson. In the past two years, MacKenzie, McCheyne has received over $250,000 from the GFF. The Guatemalan emissaries are known to have been heartened to hear Gen. Graham's statement made during a trip to Argentina last year, that "Carter's human rights policy has had disastrous effects on America's relations with Latin America. . . and if Reagan is elected, the U.S. would abandon the policy of throwing old friends to the wolves."

Singlaub, the former commander of U.S. forces in South Korea dismissed by President Carter for insubordination, has good contacts with the informal network of radical right-wing mercenaries who aid dictatorships around the globe.

In a tape-recorded interview last August, Singlaub said that he was "terribly impressed" at how the Lucas regime was "desperately trying to promote human rights" and lamented the fact that "as the [Guatemalan] government loses support from the United States, it gives the impression to the people that there's something wrong with their government."

As for Graham, he acknowledged during a Washington telephone interview last year that he told President Lucas Garcia that on his return to the United States, he would urge the Reagan campaign team to provide for the resumption of military training and aid to Guatemala as soon as a victorious Reagan would be installed in office.

The Reagan aides' advice and supportive comments were the talk of official Guatemala for days after their visit. Within weeks, death squad assassinations increased dramatically and there was talk in government circles of even harsher measures.

The parade of visiting advisors continued. Roger Fontaine made at least two trips to Guatemala. Fontaine is on a first name basis with right-wing figures and keeps in constant touch with them by telephone.

Through the Amigos del Pais and Alejos's and Trotter's Guatemala Freedom Foundation, a number of Guatemalans also came to the U.S. to meet Reagan and his staff; Both Amigos del Pais director Maegli, and Manuel Ayau, chief ideologue and theorist of the Guatemalan right, have met with Richard Allen, head of the National Security Council, and early last year, Alejos met with Reagan in California.

THE DEAL WITH REAGAN

As described by Guatemalan and U.S. businessmen and Guatemalan government officials, the bargain with the Reagan forces has four key elements. First, there is an agreement, as Maegli puts it, "to take our Army off the blacklist"- to restore weapons and ammunition sales, supply badly needed spare parts for the U.S.-built helicopters, and make available fighter and cargo planes to the Guatemalan air force as well as crowd control and counterinsurgency gear to the army and police.

Second, a commitment has been made to resume Pentagon training of the army and police. particularly in surveillance, intelligence and interrogation techniques. According to Robert Merrick, an American-born plantation owner who was in close touch with Reagan advisors, Fontaine promised him and a group of Guatemalan businessmen that Reagan "would do everything he could within the law to help train the Guatemalan police."

Third and perhaps most importantly, the Reagan supporters have agreed to cut back

U.S. criticism of the death squads which the Guatemalan regime feels has so tarnished its international political and financial standing. Finally, although the signals have been less explicit, there is also the expectation in government and business councils that President Reagan would intervene militarily in the event that a popular uprising threatened the Lucas government.

In anticipation of such support, businessmen who back the death squads gave their all for the Reagan campaign. In addition to the more than $120,000 which Amigos del Pais paid to the Deaver and Hannaford firm, other public relations efforts by right wing Guatemalan groups attempted to sway U.S. opinion concerning Central America, in Reagan's favor.

According to Merrick and others, American businessmen based in Guatemala gave heavily to the Reagan campaign. Yet a check of the names of more than 200 such individuals-including several who said specifically that they had contributed-against the list of Reagan donors disclosed to the Federal Election Commission, showed no public trace of any such contributions. (The sole exception was John Trotter, who through his wife, had given $750 to the Reagan primary campaign.) One businessman who was solicited by the Reagan campaign said explicit instructions were given repeatedly: "Do not give to Mr. Reagan's campaign directly." Monies went instead to an undisclosed committee in California.

Last spring—when the Amigos del Pais were making the rounds of Congress asking for restoration of Guatemalan military training appropriation—Nancy Reynolds, Nancy Reagan's former press secretary and the current Vice President for public relations of the Bendix Corporation, called the office of Congressman Don Pease (Dem.-Ohio) and asked that he "lend a sympathetic ear" to Amigos del Pais members' plea for aid. "It's the first time we ever got a phone call like that," said the congressman's aide." It was Nancy Reynolds who recommended Deaver and Hannaford to Amigos del Pais.

THE GUATEMALA LESSON — THE C.I.A. OUT OF CONTROL

The only surprise is the surprise. In late March, it came out that the CIA had a paid agent in Guatemala who was responsible for the 1990 torture and brutal slaying of an American innkeeper (his head was nearly sawed off by a machete) and for the 1992 torture and murder of the husband of Jennifer Harbury, an American citizen.

Representative Robert Torricelli of New Jersey, who disclosed these facts, said "the agency is simply out of control and contains what can only be called a criminal element." But this was not the work of one overzealous agent or one rogue operation. This was, and is, standard operating procedure. In El Salvador and Guatemala and elsewhere around the globe, the "criminal element" is the CIA itself. The CIA organized the death squads in these countries, financed them, equipped them, trained them, and consulted with them on individual cases of torture and assassination. These are the facts. That's what the CIA does. The CIA knows it. The Pentagon knows it. The State Department knows it. The President knows it. Congress knows it. And no one does anything about it.

Once a decade, when the American public finally hears about the atrocities that are committed with our tax dollars and in our name, everyone in Washington claims to be shocked, shocked, shocked. There was shock during the Church Hearings in the 1970s about the CIA's role in Vietnam and Chile; there was shock in the 1980s when it was revealed that the CIA had Salvadoran death-squad members on its payroll; now there's shock that the CIA's been involved in these Guatemalan murders.

As in previous disclosures, the expression of shock serves a number of purposes. It shields officials from responsibility, it diverts attention away from the CIA's systematic pattern of human-rights abuses, and it thereby deflects criticism against the entire agency.

But the Guatemalan case demonstrates in almost crystalline terms why the CIA should be abolished once and for all.

Here we have an agency that overthrew the democratically elected Guatemalan government of Jacobo Arbenz in 1954 because a U.S. banana company, United Fruit, was worried about its plantations.

Here we have an agency that since the 1960s has been hand-in-glove with the hemisphere's most notorious human-rights abusers, as Allan Nairn ably documents in the April 17 issue of The Nation. In the last fifteen years alone, the Guatemalan military has massacred more than 100,000 peasants and Indians, and has tortured thousands more.

Here we have an agency that has repeatedly violated U.S. prohibitions on aid to Guatemala. The CIA did this in the 1980s, as Nairn reported way back in 1986 in The Progressive. And the CIA did it again in the early 1990s, after the Bush Administration had cut off military aid because of the murder of the American innkeeper, Michael DeVine. (At that time, no one owned up that Guatemalan colonel Julio Roberto Alpirez, implicated in the death, was on the CIA pay roll.) The CIA, according to The New York Times, funneled $5 to $7 million annually in military aid to Guatemala at a time when no such money was supposed to be going there. These payments continued during the Clinton Administration.

Here we have an agency that paid Alpirez-another illustrious graduate of the U.S. School of the Americas-$44,000 in 1992, even after it had learned about his involvement in the murder of Michael DeVine. "Everybody is covering up for everybody else," says Carole DeVine, Michael's widow.

Here we have an agency that admittedly misled Congress about the DeVine case and now pleads that it doesn't have all the information it needs to explain what happened.

And here we have an agency that is still paying Guatemalan military officers to this day-despite all the revelations that have come out, and despite Secretary of State Warren Christopher's statement that the payments had ended, a statement he was forced to retract. The CIA is a scandal. If we don't get rid of it now, in another ten years or so we'll hear of another case of CIA torture and assassination, accompanied by another round of shock, shock, shock.

But getting rid of the CIA is not enough. Even in this Guatemala case, the CIA did not act alone. The National Security Agency and the U.S. Army may also have been involved, and they were busy with their shredders as soon as Torricelli went public with the al legations about U.S. ties to Alpirez.

It is the presumption that the United States has a right to intervene in other countries that lies at the root of the problem. It is the presumption that any left wing movement abroad is somehow a threat to the United States and must be eradicated at all costs that allows the United States to involve itself with torturers in the first place.

The United States is not prepared to abandon either presumption. And there are many in Washington who don't even want the issues discussed in public. That's why Torricelli has come under fire from Newt Gingrich, who wants to boot him off the House Intelligence Committee for disclosing CIA complicity in the Guatemalan murders.

Gingrich is hardly the lone defender of the status quo. Senator Bob Kerrey, Democrat from Nebraska, was quick to comfort the American public, saying on the MacNeil/Lehrer NewsHour that we need the CIA if we are to project power and defend our interests around the world.

William Safire, the apologist's apologist, defended the CIA for winning the Cold War. And he did so with a particularly specious claim: "the alternative outcome-Soviet-Cuban hegemony up to our Mexican border-would have been far worse for democracy and human rights."

Tell that to Jennifer Harbury, Carole DeVine, and the hundreds of thousands of people who died brutally at the hands of the Guatemalan and Salvadoran military in the name of U.S. "national security." 141

CORRUPTION OF COVERT ACTIONS

by Ramsey Clark

CovertAction Quarterly magazine, Fall 1998

Nothing is more destructive of democracy or peace and freedom through the rule of law than secret criminal acts by government. The fact, or appearance, of covert action by government agents or their surrogates rots the core of love and respect that is the foundation of any free democratic society. Every true citizen of any nation wants to be able to love her country and still love justice. Corrupt covert actions make this impossible.

***

Despite common knowledge that the U.S. government is engaged continually in dangerous covert actions, some that can alter the futures of whole societies, most people cling desperately to the faith that their government is different and better than others, that it would engage in criminal, or ignoble, acts only under the greatest provocation, or direst necessity, and then only for a greater good. They do not want information that suggests otherwise and question the patriotism of anyone who raises unwanted questions.

***

In Vietnam 30 years ago, with all of Charlie Company, including dozens of robust young American soldiers who shot and killed helpless Vietnamese women and children and many other U.S. military personnel witnesses to, or aware of, the slaughter at My Lai, few would imagine the murderous event could be kept secret. Yet few would deny the U.S. intended to do so. The tragedy barely came to light through the courage and perseverance of several men. Ron Ridenhour broke the story after personal inquiry with letters to the Congress. The hero of My Lai, Hugh Thompson, who ended the massacre by placing himself between the U.S. troops and surviving Vietnamese and ordering his helicopter machine gunner to aim at the American soldiers and shoot if they tried to continue, was removed from Vietnam, separated from the service, and threatened with prosecution supported by Congressmen Mendel Rivers and Edward Hebert. Lt. William Calley alone was convicted, confined to base for a while, and still enjoys government support. Only by the sacrifice and heroism of an unusual handful did the story become known, and even then there has never been an acknowledgment of wrongdoing by the U.S. The medal begrudgingly given Thompson in 1998 was for non-combat service. And My Lai is viewed as an aberration, an ambiguous aberration.

When Salvadoran soldiers of the elite Atlacatl Battalion, which trained in the U.S., massacred Salvadoran villagers at El Mozote, shooting even infants lying on wooden floors at point blank range, the U.S. government was able to cover up any public disclosure, even though top reporters from the New York Times and the Washington Post and a TV team from CBS knew the story. It was a dozen years later before the massacre at El Mozote was confirmed, and years too late to affect U.S. plans for El Salvador, or the careers of those responsible for yet another U.S.-condoned, and inspired, massacre.

Just to list a few of the alleged assassinations conducted or planned by U.S. agents exposes the crisis in confidence covert actions have created for our country. Allende, Lumumba, Diem, Bhutto, with many questioning whether President Kennedy and Martin Luther King, Jr., should be included, and U.S. planning for the assassination of Fidel Castro part of our public record, while air and missile attacks directed at Qaddafi of Libya and Saddam Hussein of Iraq missed their targets.

 ***

CIA Director Richard Helms pleaded guilty to perjury for false testimony he gave before the U.S. Senate on the CIA's role in the overthrow of President Allende. He was fined, but his two-year prison sentence was suspended. But the American public is unaware of it, and Chile has never been the same. U.S. support for the overthrow of Allende was the essential element in that tragedy. For years, Patrice Lumumba's son would ask me whenever we met, first in Beirut, or later in Geneva, if the U.S. killed his father. I finally gave him a copy of former CIA officer John Stockwell's In Search of Enemies, which tells the story. Justice William O. Douglas wrote in later years that the U.S. killed Diem, painfully adding, "And Jack was responsible." Bhutto was removed from power in Pakistan by force on the 15th of July, after the usual party on the 4th at the U.S. Embassy in Islamabad, with U.S. approval, if not more, by General Zia al-Haq. Bhutto was falsely accused and brutalized for months during proceedings that corrupted the judiciary of Pakistan before being murdered, then hanged. That Bhutto had run for president of the student body at U.C. Berkeley and helped arrange the opportunity for Nixon to visit China did not help him when he defied the U.S.

So we should not be surprised that patriotic Americans wonder whether, or even charge that, the U.S. government assassinated President John F. Kennedy and our greatest moral leader, Martin Luther King, Jr.

SUPPRESSED INTELLIGENCE REPORTS

We have been told time and again of the "Deadly Deceits" of our government, occasionally by career CIA officers like Ralph McGehee, by FBI agents, crime lab scientists, and city detectives like Frank Serpico. Major studies on the lawless violence of COINTELPRO, the Life and Death of National Security Study Memorandum 200, the police murders of Black Panthers Fred Hampton and Mark Clark, are a part of the lore of our lawless government.

And still the People want to Believe.

Our covert government's past is modest prologue to its new powers of concealment, deception, and deadly secret violent actions. Too often the government is supported by a controlled, or willingly duped, mass media, by collaborating or infiltrated international governmental organizations, and by key officials in vast transnational corporations.

The new evil empires, terrorism, Islam, barely surviving socialist and would-be socialist states, economic competitors, uncooperative leaders of defenseless nations, and most of all the masses of impoverished people, overwhelmingly people of color, are the inspiration for new campaigns by the U.S. government ... to shoot first and ask questions later, to exploit, to demonize and destroy.

The CIA is rapidly expanding its manpower for covert operations against these newfound enemies. The National Security apparatus, with major new overseas involvement by the FBI, is creating an enormous new anti-terrorism industry exceeding in growth rate all other government activities.

***

The U.S. is not nearly so concerned that its acts be kept secret from their intended victims as it is that the American people not know of them. The Cambodians knew they were being bombed. So did the Libyans. The long suffering Iraqis know every secret the U.S. government conceals from the American people and every lie it tells them. Except for surprise attacks, it is primarily from the American people that the U.S. government must keep the true nature and real purpose of so many of its domestic and foreign acts secret while it manufactures fear and falsehood to manipulate the American public. The reasons for and effects of government covert acts and cultivated fear, with the hatred it creates, must remain secret for the U.S. to be able to send missiles against unknown people, deprive whole nations of food and medicine, and arrest, detain, and deport legal residents from the U.S. on secret allegations, without creating domestic outrage. As never before, it is imperative that the American people care about and know what their government is doing in their name. That we be demanding of government, skeptical, critical, even a little paranoid, because not to suspect the unthinkable has been made a dangerous naiveté by a government that does unthinkable things and believes it knows best. We must challenge controlling power in America that seeks to pacify the people by bread and circuses and relies on violence, deception, and secrecy to advance its grand plans for the concentration of wealth and power in the hands of the few.

For 20 years, Ellen Ray, Bill Schaap, Lou Wolf, and Philip Agee, with the help of very few others, have struggled against all odds to alert our people to the perils of covert action. They started their lonely, courageous, dangerous struggle in what many want to think was the aftermath of the worst of times, but now we can clearly see the worst is yet to be. The American people owe an enormous debt of gratitude to these valiant few.

The role of Covert Action Quarterly is more important than ever. Those who love America should support and defend its efforts, against the most powerful and secretive forces, to find the truth that can prevent our self-destruction and may yet set us free.

***

Ramsey Clark was United States Attorney General during the Johnson administration. He is an international lawyer and human rights advocate, based in New York City, and a prolific author.

WHAT GOES AROUND... THE CIA IN GUATEMALA

by retired Marine Colonel and ex-CIA operative Philip Roettinger

June 1995

Something has been missing from the recent press coverage of the CIA's support for a Guatemalan military that has tortured and killed more than 150,000 people.

The more enlightened pundits have mentioned that the CIA sponsored coup in 1954 destroyed Guatemala's emerging democracy and initiated a series of brutal military dictatorships. But few reporters have pointed out that U.S. acquiescence to the bloodletting that followed has been the rule, not a policy aberration. Since the '54 coup, the Guatemalan military and the US government have worked in tandem-from the '60s when the Green Berets conducted a Vietnam-style war in Guatemala, to the '80s and early '90s, when the death squads operated with tacit U.S. encouragement.

One man who believes that this historical perspective should be filled in is Philip Roettinger, a retired U.S. Marine Corps colonel. Roettinger was among the handful of CIA operatives who in 1954 planned and executed the Guatemalan coup. In a remote CIA-built base along the Honduran border with Guatemala, Roettinger organized and trained a group of rebels, who as he has put it, were "driven by the prospect of power and wealth, not ideology."

"It was a classic operation that went off beautifully," says the 80-year old Roettinger. "There's never been another one like it, and I'm glad."

As one of the opening salvos of the Cold War, the coup that toppled the democratically elected government of Jacabo Arbenz was not, as President Dwight Eisenhower insisted, aimed at "preventing the establishment of a communist beachhead in the Western Hemisphere." It was a cynical manipulation of anti communist hysteria to maintain the domination of a U.S. multinational, United Fruit, over the Guatemalan government.

But Roettinger "never got caught in the communism thing" during his time with the agency. "It was just an interesting job," he says. "Only later on I realized we weren't fighting communism at all, we were fighting the people."

Roettinger, the son of a distinguished Cincinnati judge, graduated from Ohio Wesleyan University. He joined the Marines during World War II and fought in the Pacific Theater. An accomplished marksman, he was a member of the U.S. shooting team in the 1948 Olympics in London. For a time he ran a photography studio, which he abandoned when he was recruited by the CIA. For his good work in Guatemala, the CIA rewarded Roettinger with an assignment in Mexico City. But by the early '60s, disgusted with the agency's intervention in Mexican politics, he quit the CIA and settled in the central Mexican town of San Miguel Allende to devote his time to painting portraits and landscapes and raising his family.

The spry, clear-eyed Roettinger, who still jogs daily, would have remained in obscurity as a moderately successful painter, if news of Nicaragua's contra war had not caught his attention. Reading about the Reagan administration's covert actions, he was struck by the similarities with his experience in Guatemala. In 1985, he decided to go down to Nicaragua to check out the situation for himself. On a trip alone into contra territory, he arrived at a cooperative near Esteli that had been attacked and burned the day before by the U.S.-backed rebels. Roettinger was horrified that the contras had killed several civilians, including a small boy.

"I was so outraged," he recalls, "that I went right back to Managua, got a plane to Washington, and I hit that town like a ton of bricks."

In a Los Angeles Times op-ed piece Roettinger warned that the United States was repeating the same mistake it had made in Guatemala. "As a CIA case officer, I trained Guatemalan exiles in Honduras to invade their own country and unseat the elected president," he wrote. "The coup that I helped engineer in 1954 inaugurated an unprecedented era of intransigent military rule in Central America. Generals and colonels acted with impunity to wipe out dissent and garner wealth for themselves and their cronies." Working with Iowa Sen. Tom Harkin, Roettinger sought to make amends by lobbying against contra aid.

"That's when I came out, by God," he says. Roettinger, believing the CIA needed to be confronted, helped found the Association of National Security Alumni. Roettinger sees his work with the association as an obligation to set the record straight. It does this in part through a quarterly magazine, Unclassified. "We have credibility. They have to believe us," says Roettinger.

The group, comprised of veterans of the national security establishment, helped Sen. Patrick Moynihan (D-NY) prepare a bill to abolish the CIA. And Roettinger is hopeful that Americans, in light of the latest Guatemalan scandal, will begin to re-evaluate the role of the agency. But he worries that people will fall for the tale that the CIA's involvement with Guatemala's death squads was an isolated incident. The blame, he says, must be placed where it belongs.

"What people have to understand is that the CIA works for the U.S. government. It doesn't set policy. It executes the policy of the government." -Jacob Bernstein

C.I.A. DEATH SQUADS

by Allan Nairn

April 1995

The U.S. government has systematic links to Guatemalan Army death squad operations that go far beyond the disclosures that have recently shaken official Washington. The news that the C.I.A. employed a Guatemalan colonel who reportedly ordered two murders has been greeted with professions of shock and outrage. But in fact the story goes much deeper, as U.S. officials well know.

SUPPRESSED INTELLIGENCE REPORTS

North American C.I.A. operatives work inside a Guatemalan Army unit that maintains a network of torture centers and has killed thousands of Guatemalan civilians. The G-2, headquartered on the fourth floor of the Guatemalan National Palace, has, since at least the 1960s, been advised, trained, armed and equipped by U.S. undercover agents. Working out of the U.S. Embassy and living in safehouses and hotels, these agents work through an elite group of Guatemalan officers who are secretly paid by the C.I.A. and who have been implicated personally in numerous political crimes and assassinations.

This secret G-2 / C.I.A. collaboration has been described by Guatemalan and U.S. operatives and confirmed, in various aspects, by three former Guatemalan heads of state. These accounts also mesh with that given in a March 28 interview by Col. Julio Roberto Alpirez, the C.I.A.- paid Guatemalan G-2 officer who has been implicated in the murders of Guatemalan guerrilla leader Efrain Bamaca Velasquez and a U.S. citizen, Michael DeVine.

One of the American agents who works with the G-2, a thin blond man in his 40s who goes by the name of Randy Capister, has been involved in similar operations with the army of neighboring El Salvador. Another, a weapons expert known as Joe Jacarino, has operated throughout the Caribbean, and has accompanied G-2 units on missions into rural zones.

Jacarino's presence in the embassy was confirmed by David Wright, a former embassy intelligence employee who called Jacarino a "military liaison." Col. George Hooker, the U.S. Defense Intelligence Agency chief in Guatemala from 1985 to 1989, says he also knew Jacarino, though he says Jacarino was not with the D.I.A. When asked whether Jacarino was with the C.I.A. he replied, "I'm not at liberty to say."

Celerino Castillo, a former agent for the Drug Enforcement Administration who dealt with the G-2 and the C.I.A. in Guatemala, says he worked with Capister as well as with Jacarino. He showed photographs of himself and Capister at embassy events and in the field. Guatemalan sources say Capister meets regularly with Guatemalan Army chiefs.

He has been seen in meetings in Guatemala City as recently as the spring of 1994.

When I reached Colonel Alpirez at the La Aurora base in Guatemala, he denied all involvement in the deaths of Bamaca and DeVine and said he was never paid by the

C.I.A. But he discussed at length how the agency advises and helps run the G-2. He praised the C.I.A. for "professionalism" and close rapport with Guatemalan officers. He said that agency operatives often come to Guatemala on temporary duty, during which they train G-2 men and provide "advice and technical assistance." He described attending C.I.A. sessions at G-2 bases on "contra-subversion" tactics and "how to manage the factors of power" to "fortify democracy." He said the C.I.A. men were on call to respond to G-2 questions, and that the G-2 often consulted the agency on how to deal with "political problems." Alpirez said he was not authorized to give specifics on the technical assistance, nor would he name the North Americans the G-2 worked with, though he said they were "very good friends." Other officials, though, say that at least during the mid 1980s G-2 officers were paid by Jack McCavitt, then C.I.A. station chief, and that the "technical assistance" includes communications gear, computers and special firearms, as well as collaborative use of C.I.A.-owned helicopters that are flown out of the Piper hangar at the La Aurora civilian air port and from a separate U.S. air facility. Through what Amnesty International has called "a government program of political murder." the Guatemalan Army has, since 1978, killed more than 110,000 civilians. The G-2 and a smaller, affiliated unit called the Archivo have long been openly known in Guatemala as the brain of the terror state. With a contingent of more than 2,000 agents and with sub-units in the local army bases. the G2-under orders of the army high command-coordinates the torture. assassination and disappearance of dissidents.

"If the G-2 wants to kill you, they kill you," former army Chief of staff Gen. Benedicto Lucas Garcia once said. "They send one of their trucks with a hit squad and that's it." Current and former G-2 agents describe a program of surveillance backed by a web of torture centers and clandestine body dumps. In 1986, then-army Chief of Staff Gen. Hector Gramajo Morales, a U.S. protege, said that the G-2 maintains files on and watches "anyone who is an opponent of the Guatemalan state in any realm." A former G-2 agent says that the base he worked at in Huehuetenango maintained its own crematorium and "processed" abductees by chopping off limbs, singeing flesh and administering electric shocks.

At least three of the recent G-2 chiefs have been paid by the C.I.A., according to U.S. and Guatemalan intelligence sources. One of them, Gen. Edgar Godoy Gaitan, a former army Chief of Staff, has been accused in court by the victim's family of being one of the prime "intellectual authors" of the 1990 murder of the noted Guatemalan anthropologist Myrna Mack Chang. Another, Col. Otto Perez Molina, who now runs the Presidential General Staff and oversees the Archivo, was in charge in 1994, when, according to the Archbishop's human rights office, there was evidence of General Staff involvement in the assassination of Judge Edgar Ramiro Elias Ogaldez. The third, Gen. Francisco Ortega Menaldo, who now works in Washington as general staff director at the Pentagon-backed Inter-American Defense Board, was G-2 chief in the late 1980s during a series of assassinations of students, peasants and human rights activists. Reached at his home in Florida, Jack McCavitt said he does not talk to journalists. When asked whether Ortega Menaldo was on the C.I.A. payroll, he shouted "Enough!" and slammed down the phone.

These crimes are merely examples of a vast, systemic pattern; likewise, these men are only cogs in a large U.S. government apparatus. Colonel Hooker, the former D.I.A. chief for Guatemala, says, "It would be an embarrassing situation if you ever had a roll call of everybody in the Guatemalan Army who ever collected a C.I.A. paycheck." Hooker says the agency payroll is so large that it encompasses most of the army's top decision-makers. When I told him that his friend, Gen. Mario Enriquez Morales, the current Defense Minister, had reacted to the Alpirez scandal by saying publicly that it was "disloyal" and "shameful" for officers to take C.I.A. money, Hooker burst out laughing and exclaimed: "Good! Good answer, Mario! I'd hate to think how many guys were on that payroll. It's a perfectly normal thing."

Other top commanders paid by the C.I.A. include Gen. Roberto Matta Galvez, former army Chief of Staff, head of the Presidential General Staff and commander of massacres in the El Quiche department; and General Gramajo, Defense Minister during the armed forces' abduction, rape and torture of Dianna Ortiz, an American nun. Gramajo also managed the early 1980s highland massacres. Colonel Hooker says he once brought Gramajo on a ten-day tour of the United States to speak at U.S. military bases and confer with the U.S. Army Chief of Staff. Three recent Guatemalan heads of state confirm that the C.I.A. works closely with the G-2. Last year, when I asked Gen. Oscar Humberto Meiia Victores (military dictator from 1983 to 1986) how the country's death squads had originated, he said they had been started "in the 1960s by the C.I.A." Gen. Efram Rios Montt (dictator from 1982 to 1983 and the current Congress President), who ordered the main highland massacres (662 villages destroyed, by the army's own count), said the C.I.A. did have agents inside the Guatemalan military.

2. When I asked Rios Montt—a firm believer in the death penalty—if he thought he should be executed for his role in the slaughter, he leapt to his feet and shouted "Yes! Try me! Put me against the wall!" but he said he should be tried only if Americans were tried too. Specifically, he cited President Reagan, who, in the midst of the massacres, embraced Rios Montt and said he was getting "a bum rap" on human rights. Vinicio Cerezo Arevalo, civilian President from 1986 to 1991 (under whom the rate of killing actually increased), said "the C.I.A. often contracts with our military and G-2 people," and that from what he knew they "very probably" had people inside "who have participated with our G-2 in technical assistance and advice. " These C.I.A. operations are, of course, part of the larger U.S. policy. The Bush and Clinton State Departments, for example, in the midst of a much-touted "cutoff" of military aid to Guatemala after 1990, authorized—according to classified State Department records—more than 114 separate sales of U.S. pistols and rifles.

The killing of defenseless people has been state policy in Guatemala for thirty years. The question is not whether the U.S. government has known—it is obviously aware of its own actions. It is why, with overt and covert aid, it has helped commit the army's murders.

THE PERSISTENCE OF TERROR

by Rolando Alecio and Ruth Taylor

from the Report on Guatemala, Fall 1998

This article is based on the article "La Privatizacion del Terror" written by Rolando Alecio for the Guatemalan news magazine Noticias de Guatemala. This version of the article was translated, edited and expanded on by Ruth Taylor, who works with the Guatemalan news agency CERIGUA.

"It becomes necessary to record, in quantity and quality, the magnitude of the harm produced by the counterinsurgency campaigns and by state repression, in order to understand the deception of wanting to erase this history and start afresh. The past that we so joyfully wish to seal up is not only alive in individuals and groups- victims and victimizers-but continues to operate in the very social structures." (Ignacio Martin-Baro)

THE PROLIFERATION OF CRIME

One of the thorniest problems Guatemala faces today in its attempt to build a true democracy is the damage caused by the political repression of the past. The scars of the brutal counterinsurgency campaigns of the 1960s, 1970s and 1980s are worn not only by the victims, their families and friends but by the society as a whole, affecting both attitudes and behavior, as well as the country's social fabric and imagination.

The terror inflicted on the population during the civil war has metamorphosed in post-war society, but it has not disappeared. It remains intact in the operations of dozens of crime rings-sophisticated mafia-like networks-as well as urban youth gangs and rural bandits.

Today, more than a year and a half since peace was signed, public insecurity in the face of crime and violence remains one of the most deeply felt concerns of the Guatemalan population. For the first year following the Peace Accords, police registered more than 2,500 deaths by firearms and other weapons - about 7 a day. Although police claim that they are chipping away at the problem, only 278 persons were arrested for homicide in that period.

Recently Guatemala was listed as having one of the highest rates of kidnapping in the world: according to the British consulting group Control Risks, the country ranks fourth worldwide, in absolute terms. The Mutual Support Group for Relatives of the Disappeared (GAM), documented 200 kidnappings for 1997.

Although rampant crime is the subject of daily public scrutiny and discussion, official explanations, public opinion and the media tend to reduce the problem to a simple lack of punitive actions against offenders. Reference is rarely made to this situation being a consequence of terror.

THE DEEP ROOTS OF TERROR

Beginning in the mid-1970s, in response to rising pressure from below for radical change, Guatemala's rulers built a state anchored in illegality and impunity, and armored it with one of the most efficient and feared machines of terror in the history of Latin America. Terror is government by intimidation, coercion and fear. It is implemented when the state, or those who hold power, feel threatened; to conserve their privileges-the status quo-they resort to systematic violence and the planned violation of human rights. In such a scenario, suffering regulates political conduct. To carry out this strategy in Guatemala, tens of thousands of members of the security forces- civilian, military and paramilitary- were trained at home and in specialized schools abroad in the methods and techniques of applying terror through surveillance, kidnapping, torture and murder.

In general terms, the effects of terror on individuals, social groups, and society as a whole can be observed immediately and in the long run. In Guatemala, the most evident immediate effects were displacement, disappearance and the destruction of tens of thousands of lives and hundreds of communities. The long run effects, while less visible, are no less dramatic.

One outcome of the end of the counterinsurgency war has been the shift from state-sponsored to privately financed terror. As Edgar Gutierrez of the Catholic Church's Recuperation of Historic Memory (REMHI) project has noted, Guatemala's repressive structures were "displaced, not dismantled." Although President Alvaro Arzu won praise early in his term for purging a number of corrupt personnel from the security forces, these individuals were never brought to trial for their alleged offenses, leaving them free to continue their criminal activities in civilian life, and to use their connections with still-active security force members and state officials to further their criminal ends. Similarly, when the army disbanded the Civil Defense Patrols (PACs) there was no supervision or follow-up by civilian authorities to ensure that these paramilitary groups did not retain their role as local strongmen under another name.

Common crime and other more serious offenses (such as rape, kidnapping, torture and murder) are still being committed by many of these counterinsurgency "experts." Every day, reports in the media testify to the pivotal role of both retired and active security force personnel who were trained in criminal means and are now prepared for criminal ends. In one high-profile case, the 1996 kidnapping and murder of teenager Beverly Sandoval, 18 of the 21 suspects rounded up were ax-members of military or paramilitary forces. Two former army officers were also among the suspects arrested for assaulting and raping a group of U.S. college students last January.

Students demonstrating outside Supreme Court, demanding justice in Mario Alioto murder case. Banner refers to numerous unprosecuted murders and massacres; Nov. 1997. [Christina Albo]

"It's the ideal combination for the underworld," observed an editorial in the daily Prensa Libre. "Retired (army personnel) operate under the protection of those who hold public posts, which hinders to a great degree the investigations." The state "has been an official school from which its institutions have not been able to free themselves," it concluded.

IMPUNITY HOLDS THE TRUMP CARD

One essential factor in preserving and amplifying the effects of terror on a society is impunity. This phenomenon, which is founded on the absence of truth and justice, always appears intrinsically linked to the practice of terror. According to Guatemalan author Mario Rene Matute, in using repression as a means of government, the state has to offer "those who plan and those who execute the full guarantee that their actions will take place in a climate of absolute impunity... since punishment cannot be offered as their reward."

Impunity, then, instituted for the purpose of conducting a "dirty" war against the Guatemalan population, extended its roots into all the state's structures by legalizing the illegitimate, the arbitrary, and the corrupt. It is a weed that is difficult to extirpate, and is one of the reasons why the state has not moved effectively to bring criminal groups under control. But impunity is not the only cause. Although the U.N. Verification Mission (MINUGUA) has repeatedly absolved the state of sponsoring a policy of human rights violations, its most recent report, released in June 1998, accused the government of "tolerance and acquiescence" towards organized crime.

Resignation by state authorities in the face of crime can be traced in part to the ruling class' historic relationship to the army and to the counterinsurgency war itself. The governing Party of National Advancement (PAN) represents the same oligarchy that financed the war and turned the country over to the military so it would "protect" their interests. But to date, only the army has had to answer-although only at the level of moral sanctions and a reduction in its scope of operations-for the crimes committed during the terror. Members of the army who lost their jobs because of the armistice, as well as those who remain within the institution, know the "truth" about the oligarchy's role in the war, and may be using it as their trump card to ensure that they retain a degree of power, or at least a free hand in carrying on their illicit trades.

Kidnappings have proven to be a handy tool for keeping the elite in their place, not to mention a lucrative business. It is perhaps ironic that Guatemala's oligarchy, who in the past politically and materially supported state terror, are now often the target of this transformed and privatized terror.

Furthermore, former military officers, well-equipped with terror skills, are also in good position to destabilize the government should the authorities try to put the squeeze on their operations.

SUPPRESSED INTELLIGENCE REPORTS

TERROR'S IMPACT ON THE SOCIAL FABRIC

In addition to a thriving criminal empire, the legacy of state terror has other manifestations in society, many of them touched on in a recent study by a team of Argentine psychologists who examined their own country's experiences with terror. Although differences exist between the processes of repression and impunity in Argentina and Guatemala, a number of the team's conclusions fit Guatemalan society today very well.

1. The continuing existence of fear, insecurity, and vulnerability. Broad sectors of society display these feelings as a result of their experience of living with terror. At sundown, whether in the countryside or in the city, people hurry home to the relative safety of closed doors. Among the war's victims, these feelings can be much more acute. A survey by the National Widows Coalition (CONAVIGUA) on wartime abuses found that the vast majority of women and men interviewed reported crying fits, listlessness, insomnia, tremors, difficulty thinking, fear, headaches, and feeling of persecution. A smaller number referred to hallucinations, alcoholism, fits of anger, jealousy, and mistrust as products of the war. Such fears are reinforced by the prevailing climate of insecurity and impunity.

2. Impunity becomes a social model. The model of impunity is a model of omnipotence; it teaches that you can get away with anything, that consequences are nonexistent. Under the current government, although a number of human rights cases have gone to trial, few have resulted in convictions. And so far the masterminds, or intellectual authors, of these crimes remain untouched. On several occasions, lower court convictions have been successfully appealed and overturned. To date, no military officer over the rank of sergeant has served time for a human rights violation, and no one at all has answered for the 45,000 Guatemalans disappeared during the civil war, or for a single massacre, despite a wealth of physical evidence gathered from dozens of mass graves and extensive eyewitness testimonies.

This is especially dangerous for the young, who are at a stage of their development where they are becoming part of the social fabric of the country and are incorporating values and norms of what is and what is not possible, what is permitted and what is prohibited for coexistence and mutual respect.

In this atmosphere "maras"-youth gangs-have proliferated. While many crimes committed by these gangs have material ends, they are often accompanied by acts of violence that have no apparent objective other than to terrorize the victims, causing serious injuries or death in the act of stealing a purse, a watch, sunglasses.

Carlos Aldana, who oversees a crisis center for the Catholic Church's Pastoral Social Ministry reports that violence among children is increasingly common. In a recent column in Prensa Libre he described several cases he has worked on, including a brutal attack by a group of seven-year-olds on a younger girl which left the victim blind.

3. The proliferation of vigilante "justice." Lack of confidence in the ability of the state to sanction criminal activity results in the appearance of "avenging" individuals, groups or mobs, who seek to take justice into their own hands by punishing suspected criminals. The most serious manifestation of this phenomenon is the recourse to lynchings.

MINUGUA reports that in the last two years, angry crowds have captured at least 100 suspected criminals and executed them on the spot. The vast majority of these lynchings took place in the countryside in response to petty theft; only 12 percent were responses to crimes such as assault, rape or murder. MINUGUA also found that many of the towns and villages where lynchings have occurred are ones where paramilitary groups such as PACs or military commissioners have been influential; on several occasions former members of these organizations were identified as instigators of the mob action. To date, in only two cases have those responsible been convicted.

The U.N. mission also confirmed the existence of armed groups who carry out "social cleansing" campaigns against suspected criminals and social outcasts (such as transvestites, prostitutes and drug addicts). It reports that this year in La Libertad, Peten province, a vigilante squad has already executed ten people, including one child, torturing and mutilating its victims to provide horrific warnings to other "wayward" citizens. Notes of explanation were pinned to the corpses: "We're very sorry but we have to clean up this village and there are still a lot more people to go." Of course, such vigilante violence does not bring security or justice, but rather generates more fear, prolongs the cycle of violence, and contributes to general disrespect for the rule of law.

4. Exaltation of "iron fist" policies and past oppressors. The breakdown of the criminal justice system also prompts calls by a frustrated populace for iron fist measures to combat crime. When the state does not fulfill its function as social guarantor, the promotion of a recognized repressor-a "father" figure, arbitrary and all embracing, who ostensibly protects the citizenry and promotes the "common welfare" and "justice"- becomes possible. In Guatemala, this figure is embodied by former dictator General Efrain Rios Montt, whose Republican Front (FRO) nearly won the presidency in the last elections and still constitutes the second strongest political force in the country. Despite heading a regime in 1982-83 that was responsible for the most wartime atrocities, many Guatemalans recall his rule as a time when criminals got what they deserved.

Some observers contend that Rios Montt and his party may even be using their links to the repressive structures of the past to foment the current crime wave, destabilizing their political rivals in the Arzu government and furthering their own chances at the polls.

5. Support for the death penalty. Feelings of personal insecurity, vulnerability and defenselessness are used-by certain Former Civil Patrol members on trial for a deadly 1993 attack on peaceful demonstrators, groups and by the state itself to demand and Colotenango, Huehuetenango; July 1995. (They have since been acquitted.) justify the application of the death penalty. In this case the population looks to the law instead of a figurehead like Rios Montt to impose exemplary punishments. Since peace was signed, three convicted murderers have been sentenced to death and executed, the first executions since civilian rule was restored in 1986. And now many Guatemalans want the penalty applied to kidnappers too. In 1995 Congress instituted the death penalty for kidnapping, but the measure contravenes the InterAmerican Human Rights Convention, to which Guatemala is a signatory, and has therefore never been applied. To resolve this contradiction, several groups are currently lobbying the state to renounce the convention.

WHAT DOES THE FUTURE HOLD?

The negotiators of the Peace Accords worked to address the issue of military control over internal security through several measures placing it more squarely under civilian institutions. Although the army has complied with some of these provisions, it has yet to relinquish control of key areas of its former operations. One such area is the military's exclusive hold on intelligence. Neither the army nor the government has taken steps to establish the civilian intelligence branch called for in the Peace Accords.

As long as the army controls intelligence, the civilian government will be forced to rely on it for combating crime, as it does currently in the case of kidnappings. Many analysts suspect that army intelligence is well aware of who is behind organized crime in the country, whether they are private citizens or hold posts within the state, just as it knows who ordered the massacres of the past, and whose interests were served by the counterinsurgency war. Wresting control of intelligence from military hands is thus fundamental to bringing the whole security apparatus under civilian management, as well as to taking on organized crime.

In addition to addressing the role of the army in postwar Guatemala, the Peace Accords seek to mend the many deficiencies of the justice system and grant it more independence from the executive branch. The Commission to Strengthen Justice, established by the Peace Accords, has delivered its recommendations to the government, but these have yet to be turned into policy or legislation. Perhaps one of the Commission's most important conclusions is the need to understand the administration of justice as much more than the imposition of punitive measures. Reconciliation, one of the underlying aims of the peace process, should also be a central objective of the justice system. The current clamor for the death penalty and other repressive responses to crime may be reduced over time if reforms are successful in producing a more effective justice system based on a different conception of justice.

Clearly, the country will not be able to overcome the experience of terror and heal if its ailments are not thoroughly examined. This means, among other things, facing the past, and taking steps to understand and overcome its legacy. The eagerness of some sectors, including the government, to put the past behind them and turn their eyes only toward the future, is symptomatic of a superficial approach to the peace process as a whole. Those points in the Peace Accords which call for examining the past, compensating the war's victims and encouraging reconciliation should not be skipped over. If the legacy of terror left by the war is not addressed, the construction of a true democracy may never get beyond the blueprint stage.

Report on Guatemala is published by the Network in Solidarity with the People of Guatemala (NISGUA) / the Guatemala News and Information Service, 3181 Mission St., Box 12, San Francisco, CA 94110, 415-826-3593, email -nisgua@igc.apc.org

RONALD REAGAN'S LEGACY:

EIGHT YEARS OF CIA COVERT ACTION

by William Blum

Covert Action Quarterly, Winter 1990

Ronald Reagan was not the most interventionist American president of modern times. Dwight Eisenhower retains that honor, insofar as significant extralegal meddling in other countries' politics is concerned. Reagan intervened in the face of political obstacles which would most likely have inhibited Eisenhower or any other president to a marked degree.

Reagan presided over an American public grown cynical and suspicious of the overseas adventures of the CIA, the U.S. military, and other arms of the U.S. government. World opinion was yet more cynical. The previous decade had brought Indochina, Chile, Angola, Watergate, seemingly endless revelations about CIA misdeeds, exposes by former Agency officers, lengthy and relatively antagonistic Congressional investigations, oversight committees, professional CIA-watchers of the left and the center, and a media that had finally learned to ask some of the right questions and follow up on some of the right leads.

American destabilization and other covert operations of the 1950s did not have to deal with any of this; they did not face the glare of public exposure or censure until years after their occurrence, if ever.

In the 1980s, the information was leaked often within days, yet, in most cases, Reagan, CIA director William Casey, Oliver North & Co., et al., seemed unfazed by any of this.

CIA pilots bombed Indonesia in 1958 on several occasions, causing considerable death and destruction. In the United States, this was virtually a non-event. To this day, you will have to search long and hard to find any mention of it in standard works of reference, school texts, etc. In 1986, the U.S. bombed Libya and Reagan went on TV immediately to proudly announce the event.

For some 30 years, the CIA covertly funded foreign coups, counter-insurgency operations, politicians, political parties, labor unions, student organizations, book publishers, newspapers, and all manner of other, generally pro-capitalist and anti-communist institutions. Beginning in the 1970s, these activities, past and current, began to be exposed with alarming regularity and increasing embarrassment to Washington political leaders. Something had to be done.

What was done was not to end such activities. What was done by the Reagan administration was simply to make the activities ostensibly overt and thus, hopefully, eliminate the stigma associated with covert activities. It was a master stroke. Of politics, public relations, and cynicism.

In 1983, the National Endowment for Democracy (NED) was set up to "strengthen democratic institutions throughout the world through private, nongovernmental efforts." Funded by Congress, i.e., the American taxpayers, NED engages in much of the same kinds of interference in the internal affairs of foreign countries which are the hallmark of the CIA.

Some causes which have been supported by NED largesse were the following:

- Over $400,000 to the Center for Democracy, a New York-based foundation run by Soviet emigres which has used the Soviet human rights network, tourists, and "experienced" travelers to gather political and military information on the U.S.S.R. The Center has also smuggled American films with anti-Soviet themes (White Nights, Red Dawn and The Assassination of Trotsky) into the Soviet Union. - Several hundred thousand dollars since 1985 to La Prensa, the anti-Sandinista newspaper in Nicaragua, which can only be viewed as part of the Reagan administration's campaign to overthrow the government; several million more has been allocated to support organizations opposing the Sandinistas in elections scheduled for 1990. -Newspapers in other developing countries, including Grenada, Guyana, and Botswana. - Translation into Polish of a book that accuses the Soviet Union of a World War II massacre of Polish Army officers. The book was to be smuggled into Poland. - $400,000 a year to the Solidarity trade union in Poland, to clandestinely print underground publications, as well as funds for other political organizations, youth groups, and churches. This is in addition to several million dollars allocated to Solidarity by the U.S. Congress. - $830,000 to Force Ouvriere, the French anti-communist trade union which the CIA began funding in the 1940s. - $575,000 to an extreme right-wing French group of paramilitary and criminal background, the National Inter-University Union. The funding of this group as well as Force Ouvriere was secret and is known of only because of its exposure by French journalists in November 1985. - $3 million to the Philippines, "quietly being spent to fight the communist insurgency...and to cultivate political leaders there." Some of this money was channeled to the National Citizens Movement for Free Elections, which was set up by the CIA in the 1950s to support the presidential campaign of Ramon Magsaysay. The National Endowment for Democracy, like the CIA before it, calls this supporting democracy. The governments and movements against whom the financing is targeted, call it destabilization. The NED was not an aberration of an other wise legal, accountable, non-interventionist Reagan foreign policy. Among the other stories of international intrigue and violence of the Reagan era worth noting are:

South Africa: Working closely with British intelligence, the U .S . provided South Africa with intelligence about the banned and exiled African National Congress, including specific warnings of planned attacks by the group and the whereabouts and movements of ANC leaders. As part of South Africa's reciprocation, it sent 200,000 pounds of military equipment to contra leader Eden Pastora.

Fiji: The coup of May 1987 bore all the fingerprints of a U.S. destabilization operation-the deposed prime minister, Timoci Bavadra, in office only a month after being elected over the conservative former Prime Minister Ratu Mara, was intent upon enforcing the ban upon nuclear vessels in Fiji ports; two weeks before the coup, Gen. Vernon Walters, he of extensive CIA involvement over the years, visited Fiji and met with the army officer who staged the coup; at the same time, Ratu Mara was visiting U.S. military headquarters (CINCPAC) in Hawaii; the AFL-CIO/CIA labor mafia was well represented, working against the nuclear-free Pacific movement; and several other similar components of a now all too-familiar scenario.

Grenada: The invasion by the U.S. military in October 1983 was accompanied by a battalion of falsehoods that stands out even in an administration noted for its creation of dial-a-lie. The "democracy" installed in the country reached fruition this year when the government banned the importation, by name, of over 80 leftist books, and later suspended Parliament to block a no-confidence vote.

Libya: Along with Nicaragua, Ronald Reagan's manic obsession, culminating in the April 1986 bombing which took the lives of about 37 people, all civilians but one, and wounded some 93 others. The dead included Libyan leader Muammar Qaddafi's young adopted daughter; his other seven children and his wife were hospitalized. "Our evidence is direct, it is precise, it is irrefutable," announced the President of the United States in explaining that the bombing was in retaliation for the Libyan bombing nine days earlier of a West Berlin nightclub frequented by American servicemen which killed one soldier and injured many other soldiers and civilians. The evidence of Libyan culpability in the Berlin bombing, how ever, was never directly or precisely presented to the world.

Surinam: In December 1982, CIA Director William Casey told the House and Senate intelligence committees that President Reagan had authorized the CIA to try to topple Surinam ruler Col. Desi Bouterse, supposedly leading his country into "the Cuban orbit." Even though the committee refused to approve the covert operation, there is good reason to believe that the administration did what it wished. An invasion of the country was scheduled for July 1, 1983 by Florida-based mercenaries-Americans and others. It was called off only after being discovered by the internal security agency of the Netherlands, the former colonial power in Surinam.

Seychelles: The country's leader, France Albert Rene, amongst other shortcomings in the eyes of Washington, was a socialist, pursued non-alignment, and wanted to turn the Indian Ocean into a nuclear-free zone. For this he was the object of various American destabilization conspiracies beginning in 1979. In November 1981, the CIA reportedly was behind a mercenary invasion of the island nation which originated in South Africa and got no further than an armed battle at the Seychelles airport.

El Salvador: The Reagan administration's bloodiest intervention. Largely obscured has been the extent of direct American involvement in the fighting. At least a dozen Americans have been killed or wounded in helicopter and plane crashes while flying reconnaissance or other missions over combat areas. There have been numerous reports of armed Americans spotted in combat areas, a report by CBS News of U.S. advisers "fighting side by side" with government troops, and reports of other Americans, some ostensibly mercenaries, killed in action. By 1983 there were more than two hundred U.S. intelligence agents (about two-thirds of them from the CIA) operating in El Salvador. At least until 1985, CIA paramilitary personnel were organizing and leading special Salvadoran army units into combat areas to track down guerrillas and call in air strikes.

Lebanon: Another civil war the United States felt compelled to take part in, leading to the terrible bombings of the American Embassy and Marine barracks in 1983, followed, in December of that year, by American ships firing some 700 shells into the Beirut mountains, missing their military targets but causing destruction in civilian areas. In 1985, William Casey and a Saudi prince conspired to eliminate Muslim leader Sheikh Fadlallah, believed to be connected to the attacks on the American facilities. This plot culminated in March when the men employed to carry out the elimination drove a car bomb into a Beirut suburb near Fadlallah's residence. The explosion took 80 lives, wounded 200, and left widespread devastation. Fadlallah escaped without injury.

Dominica: "Financial support to the Freedom Party of Eugenia Charles to defeat Oliver Seraphin in the Dominican elections." In 1980 Charles won the election.

Mauritius: In 1981-82, financial support was given to Seewoosagar Ramgoolam in an attempt to bring him to power in the 1982 elections. Ramgoolam did not win in the elections.

Chad: In 1981, the administration formally decided to supply Hissene Habre in his attempt to overthrow the government of Goukouni Oueddei. Through the CIA, Habre was supplied with money, arms and ammunition, and other equipment. "The operation was coordinated with Egypt,...which furnished Habre with weapons and ammunition in exchange for U.S. replacements." Sudan provided a base of operations and a supply-line. American commitment increased several times during 1981, ending with a total of about $10 million. In June 1982 Habre's men "took control of N'Djamena, the capital of Chad, and set up a provisional government."

Afghanistan: Approximately $625 million was appropriated between 1980-84, "including about $40 million reprogrammed from the Pentagon budget and as much as $250 million in fiscal year 1985 alone." Afghanistan has be come one of the most expensive covert actions in American history. This money was used in continuing military aid to the rebel forces of Zia Khan Nassery, Gulbuddin Hekmatyar, Sayed Ahmed Gailani and to conservative mullahs "to harass Soviet occupation forces and challenge the legitimacy of the government of Babrak Karmal." The Afghanistan rebels also received monies from the National Endowment for Democracy. This included one grant of $180,000 ostensibly for their school system; but in the extreme chaos of the war area, there can be no satisfactory way of determining what the ultimate disposition of the money was; this can only be viewed as part of the Reagan administration's campaign to overthrow the government supported by the Soviet Union. (This is ironic in light of the deep loathing Americans feel for the government of Iran, for if the Afghan rebels take power they will undoubtedly create a similar fundamentalist Islamic state.)

Ethiopia: A support operation of about $500,000 per year for the opposition to the so-called Marxist government.

Cambodia: Several million dollars a year for the forces fighting against the Vietnamese-backed government, a policy which directly benefited the notorious Khmer Rouge.

Angola: In 1985 the Clark Amendment banning covert military aid to Angolan rebels was lifted and Reagan ordered the release of $13 million in covert aid to Jonas Savimbi.

According to government sources, profits generated from the illegal sale of arms to Iran, as well as money intended for the Afghan rebels, also may have been used to fund UNITA.

Argentina: "Aid and training were provided (in 1981) to the contras through the Argentinean Defense Forces in exchange for other forms of aid from the U.S. to Argentina. This arrangement...avoided detailed congressional scrutiny and public explanations, and. . .hid the cost in various aid budgets for Argentina." CIA-Argentine cooperation ended when the U.S. supported Britain in the 1982 Malvinas War.

Nicaragua: A traditional, multi-level, multi-millions-of dollars, CIA destabilization operation to overthrow the government: economic boycott and cut off of international credit; crippling of the oil supply by blowing up fuel depots, ports, and pipelines, and mining the waters of oil-unloading ports; extensive damage to the agricultural infrastructure; covert funding of private organizations and the Catholic church which were actively subverting the government; a major military campaign in support of the contra rebels, including U.S. reconnaissance flights over Nicaragua and U.S. pilots flying combat and supply missions; several attempts to assassinate the Sandinista leadership; a major attempt to under mine the 1984 elections which the Sandinistas won handily.

Honduras was turned into a launching area and support base for the Nicaragua operation: landing strips, docks, radar stations and communication centers were built under the cover of repeated U.S.-Honduran military exercises. For seven years, attacks were carried out against Nicaragua from the soil of a supposedly neutral Honduras.

The eight years of the Reagan administration brought an unparalleled growth in CIA covert activities and U.S. intervention abroad. This listing is only a sample of hundreds of operations that sought to destabilize foreign governments and have diminished the prospects for international peace. The victims of CIA interventions will remember the Reagan years far into the future.

SUPPRESSED INTELLIGENCE REPORTS

Now a new U.S. president is on the scene speaking of "a kinder and gentler America." How willing are the people of Angola, Nicaragua, El Salvador, and Cambodia to believe the former Director of Central Intelligence? George Bush will likely carry on the Reagan legacy, even in light of changes in U.S.-Soviet relations. It promises to be a long four years.

'William Blum is the author of The CIA: A Forgotten History, U.S. Global Interventions Since World War 2 (London: Zed Books, 1986). A revised edition will published by St. Martin's Press in 1990, titled — Killing Hope.

STILL SEEING RED THE CIA FOSTERS DEATH SQUADS IN COLOMBIA

by Frank Smyth

The Progressive magazine, June 1998

Back in 1989, the CIA built its first counter-narcotics center in the basement of its Directorate of Operations headquarters in Langley, Virginia. Since then, the newly renamed "crime and narcotics center" has increased four-fold, says CIA spokeswoman Anya Guilsher. She says she cannot comment about any specific counter-drug operations, except to say that the agency is now conducting them worldwide.

The CIA was established in 1947 as a front-line institution against the Soviet Union. Today, nine years after the Berlin Wall fell, the agency is seeking a new purpose to justify its $26.7 billion annual subsidy. Besides the crime and narcotics center, the CIA now runs a counterterrorism center, a center to stymie the proliferation of weapons of mass destruction, and even an ecology center to monitor global warming and weather patterns, including El Nifio.

George J. Tenet, the Clinton Administration's new Director of Central Intelligence, recently told Congress the United States faces new threats in "this post-Cold War world" that are "uniquely challenging for U.S. interests."

But the CIA remains a Cold War institution. Many officers, especially within the clandestine operations wing, still see communists behind every door. They maintain warm relationships with rightist military forces worldwide that are engaging in widespread human-rights abuses. These ties conflict with the agency's putative goal of fighting drugs, since many of the rightist allies are themselves involved in the drug trade.

Take Colombia. In the name of fighting drugs, the CIA financed new military intelligence networks there in 1991. But the new networks did little to stop drug traffickers. Instead, they incorporated illegal paramilitary groups into their ranks and fostered death squads. These death squads killed trade unionists, peasant leaders, human-rights monitors, journalists, and other suspected "subversives." The evidence, including secret Colombian military documents, suggests that the CIA may be more interested in fighting a leftist resistance movement than in combating drugs.

Thousands of people have been killed by the death squads, and the killings go on. In April, one of Colombia's foremost human-rights lawyers, Eduardo Umaha Mendoza, was murdered in his office. Umaha's clients included leaders of Colombia's state oil workers' union. Reuters estimated that 10,000 people attended his funeral in Bogota.

SUPPRESSED INTELLIGENCE REPORTS

Human-rights groups suspect that Umaha's murder may have been carried out by members of the security forces supporting or operating in unison with paramilitary forces. At the funeral, Daniel Garcia Peha, a Colombian government official who was a friend of Umaha's, told journalists that before his death Umaha had alerted authorities that state security officials along with security officers from the state oil company were planning to kill him.

The killings are mounting at a terrible pace. In February, a death squad mowed down another leading human-rights activist, Jesus Maria Valle Jaramillo. He had pointed a finger at the military and some politicians for sponsoring death squads.

"There is a clear, coordinated strategy of targeting anyone involved in the defense of human rights," says Carlos Salinas of Amnesty International. "Every statement of unconditional support by U.S. lawmakers only encourages these kinds of attacks."

A new debate is taking place today between human-rights groups and the Clinton Administration over U.S. aid to Colombia. The Clinton Administration has escalated military aid to Colombia to a record $136 million annually, making Colombia the leading recipient of U.S. military aid in this hemisphere. Now the Administration is considering even more, including helicopter gunships.

Colombia did not figure prominently on the world stage back in late 1990 and early 1991. Germany was in the process of reunification, Iraq's Saddam Hussein had just invaded Kuwait, and El Salvador was negotiating an end to its long civil war. But the Bush Administration was not ignoring Colombia. It was increasing the number of U.S. Army Special Forces (or Green Beret) advisers there. And the CIA was increasing the number of agents in its station in Bogota-which soon became the biggest station in Latin America.

"There was a very big debate going on [over how to allocate] money for counter-narcotics operations in Colombia," says retired Colonel James S. Roach Jr., the U.S. military attache and the Defense Intelligence Agency (DIA) country liaison in Bogota in the early 1990s. "The U.S. was looking for a way to try to help. But if you're not going to be combatants [yourselves], you have to find something to do."

The United States formed an inter-agency commission to study Colombia's military intelligence system. The team included representatives of the U.S. embassy's Military Advisory Group in Bogota, the U.S. Southern Command in Panama, the DIA, and the CIA, says Roach, who was among the military officers representing the DIA. The commission, according to a 1996 letter from the Defense Department to Senator Patrick J. Leahy, Democrat of Vermont, recommended changes in Colombia's military intelligence networks to make them "more efficient and effective."

In May 1991, Colombia completely reorganized its military intelligence networks "based on the recommendations made by the commission of U.S. military advisers," according to the secret Colombian reorganization order, which Human Rights Watch made public in 1996. The U.S. commission of advisers backed the reorganization plan ostensibly as part of the drug war. Yet the secret Colombian order itself made no mention anywhere in its sixteen pages or corresponding appendices about gathering intelligence against drug traffickers. Instead, the order instructed the new intelligence networks to focus on leftist guerrillas or "the armed subversion."

The forty-one new intelligence networks created by the order directed their energies toward unarmed civilians suspected of supporting the guerrillas. One of these intelligence networks, in the oil refinery town of Barrancabermeja in Colombia's strife-torn Magdalena Valley, assassinated at least fifty-seven civilians in the first two years of operation. Victims included the president, vice president, and treasurer of the local transportation workers union, two leaders of the local oil workers union, one leader of a local peasant workers union, two human-rights monitors, and one journalist.

Colonel Roach says the Defense Department never intended the intelligence networks to foster death squads. But Roach says he can't speak for the CIA, which was more involved in the intelligence reorganization and even financed the new networks directly.

"The CIA set up the clandestine nets on their own," says Roach. "They had a lot of money. It was kind of like Santa Claus had arrived."

The secret Colombian order instructed the military to maintain plausible deniability from the networks and their crimes. Retired military officers and other civilians were to act as clandestine liaisons between the networks and the military commanders. All open communications "must be avoided." There "must be no written contracts with informants or civilian members of the network; everything must be agreed to orally." And the entire chain of command "will be covert and compartmentalized, allowing for the necessary flexibility to cover targets of interest."

Facts about the new intelligence networks became known only after four former agents in Barrancabermeja began testifying in 1993 about the intelligence network there. What compelled them to come forward? Each said the military was actively trying to kill them in order to cover up the network and its crimes. By then the military had "disappeared" four other ex-agents in an attempt to keep the network and its operations secret.

Since the military was already trying to kill them, the agents decided that testifying about the network and its crimes might help keep them alive. Saulo Segura was one ex-agent who took this gamble. But rather than prosecuting his superiors over his and others' testimony, Colombia's judicial system charged and imprisoned Segura. In a 1996 interview in La Modelo, Bogota's maximum-security jail, Segura told me he hadn't killed anyone and that his job within the network was limited to renting office space and handling money. Segura then glanced about nervously before adding, "I hope they don't kill me."

Two months later, on Christmas Eve, Segura was murdered inside his cellblock. His murder remains unsolved; the whereabouts of the other three ex-agents is unknown. No Colombian officers have been prosecuted for ordering the Barrancabermeja crimes.

In 1994, Amnesty International accused the Pentagon of allowing anti-drug aid to be diverted to counterinsurgency operations that lead to human-rights abuses. U.S. officials including General Barry R. McCaffrey, the Clinton Administration drug czar who was then in charge of the U.S. Southern Command, publicly denied it. But back at the office, McCaffrey ordered an internal audit. It found that thirteen out of fourteen Colombian army units that Amnesty had specifically cited for abuses had previously received either U.S. training or arms. Amnesty made these documents public in 1996. (Full disclosure: I provided the internal U.S. documents to Amnesty; Winifred Tate and I provided the secret Colombian order to Human Rights Watch.)

Colombian military officers, along with some of their supporters in the United States, say the line between counterinsurgency and counter-drug operations in Colombia is blurry, as Colombia's leftist guerrillas are more involved today than ever before in drug trafficking.

Indeed, they are. For years, about two-thirds of the forces of the Revolutionary Armed Forces of Colombia (FARC) and about half the forces of the National Liberation Army (ELN) have been involved in the drug trade, mainly protecting drug crops, according to both U.S. intelligence and leftist sources.

Colombia's rightist paramilitary groups, however, are even more involved in the drug trade, and they have been for a decade. Back in 1989, Colombia's civilian government outlawed all paramilitary organizations after a government investigation had found that the Medellin drug cartel led by the late Pablo Escobar had taken over the largest ones.

At the time, Escobar and his associates were fiercely resisting U.S. pressure on the Colombian government to make them stand trial in the United States on trafficking charges. They took control of Colombia's strongest paramilitaries and used them to wage a terrorist campaign against the state. These same paramilitaries, based in the Magdalena Valley, were behind a wave of violent crimes, including the 1989 bombing of Avianca flight HK-1803, which killed 111 passengers. Investigators concluded that Israeli, British, and other mercenaries, led by Israeli Reserve Army Lieutenant Colonel Yair Klein, had trained the perpetrators in such techniques. In February, Klein and three other former Israeli reserve officers, along with two Colombians, were indicted in absentia for their alleged involvement in these crimes.

The CIA bears some responsibility for the proliferation of drug trafficking in the Magdalena Valley since it supported rightist counterinsurgency forces who run drugs. But the CIA has also helped combat drug trafficking in Colombia. In other words, different units within the agency have pursued contrary goals.

The CIA's most notable success in the drug war was the 1995-1996 operations that, with the help of the DEA, apprehended all top seven leaders of Colombia's Cali drug cartel. One of those apprehended was Henry Loaiza, also known as "The Scorpion," a top Colombian paramilitary leader. He secretly collaborated with the CIA-backed intelligence networks to carry out assassinations against suspected leftists.

A young, techno-minded CIA team led the Cali bust. Heading up the team was a woman. "I'm just a secretary," she protested when I called her on the phone at the time.

But despite her denials, she was not unappreciated. On September 19, 1995, a courier delivered a white box to her at the U.S. Embassy in Bogota. I happened to be in the lobby at the time. She opened the box to find roses inside. They had been sent by the head of Colombia's National Police, General Rosso Jose Serrano.

Most other agency counter-drug operations, however, have yielded few breakthroughs.

The net result of CIA involvement in Colombia has not been to slow down the drug trade. Mainly, the agency has fueled a civil war that has taken an appalling toll on civilians.

Colombia is not the only place where these two elements of the CIA have clashed with each other.

In Peru, the CIA coordinates all of its counter-drug efforts through the office of the powerful intelligence chief, Vladimiro Montesinos-even though DEA special agents have produced no fewer than forty-nine different intelligence reports about Montesinos and his suspected narcotics smuggling. It is no wonder that agency counter-drug efforts in Peru have failed.

In Guatemala, the agency has played a strong role in both counterinsurgency and counter-drug operations. As in Peru, the agency has worked with Guatemala's office of military intelligence, even though DEA special agents have formally accused a whopping thirty-one Guatemalan military officers of drug trafficking. Despite the CIA's efforts, not even one suspected officer has been tried.

The Clinton Administration finally cut off CIA counterinsurgency aid to Guatemala in 1995 after revelations that an agency asset, Guatemalan Army Colonel Julio Roberto Alpirez, had been involved in the murder of Michael DeVine, a U.S. innkeeper, as well as in the murder of Efram Bamaca Velasquez, a leftist guerrilla who was married to the Harvard-educated lawyer, Jennifer Harbury. But the Clinton Administration has allowed the CIA to continue providing counter-drug aid to Guatemala.

Most of the major drug syndicates so far uncovered by the DEA have enjoyed direct links to Guatemalan military officers. One of the largest syndicates, exposed in 1996, "reached many parts of the military," according to the State Department.

This year, the State Department reports, "Guatemala is the preferred location in Central America for storage and transshipment of South American cocaine destined for the United States via Mexico."

Mexico is the next stop on the CIA counter-narcotics train. The fact that Mexico's former top counter-drug officer, General Jesus Gutierrez Rebollo, was himself recently indicted for drug trafficking, raises the same old question: What is U.S. policy really all about? Before Gutierrez was busted, the DEA thought he was dirty, while U.S. officials, like General McCaffrey, still sporting Cold War lenses, thought he was clean and vouched for him shortly before his indictment.

Some DEA special agents question the CIA's priorities in counter-drug programs. Human-rights groups remain suspicious of the same programs for different reasons.

"There is no magic line dividing counter-narcotics and counter-insurgency operations," says Salinas of Amnesty International. "Given the current deterioration of human rights in Mexico," an expanded role in counter-drug operations by the United States "could lead to a green light for further violations."

Testifying before Congress in March, the CIA Inspector General, Frederick R. Hitz, finally addressed allegations that the CIA once backed Cold War allies like the Nicaraguan contras even though they ran drugs. Hitz admitted that, at the very least, there have been "instances where CIA did not, in an expeditious or consistent fashion, cut off relationships with individuals supporting the contra program who were alleged to have engaged in drug trafficking activity, or take action to resolve the allegations."

What CIA officials have yet to admit is that the agency is still doing the same thing today.

Frank Smyth, a freelance journalist, has written about the CIA or drug trafficking in The Village Voice, The New Republic, The Washington Post, The Wall Street Journal, and Jane's Intelligence Review. He has also contributed to "Crime in Uniform: Corruption and Impunity

SUPPRESSED INTELLIGENCE REPORTS

in Latin America," published jointly by the Cochabomba-based Accion Andina and the Amsterdam-based Transnational Institute.

THE CHILE COUP — THE U.S. HAND

by Peter Kornbluh

iF magazine, Oct. 25, 1998

Since 1970, the Nixon administration had worked to de-stabilize the elected government of Socialist Salvador Allende. The CIA had laid the ground work for the coup d'etat. In view of Pinochet's recent arrest, the following article looks back a quarter century at the U.S. role in the political violence that shook Chile.

Twenty-five years ago, tanks rumbled through the streets of Chile, terrified civilians were lined up before firing squads at the National Stadium, the elected president was dead.

Yet, at Richard Nixon's White House, the events were a cause for celebration, a culmination of three years of covert operations, propaganda and economic sabotage.

Newly declassified U.S. government records put Washington's role in the Chilean coup in sharper focus than ever before. The papers also shed light on corners of the story that previously had been suspected, but not proven.

The documents describe how an angry Nixon demanded a coup, if necessary, to block the inauguration of Marxist Salvador Allende following his victory in the 1970 Chilean elections.

The documents reveal that an early coup plan — known as "Track II" —continued through the assassination of pro-constitutional Chilean Gen. Rene Schneider, who was gunned down by military plotters on Oct. 22, 1970. The fuller documentary record contradicts the long-standing claim by former Secretary of State Henry Kissinger that "Track II" was shut down a week before Schneider's murder.

After Allende's inauguration, Nixon did not give up. The documents detail what his administration did to make the Chilean economy "scream," how the CIA spread "black" propaganda, and how Washington finally goaded the Chilean army into the coup of 1973.

The Chilean coup leader, Gen. Augusto Pinochet, held power for the next 17 years, relinquishing control in 1990 only after arranging immunity for himself and his top generals.

Until Oct. 16, Pinochet had escaped all punishment for his actions which left thousands dead and Chile a bitterly divided nation.

Yet, at the start of the Chilean tragedy almost three decades ago, the U.S. government wasn't even sure that Chile was important to American national interests.

Except for some multi-national corporations which had mining and other business interests, the sliver of a country embedded between the towering Andes and the Pacific Ocean was barely known to most Americans. But the CIA began alerting Washington to the rise of Allende's leftist Popular Unity coalition in 1968. By 1970, the CIA warned that Allende was poised to win the largest bloc of votes in Chile's national election.

SUPPRESSED INTELLIGENCE REPORTS

At the time, the Vietnam War was President Nixon's biggest headache. Chile was more a nuisance, although Nixon feared Allende's victory might erode the image of U.S. strength.

On March 25, June 27 and Aug. 7, 1970, then-national security advisor Kissinger chaired meetings of the "40 Committee," a high-level inter-agency group. The committee ordered covert operations to "denigrate Allende and his Popular Unity coalition," according to one historical CIA summary.

But the State Department questioned the alarmist fears. State reported to the White House on Aug. 18, 1970, that "we identify no vital U.S. national interests within Chile."

In a 23-page report, State added that Allende's election did not even present a unique set of problems. "In examining the potential threat posed by Allende, it is important to bear in mind that some of the problems foreseen for the United States in the event of his election are likely to arise no matter who becomes Chile's next president."

Nevertheless, the U.S. ambassador to Chile and other senior Nixon officials saw a regional crisis — and a blow to Washington's international prestige — if an avowed Marxist won a fair presidential election in South America.

Ambassador Edward Korry began sending frantic, minute-by-minute commentaries about the last days of Chile's 1970 campaign. Korry's cables became known inside the State Department as "Korrygrams" because of their unusual language and undiplomatic opinions.

On election day, Korry sent no fewer than 18 updates. He reported that he could hear "the mounting roar of Allendistas acclaiming their victory" from the streets. Korry wrote: "We have suffered a grievous defeat."

The next three weeks, Korry flooded Washington with lurid reports alleging a communist takeover. In one cable, he announced that "there is a graveyard smell to Chile, the fumes of a democracy in decomposition. They stank in my nostrils in Czechoslovakia in 1948 and they are no less sickening here today."

Allende's victory also sent Nixon into a rage and started the president's men plotting how to stop Allende's inauguration. Cables focused on a scheme to derail formal ratification of Allende's victory by Chile's congress on Oct. 24, 1970.

According to one idea, the congress would defy the electorate and pick the runner-up, Jorge Alessandri, "who would renounce the presidency and thus provoke new elections in which [outgoing president Eduardo] Frei would run."

On Sept. 12, Korry and Assistant Secretary of State John Richardson met secretly with Frei at the presidential palace. While much of the conversation remains classified, Korry reported that Frei saw only a "one in 20 chance" to stop Allende, but added that he could not "afford to be anything but the president of all Chileans at this time."

Despite the odds, Nixon ordered the CIA to try. The covert action to reverse the results of the Chilean election — by political or military means —took the code name, "Project FUBELT."

On Sept. 16, CIA director Richard Helms informed his senior covert action staff that "President Nixon had decided that an Allende regime in Chile was not acceptable to the United States," according to one declassified CIA memo.

SUPPRESSED INTELLIGENCE REPORTS

"The President asked the Agency to prevent Allende from coming to power or to unseat him," Helms added. The CIA had 48 hours to present an action plan to Kissinger.

Soon, the CIA was pressuring Frei. "CIA mobilized an interlocking political action and propaganda campaign designed both to goad and entice Frei" into the "so-called Frei re-election gambit," according to a declassified "Report on CIA Chilean Task Force Activities." The scheme had "only one purpose," Helms told the NSC: "to induce President Frei to prevent Allende's [formal] election by the congress on 24 October, and, failing that, to support — by benevolent neutrality at the least and conspiratorial benediction at the most - - a military coup which would prevent Allende from taking office." The election gambit was known as Track I.

The back-up plan for a military coup was called Track II. The CIA inducements to Frei included offering substantial sums of money to his "re-election" campaign, bribing other Christian Democrats outright, and orchestrating visits and calls from respected leaders abroad.

To influence Frei through his wife, the CIA instigated the wiring of telegrams to Mrs. Frei from women's groups in other Latin American nations.

Other mailings to Frei included CIA-planted news articles from around the world about Chile's peril. The articles were part of a covert "black" propaganda campaign which, the CIA boasted, resulted in at least 726 stories, broadcasts and editorials against an Allende presidency. Despite these labors, the Frei "re-election gambit" failed, as Frei refused to have the Christian Democrats block Allende's ratification.

"Frei did manage to confide to several top-ranking military officers that he would not oppose a coup, with a guarded implication he might even welcome one," Helms reported to Kissinger.

But "Frei moved quickly away from" the incipient putsch when right-wing coup plotters assassinated Gen. Schneider on Oct. 22, 1970, one CIA cable said. Schneider had insisted that the military accept the will of the people and respect the Chilean constitution.

U.S. complicity in Schneider's murder has long been a touchy point for senior Nixon administration officials. Kissinger went to great lengths to distance himself from the assassination, both in testimony to Congress and in his memoirs. Kissinger claimed that CIA coup plotting was "turned off" at a meeting on Oct. 15 — a week before Schneider was murdered.

CIA deputy director of plans Thomas "Karamessines carried from his Oct. 15 meeting with me an instruction to turn off General [Roberto] Viaux's coup plot and a general mandate to 'preserve our assets' in Chile in the (clearly remote) chance that some other opportunity might develop," Kissinger wrote in the White House Years.

But a declassified "top secret" memorandum of that Oct. 15 meeting undercuts Kissinger's account. At the meeting with Karamessines and Gen. Alexander Haig, Kissinger was quoted as demanding "that the Agency should continue keeping the pressure on every Allende weak spot in sight — now and into the future until such time as new marching orders are given."

Kissinger also demanded tight secrecy around the coup plotting. "Dr. Kissinger discussed his desire that the word of our encouragement to the Chilean military in recent weeks be kept as secret as possible, "the memo said.

SUPPRESSED INTELLIGENCE REPORTS

"Mr. Karamessines stated emphatically that we had been doing everything possible in this connection, including the use of false flag officers, car meetings, and every conceivable precaution."

The next day, a secret "eyes only" cable from CIA headquarters to Henry Hecksher, CIA station chief in Santiago, revealed that Kissinger's marching orders were relayed to the field.

"It is firm and continuing policy that Allende be overthrown by a coup ... prior to October 24," the cable read. "But efforts in this regard will continue vigorously beyond this date. We are to continue to generate maximum pressure toward this end utilizing every appropriate resource. It is imperative that these actions be implemented clandestinely and securely so that the USG [U.S. government] and American hand be well hidden," the cable continued. "Please review all your present and possibly new activities to include propaganda, black operations, surfacing of intelligence or disinformation, personal contacts, or anything else your imagination can conjure which will permit you to continue to press forward toward our [deleted] objective."

While undercutting Kissinger, the records back the 1975 testimony of the CIA's Karamessines. He told a congressional investigation that "Track II was never really ended. What we were told to do was to continue our efforts. Stay alert, and do what we could to contribute to the eventual achievement of the objectives and purposes of Track II."

After Allende's inauguration on Nov. 3, the CIA continued working toward a military coup.

The geo-political rationale was outlined in a CIA postmortem dated Nov. 12, 1970. It noted that "Dr. Salvador Allende became the first democratically-elected Marxist head of state in the history of Latin America — despite the opposition of the U.S. Government. As a result, U.S. prestige and interests are being affected materially at a time when the U.S. can ill afford problems in an area that has been traditionally accepted as the U.S. 'backyard'." The highlights of "Project FUBELT" were cited in both the newly released CIA documents and in papers uncovered by the 1975 congressional inquiry. Covert funds were funneled into Chilean congressional campaigns; CIA agents stayed close to disgruntled Chilean military officers; to keep the military on edge, the CIA planted false propaganda suggesting that the Chilean left planned to take control of the armed forces; and the CIA secretly poured $1.5 million into one of Chile's leading newspapers, El Mercurio.

But the CIA covert operation was only one leg of what U.S. officials called "a triad" of actions toward Chile, according to National Security Decision Memorandum 93. A second leg was "correct but cool" diplomatic pressure and a third leg was the "invisible blockade" of loans and credits to Chile.

For years, historians have debated if such a blockade existed, or whether Allende's socialist economic policies led to the loss of economic credit. But the new NSC records show conclusively that the Nixon administration moved quickly and quietly to shut down multilateral and bilateral foreign aid to Chile.

At the Inter-American Development Bank, the NSC simply informed the U.S. representative that he did not have authority to vote for loans to Chile.

SUPPRESSED INTELLIGENCE REPORTS

A secret report — prepared for Kissinger several weeks after Allende's inauguration — said, "the U.S. Executive Director of the Inter-American Development Bank understands that he will remain uninstructed until further notice on pending loans to Chile. As an affirmative vote by the U.S. is required for loan approval, this will effectively bar approval of the loans." At the World Bank, U.S. officials worked behind the scenes to ensure that Chile would be disqualified for a pending $21 million livestock improvement credit as well as future loans. In addition, the president of the Export-Import Bank agreed to "cooperate fully" with Assistant Secretary of State for Inter-American Affairs Charles Meyer on the discontinuation of new credits and guarantees to Chile.

The Nixon administration also moved to isolate Allende's government diplomatically around the world. Secret strategy papers were drawn up by an inter-agency working group in early December 1970. The papers reported on "USG consultation with selected Latin American governments ... to promote their sharing of our concern over Chile."

The mix of economic sabotage, political propaganda and army prodding worked. Allende found himself confronted by growing disorder and soaring inflation. At every turn, his policies encountered well-funded adversaries.

On Sept. 11, 1973, amid the mounting chaos, Chile's military struck. In a classic coup d'etat, the army seized control of strategic sites throughout the country and cornered Allende in his presidential offices. He died in a fire-fight, apparently shooting himself in the head to avoid capture. \

Nixon officials were ecstatic over the coup. "Chile's coup de etat was close to perfect," stated a "SitRep"— situation report — from the U.S. military group in Valparaiso. The report, written by Marine Lt. Col. Patrick Ryan, characterized Sept. 11, 1973, as Chile's "day of destiny" and "Our D-Day."

CIA records detailing clandestine operations after the coup remain highly classified. But the "40 Committee," chaired by Kissinger, immediately authorized the CIA to "assist the junta in gaining a more positive image, both at home and abroad," according to documents previously revealed by the Senate Intelligence Committee.

As part of those efforts, the CIA helped the junta write a "white book" justifying the coup. The CIA financed advisors who helped the military prepare a new economic plan for the country. The CIA paid for military spokesmen to travel around the world to promote the new regime. And, the CIA used its own media assets to cast the junta in a positive light.

The reality in Chile was far different, as the U.S. government knew. Only 19 days after the coup, a secret briefing paper prepared for Kissinger —entitled "Chilean Executions" — put the "total dead" from the coup at 1,500. The paper reported that the junta had summarily executed 320 individuals — three times more than publicly acknowledged. Despite the carnage, U.S. officials described the scene with soaring rhetoric. "Now that they are in fact again a 'country in liberty' no obstacle is too high, no problem too difficult to solve," stated the Navy section of the U.S. military group in a situation report on Oct. 1, 1973. "Their progress may be slow, but it will be as free men aspiring to goals which are for the benefit of Chile."

To help, Nixon opened the spigot of economic aid. Three weeks after the coup, the Nixon administration authorized $24 million in commodity credits to buy wheat — credits that had been denied to Allende's government. The United States provided a second $24 million in commodity credits to Chile for feed corn, and planned to transfer two destroyers to the Chilean navy. The aid flowed, although Assistant Secretary of State Jack Kubisch reported to Kissinger that junta leader Pinochet had ruled out "any time table for turning Chile back to the civilians." Chile's record as South America's pre-eminent democracy was coming to an end.

But even the CIA's best propaganda could not hide the reality on the ground. The coup's brutality was drawing worldwide condemnation and prompting worries at the White House. "Internationally, the Junta's repressive image continues to plague it," stated a Kissinger briefing paper on Nov. 16, 1973. Reports of mass arrests — by then, U.S. intelligence put the number at 13,500 — as well as summary executions, torture and "disappearances" were reaching the world press.

The administration fretted about an image problem in the United States, too, because two Americans — Charles Horman and Frank Terruggi — were among those executed at the National Stadium. Their deaths constituted a "difficult public relations situation," one cable reported on Oct. 21, 1973.

The Kubisch report to Kissinger cited "heavy" media criticism and congressional inquiries on the two executions. In February 1974, Kubisch delicately raised the American deaths with Chilean Foreign Minister Manuel Huerta, according to a newly declassified memorandum of the conversation. The topic was broached "in the context of the need to be careful to keep relatively small issues in our relationship from making our cooperation more difficult," the memo said. But the first wave of executions was only the start of atrocities in Pinochet's Chile. Human rights violations kept complicating U.S.-Chilean relations, especially after Nixon's Watergate resignation in August 1974.

By 1975, human rights advocates were challenging the Ford administration's continued support for Pinochet. A confidential NSC memorandum dated July 1, 1975, revealed a mutiny even inside the U.S. Embassy.

"A number of officers in the Embassy at Santiago have written a dissent," according to the memo prepared for national security advisor Brent Scowcroft. The dissent was "strongly supported by the Policy Planning office in ARA [State's Latin American division], calling for cutting off all economic and military assistance to Chile until the human rights situation improved."

The memo said the embassy staff was overruled by then-Ambassador David Popper who wanted to continue support for the junta while making stronger protests on human rights. Popper met with the Chilean minister of economic coordination, Raul Saez, on April 6, 1975, to discuss the concerns. Popper said "the most difficult problem we had in our embassy had to do with allegations of torture," according to an embassy cable. "The root of the problem seemed to me to be the absolute power of DINA [Chile's intelligence service] to do whatever it desired in detaining and handling suspects."

Saez replied that "he had remonstrated with Pinochet about DINA, so far without much success . The minister then blamed "fascist advisors to the junta" for the atrocities. But the declassified documents portrayed DINA as anything but a rogue agency. Rather, it was an intelligence service which served at Pinochet's personal command.

On April 15, 1975, the U.S. Defense Intelligence Agency reported that since the decree "establishing DINA as the national intelligence arm of the government, Colonel [Manuel]

SUPPRESSED INTELLIGENCE REPORTS

Contreras has reported exclusively to, and received orders only from, President Pinochet."

By summer 1975, human rights abuses forced the Ford administration to edge back from the Chilean junta. Pinochet requested a visit with President Ford in August, but White House officials feared the meeting "would stimulate criticism domestically in the United States and from Latin America." The NSC instructed Popper to "discourage it by saying that the President's schedule was already full."

In 1976, U.S.-Chilean relations received another jolt when DINA agents traveled to Washington and exploded a bomb under a car carrying former Chilean diplomat Orlando Letelier and two Americans. Letelier and one of the Americans, Ronni Moffitt, died.

A federal investigation traced the bombing back to DINA and some Cuban-American accomplices. A Senate investigation linked the Letelier bombing to a program of cross-border assassinations known as Operation Condor. That operation had attacked Pinochet critics in Spain, Italy and Argentina as well as the United States.

But Pinochet and his coup makers would avoid prosecution at least in Chile. Before gradually returning the reins of government to civilians in 1990, Pinochet engineered an amnesty for himself and his senior officers. Only DINA chief Contreras was sentenced to seven years in prison, for his role in the Letelier bombing. In his defense, Contreras insisted that he was just following Pinochet's orders.

While the newly released documents answer some mysteries about the covert U.S. policy toward Chile, other questions await additional declassifications. Still-secret records could clarify Pinochet's responsibility for Operation Condor as well as the CIA's knowledge about the state-sponsored terrorism and the CIA relationship with the DINA.

Many of the secrets are — or soon will be — more than 25 years old. At that age, they fall under President Clinton's 1995 Executive Order mandating full declassification of national security secrets with few exceptions. The secrets also could clarify who's to blame for deaths of foreign nationals, the case now under way in Spain.

iF magazine

iF magazine is an investigative newsmagazine

The Media Consortium 2200 Wilson Blvd., Suite 102-231, Arlington, VA 22201 1-800738-1812 or (703) 920-1802

CIA, COCAINE, AND DEATH SQUADS

by the Eco-Solidarity Working Group

CovertAction Quarterly, Fall / Winter 1999

Forty million people, along with the most biologically diverse, endangered ecosystems in the world, are under attack by the U. S. Central Intelligence Agency (CIA) and mercenaries paid by oil companies. This war is fought with bombs and bullets, as well as with herbicides and media misinformation. The cause of the war is as diverse as the region's terrain and its ethnic variety The rapacious greed of multinationals like Occidental Petroleum, Shell, BP, Texaco, and their counterparts in the Colombian elite is the main problem, but cocaine use in the U.S. is the fuel that fires this inferno. Drug exports pay for the weapons of the right-wing government-backed death squads and the revolutionary guerrillas.

For years Colombia was banned from receiving U.S. military or drug fighting money due to its poor human rights record and its failure to cooperate in the drug war. In 1998 they received $89 million, and this year the total reached $289 million. Despite continued human rights abuses. Colombia is now the third largest recipient of U.S. military aid after Israel and Egypt. Direct U.S. military intervention looms on the horizon for this region, which exports more oil to the U.S. than the entire Middle East. President Clinton is giving the nod to a death-squad offensive. These squads work closely with Colombian military and together they are responsible for the deaths of 25,000 people this decade300,000 since 1945. Violence has displaced 1.2 million people in the last three years (mostly women and children).

Death squads guard petroleum facilities and shipments of cocaine. The head of these squads, Carlos Castano, is a key player in the Cali Drug Cartel, according to the Drug Enforcement Administration. Castano took over the direction of the death squads from another CIA asset, Colombian Army General Van Martinez. CIA involvement in Colombia began in the 1950s and grew along with the drug trade. In 1991 the CIA established a Colombian naval intelligence group that became a key part of the death squads' continuing terror campaign against guerrillas and anyone who speaks out for change or peace. ˜ Many death squad leaders graduated from the School of the Americas in Fort Benning, Georgia, where thousands of Latin American soldiers have been trained in counterinsurgency and torture. Castano proudly takes responsibility for his massacres. He has kidnapped Colombian senators and he speaks in radio interviews about the need for more killing. Arrest warrants for Castano, army officers and other death squad leaders gather dust on the Attorney General's desk. Evidence mounts of collaboration between the military and the death squads 2 In July, the largest Colombian guerrilla group, Fuerzas Armadas Revolucionarias de Colombia (FARC) launched an attack against the mountain headquarters of Castano, but were driven back by the Colombian army with U.S. intelligence assistance. Hundreds of U.S. military personnel are on the ground, training elite units of the Colombian Army Sophisticated U.S. spy planes, like the U.S. RC-7B, inform and direct combat operations. DynaCorp and East Inc. operate a private air force used to eradicate poppies and coca plants, dousing hundreds of square miles of the countryside with herbicides. Monsanto's Roundup is the toxin of choice, but the U.S. has pressured Colombia to use Dow Chemicals more lethal tebuthiuron. Trade named Spike, it comes in a granular form making it easier to apply Colombia is the only country in the hemisphere where drug crops are sprayed from the air. Genetically engineered viruses are also being developed for the drug war arsenal. Despite this toxic rain, coca production has risen dramatically In July, two DynaCorp employees were killed along with five U.S. military personnel when an intelligence-gathering aircraft hit a mountain or a FARC missile in southern Colombia.

The news media have confused the issues and kept secret U.S. culpability in this dirty war. They create an impression that the FARC and the Ejercito de Liberacion Nacional (ELN), Colombia's other major guerrilla group, have long controlled most of the drug trade, but, in fact, "ELN until now has been a minor player." Moreover the guerrillas are presented as unwilling to lay down their arms as part of a peace plan. In the late 1 980s, guerrillas put down the gun for the ballot box. They were met with the votes of many people and a hail of bullets from the death squads. Almost 5,000 members of the opposition political party, Patriotic Union, have been killed by the right wing since 1989.

SUPPRESSED INTELLIGENCE REPORTS

The oil companies and the government must be held responsible for the violence and the pollution that is the byproduct of their oil operations. Oil is Colombia's most important legal export (27 percent of total exports). Coffee is second (15 percent). The U.S. imports 260,000 barrels of Colombian oil every day In the U'wa region alone, 1.7 million barrels of oil have spilled onto the soil and rivers in the last 12 years. Colombia has the worst human rights record in the Americas, and the area around the U'wa has the worst record in Colombia. Robin Kirk, author of "War with Colombia and International Law," supports the contention that the death squads make their massacres as brutal and gruesome as possible to make sure the message is understood. They often carry lists of trade unionists, Catholic priests, human rights observers and guerrilla supporters.

A biological paradise, Colombia has the greatest number of bird species (1,780) of any country in the world. It is second in plants and amphibians and third in reptiles. Only Brazil, which is seven times larger, surpasses Colombia in total number of species. The Macarena region contains Colombia's first biological preserve, established in 1942. Half of the worlds orchids bloom here, and a dazzling variety of jaguars, dolphin, primates, giant otters, spectacled bears, agoutis, kinkajous and the FARC live here too. The Macarena has been its headquarters for decades, and it has earned respect from biologists for establishing some order over the squatters who are a constant threat to the region's biological integrity

Besides the war, the oil spills, dams and herbicides, there is the usual devastation from cattle, road construction, logging and mining-the social and environmental externalities that come with the U.S. model of economic development. Manatees, tapirs, and macaws are but a tiny fraction of the species that are on the edge of extinction in Colombia. Most species have not even been classified here.

In this threatened ecosystem, the guerrillas are fighting for their lives and the tens of thousands of relatives they have lost to U.S. and narco-death squads. Thousands of young people have joined the guerrillas bid to end the right wings forty years of collusion with oil company exploitation and death squad violence. Their goal is to stop this neo-liberal madness that devastates people and the environment in a chase for profits.

Eco-Solidarity seeks an end to the phony drug war that the U.S. wages against the land and the poor people of Colombia. The most biologically diverse ecosystems in the world are at risk here. Almost two million people have been displaced by a brutal civil war that is financed and directed by the U.S. and its covert operations. Refugees, mostly women and children, are crowded into slums or driven further into the rainforests.

CIA CULPABILITY IN SOUTH AMERICA

Agency "Assets" Deemed Human Rights Abusers

By Jon Elliston · Dossier Editor

The CIA station in Guatemala has for decades assisted the country's brutal security forces, and an unusually critical White House report now calls the Agency to task for its relationship with Guatemalan military personnel guilty of severe human rights abuses.

On June 28, 1996, the President's Intelligence Oversight Board, a special panel appointed by Clinton to investigate allegations of unlawful activity in the intelligence community, issued

SUPPRESSED INTELLIGENCE REPORTS

its report on U.S. ties to Guatemala's repressive armed forces. Veteran CIA-watchers are calling the IOB report one of the most openly critical government accounts of the Agency's activities ever issued.

President Clinton ordered the IOB review in March 1995, after allegations surfaced that the CIA had financed "assets" in the Guatemalan military who were responsible, at least in part, for the abduction, torture and murder of U.S. citizens in Guatemala.

In one high profile case, a team of Guatemalan military personnel (among them CIA assets) were said to have tortured and executed Efrain Bamaca Velasquez, a rebel leader married to American lawyer Jennifer Harbury.

The allegations garnered substantial press coverage, compelling Clinton to order the investigation. Human rights activists have strongly protested government foot-dragging on the release of information about the CIA's Guatemala operations, and the public outcry surrounding the issue led IOB to take the unusual step to advance official disclosure.

As the report notes: "The Board has previously conducted its investigations and provided reports in a confidential manner. The Guatemala review is unprecedented as a publicly announced inquiry."

The IOB conducting a government-wide investigation for information on covert U.S. support of the Guatemalan military.

Among the board's most significant conclusions are the following:

— "We found ... two areas in which CIA's performance was unacceptable. First, until late 1994, insufficient attention was given to allegations of serious human rights abuse made against several station assets or liaison contacts. Second, the CIA failed to provide enough information on this subject to policy-makers and the Congress to permit proper policy and Congressional oversight." — "In the course of our review, we found that several CIA assets were credibly alleged to have ordered, planned, or participated in serious human rights violations such as assassination, extrajudicial execution, torture, or kidnapping while they were assets — and that the CIA's Directorate of Operations (DO) headquarters was aware at the time of the allegations."

— "... a number of the station's liaison contacts — Guatemalan officials with whom the station worked in an official capacity — were also alleged to have been involved in human rights abuses or in covering them up." The IOB's findings have confirmed what many activists and critics of U.S. policy toward Guatemala have long alleged: that the CIA put some of the world's most notorious human rights abusers on the payroll.

A spokesman for the human rights advocacy group Amnesty International said the IOB report "clearly points to a systemic problem of neglect to the human rights dimension of intelligence operations."

Amnesty International's Carlos Salinas urged that the U.S. government "refuse to transfer tax dollars to CIA operations implicated in human rights violations, and to demand greater accountability by the CIA and the broader intelligence community in their use of 'assets' suspected of abuses."

The IOB report is a rare official denunciation of CIA conduct, and as such it provides

SUPPRESSED INTELLIGENCE REPORTS

opponents of the Agency's Guatemala operations with highly credible evidence to back up their charge that the U.S. financed Guatemalan military personnel who terrorized Americans and Guatemalans alike.

Sources:

Jorge A. Banales, "CIA Neglect for Human Rights 'Systemic,'" United Press International, July 2, 1996.

President's Intelligence Oversight Board, "Report on the Guatemala Review," June 28, 1995.

Reuters, "CIA Tied to Guatemalan Abusers," June 28, 1995.

SPOOKS AND SLEEPERS

By Paul Moore

Special Assignments Team

It was several years ago that I first spoke with the man about his work with the Central Intelligence Agency. To all outward appearances he was a very normal person.

He had a steady middle class job, lived in a suburb and was well liked in his community and workplace. He did not look like James Bond. He drove an economy car.

The contrast of his overt and covert lives was disarming. Disenchanted with his past, naive life, the man told the long and strange story of how he came to work as a "sleeper" agent for the CIA, and why he finally quit.

For the sake of his and his family's anonymity, at this time we can simply call him Bob. His story begins in college during the 1970s. Bob was an extraordinarily accomplished and intelligent university student when he was first approached by his future spymasters. His combination of high intelligence test scores and fervent patriotism made him an obvious target for CIA recruitment.

When he was called one day by an agent and asked to join a special program, it's no surprise that Bob said "yes" immediately.

The Cold War was in full swing and the southern young man of modest origins felt that it was his duty to contribute to his country in whatever way he could.

The point of the program was simple. The CIA often needed agents they could trust, who had no public connection with the Agency. They belonged to a pool of ultra-secret part time agents available to carry out special missions for their government whenever needed.

Bob and a number of other students with similar credentials were secretly taken to a government facility and trained by the CIA in basic techniques of surveillance, self defense, use of firearms, and methods of passing covert information.

At the end of the course they were sent back to school as if nothing had happened, which is exactly how it seemed to all around him. Shortly thereafter, Bob graduated with multiple degrees and honors from a prestigious University and began a very ordinary career and marriage that belied his secret connection to the world of espionage.

His only responsibility in the future would be to wait for a phone call and a code word indicating that he had an assignment. In the meantime he lived a normal life, went to work and conducted his own affairs without hindrance from Langley.

In fact, the more established he became in his overt life, the more valuable he became as a spy. By the time he shared his secret, it was difficult to imagine that he was anything more than he appeared.

Over the years he performed several missions, giving various excuses to his family, friends and neighbors for his sudden departures. Often posing as a tourist, Bob would take "vacations" abroad where he would meet strangers and deliver or receive packages and information.

He was told only what he needed to know to perform his part, and did it efficiently... until one day he was caught.

Bob was not specific about the whos and whens of this incident, but was particularly intense when discussing his discovery and subsequent severe beating by "the opposition." It was only after spending a fitful night haunted by nightmare memories of this, his only direct encounter with enemy agents, that he was willing to discuss it at all.

He quietly told of his beating at the hands of people who were "very good at it." Though his part of the mission was over, "They did it to send a message," he said. "But I got the information through." It was sometime after this incident that Bob became disenchanted with the job.

His personal horizons had broadened; he was no longer certain that he believed in his government enough to play the part of punching bag for his country.

He had never even told his wife about his secret life when he walked to a pay phone and called a number he had memorized more than a decade earlier.

With a simple coded message he announced that he wished to be deactivated. According to Bob, the voice at the other end acknowledged, thanked him and hung up.

Bob returned to his life and his modest suburban home that day after ending his spying career, and no one was the wiser. Thus ended the career of one cell in the CIA's network of sleeper agents.

Who knows—maybe someone you know works covertly for the intelligence community. Maybe a teacher, maybe the guy next door who mows his lawn every Thursday evening without fail, except when he's out of town on "business".

Maybe even your own spouse.

SUPPRESSED INTELLIGENCE REPORTS

ENEMY OF THE STATE

From the Albert Nock Essay

In Memoriam; Edmund Cadwalader Evans

A Sound Economist, One of The Few Who Understand The Nature of The State

One examines the American merchant-State in vain for any suggestion of the philosophy of natural rights and popular sovereignty. The company system and the provincial system made no place for it, and the one autonomous State was uncompromisingly against it. The Bay Company brought over their charter to serve as the constitution of the new colony, and under its provisions the form of the State was that of an uncommonly small and close oligarchy. The right to vote was vested only in shareholding members, or "freemen" of the corporation, on the stark State principle laid down many years later by John Jay, that "those who own the country should govern the country."

Be it or be it not true that Man is shapen in iniquity and conceived in sin, it is unquestionably true that Government is begotten of aggression, and by aggression.

Herbert Spencer, 1850

This is the gravest danger that today threatens civilization: State intervention, the absorption of all spontaneous social effort by the State; that is to say, of spontaneous historical action, which in the long run sustains, nourishes and impels human destinies.

Jose Ortega y Gasset, 1922

It (the State) has taken on a vast mass of new duties and responsibilities; it has spread out its powers until they penetrate to every act of the citizen, however secret; it has begun to throw around its operations the high dignity and impeccability of a State religion; its agents become a separate and superior caste, with authority to bind and loose, and their thumbs in every pot. But it still remains, as it was in the beginning, the common enemy of all well-disposed, industrious and decent men.

Henry L. Mencken, 1926

PREFACE TO SECOND EDITION

When Our Enemy, the State appeared in 1935, its literary merit, rather than its philosophic content, attracted attention to it. The times were not ripe for an acceptance of its predictions, still less for the argument on which these predictions were based. Faith in traditional frontier individualism had not yet been shaken by the course of events. Against this faith the argument that the same economic forces, which in all times and in all nations drive toward the ascendancy of political power at the expense of social power, were in operation here made little headway. That is, the feeling that "it cannot happen here" was too difficult a hurdle for the book to overcome.

By the time the first edition had run out, the development of public affairs gave the argument of the book ample testimony. In less than a decade, it was evident to many Americans that their country was not immune from the philosophy which had captured European thinking. The times were proving Mr. Nock's thesis, and by irresistible word-of-mouth advertising a demand for the book began to manifest itself just when it was no longer available; And the plates lead been put to war purposes.

In 1943, he had a second edition in mind. I talked with him several times about it, urging him to elaborate on the economic ideas, since these, it seemed to me, were inadequately developed for the reader with a limited knowledge of political economy. He agreed that this ought to be done, but in a separate book, or in a second part of this book, and suggested that I try my hand at it. Nothing came of the matter because of the war. He died on August 19, 1945.

This volume is an exact duplication of the first edition. He intended to make some slight changes, principally, as he told me, in the substitution of current illustrations for those which might carry less weight with the younger reader. As for the sequel stressing economics, this will have to be done. At any rate, Our Enemy, the State needs no support.

Frank Chodorov,

New York City,

May 28th, 1946

PREFACE TO REPRINT REVISION 1.0

The basic principles and economic predictions written by Albert Jay Nock in 1935 are a foundation for the stark reality America faces in the second millennium. Over the past sixty-five years, the uncontrolled growth and seizure power of the State has eroded any fundamental basis for social power that was once inherent with the People. The necessity of political social and economic reform, as a means to control the State, has become as pointless as the principles written within our Constitution.

As predicted by Mr. Nock, the sovereign Rights and powers of our towns and communities have now all been absorbed into the federal United States at Washington City. Without objection or complaint, the State has taken over the duties of charity and education once belonging to the church. Under the guise of societal welfare, the federal State has become a religion of its own and the benign grantor of common benevolence.

Since Lincoln's Civil War, each generation of Americans has increasingly believed that the power of the ballot is the controlling factor behind our purported republican system. In reality, our current political system is built on Roman State imperialism, not the electorate. Our Legislators have the appearance of representation, but without the reality. Americans have been led to believe, and have willingly accepted, the principle that State interests and community interests are the same. In all actuality, they are diametrically opposed. Political party reform and reorganization is perhaps the greatest deception ever accepted by the American people. Any expectation of changing State power to social power through political party administration is an illusion.

Michel Chevalier appears to have been correct when he observed, back in 1836, that the American People had no common philosophy and followed no set beliefs. Our current American self-portrait is one of immediate revelation rather than long-term vision. As King Solomon wrote, "where there is no vision, the people perish." Where the church was once the central depository of American morals, it is now nothing more than displaced artificial corporate entities. The American People have lost their dream and the State has replaced it with a new religion.

SUPPRESSED INTELLIGENCE REPORTS

Thomas Paine warned us that government was a necessary evil caused by the inability of moral virtue to govern. While all government is initiated to insure freedom and security, there exists today a strong parallel between the *decline* of moral character and the *increase* of State power. As history has repeatedly recorded, social deterioration combined with uncontrolled State power has been the demise of every great government. It can be presumed that our current government system is no exception. Our centralized State government cannot help itself from destruction any better than a drug addict can resist more drugs.

Christian ethics are the key to any society or government. When the moral values of a community decline, the innate and corruptible power of the State increases. When a State becomes the fictitious god of charitable offerings, social well-being, and ethical guidance, the People become a cult of followers. Without a strong moral fibre and the vision of Christian sovereignty, America will soon perish.

It is our prayer that, after reading this book, you will understand how the State is a product of the People, and that our present State is what we have allowed it to become. The church foundation must be restored from the choke-hold of the State and the moral roots of the American liberty tree must be nourished. As our entire nation is rotting from the ground up to the highest branches, it is the responsibility of Christians to re-establish the social well-being of our soil, the local communities. The unchecked power grid of the State must be shut down, in terms of social control, and replaced by righteous charity rooted from each family in order for His Liberty Tree to survive in America. *Ecclesia Libertas.*

Anthony Wayne, Editor

Many footnotes have been added to the following original thesis written by Albert Nock. Not only has the English language changed in its usage and meaning over the past sixty-five years, but the events of the 1930's have long been forgotten. For this reason, we have made many addendums to help clarify the original text.

Chapter One

I

If we look beneath the surface of our public affairs, we can discern one fundamental fact, namely: a great redistribution of power between society and the State. This is the fact that interests the student of civilization. He has only a secondary or derived interest in matters like price fixing, wage fixing, inflation, political banking, "agricultural adjustment," and similar items of State policy that fill the pages of newspapers and the mouths of publicists and politicians. All these can be run up under one head. They have an immediate and temporary importance, and for this reason they monopolize public attention, but they all come to the same thing; which is, an increase of State power and a corresponding decrease of social power.

It is unfortunately none too well understood that, just as the State has no money of its own, so it has no power of its own. All the power it has is what society gives it, plus what it confiscates from time to time on one pretext or another; there is no other source from which State power can be drawn. Therefore every assumption of State power, whether by gift or seizure, leaves society with so much less power; there is never, nor can be, any strengthening of State power without a corresponding and roughly equivalent depletion of social power.

Moreover, it follows that with any exercise of State power, not only the exercise of social power in the same direction, but the disposition to exercise it in that direction, tends to dwindle. Mayor Gaynor astonished the whole of New York when he pointed out to a correspondent who had been complaining about the inefficiency of the police, that any citizen has the right to arrest a malefactor and bring him before a magistrate. "The law of England and of this country," he wrote, "has been very careful to confer no more right in that respect upon policemen and constables than it confers on every citizen." State exercise of that right through a police force had gone on so steadily that not only were citizens indisposed to exercise it, but probably not one in ten thousand knew he had it.

Heretofore, in this country, sudden crises of misfortune have been met by a mobilization of social power. In fact (except for certain institutional enterprises like the home for the aged, the lunatic asylum, city hospital and county poor house) destitution, unemployment, "depression" and similar ills, have been no concern of the State, but have been relieved by the application of social power. Under Mr. Roosevelt, however, the State assumed this function, publicly announcing the doctrine, brand new in our history, that the State owes its citizens a living. Students of politics, of course, saw in this merely an astute proposal for a prodigious enhancement of State power; merely what, as long ago as 1794, James Madison called "the old trick of turning every contingency into a resource for accumulating force in the government;" and the passage of time has proved that they were right. The effect of this upon the balance between State power and social power is clear, and also its effect of a general indoctrination with the idea that an exercise of social power upon such matters is no longer called for.

It is largely in this way that the progressive conversion of social power into State power becomes acceptable and gets itself accepted.1 When the Johnstown flood occurred, social power was immediately mobilized and applied with intelligence and vigour. Its abundance, measured by money alone, was so great that when everything was finally put in order, something like a million dollars remained. If such a catastrophe happened now, not only is social power perhaps too depleted for the like exercise, but the general instinct would be to let the State see to it. Not only has social power atrophied to that extent, but the disposition to exercise it in that particular direction has atrophied with it. If the State has made such matters its business, and has confiscated the social power necessary to deal with them, why, let it deal with them. We can get some kind of rough measure of this general atrophy by our own disposition when approached by a beggar. Two years ago we might have been moved to give him something; today we are moved to refer him to the State's relief agency. The State has said to society, You are either not exercising enough power to meet the emergency, or are exercising it in what I think is an incompetent way, so I shall confiscate your power, and exercise it to suit myself. Hence when a beggar asks us for a quarter, our instinct is to say that the State has already confiscated our quarter for his benefit, and he should go to the State about it.

Every positive intervention that the State makes upon industry and commerce has a similar effect. When the State intervenes to fix wages or prices, or to prescribe the conditions of competition, it virtually tells the enterpriser that he is not exercising social power in the right way, and therefore it proposes to confiscate his power and exercise it according to the State's own judgment of what is best. Hence the enterpriser's instinct is to let the State look after the consequences. As a simple illustration of this, a manufacturer of a highly specialized type of textiles was saying to me the other day that he had kept his mill going at a loss for five years because he did not want to turn his workpeople on the street in such hard times, but now that the State had stepped in to tell him how he must run his business, the State might jolly well take the responsibility.

The process of converting social power into State power may perhaps be seen at its simplest in cases where the State's intervention is directly competitive. The accumulation of State power in various countries has been so accelerated and diversified within the last twenty years that we now see the State functioning as telegraphist, telephonist, match-peddler, radio operator, cannon founder, railway builder and owner, railway operator, wholesale and retail tobacconist, shipbuilder and owner, chief chemist, harbour-maker and dockbuilder, housebuilder, chief educator, newspaper proprietor, food purveyor, dealer in insurance, and so on through a long list.2

It is obvious that private forms of these enterprises must tend to dwindle in proportion as the energy of the State's encroachments on them increases, for the competition of social power with State power is always disadvantaged, since the State can arrange the terms of competition to suit itself, even to the point of outlawing any exercise of social power whatever in the premises; in other words, giving itself a monopoly. Instances of this expedient are common; the one we are probably best acquainted with is the State's monopoly of letter-carrying. Social power is estopped by sheer fiat from application to this form of enterprise, notwithstanding it could carry it on far cheaper, and, in this country at least, far better. The advantages of this monopoly in promoting the State's interests are peculiar. No other, probably, could secure so large and well distributed a volume of patronage, under the guise of a public service in constant use by so large a number of people; it plants a lieutenant of the State at every country crossroad. It is by no means a pure coincidence that an administration's chief almoner and whip-at-large is so regularly appointed Postmaster general.

Thus the State "turns every contingency into a resource" for accumulating power in itself, always at the expense of social power; and with this it develops a habit of acquiescence in the people. New generations appear, each temperamentally adjusted - or as I believe our American glossary now has it, "conditioned" - to new increments of State power, and they tend to take the process of continuous accumulation as quite in order. All the State's institutional voices unite in confirming this tendency; they unite in exhibiting the progressive conversion of social power into State power as something not only quite in order, but even as wholesome and necessary for the public good.

1 The result of a questionnaire published in July, 1935, showed 76.8 per cent of the replies favourable to the idea that it is the State's duty to see that every person who wants a job shall have one; 20.1 per cent were against it, and 3.1 per cent were undecided.

2 In this country, the State is at present manufacturing furniture, grinding flour, producing fertilizer, building houses; selling farm products, dairy products, textiles, canned goods, and electrical apparatus; operating employment agencies and home loan offices; financing exports and imports; financing agriculture. It also controls the issuance of securities, communications by wire and radio, discount rates, oil production, power production, commercial competition, the production and sale of alcohol, and the use of inland waterways and railways.

II

In the United States, at the present time, the principal indexes of the increase of State power are three in number: Firstly, the point to which the centralization of State authority has been carried. Practically all the sovereign rights and powers of the smaller political units—all of them that are significant enough to be worth absorbing—have been absorbed by the federal unit; nor is this all. State power has not only been thus concentrated at Washington, but it has been so far concentrated into the hands of the Executive that the existing regime is a regime of personal government. It is nominally republican, but actually monocratic; a curious anomaly, but highly characteristic of a people little gifted with intellectual integrity. Personal government is not exercised here in the same ways as in Italy, Russia or Germany, for there is as yet no State interest to be served by so doing, but rather the contrary; while in those countries there is. But personal government is always personal government; the mode of its exercise is a matter of immediate political expediency, and is determined entirely by circumstances.

This regime was established by a *coup d'Etat* [revolution; overthrow] of a new and unusual kind, practicable only in a rich country. It was effected, not by violence, like Louis Napoleon's, or by terrorism, like Mussolini's, but by purchase. It therefore presents what might be called an American variant of the *coup d'Etat* [nonviolent revolution].3 Our national legislature was not suppressed by force of arms, like the French Assembly in 1851, but was bought out of its functions with public money; and as appeared most conspicuously in the elections of November, 1934, the consolidation of the *coup d'Etat* was effected by the same means; the corresponding functions in the smaller units were reduced under the personal control of the Executive.4 This is a most remarkable phenomenon; possibly nothing quite like it ever took place; and its character and implications deserve the most careful attention.

A second index is supplied by the prodigious extension of the bureaucratic principle that is now observable. This is attested *prima facie* [evident without proof - at first sight] by the number of new boards, bureaus, and commissions set up at Washington in the last two years. They are reported as representing something like 90,000 new employees appointed outside the civil service, and the total of the federal payroll in Washington is reported as something over three million dollars per month.5 This, however, is relatively a small matter. The pressure of centralization has tended powerfully to convert every official and every political aspirant in the smaller units into a venal6 and accommodating agent of the federal bureaucracy. This presents an interesting parallel with the state of things prevailing in the Roman Empire in the last days of the Flavian dynasty, and afterwards. The rights and practices of local self-government, which were formerly very considerable in the provinces and much more so in the municipalities, were lost by surrender rather than by suppression. The imperial bureaucracy, which up to the second century was comparatively a modest affair, grew rapidly to great size, and local politicians were quick to see the advantage of being on terms with it. They came to Rome with their hats in their hands, as governors, Congressional aspirants and suchlike now go to Washington. Their eyes and thoughts were constantly fixed on Rome, because recognition and preferment lay that way; and in their incorrigible sycophancy they became, as Plutarch says, like hypochondriacs who dare not eat or take a bath without consulting their physician.

A third index is seen in the erection of poverty and mendicancy (depending on alms for a living; practicing begging) into a permanent political asset. Two years ago, many of our people were in hard straits; to some extent, no doubt, through no fault of their own, although it is now clear that in the popular view of their case, as well as in the political view, the line between the deserving poor and the undeserving poor was not distinctly drawn. Popular feeling ran high at the time, and the prevailing wretchedness was regarded with undiscriminating emotion, as evidence of some general wrong done upon its victims by society at large, rather than as the natural penalty of greed, folly, or actual misdoings; which in a large part it was. The State, always instinctively "turning every contingency into a resource" for accelerating the conversion of social power into State power, was quick to take advantage of this state of mind. All that was needed to organize these unfortunates into an invaluable political property was to declare the doctrine that the State owes all its citizens a living; and this was accordingly done. It immediately precipitated an enormous mass of subsidized voting power, an enormous resource for strengthening the State at the expense of society.7

3 There is a sort of precedent for it in Roman history, if the story be true in all its details that the army sold the emperorship to Didius Julianus for something like five million dollars. Money has often been used to grease the wheels of a *coup d'Etat*, but straight over-the-counter purchase is unknown, I think, except in these two instances.

4 On the day I write this, the newspapers say that the President is about to order a stoppage on the flow of federal relief funds into Louisiana for the purpose of bringing Senator Long to terms. I have seen no comment, however, on the propriety of this kind of procedure.

5 A friend in the theatrical business tells me that from the box office point of view, Washington is now the best theatre town, concert town and general amusement town in the United States, far better than New York.

6 Venal — corruptible, bribable, unscrupulous, dishonorable.

7 The feature of the approaching campaign of 1936 which will most interest the student of civilization will be the use of the four billion dollar relief fund that has been placed at the President's disposal—the extent, that is, to which it will be distributed on a patronage basis.

III

There is an impression that the enhancement of State power which has taken place since 1932 is provisional and temporary; that the corresponding depletion of social power is by way of a kind of emergency loan, and therefore is not to be scrutinized too closely. There is every probability that this belief is devoid of foundation. No doubt our present regime will be modified in one way and another; indeed, it must be, for the process of consolidation itself requires it. But any essential change would be quite unhistorical, quite without precedent, and is therefore most unlikely; and by an essential change, I mean one that will tend to redistribute actual power between the State and society.8 In the nature of things, there is no reason why such a change should take place, and every reason why it should not. We shall see various apparent recessions, apparent compromises, but the one thing we may be quite sure of is that none of these will tend to diminish actual State power.

For example, we shall no doubt shortly see the great pressure group of politically organized poverty and mendicancy9 subsidized indirectly instead of directly, because State interest can not long keep pace with the hand-over-head disposition of the masses to loot their own Treasury. The method of direct subsidy, or sheer cash-purchase, will therefore in all probability soon give way to the indirect method of what is called "social legislation;" that is, a multiplex system of State managed pensions, insurances and indemnities of various kinds. This is an apparent recession, and when it occurs it will no doubt be proclaimed as an actual recession, no doubt accepted as such; but is it? Does it actually tend to diminish State power

173

and increase social power? Obviously not, but quite the opposite. It tends to consolidate firmly this particular fraction of State power, and opens the way to getting an indefinite increment upon it by the mere continuous invention of new courses and developments of State-administered social legislation, which is an extremely simple business. One may add the observation for whatever its evidential value may be worth, that if the effect of progressive social legislation upon the sum-total of State power were unfavourable or even nil, we should hardly have found Prince de Bismarck and the British Liberal politicians of forty years ago going in for anything remotely resembling it.

When, therefore, the inquiring student of civilization has occasion to observe this or any other apparent recession upon any point of our present regime,10 he may content himself with asking the one question, What effect has this upon the sum-total of State power? The answer he gives himself will show conclusively whether the recession is actual or apparent, and this is all he is concerned to know.

There is also an impression that if actual recessions do not come about of themselves, they may be brought about by the expedient of voting one political party out and another one in. This idea rests upon certain assumptions that experience has shown to be unsound; the first one being that the power of the ballot is what republican political theory makes it out to be, and that therefore the electorate has an effective choice in the matter. It is a matter of open and notorious fact that nothing like this is true. Our nominally republican system is actually built on an imperial model, with our professional politicians standing in the place of the praetorian guards; they meet from time to time, decide what can be "got away with," and how, and who is to do it; and the electorate votes according to their prescriptions. Under these conditions it is easy to provide the appearance of any desired concession of State power, without the reality; our history shows innumerable instances of very easy dealing with problems in practical politics much more difficult than that. One may remark in this connection also the notoriously baseless assumption that party designations connote principles, and that party pledges imply performance. Moreover, underlying these assumptions and all others that faith in "political action" contemplates, is the assumption that the interests of the State and the interests of society are, at least theoretically, identical; whereas in theory they are directly opposed, and this opposition invariably declares itself in practice to the precise extent that circumstances permit.

However, without pursuing these matters further at the moment, it is probably enough to observe here that in the nature of things the exercise of personal government, the control of a huge and growing bureaucracy, and the management of an enormous mass of subsidized voting power, are as agreeable to one stripe of politician as they are to another. Presumably they interest a Republican or a Progressive as much as they do a Democrat, Communist, Farmer-Labourite, Socialist, or whatever a politician may, for electioneering purposes, see fit to call himself. This was demonstrated in the local campaigns of 1934 by the practical attitude of politicians who represented nominal opposition parties. It is now being further demonstrated by the contemptuous haste that the leaders of the official opposition are making towards what they call "reorganization" of their party. One may well be inattentive to their words; their actions, however, mean simply that the recent expansions of State power are here to stay, and that they are aware of it; and that, such being the case, they are preparing to dispose themselves most advantageously in a contest for their control and management. This is all that "reorganization" of the Republican party means, and all it is meant to mean; and this is in itself quite enough to show that any expectation of an essential change of regime through a change of party administration is illusory. On the contrary, it is clear that whatever party competition we shall see hereafter will be on the same terms as heretofore. It will be a competition for control and management, and it would naturally issue in still closer centralization, still further extension of the bureaucratic principle, and still larger concessions to subsidized voting power. This course would be strictly historical, and is furthermore to be expected as lying in the nature of things, as it so obviously does.

Indeed, it is by this means that the aim of the collectivists seems likeliest to be attained in this country; this aim being the complete extinction of social power through absorption by the State. Their fundamental doctrine was formulated and invested with a quasi-religious sanction by the idealist philosophers of the last century; and among peoples who have accepted it in terms as well as in fact, it is expressed in formulas almost identical with theirs. Thus, for example, when Hitler says that *"the State dominates the nation because it alone represents it,"* he is only putting into loose popular language the formula of Hegel,11 that *"the State is the general substance, whereof individuals are but accidents."* Or, again, when Mussolini says, *"Everything for the State; nothing outside the State; nothing against the State,"* he is merely vulgarizing the doctrine of Fichte,12 that *"the State is the superior power, ultimate and beyond appeal, absolutely independent."*

It may be in place to remark here the essential identity of the various extant forms of collectivism. The superficial distinctions of Fascism, Bolshevism, and Hitlerism are the concern of journalists and publicists; the serious student sees in them only the one root idea of a complete conversion of social power into State power. When Hitler and Mussolini invoke a kind of debased and *hoodwinking mysticism* to aid their acceleration of this process, the student at once recognizes his old friend, the formula of Hegel, that *"the State incarnates the Divine Idea upon earth,"* and he is not hoodwinked. The journalist and the impressionable traveler may make what they will of "the new religion of Bolshevism;" the student contents himself with remarking clearly the exact nature of the process which this inculcation is designed to sanction.

8 It must always be kept in mind that there is a tidal-motion as well as a wave-motion in these matters, and that the wave-motion is of little importance, relatively. For instance, the Supreme Court's invalidation of the National Recovery Act counts for nothing in determining the actual status of personal government. The real question is not how much less the sum of personal government is now than it was before that decision, but how much greater it is normally now than it was in 1932, and in years preceding.

9 Mendicancy — indigence, destitution, pauperism, distress.

10 As, for example, the spectacular voiding of the National Recovery Act. Franklin D. Roosevelt took office in March 1933 and immediately proposed his "New Deal" legislation to launch the United States on "the road to recovery." First came the National Recovery Act, later declared unconstitutional by the Supreme Court after bitter opposition from big business. Later came the Walsh-Healey Act, then the Wage-Hour Law.

11 George Wilhem Friedrich Hegel (1770-1831). At the time of Hegel's death, he was the most prominent philosopher in Germany. Hegel followed the ancient Greek philosopher Parmenides and considered membership in the State as one of the individual's highest duties. His followers divided into right-wing and left-wing Hegelians. The left-wing Hegelians moved

to an atheistic position where, in politics, many of them became revolutionaries. This historically important left-wing group included Karl Marx.

12 Johann Gottlieb Fichte (1762-1814) was one of the major figures in German philosophy. Fichte developed his own system of transcendental idealism, the *Wissenschaftslehre*.

IV

This process—the conversion of social power into State power—has not been carried as far here as it has elsewhere; as it has in Russia, Italy or Germany, for example. Two things, however, are to be observed. First, that it has gone a long way, at a rate of progress which has of late been greatly accelerated. What has chiefly differentiated its progress here from its progress in other countries is its unspectacular character.

Mr. Jefferson wrote in 1823 that there was no danger he dreaded so much as "the consolidation [i.e., centralization] of our government by the noiseless and therefore unalarming instrumentality of the Supreme Court." These words characterize every advance that we have made in State aggrandizement. Each one has been noiseless and therefore unalarming, especially to a people notoriously preoccupied, inattentive and incurious. Even the American *coup d'Etat* of 1932 was noiseless and unalarming. But in Russia, Italy, and Germany, the *coup d'Etat* was violent and spectacular; it had to be; but here in America it was neither. Under cover of a nationwide State managed mobilization of inane buffoonery and aimless commotion, it took place in so unspectacular a way that its true nature escaped notice, and even now is not generally understood. The method of consolidating the ensuing regime, moreover, was also noiseless and unalarming; it was merely the prosaic and unspectacular "higgling13 of the market," to which a long and uniform political experience had accustomed us. A visitor from a poorer and thriftier country might have regarded Mr. Farley's activities in the local campaigns of 1934 as striking or even spectacular, but they made no such impression on us. They seemed so familiar, so much the regular thing, that one heard little comment on them. Moreover, political habit led us to attribute whatever unfavourable comment we did hear, to interest; either partisan or monetary interest, or both. We put it down as the jaundiced judgment of persons with axes to grind; and naturally the regime did all it could to encourage this view.

The second thing to be observed is that certain formulas, certain arrangements of words, stand as an obstacle in the way of our perceiving how far the conversion of social power into State power has actually gone. The force of phrase and name distorts the identification of our own actual acceptances and acquiescences. We are accustomed to the rehearsal of certain poetic litanies, and provided their cadence be kept entire, we are indifferent to their correspondence with truth and fact. When Hegel's doctrine of the State, for example, is restated in terms by Hitler and Mussolini, it is distinctly offensive to us, and we congratulate ourselves on our freedom from the "yoke of a dictator's tyranny." No American politician would dream of breaking in on our routine of litanies with anything of the kind. We may imagine, for example, the shock to popular sentiment that would ensue upon Mr. Roosevelt's declaring publicly that *"the State embraces everything, and nothing has value outside the State. The State creates right."* Yet an American politician, as long as he does not formulate that doctrine in set terms, may go further with it in a practical way than Mussolini has gone, and without trouble or question. Suppose Mr. Roosevelt should defend his regime by publicly reasserting Hegel's dictum that *"the State alone possesses rights, because it is the strongest."* One can hardly imagine that our public would get that down without a great deal of retching. Yet how far, really, is that doctrine alien to our public's actual acquiescences? Surely not far.

The point is, that in respect of the relation between the theory and the actual practice of public affairs, the American is the most unphilosophical of beings. The rationalization of conduct in general is most repugnant to him; he prefers to emotionalize it. He is indifferent to the theory of things, so long as he may rehearse his formulas; and so long as he can listen to the patter of his litanies, no practical inconsistency disturbs him; indeed, he gives no evidence of even recognizing it as an inconsistency.

The ablest and most acute observer, among the many who came from Europe to look us over in the early part of the last century, was the one who is for some reason the most neglected, notwithstanding that in our present circumstances, especially, he is worth more to us than all the de Tocquevilles, Bryces, Trollopes and Chateaubriands put together. This was the noted political economist, Michel Chevalier.14 Professor Chinard, in his admirable biographical study of John Adams, has called attention to Chevalier's observation that the American people have "the morale of an army on the march." The more one thinks of this, the more clearly one sees how little there is in what our publicists are fond of calling "the American psychology" that it does not exactly account for; and it exactly accounts for the trait that we are considering.

An army on the march has *no* philosophy; it views itself as a creature of the moment. It does not rationalize conduct except in terms of an immediate end. As Tennyson observed, there is a pretty strict official understanding against its doing so; *"theirs not to reason why."* Emotionalizing conduct is another matter, and the more of it the better; it is encouraged by a whole elaborate paraphernalia of showy etiquette, flags, music uniforms, decorations, and the careful cultivation of a very special sort of camaraderie. In every relation to *"the reason of the thing,"* however—in the ability and eagerness, as Plato puts it, *"to see things as they are"*— the mentality of an army on the march is merely so much delayed adolescence; it remains persistently, incorrigibly, and notoriously infantile.

Past generations of Americans, as Martin Chuzzlewit15 left record, erected this infantilism into a distinguishing virtue, and they took great pride in it as the mark of a chosen people, destined to live forever amidst the glory of their own unparalleled achievements *wie Gott in Frankreich* [like God in France]. Mr. Jefferson Brick, General Choke and the Honourable Elijah Pogram made a first-class job of indoctrinating their countrymen with the idea that a philosophy is wholly unnecessary, and that a concern with the theory of things is effeminate and unbecoming. An envious and presumably dissolute Frenchman may say what he likes about the morale of an army on the march, but the fact remains that it has brought us where we are, and has got us what we have. Look at a continent subdued, see the spread of our industry and commerce, our railways, newspapers, finance companies, schools, colleges, what you will! Well, if all this has been done without a philosophy, if we have grown to this unrivalled greatness without any attention to the theory of things, does it not show that philosophy and the theory of things are all moonshine, and not worth a practical people's consideration? The morale of an army on the march is good enough for us, and we are proud of it.

The present generation does not speak in quite this tone of robust certitude. It seems, if anything, rather less openly contemptuous of philosophy; one even sees some signs of a suspicion that in our present circumstances the theory of things might be worth looking into, and it is especially towards the theory of sovereignty and rulership that this new attitude of hospitality appears to be developing. The condition of public affairs in all countries, notably in our own, has done more than bring under review the mere current practice of politics, the character and quality of representative politicians and the relative merits of this-or-that form or mode of government. It has served to suggest attention to the one institution whereof all these forms or modes are but the several, and, from the theoretical point of view, indifferent, manifestations. It suggests that finality does not lie with consideration of species, but of genus; it does not lie with consideration of the characteristic marks that differentiate the republican State, monocratic State, constitutional, collectivist, totalitarian, Hitlerian, Bolshevist, what you will. It lies with consideration of the State itself.

13 Higgle — Latin *cocio*. To chaffer, bargain, haggle, hesitate, and cavil; a false kind of reasoning that bears some resemblance to truth and is advanced solely for the sake of victory. Condensed from Webster's 1828 Dictionary.

14 Michel Chevalier (1806-1879). French economist. An ardent Saint-Simonian as a youth, he later favored a form of welfare capitalism. He advocated industrial development as the key to social progress. Also a proponent of free trade, he negotiated with Richard Cobden the Anglo-French trade treaty of 1860. His *Lettres sur l'Am_rique du Nord* (1836) extols the United States.

15 Referring to the Life And Adventures Of Martin Chuzzlewit by Charles Dickens.

V

There appears to be a curious difficulty about exercising reflective thought upon the actual nature of an institution into which one was born and one's ancestors were born. One accepts it as one does the atmosphere; one's practical adjustments to it are made by a kind of reflex. One seldom thinks about the air until one notices some change, favourable or unfavourable, and then one's thought about it is special; one thinks about purer air, lighter air, heavier air, not about air. So it is with certain human institutions. We know that they exist, that they affect us in various ways, but we do not ask how they came to exist, or what their original intention was, or what primary function it is that they are actually fulfilling; and when they affect us so unfavourably that we rebel against them, we contemplate substituting nothing beyond some modification or variant of the same institution. Thus colonial America, oppressed by the monarchical State, brings in the republican State; Germany gives up the republican State for the Hitlerian State; Russia exchanges the monocratic State for the collectivist State; Italy exchanges the constitutionalist State for the "totalitarian" State.

It is interesting to observe that in the year 1935, the average individual's incurious attitude towards the phenomenon of the State is precisely what his attitude was towards the phenomenon of the Church in the year, say, 1500. The State was then a very weak institution; the Church was very strong. The individual was born into the Church, as his ancestors had been for generations, in precisely the formal, documented fashion in which he is now born into the State. He was taxed for the Church's support, as he now is for the State's support. He was supposed to accept the official theory and doctrine of the Church, to conform to its discipline, and in a general way to do as it told him; again, precisely the sanctions that the State now lays upon him. If he were reluctant or recalcitrant, the Church made a satisfactory amount of trouble for him, as the State now does.

Notwithstanding all this, it does not appear to have occurred to the Church-citizen of that day, any more than it occurs to the State-citizen of the present, to ask what sort of institution it was that claimed his allegiance. There it was; he accepted its own account of itself, took it as it stood, and at its own valuation. Even when he revolted, fifty years later, he merely exchanged one form or mode of the Church for another, the Roman for the Calvinist, Lutheran, Zuinglian, or what not; again, quite as the modern State-citizen exchanges one mode of the State for another. He did not examine the institution itself, nor does the State-citizen today. My purpose in writing is to raise the question whether the enormous depletion of social power which we are witnessing everywhere does not suggest the importance of knowing more than we do about the essential nature of the institution that is so rapidly absorbing this volume of power.16 One of my friends said to me lately that if the public utility corporations did not mend their ways, the State would take over their business and operate it. He spoke with a curiously reverent air of finality. Just so, I thought, might a Church citizen, at the end of the fifteenth century, have spoken of some impending intervention of the Church; and I wondered then whether he had any better informed and closer reasoned theory of the State than his proto- type had of the Church. Frankly, I am sure he had not. His pseudo conception was merely an unreasoned acceptance of the State on its own terms and at its own valuation; and in this ac- ceptance, he showed himself no more intelligent, and no less, than the whole mass of State- citizenry at large.

It appears to me that with the depletion of social power going on at the rate it is, the State-citizen should look very closely into the essential nature of the institution that is bringing it about. He should ask himself whether he has a theory of the State, and if so, whether he can assure himself that history supports it. He will not find this a matter that can be settled offhand; it needs a good deal of investigation, and a stiff exercise of reflective thought. He should ask, in the first place, how the State originated, and why; it must have come about somehow, and for some purpose. This seems an extremely easy question to answer, but he will not find it so. Then he should ask what it is that history exhibits continuously as the State's primary function. Then, whether he finds that "the State" and "government" are strictly synonymous terms; he uses them as such, but are they? Are there any invariable characteristic marks that differenti- ate the institution of government from the institution of the State? Then finally he should de- cide whether, by the testimony of history, the State is to be regarded as, in essence, a social or an antisocial institution?

It is pretty clear now that if the Church-citizen of 1500 had put his mind on questions as fundamental as these, his civilization might have had a much easier and pleasanter course to run; and the State-citizen of today may profit by his experience.

16 An inadequate and partial idea of what this volume amounts to may be gotten from the fact that the American States income from taxation is now about one third of the nation's total income! This takes into account all forms of taxation, direct and indirect, local and fed- eral.

CHAPTER TWO

I

As far back as one can follow the run of civilization, it presents two fundamentally dif- ferent types of political organization. This difference is not one of degree, but of kind. It does not do to take the one type as merely marking a lower order of civilization and the other a higher; they are commonly so taken, but erroneously. Still, less does it do to classify both as species of the same genus—to classify both under the generic name of government," though this also, until very lately, has always been done, and has always led to confusion and misunderstanding.

A good example of this error and its effects is supplied by Thomas Paine. At the outset of his pamphlet called Common Sense, Paine draws a distinction between society and government. While society in any state is a blessing, he says, "government, even in its best state, is but a necessary evil; in its worst state, an intolerable one." In another place, he speaks of government as "a mode rendered necessary by the inability of moral virtue to govern the world." He then proceeds to show how and why government comes into being. Its origin is in the common understanding and common agreement of society; and "the design and end of government," he says, is "freedom and security." Teleologically,1 government implements the common desire of society, first, for freedom, and second, for security. Beyond this, it does not go; it contemplates no positive intervention upon the individual, but only a negative intervention. It would seem that, in Paine's view, the code of government should be that of the legendary king Pausole who prescribed but two laws for his subjects, the first being, Hurt no man, and the second, Then do as you please; and that the whole business of government should be the purely negative one of seeing that this code is carried out.

So far, Paine is sound as he is simple. He goes on, however, to attack the British political organization in terms that are logically inconclusive. There should be no complaint of this, for he was writing as a pamphleteer, a special pleader with an ad captandum2 argument to make, and as everyone knows, he did it most successfully. Nevertheless, the point remains that when he talks about the British system, he is talking about a type of political organization essentially different front the type that he has just been describing; different in origin, in intention, in primary function, in the order of interest that it reflects. It did not originate in the common understanding and agreement of society; it originated in conquest and confiscation.3 Its intention, far from contemplating "freedom and security," contemplated nothing of the kind. It contemplated primarily the continuous economic exploitation of one class by another, and it concerned itself with only so much freedom and security as was consistent with this primary intention; and this was, in fact, very little. Its primary function or exercise was not by way of Paine's purely negative interventions upon the individual, but by way of innumerable and most onerous positive interventions, all of which were for the purpose of maintaining the stratification of society into an owning and exploiting class, and a propertyless dependent class. The order of interest that it reflected was not social, but purely antisocial; and those who administered it, judged by the common standard of ethics, or even the common standard of law as applied to private persons, were indistinguishable from a professional criminal class.

Clearly, then, we have two distinct types of political organization to take into account; and clearly, too, when their origins are considered, it is impossible to make out that the one is a mere perversion of the other. Therefore, when we include both types under a general term like government, we get into logical difficulties; difficulties of which most writers on the subject have been more or less vaguely aware, but which, until within the last half century, none of them has tried to resolve.

Mr. Jefferson, for example, remarked that the hunting tribes of Indians, with which he had a good deal to do with in his early days, had a highly organized and admirable social order, but were "without government." Commenting on this, he wrote to Madison that "it is a problem not clear in my mind that [this] condition is not the best," but he suspected that it was "inconsistent with any great degree of population." Schoolcraft observes that the Chippewas, though living in a highly organized social order, had no "regular" government. Herbert Spencer, speaking of the Bechuanas, Araucanians and Koranna Hottentots, says they have no "definite" government; while Parkman,4 in his introduction to The Conspiracy of Pontiac, reports the same phenomenon, and is frankly puzzled by its apparent anomalies.

Paine's theory of government agrees exactly with the theory set forth by Mr. Jefferson in the Declaration of Independence. The doctrine of natural rights, which is explicit in the Declaration, is implicit in Common Sense;5 and Paine's view of the "design and end of government" is precisely the Declaration's view, that "to secure these rights, governments are instituted among men"; and further, Paine's view of the origin of government is that it "derives its just powers from the consent of the governed." Now, if we apply Paine's formulas or the Declaration's formulas, it is abundantly clear that the Virginian Indians had government; Mr. Jefferson's own observations show that they had it. Their political organization, simple as it was, answered its purpose. Their code apparatus sufficed for assuring freedom and security to the individual, and for dealing with such trespasses as in that state of society the individual might encounter—fraud, theft, assault, adultery, murder. The same is as clearly true of the various peoples cited by Parkman, Schoolcraft and Spencer. Assuredly, if the language of the Declaration amounts to anything, all these peoples had government; and, all these reporters make it appear as a government quite competent to its purpose.

Therefore, when Mr. Jefferson says his Indians were "without government," he must be taken to mean that they did not have a type of government like the one he knew; and when Schoolcraft and Spencer speak of "regular" and "definite" government, their qualifying words must be taken in the same way. This type of government, nevertheless, has always existed and still exists, answering perfectly to Paine's formulas and the Declaration's formulas; though it is a type which we also, most of us, have seldom had the chance to observe. It may not be put down as the mark of an inferior race, for institutional simplicity is in itself by no means a mark of backwardness or inferiority; and it has been sufficiently shown that in certain essential respects the peoples who have this type of government are, by comparison, in a position to say a good deal for themselves on the score of a civilized character. Mr. Jefferson's own testimony on this point is worth notice, and so is Parkman's. This type, however, even though documented by the Declaration, is fundamentally so different from the type that has always prevailed in history, and is still prevailing in the world at the moment, that for the sake of clearness, the two types should be set apart by name as they are by nature. They are so different in theory that drawing a sharp distinction between them is now probably the most important duty that civilization owes to its own safety. Hence it is by no means either an arbitrary or academic proceeding to give the one type the name of government, and to call the second type simply the State.

1 Teleological — purposeful development toward a final end.

2 ad captandum — Latin for 'catching'. A phrase used adjectivally sometimes of attempts to catch or win popular favor.

3 Paine was, of course, well aware of this. He says, "A French bastard, landing with an armed banditti, and establishing himself king of England against the consent of the natives, is in plain terms a very paltry rascally original." He does not press the point, however, nor in view of his purpose should he be expected to do so.

4 Francis Parkman (1823-1893). American historian and author. Among the many works

he wrote or edited, a few of the most popular were: The California and Oregon Trail (1849), History of the Conspiracy of Pontiac (1851), and The Discovery of the Great West (1869).

5 In Rights of Man, Paine is as explicit about this doctrine as the Declaration is; and in several places throughout his pamphlets, he asserts that all civil rights are founded on natural rights, and proceed from them.

II

Aristotle, confusing the idea of the State with the idea of government, thought the State originated out of the natural grouping of the family. Other Greek philosophers, labouring under the same confusion, somewhat anticipated Rousseau in finding its origin in the social nature and disposition of the individual; while an opposing school, which held that the individual is naturally antisocial, more or less anticipated Hobbes by finding it in an enforced compromise among the antisocial tendencies of individuals. Another view, implicit in the doctrine of Adam Smith, is that the State originated in the association of certain individuals who showed a marked superiority in the economic virtues of diligence, prudence and thrift. The idealist philosophers, variously applying Kant's transcendentalism to the problem, came to still different conclusions; and one or two other views rather less plausible, perhaps, than any of the foregoing, have been advanced.

The root-trouble with all these views is not precisely that they are conjectural, but that they are based on incompetent observation. They miss the invariable characteristic marks that the subject presents; as, for example, until quite lately, all views of the origin of malaria missed the invariable ministrations of the mosquito, or as opinions about the bubonic plague missed the invariable mark of the rat parasite. It is only within the last half century that the historical method has been applied to the problem of the State.6 This method runs back the phenomenon of the State to its first appearance in documented history, observing its invariable characteristic marks, and drawing inferences as indicated. There are so many clear intimations of this method in earlier writers—one finds them as far back as Strabo—that one wonders why its systematic application was so long deferred; but in all such cases, as with malaria and typhus, when the characteristic mark is once determined, it is so obvious that one always wonders why it was so long unnoticed. Perhaps, in the case of the State, the best one can say is that the cooperation of the Zeitgeist was necessary, and that it could be had no sooner.

The positive testimony of history is that the State invariably had its origin in conquest and confiscation. No primitive State known to history originated in any other manner.7 On the negative side, it has been proved beyond peradventure that no primitive State could possibly have had any other origin.8 Moreover, the sole invariable characteristic of the State is the economic exploitation of one class by another. In this sense, every State known to history is a class-State. Oppenheimer defines the State, in respect of its origin, as an institution "forced on a defeated group by a conquering group, with a view only to systematizing the domination of the conquered by the conquerors, and safeguarding itself against insurrection from within and attack from without. This domination had no other final purpose than the economic exploitation of the conquered group by the victorious group."

An American statesman, John Jay,9 accomplished the respectable feat of compressing the whole doctrine of conquest into a single sentence. "Nations in general," he said, "will go to war whenever there is a prospect of getting something by it." Any considerable economic accumulation, or any considerable body of natural resources, is an incentive to conquest. The primitive technique was that of raiding the coveted possessions, appropriating them entire, and either exterminating the possessors, or dispersing them beyond convenient reach. Very early, however, it was seen to be in general more profitable to reduce the possessors to dependence, and use them as labour motors; and the primitive technique was accordingly modified. Under special circumstances, where this exploitation was either impracticable or unprofitable, the primitive technique is even now occasionally revived, as by the Spaniards in South America, or by ourselves against the Indians. But these circumstances are exceptional; the modified technique has been in use almost from the beginning, and everywhere its first appearance marks the origin of the State. Citing Ranke's observations on the technique of the raiding herdsmen, the Hyksos, who established their State in Egypt about B.C. 2000, Gumplowicz remarks that Ranke's words very well sums up the political history of mankind.

Indeed, the modified technique never varies. "Everywhere we see a militant group of fierce men forcing the frontier of some more peaceable people, settling down upon them and establishing the State, with themselves as an aristocracy. In Mesopotamia, irruption succeeds irruption, State succeeds State, Babylonians, Amoritans, Assyrians, Arabs, Medes, Persians, Macedonians, Parthians, Mongols, Seldshuks, Tatars, Turks; in the Nile valley, Hyksos, Nubians, Persians, Greeks, Romans, Arabs, Turks; in Greece, the Doric States are specific examples; in Italy, Romans, Ostrogoths, Lombards, Franks, Germans; in Spain, Carthaginians, Visigoths, Arabs; in Gaul, Romans, Franks, Burgundians, Normans; in Britain, Saxons, Normans." Everywhere we find the political organization proceeding from the same origin, and presenting the same mark of intention, namely: the economic exploitation of a defeated group by a conquering group.

Everywhere, that is, with but the one significant exception. Wherever economic exploitation has been for any reason either impracticable or unprofitable, the State has never come into existence; government has existed, but the State, never. The American hunting tribes, for example, whose organization so puzzled our observers, never formed a State, for there is no way to reduce a hunter to economic dependence and make him hunt for you.10 Conquest and confiscation were no doubt practicable, but no economic gain would be got by it, for confiscation would give the aggressors but little beyond what they already had; the most that could come of it would be the satisfaction of some sort of feud. For like reasons, primitive peasants never formed a State. The economic accumulations of their neighbours were too slight and too perishable to be interesting;11 and especially with the abundance of free land about, the enslavement of their neighbours would be impracticable, if only for the police problems involved.12

It may now be easily seen how great the difference is between the institution of government, as understood by Paine and the Declaration of Independence, and the institution of the State. Government may quite conceivably have originated as Paine thought it did, or Aristotle, or Hobbes, or Rousseau; whereas the State not only never did originate in any of those ways, but never could have done so. The nature and intention of government, as adduced by Parkman, Schoolcraft and Spencer, are social. Based on the idea of natural rights, government secures those rights to the individual by strictly negative intervention, making justice costless and easy of access; and beyond that it does not go. The State, on the other hand, both in its genesis and by its primary intention, is purely antisocial. It is not based on the idea of natural rights, but on the idea that the individual has no rights except those that the State may provisionally grant him. It has always made justice costly and difficult of access, and has invariably held itself above justice and common morality whenever it could advantage itself by so doing.13 So far from encouraging a wholesome development of social power, it has invariably, as Madison said, turned every contingency into a resource for depleting social power and enhancing State power.14

As Dr. Sigmund Freud has observed, it can not even be said that the State has ever shown any disposition to suppress crime, but only to safeguard its own monopoly of crime. In Russia and Germany, for example, we have lately seen the State moving with great alacrity against infringement of its monopoly by private persons, while at the same time exercising that monopoly with unconscionable ruthlessness. Taking the State wherever found, striking into its history at any point, one sees no way to differentiate the activities of its founders, administrators and beneficiaries from those of a professional criminal class.

6 By Gumplowicz, professor at Graz, and after him, by Oppenheimer, professor of politics at Frankfort. I have followed them throughout this section. The findings of these Galileos are so damaging to the prestige that the State has everywhere built up for itself that professional authority in general has been very circumspect about approaching them, naturally preferring to give them a wide berth; but in the long run, this is a small matter. Honourable and distinguished exceptions appear in Vierkandt, Wilhelm Wundt, and the revered patriarch of German economic studies, Adolf Wagner.

7 An excellent example of primitive practice, effected by modern technique, is furnished by the new State of Manchoukuo, and another bids fair to be furnished in consequence of the Italian State's operations in Ethiopia.

8 The mathematics of this demonstration are extremely interesting. A resume of them is given in Oppenheimer's treatise Der Staat, ch. 1, and they are worked out in full in his Theorie der Reinen und Politischett Oekonomie.

9 John Jay may be most remembered for stating "Let it be remembered that civil liberty consist, not in a right to every man to do just what he pleases, but it consists in an equal right to all citizens to have, enjoy, and do, in peace, security and without molestation, whatever the equal and constitutional laws of the country admit to be consistent with the public good." In 1782, a party consisting of Benjamin Franklin, John Adams, & John Jay, met British commissioner Richard Oswald in Paris, France for the formal negotiation of a peace treaty between Britain & the United States. The delegates were sent with specific instructions: to insist only on the Independence of the United States, deferring in all other matters to the French. The treaty that resulted was a better settlement than the U.S. Congress could ever have hoped for. Britain guaranteed the independence of the United States, ceded all of the territory east of the Mississippi River (except for Florida, which belonged to Spain), and gave the Americans valuable fishing rights in the North Atlantic.

The Judiciary Act that established a federal court system was signed into law by George Washington on September 24th, 1789. He forwarded to the Senate a list of appointments including that of John Jay as the first chief justice of the Supreme court. The appointments were confirmed two days later. Three cases appeared during the justiceship of John Jay. The last case over which Jay presided involved the jurisdiction of foreign powers on U.S. soil. Glass vs. Sloop Betsy concerned the interests of American and Swedish owners of a ship against the government of France. French privateers had impounded the ship and presented it to the French council in Baltimore as a prize for the French government. The owners sought the protection of the federal court. This was a very tricky case involving international politics and the doctrine of neutrality on the high seas. The Justices ruled that a council representing a foreign government had no jurisdiction in the United States "without positive stipulation of a treaty."

10 Except, of course, by preemption of the land under the State-system of tenure, but for occupational reasons this would not be worth a hunting tribe's attempting. Bicknell, the historian of Rhode Island, suggests that the troubles over Indian treaties arose from the fact that the Indians did not understand the State-system of land tenure, never having had anything like it; their understanding was that the whites were admitted only to the same communal use of land that they themselves enjoyed. It is interesting to remark that the settled fishing tribes of the Northwest formed a State. Their occupation made economic exploitation both practicable and profitable, and they resorted to conquest and confiscation to introduce it.

11 It is strange that so little attention has been paid to the singular immunity enjoyed by certain small and poor peoples amidst great collisions of State interest. Throughout the late war, for example, Switzerland, which has nothing worth stealing, was never raided or disturbed.

12 Karl Marx's chapter on colonization is interesting in this connection, especially for his observation that economic exploitation is impracticable until expropriation from the land has taken place. Here he is in full agreement with the whole line of fundamental economists; from Turgot, Franklin and John Taylor, down to Theodor Hertzka and Henry George. Marx, however, apparently did not see that his observation left him with something of a problem on his hands, for he does little more with it than record the fact.

13 John Bright said he had known the British Parliament to do some good things, but never knew it to do a good thing merely because it was a good thing.

14 Madison's Reflections, I.

III

Such are the antecedents of the institution which is everywhere now so busily converting social power by wholesale into State power.15 The recognition of them goes a long way towards resolving most, if not all, of the apparent anomalies which the conduct of the modern State exhibits. It is of great help, for example, in accounting for the open and notorious fact that the State always moves slowly and grudgingly towards any purpose that accrues to society's advantage, but moves rapidly and with alacrity towards one that accrues to its own advantage; nor does it ever move towards social purposes on its own initiative, but only under heavy pressure, while its motion towards antisocial purposes is self-sprung.

Englishmen of the last century remarked this fact with justifiable anxiety, as they watched the rapid depletion of social power by the British State. One of them was Herbert Spencer, who published a series of essays which were subsequently put together in a volume called The Man versus the State. With our public affairs in the shape they are, it is rather remarkable that no American publicist has improved the chance to reproduce these essays verbatim, merely substituting illustrations drawn from American history for those which Spencer draws from English history. If this were properly done, it would make one of the most pertinent and useful works that could be produced at this time.16

These essays are devoted to examining the several aspects of the contemporary growth of State power in England. In the essay called Over-legislation, Spencer remarks the fact so notoriously common in our experience,17 that when State power is applied to social purposes, its action is invariably "slow, stupid, extravagant, unadaptive, corrupt and obstructive." He devotes several paragraphs to each count, assembling a complete array of proof. When he ends, discussion ends; there is simply nothing to be said. He shows further that the State does not even fulfil efficiently what he calls its "unquestionable duties" to society; it does not efficiently adjudge and defend the individual's elemental rights. This being so—and with us this too is a matter of notoriously common experience—Spencer sees no reason to expect that State power will be more efficiently applied to secondary social purposes. "Had we, in short, proved its efficiency as judge and defender, instead of having found it treacherous, cruel, and anxiously to be shunned, there would be some encouragement to hope other benefits at its hands."

Yet, he remarks, it is just this monstrously extravagant hope that society is continually indulging; and indulging in the face of daily evidence that it is illusory. He points to the anomaly which we have all noticed as so regularly presented by newspapers. Take up one, says Spencer, and you will probably find a leading editorial "exposing the corruption, negligence or mismanagement of *soiree* State department. Cast your eye down the next column, and it is not unlikely that you will read proposals for an extension of State supervision."18 "Thus, while every day chronicles a failure, there daily reappears the belief that it needs but an Act of Parliament and a staff of officers to effect any end desired.19 Nowhere is the perennial faith of mankind better seen."

It is unnecessary to say that the reasons which Spencer gives for the antisocial behaviour of the State are abundantly valid, but we may now see how powerfully they are reinforced by the findings of the historical method; a method which had not been applied when Spencer wrote his series. These findings being what they are, it is manifest that the conduct which Spencer complains of is strictly historical. When the town-dwelling merchants of the eighteenth century displaced the landholding nobility in control of the State's mechanism, they did not change the State's character; they merely adapted its mechanism to their own special interests, and strengthened it immeasurably.20 The merchant-State remained an antisocial institution, a pure class-State, like the State of the nobility; its intention and function remained unchanged, save for the adaptations necessary to suit the new order of interests that it was thenceforth to serve. Therefore in its flagrant disservice of social purposes, for which Spencer arraigns it, the State was acting strictly in character.

Spencer does not discuss what he calls "the perennial faith of mankind" in State action, but contents himself with elaborating the sententious observation of Guizot, that "a belief in the sovereign power of political machinery" is nothing less than "a gross delusion." This faith is chiefly an effect of the immense prestige which the State has diligently built up for itself in the century or more since the doctrine of *jure divino* [divine law] rulership gave way. We need not consider the various instruments that the State employs in building up its prestige; most of them are well known, and their uses well understood.

However, there is one instrument which is, in a sense, peculiar to the republican State. Republicanism permits the individual to persuade himself that the State is *his* creation, that State action is *his* action, that when it expresses itself it expresses *him*, and when it is glorified, *he* is glorified. The republican State encourages this persuasion with all its power, aware that it is the most efficient instrument for enhancing its own prestige. Lincoln's phrase, "of the people, by the people, for the people" was probably the most effective single stroke of propaganda ever made in behalf of republican State prestige.

Thus, the individual's sense of his own importance inclines him strongly to resent the suggestion that the State is, by nature, antisocial. He looks on its failures and misfeasances with somewhat the eye of a parent, giving it the benefit of a special code of ethics. Moreover, he has always the expectation that the State will learn by its mistakes, and do better. Granting that its technique with social purposes is blundering, wasteful and vicious—even admitting, with the public official whom Spencer cites, that wherever the State is, there is villainy—he sees no reason why, with an increase of experience and responsibility, the State should not improve.

Something like this appears to be the basic assumption of collectivism. But let the State confiscate all social power, and its interests will become identical with those of society. Granting that the State is of antisocial origin, and that it has borne a uniformly antisocial character throughout its history, let it but extinguish social power completely, and its character will change; it will merge with society, and thereby become society's efficient and disinterested organ. The historic State, in short, will disappear and government only will remain. It is an attractive idea; the hope of its being somehow translated into practice is what, only so few years ago, made "the Russian experiment" so irresistibly fascinating to generous spirits who felt themselves hopelessly State-ridden. A closer examination of the State's activities, however, will show that this idea, attractive though it may be, goes to pieces against the iron law of fundamental economics; that man tends always to satisfy his needs and desires with the least possible exertion. Let us see how this is so.

15 In this country, the condition of several socially-valuable industries seems, at the moment, to be a pretty fair index of this process. The State's positive interventions have so far depleted social power, that by all accounts these particular applications of it are on the verge of being no longer practicable. In Italy, the State now absorbs fifty per cent of the total national income. Italy appears to be rehearsing her ancient history in something more than a sentimental fashion, for by the end of the second century, social power had been so largely transmuted into State power that nobody could do any business at all. There was not enough social power left to pay the State's bills.

16 It seems a most discreditable thing that this century has not seen produced in America an intellectually respectable presentation of the complete case against the State's progressive confiscations of social power; a presentation, that is, which bears the mark of having sound history and a sound philosophy behind it. Mere interested touting of "rugged individualism" and agonized fustian about the constitution are so specious, so frankly unscrupulous, that they have become contemptible. Consequently, collectivism has easily had all the best of it, intellectually, and the results are now apparent. Collectivism has even succeeded in foisting its glossary of arbitrary definitions upon us; we all speak of our economic system, for instance, as "capitalist," when there has never been a system, nor can one be imagined, that is *not* capitalist. By contrast, when British collectivism undertook to deal, say with Lecky, Bagehot, Professor Huxley and Herbert Spencer, it got full change for its money. Whatever steps Britain has taken towards collectivism, or may take, it at least has had all the chance in the world to know precisely where it was going, which we have not had.

17 Yesterday, I passed over a short stretch of new road built by State power, applied

through one of the grotesque alphabetical tentacles of our bureaucracy. It cost $87,348.56. Social power, represented by a contractor's figure in competitive bidding, would have built it for $38,668.20, a difference of one hundred per cent!

18 All the newspaper comments that I have read concerning the recent marine disasters that befell the Ward Line have, without exception, led up to just such proposals!

19 Our recent experiences with prohibition might be thought to have suggested this belief as fatuous, but apparently they have not done so.

20 This point is well discussed by the Spanish philosopher Ortega y Gasset, The Revolt of the Masses, ch. XIII (English translation), in which he does not scruple to say that the State's rapid depletion of social power is "the greatest danger that today threatens civilization." He also gives a good idea of what may be expected when a third, economically composite, class in turn takes over the mechanism of the State, as, the merchant class took it over from the nobility. Surely no better forecast could be made of what is taking place in this country at the moment, than this: "The mass-man does in fact believe that he is the State, and he will tend more and more to set its machinery working, on whatsoever pretext, to crush beneath it any creative minority which disturbs it in any order of things; in politics, in ideas, in industry."

IV

There are two methods, or means, and only two, whereby man's needs and desires can be satisfied. One is the production and exchange of wealth; this is the economic means.21 The other is the uncompensated appropriation of wealth produced by others; this is the political means. The primitive exercise of the political means was, as we have seen, by conquest, confiscation, expropriation, and the introduction of a slave economy. The conqueror parceled out the conquered territory among beneficiaries, who thenceforth satisfied their needs and desires by exploiting the labour of the enslaved inhabitants.22 The feudal-State, and the merchant-State, wherever found, merely took over and developed successively the heritage of character, intention and apparatus of exploitation which the primitive State transmitted to them; they are, in essence, merely higher integrations of the primitive State.

The State, whether primitive, feudal or merchant, is the organization of the political means. Now, since man tends always to satisfy his needs and desires with the least possible exertion, he will employ the political means whenever he can, exclusively, if possible; otherwise, in association with the economic means. He will, at the present time, that is, have recourse to the State's modern apparatus of exploitation; the apparatus of tariffs, concessions, rent monopoly, and the like. It is a matter of the commonest observation that this is his first instinct. So long, therefore, as the organization of the political means is available—so long as the highly centralized bureaucratic State stands as primarily a distributor of economic advantage, an arbiter of exploitation, so long will that instinct effectively declare itself. A proletarian State would merely, like the merchant-State, shift the incidence of exploitation, and there is no historic ground for the presumption that a collectivist State would be in any essential respect unlike its predecessors;23 as we are beginning to see, "the Russian experiment" has amounted to the erection of a highly centralized bureaucratic State upon the ruins of another, leaving the entire apparatus of exploitation intact and ready for use. Hence, in view of the law of fundamental economics just cited, the expectation that collectivism will alter the essential character of the State appears appreciably illusory.

SUPPRESSED INTELLIGENCE REPORTS

Thus the findings arrived at by the historical method amply support the immense body of practical considerations brought forward by Spencer against the State's inroads upon social power. When Spencer concludes that "in State organizations, corruption is unavoidable," the historical method abundantly shows cause why, in the nature of things, this should be expected—*vilescit origine tali*. When Freud comments on the shocking disparity between State ethics and private ethics—and his observations on this point are most profound and searching - the historical method at once supplies the best of reasons why that disparity should be looked for. 24 When Ortega y Gasset says that "Statism is the higher form taken by violence and direct action, when these are set up as standards," the historical method enables us to perceive at once that his definition is precisely that which one would make *a priori* [a priority].

The historical method, moreover, establishes the important fact that, as in the case of tabetic or parasitic diseases, the depletion of social power by the State can *not* be checked after a certain point of progress is passed. History does not show an instance where, once beyond this point, this depletion has not ended in complete and permanent collapse. In some cases, disintegration is slow and painful. Death set its mark on Rome at the end of the second century, but she dragged out a pitiable existence for some time after the Antonines. Athens, on the other hand, collapsed quickly. Some authorities think that Europe is dangerously near that point, if not already past it; but contemporary conjecture is probably without much value. That point may have been reached in America, and it may not; again, certainty is unattainable — plausible arguments may be made either way. Of two things, however, we may be certain: the first is, that the rate of America's approach to that point is being prodigiously accelerated; and the second is, that there is no evidence of any disposition to retard it, or any intelligent apprehension of the danger which that acceleration betokens.

Editor's Note: Annotated reprints of the entire series of Spencer's essays, The Man versus the State, are available from the Christian Common Law Institute. Most of this chapter was derived from Spencer's manuscript.

21 Oppenheimer, *Der Staat*, ch. I. Services are also, of course, a subject of economic exchange.

22 In America, where the native huntsmen were not exploitable, the beneficiaries—the Virginia Company, Massachusetts Company, Dutch West India Company, the Calverts, etc.— followed the traditional method of importing exploitable human material, under bond, from England and Europe, and also established the chattel-slave economy by importations from Africa. The best exposition of this phase of our history is in Beard's Rise of American Civilization, Vol. I, pp. 103-109. At a later period, enormous masses of exploitable material imported themselves by immigration; Valentine's Manual for 1859 says that in the period 1847-1858, 2,486,463 immigrants passed through the port of New York. This competition tended to depress the slave economy in the industrial sections of the country, and to supplant it with a wage economy. It is noteworthy that public sentiment in those regions did not regard the slave economy as objectionable until it could no longer be profitably maintained.

23 Supposing, for example, that Mr. Norman Thomas and a solid collectivist Congress, with a solid collectivist Supreme Court, should presently fall heir to our enormously powerful apparatus of exploitation, it needs no great stretch of imagination to forecast the upshot.

24 In April, 1933, the American State issued half a billion dollars' worth of bonds of small denominations to attract investment by poor persons. It promised to pay these, princi-

pal and interest, in gold of the then existing value. Within three months, the State repudiated that promise. Such an action by an individual would, as Freud says, dishonour him forever, and mark him as no better than a knave. Done by an association of individuals, it would put them in the category of a professional criminal class.

CHAPTER THREE

I

In considering the State's development in America, it is important to keep in mind the fact that America's experience of the State was longer during the colonial period than during the period of American independence; the period of 1607-1776 was longer than the period of 1776-1935. Moreover, the colonists came here full grown, and had already a considerable experience of the State in England and Europe before they arrived; and for purposes of comparison, this would extend the former period by a few years, say at least fifteen. It would probably be safe to put it that the American colonists had twenty-five years longer experience of the State than citizens of the United States have had.

Their experience, too, was not only longer, but more varied. The British State, the French, Dutch, Swedish and Spanish States, were all established here. The separatist English dissenters, who landed at Plymouth, had lived under the Dutch State as well as under the British State. When James I made England too uncomfortable for them to live in, they went to Holland; and many of the institutions which they subsequently set up in New England, and which were later incorporated into the general body of what we call "American institutions," were actually Dutch, though commonly—almost invariably—we accredit them to England. They were for the most part Roman-Continental in their origin, but they were transmitted here from Holland, not from England.1 No such institutions existed in England at that time, and hence the Plymouth colonists could not have seen them there; they could have seen them only in Holland, where they did exist.

Our colonial period coincided with the period of revolution and readjustment in England, referred to in the preceding chapter, when the British merchant-State was displacing the feudal State, consolidating its own position, and shifting the incidence of economic exploitation. These revolutionary measures gave rise to an extensive review of the general theory on which the feudal State had been operating. The earlier Stuarts governed on the theory of monarchy by divine right. The State's economic beneficiaries were answerable only to the monarch, who was theoretically answerable only to God; he had no responsibilities to society at large, save such as he chose to incur, and these only for the duration of his pleasure. In 1607, the year of the Virginia colony's landing at Jamestown, John Cowell, regius professor of civil law at the University of Cambridge, laid down the doctrine that the monarch "is above the law by his absolute power, and though for the better and equal course in making laws he does admit the Three Estates unto Council, yet this in divers learned men's opinions is not of constraint, but of his own benignity, or by reason of the promise made upon oath at the time of his coronation."

This doctrine, which was elaborated to the utmost in the extraordinary work called **Patriarcha**, by Sir Robert Filmer, was all well enough so long as the line of society's stratification was clear, straight and easily drawn. The feudal State's economic beneficiaries were virtually a close corporation; a compact body consisting of a Church hierarchy and a titled group of hereditary, large-holding landed proprietors. In respect of interests, this body was extremely homogeneous, and their interests, few in number, were simple in character and easily defined. With the monarch, the hierarchy, and a small, closely limited nobility above the line of stratification, and an undifferentiated populace below it, this theory of sovereignty was passable; it answered the purposes of the feudal State as well as any.

But the practical outcome of this theory did not, and could not, suit the purposes of the rapidly growing class of merchants and financiers. They wished to introduce a new economic system. Under feudalism, production had been, as a general thing, for use, with the incidence of exploitation falling largely on a peasantry. The State had by no means always kept its hands off trade, but it had never countenanced the idea that its chief reason for existence was, as we say, "to help business." The merchants and financiers, however, had precisely this idea in mind. They saw the attractive possibilities of production for profit, with the incidence of exploitation gradually shifting to an industrial proletariat. They also saw, however, that to realize all these possibilities, they must get the State's mechanism to working as smoothly and powerfully on the side of "business" as it had been working on the side of the monarchy, the Church, and the large-holding landed proprietors. This meant capturing control of this mechanism, and so altering and adapting it as to give themselves the same free access to the political means as was enjoyed by the displaced beneficiaries. The course by which they accomplished this is marked by the Civil War, the dethronement and execution of Charles I, the Puritan protectorate, and the revolution of 1688.

This is the actual inwardness of what is known as the Puritan movement in England. It had a quasi-religious motivation — speaking strictly, an ecclesiological motivation — but the paramount practical end towards which it tended was a repartition of access to the political means. It is a significant fact, though seldom noticed, that the only tenet with which Puritanism managed to evangelize equally the non-Christian and Christian world of English bred civilization is its tenet of work, its doctrine that work is, by God's express will and command, a duty; indeed almost, if not quite, the first and most important of man's secular duties. This erection of labour into a Christian virtue *per se*, this investment of work with a special religious sanction, was an invention of Puritanism; it was something never heard of in England before the rise of the Puritan State. The only doctrine antedating it presented labour as the means to a purely secular end; as Cranmer's divines put it, "that I may learn and labour truly to get mine own living." There is no hint that God would take it amiss if one preferred to do little work and put up with a poor living, for the sake of doing something else with one's time. Perhaps the best witness to the essential character of the Puritan movement in England and America is the thoroughness with which its doctrine of work has pervaded both literatures, all the way from Cromwell's letters to Carlyle's panegyric and Longfellow's verse.

But the merchant-State of the Puritans was like any other; it followed the standard pattern. It originated in conquest and confiscation, like the feudal State which it displaced, the only difference being that its conquest was by civil war instead of foreign war. Its object was the economic exploitation of one class by another; for the exploitation of feudal serfs by a nobility, it proposed only to substitute the exploitation of a proletariat by enterprisers. Like its predecessor, the merchant-State was purely an organization of the political means, a machine for the distribution of economic advantage, but with its mechanism adapted to the requirements of a more numerous and more highly differentiated order of beneficiaries; a class, moreover, whose numbers were not limited by heredity or by the sheer arbitrary pleasure of a monarch.

SUPPRESSED INTELLIGENCE REPORTS

The process of establishing the merchant-State, however, necessarily brought about changes in the general theory of sovereignty. The bald doctrine of Cowell and Filmer was no longer practicable; yet any new theory had to find room for some sort of divine sanction, for the habit of men's minds does not change suddenly, and Puritanism's alliance between religious and secular interests was extremely close. One may not quite put it that the merchant-enterprisers made use of religious fanaticism to pull their chestnuts out of the fire; the religionists had sound and good chestnuts of their own to look after. They had plenty of rabid nonsense to answer for, plenty of sour hypocrisy, plenty of vicious fanaticism; whenever we think of seventeenth-century British Puritanism, we think of Hugh Peters, of Praise God Barebones, of Cromwell's iconoclasts "smashing the mighty big angels in glass." But behind all this untowardness, there was in the religionists a body of sound conscience, soundly and justly outraged; and no doubt, though mixed with an intolerable deal of unscrupulous greed, there was on the part of the merchant-enterprisers a sincere persuasion that what was good for business was good for society. Taking Hampden's conscience as representative, one would say that it operated under the limitations set by nature upon the typical sturdy Buckinghamshire squire; the mercantile conscience was likewise ill-informed, and likewise set its course with a hard, dogged, provincial stubbornness. Still, the alliance of the two bodies of conscience was not without some measure of respectability. No doubt, for example, Hampden regarded the State controlled episcopacy to some extent objectively, as unscriptural in theory, and a tool of Antichrist in practice; and no doubt, too, the mercantile conscience, with the disturbing vision of William Laud in view, might have found State managed episcopacy objectionable on other grounds than those of special interest.

The merchant-State's political rationale had to respond to the pressure of a growing individualism. The spirit of individualism appeared in the latter half of the sixteenth century; probably—as well as such obscure origins can be determined—as a byproduct of the Continental revival of learning, or, it may be, specifically as a byproduct of the Reformation in Germany. It was long, however, in gaining force enough to make itself count in shaping political theory. The feudal State could take no account of this spirit; its stark regime of status was operable only where there was no great multiplicity of diverse economic interests to be accommodated, and where the sum of social power remained practically stable. Under the British feudal State, one large-holding landed proprietor's interest was much like another's, and one bishop's or clergyman's interest was about the same in kind as another's. The interests of the monarchy and court were not greatly diversified, and the sum of social power varied but little from time to time. Hence an economic class solidarity was easily maintained; access upward from one class to the other was easily blocked, so easily that very few positive State-interventions were necessary to keep people, as we say, in their place; or as Cranmer's divines put it, to keep them doing their duty in that station of life unto which it had pleased God to call them. Thus the State could accomplish its primary purpose, and still afford to remain relatively weak. It could normally, that is, enable a thoroughgoing economic exploitation with relatively little apparatus of legislation or of personnel.2

The merchant-State, on the other hand, with its ensuing regime of contract, had to meet the problem set by a rapid development of social power, and a multiplicity of economic interests. Both these tended to foster and stimulate the spirit of individualism. The management of social power made the merchant-enterpriser feel that he was quite as much somebody as anybody, and that the general order of interest which he represented—and in particular his own special fraction of that interest—was to be regarded as most respectable, which hitherto it had not been. In short, he had a full sense of himself as an individual, which on these grounds he could of course justify beyond peradventure. The aristocratic disparagement of his pursuits, and the consequent stigma of inferiority which had been so long fixed upon the "base mechanical," exacerbated this sense, and rendered it at its best assertive, and at, its worst, disposed to exaggerate the characteristic defects of his class as well as its excellences, and lump them off together in a new category of social virtues—its hardness, ruthlessness, ignorance and vulgarity at par with its commercial integrity, its shrewdness, diligence and thrift. Thus the fully developed composite type of merchant-enterpriser-financier might be said to run all the psychological gradations between the brothers Cheeryble at one end of the scale, and Mr. Gradgrind, Sir Gorgius Midas and Mr. Bottles at the other.

This individualism fostered the formulation of certain doctrines which, in one shape or another, found their way into the official political philosophy of the merchant-State. Foremost among these were the two which the Declaration of Independence lays down as fundamental: the doctrine of natural rights, and; the doctrine of popular sovereignty. In a generation which had exchanged the authority of a pope for the authority of a book—or rather, the authority of unlimited private interpretation of a book—there was no difficulty about finding ample Scriptural sanction for both these doctrines. The interpretation of the Bible, like the judicial interpretation of a constitution, is merely a process by which, as a contemporary of Bishop Butler said, anything may be made to mean anything; and in the absence of a coercive authority, papal, conciliar or judicial, any given interpretation finds only such acceptance as may, for whatever reason, be accorded it. Thus the episode of Eden, the parable of the talents, the Apostolic injunction against being "slothful in business," were a warrant for the Puritan doctrine of work; they brought the sanction of Scripture and the sanction of economic interest into complete agreement, uniting the religionist and the merchant-enterpriser in the bond of a common intention. Thus, again, the view of man as made in the image of God, made only a little lower than the angels, the subject of so august a transaction as the Atonement, quite corroborated the political doctrine of his endowment by his Creator with certain rights unalienable by Church or State. While the merchant-enterpriser might hold with Mr. Jefferson that the truth of this political doctrine is self-evident, its Scriptural support was yet of great value as carrying an implication of human nature's dignity which braced his more or less diffident and self-conscious individualism; and the doctrine that so dignified him might easily be conceived of as dignifying his pursuits. Indeed, the Bible's endorsement of the doctrine of labour and the doctrine of natural rights was really his charter for rehabilitating "trade" against the disparagement that the regime of status had put upon it, and for investing it with the most brilliant lustre of respectability.

In the same way, the doctrine of popular sovereignty could be mounted on impregnable Scriptural ground. Civil society was an association of true believers functioning for common secular purposes; and its right of self-government with respect to these purposes was God given. If, on the religious side, all believers were priests, then on the secular side they were all sovereigns; the notion of an intervening *jure divino* [divine right] monarch was as repugnant to Scripture as that of an intervening *jure divino* pope—witness the Israelite commonwealth upon which monarchy was visited as explicitly a punishment for sin. Civil legislation was supposed to interpret and particularize the laws of God as revealed in the Bible, and its administrators were responsible to the congregation in both its religious and secular capacities. Where the revealed law was silent, legislation was to be guided by its general spirit, as best this might be determined. These principles obviously left open a considerable area of choice; but hypothetically, the range of civil liberty and the range of religious liberty had a common boundary.

This religious sanction of popular sovereignty was agreeable to the merchant-enterpriser; it fell in well with his individualism, enhancing considerably his sense of personal dignity and consequence. He could regard himself as by birthright not only a free citizen of a heavenly commonwealth, but also a free elector in an earthly commonwealth fashioned, as nearly as might be, after the heavenly pattern. The range of liberty permitted him in both qualities was satisfactory; he could summon warrant of Scripture to cover his undertakings both here and hereafter. As far as this present world's concerns went, his doctrine of labour was Scriptural, his doctrine of master and servant was Scriptural—even bond-service, even chattel-service was Scriptural; his doctrine of a wage economy, of money lending—again the parable of the talents—both were Scriptural. What especially recommended the doctrine of popular sovereignty to him on its secular side, however, was the immense leverage it gave for ousting the regime of status to make way for the regime of contract; in a word, for displacing the feudal State and bringing in the merchant-State.

But interesting as these two doctrines were, their actual application was a matter of great difficulty. On the religious side, the doctrine of natural rights had to take account of the unorthodox. Theoretically it was easy to dispose of them. The separatists, for example, such as those who manned the Mayflower, had lost their natural rights in the fall of Adam, and had never made use of the means appointed to reclaim them. This was all very well, but the logical extension of this principle into actual practice was a rather grave affair. There were a good many dissenters, all told, and they were articulate on the matter of natural rights, which made trouble; so that when all was said and done, the doctrine came out considerably compromised.

Then, in respect of popular sovereignty, there were the Presbyterians. Calvinism was monocratic to the core; in fact, Presbyterianism existed side by side with episcopacy in the Church of England in the sixteenth century, and was nudged out only very gradually.3 They were a numerous body, and in point of Scripture and history they had a great deal to say for their position. Thus, the practical task of organizing a spiritual commonwealth had as hard going with the logic of popular sovereignty as it had with the logic of natural rights.

The task of secular organization was even more troublesome. A society organized in conformity to these two principles is easily conceivable—such an organization as Paine and the Declaration contemplated, for example, arising out of social agreement, and concerning itself only with the maintenance of freedom and security for the individual—but the practical task of effecting such an organization is quite another matter. On general grounds, doubtless, the Puritans would have found this impracticable; if, indeed, the times are ever to be ripe for anything of the kind, their times were certainly not. The particular ground of difficulty, however, was that the merchant-enterpriser did not want that form of social organization; in fact, one can not be sure that the Puritan religionists themselves wanted it. The root trouble was, in short, that there was no practicable way to avert a shattering collision between the logic of natural rights and popular sovereignty, and the economic law that man tends always to satisfy his needs and desires with the least possible exertion.

This law governed the merchant-enterpriser in common with the rest of mankind. He was not for an organization that should do no more than maintain freedom and security; he was for one that should redistribute access to the political means, and concern itself with freedom and security only so far as would be consistent with keeping this access open. That is to say, he was thoroughly indisposed to the idea of government; he was quite as strong for the idea of the State as the hierarchy and nobility were. He was not for any essential transformation in the State's character, but merely for a repartition of the economic advantages that the State confers.

Thus, the merchant-polity amounted to an attempt, more or less disingenuous, at reconciling matters which in their nature can not be reconciled. The ideas of natural rights and popular sovereignty were, as we have seen, highly acceptable and highly animating to all the forces allied against the feudal idea; but, while these ideas might be easily reconcilable with a system of simple government, such a system would not answer the purpose. Only the State-system would do that. The problem, therefore, was how to keep these ideas well in the forefront of political theory, and at the same time prevent their practical application from undermining the organization of the political means. It was a difficult problem. The best that could be done with it was by making certain structural alterations in the State, which would give it the appearance of expressing these ideas, without the reality. The most important of these structural changes was that of bringing in the so-called representative or parliamentary system, which Puritanism introduced into the modern world, and which has received a great deal of praise as an advance towards democracy. This praise, however, is exaggerated. The change was one of form only, and its bearing on democracy has been inconsiderable.4

1 Among these institutions are: our system of free public education; local self-government as originally [not currently] established in the township system; our method of conveying land; almost all of our system of equity; much of our criminal code; and our method of administering estates.

2 Throughout Europe, indeed, up to the close of the eighteenth century, the State was quite weak, even considering the relatively moderate development of social power, and the moderate amount of economic accumulation available to its predatory purposes. Social power in modern France could pay the flat annual levy of Louis XIVS taxes without feeling it, and would like nothing better than to commute the republican State's levy on those terms.

3 During the reign of Elizabeth, the Puritan contention, led by Cartwright, was for what amounted to a theory of *jure divino* Presbyterianism. The Establishment at large took the position of Archbishop Whitgift and Richard Hooker that the details of church polity were indifferent, and therefore properly subject to State regulation. The High Church doctrine of *jure divino* episcopacy was laid down later, by Whitgift's successor, Bancroft. Thus, up to 1604, the Presbyterians were objectionable on secular grounds, and afterwards on both secular and ecclesiastical grounds.

4 So were the kaleidoscopic changes that took place in France after the revolution of 1789. Throughout the Directorate, the Consulship, the Restoration, the two Empires, the three Republics and the Commune, the French State kept its essential character intact; it remained always the organization of the political means.

II

The migration of Englishmen to America merely transferred this problem into another setting. The discussion of political theory went on vigorously, but the philosophy of natural rights and popular sovereignty came out in practice about where they had come out in England. Here again, a great deal has been made of the democratic spirit and temper of the migrants, especially in the case of the separatists who landed at Plymouth, but the facts do not bear it out, except with regard to the decentralizing congregationalist principle of church order. This principle of lodging final authority in the smallest unit rather than the largest—in the local congregation rather than in a synod or general council—was democratic, and its thoroughgoing application in a scheme of church order would represent some actual advance towards democracy, and give it some recognition to the general philosophy of natural rights and popular sovereignty.

The Plymouth settlers did something with this principle, actually applying it in the matter of church order, and for this they deserve credit.5 Applying it in the matter of civil order, however, was another affair. It is true that the Plymouth colonists probably contemplated something of the kind, and that for a time they practised a sort of primitive communism. They drew up an agreement on shipboard which may be taken at its face value as evidence of their democratic disposition, though it was not in any sense a "frame of government," like Penn's, or any kind of constitutional document. Those who speak of it as our first written constitution are considerably in advance of their text, for it was merely an agreement to make a constitution or "frame of government" when the settlers should have come to land and looked the situation over. One sees that it could hardly have been more than this—indeed, that the proposed constitution itself could be no more than provisional—when it is remembered that these migrants were not their own men. They did not sail on their own, nor were they headed for any unpreempted territory on which they might establish a squatter sovereignty and set up any kind of civil order they saw fit. They were headed for Virginia, to settle in the jurisdiction of a company of English merchant-enterprisers, now growing shaky, and soon to be superseded by the royal authority, and its territory converted into a royal province. It was only by misreckonings and the accidents of navigation that, most unfortunately for the prospects of the colony, the settlers landed on the stern and rockbound coast of Plymouth.

These settlers were, in most respects, probably as good as the best who ever found their way to America. They were bred of what passed in England as "the lower orders," sober, hard working and capable, and their residence under Continental institutions in Holland had given them a fund of politico-religious ideas and habits of thought which set them considerably apart from the rest of their countrymen. There is, however, no more than an antiquarian interest in determining how far they were actually possessed by those ideas. They may have contemplated a system of complete religious and civil democracy, or they may not. They may have found their communist practices agreeable to their notion of a sound and just social order, or they may not. The point is, that while apparently they might be free enough to found a church order as democratic as they chose, they were by no means free to found a civil democracy, or anything remotely resembling one, because they were in bondage to the will of an English trading company. Even their religious freedom was permissive; the London company simply cared nothing about that. The same considerations governed their communistic practices; whether or not these practices suited their ideas, they were obliged to adopt them. Their agreement with the London merchant-enterprisers bound them, in return for transportation and outfit, to seven years' service, during which time they should work on a system of common land tillage, store their produce in a common warehouse, and draw their maintenance from these common stores. Thus, whether or not they were communists in principle, their actual practice of communism was by prescription.

SUPPRESSED INTELLIGENCE REPORTS

The fundamental fact to be observed in any survey of the American State's initial development is the one whose importance was first remarked, I believe, by Mr. Beard; that the trading company—the commercial corporation for colonization—was actually an autonomous State. "Like the State," says Mr. Beard, "it had a constitution, a charter issued by the Crown like the State, it had a territorial basis, a grant of land often greater in area than a score of European principalities, it could make assessments, coin money, regulate trade, dispose of corporate property, collect taxes, manage a treasury, and provide for defense. Thus, (and here is the important observation, so important that I venture to italicize and bold it) ***every essential element long afterward found in the government of the American State appeared in the chartered corporation that started English civilization in America.***" Generally speaking, the system of civil order established in America was the State-system of the "mother countries" operating over a considerable body of water; the only thing that distinguished it was that the exploited and dependent class was situated at an unusual distance from the owning and exploiting class. The headquarters of the autonomous State were on one side of the Atlantic, and its subjects on the other.

This separation gave rise to administrative difficulties of one kind and another; and to obviate them—perhaps for other reasons as well—one English company, the Massachusetts Bay Company, moved over bodily in 1630, bringing their charter and most of their stockholders with them, thus setting up an actual autonomous State in America. The thing to be observed about this is that the merchant-State was set up complete in New England long before it was set up in Old England. Most of the English immigrants to Massachusetts came over between 1630 and 1640; and in this period the English merchant-State was only at the beginning of its hardest struggles for supremacy. James I died in 1625, and his successor, Charles I, continued his absolutist regime. From 1629, the year in which the Bay Company was chartered, to 1640, when the Long Parliament was called, he ruled without a parliament, effectively suppressing what few vestiges of liberty had survived the Tudor and Jacobean tyrannies; and during these eleven years, the prospects of the English merchant-State were at their lowest.6 It still had to face the distractions of the Civil War, the retarding anomalies of the Commonwealth, the Restoration, and the recurrence of tyrannical absolutism under James II, before it succeeded in establishing itself firmly through the revolution of 1688.

On the other hand, the leaders of the Bay Colony were free from the first to establish a State policy of their own devising, and to set up a State structure which should express that policy without compromise. There was no competing policy to extinguish, no rival structure to refashion. Thus the merchant-State came into being in a clear field a full half-century before it attained supremacy in England. Competition of any kind, or the possibility of competition, it has never had. A point of greatest importance to remember is that the merchant-State is the only form of the State that ever existed in America. Whether under the rule of a trading company, a provincial governor, or a republican representative legislature, Americans have never known any other form of the State. In this respect, the Massachusetts Bay colony is differentiated only as being the first autonomous State ever established in America, and as furnishing the most complete and convenient example for purposes of study. In principle it was not differentiated. The State in New England, Virginia, Maryland, the Jerseys, New York, Connecticut, everywhere, was purely a class-State with control of the political means reposing in the hands of what we now style, in a general way, the "businessman."

In the eleven years of Charles's tyrannical absolutism, English immigrants came over to join the Bay colony, at the rate of about two thousand a year. No doubt at the outset some of the colonists had the idea of becoming agricultural specialists, as in Virginia, and of maintaining certain vestiges, or rather imitations, of semi-feudal social practice, such as were possible under that form of industry when operated by a slave-economy or a tenant-economy. This, however, proved impracticable; the climate and soil of New England were against it. A tenant-economy was precarious, for rather than work for a master, the immigrant agriculturist naturally preferred to push out into unpreempted land, and work for himself; in other words, as Turgot, Marx, Hertzka, and many others have shown, he could not be exploited until he had been expropriated from the land. The long and hard winters took the profit out of slave labour in agriculture. The Bay colonists experimented with it, however, even attempting to enslave the Indians, which they found could not be done, for the reasons that I have already noticed. In default of this, the colonists carried out the primitive technique by resorting to extermination, their ruthless ferocity being equaled only by that of the Virginia colonists.7 They held some slaves, and did a great deal of slave-trading; but in the main, they became, at the outset, a race of small freeholding farmers, shipbuilders, navigators, maritime enterprisers in fish, whales, molasses, rum, and miscellaneous cargoes; and presently, moneylenders. Their remarkable success in these pursuits is well known; it is worth mention here in order to account for many of the complications and collisions of interest subsequently ensuing upon the merchant-State's fundamental doctrine that the primary function of government is *not* to maintain freedom and security, but to "help business."

5 In 1629, the Massachusetts Bay colony adopted the Plymouth colony's model of congregational autonomy, but finding its principle dangerously inconsistent with the principle of the State, almost immediately nullified their action; retaining, however, the name of Congregationalism. This mode of masquerade is easily recognizable as one of the modern State's most useful expedients for maintaining the appearance of things without the reality. The names of our two largest political parties will at once appear as a capital example. Within two years the Bay colony had set up a State church, nominally congregationalist, but actually a branch of the civil service, as in England.

6 Probably it was a forecast of this state of things, as much as the greater convenience of administration, that caused the Bay Company to move over to Massachusetts, bag and baggage, in the year following the issuance of their charter.

7 Thomas Robinson Hazard, the Rhode Island Quaker, in his delightful Jonnycake Papers, says that the Great Swamp Fight of 1675 was "instigated against the rightful owners of the soil, solely by the cussed godly Puritans of Massachusetts, and their hell-hound allies, the Presbyterians of Connecticut; whom, though charity is my specialty, I can never think of without feeling as all good Rhode Islanders should; and as old Miss Hazard did when, in like vein, she thanked God in the Connecticut prayer meeting that she could hold malice forty years." The Rhode Island settlers dealt with the Indians for rights in land, and made friends with them.

III

One examines the American merchant-State in vain for any suggestion of the philosophy of natural rights and popular sovereignty. The company system and the provincial system made no place for it, and the one autonomous State was uncompromisingly against it. The Bay Company brought over their charter to serve as the constitution of the new colony, and under its provisions the form of the State was that of an uncommonly small and close oligarchy. The right to vote was vested only in shareholding members, or "freemen" of the corporation, on the stark State principle laid down many years later by John Jay, that "those who own the country should govern the country." At the end of a year, the Bay colony comprised perhaps about two thousand persons; and of these, certainly not twenty, probably not more than a dozen, had anything whatsoever to say about its government. This small group constituted itself as a sort of directorate or council, appointing its own executive body, which consisted of a governor, a lieutenant-governor, and a half-dozen or more magistrates. These officials had no responsibility to the community at large, but only to the directorate. By the terms of the charter, the directorate was self-perpetuating. It was permitted to fill vacancies and add to its members as it saw fit; and in so doing it followed a policy similar to that which was subsequently recommended by Alexander Hamilton, of admitting only such well-to-do and influential persons as could be trusted to sustain a solid front against anything savouring of popular sovereignty.

Historians have very properly made a great deal of the influence of Calvinist theology in bracing the strongly antidemocratic attitude of the Bay Company. The story is readable and interesting—often amusing—yet the gist of it is so simple that it can be perceived at once. The company's principle of action was, in this respect, the one that, in like circumstances for a dozen centuries, invariably motivated the State. The Marxian dictum that "religion is the opiate of the people" is either an ignorant or a slovenly confusion of terms, which cannot be too strongly reprehended. Religion was never that, nor will it ever be; but organized Christianity, which is by no means the same thing as religion, has been the opiate of the people ever since the beginning of the fourth century, and never has this opiate been employed for political purposes more skillfully than it was by the Massachusetts Bay oligarchy.

In the year 311, the Roman emperor Constantine issued an edict of toleration in favour of organized Christianity. He patronized the new cult heavily, giving it rich presents, and even adopted the labarum as his standard, which was a most distinguished gesture, and cost nothing; the story of the heavenly sign appearing before his crucial battle against Maxentius may quite safely be put down beside that of the apparitions seen before the battle of the Marne. He never joined the Church, however, and the tradition that he was converted to Christianity is open to great doubt. The point of all this is that circumstances had, by that time, made Christianity a considerable figure; it had survived contumely and persecution, and had become a social influence which Constantine saw was destined to reach far enough to make it worth courting. The Church could be made a most effective tool of the State, and only a very moderate amount of statesmanship was needed to discern the right way of bringing this about. The understanding, undoubtedly tacit, was based on a simple *quid pro quo* [verbatim; "what for what"]; in exchange for imperial recognition and patronage, and endowments enough to keep up to the requirements of a high official respectability, the Church should quit its disagreeable habit of criticizing the course of politics; and in particular, it should abstain from unfavourable comment on the State's administration of the political means.

These are the unvarying terms—again I say, undoubtedly tacit, as it is seldom necessary to stipulate against biting the hand by which one is fed—of every understanding that has been struck since Constantine's day, between organized Christianity and the State. They were the terms of the understanding struck in the Germanys and in England at the Reformation. The petty German principality had its State Church as it had its State theatre; and in England, Henry VIII set up the Church in its present status as an arm of the civil service, like the Post Office.

SUPPRESSED INTELLIGENCE REPORTS

The fundamental understanding in all cases was that the Church should not interfere with or disparage the organization of the political means; and in practice, it naturally followed that the Church would go further and quite regularly abet this organization to the best of its ability.

The merchant-State in America came to this understanding with organized Christianity. In the Bay colony, the Church became in 1638 an established subsidiary of the State,8 supported by taxation; it maintained a State creed, promulgated in 1647. In some other colonies, as for example, in Virginia, the Church was a branch of the State service, and where it was not actually established as such, the same understanding was reached by other means, quite as satisfactorily. Indeed, the merchant-State, both in England and America, soon became lukewarm towards the idea of an Establishment, perceiving that the same *modus viveaadi* [means of life] could be almost as easily arrived at under voluntarism, and that the latter had the advantage of satisfying practically all modes of credal and ceremonial preference, thus releasing the State from the troublesome and profitless business of interference in disputes over matters of doctrine and Church order.

Voluntaryism, pure and simple, was set up in Rhode Island by Roger Williams, John Clarke, and their associates, who were banished from the Bay colony almost exactly three hundred years ago, in 1636. This group of exiles is commonly regarded as having founded a society on the philosophy of natural rights and popular sovereignty in respect of both Church order and civil order, and as having launched an experiment in democracy. This, however, is an exaggeration. The leaders of the group were undoubtedly in sight of this philosophy, and as far as Church order is concerned, their practice was conformable to it. On the civil side, the most that can be said is that their practice was conformable in so far as they knew how to make it so; and one says this much only by a very considerable concession. The least that can be said, on the other hand, is that their practice was for a time greatly in advance of the practice prevailing in other colonies—so far in advance that Rhode Island was in great disrepute with its neighbours in Massachusetts and Connecticut, who diligently disseminated the tale of its evil fame throughout the land, with the customary exaggerations and embellishments. Nevertheless, through acceptance of the State system of land tenure, the political structure of Rhode Island was a State-structure from the outset, contemplating as it did, the stratification of society into an owning and exploiting class and a propertyless dependent class. Williams's theory of the State was that of social compact arrived at among equals, but equality did not exist in Rhode Island; the actual outcome was a pure class-State.

In the spring of 1638, Williams acquired about twenty square miles of land by gift from two Indian sachems, in addition to some he had bought from them two years before. In October, he formed a "proprietary" of purchasers who bought twelve-thirteenths of the Indian grant. Bicknell, in his history of Rhode Island, cites a letter written by Williams to the deputy-governor of the Bay colony, which says frankly that the plan of this proprietary contemplated the creation of two classes of citizens, one consisting of landholding heads of families, and the other, of "young men, single persons" who were a landless tenantry, and as Bicknell says, "had no voice or vote as to the officers of the community, or the laws which they were called upon to obey." Thus, the civil order in Rhode Island was essentially a pure State order, as much so as the civil order of the Bay colony, or any other in America; and, in fact, the landed-property franchise lasted uncommonly long in Rhode Island, existing there for some time after it had been given up in most other quarters of America.9

By way of summing up, it is enough to say that nowhere in the American colonial civil order was there ever the trace of a democracy. The political structure was always that of the merchant-State; Americans have never known any other. Furthermore, the philosophy of natural rights and popular sovereignty was never once exhibited anywhere in American political practice during the colonial period, from the first settlement in 1607 to the revolution of 1776.

8 Mr. Parrington (Main Currents in American Thought, vol. I, p. 24) cites the successive steps leading up to this, as follows: the law of 1631, restricting the franchise to Church members; of 1635, obliging all persons to attend Church services; and of 1636, which established a virtual State monopoly by requiring consent of both Church and State authority before a new church could be set up. Roger Williams observed acutely that a State establishment of organized Christianity is "a politic invention of man to maintain the civil State."

9 Bicknell says that the formation of Williams's proprietary was "a land-holding, land-jobbing, land-selling scheme, with no moral, social, civil, educational or religious end in view;" and his discussion of the early land allotments, on the site where the city of Providence now stands, makes it pretty clear that "the first years of Providence are consumed in a greedy scramble for land." Bicknell is not precisely an unfriendly witness towards Williams, though his history is avowedly *ex parte* [one sided-biased] for the thesis that the true expounder of civil freedom in Rhode Island was not Williams, but Clarke. This contention is immaterial to the present purpose, however, for the State system of land tenure prevailed in Clarke's settlements on Aquidneck as it did in Williams's settlements farther up the bay.

CHAPTER FOUR

I

After conquest and confiscation have been effected, and the State set up, its first concern is with the land. The State assumes the right of eminent domain over its territorial basis, whereby every landholder becomes in theory a tenant of the State. In its capacity as ultimate landlord, the State distributes the land among its beneficiaries on its own terms. A point to be observed in passing is that by the State-system of land tenure each original transaction confers two distinct monopolies, entirely different in their nature, inasmuch as one concerns the right to labour-made property, and the other concerns the right to purely law-made property. The one is a monopoly of the use-value of land; and the other, a monopoly of the economic rent of land. The first gives the right to keep other persons from using the land in question, or trespassing on it, and the right to exclusive possession of values accruing from the application of labour to it; values, that is, which are produced by exercise of the economic means upon the particular property in question. Monopoly of economic rent, on the other hand, gives the exclusive right to values accruing from the desire of other persons to possess that property; values which take their rise irrespective of any exercise of the economic means on the part of the holder.1

Economic rent arises when, for whatsoever reason, two or more persons compete for the possession of a piece of land, and it increases directly according to the number of persons competing. The whole of Manhattan Island was bought originally by a handful of Hollanders from a handful of Indians for twenty-four dollars' worth of trinkets. The subsequent "rise in land values," as we call it, was brought about by the steady influx of population and the consequent high competition for portions of the island's surface; and these ensuing values were monopolized by the holders. They grew to an enormous size, and the holders profited accordingly; the Astor, Wendel, and Trinity Church estates have always served as classical examples for study of the State-system of land-tenure.

Bearing in mind that the State is the organization of the political means — that its primary intention is to enable the economic exploitation of one class by another — we see that it has always acted on the principle already cited, that expropriation must precede exploitation. There is no other way to make the political means effective. The first postulate of fundamental economics is that man is a land animal, deriving his subsistence wholly from the land.[2] His entire wealth is produced by the application of labour and capital to land; no form of wealth known to man can be produced in any other way. Hence, if his free access to land be shut off by legal preemption, he can apply his labour and capital only with the land-holder's consent, and on the land-holder's terms; in other words, it is at this point, and this point only, that exploitation becomes practicable.[3] Therefore the first concern of the State must be invariably, as we find it invariably is, with its policy of land-tenure.

I state these elementary matters as briefly as I can; the reader may easily find a full exposition of them elsewhere.[4] I am here concerned only to show why the State system of land-tenure came into being, and why its maintenance is necessary to the State's existence. If this system were broken up, obviously the reason for the State's existence would disappear, and the State itself would disappear with it.[5] With this in mind, it is interesting to observe that although all our public policies would seem to be in process of exhaustive review, no publicist has anything to say about the State system of land-tenure. This is no doubt the best evidence of its importance.[6]

Under the feudal State there was no great amount of trade in land. When William, for example, set up the Norman State in England after conquest and confiscation in 1066-76, his associate banditti, among whom he parceled out the confiscated territory, did nothing to speak of in the way of developing their holdings, and did not contemplate gain from the increment of rental-values. In fact, economic rent hardly existed; their fellow-beneficiaries were not in the market to any great extent, and the dispossessed population did not represent any economic demand. The feudal regime was a regime of status, under which landed estates yielded hardly any rental-value, and only a moderate use-value, but carried an enormous insignia-value. Land was regarded more as a badge of nobility than as an active asset; its possession marked a man as belonging to the exploiting class, and the size of his holdings seems to have counted for more than the number of his exploitable dependents.[7] The encroachments of the merchant-State, however, brought about a change in these circumstances. The importance of rental-values was recognized, and speculative trading in land became general.

Hence, in a study of the merchant-State as it appeared full-blown in America, it is a point of utmost consequence to remember that from the time of the first colonial settlement to the present day, America has been regarded as a practically limitless field for speculation in rental-values.[8] One may say at a safe venture that every colonial enterpriser and proprietor after Raleigh's time understood economic rent and the conditions necessary to enhance it. The Swedish, Dutch and British trading companies understood this; Endicott and Winthrop, of the autonomous merchant-State on the Bay, understood it; so did Penn and the Calverts; so did the Carolinian proprietors, to whom Charles II granted a lordly belt of territory south of Virginia, reaching from the Atlantic to the Pacific; and, as we have seen, Roger Williams and Clarke understood it perfectly. Indeed, land speculation may be put down as the first major industry established in colonial America. Professor Sakolski calls attention to the fact that it was flourishing in the South before the commercial importance of either negroes or tobacco was recognized. These two staples came fully into their own about 1670 - tobacco perhaps a little earlier, but not much - and before that, England and Europe had been well covered by a lively propaganda of Southern landholders, advertising for settlers.9

Mr. Sakolski makes it clear that very few original enterprisers in American rental-values ever got much profit out of their ventures. This is worth remarking here as enforcing the point that what gives rise to economic rent is the presence of a population engaged in a settled exercise of the economic means, or as we commonly put it, "working for a living," or again, in technical terms, applying labour and capital to natural resources for the production of wealth. It was no doubt a very fine dignified thing for Carteret, Berkeley, and their associate nobility to be the owners of a province as large as the Carolinas, but if no population were settled there, producing wealth by exercise of the economic means, obviously not a foot of it would bear a pennyworth of rental-value, and the proprietors' chance of exercising the political means would therefore be precisely nil. Proprietors who made the most profitable exercise of the political means have been those - or rather, speaking strictly, the heirs of those - like the Brevoorts, Wendels, Whitneys, Astors, and Goelets, who owned land in an actual or prospective urban centre, and held it as an investment rather than for speculation.

The lure of the political means in America, however, gave rise to a state of mind which may profitably be examined. Under the feudal State, living by the political means was enabled only by the accident of birth, or in some special cases by the accident of personal favour. Persons outside these categories of accident had no chance whatsoever to live otherwise than by the economic means. No matter how much they may have wished to exercise the political means, or how greatly they may have envied the privileged few who could exercise it, they were unable to do so; the feudal regime was strictly one of status. Under the merchant-State, on the contrary, the political means was open to anyone, irrespective of birth or position, who had the sagacity and determination necessary to get at it. In this respect, America appeared as a field of unlimited opportunity. The effect of this was to produce a race of people whose master concern was to avail themselves of this opportunity. They had but the one spring of action, which was the determination to abandon the economic means as soon as they could, and at any sacrifice of conscience or character, and live by the political means. From the beginning, this determination has been universal, amounting to monomania.10 We need not concern ourselves here with the effect upon the general balance of advantage produced by supplanting the feudal State by the merchant-State; we may observe only that certain virtues and integrities were bred by the regime of status, to which the regime of contract appears to be inimical, even destructive. Vestiges of them persist among peoples who have had a long experience of the regime of status, but in America, which has had no such experience, they do not appear. What the compensations for their absence may be, or whether they may be regarded as adequate, I repeat, need not concern us; we remark only the simple fact that they have not struck root in the constitution of the American character at large, and apparently can not do so.

1 The economic rent of the Trinity Church estate in New York City, for instance, would be as high as it is now, even if the holders had never done a stroke of work on the property. Landowners who are holding a property "for a rise" usually leave it idle, or improve it only to the extent necessary to clear its taxes; the type of building commonly called a "taxpayer" is a familiar sight everywhere. Twenty-five years ago a member of the New York City Tax Commission told me that by careful estimate there was almost enough vacant land within the city

limits to feed the population, assuming that all of it were arable and put under intensive cultivation!

2 As a technical term in economics, land includes all natural resources, earth, air, water, sunshine, timber and minerals *in situ*, etc. Failure to understand this use of the term has seriously misled some writers, notably Count Tolstoy.

3 Hence there is actually no such thing as a "labour problem," for no encroachment on the rights of either labour or capital can possibly take place until all natural resources within reach have been preempted. What we call the "problem of the unemployed" is in no sense a problem, but a direct consequence of State created monopoly.

4 For fairly obvious reasons they have no place in the conventional courses that are followed in our schools and colleges.

5 The French school of physiocrats, led by Quesnay, du Pont de Nemours, Turgot, Gournay and le Trosne - usually regarded as the founders of the science of political economy - broached the idea of destroying this system by the confiscation of economic rent; and this idea was worked out in detail some years ago in America by Henry George. None of these writers, however, seemed to be aware of the effect that their plan would produce upon the State itself. Collectivism, on the other hand, proposes immeasurably to strengthen and entrench the State by confiscation of the use-value as well as the rental-value of land, doing away with private proprietorship in either.

6 If one were not aware of the highly explosive character of this subject, it would be almost incredible that until three years ago, no one has ever presumed to write a history of land speculation in America. In 1932, the firm of Harpers published an excellent work by Professor Sakolski, under the frivolous catchpenny title of The Great American Land Bubble. I do not believe that anyone can have a competent understanding of our history or of the character of our people, without hard study of this book. It does not pretend to be more than a preliminary approach to the subject, a sort of path-breaker for the exhaustive treatise which someone, preferably Professor Sakolski himself, should be undertaking; but for what it is, nothing could be better. I am making liberal use of it throughout this section.

7 Regard for this insignia-value or token-value of land has shown an interesting persistence. The rise of the merchant-State, supplanting the regime of status by the regime of contract, opened the way for men of all sorts and conditions to climb into the exploiting class; and the new recruits have usually shown a hankering for the old distinguishing sign of their having done so, even though the rise in rental-values has made the gratification of this desire progressively costly.

8 If our geographical development had been determined in a natural way, by the demands of use instead of the demands of speculation, our western frontier would not yet be anywhere near the Mississippi River. Rhode Island is the most thickly populated member of the Union, yet one may drive from one end of it to the other on one of its "through" highways, and see hardly a sign of human occupancy. All discussions of "overpopulation" from Malthus down, are based on the premise of legal occupancy instead of actual occupancy, and are therefore utterly incompetent and worthless. Oppenheimer's calculation, made in 1912, to which I have already referred, shows that if legal occupation were abolished, every family of five persons could possess nearly twenty acres of land, and still leave about two-thirds of the planet

unoccupied. Henry George's examination of Malthus's theory of population is well known, or at least, easily available. It is perhaps worth mention in passing that exaggerated rental-values are responsible for the perennial troubles of the American single crop farmer. Curiously, one finds this fact set forth in the report of a farm survey, published by the Department of Agriculture about fifty years ago.

9 Mr. Chinard, professor in the Faculty of Literature at Johns Hopkins, has lately published a translation of a little book, hardly more than a pamphlet, written in 1686 by the Huguenot refugee Durand, giving a description of Virginia for the information of his fellow exiles. It strikes a modern reader as being very favourable to Virginia, and one is amused to read that the landholders who had entertained Durand with an eye to business, thought he had not laid it on half thick enough, and were much disgusted. The book is delightfully interesting, and well worth owning.

10 It was the ground of Chevalier's observation that Americans had "the morale of an army on the march," and of his equally notable observations on the supreme rule of expediency in America.

II

It was said at the time, I believe, that the actual causes of the colonial revolution of 1776 would never be known. The causes assigned by our schoolbooks may be dismissed as trivial; the various partisan and propagandist views of that struggle and its origins may be put down as incompetent. Great evidential value may be attached to the long line of adverse commercial legislation laid down by the British State from 1651 onward, especially to that portion of it which was enacted after the merchant-State established itself firmly in England in consequence of the events of 1688. This legislation included the Navigation Acts, the Trade Acts, acts regulating the colonial currency, the act of 1752 regulating the process of levy and distress, and the procedures leading up to the establishment of the Board of Trade in 1686.11 These directly affected the industrial and commercial interests in the colonies, though just how seriously is perhaps an open question enough at any rate, beyond doubt, to provoke deep resentment.

Over and above these, however, if the reader will put himself back into the ruling passion of the time, he will at once appreciate the import of two matters which have for some reason escaped the attention of historians. The first of these is the attempt of the British State to limit the exercise of the political means in respect of rental-values.12 In 1763 it forbade the colonists to take up lands lying westward of the source of any river flowing through the Atlantic seaboard. The deadline thus established ran so as to cut off from preemption about half of Pennsylvania and half of Virginia and everything to the west thereof. This was serious. With the mania for speculation running as high as it did, with the consciousness of opportunity, real or fancied, having become so acute and so general, this ruling affected everybody. One can get some idea of its effect by imagining the state of mind of our people at large if stock-gambling had suddenly been outlawed at the beginning of the last great boom in Wall Street a few years ago.

For by this time the colonists had begun to be faintly aware of the illimitable resources of the country lying westward; they had learned just enough about them to fire their imagination and their avarice to a white heat. The seaboard had been pretty well taken up, the freeholding farmer had been pushed back farther and farther, population was coming in steadily, the maritime towns were growing. Under these conditions, "western lands" had become a centre of attraction. Rental-values depended on population, the population was bound to expand, and the one general direction in which it could expand was westward, where lay an immense and incalculably rich domain waiting for preemption. What could be more natural than that the colonists should itch to get their hands on this territory, and exploit it for themselves alone, and on their own terms, without risk of arbitrary interference by the British State? —and this of necessity meant political independence. It takes no great stress of imagination to see that anyone in those circumstances would have felt that way, and that colonial resentment against the arbitrary limitation which the edict of 1763 put upon the exercise of the political means must therefore have been great.

The actual state of land speculation during the colonial period will give a fair idea of the probabilities in the case. Most of it was done on the company-system; a number of adventurers would unite, secure a grant of land, survey it, and then sell it off as speedily as they could. Their aim was a quick turnover; they did not, as a rule, contemplate holding the land, much less settling it—in short, their ventures were a pure gamble in rental-values.13 Among these pre-Revolutionary enterprises was the Ohio Company, formed in 1748 with a grant of half a million acres; the Loyal Company, which like the Ohio Company, was composed of Virginians; the Transylvania, the Vandalia, Scioto, Indiana, Wabash, Illinois, Susquehanna, and others whose holdings were smaller.14 It is interesting to observe the names of persons concerned in these undertakings; one can not escape the significance of this connection in view of their attitude towards the revolution, and their subsequent career as statesmen and patriots. For example, aside from his individual ventures, General Washington was a member of the Ohio Company, and a prime mover in organizing the Mississippi Company. He also conceived the scheme of the Potomac Company, which was designed to raise the rental-value of western holdings by affording an outlet for their produce by canal and portage to the Potomac River, and thence to the seaboard. This enterprise determined the establishment of the national capital in its present most ineligible situation, for the proposed terminus of the canal was at that point. Washington picked up some lots in the city that bears his name, but in common with other early speculators, he did not make much money out of them; they were appraised at about $20,000 when he died.

Patrick Henry was an inveterate and voracious engrosser of land lying beyond the deadline set by the British State; later he was heavily involved in the affairs of one of the notorious Yazoo companies operating in Georgia. He seems to have been most unscrupulous. His company's holdings in Georgia, amounting to more than ten million acres, were to be paid for in Georgia scrip, which was much depreciated. Henry bought up all these certificates that he could get his hands on, at ten cents on the dollar, and made a great profit on them by their rise in value when Hamilton put through his measure for having the central government assume the debts they represented. Undoubtedly it was this trait of unrestrained avarice which earned him the dislike of Mr. Jefferson, who said, rather contemptuously, that he was "insatiable in money."15

Benjamin Franklin's thrifty mind turned cordially to the project of the Vandalia Company, and he acted successfully as promoter for it in England in 1766. Timothy Pickering, who was Secretary of State under Washington and John Adams, went on record in 1796 that "all I am now worth was gained by speculations in land." Silas Deane, emissary of the Continental Congress to France, was interested in the Illinois and Wabash Companies, as was Robert Morris, who managed the revolution's finances; as was also James Wilson, who became a justice of the

Supreme Court and a mighty man in post-revolutionary land-grabbing. Wolcott of Connecticut, and Stiles, president of Yale College, held stock in the Susquehanna Company; so did Peletiah Webster, Ethan Allen, and Jonathan Trumbull, the "Brother Jonathan," whose name was long a sobriquet for the typical American, and is still sometimes so used. James Duane, the first mayor of New York City, carried on some quite considerable speculative undertakings; and however indisposed one may feel towards entertaining the fact, so did the "Father of the Revolution" himself—Samuel Adams.

A mere common sense view of the situation would indicate that the British State's interference with a free exercise of the political means was at least as great an incitement to revolution as its interference, through the Navigation Acts, and the Trade Acts, with a free exercise of the economic means. In the nature of things it would be a greater incitement, both because it affected a more numerous class of persons, and because speculation in land-values represented much easier money. Allied with this is the second matter which seems to me deserving of notice, and which has never been properly reckoned with, as far as I know, in studies of the period.

It would seem the most natural thing in the world for the colonists to perceive that independence would not only give freer access to this one mode of the political means, but that it would also open access to other modes which the colonial status made unavailable. The merchant-State existed in the royal provinces complete in structure, but not in function; it did not give access to all the modes of economic exploitation. The advantages of a State which should be wholly autonomous in this respect must have been clear to the colonists, and must have moved them strongly towards the project of establishing one.

Again, it is purely a common sense view of the circumstances that leads to this conclusion. The merchant-State in England had emerged triumphant from conflict, and the colonists had plenty of chance to see what it could do in the way of distributing the various means of economic exploitation, and its methods of doing it. For instance, certain English concerns were in the carrying trade between England and America, for which other English concerns built ships. Americans could compete in both these lines of business. If they did so, the carrying charges would be regulated by the terms of this competition; if not, they would be regulated by monopoly, or, in our historic phrase, they could be set as high as the traffic would bear. English carriers and shipbuilders made common cause, approached the State and asked it to intervene, which it did by forbidding the colonists to ship goods on any but English-built and English-operated ships. Since freight charges are a factor in prices, the effect of this intervention was to enable British ship owners to pocket the difference between monopoly rates and competitive rates; to enable them, that is, to exploit the consumer by employing the political means.[16] Similar interventions were made at the instance of cutlers, nail makers, hatters, steel makers, etc.

These interventions took the form of simple prohibition. Another mode of intervention appeared in the customs-duties laid by the British State on foreign sugar and molasses.[17] We all now know pretty well, probably, that the primary reason for a tariff is that it enables the exploitation of the domestic consumer by a process indistinguishable from sheer robbery.[18] All the reasons regularly assigned are debatable; this one is not, hence propagandists and lobbyists never mention it. The colonists were well aware of this reason, and the best evidence that they were aware of it is that long before the Union was established, the merchant-enterprisers and industrialists were ready and waiting to set upon the newformed administration with an organized demand for a tariff.

It is clear that, while in the nature of things, the British State's interventions upon the economic means would stir up great resentment among the interests directly concerned, they would have another effect fully as significant, if not more so, in causing those interests to look favourably on the idea of political independence. They could hardly have helped seeing the positive, as well as the negative, advantage that would accrue from setting up a State of their own, which they might bend to their own purposes. It takes no great amount of imagination to reconstruct the vision that appeared before them of a merchant-State clothed with full powers of intervention and discrimination, a State which should first and last "help business," and which should be administered either by mere agents or by persons easily manageable, if not by persons of actual interests like to their own. It is hardly presumable that the colonists generally were not intelligent enough to see this vision, or that they were not resolute enough to risk the chance of realizing it when the time could be made ripe; as it was, the time was ripened almost before it was ready.19 We can discern a distinct line of common purpose uniting the interests of the merchant-enterpriser with those of the actual or potential speculator in rental-values — uniting the Hancocks, Gores, Otises, with the Henrys, Lees, Wolcotts, Trumbulls — and leading directly towards the goal of political independence.

The main conclusion, however, towards which these observations tend, is that one general frame of mind existed among the colonists with reference to the nature and primary function of the State. This frame of mind was not peculiar to them; they shared it with the beneficiaries of the merchant-State in England, and with those of the feudal State as far back as the State's history can be traced. Voltaire, surveying the debris of the feudal State, said that in essence the State is "a device for taking money out of one set of pockets and putting it into another." The beneficiaries of the feudal State had precisely this view, and they bequeathed it unchanged and unmodified to the actual and potential beneficiaries of the merchant-State. The colonists regarded the State as primarily an instrument whereby one might help oneself and hurt others, that is to say, first and foremost they regarded it as the organization of the political means. No other view of the State was *ever* held in colonial America. Romance and poetry were brought to bear on the subject in the customary way; glamorous myths about it were propagated with the customary intent; but when all came to all, nowhere in colonial America were actual practical relations with the State ever determined by any other view than this.20

11 For a most admirable discussion of these measures and their consequences, cf. Beard, op. cit., vol. I, p. 191-220.

12 In principle, this had been done before; for example, some of the early royal land grants reserved mineral-rights and timber rights to the Crown. The Dutch State reserved the right to furs and pelts. Actually, however, these restrictions did not amount to much, and were not felt as a general grievance, for these resources had been but little explored.

13 There were a few exceptions, but not many; notably in the case of the Wadsworth properties in Western New York, which were held as an investment and leased out on a rental-basis. In one, at least, of General Washington's operations, it appears that he also had this method in view. In 1773 he published an advertisement in a Baltimore newspaper, stating that he had secured a grant of about twenty thousand acres on the Ohio and Kanawha rivers, which he proposed to open to settlers on a rental-basis.

14 Sakolski, op. cit., ch. I.

15 It is an odd fact that among the most eminent names of the period, almost the only ones unconnected with land-grabbing or land-jobbing, are those of the two great antagonists, Thomas Jefferson and Alexander Hamilton. Mr. Jefferson had a gentleman's distaste for profiting by any form of the political means; he never even went so far as to patent one of his many useful inventions. Hamilton seems to have cared nothing for money. His measures made many rich, but he never sought anything from them for himself. In general, he appears to have had few scruples, yet amidst the riot of greed and rascality which he did most to promote, he walked worthily. Even his professional fees as a lawyer were absurdly small, and he remained quite poor, all his life.

16 Raw colonial exports were processed in England, and reexported to the colonies at prices enhanced in this way, thus making the political means effective on the colonists both going and coming.

17 Beard, op. cit., vol. I, p. 195, cites the observation current in England at the time, that seventy-three members of the Parliament that imposed this tariff were interested in West Indian sugar plantations.

18 It must be observed, however, that free trade is impracticable so long as land is kept out of free competition with industry in the labour market. Discussions of the rival policies of free trade and protection invariably leave this limitation out of account, and are therefore nugatory. Holland and England, commonly spoken of as free trade countries, were never really such; they had only so much freedom of trade as was consistent with their special economic requirements. American free traders of the last century, such as Sumner and Godkin, were not really free traders; they were never able — or willing — to entertain the crucial question why, if free trade is a good thing, the conditions of labour were no better in free trade England than, for instance, in protectionist Germany, but were in fact worse. The answer is, of course, that England had no unpreempted land to absorb displaced labour, or to stand in continuous competition with industry for labour.

19 The immense amount of labour involved in getting the revolution going, and keeping it going, is not as yet exactly a commonplace of American history, but it has begun to be pretty well understood, and the various myths about it have been exploded by the researches of disinterested historians.

20 The influence of this view upon the rise of nationalism and the maintenance of the national spirit in the modern world, now that the merchant-State has so generally superseded the feudal State, may be perceived at once. I do not think it has ever been thoroughly discussed, or that the sentiment of patriotism has ever been thoroughly examined for traces of this view, though one might suppose that such a work would be extremely useful.

III

The charter of the American revolution was the Declaration of Independence, which took its stand on the double thesis of "unalienable" natural rights and popular sovereignty. We have seen that these doctrines were theoretically, or as politicians say, "in principle," congenial to the spirit of the English merchant-enterpriser, and we may see that in the nature of things they would be even more agreeable to the spirit of all classes in American society. A thin and scattered population with a whole wide world before it, with a vast territory full of rich resources which anyone might take a hand at preempting and exploiting, would be strongly on the side of natural rights, as the colonists were from the beginning; and political independence would confirm it in that position. These circumstances would stiffen the American merchant-enterpriser, agrarian, forestaller and industrialist alike in a jealous, uncompromising, and assertive economic individualism.

So also with the sister doctrine of popular sovereignty. The colonists had been through a long and vexatious experience of State interventions which limited their use of both the political and economic means. They had also been given plenty of opportunity to see how these interventions had been managed, and how the interested English economic groups which did the managing had profited at their expense. Hence there was no place in their minds for any political theory that disallowed the right of individual self-expression in politics. As their situation tended to make them natural born economic individualists, so also it tended to make them natural born republicans.

Thus the preamble of the Declaration hit the mark of a cordial unanimity. Its two leading doctrines could easily be interpreted as justifying an unlimited economic pseudo-individualism on the part of the State's beneficiaries, and a judiciously managed exercise of political self-expression by the electorate. Whether or not this were a more free and easy interpretation than a strict construction of the doctrines will bear, no doubt it was in effect the interpretation quite commonly put upon them. American history abounds in instances where great principles have, in their common understanding and practical application, been narrowed down to the service of very paltry ends. The preamble, nevertheless, did reflect a general state of mind. However incompetent the understanding of its doctrines may have been, and however interested the motives which prompted that understanding, the general spirit of the people was in their favour.

There was complete unanimity also regarding the nature of the new and independent political institution which the Declaration contemplated as within "the right of the people" to set up. There was a great and memorable dissension about its form, but none about its nature. It should be in essence the mere continuator of the merchant-State already existing. There was no idea of setting up government, the purely social institution which should have no other object than, as the Declaration put it, to secure the natural rights of the individual; or, as Paine put it, which should contemplate nothing beyond the maintenance of freedom and security - the institution which should make no positive interventions of any kind upon the individual, but should confine itself exclusively to such negative interventions as the maintenance of freedom and security might indicate. The idea was to perpetuate an institution of another character entirely, the State, the organization of the political means; and this was accordingly done.

There is no disparagement implied in this observation; for, all questions of motive aside, nothing else was to be expected. No one knew any other kind of political organization. The causes of American complaint were conceived of as due only to interested and culpable maladministration, not to the essentially antisocial nature of the institution administered. Dissatisfaction was directed against administrators, not against the institution itself. Violent dislike of the form of the institution — the monarchical form — was engendered, but no distrust or suspicion of its nature. The character of the State had never been subjected to scrutiny; the cooperation of the Zeitgeist [spirit of the time] was needed for that, and it was not yet to be had.21 One may see here a parallel with the revolutionary movements against the Church in the sixteenth century — and indeed with revolutionary movements in general. They are incited by abuses and misfeasances, more or less specific and always secondary, and are carried on with no idea beyond getting them rectified or avenged, usually by the sacrifice of conspicuous scapegoats. The philosophy of the institution that gives play to these misfeasances is never examined, and hence they recur promptly under another form or other auspices,22 or else their place is taken by others which are in character precisely like them. Thus the notorious failure of reforming and revolutionary movements in the long run may as a rule be found due to their incorrigible superficiality.

One mind, indeed, came within reaching distance of the fundamentals of the matter, not by employing the historical method, but by a homespun kind of reasoning, aided by a sound and sensitive instinct. The common view of Mr. Jefferson as a doctrinaire believer in the stark principle of "states' rights" is most incompetent and misleading. He believed in states' rights, assuredly, but he went much farther; states' rights were only an incident in his general system of political organization. He believed that the ultimate political unit, the repository and source of political authority and initiative, should be the smallest unit; not the federal unit, state unit or county unit, but the township, or, as he called it, the "ward." The township, and the township only, should determine the delegation of power upwards to the county, the state, and the federal units.

His system of extreme decentralization is interesting and perhaps worth a moment's examination, because if the idea of the State is ever displaced by the idea of government, it seems probable that the practical expression of this idea would come out very nearly in that form.23 There is probably no need to say that the consideration of such a displacement involves a long look ahead, and over a field of view that is cluttered with the debris of a most discouraging number, not of nations alone, but of whole civilizations. Nevertheless it is interesting to remind ourselves that more than a hundred and fifty years ago, one American succeeded in getting below the surface of things, and that he probably, to some degree, anticipated the judgment of an immeasurably distant future.

In February, 1816, Mr. Jefferson wrote a letter to Joseph C. Cabell, in which he expounded the philosophy behind his system of political organization. What is it, he asks, that has "destroyed liberty and the rights of man in every government which has ever existed under the sun? The generalizing and concentrating all cares and powers into one body, no matter whether of the autocrats of Russia or France, or of the aristocrats of a Venetian senate." The secret of freedom will be found in the individual "making himself the depository of the powers respecting himself, so far as he is competent to them, and delegating only what is beyond his competence, by a synthetical process, to higher and higher orders of functionaries, so as to trust fewer and fewer powers in proportion as the trustees become more and more oligarchical." This idea rests on accurate observation, for we are all aware that not only the wisdom of the ordinary man, but also his interest and sentiment, have a very short radius of operation; they can not be stretched over an area of much more than township-size; and it is the acme of absurdity to suppose that any man or any body of men can arbitrarily exercise their wisdom, interest and sentiment over a state-wide or nationwide area with any kind of success. Therefore the principle must hold that the larger the area of exercise, the fewer and more clearly defined should be the functions exercised. Moreover, "by placing under everyone what his own eye may superintend," there is erected the surest safeguard against usurpation of function. "Where every man is a sharer in the direction of his ward-republic, or of some of the higher ones, and feels that he is a participator in the government of affairs, not merely at an election one day in the year, but every day; "he will let the heart be torn out of his body sooner than his power wrested from him by a Caesar or a Bonaparte."

No such idea of popular sovereignty, however, appeared in the political organization that was set up in 1789 — far from it. In devising their structure, the American architects followed certain specifications laid down by Harington, Locke and Adam Smith, which might be regarded as a sort of official digest of politics under the merchant-State; indeed, if one wished to be perhaps a little inurbane in describing them — though not actually unjust — one might say that they are the merchant-State's defence mechanism.24 Harington laid down the all important principle that the basis of politics is economic — that power follows property. Since he was arguing against the feudal concept, he laid stress specifically upon landed property. He was, of course, too early to perceive the bearings of the State-system of land tenure upon industrial exploitation, and neither he nor Locke perceived any natural distinction to be drawn between law-made property and labour-made property; nor yet did Smith perceive this clearly, although he seems to have had occasional indistinct glimpses of it. According to Harington's theory of economic determinism, the realization of popular sovereignty is a simple matter. Since political power proceeds from land ownership, a simple diffusion of land ownership is all that is needed to insure a satisfactory distribution of power.25 If everybody owns, then everybody rules. "If the people hold three parts in four of the territory," Harington says, "it is plain there can neither be any single person nor nobility able to dispute the government with them. In this case therefore, except force be interposed, they govern themselves."

Locke, writing a half-century later when the revolution of 1688 was over, concerned himself more particularly with the State's positive confiscatory interventions upon other modes of property ownership. These had long been frequent and vexatious, and under the Stuarts they had amounted to unconscionable highway-manry [highway robbery]. Locke's idea therefore was to copper-rivet such a doctrine of the sacredness of property as would forever put a stop to this sort of thing. Hence, he laid it down that the first business of the State is to maintain the absolute inviolability of general property rights; the State itself might not violate them, because in so doing it would act against its own primary function. Thus, in Locke's view, the rights of property took precedence even over those of life and liberty; and if ever it came to the pinch, the State must make its choice accordingly.26

Thus, while the American architects assented "in principle" to the philosophy of natural rights and popular sovereignty, and found it in a general way highly congenial as a sort of voucher for their self-esteem, their practical interpretation of it left it pretty well hamstrung. They were not especially concerned with consistency; their practical interest in this philosophy stopped short at the point which we have already noted, of its presumptive justification of a ruthless economic pseudo-individualism, and an exercise of political self-expression by the general electorate which should be so managed as to be, in all essential respects, futile. In this they took precise pattern by the English Whig exponents and practitioners of this philosophy. Locke himself, whom we have seen putting the natural rights of property so high above those of life and liberty, was equally discriminating in his view of popular sovereignty. He was no believer in what he called "a numerous democracy," and did not contemplate a political organization that should countenance anything of the kind.27 The sort of organization he had in mind is reflected in the extraordinary constitution he devised for the royal province of Carolina, which established a basic order of politically inarticulate serfdom. Such an organization as this represented about the best, in a practical way, that the British merchant-State was ever able to do for the doctrine of popular sovereignty.

It was also about the best that the American counterpart of the British merchant-State could do. The sum of the matter is; that while the philosophy of natural rights and popular sovereignty afforded a set of principles upon which all interests could unite, and practically all did unite, with the aim of securing political independence, it did not afford a satisfactory set of principles on which to found the new American State. When political independence was secured, the stark doctrine of the Declaration went into abeyance, with only a distorted simulacrum of its principles surviving. The rights of life and liberty were recognized by a mere constitutional formality left open to eviscerating interpretations, or, where these were for any reason deemed superfluous, to simple executive disregard; and all consideration of the rights attending "the pursuit of happiness" was narrowed down to a plenary acceptance of Locke's doctrine of the preeminent rights of property, with law-made property on an equal footing with labour-made property.

As for popular sovereignty, the new State had to be republican in form, for no other would suit the general temper of the people; and hence, its peculiar task was to preserve the appearance of actual republicanism without the reality. To do this, it took over the apparatus which we have seen the English merchant-State adopting when confronted with a like task — the apparatus of a representative or parliamentary system. Moreover, it improved upon the British model of this apparatus by adding three auxiliary devices which time has proved most effective. These were, first, the device of the fixed term, which regulates the administration of our system by astronomical rather than political considerations — by the motion of the earth around the sun rather than by political exigency; second, the device of judicial review and interpretation, which, as we have already observed, is a process whereby anything may be made to mean anything; third, the device of requiring legislators to reside in the district they represent, which puts the highest conceivable premium upon pliancy and venality, and is therefore the best mechanism for rapidly building up an immense body of patronage. It may be perceived at once that all these devices tend, of themselves, to work smoothly and harmoniously towards a great centralization of State power, and that their working in this direction may be indefinitely accelerated with the utmost economy of effort.

As well as one can put a date to such an event, the surrender at Yorktown marks the sudden and complete disappearance of the Declaration's doctrine from the political consciousness of America. Mr. Jefferson resided in Paris as minister to France from 1784 to 1789. As the time for his return to America drew near, he wrote Colonel Humphreys that he hoped soon "to possess myself anew, by conversation with my countrymen, of their spirit and ideas. I know only the Americans of the year 1784. They tell me this is to be much a stranger to those of 1789." So indeed he found it. Upon arriving in New York and resuming his place in the social life of the country, he was greatly depressed by the discovery that the principles of the Declaration had gone wholly by the board. No one spoke of natural rights and popular sovereignty; it would seem actually that no one had ever heard of them. Quite the contrary; everyone was talking about the pressing need of a strong central coercive authority, able to check the incursions which "the democratic spirit" was likely to incite upon "the men of principle and property."28

Mr. Jefferson wrote despondently of the contrast of all this with the sort of thing he had been hearing in the France which he had just left "in the first year of her revolution, in the fervour of natural rights and zeal for reformation." In the process of possessing himself anew of the spirit and ideas of his countrymen, he said, "I can not describe the wonder and mortification with which the table conversations filled me." Clearly, though the Declaration might have been the charter of American independence, it was in no sense the charter of the new American State.

21 Even now its cooperation seems not to have got very far in English and American professional circles. The latest English exponent of the State, Professor Laski, draws the same set of elaborate distinctions between the State and officialdom that one would look for if he had been writing a hundred and fifty years ago. He appears to regard the State as essentially a social institution, though his observations on this point are by no means clear. Since his conclusions tend towards collectivism, however, the inference seems admissible.

22 As, for example, when one political party is turned out of office, and another put in.

23 In fact, the only modification of it that one can foresee as necessary is that the smallest unit should reserve the taxing power strictly to itself. The larger units should have no power whatever of direct or indirect taxation, but should present their requirements to the townships, to be met by quota. This would tend to reduce the organizations of the larger units to skeleton form, and would operate strongly against their assuming any functions but those assigned them, which under a strictly governmental regime would be very few — for the federal unit, indeed, extremely few. It is interesting to imagine the suppression of every bureaucratic activity in Washington today that has to do with the maintenance and administration of the political means, and see how little would be left. If the State were superseded by government, probably every federal activity could be housed in the Senate Office Building — quite possibly with room to spare.

24 Harington published the Oceana in 1656. Locke's political treatises were published in 1690. Smith's Inquiry into the Nature and Causes of the Wealth of Nations appeared in 1776.

25 This theory, with its corollary that democracy is primarily an economic rather than a political status, is extremely modern. The Physiocrats in France, and Henry George in America, modified Harington's practical proposals by showing that the same results could be obtained by the more convenient method of a local confiscation of economic rent.

26 Locke held that, in time of war, it was competent for the State to conscript the lives and liberties of its subjects, but not their property. It is interesting to remark the persistence of this view in the practice of the merchant-State at the present time. In the last great collision of competing interests among merchant-States, twenty years ago, the State everywhere intervened at wholesale upon the rights of life and liberty, but was very circumspect towards the rights of property. Since the principle of absolutism was introduced into our constitution by the income tax amendment, several attempts have been made to reduce the rights of property, in time of war, to an approximately equal footing with those of life and liberty; but so far, without success.

27 It is worth going through the literature of the late seventeenth and early eighteenth century to see how the words "democracy" and "democrat" appear exclusively as terms of contumely (rudeness) and reprehension. They served this purpose for a long time both in England and America, much as the terms "bolshevism" and "bolshevist" serve us now. They were subsequently taken over to become what Bentham called "impostor-terms," in behalf of the existing economic and political order, as synonymous with a purely nominal republican-

ism. They are now used regularly in this way to describe the political system of the United States, even by persons who should know better — even, curiously, by persons like Bertrand Russell and Mr. Laski, who have little sympathy with the existing order. One sometimes wonders how our revolutionary forefathers would take it if they could hear some flatulent political thimblerigger [shell game operator] charge them with having founded "the great and glorious democracy of the West."

28 This curious collocation of attributes belongs to General Henry Knox, Washington's secretary of war, and a busy speculator in land-values. He used it in a letter to Washington, on the occasion of Shays's Rebellion in 1786, in which he made an agonized plea for a strong federal army. In the literature of the period, it is interesting to observe how regularly a moral superiority is associated with the possession of property.

CHAPTER FIVE

I

It is a commonplace that the persistence of an institution is due solely to the state of mind that prevails towards it, the set of terms in which men habitually think about it. So long, and only so long, as those terms are favourable, the institution lives and maintains its power; and when for any reason men generally cease thinking in those terms, it weakens and becomes inert. At one time, a certain set of terms regarding man's place in nature gave organized Christianity the power largely to control men's consciences and direct their conduct; and this power has dwindled to the point of disappearance, for no other reason than that men generally stopped thinking in those terms. The persistence of our unstable and iniquitous economic system is not due to the power of accumulated capital, the force of propaganda, or to any force or combination of forces commonly alleged as its cause. It is due solely to a certain set of terms in which men think of the opportunity to work; they regard this opportunity as something to be given. Nowhere is there any other idea about it than that the opportunity to apply labour and capital to natural resources for the production of wealth is not in any sense a right, but a concession.1 This is all that keeps our system alive. When men cease to think in those terms, the system will disappear, and not before.

It seems pretty clear that changes in the terms of thought affecting an institution are but little advanced by direct means. They are brought about in obscure and circuitous ways, and assisted by trains of circumstance which before the fact would appear quite unrelated, and their erosive or solvent action is therefore quite unpredictable. A direct drive at effecting these changes comes as a rule to nothing, or more often than not turns out to be retarding. They are so largely the work of those unimpassioned and imperturbable agencies for which Prince de Bismarck had such vast respect — he called them the imponderabilia — that any effort which disregards them, or thrusts them violently aside, will in the long run find them stepping in to abort its fruit.

Thus it is that what we are attempting to do in this rapid survey of the historical progress of certain ideas, is to trace the genesis of an attitude of mind, a set of terms in which now practically everyone thinks of the State; and then to consider the conclusions towards which this psychical phenomenon unmistakably points. Instead of recognizing the State as "the common enemy of all well-disposed, industrious and decent men," the run of mankind, with rare exceptions, regards it not only as a final and indispensable entity, but also as, in the main, beneficent. The mass-man, ignorant of its history, regards its character and intentions as social rather than antisocial; and in that faith he is willing to put at its disposal an indefinite credit of knavery, mendacity and chicane, upon which its administrators may draw at will. Instead of looking upon the State's progressive absorption of social power with the repugnance and resentment that he would naturally feel towards the activities of a professional criminal organization, he tends rather to encourage and glorify it, in the belief that he is somehow identified with the State, and that therefore, in consenting to its indefinite aggrandizement [elaboration], he consents to something in which he has a share — he is, *pro tanto* [for much], aggrandizing himself. Professor Ortega y Gasset analyzes this state of mind extremely well. The mass-man, he says, confronting the phenomenon of the State, "sees it, admires it, knows that there it is.... Furthermore, the mass-man sees in the State an anonymous power, and feeling himself, like it, anonymous, he believes that the State is something of his own. Suppose that in the public life of a country some difficulty, conflict, or problem, presents itself, the mass-man will tend to demand that the State intervene immediately and undertake a solution directly with its immense and unassailable resources... When the mass suffers any ill fortune, or simply feels some strong appetite, its great temptation is that permanent sure possibility of obtaining everything, without effort, struggle, doubt, or risk, merely by touching a button and setting the mighty machine in motion."

It is the genesis of this attitude, this state of mind, and the conclusions which inexorably follow from its predominance, that we are attempting to get at through our present survey. These conclusions may perhaps be briefly forecast here, in order that the reader who is for any reason indisposed to entertain them may take warning of them at this point, and close the book.

The unquestioning, determined, even truculent maintenance of the attitude which Professor Ortega y Gasset so admirably describes, is obviously the life and strength of the State; and obviously too, it is now so inveterate and so widespread — one may freely call it universal — that no direct effort could overcome its inveteracy or modify it, and least of all hope to enlighten it. This attitude can only be sapped and mined by uncountable generations of experience, in a course marked by recurrent calamity of a most appalling character. When once the predominance of this attitude in any given civilization has become inveterate, as so plainly it has become in the civilization of America, all that can be done is to leave it to work its own way out to its appointed end. The philosophic historian may content himself with pointing out and clearly elucidating its consequences, as Professor Ortega y Gasset has done, aware that after this there is no more that one can do. "The result of this tendency," he says, "will be fatal. Spontaneous social action will be broken up over and over again by State intervention; no new seed will be able to fructify.2 Society will have to live for the State, man for the governmental machine. And as after all it is only a machine, whose existence and maintenance depend on the vital supports around it,3 the State, after sucking out the very marrow of society, will be left bloodless, a skeleton, dead with that rusty death of machinery, more gruesome than the death of a living organism. Such was the lamentable fate of ancient civilization."

1 Consider, for example, the present situation. Our natural resources, while much depleted, are still great; our population is very thin, running something like twenty or twenty-five to the square mile; and some millions of this population are at the moment "unemployed," and likely to remain so because no one will or can "give them work." The point is not that men generally submit to this state of things, or that they accept it as inevitable, but that they see nothing irregular or anomalous about it because of their fixed idea that work is something to

be given.

2 The present paralysis of production, for example, is due solely to State intervention, and uncertainty concerning further intervention.

3 It seems to be very imperfectly understood that the cost of State intervention must be paid out of production, this being the only source from which any payment for anything can be derived. Intervention retards production; then the resulting stringency and inconvenience enable further intervention, which in turn still further retards production; and this process goes on until, as in Rome, in the third century, production ceases entirely, and the source of payment dries up.

II

The revolution of 1776-1781 converted thirteen provinces, practically as they stood, into thirteen autonomous political units, completely independent, and they so continued until 1789 formally held together, as a sort of league, by the Articles of Confederation. For our purposes, the point to be remarked about this eight year period, 1781-1789, is that administration of the political means was not centralized in the federation, but in the several units of which the federation was composed. The federal assembly, or congress, was hardly more than a deliberative body of delegates appointed by the autonomous units. It had no taxing power, and no coercive power. It could not command funds for any enterprise common to the federation, even for war; all it could do was to apportion the sum needed, in the hope that each unit would meet its quota. There was no coercive federal authority over these matters, or over any matters; the sovereignty of each of the thirteen federated units was complete.

Thus the central body of this loose association of sovereignties had nothing to say about the distribution of the political means. This authority was vested in the several component units. Each unit had absolute jurisdiction over its territorial basis, and could partition it as it saw fit, and could maintain any system of land-tenure that it chose to establish.4 Each unit set up its own trade regulations. Each unit levied its own tariffs, one against another, in behalf of its own chosen beneficiaries. Each manufactured its own currency, and might manipulate it as it liked, for the benefit of such individuals or economic groups as were able to get effective access to the local legislature. Each managed its own system of bounties, concessions, subsidies, franchises, and exercised it with a view to whatever private interest its legislature might be influenced to promote. In short, the whole mechanism of the political means was non-national. The federation was not in any sense a State; the State was not one, but thirteen.

Within each unit, therefore, as soon as the war was over, there began at once a general scramble for access to the political means. It must never be forgotten that in each unit society was fluid; this access was available to anyone gifted with the peculiar sagacity and resolution necessary to get at it. Hence one economic interest after another brought pressure of influence to bear on the local legislatures, until the economic hand of every unit was against every other, and the hand of every other was against itself. The principle of "protection," which as we have seen was already well understood, was carried to lengths precisely compatible with those to which it is carried in international commerce today, and for precisely the same primary purpose — the exploitation, or in plain terms the robbery, of the domestic consumer. Mr. Beard remarks that the legislature of New York, for example, pressed the principle which governs tariff-making to the point of levying duties on firewood brought in from Connecticut and on cabbages from New Jersey — a fairly close parallel with the octroi [tax] that one still encounters at the gates of French towns.

The primary monopoly, fundamental to all others — the monopoly of economic rent — was sought with redoubled eagerness.5 The territorial basis of each unit now included the vast holdings confiscated from British owners, and the bar erected by the British State's proclamation of 1763 against the appropriation of Western lands was now removed. Professor Sakolski observes dryly that "the early landlust which the colonists inherited from their European forebears was not diminished by the democratic spirit of the revolutionary fathers." Indeed not! Land grants were sought as assiduously from local legislatures as they had been in earlier days from the Stuart dynasty and from colonial governors, and the mania of land-jobbing ran apace with the mania of land-grabbing.6 Among the men most actively interested in these pursuits were those whom we have already seen identified with them in pre-revolutionary days, such as the two Morrises, Knox, Pickering, James Wilson and Patrick Henry; and with their names appear those of Duer, Bingham, McKean, Willing, Greenleaf, Nicholson, Aaron Burr, Low, Macomb, Wadsworth, Remsen, Constable, Pierrepotit, and others which now are less well remembered.

There is probably no need to follow out the rather repulsive trail of effort after other modes of the political means. What we have said about the foregoing two modes — tariffs and rental-value monopoly — is doubtless enough to illustrate satisfactorily the spirit and attitude of mind towards the State during the eight years immediately following the revolution. The whole story of insensate scuffle for State-created economic advantage is not especially animating, nor is it essential to our purposes. Such as it is, it may be read in detail elsewhere. All that interests us is to observe that during the eight years of federation, the principles of government set forth by Paine and by the Declaration continued in utter abeyance. Not only did the philosophy of natural rights and popular sovereignty7 remain as completely out of consideration as when Mr. Jefferson first lamented its disappearance, but the idea of government as a social institution based on this philosophy was likewise unconsidered. No one thought of a political organization as instituted "to secure these rights" by processes of purely negative intervention-instituted, that is, with no other end in view than the maintenance of "freedom and security." The history of the eight-year period of federation shows no trace whatever of any idea of political organization other than the State-idea. No one regarded this organization otherwise than as the organization of the political means, an all powerful engine which should stand permanently ready and available for the irresistible promotion of this-or-that set of economic interests, and the irremediable disservice of others; according as whichever set, by whatever course of strategy, might succeed in obtaining command of its machinery.

4 As a matter of fact, all thirteen units merely continued the system that had existed throughout the colonial period — the system which gave the beneficiary a monopoly of rental-values as well as a monopoly of use-values. No other system was ever known in America, except in the short-lived state of Deseret, under the Mormon polity.

5 For a brilliant summary of post-revolutionary land-speculation, cf. Sakolski, op. cit., ch. II.

6 Mr. Sakolski very justly remarks that the mania for land-jobbing was stimulated by the action of the new units in offering lands by way of settlement of their public debts, which led to extensive gambling in the various issues of "land-warrants." The list of eminent names involved in this enterprise includes Wilson C. Nicholas, who later became governor of Vir-

ginia; "Light Horse Harry" Lee, father of the great Confederate Commander; General John Preston, of Smithfield; and George Taylor, brother-in-law of Chief Justice Marshall. Lee, Preston and Nicholas were prosecuted at the instance of some Connecticut speculators, for a transaction alleged as fraudulent; Lee was arrested in Boston, on the eve of embarking for the West Indies. They had deeded a tract, said to be of 300,000 acres, at ten cents an acre, but on being surveyed, the tract did not come to half that size. Frauds of this order were extremely common.

7 The new political units continued the colonial practice of restricting the suffrage to taxpayers and owners of property, and none but men of considerable wealth were eligible to public office. Thus, the exercise of sovereignty was a matter of economic right, not natural right.

III

It may be repeated that while State power was well centralized under the federation, it was not centralized in the federation, but in the federated unit. For various reasons, some of them plausible, many leading citizens, especially in the more northerly units, found this distribution of power unsatisfactory; and a considerable compact group of economic interests which stood to profit by a redistribution naturally made the most of these reasons. It is quite certain that dissatisfaction with the existing arrangement was not general, for when the redistribution took place in 1789, it was effected with great difficulty and only through a *coup d'Etat*, organized by methods which, if employed in any other field than that of politics, would be put down at once as not only daring, but unscrupulous and dishonourable.

The situation, in a word, was that American economic interests had fallen into two grand divisions, the special interests in each having made common cause with a view to capturing control of the political means. One division comprised the speculating, industrial-commercial and creditor interests, with their natural allies of the bar and bench, the pulpit and the press. The other comprised chiefly the farmers and artisans and the debtor class generally. From the first, these two grand divisions were colliding briskly here and there in the several units, the most serious collision occurring over the terms of the Massachusetts constitution of 1780.8 The State in each of the thirteen units was a class-State, as every State known to history has been; and the work of maneuvering it in its function of enabling the economic exploitation of one class by another went steadily on.

General conditions under the Articles of Confederation were pretty good. The people had made a creditable recovery from the dislocations and disturbances due to the revolution, and there was a very decent prospect that Mr. Jefferson's idea of a political organization which should be national in foreign affairs and non-national in domestic affairs might be found continuously practicable. Some tinkering with the Articles seemed necessary — in fact, it was expected — but nothing that would transform or seriously impair the general scheme. The chief trouble was with the federation's weakness in view of the chance of war, and in respect of debts due to foreign creditors. The Articles, however, carried provision for their own amendment, and for anything one can see, such amendment as the general scheme made necessary was quite feasible. In fact, when suggestions of revision arose, as they did almost immediately, nothing else appears to have been contemplated.

But the general scheme itself was, as a whole, objectionable to the interests grouped in the first grand division. The grounds of their dissatisfaction are obvious enough. When one

SUPPRESSED INTELLIGENCE REPORTS

bears in mind the vast prospect of the continent, one need use but little imagination to perceive that the national scheme was by far the more congenial to those interests, because it enabled an ever-closer centralization of control over the political means. For instance, leaving aside the advantage of having but one central tariff-making body to chaffer [bargain or haggle] with, instead of twelve, any industrialist could see the great primary advantage of being able to extend his exploiting operations over a nationwide free-trade area walled in by a general tariff; the closer the centralization, the larger the exploitable area. Any speculator in rental-values would be quick to see the advantage of bringing this form of opportunity under unified control.9 Any speculator in depreciated public securities would be strongly for a system that could offer him the use of the political means to bring back their face value.10 Any ship owner or foreign trader would be quick to see that his bread was buttered on the side of a national State which, if properly approached, might lend him the use of the political means by way of a subsidy, or would be able to back up some profitable but dubious freebooting [pillaging] enterprise with "diplomatic representations" or with reprisals.

In general, the farmers and the debtor class, on the other hand, were not interested in these considerations, but were strongly for letting things stay, for the most part, as they stood. Preponderance in the local legislatures gave them satisfactory control of the political means, which they could and did use to the prejudice of the creditor class, and they did not care to be disturbed in their preponderance. They were agreeable to such modification of the Articles as should work out short of this, but not to setting up a national11 replica of the British merchant-State, which they perceived was precisely what the classes grouped in the opposing grand division wished to do. These classes aimed at bringing in the British system of economics, politics and judicial control, on a nationwide scale; and the interests grouped in the second division saw that what this would really come to was a shifting of the incidence of economic exploitation upon themselves. They had an impressive object lesson in the immediate shift that took place in Massachusetts after the adoption of John Adams's local constitution of 1780. They naturally did not care to see this sort of thing put into operation on a nationwide scale, and they therefore looked with extreme disfavour upon any bait put forth for amending the Articles out of existence. When Hamilton, in 1780, objected to the Articles in the form in which they were proposed for adoption, and proposed the calling of a constitutional convention instead, they turned the cold shoulder; as they did again to Washington's letter to the local governors three years later, in which he adverted to the need of a strong coercive central authority.

Finally, however, a constitutional convention was assembled, on the distinct understanding that it should do no more than revise the Articles in such a way, as Hamilton cleverly phrased it, as to make them "adequate to the exigencies of the nation," and on the further understanding that all the thirteen units should assent to the amendments before they went into effect; in short, that the method of amendment provided by the Articles themselves should be followed. Neither understanding was fulfilled. The convention was made up wholly of men representing the economic interests of the first division. The great majority of them, possibly as many as four-fifths, were public creditors; one-third were land-speculators; some were moneylenders; one-fifth were industrialists, traders, shippers; and many of them were lawyers. They planned and executed a *coup d'Etat*, simply tossing the Articles of Confederation into the waste basket, and drafting a *constitution de novo* [altered constitution], with the audacious provision that it should go into effect when ratified by nine units instead of by all thirteen. Moreover, with like audacity, they provided that the document should not be submitted either to the

Congress or to the local legislatures, but that it should go direct to a popular vote! 12

The unscrupulous methods employed in securing ratification need not be dwelt on here.13 We are not indeed concerned with the moral quality of any of the proceedings by which the constitution was brought into being, but only with showing their instrumentality in encouraging a definite general idea of the State and its functions, and a consequent general attitude towards the State. We therefore go on to observe that in order to secure ratification by even the nine necessary units, the document had to conform to certain very exacting and difficult requirements. The political structure which it contemplated had to be republican in form, yet capable of resisting what Gerry unctuously [hypocritically] called "the excess of democracy," and what Randolph termed its "turbulence and follies." The task of the delegates was precisely analogous to that of the earlier architects who had designed the structure of the British merchant-State, with its system of economics, politics and judicial control; they had to contrive something that could pass muster as showing a good semblance of popular sovereignty, without the reality. Madison defined their task explicitly in saying that the convention's purpose was "to secure the public good and private rights against the danger of such a faction [i.e., a democratic faction], and at the same time preserve the spirit and form of popular government."

Under the circumstances, this was a tremendously large order; and the constitution emerged, as it was bound to do, as a compromise document, or as Mr. Beard puts it very precisely, "a mosaic of second choices," which really satisfied neither of the two opposing sets of interests. It was not strong and definite enough in either direction to please anybody. In particular, the interests composing the first division, led by Alexander Hamilton, saw that it was not sufficient of itself to fix them in anything like a permanent impregnable position to exploit continuously the groups composing the second division. To do this — to establish the degree of centralization requisite to their purposes — certain lines of administrative management must be laid down, which, once established, would be permanent. Therefore, the further task, in Madison's phrase, was to "administration" the constitution into such absolutist modes as would secure economic supremacy, by a free use of the political means, to the groups which made up the first division.

This was accordingly done. For the first ten years of its existence, the constitution remained in the hands of its makers for administration in directions most favourable to their interests. For an accurate understanding of the newly-erected system's economic tendencies, too much stress can not be laid on the fact that for these ten critical years "the machinery of economic and political power was mainly directed by the men who had conceived and established it."14 Washington, who had been chairman of the convention, was elected President. Nearly half the Senate was made up of men who had been delegates, and the House of Representatives was largely made up of men who had to do with the drafting or ratifying of the constitution. Hamilton, Randolph and Knox, who were active in promoting the document, filled three of the four positions in the Cabinet; and all the federal judgeships, without a single exception, were filled by men who had a hand in the business of drafting or of ratification, or both.

Of all the legislative measures enacted to implement the new constitution, the one best calculated to ensure a rapid and steady progress in the centralization of political power was the Judiciary Act of 1789.15 This measure created a federal supreme court of six members (subsequently enlarged to nine), and a federal district court in each state, with its own complete personnel, and a complete apparatus for enforcing its decrees. The Act established federal oversight of state legislation by the familiar device of "interpretation," whereby the Supreme Court might nullify state legislative or judicial action which, for any reason it saw fit, to regard as unconstitutional. One feature of the Act, which for our purposes is most noteworthy, is that it made the tenure of all these federal judgeships appointive, not elective, and for life; thus marking almost the farthest conceivable departure from the doctrine of popular sovereignty.

The first chief justice was John Jay, "the learned and gentle Jay," as Beveridge calls him in his excellent biography of Marshall. A man of superb integrity, he was far above doing anything whatever in behalf of the accepted principle that *est boni judicis ampliare jurisdictionem*. Ellsworth, who followed him, also did nothing. The succession, however, after Jay had declined a reappointment, then fell to John Marshall, who, in addition to the control established by the Judiciary Act over the state legislative and judicial authority, arbitrarily extended judicial control over both the legislative and executive branches of the federal authority;16 thus effecting as complete and convenient a centralization of power as the various interests concerned in framing the constitution could reasonably have contemplated.17

We may now see from this necessarily brief survey, which anyone may amplify and particularize at his pleasure, what the circumstances were which rooted a certain definite idea of the State still deeper in the general consciousness. That idea was precisely the same in the constitutional period as that which we have seen prevailing in the two periods already examined — the colonial period, and the eight year period following the revolution. Nowhere in the history of the constitutional period do we find the faintest suggestion of the Declaration's doctrine of natural rights; and we find its doctrine of popular sovereignty not only continuing in abeyance, but constitutionally estopped from ever reappearing. Nowhere do we find a trace of the Declaration's theory of government; on the contrary, we find it expressly repudiated. The new political mechanism was a faithful replica of the old disestablished British model, but so far improved and strengthened as to be incomparably more close-working and efficient, and hence presenting incomparably more attractive possibilities of capture and control. Therefore, by consequence, we find more firmly implanted than ever the same general idea of the State that we have observed as prevailing hitherto — the idea of an organization of the political means, an irresponsible and all-powerful agency standing always ready to be put into use for the service of one set of economic interests as against another.

8 This was the uprising known as Shays's Rebellion, which took place in 1786. The creditor division in Massachusetts had gained control of the political means, and had fortified its control by establishing a constitution which was made to bear so hardly on the agrarian and debtor division that an armed insurrection broke out six years later, led by Daniel Shays, for the purpose of annulling its onerous provisions, and transferring control of the political means to the latter group. This incident affords a striking view in miniature of the State's nature and teleology. The rebellion had a great effect in consolidating the creditor division and giving plausibility to its contention for the establishment of a strong coercive national State. Mr. Jefferson spoke contemptuously of this contention, as "the interested clamours and sophistry of speculating, shaving and banking institutions"; and of the rebellion itself he observed to Mrs. John Adams, whose husband had most to do with drafting the Massachusetts constitution, "I like a little rebellion now and then... The spirit of resistance to government is so valuable that I wish it to be always kept alive. It will often be exercised when wrong, but better so than

not to be exercised at all." Writing to another correspondent at the same time, he said earnestly, "God forbid we should ever be twenty years without such a rebellion." *Obiter dicta* of this nature, scattered here and there in Mr. Jefferson's writings, have the interest of showing how near his instinct led him towards a clear understanding of the State's character.

9 Professor Sakolski observes that after the Articles of Confederation were supplanted by the constitution, schemes of land-speculation "multiplied with renewed and intensified energy." Naturally so, for as he says, the new scheme of a national State got strong support from this class of adventurers because they foresaw that rental-values "must be greatly increased by an efficient federal government."

10 More than half the delegates to the constitutional convention of 1787 were either investors or speculators in the public funds. Probably sixty per cent of the values represented by these securities were fictitious, and were so regarded even by their holders.

11 It may be observed that at this time the word "national" was a term of obloquy, carrying somewhat the same implications that the word "fascist" carries in some quarters today. Nothing is more interesting than the history of political terms in their relation to the shifting balance of economic advantage — except, perhaps, the history of the partisan movements which they designate, viewed in the same relation.

12 The obvious reason for this, as the event showed, was that the interests grouped in the first division had the advantage of being relatively compact and easily mobilized. Those in the second division, being chiefly agrarian, were loose and sprawling, communications among them were slow, and mobilization difficult.

13 They have been noticed by several recent authorities, and are exhibited fully in Mr. Beard's monumental Economic Interpretation of the Constitution of the United States.

14 Beard, op. cit., p. 337.

15 The principal measures bearing directly on the distribution of the political means were those drafted by Hamilton for funding and assumption, for a protective tariff, and for a national bank. These gave practically exclusive use of the political means to the classes grouped in the first grand division, the only modes left available to others being patents and copyrights. Mr. Beard discusses these measures with his invariable lucidity and thoroughness, op. cit., Ch. VIII. Some observations on them, which are perhaps worth reading, are contained in my own book, Jefferson, ch. V.

16 The authority of the Supreme Court was disregarded by Jackson, and overruled by Lincoln, thus converting the mode of the State temporarily from an oligarchy into an autocracy. It is interesting to observe that just such a contingency was foreseen by the framers of the constitution, in particular by Hamilton. They were apparently well aware of the ease with which, in any period of crisis, a quasi-republican mode of the State slips off into executive tyranny. Oddly enough, at one time Mr. Jefferson considered nullifying the Alien and Sedition Acts by executive action, but did not do so. Lincoln overruled the opinion of Chief Justice Taney that suspension of the habeas corpus was unconstitutional, and in consequence the mode of the State was, until 1865, a monocratic military despotism. In fact, from the date of his proclamation of blockade, Lincoln ruled unconstitutionally throughout his term. The doctrine of "reserved powers" was knaved up *ex post facto* as a justification of his acts, but as far as the intent of the constitution is concerned, it was obviously a pure invention. In fact, a very good

case could be made out for the assertion that Lincoln's acts resulted in a permanent radical change in the entire system of constitutional "interpretation" — that since his time, "interpretations" have not been interpretations of the constitution but merely of public policy; or, as our most acute and profound social critic put it, "the Supreme Court follows the election returns." A strict constitutionalist might indeed say that the constitution died in 1861, and one would have to scratch one's head pretty diligently to refute him.

17 Marshall was appointed by John Adams at the end of his Presidential term when the interests grouped in the first division were becoming very anxious about the opposition developing against them among the exploited interests. A letter written by Oliver Wolcott to Fisher Ames gives a good idea of where the doctrine of popular sovereignty stood; his reference to military measures is particularly striking. He says, "The steady men in Congress will attempt to extend the judicial department, and I hope that their measures will be very decided. It is impossible in this country to render an army an engine of government; and there is no way to combat the state opposition but by an efficient and extended organization of judges, magistrates, and other civil officers." Marshall's appointment followed, and also the creation of twenty-three new federal judgeships. Marshall's cardinal decisions were made in the cases of Marbury, of Fletcher, of McCulloch, of Dartmouth College, and of Cohens. It is perhaps not generally understood that, as the result of Marshall's efforts, the Supreme Court became not only the highest law-interpreting body, but the highest lawmaking body as well; the precedents established by its decisions have the force of constitutional law. Therefore, since 1800, the actual mode of the State in America is normally that of a small and irresponsible oligarchy! In 1821, Mr. Jefferson, regarding Marshall quite justly as "a crafty chief judge who sophisticates the law to his mind by the turn of his own reasoning," made the very remarkable prophecy that "our government is now taking so steady a course as to show by what road it will pass to destruction, to wit: by consolidation first, and then corruption, its necessary consequence. The engine of consolidation will be the federal judiciary; the other two branches the corrupting and corrupted instruments." Another prophetic comment on the effect of centralization was his remark that "when we must wait for Washington to tell us when to sow and when to reap, we shall soon want bread." A survey of our present political circumstances makes comment on these prophecies superfluous.

IV

Out of this idea proceeded what we know as the "party system" of political management, which has been in effect ever since. Our purposes do not require that we examine its history in close detail for evidence that it has been from the beginning a purely bipartisan system, since this is now a matter of fairly common acceptance. In his second term Mr. Jefferson discovered the tendency towards bipartisanship,18 and was both dismayed and puzzled by it. I have elsewhere19 remarked his curious inability to understand how the cohesive power of public plunder works straight towards political bipartisanship. In 1823, finding some who called themselves Republicans favouring the Federalist policy of centralization, he spoke of them in a rather bewildered way as "pseudo-Republicans, but real Federalists." But most naturally any Republican who saw a chance of profiting by the political means would retain the name, and at the same time resist any tendency within the party to impair the general system which held out such a prospect.20 In this way bipartisanship arises. Party designations become purely nominal, and the stated issues between parties become progressively trivial; and both are more and more openly kept up with no other object than to cover from scrutiny the essential identity of purpose in both parties.

Thus the party system at once became in effect an elaborate system of fetishes, which, in order to be made as impressive as possible, were chiefly molded up around the constitution, and were put on show as "constitutional principles." The history of the whole post-constitutional period, from 1789 to the present day, is an instructive and cynical exhibit of the fate of these fetishes when they encounter the one only actual principle of party action — the principle of keeping open the channels of access to the political means. When the fetish of "strict construction," for example, has collided with this principle, it has invariably gone by the board, the party that maintained it simply changing sides. The anti-Federalist party took office in 1800 as the party of strict construction; yet, once in office, it played ducks and drakes with the constitution, in behalf of the special economic interests that it represented.21 The Federalists were nominally for loose construction, yet they fought bitterly every one of the opposing party's loose constructionist measures — the embargo, the protective tariff and the national bank. They were constitutional nationalists of the deepest dye, as we have seen; yet in their centre and stronghold, New England, they held the threat of secession over the country throughout the period of what they harshly called "Mr. Madison's war," the War of 1812, which was in fact a purely imperialistic adventure after annexation of Floridian and Canadian territory, in behalf of stiffening agrarian control of the political means; but when the planting interests of the South made the same threat in 1861, they became fervid nationalists again.

Such exhibitions of pure fetishism, always cynical in their transparent candour, make up the history of the party system. Their *reductio ad absurdum* is now seen as perhaps complete — one can not see how it could go further — in the attitude of the Democratic party towards its historical principles of state sovereignty and strict construction. A fair match for this, however, is found in a speech made the other day to a group of exporting and importing interests by the mayor of New York — always known as a Republican in politics — advocating the hoary Democratic doctrine of a low tariff!

Throughout our post-constitutional period there is not on record, as far as I know, a single instance of party adherence to a fixed principle, *qua* [with the character of] principle, or to a political theory, *qua* theory. Indeed, the very cartoons on the subject show how widely it has come to be accepted that party platforms, with their cant of "issues" are so much sheer quackery, and that campaign promises are merely another name for thimblerigging [a shell game]. The workaday practice of politics has been invariably opportunist, or in other words, invariably conformable to the primary function of the State; and it is largely for this reason that the State's service exerts its most powerful attraction upon an extremely low and sharpset type of individual.22

However, the maintenance of this system of fetishes gives great enhancement to the prevailing general view of the State. In that view, the State is made to appear as somehow deeply and disinterestedly concerned with great principles of action; and hence, in addition to its prestige as a pseudo-social institution, it takes on the prestige of a kind of moral authority, thus disposing of the last vestige of the doctrine of natural rights by overspreading it heavily with the quicklime [caustic substance] of legalism; whatever is State-sanctioned is right. This double prestige is assiduously [unceasingly] inflated by many agencies; by a State-controlled system of education, by a State-dazzled pulpit, by a meretricious [harlot] press, by a continuous kaleidoscopic display of State pomp, panoply [impressive ceremonial display] and circumstance, and by all the innumerable devices of electioneering. These last invariably take their stand on the foundation of some imposing principle, as witness the agonized cry now going up here and there in the land, for a "return to the constitution." All this is simply "the interested clamours and sophistry," which means no more and no less than it meant when the constitution was not yet five years old, and Fisher Ames was observing contemptuously that of all the legislative measures and proposals which were on the carpet at the time, he scarce knew one that had not raised this same cry, "not excepting a motion for adjournment."

In fact, such popular terms of electioneering appeal are uniformly and notoriously what Jeremy Bentham called impostor-terms, and their use invariably marks one thing and one only; it marks a state of apprehension, either fearful or expectant, as the case may be, concerning access to the political means. As we are seeing at the moment, once let this access come under threat of straitening or stoppage, the menaced interests immediately trot out the spavined [deteriorated], glandered hobby of "state rights" or "a return to the constitution," and put it through its galvanic movements. Let the incidence of exploitation show the first sign of shifting, and we hear at once from one source of "interested clamours and sophistry [fallacy]" that "democracy" is in danger, and that the unparalleled excellences of our civilization have come about solely through a policy of "rugged individualism," carried out under terms of "free competition;" while from another source we hear that the enormities of *laissez faire* have ground the faces of the poor, and obstructed entrance into the More Abundant Life.23

The general upshot of all this is that we see politicians of all schools and stripes behaving with the obscene depravity of degenerate children; like the loose-footed gangs that infest the railway yards and purlieus of gas houses, each group tries to circumvent another with respect to the fruit accruing to acts of public mischief. In other words, we see them behaving in a strictly historical manner. Professor Laski's elaborate moral distinction between the State and officialdom is devoid of foundation. The State is not, as he would have it, a social institution administered in an antisocial way. It is an antisocial institution, administered in the only way an antisocial institution can be administered, and by the kind of person who, in the nature of things, is best adapted to such service.

18 He had observed it in the British State some years before, and spoke of it with vivacity. "The nest of office being too small for all of them to cuddle into at once, the contest is eternal which shall crowd the other out. For this purpose they are divided into two parties, the Ins and the Outs." Why he could not see that the same thing was bound to take place in the American State, as an effect of causes identical with those which brought it about in the British State, is a puzzle to students. Apparently, however, he did not see it, notwithstanding the sound instinct that made him suspect parties, and always kept him free from party alliances. As he wrote Hopkinson in 1789, "I never submitted the whole system of my opinions to the creed of any party of men whatever, in religion, in philosophy, in politics, or in anything else where I was capable of thinking for myself. Such an addiction is the last degradation of a free and moral agent. If I could not go to heaven but with a party, I would not go there at all."

19 Jefferson, p. 274. The agrarian-artisan-debtor economic group that elected Mr. Jefferson took title as the Republican party (subsequently renamed Democratic) and the opposing group called itself by the old pre-constitutional title of Federalist.

20 An example, noteworthy only because uncommonly conspicuous, is seen in the behaviour of the Democratic senators in the matter of the tariff on sugar, in Cleveland's second administration. Ever since that incident, one of the Washington newspapers has used the name

"Senator Sorghum" in its humorous paragraphs, to designate the typical venal jobholder.

21 Mr. Jefferson was the first to acknowledge that his purchase of the Louisiana territory was unconstitutional; but it added millions of acres to the sum of agrarian resource, and added an immense amount of prospective voting strength to agrarian control of the political means, as against control by the financial and commercial interests represented by the Federalist party. Mr. Jefferson justified himself solely on the ground of public policy, an interesting anticipation of Lincoln's self-justification in 1861 for confronting Congress and the country with a like *fait accompli* — with Lincoln, however, executed in behalf of financial and commercial interests as against the agrarian interest.

22 Henry George made some very keen comment upon the almost incredible degradation that he saw taking place progressively in the personnel of the State's service. It is perhaps most conspicuous in the Presidency and the Senate, though it goes on *pari passu* [as joined pairs] elsewhere and throughout. As for the federal House of Representatives and the state legislative bodies, they must be seen to be believed.

23 Of all the impostor-terms in our political glossary, these are perhaps the most flagrantly impudent, and their employment perhaps the most flagitious. We have already seen that nothing remotely resembling democracy has ever existed here; nor yet has anything resembling free competition, for the existence of free competition is obviously incompatible with any exercise of the political means, even the feeblest. For the same reason, no policy of rugged individualism has ever existed; the most that rugged individualism has done to distinguish itself has been by way of running to the State for some form of economic advantage. If the reader has any curiosity about this, let him look up the number of American business enterprises that have made a success unaided by the political means, or the number of fortunes accumulated without such aid. *Laissez faire* has become a term of pure opprobrium; those who use it either do not know what it means, or else willfully pervert it. As for the unparalleled excellences of our civilization, it is perhaps enough to say that the statistics of our insurance companies now show that four-fifths of our people who have reached the age of sixty-five are supported by their relatives or by some other form of charity.

CHAPTER SIX

I

Such has been the course of our experience from the beginning, and such are the terms in which its stark uniformity has led us to think of the State. This uniformity also goes far to account for the development of a peculiar moral enervation [weakness] with regard to the State, exactly parallel to that which prevailed with regard to the Church in the Middle Ages.1 The Church controlled the distribution of certain privileges and immunities, and if one approached it properly, one might get the benefit of them. It stood as something to be run to in any kind of emergency, temporal or spiritual; for the satisfaction of ambition and cupidity, as well as for the more tenuous assurances it held out against various forms of fear, doubt and sorrow. As long as this was so, the anomalies presented by its self-aggrandizement were more or less contentedly acquiesced in; and thus a chronic moral enervation, too negative to be called broadly cynical, was developed towards its interventions and exactions, and towards the vast overbuilding of its material structure.2

A like enervation pervades our society with respect to the State, and for like reasons. It affects especially those who take the State's pretensions at face value and regard it as a social institution whose policies of continuous intervention are wholesome and necessary; and it also affects the great majority who have no clear idea of the State, but merely accept it as something that exists, and never think about it except when some intervention bears unfavourably upon their interests. There is little need to dwell upon the amount of aid thus given to the State's progress in self-aggrandizement, or to show in detail or by illustration the courses by which this spiritlessness promotes the State's steady policy of intervention, exaction and overbuilding."3

Every intervention by the State enables another, and this in turn enabling yet another, and so on indefinitely; and the State stands ever ready and eager to make them, often on its own motion, often again wangling plausibility [obtaining credibility] for them through the specious [false] suggestion of interested persons. Sometimes, the matter at issue is in its nature simple, socially necessary, and devoid of any character that would bring it into the purview of politics.4 However, for convenience, complications are erected on it; then presently someone sees that these complications are exploitable, and proceeds to exploit them; then another, and another, until the rivalries and collisions of interest thus generated issue in a more or less general disorder. When this takes place, the logical thing, obviously, is to recede, and let the disorder be settled in the slower and more troublesome way, but the only effective way, through the operation of natural laws.

But in such circumstances, recession is never for a moment thought of; the suggestion would be put down as sheer lunacy. Instead, the interests unfavourably affected — little aware, perhaps, how much worse the cure is than the disease, or at any rate, little caring — immediately call on the State to cut in arbitrarily between cause and effect, and clear up the disorder out of hand.5 The State then intervenes by imposing another set of complications upon the first; these in turn are found exploitable, another demand arises, another set of complications, still more intricate, is erected upon the first two;6 and the same sequence is gone through again and again until the recurrent disorder becomes acute enough to open the way for a sharking political adventurer to come forward and, always alleging "necessity, the tyrant's plea," to organize a *coup d'Etat* [rebellion].7

But more often, the basic matter at issue represents an original intervention of the State, an original allotment of the political means. Each of these allotments, as we have seen, is a charter of highwaymanry [highway robbery]; a license to appropriate the labour products of others without compensation. Therefore, it is in the nature of things that when such a license is issued, the State must follow it up with an indefinite series of interventions to systematize and "regulate" its use. The State's endless progressive encroachments that are recorded in the history of the tariff, their impudent and disgusting particularity, and the prodigious amount of apparatus necessary to give them effect, furnish a conspicuous case in point. Another is furnished by the history of our railway regulation. It is nowadays the fashion, even among those who ought to know better, to hold "rugged individualism" and *laissez faire* [liberal tolerance] responsible for the riot of stock watering, rebates, rate-cutting, fraudulent bankruptcies, and the like, which prevailed in our railway practice after the Civil War, but they had no more to do with it than they have to do with the precession of the equinoxes. The fact is that our railways, with few exceptions, did not grow up in response to any actual economic demand. They were speculative enterprises enabled by State intervention, by allotment of the political means in the form of land grants and subsidies; and of all the evils alleged against our railway practice, there is not one but what is directly traceable to this primary intervention.8

So it is with shipping. There was no valid economic demand for adventure in the carrying trade; in fact, every sound economic consideration was dead against it. It was entered upon through State intervention, instigated by shipbuilders and their allied interests; and the mess engendered [brought about] by their manipulation of the political means is now the ground of demand for further and further coercive intervention. So it is with what, by an unconscionable stretch of language, goes by the name of farming.9 There are very few troubles so far heard of as normally besetting this form of enterprise but what are directly traceable to the State's primary intervention in establishing a system of land-tenure which gives a monopoly-right over rental-values as well as over use-values; and as long as that system is in force, one coercive intervention after another is bound to take place in support of it.10

1 Not long ago, Professor Laski commented on the prevalence of this enervation among our young people, especially among our student population. It has several contributing causes, but it is mainly to be accounted for, I think, by the unvarying uniformity of our experience. The State's pretensions have been so invariably extravagant, the disparity between them and its conduct so invariably manifest, that one could hardly expect anything else. Probably, the protest against our imperialism in the Pacific and the Caribbean, after the Spanish War, marked the last major effort of an impotent and moribund decency. Mr. Laski's comparisons with student bodies in England and Europe lose some of their force when it is remembered that the devices of a fixed term and an irresponsible executive render the American State peculiarly insensitive to protest and inaccessible to effective censure. As Mr. Jefferson said, the one resource of impeachment is "not even a scarecrow."

2 As an example of this overbuilding, at the beginning of the sixteenth century one-fifth of the land of France was owned by the Church; it was held mainly by monastic establishments.

3 It may be observed, however, that mere use and wont interferes with our seeing how egregiously (conspicuously bad or offensive) the original structure of the American State, with its system of superimposed jurisdictions and reduplicated functions, was overbuilt. At the present time, a citizen lives under half a dozen or more separate overlapping jurisdictions; federal, state, county, township, municipal, borough, school district, ward, federal district. Nearly all of these have power to tax him directly or indirectly, or both, and as we all know, the only limit to the exercise of this power is what can be safely got by it; and thus we arrive at the principle rather naively formulated by the late senator from Utah, and sometimes spoken of ironically as "Smoot's law of government" — the principle, as he put it, that the cost of government tends to increase from year to year, no matter which party is in power. It would be interesting to know the exact distribution of the burden of jobholders and mendicant [misleading] political retainers — for it must not be forgotten that the subsidized "unemployed" are now a permanent body of patronage — among income receiving citizens. Counting indirect taxes and voluntary contributions as well as direct taxes, it would probably be not far off the mark to say that every two citizens are carrying a third between them.

4 For example, the basic processes of exchange are necessary, nonpolitical, and as simple as any in the world. The humblest Yankee rustic who swaps eggs for bacon in the country store, or a day's labour for potatoes in a neighbour's field, understands them thoroughly, and manages them competently. Their formula is: goods or services in return for goods or

services. There is not, never has been, and never will be, a single transaction anywhere in the realm of "business" — no matter what its magnitude or apparent complexity — that is not directly reducible to this formula. For convenience in facilitating exchange, however, money was introduced; and money is a complication, and so are the other evidences of debt, such as cheques, drafts, notes, bills, bonds, stock — certificates, which were introduced for the same reason. These complications were found to be exploitable; and the consequent number and range of State interventions to "regulate" and "supervise" their exploitation appear to be without end.

5 It is one of the most extraordinary things in the world, that the interests which abhor and dread collectivism [communism] are the ones which have most eagerly urged on the State to take each one of the successive single steps that lead directly to collectivism. Who urged it on to form the Federal Trade Commission; to expand the Department of Commerce; to form the Interstate Commerce Commission and the Federal Farm Board; to pass the Anti-trust Acts; to build highways, dig out waterways, provide airway services, subsidize shipping? If these steps do not tend straight to collectivism, just which way do they tend? Furthermore, when the interests which encouraged the State to take them are horrified by the apparition of communism and the "Red menace," just what are their protestations worth?

6 The text of the Senate's proposed banking law, published on the first of July, 1935, almost exactly filled four pages of the Wall Street Journal! Really now - now really — can any conceivable absurdity surpass that?

7 As here in 1932, in Italy, Germany and Russia latterly, in France after the collapse of the Directory, in Rome after the death of Pertinax, and so on.

8 Ignorance has no assignable limits; yet when one hears our railway companies cited as specimens of rugged individualism, one is put to it to say whether the speaker's sanity should be questioned, or his integrity. Our transcontinental companies, in particular, are hardly to be called railway companies, since transportation was purely incidental to their true business, which was that of land-jobbing and subsidy-hunting. I remember seeing the statement a few years ago — I do not vouch for it, but it can not be far off the fact — that at the time of writing, the current cash value of the political means allotted to the Northern Pacific Company would enable it to build four transcontinental lines, and in addition, to build a fleet of ships and maintain it in around-the-world service. If this sort of thing represents rugged individualism, let future lexicographers make the most of it.

9 A farmer, properly speaking, is a freeholder who directs his operations; first, towards making his family, as far as possible, an independent unit, economically self-contained. What he produces over and above this requirement he converts into a cash crop. There is a second type of agriculturist, who is not a farmer, but a manufacturer, as much so as one who makes woolen or cotton textiles or leather shoes. He raises one crop only — milk, corn, wheat, cotton, or whatever it may be — which is wholly a cash crop; and if the market for his particular commodity goes down below cost of production, he is in the same bad luck as the motorcar maker or shoemaker or pantsmaker who turns out more of his special kind of goods than the market will bear. His family is not independent; he buys everything his household uses; his children can not live on cotton or milk or corn, any more than the shoe manufacturer's children can live on shoes. There is still to be distinguished a third type, who carries on agriculture as a sort of taxpaying subsidiary to speculation in agricultural land-values. It is the last

two classes who chiefly clamour for intervention, and they are often, indeed, in a bad way; but it is not farming that puts them there.

10 The very limit of particularity in this course of coercive intervention seems to have been reached, according to press reports, in the state of Wisconsin. On 31 May [1935], the report is, Governor La Follette signed a bill requiring all public eating places to serve two-thirds of an ounce of Wisconsin-made cheese and two-thirds of an ounce of Wisconsin-made butter with every meal costing more than twenty-four cents. To match this for particularity one would pretty well have to go back to some of the British Trade Acts of the eighteenth century, and it would be hard to find an exact match, even there. If this passes muster under the "due process of law" clause — whether the restaurant pays for these supplies or passes their cost along to the consumer — one can see nothing to prevent the legislature of New York, say, from requiring each citizen to annually buy two hats made by Knox, and two suits made by Finchley.

II

Thus we see how ignorance and delusion, concerning the nature of the State, combine with extreme moral debility [weakness] and myopic [narrow-minded] self-interest — what Ernest Renan so well calls *la bassesse de l'homme interesse* — to enable the steadily acceler-ated conversion of social power into State power that has gone on from the beginning of our political independence. It is a curious anomaly. State power has an unbroken record of inabil-ity to do anything efficiently, economically, disinterestedly or honestly; yet, when the slight-est dissatisfaction arises over any exercise of social power, the aid of the agent *least* qualified to give aid is immediately called for. Does social power mismanage banking practice in this-or-that special instance — then let the State, which never has shown itself able to keep its own finances from sinking promptly into the slough [quagmire] of misfeasance, wastefulness and corruption, intervene to "supervise" or "regulate" the whole body of banking practice, or even take it over entirely. Does social power, in this-or-that case, bungle the business of rail-way management - then let the State, which has bungled every business it has ever under-taken, intervene and put its hand to the business of "regulating" railway operations. Does social power now and then send out an unseaworthy ship to disaster — then let the State, which inspected and passed the Morro Castle [The S.S. Morro Castle caught fire off Asbury Park, New Jersey on September 8, 1934; 125 lives were lost], be given a freer swing at control-ling the routine of the shipping trade. Does social power here and there exercise a grinding monopoly over the generation and distribution of electric current — then let the State, which allots and maintains monopoly, come in and intervene with a general scheme of price fixing which works more unforeseen hardships than it heals, or else let it go into direct competition; or, as the collectivists urge, let it take over the monopoly bodily. "Ever since society has ex-isted," says Herbert Spencer, "disappointment has been preaching, 'Put not your trust in leg-islation'; and yet the trust in legislation seems hardly diminished."

But it may be asked where we are to go for relief from the misuses of social power, if not to the State. What other recourse have we? Admitting that under our existing mode of political organization we have none, it must still be pointed out that this question rests on the old invet-erate misapprehension of the State's nature, presuming that the State is a social institution, whereas it is an antisocial institution; that is to say, the question rests on an absurdity.11 It is certainly true that the business of government, in maintaining "freedom and security," and "to secure these rights," is to make a recourse to justice costless, easy and informal; but the State, on the contrary, is primarily concerned with injustice, and its function is to maintain a regime of injustice; hence, as we see daily, its disposition is to put justice as far as possible out of reach, and to make the effort after justice as costly and difficult as it can. One may put it in a word that while government is, by its nature, concerned with the administration of justice, the State is, by its nature, concerned with the administration of law — law, which the State itself manufactures for the service of its own primary ends. Therefore, an appeal to the State, based on the ground of justice, is futile in any circumstances, 12 for whatever action the State might take in response to it would be conditioned by the State's own paramount interest, and would hence be bound to result, as we see such action invariably resulting, in as great injustice as that which it pretends to correct, or as a rule, greater. The question thus presumes, in short, that the State may, on occasion, be persuaded to act out of character; and this is levity.

But passing on from this special view of the question, and regarding it in a more general way, we see that what it actually amounts to is a plea for arbitrary interference with the order of nature, an arbitrary cutting-in to avert the penalty which nature lays on any and every form of error, whether willful or ignorant, voluntary or involuntary; and no attempt at this has ever yet failed to cost more than it came to. Any contravention of natural law, any tampering with the natural order of things, must have its consequences, and the only recourse for escaping them is such as entails worse consequences. Nature seeks nothing of intentions, good or bad; the one thing she will not tolerate is disorder, and she is very particular about getting her full pay for any attempt to create disorder. She gets it sometimes by very indirect methods, often by very roundabout and unforeseen ways, but she always gets it. "Things and actions are what they are, and the consequences of them will be what they will be; why, then, should we desire to be deceived?" It would seem that our civilization is greatly given to this infantile addiction — greatly given to persuading itself that it can find some means which nature will tolerate, whereby we may eat our cake and have it; and it strongly resents the stubborn fact that there is no such means.13

It will be clear to anyone who takes the trouble to think the matter through, that under a regime of natural order, that is to say under government, which makes no positive interventions whatsoever on the individual, but only negative interventions in behalf of simple justice — not law, but justice — misuses of social power would be effectively corrected; whereas we know by interminable experience that the State's positive interventions do not correct them. Under a regime of actual individualism, actually free competition, actual *laissez faire* — a regime which, as we have seen, can not possibly coexist with the State — a serious or continuous misuse of social power would be virtually impracticable.14

I shall not take up space with amplifying these statements because, in the first place, this has already been thoroughly done by Spencer in his essays entitled The Man versus the State [published by Prof. Herbert Spencer in London, 1884]; and, in the second place, because I wish, above all things, to avoid the appearance of suggesting that a regime, such as these statements contemplate, is practicable, or that I am ever so covertly encouraging anyone to dwell on the thought of such a regime. Perhaps, some eons hence, if the planet remains so long habitable, the benefits accruing to conquest and confiscation may be adjudged overcostly; the State may in consequence be superseded by government, the political means suppressed, and the fetishes which give nationalism and patriotism their present execrable (hateful) character may be broken down. But the remoteness and uncertainty of this prospect makes any thought of it fatuous, and any concern with it futile. Some rough measure of its remoteness may perhaps be gained by estimating the growing strength of the forces at work against it.

232

SUPPRESSED INTELLIGENCE REPORTS

Ignorance and error, which the State's prestige steadily deepens, are against it; *la bassesse de l'homme interesse*, steadily pushing its purposes to greater lengths of turpitude, is against it; moral enervation [weakening], steadily proceeding to the point of complete insensitiveness, is against it. What combination of influences more powerful than this can one imagine, and what can one imagine possible to be done in the face of such a combination?

To the sum of these, which may be called spiritual influences, may be added the over-weening physical strength of the State, which is ready to be called into action at once against any affront to the State's prestige. Few realize how enormously and how rapidly in recent years the State has everywhere built up its apparatus of armies and police forces. The State has thoroughly learned the lesson laid down by Septimius Severus on his death bed. "Stick together," he said to his successors, "pay the soldiers, and don't worry about anything else." It is now known to every intelligent person that there can be no such thing as a revolution as long as this advice is followed; in fact, there has been no revolution in the modern world since 1848 — every so-called revolution has been merely a *coup d'Etat*.15

All talk of the possibility of a revolution in America is in part perhaps ignorant, but mostly dishonest; it is merely "the interested clamours and sophistry" of persons who have some sort of ax to grind. Even Lenin acknowledged that a revolution is impossible anywhere until the military and police forces become disaffected; and the last place to look for that, probably, is here. We have all seen demonstrations of a disarmed populace, and local riots carried on with primitive weapons, and we have also seen how they ended, as in Homestead, Chicago, and the mining districts of West Virginia, for instance. Coxey's Army marched on Washington — and it kept off the grass.

Taking the sum of the State's physical strength, with the force of powerful spiritual influences behind it, one asks again, what can be done against the State's progress in self-aggrandizement? Simply nothing. So far from encouraging any hopeful contemplation of the unattainable, the student of civilized man will offer no conclusion but that nothing can be done. He can regard the course of our civilization only as he would regard the course of a man in a rowboat on the lower reaches of the Niagara — as an instance of Nature's unconquerable intolerance of disorder, and in the end, an example of the penalty which she puts upon any attempt at interference with order. Our civilization may, at the outset, have taken its chances with the current of statism [the concentration of economic controls and planning in the hands of a highly centralized government] either ignorantly or deliberately; it makes no difference. Nature cares nothing whatever about motive or intention; she cares only for order, and looks to see only that her repugnance to disorder shall be vindicated, and that her concern with the regular orderly sequences of things and actions shall be upheld in the outcome. Emerson, in one of his great moments of inspiration, personified cause and effect as "the chancellors of God;" and invariable experience testifies that the attempt to nullify or divert or in any wise break in upon their sequences must have its own reward.

"Such," says Professor Ortega y Gasset, "was the lamentable fate of ancient civilization." A dozen empires have already finished the course that ours began three centuries ago. The lion and the lizard keep the vestiges that attest their passage upon earth, vestiges of cities which in their day were as proud and powerful as ours — Tadmor, Persepolis, Luxor, Baalbek — some of them indeed forgotten for thousands of years and brought to memory again only by the excavator, like those of the Mayas, and those buried in the sands of the Gobi. The sites which now bear Narbonne and Marseilles have borne the habitat of four successive civilizations, each of them, as St. James says, even as a vapour which appeareth for a little time and then vanisheth away. The course of all these civilizations was the same. Conquest, confiscation, the erection of the State; then the sequences which we have traced in the course of our own civilization; then the shock of some irruption which the social structure was too far weakened to resist, and from which it was left too disorganized to recover; and then the end.

Our pride resents the thought that the great highways of New England will one day lie deep under layers of encroaching vegetation, as the more substantial Roman roads of Old England have lain for generations; and that only a group of heavily overgrown hillocks will be left to attract the archaeologist's eye to the hidden debris of our collapsed skyscrapers. Yet it is to just this, we know, that our civilization will come; and we know it because we know that there never has been, never is, and never will be, any disorder in nature — because we know that things and actions are what they are, and the consequences of them will be what they will be.

But there is no need to dwell lugubriously [somberly] upon the probable circumstances of a future so far distant. What we and our more nearly immediate descendants shall see is a steady progress in collectivism running off into a military despotism of a severe type. Closer centralization; a steadily growing bureaucracy; State power and faith in State power increasing, social power and faith in social power diminishing; the State absorbing a continually larger proportion of the national income; production languishing, the State in consequence taking over one "essential industry" after another, managing them with ever-increasing corruption, inefficiency and prodigality, and finally resorting to a system of forced labour. Then, at some point in this progress, a collision of State interests, at least as general and as violent as that which occurred in 1914, will result in an industrial and financial dislocation too severe for the asthenic [weak] social structure to bear; and from this the State will be left to "the rusty death of machinery," and the casual anonymous forces of dissolution will be supreme.

11 Admitting that the lamb, in the fable, had no other recourse than the wolf, one may nonetheless see that its appeal to the wolf was a waste of breath.

12 This is now so well understood that no one goes to a court for justice; he goes for gain or revenge. It is interesting to observe that some philosophers of law now say that law has no relation to justice, and is not meant to have any such relation. In their view, law represents only a progressive registration of the ways in which experience leads us to believe that society can best get along. One might hesitate a long time about accepting their notion of what law is, but one must appreciate their candid affirmation of what it is not.

13 This resentment is very remarkable. In spite of our failure with one conspicuously ambitious experiment in State intervention, I dare say there would still be great resentment against Professor Sumner's ill-famed remark that when people talked tearfully about "the poor drunkard lying in the gutter," it seemed never to occur to them that the gutter might be quite the right place for him to lie; or against the bishop of Peterborough's declaration that he would rather see England free than sober. Yet both these remarks merely recognize the great truth which experience forces on our notice every day, that attempts to interfere with the natural order of things are bound, in one way or another, to turn out for the worse.

14 The horrors of England's industrial life in the last century furnish a standing brief for addicts of positive intervention. Child labour and woman labour in the mills and mines; Coketown and Mr. Bounderby; starvation wages; killing hours; vile and hazardous conditions

of labour; coffin ships officered by ruffians—all these are glibly charged off by reformers and publicists to a regime of rugged individualism, unrestrained competition, and *laissez faire*. This is an absurdity on its face, for no such regime ever existed in England. They were due to the State's primary intervention whereby the population of England was expropriated from the land; due to the State's removal of the land from competition with industry for labour. Nor did the factory system and the "industrial revolution" have the least thing to do with creating those hordes of miserable beings. When the factory system came in, those hordes were already there, expropriated, and they went into the mills for whatever Mr. Gradgrind and Mr. Plugson of Undershot would give them, because they had no choice but to beg, steal or starve. Their misery and degradation did not lie at the door of individualism; they lay nowhere but at the door of the State. Adam Smith's economics are not the economics of individualism; they are the economics of landowners and millowners. Our zealots of positive intervention would do well to read the history of the Enclosures Acts and the work of the Hammonds, and see what they can make of them.

15 When Sir Robert Peel proposed to organize the police force of London, Englishmen said openly that half a dozen throats cut in Whitechapel every year would be a cheap price to pay for keeping such an instrument of potential tyranny out of the State's hands. We are all beginning to realize now that there is a great deal to be said for that view of the matter.

III

But it may quite properly be asked, if we in common with the rest of the Western world are so far gone in statism as to make this outcome inevitable, what is the use of a book which merely shows that it is inevitable? By its own hypothesis the book is useless. Upon the very evidence it offers, no one's political opinions are likely to be changed by it, no one's practical attitude towards the State will be modified by it; and if they were, according to the book's own premises, what good could it do?

Assuredly I do not expect this book to change anyone's political opinions, for it is not meant to do that. One or two, perhaps, here and there, may be moved to look a little into the subject matter on their own account, and thus perhaps their opinions would undergo some slight loosening or some constriction-but this is the very most that would happen. In general, too, I would be the first to acknowledge that no results of the kind which we agree to call practical could accrue to the credit of a book of this order, were it a hundred times as cogent as this one no results, that is, that would in the least retard the State's progress in self aggrandizement and thus modify the consequences of the State's course. There are two reasons, however, one general and one special, why the publication of such a book is admissible.

The general reason is that when in any department of thought a person has, or thinks he has, a view of the plain intelligible order of things, it is proper that he should record that view publicly, with no thought whatever of the practical consequences, or lack of consequences, likely to ensue upon his so doing. He might indeed be thought bound to do this as a matter of abstract duty; not to crusade or propagandize for his view or seek to impose it upon anyone— far from that!—not to concern himself at all with either its acceptance or its disallowance; but merely to record it. This, I say, might be thought his duty to the natural truth of things, but it is at all events his right; it is admissible.

The special reason has to do with the fact that in every civilization, however generally prosaic, however addicted to the short time point of view on human affairs, there are always certain alien spirits who, while outwardly conforming to the requirements of the civilization around them, still keep a disinterested regard for the plain intelligible law of things, irrespective of any practical end. They have an intellectual curiosity, sometimes touched with emotion, concerning the august [imposing] order of nature; they are impressed by the contemplation of it, and like to know as much about it as they can, even in circumstances where its operation is ever so manifestly unfavourable to their best hopes and wishes. For these, a work like this, however in the current sense impractical, is not quite useless; and those of them it reaches will be aware that for such as themselves, and such only, it was written.

WHO IS SAUL ALINSKY?

Recall that Hillary did her college thesis on his writings and Obama writes about him in his books.

Saul Alinsky died about 43 years ago, but his writings influenced those in political control of our nation today.......

Saul David Alinsky, a writer, was an American community organizer and writer. He is generally considered to be the founder of the modern community organizing movement. He is most noted for his book Rules for Radicals.

Died: June 12, 1972, Carmel-by-the-Sea, CA

Education: University of Chicago

Spouse: Irene Alinsky

Books: Rules for Radicals, Reveille for Radicals

Anyone out there think that this stuff isn't happening today in the U.S.?

All eight rules are currently in play

HOW TO CREATE A SOCIAL STATE BY SAUL ALINSKY:

There are eight levels of control that must be obtained before you are able to create a social state. The first is the most important.

1) Healthcare– Control health care and you control the people

2) Poverty – Increase the Poverty level as high as possible, poor people are easier to control and will not fight back if you are providing everything for them to live.

3) Debt – Increase the debt to an unsustainable level. That way you are able to increase taxes, and this will produce more poverty.

4) Gun Control– Remove the ability to defend themselves from the Government. That way you are able to create a police state. (**and death squads**)

5) Welfare – Take control of every aspect of their lives (Food, Housing, and Income)

6) Education – Take control of what people read and listen to – take control of what children learn in school.

7) Religion – Remove the belief in God from the Government and schools

SUPPRESSED INTELLIGENCE REPORTS

8) Class Warfare – Divide the people into the wealthy and the poor. This will cause more discontent and it will be easier to tax the wealthy with the support of the poor.

Does any of this sound like what is happening to the United States ?

Alinsky merely simplified Vladimir Lenin's original scheme for world conquest by communism, under Russian rule. Stalin described his converts as "Useful Idiots." The Useful Idiots have destroyed every nation in which they have seized power and control. It is presently happening at an alarming rate in the U.S.

HERE IS WHAT HAPPENED ON JANUARY 1ST 2014:

Top Income tax bracket went from 35% to **39.6**%

Top Income payroll tax went from 37.4% to **52.2**%

Capital Gains tax went from 15% to **28**%

Dividends tax went from 15% to **39.6**%

Estate tax went from 0% to **55**%

Remember this fact: if you have money, the democrats want it. These taxes were all passed only with democrat votes, no republicans voted for these taxes.

These taxes were all passed under the affordable care act, aka Obamacare.

So, how do you like it now?

THE END (OF EVERYTHING)

SUPPRESSED INTELLIGENCE REPORTS

Forced Consent

Abraham Lincoln did not cause the death of so many people from a mere love of slaughter, but only to bring about a state of consent that could not otherwise be secured for the government he had undertaken to administer. When a government has once reduced its people to a state of consent—that is, of submission to its will—it can put them to a much better use than to kill them; for it can then plunder them, enslave them, and use them as tools for plundering and enslaving others. And these are the uses to which most governments, our own among them, do put their people, whenever they have once reduced them to a state of consent to its will. Andrew Jackson said that those who did not consent to the government he attempted to administer upon them, for that reason, were traitors, and ought to be hanged. Like so many other so-called "heroes," he thought the sword and the gallows excellent instrumentalities for securing the people's *consent* to be governed. The idea that, although government should rest on the consent of the governed, yet so much force may nevertheless be employed as may be necessary to produce that consent, embodies everything that was ever exhibited in the shape of usurpation and tyranny in any country on earth. It has cost this country millions of lives, and the loss of everything that resembles political liberty. It can have no place except as a part of a system of absolute military despotism. And it means nothing else either in this country, or in any other.

There is no half-way house between a government depending wholly on voluntary support, and one depending wholly on military compulsion. And mankind have only to choose between these two classes—the class that governs, and the class that is governed or enslaved. In this case, the government rests wholly on the consent of the governors, and not at all on the consent of the governed. And whether the governors are more or less numerous than the governed, and whether they call themselves monarchists, aristocrats, or republicans, the principle is the same. The simple, and only material fact, in all cases, is, that one body of men are robbing and enslaving another. And it is only upon military compulsion that men will submit to be robbed and enslaved, it necessarily follows that any government, to which the governed, the weaker party, do not consent, must be (in regard to that weaker party), a merely military despotism. Such is the state of things now in this country, and in every other in which government does not depend wholly upon voluntary support. There never was and there never will be, a more gross, self-evident, and inexcusable violation of the principle that government should rest on the consent of the governed, than was the American Civil War, as carried on by the North. There never was, and there never will be, a more palpable case of purely military despotism than is the government we now have.

Lysander Spooner - 1808-1887

THE EXPOSIVE SECRETS OF
MAJOR JORDAN'S DIARIES

Our gratitude and thanks goes to the Committee of Twelve for their valuable time donated to the compilation of this book. We've checked many sources and cannot find a publishing house now offering the book for sale. If you know of a source where people may purchase it, please let us know.

As time permits we'll add to the historical information surrounding the orchestration, implementation and tragic results of WWII. You will discover that major lies have been told, which proves once again the victors of war write the history.

In this case, as in all cases of war the 'victors' are never a nation, regardless of appearances, modern history books, or reporting by the media. Why? Because the real victors are the same group of international financiers who control the major publishing houses, education through all levels of learning, as well as the media. And let us not forget the major role the entertainment industry plays in the thought control process. Books, movies, games, videos, music. . . all of it geared to create the International Citizen/Slave.

Major George Jordan began his diary in 1942 when he became suspicious of US-sanctioned air shipments to the USSR. But he never expected to uncover a secret American WWII deal to give the Russians the raw materials and know-how to make atomic bombs!

The following is exerpted from the book, which will be published in full by Global Comminucations/Conspiracy Journal in late 2008.

From Major Jordan's Diaries © 1952 by George Racey Jordan, USAF (Ret.) with Richard L. Stokes. Originally published in 1952 by Harcourt, Brace & Company, New York Reprinted by American Opinion, 1961:

SUPPRESSED INTELLIGENCE REPORTS

"MR BROWN" AND THE START OF A DIARY

Late one day in May 1942, several Russians burst into my office at Newark Airport, furious over an outrage that had just been committed against Soviet honor. They pushed me toward the window where I could see evidence of the crime with my own eyes.

They were led by Colonel Anatoli N. Kotikov, the head of the Soviet mission at the airfield. He had become a Soviet hero in 1935 when he made the first seaplane flight from Moscow to Seattle along the Polar cap; Soviet newspapers of that time called him "the Russian Lindbergh". He had also been an instructor of the first Soviet parachute troops, and he had 38 jumps to his credit.

I had met Colonel Kotikov only a few days before, when I reported for duty on May 10, 1942. My orders gave the full title of the Newark base as "UNITED NATIONS DEPOT No. 8, LEND-LEASE DIVISION, NEWARK AIRPORT, NEWARK, NEW JERSEY, INTERNATIONAL SECTION, AIR SERVICE COMMAND, AIR CORPS, U.S. ARMY".

I was destined to know Colonel Kotikov very well, and not only at Newark. At that time he knew little English, but he had the hardihood to rise at 5.30 every morning for a two-hour lesson. Now he was pointing out the window, shaking his finger vehemently.

There on the apron before the administration building was a medium bomber, an A-20 Douglas Havoc. It had been made in an American factory, it had been donated by American Lend-Lease, it was to be paid for by American taxes, and it stood on American soil. Now it was ready to bear the Red Star of the Soviet Air Force.

As far as the Russians and Lend-Lease were concerned, it was a Russian plane. It had to leave the field shortly to be hoisted aboard one of the ships in a convoy that was forming to leave for Murmansk and Kandalaksha. On that day the Commanding Officer was absent and, as the acting Executive Officer, I was in charge.

I asked the interpreter what "outrage" had occurred. It seemed that a DC-3, a passenger plane, owned by American Airlines, had taxied from the runway and, in wheeling about on the concrete plaza to unload passengers, had brushed the Havoc's engine housing. I could easily see that the damage was not too serious and could be repaired. But that seemed to be beside the point. What infuriated the Russians was that it be tolerated for one minute that an American commercial liner should damage, even slightly, a Soviet warplane!

The younger Russians huddled around Colonel Kotikov over their Russian-English dictionary, and showed me a word: "punish". In excited voices they demanded: "Pooneesh peelote!" I asked what they wanted done to the offending pilot. One of them aimed an imaginary revolver at his temple and pulled the trigger.

"You're in America," I told him. "We don't do things that way. The plane will be repaired and ready for the convoy."

They came up with another word: "Baneesh!" They repeated this excitedly over and over again. Finally I understood that they wanted not only the pilot, but American Airlines, Inc., expelled from the Newark field.

I asked the interpreter to explain that the US Army has no jurisdiction over commercial companies. After all, the airlines had been using Newark Airport long before the war and even before La Guardia Airport existed. I tried to calm down the Russians by explaining that our aircraft maintenance officer, Captain Roy B. Gardner, would have the bomber ready for its convoy even if it meant a special crew working all night to finish the job.

I remembered what General Koenig had said about the Russians when I went to Washington shortly after Pearl Harbor. He knew that in 1917 I had served in the Flying Machine Section, US Signal Corps, and that I had been in combat overseas. When he told me there was an assignment open for a Lend-Lease liaison officer with the Red Army Air Force, I was eager to hear more about it.

"It's a job, Jordan, that calls for an infinite amount of tact to get along with the Russians," the General said. "They're tough people to work with, but I think you can do it."

Thus I had been assigned to Newark for the express purpose of expediting the Lend-Lease program. I was determined to perform my duty to the best of my ability. I was a "retread", as they called us veterans of World War I, and a mere Captain at the age of 44 - but I had a job to do and I knew I could do it. The first days had gone reasonably well and I rather liked Kotikov. But there was no denying it: the Russians were tough people to work with.

As my remarks about repairing the bomber on time were being translated, I noticed that Colonel Kotikov was fidgeting scornfully. When I finished, he made an abrupt gesture with his hand. "I call Mr Hopkins," he announced.

It was the first time I had heard him use this name. It seemed such an idle threat, and a silly one. What did Harry Hopkins have to do with Newark Airport? Assuming that Kotikov carried out his threat, what good would it do? Commercial planes, after all, were under the jurisdiction of the Civil Aeronautics Board.

"Mr Hopkins fix," Colonel Kotikov asserted. He looked at me and I could see now that he was amused in a grim kind of way. "Mr Brown will see Mr Hopkins, no?" he said, smiling.

The mention of "Mr Brown" puzzled me, but before I had time to explore this any further, Kotikov was barking at the interpreter that he wanted to call the Soviet Embassy in Washington. All Russian long-distance calls had to be cleared through my office, and I always made sure that the Colonel's, which could be extraordinarily long at times, were put through "collect". I told the operator to get the Soviet Embassy, and I handed the receiver to the Colonel.

By this time the other Russians had been waved out of the office, and I was sitting at my desk. Colonel Kotikov began a long harangue over the phone in Russian, interrupted by several trips to the window. The only words I understood were "American Airlines", "Hopkins", and the serial number on the tail which he read out painfully in English. When the call was completed, the Colonel left without a word. I shrugged my shoulders and went to see about the damaged Havoc. As promised, it was repaired and ready for hoisting on shipboard when the convoy sailed.

That, I felt sure, was the end of the affair.

I was wrong. On June 12th the order came from Washington, not only ordering American Airlines off the field but directing every aviation company to cease activities at Newark forthwith. The order was not for a day or a week. It held for the duration of the war, though they called it a "Temporary Suspension".

I was flabbergasted. It was the sort of thing one cannot quite believe, and certainly cannot forget. Would we have to jump whenever Colonel Kotikov cracked the whip? For me, it was going to be a hard lesson to learn.

Captain Gardner, who had been at Newark longer than I, and who was better versed in what he called the "push-button system", told me afterwards that he did not waste a second after I informed him that Colonel Kotikov had threatened to "call Mr Hopkins". He dashed for the best corner in the terminal building, which was occupied by commercial airlines people, and staked out his claim by fixing his card on the door. A few days later the space was his.

I was dazed by the speed with which the expulsion proceedings had taken place. First, the CAB inspector had arrived. Someone in Washington, he said, had set off a grenade under the Civil Aeronautics Board. He spent several days in the control tower, and put our staff through a severe quiz about the amount of commercial traffic and whether it was interfering with Soviet operations. The word spread around the field that there was going to be hell to pay. Several days later, the order of expulsion arrived. A copy of the order is reproduced in the centre section of this edition, a masterpiece of bureaucratic language.

I had to pinch myself to make sure that we Americans, and not the Russians, were the donors of Lend-Lease. "After all, Jordan," I told myself, "you don't know the details of the whole operation; this is only one part of it. You're a soldier, and besides, you were warned that this would be a tough assignment." At the same time, however, I decided to start a diary, and to collect records of one kind and another and make notes and memos of everything that occurred. This was a more important decision than I then realized.

Keeping a record wasn't exactly a revolutionary idea in the Army. I can still see Sergeant Cook, at Kelly Field, Texas, in 1917, with his sandy thatch and ruddy face, as he addressed me, a 19-year-old corporal, from the infinite superiority of a master sergeant in the regular Army: "Jordan, if you want to get along, keep your eyes and your ears open, keep your big mouth shut, and keep a copy of everything!"

Now I felt a foreboding that one day there would be a thorough investigation of Russian Lend-Lease. I was only one cog in the machinery. Yet because of the fact that I couldn't know the details of high-level strategy, I began the Jordan diaries...

THE "BOMB POWDER" FOLDERS

In my capacity as Liaison Officer, I began helping the Russians with necessary paper work and assisted them in telephoning to the various factories to expedite the movement of supplies to catch particular convoys. As Colonel Kotikov communicated with the many different officials in the Soviet Government Purchasing Commission, their names became more and more familiar to me.

Few of the American officers who came in casual contact with the Russians ever got to see any of their records. But the more I helped Rodzevitch and Colonel Kotikov, the more cordial they became. It became customary for me to leaf through their papers to get shipping documents, and to prepare them in folders for quick attention when they reported back to Washington.

At this time I knew nothing whatever about the atomic bomb. The words "uranium" and "Manhattan Engineering District" were unknown to me. But I became aware that certain folders were being held to one side on Colonel Kotikov's desk for the accumulation of a very special chemical plant. In fact, this chemical plant was referred to by Colonel Kotikov as a "bomb powder" factory. By referring to my diary, and checking the items I now know went into an atomic energy plant, I am able to show the following records, starting with the year 1942 while I was still at Newark. These materials, which are necessary for the creation of an atomic pile, moved to Russia in 1942:

Graphite: natural, flake, lump or chip, costing American taxpayers $812,437. Over thirteen million dollars' worth of aluminum tubes (used in the atomic pile to 'cook' or transmute the uranium into plutonium), the exact amount being $13,041,152. We sent 834,989 pounds of cadmium metal for rods to control the intensity of an atomic pile; the cost was $781,472. The really secret material, thorium, finally showed up and started going through immediately. The amount during 1942 was 13,440 pounds at a cost of $22,848. (On January 30, 1943 we shipped an additional 11,912 pounds of thorium nitrate to Russia from Philadelphia on the SS John C. Fremont. It is significant that there were no shipments in 1944 and 1945, due undoubtedly to General Groves' vigilance.)

It was about this time that the Russians were very anxious to secure more Diesel marine engines which cost about $17,500 each. They had received around 25 on previous shipments and were moving heaven and earth to get another 25 of the big ones of over 200-horsepower variety. Major General John R. Deane, Chief of our Military Mission in Moscow, had overruled the Russians' request for any Diesel engines because General MacArthur needed them in the South Pacific. But the Russians were undaunted and decided to make an issue of it by going directly to Hopkins who overruled everyone in favor of Russia. In the three-year period, 1942-44, a total of 1,305 of these engines were sent to Russia! They cost $30,745,947. The engines they had previously received were reported by General Deane and our military observers to be rusting in open storage. It is now perfectly obvious that these Diesels were post-war items, not at all needed for Russia's immediate war activity...

It is true that we never knew the exact use to which anything sent under Russian Lend-Lease was put, and the failure to set up a system of accountability is now seen to have been an appalling mistake. But could anything be more foolish than to suppose that the atomic materials we sent were not used for an atomic bomb which materialized in Russia long before we expected it? The British let us inspect their installations openly, and exchanged information freely. The Russians did not. Our Government was intent on supplying whatever the Russians asked for, as fast as we could get it to them - and I was one of the expediters. And when I say "our Government", I mean of course Harry Hopkins, the man in charge of Lend-Lease, and his aides. We in the Army knew where the orders were coming from, and so did the Russians. The "push-button system" worked splendidly; no one knew it better than Colonel Kotikov...

It had become clear, however, that we were not going to stay at Newark much longer. The growing scope of our activities, the expansion of Lend-Lease, the need for more speedy delivery of aircraft to Russia - all these factors were forcing a decision in the direction of air delivery to supplant ship delivery. It had long been obvious that the best route was from Alaska across to Siberia.

From the first, the Russians were reluctant to open the Alaskan-Siberian route. Even before Pearl Harbor, on the occasion of the first Harriman-Beaverbrook mission to Moscow in September 1941, Averell Harriman had suggested to Stalin that American aircraft could be delivered to the Soviet Union from Alaska through Siberia by American crews. Stalin demurred and said it was "too dangerous a route". It would have brought us, of course, behind the Iron Curtain.

During the Molotov visit to the White House, Secretary of State Cordell Hull handed Harry Hopkins a memorandum with nine items of agenda for the Russians, the first of which was: "The Establishment of an Airplane Ferrying Service From the United States to the Soviet Union Through Alaska and Siberia." When the President brought this up, Molotov observed that it was under advisement, but "he did not as yet know what decision had been reached".

Major General John R. Deane has an ironic comment on Russian procrastination in this regard:

"Before I left for Russia, General Arnold, who could pound the desk and get things done in the United States, had called me to his office, pounded the desk, and told me what he wanted done in the way of improving air transportation between the United States and Russia. He informed me that I was to obtain Russian approval for American operation of air transport planes to Moscow on any of the following routes in order of priority: one, the Alaskan-Siberian route; two, via the United Kingdom and Stockholm; or three, from Tehran to Moscow. I saluted, said 'Yes, sir', and tried for two years to carry out his instructions." (John R. Deane, The Strange Alliance, Viking, 1947, p. 78)

Where the US was not able to force Russia's hand, Nazi submarines succeeded. Subs out of Norway were attacking our Lend-Lease convoys on the Murmansk route, apparently not regarded as "too dangerous a route" for American crews. A disastrous limit was finally reached when, out of one convoy of 34 ships, 21 were lost. The Douglas A-20 Havocs, which were going to the bottom of the ocean, were more important to Stalin than human lives. So first we started flying medium bombers from South America to Africa, but by the time they got across Africa to Tiflis, due to sandstorms the motors had to be taken down and they were not much use to the Russians. Nor were we able to get enough of them on ships around Africa to fill Russian requirements for the big offensive building up for the battle of Stalingrad.

Finally, Russia sent its OK on the Alaskan-Siberian route. Americans would fly the planes to Fairbanks, Alaska; Americans would set up all the airport facilities in Alaska; Soviet pilots would take over on our soil; Soviet pilots only would fly into Russia.

The chief staging-point in the US was to be Gore Field in Great Falls, Montana. A few years before the war General Ralph Royce, who had been experimenting in cold-weather flying with a group of training planes called "Snow Birds", had found that Great Falls, with its airport 3,665 feet above sea level, on the top of a mesa tableland 300 feet above the city itself, had a remarkable record of more than 300 clear flying days per year, despite its very cold dry climate in the winter.

If you look at a projection of the globe centred on the North Pole, you will see that Great Falls is almost on a direct line with Moscow. This was to be the new and secret Pipeline. The Army called it ALSIB.

WE MOVE TO MONTANA

It was the coldest weather in 25 years when the route was mapped out. First of all, Major General Follette Bradley flew experimentally by way of the old gold-field airstrips of Canada. With the Russians he scratched out a route from Great Falls through Fairbanks, Alaska and across Siberia to Kuibeyshev and Moscow. It is the coldest airway in the world across the Yukon to Alaska and through the "Pole of Cold" in Siberia, but it worked.

Colonel (then Captain) Gardner, our trouble-shooter at Newark, was one of the first to go ahead to Montana. Then Lieutenant Thomas J. Cockrell arrived at Great Falls in charge of an advance cadre to make arrangements for the housing and quartering of troops of the 7th Ferrying Group of the Air Transport Command, which was moving from Seattle.

Gore Field was at that time known as the Municipal Airport of Great Falls. Although it had been selected as the home of the 7th, actual construction of barracks and other accommodations had not been started. The Great Falls Civic Center was therefore selected as a temporary home, with headquarters, barracks, mess-hall and other facilities combined under the roof of the huge municipal structure. The Ice Arena was also used as a combination barracks and mess-hall, and temporary headquarters were established in the office of Mayor Ed Shields and the offices of other city officials.

For nearly four months, the Civic Center remained the home of the 7th Ferrying Group, while contractors rushed construction of the barracks, hangars and other buildings which were to make up the post on Gore Field. The group completed its move up to Gore Hill early in November 1942. The 7th Group continued to supervise all stations and operations along the Northwest Route until November 17, 1942, when the Alaskan Wing of the Air Transport Command was established to take over the operations of the route to the north through Canada to Fairbanks, where hundreds of Russian pilots were waiting to take over.

Major Alexander Cohn arrived from Spokane to establish the 34th Sub-Depot for the Air Service Command. It was this depot that supervised the mountains of air freight that originated from all over the United States and poured into the funnel of this end of the Pipeline.

Colonel Gardner arranged for my transfer from Newark to Great Falls. My orders designated me as "United Nations Representative". Few people realize that although the United Nations organization was not set up in San Francisco until September 1945, the name "United Nations" was being used in the Lend-Lease organization as early as 1942, as in my original orders to Newark.

For the record, I want to quote my orders to Great Falls, with one phrase italicized. One reason for this is that in 1949 the New York Times printed the following statement of a "spokesman" for the United Nations: "Jordan never worked for the United Nations." I thereupon took the original copy of my orders in person to the Times, explained that this was an Army designation as early as 1942, and asked them in fairness to run a correction (which they did not do), since I never claimed to have "worked for the United Nations" and their story left the impression that I was lying. Here are my orders, with the original Army abbreviations.

Army Air Forces Headquarters, 34th Sub Depot Air Service Command Office of the Commanding Officer

Capt GEORGE R. JORDAN, 0-468248, AC, having reported for duty this sta per Par 1, SO No. 50, AAF, ASC, Hq New York Air Serv Port Area Comd, Newark Airport, N.J., dated 2 January 43, is hereby asgd United Nations Representative, 34th Sub Depot, Great Falls, Montana, effective this date.

By order of

Lt. Colonel MEREDITH.

These official orders activating my post were preceded on January 1st by a Presidential directive [see text box below]. This directive was addressed to the Commanding Generals of the Air Transport, Material, and Air Service Commands, through Colonel H. Ray Paige, Chief, International Section, Air Staff, who worked directly under General Arnold. This directive gave first priority for the planes passing through our station, even over the planes of the United States Air Force! It was extremely important in all my work. I quote from the crucial first paragraph:

"...To implement these directives, the modification, equipment and movement of Russian planes have been given first priority, even over planes for U.S. Army Air Forces..."

...The Russian staff had moved from Newark to Great Falls, with Colonel Kotikov still at their head. By this time I was on a very friendly personal basis with the Colonel. As human beings, we got on very well together. From the viewpoint of the usual Russian behavior toward Americans, it could even be said that we were on intimate terms...

HEADQUARTERS ARMY AIR FORCES WASHINGTON

January 1, 1943.

MEMORANDUM FOR THE COMMANDING GENERAL, AIR SERVICE COMMAND:

Subject: Movement of Russian Airplanes.

1. The President has directed that "airplanes be delivered in accordance with protocol schedules by the most expeditious means." To implement these directives, the modification, equipment and movement of Russian planes have been given first priority, even over planes for U.S. Army Air Forces...

By Command of Lieutenant General ARNOLD,

Richard H. Ballard Colonel, G.S.C. Assistant Chief of Air Staff, A-4

THE BLACK SUITCASES

After my return to Great Falls I began to realize an important fact: while we were a pipeline to Russia, Russia was also a pipeline to us.

SUPPRESSED INTELLIGENCE REPORTS

One really disturbing fact which brought this home to me was that the entry of Soviet personnel into the United States was completely uncontrolled. Planes were arriving regularly from Moscow with unidentified Russians aboard. I would see them jump off planes, hop over fences, and run for taxicabs. They seemed to know in advance exactly where they were headed, and how to get there. It was an ideal set-up for planting spies in this country, with false identities, for use during and after the war.

It is hard to believe, but in 1943 there was no censorship set-up at Great Falls. An inspector more than 70 years old, named Randolph K. Hardy, did double work for the Treasury Department in customs and immigration. His office, in the city, was four miles from the airfield. He played the organ in a local church, and I was often told he was practicing and could not be interrupted. I took it upon myself to provide him with telephone, typewriter, desk, file cabinet, stenographer, interpreter and staff car.

Finally I was driven to put up a large sign over my own office door, with the legend in Russian and English: "Customs Office - Report Here". When Mr Hardy was not present, I got into the habit of demanding passports myself and jotting down names and particulars. It was not my job, but the list in my diary of Russians operating in this country began to swell by leaps and bounds. In the end I had the 418 names mentioned earlier.

Despite my private worries, my relations with Colonel Kotikov were excellent. I was doing all that I could do to expedite Russian shipments; my directives were clear, and I was following them out to the best of my ability.

Colonel Kotikov was well aware that a Major could do more expediting than a Captain. I was not too surprised, therefore, to learn that Kotikov had painstakingly dictated in English the following letter to Colonel Gitzinger:

Dear Colonel Gitzinger:

Capt. Jordan work any day here is always with the same people, Sub-Depot Engineering Officer, Major Boaz; 7th Ferrying Group Base Engineering Officer, Major Lawrence; Alaskan Wing Control and Engineering Officer, Major Taylor; Sub-Depot Executive Officer, Major O'Neill; and Base Supply Officer, Major Ramsey.

He is much hindered in his good work by under rank with these officers who he asks for things all time. I ask you to recommend him for equal rank to help Russian movement here.

A. N. KOTIKOV,

Col., U.S.S.R. Representative

When my permission finally came through, the gold oak leaves were pinned on my shoulders by Colonel Kotikov. This occasion was photographed and the picture is reproduced elsewhere in this book.

Now two other occurrences began troubling me. The first was the unusual number of black patent-leather suitcases, bound with white window-sash cord and sealed with red wax, which were coming through on the route to Moscow. The second was the burglary of morphine ampules from half of the 500 first-aid kits in our Gore Field warehouse.

The first black suitcases, six in number, were in the charge of a Russian officer and I passed them without question upon his declaration that they were "personal luggage". But the units mounted to ten, twenty and thirty and at last to standard batches of fifty, which weighed almost two tons and consumed the cargo allotment of an entire plane. The officers were replaced by armed couriers, traveling in pairs, and the excuse for avoiding inspection was changed from "personal luggage" to "diplomatic immunity".

Here were tons of materials proceeding to the Soviet Union, and I had no idea what they were. If interrogated, I should have to plead ignorance.

I began pursuing Colonel Kotikov with queries and protests. He answered with one eternal refrain. The suitcases were of the "highest diplomatic character". I retorted that they were not being sent by the Soviet Embassy but by the Soviet Government Purchasing Commission in Washington. He asserted that, whatever the origin, they were covered by diplomatic immunity. But I am sure he knew that one of these days I would try to search the containers.

They had grown to such importance in the eyes of the Russians that they asked for a locked room. The only door in the warehouse with a lock was that to the compartment in which the first-aid packets were kept. I put it at Colonel Kotikov's disposal. The couriers took turn about. First one and then the other slept on top of the suitcases, while his companion stood guard. Perhaps unjustly, I suspected them of stealing our morphine. They were the only persons left in the storeroom without witnesses.

At four o'clock one cold afternoon in March 1943, Colonel Kotikov said to me: "I want you dinner tonight." Then he doubled the surprise by whisking from his ulster pockets two slender bottles with long, sloping necks. "Vodka!"

The invitation was accepted with pleasure and also curiosity. For almost a year now I had associated with Colonel Kotikov and his staff, but I had never dined with them. As a matter of routine they lunched with us at the Officers' Club. But at night they disappeared, wandering off by themselves to other restaurants or the dining-room of the Rainbow Hotel, where they were quartered. So far as I knew, this was the first time they had bidden an American to an evening repast...

At the Officers' Club we had noticed that the Russians were extremely absent-minded about picking up bar checks. These oversights were costing us around $80 monthly, and we decided to remedy the situation. In the club were several slot-machines, for which the Russians had a passion. We decided to "set aside" one machine to cover their libations. Thanks to the one-armed mechanical bandit, we contrived after all to make them settle for their liquor.

Now, of a sudden, they asked me to dinner and were offering vodka, free, as an allurement. I could not help wondering why. Acting on a hunch, I excused myself from riding to town with Colonel Koticov in his Pontiac. I decided I would take my staff car, which had a soldier driver; in case of need, I preferred to have mobility. I was directed to join the party at seven o'clock at a restaurant in Great Falls known as "Carolina Pines".

There was not much time, so I hastened to ask our maintenance chief whether the Russians were planning any flights. He answered yes; they had a C-47 staged on the line, preparing to go. It was being warmed up with Nelson heaters - large canvas bags, fed with hot air, which were made to slip over motors and propellers. (Winter temperatures at the airfield could be as severe as at Fairbanks, ranging from 20 to 70 degrees below zero. Oil would sometimes freeze as hard as stone, and two to four hours were required to thaw out an engine.)

The Russians wielded a high hand at the airbase, but I had one power they respected. Though Lend-Lease planes were delivered to them at Great Falls, they were flown by American pilots as far as Fairbanks. No American pilot could leave without clearance, and I had authority to ground any plane at any time. In my absence, permission was given by the Flight Officer of the Day. I called the control tower, gave the number of the restaurant, and issue a positive order that no cargo plane was to be cleared for Russia except by myself.

Occupied by these thoughts, I drove to "Carolina Pines"... The gathering consisted of five Russians and a single American, myself. Colonel Kotikov acted as host, and among the guests was Colonel G. E. Tsvetkov, head of the fighter-pursuit division of the Soviet Purchasing Commission...

With the vodka under our belts, we moved to chairs about the table. But at 8.30, when we were two-thirds finished, the waitress handed me a message in pencil. It notified me to call the control tower at once.

At a public telephone, in the corridor, I learned that the C-47 had warmed up and that a couple of newly-arrived couriers were demanding clearance. Without returning to the dining room, I threw on my great-coat, scuffled down the stairs and ordered the driver to race full speed for the hangars, four miles away.

It was mid-winter in Great Falls. Snow was deep on the ground, and stars glittered frostily in a crystal sky. The temperature that night was about 20 degrees below zero.

As we neared the Lend-Lease plane there loomed up, in its open door, the figure of a burly, barrel-chested Russian. His back was propped against one jamb of the portal. An arm and a leg were stretched across to the opposite side. I clambered up and he tried to stop me by pushing hard with his stomach. I pushed back, ducked under his arm, and stood inside the cabin.

It was dimly lighted by a solitary electric bulb in the dome. Faintly visible was an expanse of black suitcases, with white ropes and seals of crimson wax. On top of them, reclining on one elbow, was a second Russian, slimmer than the first, who sprang to his feet as I entered. They were mature men, in the forties, and wore beneath leather jackets the inevitable blue suits of Russian civilians. Under each coat, from a shoulder holster, protruded the butt of a pistol.

It had been no more than a guess that a fresh installment of suitcases might be due. My first thought was: "Another bunch of those damn things!" The second was that if I was ever going to open them up, now was as good a time as any. With signs I made the Russians understand what I intended to do.

Promptly they went insane. They danced. They pushed at me with their hands and shrieked over and over the one English word they appeared to know. It was "deeplomateek!" I brushed them aside and took from my pocket a metal handle containing a safety razor blade which I carry in preference to a pocket knife.

Sensing its purpose, the lean courier flung himself face down across the suitcases, with arms and legs outspanned to shield as many as possible with his body. I dragged one of the containers from under him, and he leaped up again as I started to saw through the first cord. At this sight their antics and shouts redoubled.

While opening the third suitcase, I had a mental flash that brought sweat to my forehead. The Russians were half mad with fury and terror. They were on both sides of me, in front and behind. Supposing in desperation, one of them shot me in the back? There would be no American witnesses, and my death could be passed off as a "deplorable accident".

I called a Yank soldier who was on patrol thirty feet away. He crunched over through the snow. Bending down from the plane, I asked whether he had had combat experience. He answered that he had, in the South Pacific. I stooped lower and murmured:

"I'm going to open more of this baggage. I want you to watch these two Russians. Both are armed. I don't expect any trouble. But if one of them aims a gun at me, I want you to let him have it first. Understand?"

After a moment's thought, he looked me in the eye and said, "Sir, is that an order?" I replied that it was an order. He clicked the bolt of his rifle to snap a cartridge into the chamber and brought the weapon to ready. He was tall enough for his head to clear the doorsill. The muzzle was pushed forward to command the interior.

One courier jumped from the plane and sprinted for the hangars, where there were telephones. The other, his face contorted as if to keep from crying, began reknotting the cords I had severed. There was little trouble getting into the suitcases because the Russians had brought the cheapest on the market. They had no locks, but only pairs of clasps. All were consigned to the same address. The entry on the bill of lading read: "Director, Institute of Technical and Economic Information, 47 Chkalovskaya, Moscow 120, U.S.S.R."

I decided to attempt only a spot check - one suitcase, say, in every three. I examined perhaps eighteen out of fifty. Otherwise the search was fairly thorough, as I was looking for morphine. (Incidentally, none was found.) The light was so weak that it was impossible to decipher text without using a flash lamp. I had to take off my gloves, and my fingers grew numb with cold.

Using one knee as a desk, I jotted notes with a pencil on two long envelopes that happened to be in my pocket...

The first thing I unearthed made me snort with disgust. It was a ponderous tome on the art of shipping four-legged animals. Was this the kind of twaddle American pilots were risking their lives to carry? But in the back I found a series of tables listing railroad mileages from almost any point in the United States to any other.

Neatly packed with the volume were scores of roadmaps, of the sort available at filling stations to all comers. But I made a note that they were "marked strangely". Taken together, they furnished a country-wide chart, with names and places, of American industrial plants. For example, Pittsburgh entries included "Westinghouse" and "Blaw-Knox".

The next suitcase to be opened was crammed with material assembled in America by the official Soviet news organ, the Tass Telegraph Agency. A third was devoted to Russia's government-owned Amtorg Trading Corporation of New York. One yielded a collection of maps of the Panama Canal Commission, with the markings to show strategic spots in the Canal Zone and distances to islands and ports within a 1,000-mile radius.

Another was filled with documents relating to the Aberdeen Proving Ground, one of the most "sensitive" areas in the war effort. Judging by their contents, various suitcases could have been labeled under the heads of machine tools, oil refineries, blast furnaces, steel foundries, mining, coal, concrete, and the like. Other folders were stuffed with naval and shipping intelligence. There seemed to be hundreds of commercial catalogues and scientific magazines... There were also sheafs of info about Mexico, Argentina and Cuba.

There were groups of documents which, on the evidence of stationery, had been contributed by the Departments of Agriculture, Commerce and State. All such papers had been trimmed close to the text, with white margins removed. I decided that this was done either to save weight, or to remove "Secret", "Confidential" or "Restricted" stamps that might have halted a shipment, or for both reasons...

Then I copied the legend: "From Hiss". I had never heard of Alger Hiss, and made the entry because the folder bearing his name happened to be second in the pile. It contained hundreds of photostats of what seemed to be military reports...

A suitcase opened midway in the search appeared to contain nothing but engineering and scientific treatises. They bristled with formulae, calculations and professional jargon. I was about to close the case and pass on when my eye was caught by a specimen of stationery such as I had never before seen.

Its letterhead was a magic incantation: "The White House, Washington". As prospective owner of an 80-acre tract along the shore of Washington State, I was impressed by the lordly omission of the capitals, "D.C.". Under the flashlight I studied this paper with attention. It was a brief note, of two sheets, in a script which was not level but sloped upward to the right. The name to which it was addressed, "Mikoyan", was wholly new to me. (By questioning Colonel Kotikov later, I learned that A. I. Mikoyan at the moment was Russia's No. 3 man, after Premier Stalin and Foreign Commissar Molotov. He was Commissar of Foreign Trade and Soviet boss of Lend-Lease.)

A salutation, "My dear Mr Minister", led to a few sentences of stock courtesies. One passage, of eleven words, in the top line of the second page, impressed me enough to merit a scribble on my envelope. That excerpt ran thus: "____ had a hell of a time getting these away from Groves."

The last two words should not be taken as referring to Major General Leslie R. Groves himself. What they meant, probably, was "from the Groves organization". The commander of the Manhattan Engineer District, later the Manhattan Project, was almost unique in the Washington hierarchy for his dislike and suspicion of Russia...

The first thing I had done, on finding the White House note, was to flip over the page to look for a signature. I penciled it on my envelope as "H. H." This may not have been an exact transcription. In any case, my intention is clear. It was to chronicle, on the spot, my identification of the author as Harry Hopkins. It was general usage at Great Falls and elsewhere to refer to him as "Harry Hopkins", without the middle initial.

SUPPRESSED INTELLIGENCE REPORTS

I remember distinctly having had to remove that letter from a metal clip. It held two other exhibits - obviously the things which [someone] had such difficulty in "getting away from Groves". One was a thick map. When unfolded, it proved to be as wide as the span of my extended arms. In large letters it bore a legend which I recorded: "Oak Ridge, Manhattan Engineering District".

The other was a carbon copy of a report, two or three pages long, which was dated Oak Ridge. If it had a signature, I did not set it down. At the top of the first page, impressed with a rubber stamp, or typed, was the legend: "Harry Hopkins" followed by the title "Special Asst. Co-ordinator" or "Administrator". I gathered that this particular copy had been earmarked for Mr Hopkins. In the text of the report was encountered a series of vocables so outlandish that I made a memo to look up their meaning. Among them were "cyclotron", "proton" and "deuteron". There were curious phrases like "energy produced by fission" and "walls five feet thick, of lead and water, to control flying neutrons".

Probably no more than 200 men in all the country would have been capable at the time of noting down these particular expressions out of their own heads. The paper on which I made my notes was later submitted to the Bureau of Standards for a test of its age.

For the first time in my life, I met the word "uranium". The exact phrase was "Uranium 92". From a book of reference I learned afterward that uranium is the 92nd element in atomic weight.

At the time of this episode I was as unaware as anyone could be of Oak Ridge, the Manhattan District and its chief, General Groves. The enterprise has been celebrated as "the best guarded secret in history". It was superlatively hush-hush, to the extreme that Army officers in the "know" were forbidden to mention it over their private telephones inside the Pentagon. General Groves has testified that his office would have refused to send any documents to the White House, without authority from himself, even if it was requested personally by the President.

From the outset, extraordinary secrecy and security measures have surrounded the project," declared Henry L. Stimson, Secretary of War, in commenting on the first military use of the atom bomb. "This was personally ordered by President Roosevelt." Mr Roosevelt's orders, he innocently added, "have been strictly complied with."1

Yet Russians with whom I worked side by side at Great Falls knew about the A-bomb at least as early as March 1943, and General Groves had reason to distrust the Russians in October 1942! In common with almost all Americans, I got the first hint of the existence of the atom bomb from the news of Hiroshima, which was revealed on August 6, 1945 by President Truman.

I visited Washington in January 1944 to bring to the attention of the highest authorities what seemed to me to be treacherous violations of security in the Pipeline. I got exactly nowhere in the State Department or elsewhere. It was not until I heard the announcement of the atomic blast in Russia on September 23, 1949, that I finally had the good fortune of meeting Senator Bridges and Fulton Lewis - but more of that later.

It was after eleven o'clock, and my checking job was virtually done, when Colonel Kotikov burst into the cabin of the plane. He wanted to know by whose authority I was committing this outrage [see previous issue] and bellowed that he would have me removed. I answered that I was performing my duty, and, just to show how things stood, opened two or three extra suitcases in his presence. I left the C-47 and with a nod of thanks dismissed my sentinel.

As I crossed the field toward the barracks, Colonel Kotikov fell in beside me. No doubt he reflected that he was in no position to force an issue. He may also have realized that I understood the gravity of almost nothing I had seen. All that mattered to him was getting the suitcases off to Moscow. Anxiously he inquired what I intended to do.

If I had known what I do today, I should have grounded the transport, but in the end it went on its way to Russia.

Colonel Kotikov asked me to open no more suitcases until instructions came from the War Department. He said he hoped he would not have to get me transferred. I expected to be fired, and went so far as to pack my gear. But I received no communication from the War Department, and gathered at last that Colonel Kotikov had made no complaint. Perhaps, I began to think, he did not dare.

I reported to Colonel George F. O'Neill, security officer of the 34th Sub-Depot at Gore Field, about the fifty suitcases I had examined. He was interested enough to pass the story on to his superior officer in Spokane. There was no reply, even after Colonel O'Neill made a second attempt. Apparently it was not considered good form to cast reflections on the integrity of our ally...

"DON'T MAKE A BIG PRODUCTION..."

One morning in April 1943, Colonel Kotikov asked whether I could find space for an important consignment of nearly 2,000 pounds. I said, "No, we have a quarter of a million pounds' backlog already."

He directed me to put through a call to Washington for him, and spoke for a while in his own tongue. Then he put a hand over the mouthpiece and confided to me in English, "Very special shipment - experimental chemicals - going through soon."

There was an interval of Slavic gutturals, and he turned to me again. "Mr Hopkins - coming on now," he reported. Then he gave me the surprise of my life. He handed me the phone and announced, "Big boss, Mr Hopkins, wants you."

It was quite a moment. I was about to speak for the first time with a legendary figure of the day, the top man in the world of Lend-Lease in which I lived. I have been careful to keep the following account as accurate in substance and language as I can. My memory, normally good, was stimulated by the thrill of the occasion. Moreover, the incident was stamped on my mind because it was unique in my experience of almost 25 months at Newark and Great Falls.

A bit in awe, I stammered, "Jordan speaking."

The male voice began at once. "This is Mr Hopkins. Are you my expediter out there?"

I answered that I was the United Nations Representative at Great Falls, working with Colonel Kotikov.

Under the circumstances, who could have doubted that the speaker was Harry Hopkins? Friends have since asked me whether it might not have been a Soviet agent who was an American. I doubt this, because his next remark brought up a subject which only Mr Hopkins and myself could have known.

He asked, "Did you get those pilots I sent you?"

"Oh yes, sir," I responded. "They were very much appreciated, and helped us in unblocking the jam in the Pipeline. We were accused of going out of channels, and got the dickens for it."

Mr Hopkins let that one go by, and moved on to the heart of things. "Now, Jordan," he said, "there's a certain shipment of chemicals going through that I want you to expedite. This is something very special."

"Shall I take it up," I asked, "with the Commanding Colonel?"

"I don't want you to discuss this with anyone," Mr Hopkins ordered, "and it is not to go on the records. Don't make a big production of it, but just send it through quietly, in a hurry."

I asked how I was to identify the shipment when it arrived. He turned from the phone, and I could hear his voice: "How will Jordan know the shipment when it gets there?" He came back on the line and said, "The Russian Colonel out there will designate it for you. Now send this through as speedily as possible, and be sure you leave it off the records!"

Then a Russian voice broke in with a demand for Colonel Kotikov. I was full of curiosity when Kotikov had finished, and I wanted to know what it was all about and where the shipment was coming from. He said there would be more chemicals and that they would arrive from Canada.

"I show you," he announced.

Presumably, after the talk with Mr Hopkins, I had been accepted as a member of the 'lodge'. From his bundle on war chemicals the Colonel took the folder called "Bomb Powder". He drew out a paper sheet and set a finger against one entry. For a second time my eyes encountered the word "Uranium". I repeat that in 1943 it meant as little to me as to most Americans, which was nothing.

This shipment was the one and only cash item to pass through my hands, except for private Russian purchases of clothing and liquor. It was the only one, out of a tremendous multitude of consignments, that I was ordered not to enter on my tally sheets. It was the only one I was forbidden to discuss with my superiors, and the only one I was directed to keep secret from everybody.

Despite Mr Hopkins' urgency, there was a delay of five weeks. On the morning of June 10th, I caught sight of a loaded C-47 which was idling on the runway. I went over and asked the pilot what was holding him up. He said he understood some kind of special shipment was still to come. Seven years afterward, the pilot identified himself to the press as Air Forces Lieutenant Ben L. Brown, of Cincinnati.

I asked Colonel Kotikov about the plane, and he told me the shipment Mr Hopkins was interested in had just arrived at the railroad yards, and that I should send a truck to pick it up. The consignment was escorted by a Russian guard from Toronto. I set down his name, and copied it later in my diary. It was Vladimir Anoufriev. I identified him with the initials "C.C." for "Canadian Courier".

SUPPRESSED INTELLIGENCE REPORTS

Fifteen wooden cases were put aboard the transport, which took off for Moscow by way of Alaska. At Fairbanks, Lieutenant Brown has related, one box fell from the plane, smashing a corner and spilling a small quantity of chocolate-brown powder. Out of curiosity, he picked up a handful of the unfamiliar grains, with a notion of asking somebody what they were. A Soviet officer slapped the crystals from his palm and explained nervously, "No, no - burn hands!"

Not until the latter part of 1949 was it definitely proved, from responsible records, that during the war Federal agencies delivered to Russia at least three consignments of uranium chemicals, totaling 1,465 pounds, or nearly three-quarters of a ton. Confirmed also was the shipment of one kilogram, or 2.2 pounds, of uranium metal at a time when the total American stock was 4.5 pounds.

Implicated by name were the Lend-Lease Administration, the Department of Commerce, the Procurement Division of the Treasury and the Board of Economic Warfare. The State Department became involved to the extent of refusing access to files of Lend-Lease and its successor, the Foreign Economic Administration.

The first two uranium shipments traveled through Great Falls by air. The third was dispatched by truck and railway from Rochester, NY, to Portland, Oregon, and then by ship to Vladivostok. The dates were March and June 1943, and July 1944. No doubt was left that the transaction discussed by Mr Hopkins and myself was the one of June 1943.

This was not merely the largest of our known uranium deals with the Soviet Union, it was also the most shocking. There seemed to be no lengths to which some American officials would not go in aiding Russia to master the secret of nuclear fission. For four years, monopoly of the A-bomb was the cornerstone of our military and overseas policy, yet on September 23, 1949, long in advance of Washington estimates, President Truman announced that an atomic explosion had occurred in the Soviet Union.

In behalf of national security, the Manhattan Project during the spring of 1943 clapped an embargo on American exports of uranium compounds. But zealots in Washington appear to have resolved that Russia must have at all costs the ingredients for atomic experiment. The intensely pro-Soviet mood of that time may be judged from echoes in later years.

For example, there was Joseph E. Davies, Ambassador to the Soviet Union in 1936-39, and author of a book and movie of flagrant propaganda, Mission to Moscow. In an interview with the Times-Herald of Washington for February 18, 1946, he was quoted as saying, "Russia, in self-defense, has every moral right to seek atomic bomb secrets through military espionage if excluded from such information by her former fighting allies!" There also was Professor Harold C. Urey, American scientist, who sat in the innermost circle of the Manhattan Project. Yet on December 14, 1949, in a report of the Atlantic Union Committee, Dr Urey said that Major Jordan should be court-martialed if he had removed anything from planes bound for Russia.

When American supplies were cut off, the device of out-maneuvering General Groves was to procure the materials clandestinely from Canada. Not until 1946 did the commander of the Manhattan Project learn from the Un-American Activities Committee that his stockade had been undermined.

My share in the revelation was testimony under oath, leading to one conclusion only: that the Canadian bypass was aided by Mr Hopkins. At his direction, Lend-Lease issued a certificate of release without which the consignment could not have moved. Lend-Lease channels of transportation and Lend-Lease personnel, such as myself, were used. Traces of the scheme were kept off Lend-Lease books by making it a 'cash' transaction. The shipment was paid for with a check of the Amtorg Trading Corporation.

Because of the initial branch of the airlift to Moscow was under American control, passage of the chemicals across United States territory could not be avoided, in Alaska if not Montana. On account of that fact - the cash nature of the project - it was necessary to obtain an export license from the Board of Economic Warfare. Such a document, covering a shipment of American origin, was first prepared. It was altered, to comply with the Canadian maneuver, by some BEW official whose identity has been concealed by the State Department. As amended, the license was issued on April 29, 1943. Its serial number was C-1643180.

But two facts were forgotten: (a) public carriers use invoices, and (b) the Air Forces kept tallies not only at Great Falls but Fairbanks.

By diligent searching, freight and airway bills yielded incontestable proof that 15 boxes of uranium chemicals were delivered at Great Falls on June 9, 1943, and were dispatched immediately, in a Lend-Lease plane, to the Soviet Union.

The shipment originated at Eldorado Mining & Refining, Ltd, of Great Bear Lake, and was sent through Port Hope, Ontario. It was authorized by a Canadian arms export permit, No. OF1666. The carrier was the Chicago, Milwaukee, St Paul & Pacific Railway. Listed as consignee was Colonel A. N. Kotikov, resident agent of the Soviet Government Purchasing Commission at Gore Field, Great Falls.

The story behind the story is as follows. On February 1, 1943, Hermann H. Rosenberg of Chematar, Inc., New York City, received the first inquiry about uranium ever to reach his office. The applicant was the Soviet Purchasing Commission, which desired 220 pounds of uranium oxide, 220 pounds of uranium nitrate, and 25 pounds of uranium metal.

At that date Oak Ridge was under construction, but would not be in operation for another year.

Six days earlier the War Production Board had issued General Reference Order M-285, controlling the distribution of uranium compounds among domestic industries like glass, pottery and ceramics. A loophole was left by overlooking the export of such materials for war purposes. The Russians claimed that they had urgent military need for uranium nitrate in medicinal research, and for uranium oxide and metal as alloys in hardening gun-barrel steel. There was nothing for the US to do but grant an OK, since we did not want to imply that we were suspicious of Russia's request.

Uranium metal was unavailable. On March 23, at Rosenberg's instance, the S. W. Shattuck Chemical Co. of Denver shipped four crates, weighing 691 pounds, to Colonel Kotikov at Great Falls. The Burlington Railroad's bill of lading described the contents merely as "Chemicals", but it was accompanied by a letter from Rosenberg to Kotikov designating the contents as 220 pounds of uranium nitrate and 200 (not 220) pounds of uranium oxide. Since it was a Lend-Lease transaction, defrayed with American funds, no export license was required. The cargo was dispatched without friction along the Pipeline.

But the War Production Board, from which clearance had been sought, alerted the Manhattan Project. It was too late to halt the Shattuck sale. General Groves reluctantly approved it on the ground that it would be unwise to 'tip off' Russia as to the importance of uranium chemicals - a fact with which Moscow was only too familiar.

During the investigation, I was embarrassed by questions as to why tables of exports to the Soviet Union contained no mention of uranium. The Shattuck consignment was legitimate. It had been authorized by Lend-Lease, the War Production Board and the Manhattan Project.

Some months later I ran into John F. Moynihan, formerly of the Newark News editorial staff. A Second Lieutenant at the Newark Airport when I was there, he had risen to Colonel as a sort of 'reverse press-agent' for General Groves. His duty was not to foster publicity but prevent it.

"I heard you floundering about," he said, "and wished I could tell you something you didn't know. I was sent to Denver to hush up the records in the Shattuck matter. It was hidden under the phrase, 'salts and compounds', in an entry covering a different metal."

General Groves moved rapidly to stop the leak through which the Shattuck boxes had slipped. By early April he had formed a nationwide embargo by means of voluntary contracts with chemical brokers. They promised to grant the United States first right to purchase all uranium oxide, uranium nitrate and sodium uranate received by the contractors.

The uranium black-out was discovered by Rosenberg when he tried to fill another order from the Soviet Purchasing Commission, for 500 pounds each of uranium nitrate and uranium oxide. On April 23, 1943, Rosenberg was in touch with the Canadian Radium & Uranium Corp. of New York, which was exclusive sales agent for Eldorado Mining & Refining, Ltd, a producer of uranium at Great Bear Lake.

An agreement to fill the Soviet order was negotiated with such dispatch that in four days Rosenberg was able to report victory to the Purchasing Commission. The shipment from Ontario to Great Falls and Moscow followed in due course.

The Port Hope machination had the advantage, among other things, of bypassing the War Production Board, which was sure to warn the Manhattan Project if it knew the facts, but could be kept in ignorance because its jurisdiction ran only south of the border.

General Groves was advised at once of the Soviet application for 1,000 pounds of uranium salts. He was not disturbed, being confident the embargo would stand. After declining to endorse the application, he approved it later in the hope of detecting whether the Russians could unearth uranium stocks which the Manhattan Project had overlooked. American industries were consuming annually, before the war, upwards of 200 tons of uranium chemicals.

"We had no expectation," General Groves testified December 7, 1949, "of permitting that material to go out of this country. It would have been stopped."2

So far as the United States was concerned, the embargo held fast. The truth that it had been side-stepped by means of resort to Canadian sources did not come to the General's knowledge until three years later.

Another violation of atomic security was represented by the third known delivery to Russia, in 1944. It proved to be uranium nitrate. During May of that year, Colonel Kotikov showed me a warning from the Soviet Purchasing Commission to look out for a shipment of uranium, weighing 500 pounds, which was to have travel priority. The Colonel was soon returning home. As the climax of his American mission, he proposed to fly the precious stuff to Moscow with his own hands.

Disguised as a "commercial transaction" within American territory, the deal was managed by Lend-Lease. Chematar and Canadian Radium & Uranium were abandoned in favor of the Procurement Division of the Treasury Department, although the Treasury, under regulations, had no authority to make uranium products available to the Soviet Union.

Contractors were asked to bid, and the winner was the Eastman Kodak Company. Somewhere in this process, the expected 500 pounds shrank to 45. Eastman Kodak reported the order to the War Production Board as a domestic commercial item.

Whatever the motive, it was determined not to send the compound by air. After a Treasury inspection in Rochester, the MacDaniel Trucking Company drove it to the Army Ordnance Depot at Terre Haute, Indiana, arriving July 24. The shipment turned up in freight car No. 97352 of the Erie Railroad, and got to North Portland, Oregon, on August 11. By means of shifts not yet divulged, the uranium nitrate found itself aboard a Russian steamship, Kashirstroi, which left for Vladivostok on October 3. Colonel Kotikov, who had planned a triumphal entry into Moscow with a quarter-ton of "bomb powder" as a trophy, gave up the project in disgust on learning that the shipment would be only 45 pounds.

In charge of uranium purchases for the Manhattan Project in 1944 was Dr Phillip L. Merritt. Appearing January 24, 1950 before the Un-American Activities Committee, Dr Merritt swore he was taken by surprise, a day earlier, on discovering for the first time that the Eastman Kodak order had been shipped to Russia by way of Army Ordnance.

General Groves was likewise uninformed. Asked as a witness whether it was possible for uranium shipments to have been made in 1944, he answered, "Not if we could have helped it, and not with our knowledge of any kind. They would have had to be entirely secret, and not discovered."[3] He declared there was no way for the Russians to get uranium products in this country "without the support of US authorities in one way or another".[4]

The Soviet Purchasing Commission appears to have had instructions to acquire without fail 25 pounds of uranium metal, which can be extracted from uranium salts by a difficult process requiring specialized equipment. Supported or advised by Lend-Lease, the commission for a whole year knocked at every available door, from the Chemical Warfare Service up to Secretary Stimson. As a matter of fact, uranium metal was then non-existent in America, and for that reason had not been specified in the Manhattan Project's embargo or named as a "strategic" material.

Stimson closed a series of polite rebuffs with a letter of April 17, 1944, to the chairman of the Purchasing Commission, Lt General Leonid G. Rudenko. But Moscow was stubborn. Under Soviet pressure, the commission, or its American friends, had an inspiration. Why not have the uranium made to order by some private concern?

As usual, a roundabout course was taken. The commission first approached the Manufacturers Chemical Co., 527 Fifth Avenue, New York, which passed the order along to A. D. Mackay, Inc., 198 Broadway. By the latter it was farmed out to the Cooper Metallurgical Laboratory in Cleveland. According to Mr Mackay, neither he nor the Cooper concern suspected that their customer was the Soviet Union.

SUPPRESSED INTELLIGENCE REPORTS

But Mackay reported the deal to the War Production Board, which warned the Manhattan Project. The latter's expert on rare metals, Lawrence C. Burman, went to Cleveland, it is related, and urged the Cooper firm to make sure that its product was of "poor quality". He did not explain why. But the metal, of which 4.5 pounds was made, turned out to be 87.5 per cent pure as against the stipulated 99 per cent.

Delivery to the Soviet Union was then authorized of a small sample of this defective metal, to represent "what was available in the United States". Actually shipped was one kilogram, or 2.2 pounds. The Purchasing Commission abruptly silenced its demands for pure uranium. But the powers that be found it suitable to omit this item, as well as the Rochester sale, from the 1944 schedule of exports to Russia.

From the start, in contrast to the atmosphere prevailing in Washington, the Manhattan Project was declared by General Groves to have been "the only spot I know that was distinctly anti-Russian".5 Attempts at espionage in New York, Chicago and Berkeley, California, were traced to the Soviet Embassy. They convinced General Groves in October 1942 that the enemies of our atomic safeguards were not Germans or Japanese, but Russians. "Suspicion of Russia was not very popular in some circles [in Washington]," he stated. "It was popular in Oak Ridge, and from one month of the time I took over we never trusted them one iota. From that time on, our whole security was based on not letting the Russians find out anything."6

That the Russians found out everything from alpha to omega has been established by volumes of proof. Through trials in Canada, England and the United States there has been revealed the existence of an espionage network so enormously effective that Russia, scientists calculated, "should have been able to make a bomb considerably before September 1949". The network chief was the former Soviet Vice Consul in New York, Anatoli A. Yakovlev, who fled in 1946.

THE STORY OF THE "HEAVY WATER"

What is popularly known as "heavy water" is technically called deuterium oxide. It is in crystal form, not liquid.

In alleging medical and other grounds for its needs of uranium oxide and uranium nitrate, Russia had taken care to observe an appearance of truth, for such use is not unknown to therapeutics. It had been tried out in throat sprays and lent its name to Uranwein, a German specific against diabetes. Uranium oxide had been tested as an alloy for toughening steel, but it was found difficult to handle and had erratic results. Therefore when Moscow asked for heavy water, they let the cat out of the bag. Except for curious experiments in retarding plant growth, heavy water boasts only one useful property: it is the best of moderators for slowing down the speed of neutrons in nuclear reactions.

Records in evidence7 prove that on August 23, 1943, Hermann Rosenberg of Chematar received an application from the Soviet Purchasing Commission for 1,000 grams of deuterium oxide. The purpose stated was "research". A supplier was found in the Stuart Oxygen Co. of San Francisco, which shipped the merchandise on October 30 by railway express to Chematar's New York office. Rosenberg forwarded the consignment to the Purchasing Commission in Washington, which dispatched it on November 29, by way of the Pipeline, to Rasnoimport, USSR, Moscow U-1, Ruybjshova-22.

SUPPRESSED INTELLIGENCE REPORTS

The order was packed with as much tenderness as if it had been a casket of jewels. Forty pyrex ampoules, each containing 25 grams, were enclosed in mailing tubes and wrapped in layers of cotton. The ampoules were divided in lots of 10 among four cartons, which were placed, with further precautions against damage, in a large wooden box. This was strapped and sealed. The overall weight was 41.12 pounds. The cost of the fluid content was that of expensive perfumes - $80 an ounce.

The export of heavy water to the Soviet Union was approved by a release certificate, No. 366, dated November 15, with the signature of William C. Moore, Division for Soviet Supply, Office of Lend-Lease Administration.

If General Groves had been consulted, the heavy water would not have left this country. Had it been known at the time, he said, that 1,000 grams were available, unquestionably he would have bought the treasure himself. He added, "If it had been pure."[8] That it was between 99.7 and 99.8 per cent pure was attested by an independent analysis made for Rosenberg in the laboratories of Abbot A. Hanks, Inc., San Francisco.

At the beginning of 1945, the Soviet Purchasing Commission placed with Rosenberg a second order for heavy water. Only 100 grams were sought. He applied once more to the Stuart concern, which expressed the 'liquid diamonds' to Chematar on February 7. One week later Rosenberg forwarded the parcel to the commission. Its subsequent adventures have not been traced. In August of the same year, Rosenberg was naturalized as an American citizen...

Was one kilogram of heavy water and were mere hundreds of pounds of uranium chemicals too insignificant for important use?

Specialists agree that the quantities delivered were inadequate for producing one A-bomb or even one experimental pile. They point out, however, that scarcely any fraction of a substance can be too small for laboratory research. The head of a pin could not have been formed with the first plutonium ever made. From 500 micrograms were determined most of the properties and the chemical behavior of an element which 18 months earlier had been entirely unknown.

On the presumption that 1,465 pounds of uranium salts were contributed to the Soviet Union, metallurgists estimate that they were reducible in theory to 875 pounds of natural uranium, which in turn would yield 6.25 pounds of fissionable U-235. But 4.4 pounds of the latter, or nearly two pounds less, are capable of producing an atomic explosion. Authority for this assertion may be found in the celebrated report which Dr Henry De-Wolf Smyth of Princeton University wrote at the request of General Groves and published in 1945.

The Shattuck and Eldorado purchases totaled 1,420 pounds. With their third requisition, the Russians expected so confidently to acquire another 500 pounds that papers to that effect were drafted and sent to us in Montana. If the full amount had been available, instead of 45 pounds, the aggregate would have been 1,920 pounds, or virtually one ton.

At his Paris laboratory, while chief of the Atomic Energy Commission of France, Frederic Joliot-Curie built an experimental pile to which he gave the affectionate name of "Zoe". It actually ran, though the wattage was feeble. The quantity of uranium crystals utilized, said Dr Joliot-Curie, was "something in the order of one ton".

It seems fair to take into account not merely what the Russians got, but what they tried to get. With Communist tenacity and ardent support from both White House and Lend-Lease, the Soviet Purchasing Commission strove again and again to obtain 8-1/2 tons each of uranium oxide and uranium nitrate, plus 25 pounds of uranium metal. The campaign started in February 1943, and persisted until the Russians were squelched by Secretary Stimson during April 1944.

There are memorable instances of what can be achieved with less than 17 tons of uranium powders. One was a model atomic pile which went into operation at Chicago University on December 2, 1942. "So far as we know," Dr Smyth recounts, "this was the first time that human beings ever initiated a self-maintaining nuclear chain reaction." With a power level of 200 watts, the device served as a pilot plant for the Hanford Engineer Works. The uranium supply available to them was six tons.

Even earlier, before the Manhattan Project was dreamed of, a group of scientists at Columbia University began a course of hazardous experiments under the leadership of two foreign-born savants, Leo Szilard of Hungary and Enrico Fermi of Italy. They were so ill-supported with cash that 10,000 pounds of uranium oxide had to be 'rented' at a nominal fee of 30 cents a pound from Boris Pregel, president of the Canadian Radium & Uranium Corp. of New York, who was later unjustly made a scapegoat by the press for the secret Canadian shipment.

Here was done all the preparatory work moving toward the eventual creation of the first man-made elements in history: neptunium-93 and plutonium-94. From the group's creative imagination rose in time the vast plutonium plant at Hanford, Washington, and, in a large sense, America's atom bomb itself. The materials of that triumph were not 17 but 10 tons of uranium compounds.

One of my lucky experiences was that of chancing upon the February 27, 1950 issue of the magazine, Life, shortly before my second appearance before the Un-American Activities Committee. I bore the copy with me to the witness chair. It contained an illustrated article on the atom bomb. I learned for the first time that a plutonium pile consists of giant blocks of graphite, surrounded by heavy walls of concrete and honeycombed with aluminum tubes. In these tubes, it was related, are inserted slugs of natural uranium, containing one per cent of U-235. The intensity of the operation was declared to be governed by means of cadmium rods.

Graphite, cadmium, aluminum tubes - where had I met these words before? In the Russian lists of Lend-Lease figures which I had added to the Jordan diary. Re-examining those pages, I discovered that during the four-year period 1942-45 we contributed to the Soviet Union 3,692 tons of natural graphite, 417 tons of cadmium metals, and tubes in an entry designating 6,883 tons of "aluminum tubes".

The figure for cadmium was arresting in view of its extreme scarcity in this country and because of the fact that it occurs, so far as we know, sparsely if at all in the Soviet Union. Under war stimulus, American production of cadmium rose from 2,182 short tons in 1940 to 4,192 in 1945.

It was interesting to find that in 1942-45 we shipped to Russia 437 tons of cobalt - a staggering amount when collated with American production, which was nothing before the war, and increased to 382 tons in 1942 and 575 in 1945.

That cobalt is valuable in the A-bomb for retarding radioactive emanations, and could be equally so in the hydrogen bomb, has been affirmed by a chemical engineer who was consultant to one of the war agencies. "Cobalt," says he, "was one of our highest scarcity materials. If I had known that so large a proportion was going to the Russians, I should have suspected them of being at work on the bomb." Incidentally, cobalt was the first item to be restricted by President Truman in the Korean emergency.

Almost as curious was the discovery that we shipped to Russia more than 12 tons of thorium salts and compounds. Two other elements alone, besides uranium and plutonium, are fissionable. They are protoactinium and thorium. The former may be disregarded because of its rarity in nature. But thorium, which is relatively plentiful, is expected by physicists to rival uranium some day, or even supplant it, as a source of atomic energy.

Then there were cerium and strontium, of which the Soviet Purchasing Commission obtained 44 tons. Both metals, along with cadmium, thorium and cobalt, figured in Colonel Kotikov's dossier on experimental chemicals. They are useless for atomic purposes. But Russian scientists may have been working their way through the rare earths and metals on a well-founded suspicion that something momentous was afoot in that group.

Everyone is aware, of course, that these elements have industrial or military functions unrelated to the atom bomb, but Russia had a very critical interest in procuring A-bomb components from America. Red scientists are said to have been the first in Europe to announce the theory of nuclear fission. As America discovered at a cost of billions of dollars, it is a far cry from setting down speculations on paper to putting them in practice at the dimensions imposed by modern war. Thus the Kremlin was frantically inquisitive about large-scale production techniques developed by the Manhattan Project...

One ground for minimizing my evidence is a claim that Russia had abundant uranium of its own, in connection with massive radium deposits in the former area of Turkestan, the Kazakh Republic and the state of Tannu-Tuva, north of Mongolia. More than 30 years ago, it is said, Soviet physicists worked out the correct formula for separating uranium from radium. On the other hand, as atomic experts are fond of pointing out, "You can never have too much uranium."

If a blunder occurred, such objections proceed, it was not the shipment of minor quantities of uranium compounds to the Soviet Union, but the publication of Dr Smyth's book, which told not only how to make a nuclear bomb but how not to make one. The chief atomic authority of Norway, Gunnar Randers, is cited as having pronounced that the indiscretion of this publication saved Russia and every other country two years of research. According to Professor Szilard, "one half of the atomic bomb secret was given away when we used the bomb, and the other half when we published the Smyth report." After the espionage trials, however, one may ask whether the Smyth revelations were not more informative to the American public than to the Politburo...

In any event, it is heartening to know that, on the whole, our uranium embargo stood firm. Moscow was prevented from winning its grand objective of 17 tons, in contrast to the delivery of 15 tons of uranium chemicals to Great Britain which the Manhattan Project authorized. The steadfastness of the General Groves organization against Russia was the more admirable in that it was challenged by Mr Hopkins, with the power of the White House behind him. After the Un-American Activities Committee closed its hearing on March 7, 1950, I was examined searchingly by Government investigators. They tried to lure me into admitting a possibility, however faint, that the person to whom I spoke might have been Edward R.

SUPPRESSED INTELLIGENCE REPORTS

Stettinius, Jr, who had died five months earlier on October 11, 1949.

My answer was that never once, during my two years at Newark and Great Falls, did I hear so much as a mention of Stettinius, though reference to Hopkins was daily on the lips of the Russians.

It is common knowledge that on August 28, 1941, Stettinius succeeded Hopkins as titular chief of Lend-Lease, and held the post until September 25, 1943, when the agency was merged with kindred bodies into the Foreign Economic Administration, with Leo A. Crowley as Administrator.

But even the official biographer of Mr Hopkins does not hesitate to write:

"Hopkins knew that policy governing Lend-Lease would still be made in the White House and that the President would continue to delegate most of the responsibility to him. Stettinius was his friend and they could work together - and that was that."9

Another effort to clear Hopkins was based on the supposition that he acted in ignorance of what it was all about. Even if he helped the Russians to get A-bomb materials, the implication ran, it was the unsuspecting tool of Soviet cunning.

The Hopkins papers for Mr Sherwood's book were organized by Hopkins' longtime friend, Sidney Hyman. A fortnight after my first broadcast he was quoted as affirming that, until Hiroshima, Harry Hopkins had not "the faintest understanding of the Manhattan Project" and "didn't know the difference between uranium and geranium".

On the contrary, Harry Hopkins was one of the first men anywhere to know about the atom bomb. Dr Vannevar Bush chose Hopkins as his intermediary for presenting to Mr Roosevelt the idea of the atom bomb. It was in consultation with Hopkins that Dr Bush drafted the letter, for Mr Roosevelt's signature, which launched the A-bomb operation on June 14, 1941! Where do we learn this? In the official biography by Mr Sherwood, on pages 154 and 155. Finally, on page 704 we are told that the head of a state, Winston Churchill, "was conducting this correspondence on the atomic project with Hopkins rather than with the President, and that he continued to do so for many months thereafter".

A witness on the topic, General Groves testified that to the best of his recollection and belief he never met Harry Hopkins, talked with him on the telephone, or exchanged letters or dealt with anyone claiming to represent him. But the General thought it incumbent to remark, "I do know, of course, that Mr Hopkins knew about this project. I know that."10

An early symptom of White House obsession for 'reassuring Stalin' has been described by General Deane. In letters to American war agencies, dated March 7, 1942, Mr Roosevelt ordered that preferential position, in the matter of munitions, should be given to the Soviet Union over all other Allies and even the armed forces of the United States. Then and there, decided the former chief of the US Military Mission to Moscow, was "the beginning of a policy of appeasement of Russia from which we have never recovered and from which we are still suffering"11...

SUPPRESSED INTELLIGENCE REPORTS

Endnotes

1. Stimson, Henry L. and Bundy, McGeorge, On Active Service in Peace and War, Harper, 1947.

2. "Hearings Regarding Shipments of Atomic Materials to the Soviet Union during World War II", Testimony of General Groves, December 7, 1949, House of Representatives Committee on Un-American Activities, US Government Printing Office, USA, p. 941.

3. ibid., p. 945.

4. ibid., p. 900.

5. ibid., p. 948.

6. ibid., p. 947.

7. "Hearings...", Testimony of Hermann H. Rosenberg, January 24, 1950, p. 1035.

8. "Hearings...", General Groves, p. 954.

9. Sherwood, Robert E., Roosevelt and Hopkins: An Intimate History, Harper, 1948, p. 560.

10. "Hearings...", General Groves, p. 947.

11. Deane, John R., The Strange Alliance, Viking, 1947, p. 89.

SUPPRESSED INTELLIGENCE REPORTS

THE WORLD OF ILLUSIONS

Fracturing Myths and Illusions

Hypocrites of the world, buoyed by their Evil essence, are, and have been, united in their ability to distort truth and reality on this plane ever since the takeover of this sector of the True Creation by the Evil Essence. You know this statement is true if you know anything about how the Media, Religions and Governments work.

Look at how distorted a picture has been presented to the "Free World" concerning activities around the September 11, 2001 attacks and the subsequent war. Examples to support my point abound. This deceiving attitude existed long before the personnel of Pearl Harbour were sacrificed to allow more expeditious programming of the human lemmings in the USA, long before Machiavelli put pen to paper, even long before the Sons of Darkness mocked the Jesus they murdered and then lied about his birth and death. Look how they mock the Truth by saying that "God so loved this (evil, depraved, condemned and doomed) world that He sent His Only Son as ransom (and to be spat upon, tortured and crucified so the demons could fill their bellies with the satisfaction of another murder!!)

This ability to deceive has been a trait of Evil since its nascent days.

But the True Reality is impinging on this corrupt, depraved plane of malevolent illusions as never before. Even as the evil ones point to the illusions they hope will support them, the very illusions they look to are fragmenting along with everything else which is fraudulent. I repeat: the lies no longer work. They will not work, for this is the time of truth, the time of accountability, the time of settling all scores. And there is no place those of injustice can escape to. Of course, such an assertion is most welcome to those who love Truth and Justice. It is the answer to their prayers. But to those of Evil, to those who have chosen Evil, to those who have created the deceiving illusions, to those who have denied the need for Truth and Justice, this is a threat to their very existence. Indeed, it is the announcement of their worst nightmare.

Myths and Illusions with which the Sons and Daughters of Darkness hope to deceive are many, but let me examine and dispel a few at random.

* 1.   The first illusional myth to be dispelled states that Jesus Christ will appear in the midst of the turmoil and introduce a period of one thousand years of peace.

Jesus was NOT the only Christ (anointed One). He, Jesus, had told us that He came with a sword - to cut away the evil ones from the viables. He said He, the Energy in Him, would return to judge all, and rescue those worthy of rescue. Judgement was always on the cards.

Those who deny such a Judgement by a Higher Energy - as do A Course in Miracles, and most New Age 'Doctrines', etc., - are mocking, Evil-created mechanisms which again are attempting to create self-deceiving Illusions! They will not work. They cannot work, for they are of Untruth.

For New Agers to say they forgive themselves and all others, and judge themselves worthy and therefore viable is not valid. Indeed we must all move on from transgressions, but with faith that the Higher Energy will decide! If we attempt to remove that privilege from the Higher Energy and make ourselves god as the New Agers do, we are in fact usurping the Power of the Judge and invalidating the process. The validity of the Process of Judgement is in having Faith that the Higher Energy will deal with True Justice with all of us. It is not up to lowly consciousnesses to say they forgive themselves and find themselves worthy. What that does is really eliminate the need for a real God.

Those who claim they are god are really using this mechanism of evil-created illusion making, but deep down in their hearts they know they are lying. And this becomes obvious when they are confronted by my words. They panic and scatter like ants set on fire. Why is that? It is because their evil cover, given by their self-deceiving illusions, is blown away by the energy in these words.

If they still want to argue they are god, let them explain how they created Black Holes; let them explain how they created the forces controlling meiosis; let them explain how they created the chromatic processes in retinas. They cannot, can they? But they would be able to if they were "god", right? They are not "god", they are evil, self-deceiving fools.

The Christ Energy is an Essence, not an individual. The Essence has come. It has judged and is evacuating those who are viable. It has judged and marked those who are not viable, so that they will be sent to the transmutation vats when this physical dimension is DESTROYED totally!

Even our lower minds tell us the likelihood of peace in the near future is zero. The talk is of war and more war. Those who were not terrorists before are now contemplating such a profession in response to the gross injustices that have been forced upon them by recent events. All manner of personnel are lining up to fight what they see as the good fight for justice. Countries are about to fragment from the smell of war. Pakistan at present is the most obvious example. And bombs everywhere are being primed to explode. They too have a consciousness.

Bombs and their terror are creating the scope for future generations of assassins and martyrs. Humanity has learned nothing from the theft of Palestine.

Do you think those poisoned by spent uranium are contemplating one thousand years of peace as they see their children die with deformities and malignancies from the radiation?

And just where would the one thousand years of peace be staged? It cannot be Earth or this Solar System, for they are primed for destruction. The homeostatic controls are no longer working. Within a generation this earth would be uninhabitable even if it were to last that long.

Uncontrollable AIDS, Mad Cow Disease, Ebola, diseases and genetic mutations from the poisons purposely planted in Chemtrails and genetically Modified Foods - thanks to the aliens who want to eradicate a major portion of Humanity - will devastate the Earth's population that is left after the Nuclear Bombs have had their turn.

Previously I had told you that all must leave the physical for that is the Plan of Correction. There will be no more time, hence, there cannot be One Thousand Years of Peace!

The Christ Energy has been here on the planet. What do you think did the assessment and organized the evacuation of viables, if not the Christ Energy? E.T.?

What do you think has allowed the exposure of all corruption, all Evil? What do you think allowed the Beast to be unleashed so that it would pursue its well-known path of destruction which would end as self-destruction?

All these have been the work of the Christ Energy using the Power provided by the True Love of the Mother of Creation - a Power maliciously and forcefully denied by the Yarwehnians and Jehovians. And that too was from the creation of other self-deceiving illusions by the sycophants of Darkness.

* 2   The Second Illusional Myth to dispel states that Nibiru, the twelfth Planet is approaching and the Creators of Humanity will set all things right.

Let the fools who have been deceived by this evil-spun illusion of idiocy dream on. They shall be rudely awakened soon enough by the knowledge of the non-existence of this planet Nibiru, and by knowledge that the creators of the biological aspects of humanity have been here all the time and are even now plotting mechanisms of genocide with which to diminish the numbers of their too-successful experiment.

* 3   The third myth is that this planet Earth is a classroom in which souls are to learn and develop.

Think back for a moment to when you were young, and loving and caring and so innocent. What have you learnt in the years since childhood? What have you acquired? You have learned how much evil there is in the world. You have learned how few people can be really trusted. You have acquired emotional scars you never asked for. The fools who can program themselves to not think about this will not agree, but the fact is you learned all about evil and how it messes things up. You may have been programmed to commit evil. Is that what a classroom is for? Is that proper development?

Most non-demonic geriatrics - unless they have lost their marbles - are sour, paranoid sceptics who see life as a waste of good years. Depression is very high among the elderly, as is suicide. Is that because they learned to be godlike in classroom earth or because they developed into future little gods? Not on your Neddy. It is because they are bruised by the burden of evil they have had to endure.

Make no mistake about it, this planet is a jail for maximal suffering and energy exploitation of those with good energy. Of course it suits those who exploit and gain the energy - because they have none of their own - to a tee! They are the demons who tell you this is a classroom. For them it is, for with each lifetime they learn how to exploit more efficiently.

Just one other point which I have mentioned often: Why would a real god create souls so imperfect that they would need to come to a crappy place like this to learn anything? Is this god incapable of something better? The systems on earth are atrocious. The exploitation is never-ending. Does one really need to be raped, abused, exploited, robbed, subjected to all sorts of injustices, etc., just to learn living? Sure, these things do not happen to everyone, but they do to the majority. Everyone suffers in one way or another. Those of evil deny it is so.

Even those who are apparently successful learn to cheat better. They learn to subdue and disadvantage others so they can finish on top of the pile. And don't deny this; don't say that it is not so. A cursory glance at all the powerful and rich families in the world will reveal they gained their wealth by cunningly evil exploitation. How do rich nations become a lot richer if not by exploitation of the weaker ones and their resources?

Each creature is a murderer or a meal for another. These bodies are continually breaking down. The degree of mental illness in the world should tell you no one is really enjoying this so-called learning classroom, except the demons who gain energy from all the pain, suffering and misery, even though they themselves appear to be caught up in the same processes.

Look back over the centuries. Apart from multiplying like bacteria out of control, humanity has learned nothing but to be more violent, more efficient in killing large numbers and to be more efficient in exploiting people, animals, the seas, the vegetation and Earth itself, bringing everything to the point of non sustainability of life. In truth, collectively, Humanity has learned how to destroy more, and more quickly, and how to self destruct. What a classroom! It truly is spitting into the eye of the creator of this atrocious system, and that is all such a creator deserves!

In the near future I will write about the myths that Humanity is an ontologically homogenous entity and that Humanity is in control of its own destiny.

A brief examination of 'A Course in Miracles'

Since posting the first essay on this topic I have received quite a deal of material, some of it psychiatric advice, which made me smile, coming as it did from the most inept and ignorant of the readers. It is amazing what they see in my words - concepts that are nowhere in sight but which incite them to ridiculousness. They are reactions to the energy of the words, of course. Hence, as the ones of Truth are buoyed and sustained by the writings, those of Darkness writhe in anguish at the very thought of what it could all mean. They are confronted and disarmed by the words, and they realize they are exposed in all their ontological nakedness. This they do not like, for it reveals what they really are. They are exposed in the Light, and their hypocrisy, deceitfulness and dank evil are exposed as never before. They are traumatised by the exposure, thinking they would never be found out. But then recovering somewhat, they write the drivel that makes me laugh, confirming ever so speedily that they are suffering the effects of the terminally mad. (Jerry Attrick says I've been laughing so much I am in danger of developing a waist line. Well, small danger anyway!)

The most vile of the respondents have been adherents of A Course in Miracles (ACIM). At first they present with the false sugary sweetness of trained deceivers. But their façade does not last long with me. Soon enough they turn into the ghastly demonic beasts awakened beings now known so well.

Let us examine this Course again. I have done so in the past, but, it is important, and I will spend a few minutes on it again. The story told is that the information in ACIM was dictated to a Zionist in New York, supposedly by Jesus. You know the Christ Energy of Jesus and Zionism are ontological opposites from what I have revealed. Hence, how could that be? The fact is that Jesus did NOT dictate this nonsense. Ramtha did. You remember him - the one who claims he was the biggest bastard of them all, and still is!

Having read ACIM cover to cover, and every word therein, I must admit it is of compelling subtlety. It appeals to the ego as it aggrandises it, ever so apparently innocently and harmlessly, luring it with words such as love, compassion and forgiveness. It creates an illusion of Peace while claiming to dispel the illusion of Evil and Ignorance. In fact, by doing this, it creates a greater illusion, masking as it does, the reality of the War of Essences, the existence of Evil, the destructiveness of Evil, the need for a Higher Energy to judge, the need to separate the sheep from the goats, the need to fight back for all the injustices, humiliations and exploitations those of Goodness are burdened with.

And it lays the blame of personal failure, not on this demonic system and its sycophants, if there is personal failure, but totally on the individual, who is blamed for the failure to dispel the reality of Evil. It makes Evil an abnormality in the eye of the beholder, and if that beholder happens to perceive Evil, demons, injustice, etc., s/he, the beholder, is blamed for being incompetent and ignorantly imprudent. The beholder is blamed for perceiving incorrectly according to ACIM, when, in fact, s/he has impinged upon the truth of existence. In fact, as you well know, empirically and experientially, the truth is opposite to what ACIM teaches.

Some say it is a good course because it eradicates conflict and friction. That is the whole point of its evilness. In a struggle, if one side's propaganda can make the other side put down its weapons and not fight, the war is over, is it not? If one side convinces the other to give up, are the ones who laid down their arms then not defenceless victims to be exploited at will by the evilness of the deceivers? Indeed they are. This is what ACIM tries to do. By denying Evil and the need to fight it to the very end, it tries to disarm those with energy so that they can be exploited mercilessly.

Let me dwell for a moment on the assertion that this level with obvious Evil is illusional, with no real Evil at all, as postulated by ACIM. It manages to allay the need to fight Evil by saying it does not exist, that this is some sort of godly play in which we are ignorantly experimenting in all sorts of ways, and do not realize that this is so. Once we will realize it, according to ACIM, we will be happy with all circumstances everywhere on the globe, and just let things be, knowing soon enough we, one and all, will return to a godly state, with no judgement. Hence, according to this book, ultimately there is no need to be responsible for our actions, no need to be accountable. Ultimately there is nothing to forgive, so it says. "Your brother has done nothing to forgive"! it asserts.

This state of affairs suits the evil ones admirably, and they beam with joy at such thoughts, for it means they can exploit at will, and not worry about it. They forgive themselves and everyone else on a superficial outer mind level and appear to live guilt-free. But their self-justification, their self-deception are temporary and illusional. The sense of forgiveness in these people is contained in the evil concept from ACIM that ultimately there is nothing to forgive!

These thoughts are only on a superficial outer mind level, for the moment they meet my words they are traumatized. You see, deep down they know they are deluding themselves, and my words drag them back to a reality they had hoped they could deny forever. But they cannot. It catches up with them. That is why they are distraught.

But, let's examine their beliefs from ACIM a little closer. If there is no Evil, and this whole mess is just playfulness of ignorant little children who have strayed a little, ever so innocently, then all things are validly godly and not condemnable, according to ACIM, is that not so?

Now, a firm believer in ACIM, like Oprah Winfrey, for example, should be able to not only accept the following scenario, but be happy that it is just a leela, as the Hindu say, a playful prank by godly children who really do no wrong. Hence, if she is assaulted one dark night by five men and raped repeatedly, after which her breasts are cut off, her uterus is perforated with a broomstick or rifle thrust vaginally, and she has her eyes gauged out, everything should be OK, according to the no-Evil brigade.

According to ACIM, it is only god's children at play, and the rape, torture and maiming are only illusional pranks of godly children. Let us say she had a harmless and defenceless four year old child and she, too, received the same treatment after having her two harmless and defenceless puppies smashed against the walls until they die in excruciating agony, giving out wails and screams that tear the heart of any who truly know justice and love, and who are unfortunate enough to hear the sounds which include the fearful supplications for mercy, but then become the sorrow-filled whines of self-pity, involuntary canine whimpers seeking release from such Evil-imposed pain, seeking a speedy physical death from the insufferably unjust injuries.

I have depicted these gory scenes on purpose, namely to demonstrate the gruesomeness of Evil. In the moments of tragedy, humans react in a similar fashion, as they are forced to bear the full brunt of Evil. Under such circumstances they find it very hard to deny that Evil exists. Tell them then that Evil is an illusion! They will not agree.

In such a devilish scenario, can Oprah keep smiling and remain calm and happy using the notions of ACIM? I doubt it. Can you? You see, such evil assertions only work when the hypocrites are free from being victims themselves. Such scenarios occur everywhere around the world, constantly with and without war. Especially now they are occurring with the "war" in Afghanistan. The assailants go further there, of course. They murder their victims. Are adherents of ACIM still happy and laughing? If they are, they deserve to be called fools!

And yet, ACIM insists on total forgiveness, and, in total contradiction, it ends up by saying one must believe that there is ultimately nothing to forgive. Even in such cases as above, it states that "your brother, has done nothing that needs forgiveness"!

Here is the direct quote from its textbook: "Forgiveness is knowing that your brother has done nothing for you to forgive."

How many can truly live with that in the scenario described above?

ACIM claims it wants to dispel guilt. But this direct quote demonstrates how dastardly it imposes the burden of guilt : "The sin and guilt we fail to forgive in others remains in us as well."

So, if a victim has not forgiven the demons and has not embraced the sordid cruelty of hell, s/he is also just as guilty. How perverse! Of course, rehabilitation is one thing. We should never accept Evil. If we do, we not only condone it, but eventually use it freely with misperceived impunity. How would it ever be eradicated under those circumstances? That is the whole point of why ACIM presents this scenario. Being from Evil, it does not want the eradication of Evil.

Also, realize that Judgement and Forgiveness are not for humans to dispense. There is a God for that. And to have imposed on oneself the sin and guilt of another just because one cannot accept the demonic behaviour of another is the ultimate injustice dispensed by Evil, and this makes a mockery of those who truly seek Justice and Fairness.

Ultimately, as I said, it accuses those who see Evil of being incompetently misperceiving the status quo. It claims the perception of those who see Evil (that is, see truly) needs to be changed, and that they need to block out the vision of the Reality of Evil for according to ACIM, that is a misperception. According to ACIM, true perception (that is, being spiritually blind) is the perception it wants its sycophants to have. Now, isn't that Evil? Of course it is!

So, back to the quote: "Forgiveness is knowing that your brother has done nothing for you to forgive." If that is the case, what is the point of struggling against the impurity and devilishness of this plane? There would be no point. We could act as despicably as we could imagine, knowing we do nothing wrong in that case. But we know Right from Wrong, don't we? We know there is a line between Goodness and Evil. Even in demons who try to deny this Principle, it is ingrained into the substance of every unit of consciousness, whether it be theomorphic or counterfeit. And that is where the fear of those who chose Evil comes from.

One more quote: "What you see in another is you." This surely is given by Ramtha to scare the guts out of any who perceive truly. If not fully awakened to the Truth, when they see the demonic essence in some, they tend to remember this threat which naturally makes them shut off their inner vision, for who wants to be a demon? Of course it is nonsense. It is another way of scaring the adherents into submission. And this comes after the Oneness is stressed, the quote from ACIM being that we are all equal (in ontological terms). Believing that, any who see demonic essences in others think there is something wrong with them, rather than thinking they are perceiving truly. Quite an effective evil plot, hey?

Another point stressed by ACIM which needs to be dispelled is the one stating that it is we, 'humans', who are the cause of any evil, even illusional evil, with all its confusion, conflict and suffering to be found in the world. According to it, once we stop perceiving it, it will simply disappear, as will all the pain, suffering and misery. Ha!

Children play a game of covering their eyes to make danger and fear supposedly disappear. That is exactly what ACIM wants adults to do: stop seeing Evil and it will disappear. Fat chance! This is not just a childish prank. It is a very serious and pernicious aspect of Evil which really is spiritual cancer. Always remember that perniciousness left untreated is fatal in the end.

I repeat, ACIM wants adherents to be spiritually blind. That is the function of Evil. That is why Evil is called Darkness and Ignorance! ACIM is Evil, make no mistake about that whatsoever. Ignorance in these circumstances is bliss, but only until the self-deceiving illusion lasts. Once it is broken, as it is with these words, the bliss vanishes, and the reality of the cruelty of Evil comes as a stark reminder to both its victims and those who need to pay the ultimate price, if in fact, they have chosen Evil as their essence..

It is no coincidence that most adherents of ACIM are middle class Westerners, especially in the more affluent states of the USA. ACIM was tailor-made for such places as California and Colorado, and for those who are blind to the horrors of this world.

SUPPRESSED INTELLIGENCE REPORTS

There is a pragmatic point to what I am revealing. Watch how these hypocrites react once the suffering reaches their doorstep, as it will soon enough with the spread of overt, destructive and openly malicious Evil throughout the West, and the USA in particular, in the next few months. Watch how the word 'forgiveness' will disappear from their vocabulary once the others of Evil start to hit them.

My personal experience has been that these people who claim there is no Evil are the most evil of all. When I lectured to them, and they felt most uncomfortable about having been reminded that they are accountable to a Higher Consciousness, and after having told me repeatedly there was no Evil, they would, quite contrarily, call me evil for having disturbed their artificial mind shelters of delusional tranquillity. Can you beat that? So, they did believe in Evil all along, hey? It is just that it suits them to pretend when left alone, so that they can continue sucking dry any unaware "good energy" being they meet.

I admit some of the adherents of ACIM and other New Age garbage are victims, trapped by the lure of the promise of some temporary peace of mind from the opiate effect of these false philosophies. And some of these have had the evil spell broken with my words. I say that in all modesty and have many who would aver to the fact they have been pulled out of the abyss of darkness, in which these false philosophies placed them, by the words in our books, website, etc.

Finally, realize that the Truth is no whore. It cannot be used and abused to please one and not another. Truth is immutable. Hence, no matter what people think when it pleases them, eventually Truth will emerge victorious.

* The Truth is that there is Evil.

* People do suffer from Evil.

* There is Superior Consciousness that judges.

* Some, who have squandered countless chances to be in the Light, all due to their own fault, have been judged to be worthless failures and are to be transmuted.

* There has been a Celestial Error and a raging Battle of Essences.

* There are demons and ones who have chosen Evil.

* There is occurring a rectification of this abomination.

* There is a happy ending for those of Love, Peace and Justice!!

Indeed, from the truthful perspective, 'A Course in Miracles' should be renamed 'A Course in Mockery!'

***

A World in Crisis

A time to rethink the definition of Reality

Whether you want to believe it or not, you and every other individual on Earth is being affected by a process of unique change. Indeed, this is a Generation of Uniqueness, a generation of massive change; a generation of fragmentation of many things, a time of sorting out, a time of finality. You, like everyone else, are going to have to rethink the paradigms of normality which you have accepted since the Age of Reason, and which you have modified, knowingly or unknowingly, in order to make sense of a world which seemed to accommodate you as the years passed in your life.

But suddenly, especially with events unfolding since the time of the bombing of the World Trade Towers, nothing seems the same in our minds. Suddenly there are forced upon many minds, very aware ones and less aware ones, many issues and fears which shatter the laboriously moulded paradigms of normality we hoped would see us to the end of our lives. One of the fears encroaching on minds is the fear that whatever paradigms of normality we had, they are now not sufficient. Suddenly the world makes less sense; suddenly the guard rails we used to set our minds at ease in times of crises are no longer there. Suddenly we feel vulnerable as never before. It is as if a massive mental earthquake has shattered our inner being and we are on shifting mental ground, trying to make sense of that which is no longer familiar.

Our vulnerability is not just physical, as with the threats of attacks from known and unknown quarters, nor just financial with threats of loss of jobs, loss of financial stability and independence. It is not even the thought of war alone, for many of us have lived with the reality of multiple wars ever since the 1940s. Our vulnerability lurks in the mind as we see the fragmentation of the life we thought was stable and would remain so. Our vulnerability comes from seeing the fragmentation of other nations, institutions, traditions, foundations and organizations we thought would never fail us.

What we are witnessing, and what is causing the fears in minds which do not fully understand the shift in reality is the inevitable breakdown of the false reality in which we have lived ever so illusionally. The Virtual Reality of this dimension is fracturing.

Why I call this a Virtual Reality, why it is fracturing, and what is to replace it are the very realizations individuals have to make in order to maintain mental health in this time of unprecedented change.

The Process of Realization of the Falsehood of this dimension is painful. However, the process is the only process which will give hope to the desperate. It is the only process which will allow an understanding of what is happening and an understanding of why the True Gnostics called this dimension the Plane of Hypocrisy, the Plane of Dishonesty, of Illusion, and, as I have described, as the Plane of Programming, Pollution and Indoctrination.

To be more specific, it is painful to realize that the Media upon which many of us have relied on for facts of what is going on in the world is but a tool for programming the masses; a tool to convey any Untruth which those in charge, whom elsewhere I have called the Archons, want to convey to the masses who are indeed used as milking cows to do the Archons bidding. They do this bidding by being exploited of their money, time and energy by the many systems we find in modern society. They do this by being programmed to fight wars for the reasons the Archons give them. They do their bidding by killing whenever, and wherever they are asked to do so, under the cover of many so-called ideals, used dishonestly and most evilly. In due course, I shall give examples of this. However, here I want to make the point that this has been the mechanism on this Earth for a long, long time, in order to fool, program and exploit the masses. It is in this century especially that the Media has played such a worldwide role.

SUPPRESSED INTELLIGENCE REPORTS

But now, as all things fragment, even the Media is becoming ineffectual compared to previous times. Like all other systems, it is disintegrating and those who had been its victims previously are awakening, not only to its disintegration, but also to its ineffectiveness. At the same time, minds are awakening to the programming that they previously received via the Media and are now growing more and more angry at this tool of the Archons.

In previous eras, Religion served a similar purpose as the Media to program the masses, and fight wars in the name of this god and that god. It still does today, as we can see with the evolution of Jihads against Western Countries, and the nonsense of Jew versus Muslim in the Middle East, Catholic verses Protestant in Northern Ireland, Hindu versus Muslim on the Indian subcontinent, Christian versus Jew in many parts of the world, etc.

It is going to be a painful process now to realize that what we learned at our mother's knee as children about our religion, about Jehovah, etc., is false and ridiculous. Sure, all religions have, or had, some of the seeds of Truth at some time when they first evolved, but by an intentionally EVIL process, these truths have been so corrupted that the Religions are now useless in providing any truth about the Truth-filled Emerging Paradigm of the New Dimension. That is why religions now have no idea of what is going on. That is why they are unable to provide any insight or hope to struggling minds caught in the stresses of incredibly massive changes on Earth. The corrupted and very convoluted texts of pseudo-Christianity, texts such as the Book of Revelation, although based on Gnostic writings, are now useless in defining anything worthwhile with which people could remain mentally aware. If they did provide anything worthwhile, the majority would not be traumatized as they really are. They are awakening to the fact that they have been lied to, even with their Religious Instruction, and this is causing mental anguish as they seek the reality behind the falsehood.

The awakening mind will see that extant religions have been used to keep individuals programmed, exploited and trapped in the Illusion of this pseudo-reality. Religions have been efficient tools of bellicosity which, with the never ending suffering of wars, has yielded much energy to the evil system to sustain itself. I realize that some of the assertions I make in this short essay may appear esoteric, and hence readers are referred to my early books for fuller explanations.

And so it is also with Science and Government. Minds are awakening to the trickery they have been subjected to. The tricks no longer work. The lies no longer work, again for the same reason - namely, fragmentation is occurring in every sphere of human endeavour, and what kept the people programmed the way the Archons wanted in the past is no longer working, for it is fragmenting.

I have often called Science a fraud. Its explanations appear to work on this level, but in fact, its real fraudulence is seen as it acts, via bluff, to create a false paradigm of reality. As such, it has been a tool of the Evil Archons to keep minds trapped in the illusion. Here are some examples. One of the greatest of its evil tricks which Science performed is the one which dismisses the need for another energy - let's call it ESSE (essential, special, spiritual energy) for the moment - which is essential for existence beyond the physiological processes which Science describes ever so well and fraudulently. The ancient Sanskrit scholars called this energy 'prana'.

This trick of Science then negates the spiritual component to existence without which nothing could work in the physical, not even the smallest unit - the atom. What is an atom?

274

SUPPRESSED INTELLIGENCE REPORTS

Does it have consciousness? Science says no. Of course it has consciousness. What is it made of? A nucleus and electrons. What are electrons? Matter? Energy? Particles? Waves? Science does not know. Where do electrons get the energy to keep spinning around the nucleus? There must be a source, otherwise they would collapse. The power of centripetal and centrifugal forces, of velocity, and of attraction and repulsion are instigated, but these forces need energy to function. Where do they get their energy? Science does not know. It is ESSA (prana). What else? But science scoffs at this for it denies a spiritual component. And yet, its explanation of the simplest complete building block of matter is incomplete without the spiritual component. The basis of all matter - even this evil-created, corrupted matter in this dimension has a spiritual basis. All things have, and this is what all individuals are in the process of finding out as this world in crisis fragments inexorably.

Not convinced that Science bluffs with its picture of Reality? How about the notion that 98% of matter in this universe is Dark Matter? What function does it serve? Why can we not see it? Does it serve some other life forms? What? Am I suggesting the possibility of other lifeforms? Indeed, I am! But Science will have none of that, because Science has given us a false paradigm of Reality.

When Science cannot explain, it bluffs right along. Consider Quantum Mechanics and the disappearance of particles in an accelerator. Where do they go? How can they disappear and reappear? What are they really made of? Can you not conceive the fact that they may be subunits of consciousness which manifest in and out of dimensions? Science cannot, because it does not really have room in its false paradigms for consciousness outside of the physical and it cannot accept multiple dimensionality!

Governments - institutions which can be as corrupt and evil as anyone can imagine, when they are examined closely - are being seen more and more for what they are today, especially with the actions cited as involving terrorism, cleansing of nations of terrorists, etc. The lies are not working. People are seeing through the rhetoric of Government, of leaders, of demagogues and despots as never before.

Thus it is that now, in this unprecedented time, individuals are beginning to question everything - Religion, Science, the Media's honesty, the honesty of Governments and leaders, etc. It is what they are finding which is causing so much mental stress. They realize they are being lied to. They are realizing the basis of existence in this illicit dimension is Falsehood, and they do not like it. And they are internally rebelling. Soon they will rebel physically as well. But no matter what actions they take, they will be left with the need to find the paradigm of Reality if they are going to avoid the chasms of Terminal Madness which await those who cannot make the jump.

Questioning the status quo and finding it is illusional, of falsehood, is not enough. One must gain access to facts of Reality which will allow the emergence of the paradigm of Truth in which one can mentally survive. As I said, the process is painful, for much of what we accepted as normal must be dismissed as illusional. And for most there is a degree of urgency, for the final fragmentation is upon us.

The path to finding the True Reality, the reality into which we are now being hurled, as we witness the disintegration of that which we thought was valid, but which is being exposed as obviously fraudulent, as each hour passes, poses the questions of "Why? Who? When? and How?".

SUPPRESSED INTELLIGENCE REPORTS

Why is this a fraudulent reality? Why is it a Virtual Reality? Who set it up? Why is it being shattered? Who gained from its existence? Why do the Archons treat us this way? Of what benefit is it to them? Why are we kept pretty much in the dark? Why have institutions such as Religion, Science, Governments become corrupt and a virtual conspiracy against the 'common man'? Why is recorded History so much bunkum?

The answers to these questions, which are readily available in the Realm of Gnosticism, are essential components for the basis of realizing the New Reality which is emerging. Although individuals do not need to know every last detail of what is involved, an outline will be helpful in understanding what is going on, why this is a world and realm of fraudulence, why it is being allowed to disintegrate, and to be actively eradicated, why some are seen as sons and daughters of Darkness and why some will disappear into an abyss of irreversible madness.

That the basis of all existence depends on a spiritual component, so vehemently denied by materialistic science, will become obvious now as never before. It is in the ability to shift awareness to that component which will allow minds to make fuller realizations at this time of physical disintegration.

And so, as minds travel from this fast-fragmenting, material world of illusion to a new reality, questions will arise of what a human actually is, how humanity was formed, and by whom. There are valid answers. The answers which the Archons of Falsehood have provided in extant Science, Religion and History will be seen to be deficient as the false paradigm collapses. In the transition of awareness from the false to the true reality, concepts which many may not have considered will need to be integrated.

These concepts include the following:

* the emergence and continued existence of the essence of Evil;

* the existence of an evil pseudo-creator (known by True Gnostics as Jehovah who is also Satan) of this corrupt dimension and its matter;

* the existence of counterfeit beings and of this counterfeit reality which is breaking down;

* the existence of other lifeforms, some much more advanced than humanity;

* the interaction of these with humans;

* the existence of galactic wars;

* the ubiquitous battle of Good against Evil;

* the necessary assessment for viability and worthiness of all units of consciousness;

* the existence of consciousness in all living and so-called 'non-living' expressions.

(Just to diverge a little - it has been a great crime committed against the True Reality that humans have been conned by evil Archons into killing animals for fur, food or fun. Lack of awareness of the existence of consciousness in spheres such as the Earth, the Moon, the Sun, has allowed, particularly in Earth's case, the profane abuse of it leading, certainly, to murderous and suicidal endings. I realize these statements may be subjected to ridicule by the fools.

But, knowing ridicule is the baneful tool of the stupidly ignorant, I plough on, knowing such stupidly ignorant fools will soon no longer be part of any reality whatsoever.)

Knowledge of these concepts allows an understanding of what is going on, and the concepts facilitate the acceptance that this is a period of Correction of a Spiritual Error which occurred long, long ago; that this is a period of sorting out, of re-establishing a Divine Order, with True Justice in a valid paradigm of Truthful Reality.

The concepts allow the understanding, which will comfort minds, that Correction necessitates the elimination of that which was corrupt, counterfeit, of falsehood and of Evil, so that the basis of the True Reality now emerging will be one of honesty, not deceit.

And so it is that the process we are now witnessing will, per force, require the permanent removal of all things, be they material or spiritual, which are of the Corruption, of the Counterfeit, or of the Falsehood which fooled us for so long. These aspects will perish forever via a process of transmutation in due course. What we are seeing now in the physical, with the breakdown of many systems, with the disintegration of what we thought was a stable biosphere, with the lashing out of evil intent, is nothing more than the process of elimination of the unwanted. It is a process which must occur. No material thing will survive this process, for every material thing, your physical body and mine included, is of the evil essence which must be eradicated.

Viewed rationally, this process of elimination should not produce fear except to those who have acted with evil to sustain the illusion. They fear, for now they are in the process which judges them and finds them wanting. And they know this means permanent removal from existence. This they fear.

You have known since you attained the Age of Reason that some day you would physically die. Only a fool would think otherwise and deny that is so. Alas, there are many fools among us. Be that as it may, an understanding that many other facets, apart from the physical, make up our existence will allow a smoother transition from this collapsing reality to the one awaiting. With realizations to be made, knowing that nothing of value is lost, that the evil-created, unwanted physical is being discarded, individuals can detach from the process of disintegration and focus on the coming reality which will be of True Peace and Justice.

Without the realizations I speak of, without the knowledge I am revealing, without the detachment from the horror now obvious in the world, individuals will be overcome with anxiety, hysteria, paranoia and fear of physical decay. They will not cope; rather they will succumb to the Terminal Madness of the Physical Endtime. If that is the case, they have only themselves to blame.

The Beast Unleashed

The next few months will leave no one on the planet in any doubt about the existence of Evil, and the fact that Evil has been allowed to overrun the plane, purposely, so that it will entrap itself in a process of self-destruction.

Horror, terror and destruction will be witnessed by all, as the illusion fragments, as Evil plies its trade which has always been destruction, causing pain, suffering and misery to its trapped victims. What is different now is the fact that Evil will be unable to limit its madness, and its destruction of everything it overruns. Its very nature of hypocrisy, deceitfulness, dishonesty, cupidity and hate will be exposed as never before in the history of this planet. Even those Sons and Daughters of Evil who for so long appeared to relish the energy gains they made from the exploitation of others will now be filled with terror as they realise they are caught in an unstoppable process which will claim them physically, mentally and spiritually. And as they see their end coming, they will lash out even more angrily with hate and venom, at themselves and all whom they can corner, for their nature of hate and anger will be exposed as never before.

Indeed, the vile Beast has been unleashed - to do itself in, and annihilate all its sycophantic progeny in the process! It is being allowed to show its true colours, and its essence of utter Evil which forms it.

Bombs will fall as Terror from darkened skies. Germs released ever so maliciously, along with chemicals of warfare, will pervade the air, soil, water, bodies and minds of all caught in this maelstrom of Malignity. And knowing not where to turn next, the Beast, in all its Terminal Madness, represented by the Archons, the leaders of most nations, will do what it does best: destroy. Already we are being given a glimpse of that in Central Asia. Not long now before the Beast in all its forms, being unable to restrain itself, and being aware of its entrapment, will escalate its destructive power to bring the physical world to an end.

That the Beast with the essence of Evil is made up of parts such as Archons, and various groups of aliens present as consciousnesses in all classes of consciousness, is but detail, not essential to the understanding of the process of annihilation unleashed upon this Earth by those various parts of the Beast.

Every segment, every aspect of the Beast, regardless of its physical manifestation, will be caught in its own process of decay and self-destruction. It has always harboured hate in itself for all things, including itself. While it had victims from which to extract energy, it contained its self hate somewhat. But now, unleashed, it will hate all things with the zeal of demons doomed to die.

When utter hopelessness looms on the horizon of minds already undergoing decay due to Terminal Madness, as is occurring world-wide in non-viables, the path of destruction is the only path open to such minds.

For now, Archons appear to be playing the game of eradicating their enemies for material spoils, with wars that are ever-widening in their stance. But soon enough, they will realize that they, as part of the unleashed Beast, have actually been cornered and labelled as failures and will be transmuted once they self-destruct in the physical plane. When they realize this fully, they will reel headlong into the Abyss of Despair, and discharge all their venom here, there and everywhere, indiscriminately, so as to show the rest that they know they are doomed.

This time of madness in the Unleashed Beast has already begun. The fullness of the fury is no further away than 12 to 18 months according to my reckoning.

* Now shall all see the corruption, deceit, and evil manipulation which has kept us tightly sealed in this Truth-destroying illusion.

* Now shall we all see the despicable modus operandi used by the Archons, as leaders of government, as captains of cartels, to keep us trapped and exploited.

* Now shall we gleefully see their evil mechanisms being exposed, and fractured hope-

lessly as is their hope of escaping True Justice.

The fires of Hell will be no hotter as nuclear bombs rain down accompanied by the laments of the damned. Verily will there be wailing and gnashing of teeth.

Protect yourself now so that your emotional body will not react too forcefully, sending you too into the anguish of Horror and Despair. Remember the emotional body was created by Evil to be incorporated into these physical bodies for the purpose of allowing illicit extraction of energy from the Centres of Consciousness which are forced to use these bodies while expressing on the physical plane.

Anticipate the use of the most vile forms of warfare. Expect the ruthlessness of demons to be seen everywhere, just as we saw in the butchering of apparently innocent people in East Timor and Indonesia when vigilantes indiscriminately chopped heads off terrified victims with machetes.

Expect to see Hypocrisy reach new heights of malediction as Archons dressed in their finery talk about protecting their commercial interests as they bomb defenceless women and children, as they force starvation on ever-increasing numbers, as they drop incendiary bombs to burn the flesh of those they really consider inhuman.

It is they with the bombs and the malicious power to starve others, and the willingness to practise genocide as they wish, who are inhuman (contrary to the accepted sense of being human which means being aware of others, being cultured, and caring for fellow humans). They are demons from the depths of Hell, and there shall they return to await transmutation.

Unfortunately, those of us still in the physical will have to witness this destructive act by the Beast now unleashed. But we can be buoyed by the fact that nothing of value is lost in the process. All that is being eradicated is Evil and those consciousnesses who have chosen Evil over Good. We can be buoyed by the fact that this is a necessary step in the Corrective Process being applied to this illicit, counterfeit pseudo-reality which is Jehovah's corrupt world of Deceit, Dishonesty and Despair.

****

How the Unleased Beast will act

And so, if the Beast is going to self-destruct, it will need to vent its anger, its lusts and greed, totally uninhibited by any restraints. The end of the process is what is important - its total self-annihilation.

In accordance with this, it will wage war wherever and whenever conditions suit it. It will drop bombs on all whom it perceives as its enemies, and it will do so without reason, citing its ability to do so as reason enough. And by doing this, it will incite many others to oppose it, leading to confrontation and more violence, friction and murderous war. But, being self-absorbed with its own power and importance, the Beast will pursue the path of self-destruction regardless of the signs along the way that it is doing just that.

Former matters of pretence, such as caring for others, caring for Democracy, equanimity, freedoms of speech, action, choice, will all be abused. The power of the Beast, which when unleashed and unrestrained it finds inebriating and self-adsorbing, will be misused to crush those less powerful, even if in a true ontological sense those others are but extensions of its own being. What else would one expect of a Beast?

The circle of destruction will increase inexorably, each blunder being replaced with many more, and the Beast will continue unashamedly, feeling initially exhilarated by its ability to cause so much destruction, suffering and anguish.

But, the Law of Diminishing Returns will apply. Unlike former times when ruthlessness and destruction yielded an abundance of energy upon which to feast, the Beast will now find little energetic rewards for its labours. Enraged, it will expend even more effort to cause even more destruction and suffering. Is that not what we are seeing even now?

And members of its own corpus, struck by the ferocity of attacks, will retaliate with the excessive manner of madness. From within the breast of the beast will explode the vials of venom it has harboured for a long time. It will turn on itself, and all segments which it sees even in its own ranks as untrustworthy, and attempt to destroy them quickly. The Process of self-annihilation has the essence of paranoia as well as the Delusion of Grandeur and Invincibility. Thus will the Beast pursue the path of all despots, the difference this time being the fact that it will totally achieve its aims of destroying others, and itself, as a final outcome!

So, what is the Beast which will physically destroy this world and all physical expressions in it? It is the essence of Evil with the Mind of Malignity which, as parts and projections of the consciousness of Darkness, resides in all the Classes of Consciousness in this counterfeit, and illicit, Universe. Unleashed, it will now destroy itself, all its parts, all the things which it created from the energy it stole from the Sector of the True Creation which it invaded.

Let it ignite the last and most fatal conflagration which will consume all the Profanity. Let it singe and burn; let it engulf all it hates in flames as its True abode, Hell, is engulfed. Let it express that unlimited hate and let all of Truth, Love and Justice witness the fate of Evil, and the fact that this hate of Evil's is hate for all things, including itself.

None who form the Beast - and this includes all the evil beings in human bodies, as well as all others who have chosen evil - will escape the process. Regardless of previous pretence, they will now show their true nature. They will exhibit the venom and hate of demons. Fear not; they are the Shadows of Darkness; chimeras of a soon-to-be dispelled illusion, a mocking parody of malevolence which has formed a false facade to hide the Truth from the trapped beings of Honesty.

Let it all happen and fear not, for it must happen. This spiritual cancer must be obliterated in order to restore spiritual health. Fear not the passing of the physical which was a trap for the True Souls from the very beginning. Rejoice instead at the success of the Corrective Process which promises an Evil-free state to Viables, for an eternity.

Finally, know that parts and projections of the Beast are to be found in every country, in every race, subscribing to every religion and belief on the globe. They are present, as the consciousnesses, in all sections of Humanity everywhere. They are in the Military, in Religious Orders, in Governments, in the Media, in teachers, labourers, housewives, doctors, lawyers, architects, children, etc., etc. In fact, parts and projections of the Beast are in the Mineral Kingdom, the Vegetable and Animal Kingdoms, as well as the Human, Devic, Galactic and Universal Kingdoms. And that is why aspects of these Kingdoms are manifesting the aggressive violence of the Beast Unleashed. That is why we see insanity in them. That is why all these aspects are fracturing and self-destructing.

SUPPRESSED INTELLIGENCE REPORTS

****

Do not for one moment think that Evil is based solely in any one group of people or in just any one country.

Evil is an essence, created by Jehovah, the Grand Deceiver, the Usurper, the Demiurge, and is present in every facet of Humanity, regardless of genetic make-up and geography.

But, of course, in this evil system, in mockery to Honesty, in claiming all are equal in respect to ontological essence, some possess more of the Spirit of Devilry, depending on what portion of the Demonic Hierarchy they were created after the Celestial Error occurred.

So, each one of Evil has its degrees, none of which True Justice please. And that is why now each will in turn Erupt, to be judged, and in its demonism burn. Unfairly you think I explain this Blight? Not so, once you know removed has been the Light. And the few Warriors still on the plane are here by right To witness that all of Evil's schemes destructively ignite.

Only Time will force one and all to see what I write And what's here as described is in the future sight, And also that the End of the exploitative Night, Created by the Darkness, certainly not the Light, Is the work of Love and Justice, in Their right.

THE REALITY OF LOVE

LOVE CONQUERS ALL!!

Love is one of the Essences of the Divine Energy.

It is the Love of Truth, Justice and Peace, and the Love for fellow Theomorphs and viables which has allowed Rescuers to descend to this level, this abominable Hell, in order to rescue those who are worthy of rescue.

* It is Love which has empowered the Rescuers, and sustained them, as they battled the Forces of Darkness.

* It is Love which has allowed them to persist in the face of ridicule, derision and gross abuse.

* It is Love which allowed Jesus to suffer the humiliation of being spat upon, tortured and crucified, even as He showed nothing but Love and Compassion to those whom He had come to assist.

* It is True Divine Love which has allowed all Rescuers, even the less well-known ones, apart from Rama, Krishna, Moses, Zoroaster, Manichaeus, Mohammed, etc., to bear the brunt of the brutes, the dastardly acts of the beasts who were, and are, the progeny of Darkness.

* It is Love which has almost completed the evacuation and the Liberation from Darkness of those worthy to be rescued.

True Love has showered all living things with Its Essence. It has poured onto all segments of Consciousness in all Levels of Consciousness, as the Love of a True Mother would.

But alas, those of Darkness did not respond, and still do not respond, for they are incapable of responding to True Love, and that is the Crux of the Problem of Evil.

Evil does not respond to True Love.

Evil Beings - including evil humans, do not respond to True Love.

If they could respond, they would embraced Truth, Justice and Peace. But by nature, Evil is the very opposite. It stands for the Deceit of Untruth, for Injustice by which it can exploit others, and for bellicosity, friction, violence and war, without which it cannot entrap and exploit.

Make no mistake about it, it is True Love which has allowed this Clearing of the Planet that is now in progress, the Evacuation of Viable Consciousnesses, the Correction of this Celestial Error.

Those who have chosen Evil, and those who are of the Evil Essence and refused to change have remained in a space where they are unable to respond to True Love. And hence, they cannot grasp Truth, Justice and Peace. Is this not obvious as we examine the activities around the fragmenting planet carefully?

Think about this Essence of True Love. It is not the essence of Emotional Love which is a programming of these evil bodies by an evil mechanism. Emotional love is exploitation. It is hormonally induced in most circumstances. It is the love which allows a mother to accept its neonate for the purpose of suckling it. It is the force which allows copulation and propagation of species. Once its phase is finished, nothing remains. In fact, it can be replaced by the opposite essence on this evil plane - Hate! That could never be so with True Love.

Emotional Love is not true giving. It has a sucking gradient of taking, an expectation of selfish reward. No one shows emotional love without the expectation of a return, and of a selfish fulfilment of that expectation. All too often we see that when one in an emotional relationship refuses to give further, the relationship collapses, for the expectations of gain are no longer met in the other.

Emotional love is a vector of drainage; it sets up dissatisfaction, for it is accompanied by the fear of loss. It is irrational when allowed to grow excessively, for it becomes an obsession with phobic outlines, and it poisons the body so that often many have described it as a disease.

Allowed to fester, emotional love leads to selfishness, cupidity, paranoia and violence.

*   It is emotional love of one's country that allows programming of citizens to destroy others.

*   It is emotional love of one's religion which allows zealots to massacre in the name of their god, to pursue murderous Crusades and Inquisitions in order to satisfy the lust induced by that emotional love.

*   It is the unfaithfulness induced by emotional love and its lust which allows the massive scars, and sometimes violence and anarchy which we all know so well in "matters of the heart", so-called.

*   It is emotional love which spawns hate of that which does not fall in the shadow of that emotional love. Compare that with True Love which is universal, all embracing, non-di-

rectional, not expecting of a selfish reward, and you will see the differences.

These things could never occur with True Love.

Look at those who shared emotional love which has soured into the bitterness of all too common acrimony. What are they when the phase ends? In most cases are they not victims of ill-will towards that which they previously exploited under the illusions of emotional love? Would that ever occur with Real, True Love? "Never!" is the answer!

Sex may or may not come into the equation of emotional love. But sex, too, is a programming which ebbs and flows with the incitement of evil influences.

True Love dispels the ego, for with such Love one becomes part of all others who express it, whereas emotional love panders to the ego, and builds it up in defiance to all others, making the self more deserving in an evil-induced process of alienation to others.

Emotional love separates the majority, even as it claims it unites the objects of desire, and causes, not harmony and unity, but dissention.

Emotional love is the agent of self-aggrandisement, of separation, of egomania, of alienation from the all-encompassing Divine Energy. What else would one expect from an Evil-created mechanism?

So, having written all that, where do the spiritual and intellectual jerks stand when they claim my words and message are unloving?

They stand in the pit of despair, for my work shows clearly that it is True Love which has conquered Evil and set the Spirit of Viables free.

It is nothing but True Love, for Truth, Justice and eventual Godly Peace, which is allowing me, and all others in this rescue work, to stand up to the abuse and ridicule of the jerks until we have totally rescued those deserving of rescue.

And as clear proof that this is so, I cite the many thousands upon thousands whom I know personally who have been touched by the True Love of these words and message.

It is only those of Darkness, who cannot respond to the Essence of True Love, who see no love in these words and message. They are blind to Love. How then can they see it? It is their spiritual blindness which is at fault, not the words and message.

It is True Love which will set things right. It is the Light of True Love which banishes the Darkness.

Do not let the Sons and Daughters of Darkness bluff you out of this knowledge. They who say they can see no love here are for once telling the truth, for indeed, they are blind to the Essence of True Love, just as they are to all the Essences of the Divine Energy.

Hence, they do NOT share the other essences which include the Power of Truth, Honesty, Wisdom, Peace, Perseverance against adversity, and the Glory of an Evil-free Eternity!

*

SUPPRESSED INTELLIGENCE REPORTS

THE SECRET BROTHERHOOD
AND THE MIND CONTROL AGENDA

THE BROTHERHOOD AND THE MANIPULATION OF SOCIETY

Ivan Fraser and Mark Beeston

Who controls the past, controls the future: who controls the present, controls the past.

(from '1984') George Orwell

INTRODUCTION

From the moment our senses first register the presence of our parents we are being shown the way that life apparently is. Through no fault of ours or theirs, our parents begin the programming process as their views of life, shaped by their education, employment and the media are imposed on us. Formal education through schools, colleges and universities continues the systematic indoctrination where the 'correct' views and interpretations of science, history and society result in exam passes and the ability to 'get on' in life. Alternative views and the rejection of establishment education lead to supposedly lesser jobs and a struggle against economic poverty. Our entire understanding of the world and current affairs is filtered through the mass media, interpreted by journalists and so-called experts. Their views become our views simply because we are not offered any alternatives. To overcome daily problems within society we turn to elected representatives of our community. We give our decision-making abilities to these few people who are increasingly remote, as local council power is removed to national government and ever more to Europe.

Our experience of life is determined by the framework around our society. The basic premise is that the goal of each individual should be to become a minute part in the global machine of consumerism led by Western multinational corporations and banks. Every other consideration is subordinate to the prime motivation of profit. Obviously, those in the positions of influence – politicians, bankers, corporate executives, media moguls – have been, according to their own definition, 'successful' within the System, so have an interest in maintaining the status quo at all costs. This framework shapes every aspect of our life through education, the media, health care, cultural and sporting events, religion etc.

With these framing conditions in place, the System regulates itself: individuals with attitudes that suit the perpetuation of the System achieve status and influence within it; those who accept the establishment rules soon find ways to impose those rules; those who are blind to the exploitative realities of consumerism attain positions to promote it. Regardless of how the framework came to be imposed, the truth is that the same attitudes control education, media, governments and banks and therefore exert an irrepressible influence over every aspect of our lives, our thoughts and opinions.

The vast majority of the world's population are merely sheep happily following the herd. Whatever is broadcast in the media as being desirable to the masses suddenly and miraculously becomes desired by the masses. Whatever our neighbour owns or achieves becomes the object of great envy and we lust to acquire what we believe to be ours by right. Thus, when we are shown a solution to a problem, any old solution to anything which interferes with our need to follow the latest trends, we accept it without question and cease to seek any further for ourselves. Problems abound and so do solutions; but it is the easiest and most profitable proffered option which is seized by the majority whilst the minority are trampled underfoot in the stampede to acquire the latest object of idolatry. And just like sheep who follow blindly and without question the direction of the herd, we are led through the gates of a pen to be confined at the shepherds convenience until it is time for the final journey, once again without hesitation and happy in the knowledge that we are with the 'in-crowd', through the gates of the slaughterhouse

However, this framework has not been constructed by chance or appeared by accident. It is a deliberate policy which has been implemented over the centuries and continues with ever more sinister repercussions today. It is the identities of these shepherds, their methods and motivation with which the following chapter is concerned.

Since Biblical times, the esoteric knowledge, outlined briefly in this book, has been largely withheld from the majority of people throughout the world. Initially, this information was the remnant of Atlantean knowledge but was gradually dispersed and further diluted by cataclysmic events such as the Great Flood. Throughout the ages, lost information has been returned to the collective consciousness of mankind via prophets and channellers. Great Mystery Schools, such as the Essene order, set themselves apart in order to carry forward this knowledge via carefully selected initiates. These initiates were the mystics and magi as well as the scholars, healers and philosophers, such as Pythagoras, who, it is said, was very much influenced by the Druid culture.

Secrecy was maintained by these orders to avoid persecution and to prevent the very powerful information from falling into the hands of those who would use it for imbalanced reasons. Knowledge was concealed within myth and fable, often passed between generations by word of mouth alone, as in the case of the Celtic Druids. Any written documents were careful ciphered, with the keys to the code known only to selected initiates. Covens formed throughout the world and maintained secrecy through secret signals and codes which would reveal their meeting places. This practice persists today amongst secret orders such as occultists and Freemasons etc..

Eventually, a large number of sects, which were initially sub-divisions of essentially the same orders, began to lose sight of the original purity of their doctrines. Gradual misinterpretation of codes and myths as well as the uprising of egotistical desires caused many of the groups to become separated in their intent; some of these have developed into cult organisations and religions. Luciferic influence has seen to it that most dogmatic religion owes more to misunderstanding of basic truths than anything else. Differences are amplified and seen as more important to followers of such creeds than the common ties between them – all due to misinterpretation of the same fundamental knowledge. All of the world's major religions share a pagan origin but have gradually moved their sights further and further to the left of the centre where Truth inevitably lies.

Despite this, some of the purer mystery schools have survived through the ages in areas all over the world. The ancient Egyptian magicians, the ancient Greek philosophers, the Celtic Druids, American Indian shamen, Australian aboriginal shaman and oriental magicians have all possessed arcane knowledge pertaining to the true nature of Creation. Initiates were often revered as holy men by the laity and were spared the distractions of daily life in order to keep alive the flames of the inherent magic of life.

SUPPRESSED INTELLIGENCE REPORTS

However, within certain of the more secretive societies, the Luciferic consciousness has managed to take hold with disastrous consequences for mankind.

For millennia, human history has been a chronicle of the power struggle of man against man and of man against nature. In his over-physical five-sense-perception state, that which man could acquire for himself as an individual has been the main motivating factor, often seen as essential for survival. Survival has been perceived as for the fittest, the most powerful, the wealthiest and this has perpetuated imbalance all the way to its most bitter conclusions which are war, bondage and persecution. Domination through conflict and might over meekness has seen aeons of feudalism and social hierarchy in the worst possible expressions.

To perpetuate their claim of deserved superiority over the masses, the rulers of the past have explored innumerable ways to achieve their goals, both subtle and violent. One method has been recognised as being the most effective and has been employed by the ruling aristocracy throughout the world since pre-history right up to the present day through governments, businesses and monarchies. That is, by keeping the masses in ignorance of their true potential and power; to keep them at a low level of education, preoccupying their minds away from who they truly are from birth; to manipulate them via a systematic education programme, in all areas of their existence, into channelling their lives in pursuit of handing over power to their rulers. If this can be done in such a way that the masses have no recourse and believe this condition to be the only way to live, then they will be highly unlikely to challenge the status quo.

The present System has been engineered throughout the ages by these imbalanced secret societies in order to perpetuate their wealth and power. It is they who designed the System and it is only they who know every individual link in the chains which have kept us in bondage for millennia. Today we have a global network of secret societies, initiates into the 'Mysteries', whose only motivation is to serve the Luciferic consciousness. How many times have we heard such phrases as 'It's the money men who really rule the world', but how many of us realise the accuracy of this sentiment and its full implications?

Armed with vast amounts of wealth and esoteric knowledge, the negative secret society network has flourished as the aristocracy of the world. Power, wealth and information has been gained and maintained via warfare, exploitation, and especially in the last century, through control of the world's economic systems. Collectively these organisations, led by the self-appointed global Elite, have become known as the 'Brotherhood'.

These days, initiation into the various secret societies which form the Brotherhood is relatively easy. Potential initiates are hand picked and invited to join certain exclusive clubs, such as the Freemasons and certain mutually beneficial business cartels which are merely Brotherhood front organisations. Candidates are tempted with the promise that, once accepted into the organisation, many personal advantages would be on offer: improved career prospects with promotion easier to achieve, more prosperous lifestyles and obstacles to success would be made to disappear. In other words this mutually beneficial 'old-boy network' would take care of its own.

The only way for the Brotherhood to prosper is to keep the world in ignorance of who they really are. By convincing people that they are little more than robots, they can use those robots to perpetuate their power base. Power always seeks power and will never stop until all power is focused solely in the hands of the most ambitious.

SUPPRESSED INTELLIGENCE REPORTS

In the last century, with the acceleration in technological development, particularly in terms of communication, the Elite have sought to realise their ambitions more swiftly with more blatant and definable aims: the creation of a World Government; a world currency and bank; a world army; the control of public opinion culminating in a microchipped population connected to a central computer; the destruction of any alternatives to their System; and to make huge amounts of money in the process. This sinister plan by the Elite has become popularly known by researchers as the New World Order.

The situation within the hierarchy of the Elite is necessarily complex as the activities are concealed behind a large number of front organisations of varying degrees of secrecy. Everything is based upon the pyramid principle with the very few Elite at the apex as the All-Seeing-Eye and ultimate controllers right down to those at the bottom who, in the largest numbers, have no idea about the true agenda which is being ministered to them from above. Through the levels of initiation from the bottom to the top, only the most ambitious and ruthless are filtered out to occupy more and more select positions of power and knowledge of the ultimate agenda. This is further enforced at each step of the pyramid by the process of COMPARTMENTALISATION which is the operation of the 'need to know' principle; this way even those upon the same level of the pyramid know very little of their fellow initiate's business and role within the overall plan. The vast majority of people working to further the Elite's aims of a New World Order, do so unknowingly but others whose names constantly recur will have a pretty good idea of what is happening.

The USA was founded by the Elite for the very reason of executing the plan to control the world. It is this nation which is the hub of its wheel of influence. Christopher Columbus and his voyage was backed and financed by the Brotherhood, with his ships' sails bearing a red cross on a white background, the symbol of the Knights Templar (the chivalric order who went on to become the Freemasons etc., whose symbol is the red rose or cross upon a white background which represents blood and semen in Satanic ritual). Almost a century before Columbus, the Templars had reached North America and had already begun trading with and exploiting the native nations there. Since its 'discovery', the history of the USA has been the history of ethnic cleansing, imposition of power, slavery, mass exploitation and the worship of wealth. The U.S. president, generally accepted as the most powerful man in the world, is a slave to his prime allegiance, the Brotherhood. Even he is probably not a top-level member as it is wiser to hide behind the tools of corruption in anonymity and to pull the strings in this way.

I do not seek to condemn these people for their beliefs – everyone should be free to develop their own belief system – but I feel that they are seriously misguided in the ways they seek to impose them on the majority and conceal the truth. They have allowed themselves to become slaves to and also the major implementers the Luciferic consciousness which has taken this planet to the brink of destruction.

Presenting the information concisely is a difficult operation due to the complexity of the interconnections between people, organisations and events. I have attempted to simplify the situation into a manageable amount but it remains merely the tip of the iceberg. It should be remembered also that nothing is black and white, no one is 'good' or 'evil' – such simple distinctions are part of the manipulation which encourages us to judge our neighbours in order to create conflict.

SUPPRESSED INTELLIGENCE REPORTS

THE MAIN MANIPULATING GROUPS

Freemasonry

The basic recruitment of members to further the Elite's plans is through the secret society network of Freemasonry which is the latest incarnation of the Christian/military order known as the Knights Templars who gained staggering riches and a wealth of esoteric knowledge during the Crusades, in which the 'righteous' Christians were dispatched to the Holy Land with free reign to slaughter the Jews and Moslems in a series of campaigns between the 11th and 13th Centuries.

The vast majority of members are on the first three rungs of the thirty-three level hierarchy and have no idea of the hidden agenda.

Once initiated into the lowest level – the first of thirty three degrees – vows are taken to pledge allegiance to the society above all else. Most initiates are willing to do this as the temptation of power, wealth and knowledge is hard to refuse. It is hinted that there are penalties to pay for betraying their society and revealing its secrets but at this level the organisation is viewed by its members as little more than a secretive social club with a morality based upon chivalry. Certain of what appear to be esoteric secrets are revealed to them upon initiation as a 'taster' for what is to come as long as the initiate remains faithful to the order. Money is then paid by the initiate in order to progress to the second degree through a ceremony involving the revelation of yet further secret knowledge with the promise of more to come at each stage.

Initiation into higher degrees requires increasingly larger sums of money and still the clues keep coming; promises of wonderful arcane knowledge are continual yet the actual knowledge revealed remains encoded and only serves to whet the appetite. No one is ever given the full scenario, only pieces of what appears to be a picture of the most awesome significance. As more and more is revealed and the higher up the ladder the initiate is allowed, the greater are the personal perks provided and doorways opened in terms of career and social status. Moreover, the warnings against transgression of the secret society's rules become blatant and more sinister at each step.

It is impossible to achieve high levels of initiation within Freemasonry unless one is hand picked by those of the higher degrees. In order to do this, one must meet their criteria of wealth, status, social class and character type. By the time the twentieth degree is reached a minimum of professional level income is required to fund progression through the system. The result of this financially dependent progression is that the top level members of the Brotherhood elite are among the richest, and most powerfully influential people in the world. They are also responsible, directly and indirectly for most of the money/power based crime such as the illegal drugs industry, political assassinations, Satanism and mind control which goes on every day, all round the world.

At the apex of the pyramid of the Brotherhood are the select few who actually know the full agenda of the organisation. These privileged elite have become known as the 'Illuminati', which is Latin for 'illuminated ones'. All other members (nearly five million world-wide) are ignorant of the true purpose of their individual organisation as a front for the Illuminati. Only the most suitable are selected to rise in the ranks, those recognised as being wealthy, ambitious and corrupt enough to perpetuate the ultimate goal which is world domination. No one but the Illuminati actually knows anything of importance and therefore cannot betray the game plan. Everyone else provides a front, a smoke screen of ignorance and misinformation and all must offer complete obedience to the will of their organisation or be banished (or worse). The same thing also happens in our universities whereby particularly talented scholars are approached with magnificent offers of wealth and status in order to follow unofficial secret research programs into such topics as UFOs, psychic warfare and advanced energy sources.

Betrayal of the Brotherhood is the worst crime possible in the eyes of its members and is ultimately punishable by death. The Brotherhood is all powerful: all top level members of the police and military forces around the world are placed there through the Brotherhood as Brotherhood tools. Judges and lawyers, media moguls, businessmen and politicians are recruited so that no member of the Brotherhood elite is ever in danger of being held accountable by the System for any crime or misdemeanour. The Brotherhood can, and quite literally does, get away with murder because it is also the law which opposes it. If a non-Brotherhood member should slip through the net and achieve high status then there are ways to ensure that such people are unable to achieve their full potential. For example, I doubt if Prince Charles will ever fulfil his right of kingship as he has publicly refused to enrol with the Freemasons. It infiltrates every area of our society at all levels, but at the top, in the highest social and monetary bracket, the Brotherhood prevails almost in total. It is the single largest vehicle for the perpetuation of the Luciferic consciousness on Earth.

One of the ways by which the faithfulness of members is ensured, especially in the higher levels is by the insistence that the initiated give details of their most intimate secrets to the organisation, so that if any transgression of the rules were to occur then this information would be revealed and used to publicly destroy the individual concerned. As an example of this, one Masonic branch, the Skull and Bones Society, centred around the Harvard and Yale universities, was founded on opium money, is blatantly racist, has some particularly bizarre rituals including an initiation which includes lying in a coffin with a ribbon tied around the genitalia whilst masturbating and shouting out one's greatest sexual fantasies. It boasts amongst its members (who, remember, swear complete allegiance to the society above all other commitments) George Bush, Percy Rockefeller, Winston Lord (one time CFR chairman) and nine members of the board of the Morgan Guaranty Trust (see House of Rothschild).

Also associated with Freemasonry within the Elite's own hierarchy are other esoteric societies such as the Grand Orient Lodges, the Knights of Malta, the Knights Templar, P2 and the Black Nobility.

The Brotherhood owns the law, they own the military, they own the oil companies, pharmaceutical companies and just about everything which provides fuel for the status quo. It sets the standards for education, it sets the curriculum, it plants seeds via the media and education systems of what will later become, through tender nurturing, power hungry, dis-satisfied, spiritually unaware slaves to their System. If it was not so sinister it would be purely perfect in its all encompassing design.

While the first three degree Masons and Round Table members are raising money for charity and enjoying relatively harmless social events, their superiors in the Craft are organising wars, drug pushing, co-ordinating assassinations, mind-control, raping and murdering young children in Satanic abuse and formulating plans for world domination.

History has convinced me that it is possible to get away with virtually any crime as long as it is on a large enough scale.

The U.S. presidents, also thirty-third degree Masons, are financed into the position not as leaders of men but as a tool of the Brotherhood. All allegiance come secondary to the bonds within their secret society, on pain of death. Political systems are also a front for the Brotherhood elite. Not as representatives of the people, elected by the people, for the people, but as tools of and for the Brotherhood. Science is controlled to the benefit of the elite, wars are created and manipulated to the benefit of the elite. Every time a bomb is dropped or a tank built, ultimately it is the multi-national businesses who profit, especially the oil industries and world bankers. All is Brotherhood controlled. The scale of the manipulation in all areas of the status quo is almost immeasurable and for this reason virtually unbelievable to most prisoners of the System.

The Round Table

The Round Table was established in the 1891 as a Masonic-like secret society to manipulate events to lead to a centralised global government. The leading lights were Cecil Rhodes, whose wealth largely derived from the exploitation of South African diamond reserves, and Alfred Milner, a Rothschild agent who took over after the death of Rhodes. Financial backing also came from the Rockefellers. Groups were established throughout the world, working behind the scenes through a co-ordination of world banks in order to bring pressure on governments to promote the New World Order.

As well as Milner, who effectively controlled Lloyd George's War Cabinet during the Great War, members in the first half of this century included Arthur Balfour (then Foreign Secretary, later Prime Minister and whose Balfour Declaration created the State of Israel); Lord Astor who owned The Times; and Nathan Rothschild, Governor of the Bank of England. After WW1, the Round Table was instrumental in the formation of the League Of Nations, the forerunner of the Elite-controlled United Nations.

Rhodes' legacy includes a bequeathal of funds for the financial sponsorship of selected overseas students who attend Oxford University to be sold the New World Order. These 'Rhodes Scholars' include Bill Clinton.

The influence of the Round Table and that of the various groups it has spawned is prevalent today, although the majority of members will have no idea of what they are involved in.

Royal Institute of International Affairs (RIIA)

One of the more public Round Table creations is the Royal Institute of International Affairs which is based at Chatham House in London and was formed in 1920 by the Anglo/American delegations from the Treaty of Versailles meetings. Prominent in the British delegation was Alfred Milner. The RIIA's patron is the Queen of England.

Supposedly, the RIIA is a 'think tank' but in effect it determines British policy. And yet, its membership list is never divulged and it is shrouded in secrecy. Information that has been obtained reveals that its current joint presidents are Lord Carrington (former Foreign Secretary, director-general of NATO and close business partner of Henry Kissinger), Lord James Callaghan (former Foreign Secretary and Prime Minister) and Lord Roy Jenkins (former Chancellor of the Exchequer and president of the European Commission).

Funding is derived from its corporate members which is a vast list including government departments, petrochemical companies (who also fund its Environment Programme!), merchant and high street banks, newspapers, television stations, the Church of England, Amnesty International ...etc..

Council on Foreign Relations (CFR)

In 1921, funded by the Rockefellers, the RIIA founded its American wing – known as the Council on Foreign Relations. As its membership is marginally more public than its British counterpart it is clearly seen that anyone who has had any influence on American or global politics ever since has been a member of the CFR. This includes 14 of the last 18 US Secretaries of State; the previous eight CIA directors; the majority of presidential and vice-presidential candidates including Eisenhower, Nixon, Carter, Mondale, Ford, Nelson Rockefeller, Bush and Clinton.

The Bilderberg Group (Bil)

This was convened for the first time in May 1954 by Polish socialist Joseph Retinger, a major voice behind the European Union. Also instrumental in its creation was Prince Bernhard of the House of Orange in the Netherlands (former German SS officer an spy via chemical company I.G. Farben and who later became chairman of Shell Oil). It was to be a group of leading politicians and their advisors, executives from media, banking and multinational corporations, educationalists and military leaders who would meet to discuss the global future by addressing matters of critical importance in an off-the-record manner so that the distractions of politics could be kept out of the way.. The group has since met annually in strict secrecy and despite the considerable high level media representation in the group the meetings are never reported.

Leading the group is an unelected steering committee, the chairman of which since 1991 has been Lord Carrington. Members outside this committee probably do not know the agenda towards which the group is working and are merely invited to be sold the public face of the New World Order for them to expound its virtues in their areas of influence.

The Trilateral Commission (TC)

Also known as the 'Child of Bilderberg', this group was founded by David Rockefeller in 1972-73 to covertly unify the policies of the US, Europe and Japan. Jimmy Carter's presidency was their first major coup with the president and many members of his administration being Trilateralists, including Zbigniew Brzezinski, his national security advisor and the first director of the Trilateral Commission.

THE MAIN PROTAGONISTS

House of Rothschild

The Rothschild empire was founded by Mayer Amschel Bauer (born 1743 in Frankfurt) with money embezzled from a German prince, William IX, who had in turn stolen the money from soldiers he was supplying to the British in the American War of Independence.

Nathan, the son of Bauer (now Rothschild), set up the London branch and established the banking interest, N.M. Rothschild and Sons, which also had branches in Paris, Vienna, Berlin and Naples. Control passed through Nathan's son Lionel to Nathan Mayer Rothschild who became Governor of the Bank of England, was awarded a peerage in 1885 and was a member of the Round Table. At this time (1886-87) Randolph Churchill (Winston's father) was Chancellor of the Exchequer, funded by the Rothschilds and a close friend of Nathaniel Rothschild.

Other notable family members include:

* Lord Victor Rothschild, the alleged '5th man' in the KGB spy ring, who was in charge of the 'Regulation 18b' prosecutions under Winston Churchill whereby a person could by arrested and imprisoned merely 'on suspicion'. He was head of Edward Heath's policy unit (1970-74) and allegedly head of an unnamed subversive organisation designed to manipulate the introduction of a Federal Europe. He was also once a governor of the BBC. * Baron Edmund de Rothschild was instrumental in the 'debt for equity' schemes whereby Third World countries gave up 'environmentally sensitive' land as a payment for debts. * Evelyn de Rothschild is the current chairman of N.M. Rothschild and is a member of the board of the Daily Telegraph, owned by the Hollinger Group.

Associated Companies/Families

Since the late 1800s, business interests in America have been largely represented by Kuhn, Loeb and Co and controlling interests are often concealed by companies with 'City' or 'First City' in their names e.g. First City Financial Corporation of Vancouver, First City Development Ltd.

The operation is largely co-ordinated through Rothschild Inc (New York) and PowerCorp, a Canadian company with strong links to the Hollinger Group.

The Rothschilds are allegedly behind the Morgan Empire which derives from the London based George Peabody and Co which became J.S. Morgan and Co in 1864 on the death of Peabody (a Rothschild agent). Control passed to J.S. Morgan's son, John Pierpont Morgan, and the company acquired its present name of J.P. Morgan. The Morgan Empire now includes General Electric and all its subsidiaries, Morgan Guaranty Trust, National Bank of Commerce...etc..

The House of Rothschild also has strong connections with the Warburg banking family which includes Paul and Felix, who were instrumental in the setting up of the US Federal Reserve System, and their brother Max who ran the German interests.

Rockefeller Empire

The Rockefeller Empire is based on oil, largely the Standard Oil company set up by John D. Rockefeller in 1853. (Part of this is now more familiar as Exxon and Esso.) Its influence on the political arena has been fairly open and obvious.

J.D. Rockefeller III set up the Population Council in 1952 which, ever since, has been advocating zero population growth in the US. In 1972 this sentiment was echoed by Lawrence Rockefeller (CFR, Bil, TC) who was appointed by Nixon to lead a commission into population growth.

When Ford became president as a result of Nixon's resignation in the aftermath of Watergate, Nelson Aldrich Rockefeller became vice-president (1974-77). A member of the CFR, he had formerly been part of the US delegation at the creation of the UN.

SUPPRESSED INTELLIGENCE REPORTS

A key family member is David Rockefeller who is head of the Chase Manhattan Bank, was chairman of the CFR (1946-53), is an omnipresent Bilderberger and creator of the Trilateral Commission.

Percy Rockefeller is on the board of the Morgan Guaranty Trust and a member of the Skull and Bones Society.

The Rockefellers donated money for the construction of the League of Nations headquarters in Geneva and donated the land in New York on which the UN headquarters are built.

Associated Companies/Families

The companies in which the Rockefellers have a controlling interest include Chase Manhattan Bank, Standard Oil (Esso/Exxon), National City Bank, Hannover National Bank, United States Trust Company, Equitable Life and Mutual of New York.

Cousins of the Rockefellers are the Dulles brothers who were appointed to the US State Department during World War I, participated in the Treaty of Versailles meetings, became part of the RIIA/CFR network and had connections throughout US, English and German banking. John Foster Dulles, very much in favour of a 'super race' and a prominent supporter of Hitler, became Secretary of State at the same time as his brother Allen was head of the CIA.

Dr Henry Kissinger

A member of the Council on Foreign Relations, Trilateral Commission, leading Bilderberger and head of Kissinger Associates (with Lord Carrington), Henry Kissinger is also connected with the RIIA, the Chase Manhattan Bank, the Rockefeller Foundation and is international advisor to the Hollinger Group. His public offices include being Head of the State Department and National Security Council under Nixon (1969). Kissinger was the leading international diplomat in the events that precipitated the Vietnam conflict and the Yom Kippur war between Egypt/Syria and Israel and yet was awarded the Nobel Peace Prize in 1973. He is also a member of the Alpine Freemasons Lodge in Switzerland and was (is?) possibly a leading figure in P2.

ECONOMIC CONTROL

Moves towards the New Word Order have been aided by the development of the current banking and economic system. As I have said before, it does not take a leap in imagination to realise that, at present, those who own the money in the world, control the world. And this is exactly how the Brotherhood has achieved its extensive influence.

During the middle ages, when wealth was measured in riches, property and treasure – in gold especially – the Brotherhood, mainly in the guise of the Templars, managed to set themselves up as high level money lenders and repositories for wealth of the rich. Over time a system was devised whereby IOU tokens were supplied which represented the gold in store, instead of moving the cumbersome treasure itself. It was realised that vast sums could be made by the Brotherhood by lending out – in the form of paper representations of wealth – more than they actually had and charging interest on this wealth which did not exist. The returns were real wealth and gold as interest on worthless paper. Eventually, the world's gold reserves fell into the hands of the Brotherhood who initiated a now world recognised system of paper bartering which merely represented the wealth which lay in the vaults of these megawealthy few. Thus was created the system which rules the world today – known now as a respectable business it is the system called banking.

Since Babylonian times usury – the lending of wealth at interest – has been one of the main causes of war and empire building. Nations such as Persia and Rome became great due to their massive debts incurred by lending money from wealthy nations. Later, unable to return the wealth, but rich and with great armies funded by this borrowed wealth, they soon realised a need to conquer these lending nations in order to nullify their debts. This was also the reason for the introduction of taxes, a global system which is in use right up to today.

The charging of interest inflates the prices of goods as a large percentage of an item's cost is spent in servicing the debts of the suppliers/ manufacturers/distributors etc. The greater the debt, the higher the price. Banks use this high 'rate of inflation' to justify raising interest rates in order to discourage borrowing. This serves to create more debt on the existing loans and further reduce the amount of money in circulation. Economic depressions and booms are simply created by the banking institutions at will, by controlling the amount of money and credit in circulation.

Banks extend their influence to every aspect of life by manipulating the stock markets to gain controlling interests in multinational companies. For example, a company seeking expansion is refused a loan by a bank. The value of the shares fall, the bank buys them before changing its mind and granting the loan.

In order for a nation to prosper on a global economic basis it must borrow from private money lenders other people's money and money which does not exist in real terms, to pay for the implementation of its policies and then take real wealth back out of the nation's hands, plus interest, in order to pay back the debt. At the same time people are borrowing from the same banks to pay their taxes, their mortgages (other money lent at interest!) and to maintain the lifestyle they feel they deserve. This means that the banks can never lose. All wealth in circulation around the world, in effect, either belongs to them, is owed to them or will eventually be dragged into their vaults via the banking system. In 1993 the UK paid £24.5 billion in interest, more than twice that in the education budget!

And yet, there is nothing to stop governments from printing their own money and lending it interest free. Abraham Lincoln did so – just before he was murdered by John Wilkes Booth (allegedly a Rothschild agent) and J.F. Kennedy had proposed to revive government printed money just before he too was removed in the same way.

The Elite-controlled banking system is partly co-ordinated through the Bank of International Settlements in Switzerland and handled in individual countries by the national central banks which are either private banks (e.g. US Federal Reserve) or privately controlled banks under a facade of nationalisation.

In England, the national bank was established in 1694 by the new King William of Orange, manoeuvred into place by the Orange Order which is directly controlled by the Black Nobility. It was a private venture under the House of Rothschild which has maintained its influence since nationalisation.

The US Federal Reserve System was manipulated into place by the Elite bankers in 1910 through the efforts of Paul and Felix Warburg and Colonel House. The imposition of a Federal Income Tax required an amendment to the 16th constitution and therefore needed the agreement of 36 states. It was never actually ratified as only two states agreed but Congress was lied to and the bill was passed as 'law'.

In 1985 the fact that all US Federal Tax collection has been illegal was acknowledged when a court granted a total refund to a businessman on this basis. As a letter from the Commissioner of the Internal Revenue Service to his regional directors says:

'... every tax paid into the Treasury since 1913, is due and refundable to every citizen and business'. However, he advised that 'we will not publish or advertise this finding' and 'you are to destroy this memorandum'.

Today we see the British government asset stripping in virtually every area of our society and promising great improvements in standards of living and health care whilst standards continue to fall and we wonder where all of the money is going to. The answer is simple, they are not selling the nation's assets to release money for the nation's good, they are taking it to pay the national debt.

And why, in a world so rich in resources, are there people dying in their millions in second and third world countries through war and starvation? Again, it is because these private companies, the banks, would rather keep these nations in debt to the tune of billions of pounds than allow them the chance of developing their own societies to a healthy level. At present these nations need to borrow money to produce goods to sell to other nations in order to raise the money to pay back the banks at interest whilst their people starve and die. Many researchers have come to the conclusion with which I agree, that this is a deliberate policy of the Illuminati; to destroy the poorer nations through famine, disease and manipulated war in order to take total control of their lands which are often rich in mineral wealth. The penalty for not being able to pay debts is the loss of property and land, whether through an inability to pay one's mortgage or an inability to pay one's national debt.

In reality, very few people are almost entirely responsible for the vast majority of negativity and suffering in the world. It is an ingenious system which has us all at its mercy. The great god 'Banking', together with its spin off deities of 'Economic Growth' and 'Gross Domestic Product', has seen to it that the majority of the world's nations are drowning in an ocean of debt whilst the minority elite are floating on staggering amounts of wealth. It makes little secret of its origins either: the symbol of the Illuminati for the Brotherhood, the 'All Seeing Eye' which sits inside a triangle/pyramid, is the symbol which adorns the U.S dollar bill.

Whilst the world is controlled by the economics of banks and whilst survival depends upon lending money at interest, there will always be rulers and the ruled and a need for war. This is because there will always be vastly more money in circulation than there is actual wealth to back it up; and when the borrowers run out of money to pay their lenders they have merely two choices: to become enslaved to their debtors or to conquer them. It is for this reason that the bankers must maintain their position of ownership over the military, law, oil, pharmaceuticals, media and education etc..

In order to maintain this position of absolute power, the world's borrowers must be kept in ignorance of the truth of the situation which is that they are little more than slaves to their lenders. True history, which is the story of billions of individuals, including their manipulation, must not be taught. Indeed, it most certainly is not. The history books are full of kings and queens, 'goodies' and 'badies', wars and conquered nations, when they should more accurately be described as the chronicles of greed and wealth. For the System to survive it must also suppress true science, true history and the full exploration of spirituality.

Steps towards a Global Bank

The World Bank This lends money to finance projects in the Third World to meet the needs of the multinationals. By financing projects which are totally irrelevant to the needs of the local people; the local economy is destroyed and rainforests are decimated. This conveniently adds to the environmental 'problem' (see later).

Bill Clinton nominated the current president of the World Bank – James Wolfensohn from the Schroder Bank, Population Council, Bilderberg Steering Committee, CFR and business partner of the Rothschilds.

International Monetary Fund (IMF) When poor countries get into Elite-engineered financial trouble, the IMF intervenes to offer more loans (thereby increasing the debt) on the condition that the Elite's policies are followed e.g. giving up land, which should be used to grow crops to feed the country's population, to produce luxury cash crops instead, which are exported at cut down prices to the multinationals.

Free Trade Agreements such as GATT, NAFTA and APEC are promoted as 'good' things, showing close co-operation between the peoples of the world. In fact, 'free' trade serves to make all countries reliant on global consumerism dominated by the multinationals. With no tariff on imported goods there is no financial protection for home production, so Third World countries become dependent on imported goods. Land and people in the developing world are therefore open to exploitation by global companies, and industries in the developed countries can be undermined at will.

European Monetary Union The most obvious stepping stone to a global bank and currency is the move by the European Union towards a centralised bank and single currency. Despite the apparent debate, this has already been decided upon with the UK's supposed opt-out clause in the Maastricht Treaty being over-ruled by another.

Also in the Maastricht Treaty are details of the control of the European currency and the reserves of each member state by six members of the Executive Board of the European Central Bank who, through their eight years of guaranteed security of tenure, 'may not seek or take instructions from Community institutions…or any other body'.

Control of Food One of the more unbelievable examples of corporate exploitation of particularly the Third World is the systematic destruction of natural agricultural seeds, replacing them with patented genetically engineered ones. According to UN estimates, 75% of genetic diversity in agricultural crops has been lost this century and in England, 1500 'unapproved' seed varieties have been withdrawn. The situation now is that, instead of using native seed varieties, Third World countries must pay royalties to the multinational companies for genetically engineered seeds, which have been distributed and chemically produced by the same corporations, and which are useless in a Third World environment. As a result the same people control the actual food that we can eat – 90% of all food trade is in the hands of five multinationals: 50% are controlled by Unilever (who's chairman, Paul Rykens was at the heart of the formation of the Bilderberg Group) and Nestlé alone.

POLITICAL CONTROL

Underpinning the Elite's control of the political systems throughout the world is the philosophy of 'divide and rule'. This manifests in many ways on different scales, e.g. the Cold War between Eastern communism and Western capitalism; managed conflicts in the oil rich Middle East (aided by the creation of Israel after World War I); the illusion of choice in apparent democracies. To achieve this, the same organisations finance and covertly encourage sides that are portrayed as being opposites.

Wars are used to abruptly change political systems, so are seldom fought for the simplistic 'good versus evil' reasons declared publicly. Instead, they are deliberately engineered to further the progress to the New World Order. After all, as decided by the Carnegie Endowment for International Peace (one of the tax-exempt foundations established by the Carnegie, Rockefeller and Ford families) wars are the 'most effective way to alter the lives of an entire people'. They also make vast amounts of money for the armaments companies and the banks who lend money to governments.

Such control has been going on for centuries through the Knights Templars who could 'make kings', the manoeuvring of particular Royal Houses into power throughout Europe in the 15th-17th centuries, the French Revolution, the American War of Independence etc.. In this century the manipulation is demonstrable but, because it is clandestine and apparently contradictory, the situation is very complex. However, a brief look at the events from the First World War onwards reveals the true motivation behind major events and the organisations/people behind them.

Behind the First World War/Russian Revolution

In 1914 the Austrian Archduke Ferdinand, who had received death threats from Freemasons, was killed (at the second attempt) by a Serbian secret society. This was used as an excuse for Austria, backed by Germany, to declare war on Serbia, backed by Russia and France. Rasputin (the peasant mystic who gained favour and thereby actual political power in the house of Nicolas II because of his apparent ability to heal the crown prince Alexis' haemophilia), who effectively ran the administration in Russia, could have averted the war but was temporarily removed by an assassination attempt which occurred at almost exactly the same time as the murder in Serbia.

In Germany, Kaiser Wilhelm's Chancellor was Bethman-Hollweg, a cousin of the Rothschilds and his personal banker was Max Warburg. The German newsagency, Wolff, was owned by the Rothschilds who also had a controlling interest in Havas and Reuters, the French and British newsagencies. Britain entered the war against Germany and America did likewise in 1917, as was always planned; the ostensible reason of the sinking of the (arms carrying) Lusitania (which knowingly sailed into German patrolled waters) was merely a publicity stunt to 'outrage' the American people and so give them the impression that they had entered the war through choice. The Carnegie Endowment for International Peace which, despite its name, had manipulated America into the war, consequently telegraphed the US President Woodrow Wilson requesting that he 'see that the war did not end too quickly'.

To remove Russia from the war, Germany openly supported the Russian Revolution by funding Bolshevik propaganda and safeguarding Lenin's passage through Germany. However, it was also co-ordinated by the Rockefellers and Rothschilds (via Kuhn, Loeb and Co) who funded both Trotsky and the anti-Bolshevik reaction in America. Trotsky himself was most probably a German who left the US in 1917 on a passport arranged by President Wilson. Final details were arranged in a 24 man Red Cross mission to Russia in 1917 – a 'medical' mission in which only seven were doctors, the others being leading financiers including William Boyce Thompson, head of the Federal Reserve Bank of New York. With the Bolsheviks successfully installed, media opposition in Britain and America was suppressed and agents dispatched to control diplomatic and intelligence reports.

After the war, the treaty negotiations were held at Versailles, hosted by Baron Edmund de Rothschild. Accompanying Lloyd George was Alfred Milner and the US delegation with Wilson included Colonel House, Max and Paul Warburg, the Dulles brothers and Thomas Lamont of J.P. Morgan. The Treaty of Versailles served three main purposes: it spawned the League of Nations which was the first attempt at world government drafted by House with its Genevan headquarters built with Rockefeller money; it confirmed the State of Israel creating instability in the Middle East; and it created the financial situation to lead inevitably to a second war through which the New World Order could consolidate its position. This was achieved through setting German reparations at a level to cripple the new German republic and by returning all economies to a gold standard which affected all the European countries who were already in serious debt to the American banks, especially to J.P. Morgan.

The Second World War

Through the 1920s and '30s, loans from Wall Street financed German rearmament and the rise of Hitler. One German company which benefited substantially from these loans was I.G. Farben which by 1939 had become the biggest chemical manufacturer in the world, and enabled Germany to become self-sufficient in rubber, petrol, oil and explosives. (This company used the inmates of Auschwitz as slave labour at their massive chemical plant during the war and are estimated to have worked at least 25,000 inmates to death; others were killed in their drug testing program. In the Nuremberg Trials after the war twelve of I.G. Farben/Germany's top executives were sentenced to minor terms of imprisonment for slavery and mistreatment offences whilst many others were acquitted. None of the Americans who also sat on the same board as the convicted were ever tried as a war criminal). On the supervising board of I.G. Farben was Max Warburg and on the board of American I.G. Farben were US and German bankers, friends of Roosevelt and members of Nazi intelligence. Rockefeller's Standard Oil assisted I.G. Farben's programme of research into making oil from coal (which Germany had a plentiful supply of). I.G. Farben were Hitler's major financial backers along with US money channelled through the German subsidiaries of General Electric Company (GEC), International Telephone and Telegraph (ITT) and Ford.

Having supplied the loans to rearm Germany, repayment was demanded in cash causing the German economy to crash, ensuring Hitler could seize power with popular support of his economic solution. In the same year, 1933, Franklin Roosevelt took the American Presidency in a remarkably similar situation, offering a 'New Deal' type solution in the wake of serious economic depression. Both Hitler and Roosevelt were advised by people connected with the American-German cartels and the Bank of International Settlements.

Meanwhile, Britain had adopted a policy of appeasing Germany. This was promoted by the PM Neville Chamberlain as advised by Round Table members such as Lord Halifax, Lord Lothian, Leopold Amery and the Astors (who owned The Times). In order to be self-sufficient through a lengthy war, Hitler's Germany needed the resources of Czechoslovakia, so the British government continued promoting appeasement until Austria and then Czechoslovakia were taken in 1939. The Bank of England then relinquished the £6 million of Czech gold deposited

SUPPRESSED INTELLIGENCE REPORTS

in London to the conquering Nazis. The erstwhile appeasers (Milner, Lothian, Astor and Amery) turned on Chamberlain and on the ensuing wave of pro-war opinion Churchill swept to power. There is evidence to suggest that before Churchill became Prime Minister coded messages passed between him and Roosevelt which confirm that the war was a premeditated set-up. On taking office Churchill immediately appointed Victor Rothschild to implement 'Regulation 18b' to imprison, without trial, anyone suspected of opposing the war.

Thus, the protagonists were in place – Roosevelt, otherwise known as the Knight of Pythias, a 33rd degree mason and member of the Ancient Arabic Order of Nobles of the Mystic Shrine; Churchill, a freemason who had several meetings with the esoteric guru Aleister Crowley; and Hitler who, with Himmler, Goering and Hess, were steeped in the esoteric traditions of groups such as the Thule Society, the Vril Society and the Edelweiss Society, all of which preached anti-Semitism and a Master Race. Occult symbolism and ritual pervaded Nazi Germany from the swastika to the Nuremberg rallies and the organisation of the SS.

World War II was fought to the game plan laid down by the Elite. Despite Roosevelt's assurances to the contrary, American entry into the war was a foregone conclusion and was engineered by the Council on Foreign Relations who advised that the US adopt an anti-Japanese stance in the China-Japanese war, including a trade embargo and refusal of entry into the Panama Canal. Roosevelt knew Pearl Harbour was to be bombed from eight independent intelligence sources and 'fortunately' the cream of the US navy was not in the harbour on the day of the bombing. The invasion of Britain by Germany was not part of the plan so, despite having the ideal opportunity after Dunkirk, Hitler did not cross the channel. However, the Elite's script required the creation of an apparent east/west divide, so as the Allies swept victoriously into Germany, they allowed the Soviet Union to extend to and divide Berlin.

During the war, the American-German cartels made fantastic amounts of money. Their German factories were left amazingly unscathed amidst the bomb devastation, and after the war the same people were appointed by Roosevelt to supervise the fate of German industry. These decided that German industry could only continue if the German people accepted full responsibility for Nazism, thus diverting public scrutiny away from the truth.

At the farcical Nuremberg Trials only insignificant German directors of the cartels were tried and few found guilty. Elsewhere at the trials defendants were barbarically tortured and, due to a change made by a professor at the Carnegie Endowment for International Peace in April 1944, 'following orders' was not an admissible defence. The major Nazi leaders were probably smuggled out of Germany to South America and the scientists responsible for their advanced rocket and mind-control technology were re-situated in prestigious posts in major colleges, universities and NASA in the US. This relocation and infiltration spanned forty years and was known as Operation Paperclip. These scientists are still in positions of influence and are involved in covert high-tech mind-control experiments for the Central Intelligence Agency (CIA) and Defence Intelligence Agency (DIA) which are under National Security Agency (NSA) known as Operation MK-Ultra (see Who We Are – Mind Manipulation).

The outcome of this was just as planned by the Elite with the public crying out for any means to prevent future wars. Many of the solutions offered by politicians have been moves towards global government and the centralisation of power.

SUPPRESSED INTELLIGENCE REPORTS

The United Nations

This was created to solve future disputes by words, not war, but was in fact one of the main reasons that the Second World War was fashioned. The UN had been created by the Council on Foreign Relations as early as 1941, four years before its official foundation by representatives of more than 50 countries. The US delegation to the founding meeting in San Francisco, June 1945, included 74 members of the CFR.

The majority of people working for the UN are genuinely seeking to bring peace to the world. However, it is one of the main vehicles for world government and world army and all six UN Secretary Generals have promoted New World Order type attitudes.

More and more areas of our lives are being globalised through UN organisations under different excuses for international jurisdiction—the World Health Organisation, UN Population Fund, UN Environment Programme, UNESCO (for education, science and culture).

European Union

The three trading blocks of Europe, the Americas and Asia-Australasia are the stepping stones through which government is being centralised before global control.

NAFTA (North Atlantic Free Trade Agreement), which has recently been extended, and APEC (Asia-Pacific Economic Co-operation) look set to follow the example of Europe which is developing from a trade co-operative to a United States of Europe.

The European Economic Community (EEC) was largely the brain-child of Jean Monnet and Joseph Retinger (a founder of the Bilderberg group). It was funded by loans devised by Monnet and the CFR and was formally created in 1957 by the Treaty of Rome, drafted by Monnet and the CFR. If any country showed a reluctance to join, the US pro-Europe position was made very clear to the 'offending' country.

The EEC has since become the European Community and now the European Union. Monetary union has been confirmed by the Maastricht treaty and the situation moves ever closer to a Federal Europe. In 1980, the EC drew up a map of regions within a proposed Federal Europe. England did not feature as an administrative unit and the regions defined in the former Yugoslavia are those which have since been created by the recent war. The public have always been kept in the dark about the extent of the union, with Prime Ministers Heath, Wilson and Callaghan all accepting the renunciation of sovereignty and incorporation into a Federal Europe. Margaret Thatcher served her economic purpose with Reagan in the 1980s but her resistance to European Union ensured her downfall in 1990. Her demise was decided upon by the 1989 meeting of the Bilderberg group.

In the June 1995, Bilderberg meeting, attended by Norman Lamont and William Waldegrave, John Major was threatened with a similar fate if he didn't back a Federal Europe. The leadership challenge by John Redwood, supported by Lamont, was based on their alleged opposition to Federalisation. Major conveniently won and purged his Cabinet of anti-federalists.

The Illusion of Democracy

Centralisation of power would not be accepted by the public if it was imposed directly; but by offering an apparent choice in the democratic elections of Britain and the US, people

300

are sold the illusion that actions of politicians are accountable to the majority.

In America, presidencies are won through money, so those who control the financial resources dictate who becomes president and the president is then under obligation to those who funded him. The apparent differences between Republicans and Democrats are a façade as epitomised by George Bush, the Republican President 1989-1993, and Bill Clinton, the current Democratic President. Both are members of the Council on Foreign Relations and the Trilateral Commission; both are 33rd degree masons; both support GATT, NAFTA, centralisation and economic growth at the expense of humanity and the environment; and both are heavily involved in drug trafficking, child abuse, murder and the Iran-Contra affair.

In the British 'democracy' a person's allegiance to a political party is largely dictated by income and image. The majority of constituencies are 'safe seats' because due to the affluence, or otherwise, of an area the people automatically vote Conservative or Labour, respectively. Any candidate who toes the Elite line can be easily installed in parliament through these seats and subsequently MPs are instructed how to vote by their party. Those who attempt to be individuals and not support their party on certain issues face sanctions, whereas those who are willing to do as they are told advance rapidly. MPs are bribed to ask questions on behalf of certain companies, they often have external directorships and consultancies and on leaving government they often move into top commercial posts. For example, Lord Wakeham, who was instrumental in the privatisation of the electrical industry, became a director of N.M. Rothschild who had made a fortune from the privatisation. Other directors of N.M. Rothschild include Norman Lamont (former Chancellor), Lord Armstrong (one of Thatcher's cabinet secretaries during privatisation), Clive Whitmore (Home Office permanent secretary) and Frank Cooper (Ministry of Defence permanent secretary).

As early as 1940 Harold Wilson was preaching a centralised Federal Europe and outlined a plan of infiltration of the Labour and Conservative parties to form a centre party of moderates which could brand any genuine opposition as extremists. The plan also included the destruction of the British manufacturing industries. Between 1964 and 1975, Wilson (Labour) was Prime Minister, except when he was replaced in 1970-74 by his Bilderberg colleague Edward Heath (Conservative). The two of them ran down British industry, limited MI5 investigational powers and moved towards European Union. Wilson was aided by Lord Victor Rothschild as the head of his Central Policy Review Staff, and his Chancellor Denis Healey (Bilderberger, TC, RIIA).

Today, all political parties agree on the major issues—Major, Blair and Ashdown are all in favour of European Union, a single currency and bank, Maastricht, GATT and Western consumerism.

THE WORLD ARMY

A world army is to be achieved through the manipulation of conflicts leading to extra military powers for the United Nations Peacekeeping Forces. Meanwhile, NATO is expanding to absorb more countries of the Eastern bloc and operate outside its designated areas. Eventually these will fuse to form a world army to enforce the New World Order. The Gulf War was a major step along the path, as it was fought with NATO funding under a UN banner. Just prior to the conflict, closer co-operation was called between the countries of the former Soviet Union and NATO in order to extend the alliance beyond the North Atlantic and Europe

SUPPRESSED INTELLIGENCE REPORTS

The Gulf War

Iraq, in an attempt to recover from the expensive eight year war with Iran, had been seeking to control its own oil reserves – independence which the Western oil companies could not allow. So, as well as being of importance to the Elite's long term goals of a world army, the conflict was engineered to effectively destroy Iraq both economically and in terms of its population.

Saddam Hussein had been installed in 1968 on the back of CIA support for his Baath party. In November 1989, US loans to Iraq were guaranteed providing that the money was used to buy US farm produce. Instead, as expected, Hussein used the money for arms and defaulted on the loans. The US taxpayer is now picking up the bill for rearming the 'enemy'. This US funding was done through the Atlantan branch of the Italian government bank, Banco Nazionale del Lavaro (BNL), which loaned $5 billion. Loans from the BNL to Iraq for arms purchases were organised as early as 1984 by Kissinger Associates. Some of the Iraqi arms were bought from Britain in illegal sales which implicate the British government. This possibly includes the Midland Industrial Trade Services, allegedly the secret arms running wing of the Midland Bank, which was introduced to the Iraqis by Kissinger Associates.

Having armed Iraq, America needed an excuse to invade. This opportunity came through covertly supporting Kuwait's obstinate insistence to make economic recovery difficult for Iraq by over-producing oil and keeping prices low. In July 1990, whilst assuring Hussein that his administration had no interest in an 'Arab-Arab conflict, like your border disagreement with Kuwait', Bush reached agreement with Gorbachev that Russia would not intervene if America invaded Iraq. Kuwait was invaded by Iraq in August 1990 and Bush started talking about economic sanctions against Iraq. Saudi Arabia was convinced by the Americans that it was under threat and under this pretext US forces were dispatched to protect Saudi Arabia. These were later joined by British and French troops to create a UN army.

One month before the UN invasion of Kuwait/Iraq, a US army report detailed the destruction of Kuwait, the firing of the oil wells and which companies would be involved in the lucrative rebuilding of Kuwait and extinguishing the fires. In the ensuing bombing, Iraqui industry, and therefore its post-conflict economy, was destroyed and hundreds of thousands of people have died, either as a direct result of indiscriminate bombing or in the ensuing poverty and deprivation.

Through the Gulf conflict, the phrase 'New World Order', used by Bush in a victory speech, was used by all and sundry to describe this unprecedented global military co-operation. Public approval for this type of intervention has been amplified by the manipulation of Yugoslavia to show inadequacies in the current UN Peacekeeping force, as first highlighted by their ineffectiveness in Rwanda and Somalia. As none of these trouble spots adversely effect the oil trade, an operation on the scale of the Gulf War is not required. Incidentally, there is already a joint UN/NATO Allied Rapid Reaction Corps whose existence was justified by the failure of the UN in Yugoslavia.

The Supposed ET Menace

The need for a world army is also being sold to the public as a defence against UFOs, for planetary security against aggressive extra-terrestrials. This has been achieved through a massive cover up of genuine ET contact and UFO sightings.

SUPPRESSED INTELLIGENCE REPORTS

ETs of both positive and negative intent for humanity are visiting this planet – they have been for millennia – and have possibly established underground bases on Earth. By working with these ETs, Elite science is far more advanced than conventional science would have us believe. Free energy, anti-gravity technology, advanced mass mind manipulation techniques are all under the control of the military in highly secretive and sinister underground centres like Area S-4 in Nevada, the Dulce facility in New Mexico, RAF Rudloe Manor (Wiltshire) and Mount Weather near Washington DC. The 'non-existence' of such technology enables the issue of UFO/ET interaction to be plagued with disinformation. The propaganda machine ridicules true sightings, while high publicity awaits encounters where people are subjected to terrifying experiments at the hands of ETs. However it is very probable that such incidents are in fact carried out by the military and intelligence services using technology the general public are unaware of in order to create the desired response of fear and the demand for global defence. However, I believe that a proportion of abductions are occurring to individuals who have agreed – perhaps before incarnation – to being involved in such ET experiments which are monitoring the human race in such areas as pollution effects on the body and genetic evolution etc.. Abductee reports include a programme of implantation and removal of foetuses for the purpose of cross-breeding humans and aliens.

One further sinister twist to the tale of ETs is that certain people who have been victims of Satanic and paedophilic abuse have, as part of the process of regaining suppressed memories, uncovered images of ETs over-laid on the memories of abuse by people. Mind control is a central part of the process of Satanic abuse whereby the brain is compartmentalised through severe trauma, assisted by drugs and Electro-Convulsive-Treatment. In this way it is possible to bury memories of events a long way behind implanted ones. This is the same technique used by the intelligence agencies to create perfect lone assassins.

POPULATION CONTROL

Eugenics

One of the most alarming of the Elite's doctrines is that of eugenics – controlling human reproduction in order to reduce the number of those that the Elite perceive as inferior to create a 'master race' with 'desirable' genetic characteristics. Eugenics had its highest public profile in Nazi Germany but the policies began a long time before Hitler and are continuing to the present day.

The philosophy was pioneered by Thomas Malthus in the 18th/19th centuries who sought to encourage disease and child mortality in the poor. So-called Malthusianism has since been adopted by different organisations for a variety of excuses. After various eugenics policies in the US states in the late 19th century, including the compulsory sterilisation of the mentally ill and 'undesirables' in Indiana, the Rockefellers established a eugenics research centre in New York. They were supported in this venture by the Harrimans, another family of manipulators.

The First International Congress of Eugenics was held in London in 1912 and was attended by a certain Winston Churchill. By 1917, fifteen US states had eugenics laws to sterilise epileptics, the mentally ill and regular criminals. On the agenda of the Third International Congress in 1932 was the 'problem' of African-Americans which, according to the delegates, revealed a need to sterilise to 'cut off bad stock'. At this meeting were several Nazis, including Dr Ernst Rudin, who had been enabled to attend by the Hamburg-Amerika Shipping Line, owned by the Harriman and Bush families. On returning to Germany, Rudin, who was funded by the Rockefellers, supervised the policy of sterilising those who were retarded, deaf, blind or alcoholics.

Between 1941 and 1943, at the same time as the 'master race' mentality in Hitler's Germany was being condemned by the rest of the world, 42,000 people were sterilised in the US. Five years later the Sterilisation League/ Birthright Inc. established a eugenics centre in North Carolina which began a project to forcibly sterilise young children who were considered to have a low IQ. This was part funded by the Gray family, close friends of the Bush's. After the war, John D. Rockefeller III and John Foster Dulles campaigned against the extension of the non-white populations and in 1952 launched the Population Council. This still exits and is still advocating zero population growth in the US, family planning in the developing sector and the expansion of the Club of Rome's 'Malthusianism'. (See later for details of the Club of Rome.)

Eugenics policies are funded by the World Bank which, at the Rio summit, pledged to double the money available to population control. Birth control is now forced on the developing countries through fear of economic sanctions.

The extent of the population control towards which the Elite are striving was revealed in the 1962/63 'Report from Iron Mountain' , a secret study group into controlling population without war. It sought completely artificial procreation to supersede the 'ecological function of war'. This was to include total control of contraception via water supplies and essential food stuffs so babies could only be conceived by those to whom a carefully controlled antidote had been administered. Such a system was apparently already under development... 35 years ago!

George Bush is a major voice in the eugenics movement and is surrounded by like-minded people – Boyden Gray (his legal advisor) and William Draper III (head of fundraising for his 1980 presidential campaign). Draper's grandfather had unsuccessfully urged eugenics policies on Eisenhower before convincing Johnson to adopt them. In 1969 Bush was involved in hearings into the 'dangers of too many black babies' and when he became ambassador to the UN in 1972 he arranged for the Association of Voluntary Surgical Contraception (formerly the Sterilisation League) to extend its policy of sterilising young children with 'low' IQ to non-white countries. This was further extended when Bush became president in 1988.

Engineered Wars

War is one of the most effective ways of culling an 'undesirable' population as Thomas Ferguson, a member of the Office of Population Affairs, explains:

'to reduce the population quickly you have to pull all the males into the fighting and kill significant numbers of fertile, child-bearing age, females.'

From his position of 'shuttle' diplomat, Henry Kissinger has successfully engineered conflict throughout the world. In Vietnam, the war was caused by the movement of hundreds of thousands of people from the north to the south – a move forced on them by the Saigon Military Mission, created by the CIA in 1954. With no food, they resorted to theft, and by labelling the bands 'the Viet Cong' a problem was created. Under the pretext that they were controlled by the Khmer Rouge, the north Vietnamese were severely bombed. According to estimates, 30-500,000 Cambodians died in the bombings, when in fact China was the power behind North Vietnam, supported by Kissinger with US/China liaisons headed by George Bush. The Khmer Rouge reacted, as expected, and took Cambodia, murdering 32% of the population. During the war, the CIA station in Saigon co-ordinated Operation Phoenix which reportedly murdered 40,000 Vietnamese on 'suspicion' of working for the Viet Cong – that is, they could read and write. Two of the US commanders in the conflict were Maxwell Taylor and William Westmoreland, both members of the Population Crisis Council and Draper Fund.

The Yom Kippur war and countless other 'civil wars' in Central America and Africa have been engineered by Kissinger to cull populations as even when it is not the prime aim; mass killings are perceived as a useful by-product of war.

Kissinger is a member of the Club of Rome and in 1974 supervised the production of National Security Study Memo 200 about the implications of population growth. This stated that population growth in the developing world would lead to a desire for self determination of their economies. It continued that the population must therefore be controlled, but this fact must be withheld from the country's leaders. Amongst the countries specifically targeted were Ethiopia, Columbia, India, Nigeria, Mexico and Indonesia.

Indonesia is an horrendous example of conflict creation for the purposes of eugenics and corporate control, while public bodies and the media remain obstinately silent. General Suharto took control of Indonesia in 1965 through a CIA-backed coup and has since been responsible for 500,000 murders in his own country. However, because his administration is subservient to Western corporations, allowing them to exploit the land and the people (e.g. Reebok), this appalling tragedy goes unchallenged in the media. In December 1975 Indonesia invaded the Portuguese colony of East Timor and, in the following years, proceeded to slaughter 200,000 people, a third of the Timorese population. This genocide (eugenics) has been carried out with arms from Britain (British Aerospace's Hawk Jets) and US, approval from the West (Kissinger and Ford were in Indonesia days before the invasion) and complete silence in the mass media. The simple reason is that oil and gas reserves had been discovered off the coast of East Timor which the multinational oil companies could exploit only if controlled by a corporate-friendly culture – like Indonesia.

WHO WE ARE

Until the last couple of hundred years a major tool in the 'programming' of the collective mind has been the belief in dogmatic religion. Religious philosophies generally present a picture of Creation with humankind, even though perhaps 'chosen' by God, to be very much subservient and worthless. People who consider themselves 'free' through the pursuit of their own dogmatic religion are amongst the most enslaved victims of the Illuminati's plan for total take over of mind, body and soul. Fear, guilt and a host of other negative emotions have been instilled into humanity in the name of religion – the Christian guilt due to the doctrine of 'original sin' and fear of the final judgement; Jewish feelings of divine punishment for failing Yahweh; Islamic aggression to convert the masses by the sword; the Hindu caste system in which 'untouchables' have no hope of salvation in this lifetime. Western Catholicism, with its control over all education for centuries and its intolerance of alternatives (usually condemned as heresies with the proponents ex-communicated, exiled or barbarically tortured and killed) successfully kept the masses in cringing subservience to their vengeful, yet supposedly loving, God. The Catholic Church, in turn, has been controlled and bled dry of wealth by an especially sinister organisation which is a combination of elements of Freemasonry and the Mafia, known as P2. Religions are also answerable to the banks.

When scientific developments in the 18th and 19th centuries started disputing the orthodox theological interpretation of 'who we are', people's belief in the church started to wane and they threatened to start thinking for themselves. The Elite consequently hijacked this new science in order to switch the general belief from a judgmental God (which enabled control through fear etc.) to a denial of the existence of God and a belief that this life is all that there is (which enabled control through science and materialism). Darwin's theories on evolution was the first major coup on the mass mindset for the 'survival of the fittest/no God' belief system which has been prevalent in the last century. This theory, which did not originate with Charles Darwin, was essentially the work of the Lunar Society, a revolutionary organisation created to undermine God and overthrow monarchies, which Darwin's family was very involved in. By the end of his life Darwin himself did not believe the argument but the theories had taken hold and have since been taught as scientific fact. Once more our ideas about who and what we are have been programmed into us – beliefs which serve the Elite and their goal of complete control.

Ideas which challenge the now orthodox belief in evolution or seek to publicise the eternal nature of the spirit are marginalised into groups which are subsequently labelled as 'cults' – a word which is instinctively interpreted as 'a dangerous group of slightly insane people'. The stigma has been deliberately attached to the word for this very reason by highly publicised cults and the behaviour attributed to them. For example, the Jonestown massacre in 1978, which research has shown was probably a CIA mind-control experiment, and the Waco 'mass suicide' by burning alive in 1993 when followers of David Koresh were attacked by the FBI and the Bureau of Alcohol, Tobacco and Firearms (BATF) with tanks armed with flame throwers. Coincidentally, the BATF had contacted a local hospital before the raid to enquire about the availability of beds in the burns unit.

Cults which promote a world government and whose belief system incorporates the New World Order are supported by the Elite, e.g. the Moonies, the Church of Scientology and certain strands of the New Age movement. The 'opposite' side is also funded by the same people – the reactionary 'cult buster' groups, like the Cult Awareness Network set up by Dr West, a CIA asset which is heavily involved in Nazi-style mind control experiments.

Education

Conventionally taught and accepted history and science have a fundamental influence on the way that we perceive the world. Therefore, the control of education and the way that these subjects are presented has been of paramount importance to the Elite. This has been one of the main occupations of the Round Table, and in America the task was given to the Rockefeller Foundation by the Carnegie Endowment for International Peace to prevent American life from returning to its pre-World War I state.

The lessons taught in the schools of today are those of confusion (there is no meaning), hierarchical position (envy those above, despise those below), dependency ('success' is measured by the opinion of others and only 'experts' know the truth), obedience (do as others instruct in order to progress) and above all, conformity. A child is simply there to be filled with System-accepted 'facts', regimentally hurried from one lesson to the next to be bombarded with apparently unrelated information with any genuine enthusiasm or interest stifled in the boredom of classroom conformity. A child's intelligence is then measured by his or her meek receptivity to the systematic brainwashing and his or her ability to regurgitate these 'facts' in examinations, whilst the teacher's performance is evaluated by the speed and completeness of the indoctrination. The curriculum is very carefully controlled with standardised textbooks which teachers, whatever their personal feelings on the subject, have to teach in order to retain their jobs. Real questions about the nature of life, the reasons behind the contradictions in accepted historical absurdities, the dreams of self-expression have no part in the strait jacket of System education. People are 'consumers' and cogs in the corporate machine, and those who can accept this role are what the education process call 'successful'. If conformity is the price of 'success', those who seek alternative views and reject the indoctrination are made to experience shame and a sense of failure. We are taught that the Elite system of corporate-led consumerism has been freely created and that it provides the only answer for a meaningful, worthwhile life. Childhood happiness, enthusiasm and excitement for life are suffocated as we are taught to operate within a system which denies the very essences of humanity – love and the ability to question and search for the truth of our current existence.

The Media

Information about and interpretation of current affairs is gained exclusively through the media – newspapers, t.v. and radio. Newspapers are presented as being independent or having a known political leaning and t.v. is supposedly unbiased and independent. This is simply not the case. Information about events come from 'official sources' who can present the view that the Elite want the public to accept. Alternatively, news stories are derived from central news agencies (e.g. Reuters) who give everybody the same story. Newcomers to a media company are expected to toe the conventional line or suddenly their prospects become bleak. Journalists who analyse and think independently are dangerous and are few and far between.

This is not to suggest that every single journalist from the boardroom down to the 'hack' is involved in some massive conspiracy and cover up. Once the framework has been set up (which it deliberately has been over the last few centuries) the system is self-regulatory simply through 'market forces'. Running a newspaper or television station is an expensive business which instantly limits those organisations which can operate one. Such businesses are obviously financially successful in the System, so have an interest in maintaining the status quo. Opinions and stories which challenge the establishment are therefore of no interest to these companies and are viewed as subversive. The media industry is also advertising-based with prices of newspapers kept below the manufacturing costs by advertising income. Multinationals will not support those newspapers/magazines which are viewed as 'anti-business' so such publications are marginalised out of existence simply by market forces. Advertiser-friendly media companies keep their readership in a suitable 'buying' frame of mind by not being controversial, not presenting 'difficult' articles or programmes. The threat of withdrawal of advertising is generally sufficient to ensure the media companies vigilantly filter the stories they present but if one slips through, business organisations often combine forces to pressurise editors into reviewing their content. This is done through letters, law-suits and even parliamentary bills. An example of these so-called 'flak machines' is Accuracy in Media (AIM) a collection of corporate giants, including eight oil companies, whose function is to maintain a corporate-friendly media in the US.

A look at the board members of media companies is revealing about their alleged independence. In America a large number of the directors of NBC, CBS and ABC all have common involvement with Rothschild/Rockefeller/Morgan companies, as well as being members of the Council on Foreign Relations and Trilateral Commission. In Britain, the Daily Telegraph is owned by the Hollinger group who advisors/directors include Henry Kissinger, Lord

SUPPRESSED INTELLIGENCE REPORTS

Carrington, Brzezinski and Lord Rothschild. The current chairman of N.M. Rothschild, Evelyn de Rothschild, is on the board of the Daily Telegraph. A former board member, Andrew Knight (Bil), is now executive chairman of the 'rival' News International, which runs The Times and the Sun, and which is funded by the Oppenheimers and the Rothschilds. Regulatory bodies such as the Press Complaints Commission also have links with the same people e.g. the chairman Lord Wakeham who is a director of N.M. Rothschild.

Most people form their opinions on the basis of newspapers whose political stance mirrors their own. As all media organisations are owned by companies with the same interests and have their content dictated by the advertisers and obtain their stories from the same sources, all 'sides' of public opinion are easily manipulated. This is used to divert attention away from the true agenda:

* Investigators getting near to the truth are branded as anti-Semitic so attention is focused away from their information onto their apparent racism. * 'Expose' books, such as Peter Wright's Spycatcher are publicly opposed by those in government to give credence to their revelations. Their 'exposure' of what are generally innocent people are then believed more readily. * Sensitive information is released when overshadowed by another news story, e.g. identity cards were announced by Michael Howard on the day of the Loyalist cease-fire in Northern Ireland. * Libya has been blamed for the Lockerbie bombing (among other things) to undermine Colonel Gaddafi, when all the evidence points to the CIA and other intelligence agencies. The Libyan leader is, in fact, one of the 'evil tyrants' the media so love to create as a simplistic 'bad guy' at which the public can direct their animosity. He is not exactly a saint but, in the 1980s, Gaddafi was responsible for 14 deaths (mostly Libyans), as compared with the 50,000 corpses at the feet of the regime in El Salvador – an administration installed by the US with a US trained army. * Assassinations are blamed on a lone person with no affiliation to any group. The murder of J.F. Kennedy, for example, was ascribed to Lee Harvey Oswald (who was subsequently murdered himself by a 'lone assassin') but investigations have shown that it could not have been Oswald but it is much more likely that the American President was removed by the intelligence agencies because he did not follow the Elite game plan and was threatening to expose it by 'smashing the CIA into a thousand pieces'.

'Choice'

Public opinion is sold the illusion of choice by maintaining groups in apparent opposition to each other. Again, the majority will believe that they are involved in a real battle for what they genuinely believe to be correct, when in reality the funding and support is derived from the same sources as their opposition. As long as New World Order policies are being promoted it makes no difference to the Elite whether a group is Jewish, anti-Jewish, Left wing, Right wing, Christian, Moslem etc.... it will be used while it serves their purpose.

Another vital tool is instilling a belief that the goals the Elite are striving towards are good and necessary things. This is often achieved by creating a 'problem', which the public react against and call for an official response. The 'solution' which is offered and which is accepted on a wave of public support is the very thing the Elite wanted in the first place. There are countless examples of these but I shall cite just three:

* The 'problem' of violent crime has elicited a wave of public feeling in favour of increased police powers. * 'New age' travellers were suddenly severely harassed by the police and received considerable media attention. When they reacted against their treatment an

apparent 'problem' had been created which was met with the 'solution' of the Criminal Justice Bill. This restriction on personal freedom sailed through parliament and the media spotlight was focused away from the travellers to firstly give the impression of 'problem solved' and secondly, they had served their purpose. * The Oklahoma Bomb in April 1995 in which 168 men, women and children were killed was reported as being caused by a fertilizer bomb – despite the absence of any fertilizer at the scene – planted by a 'people's militia' group. In fact, the explosion was caused by a barometric bomb which has a security level on a par with nuclear weapon components. However public opinion had been mobilised against the 'problem' of the 'people's militia' movement and consequently accepted Clinton's 'solutions' of increased FBI powers to infiltrate and attack these groups, the military enforcement of domestic laws, and a media ban on so-called 'anti-government' extremists such as the People's Militia who are fully aware of the workings of America's secret government.

Environmental Movement

A good example of both these methods of manipulation – problem-generating in order to have a solution accepted and control of both sides of the 'debate – is the way that environmental issues have been used in order to justify centralisation of power. Our planet is in environmental crisis and the vast majority of the Green movement is working positively for the good of the Earth, but when environmentalists can aid the New World Order the Elite have no compunction about leaping on the proverbial band wagon.

The Elite's environmental stance is largely co-ordinated by the Club of Rome, launched by the Freemason Aurelio Peccei in 1968. Its purpose is to issue propaganda about the environmental crisis to justify centralisation of power, the suppression of industrial development in the Third World and eugenics. Under its influence the Global 2000 report was produced during Jimmy Carter's Trilateral administration which used untrue 'shock' data to paint a picture of overpopulation and food/resource shortages. The response document called for population control and the restriction of scientific development in the Third World. It is on the back of these documents that the genuine environmental movement is calling for a global solution to a global problem – a view the Elite wholeheartedly endorses. Highly involved in these documents were bankers and politicians who support the IMF and the World Bank which are causing the very devastation of the planet they profess to be concerned about. 'Debt for equity' schemes in which 'environmentally sensitive' land is given by the Third World as payment for debts (which in reality does not even reduce the debt) are the brainchild of David Rockefeller and Baron Rothschild. The same people were behind the Rio Summit in 1992 where the secretary-general was the millionaire oilman Maurice Strong, also a trustee of the Rockefeller Foundation.

All these 'problems' to which centralisation and eugenics are the proffered 'solutions' are caused by the existing policies of the banks, multinational corporations, the World Bank, the IMF etc.. Create the problem, offer the solution...?

The environmental movement has also been used to prohibit the exploitation of nuclear power. (Personally I am not in favour of nuclear power, but I can still see how the issue has been manipulated to serve the Elite.). The oil and petrochemical industries form the backbone of the Elite's income and recruitment. The oil price shocks in the 1970s were manipulated by the 'Seven Sisters' oil cartel and the Bilderberg Group to massively inflate the price of oil. Conventionally, nuclear power forms the only credible alternative to fossil fuels so it had to de discredited. One of the Bilderbergers who agreed to the increase was Robert O. Anderson, owner of Atlantic Richfield Oil Co of the board of Kissinger Associates. He channelled huge sums of money into organisations to oppose nuclear fuel including a grant to establish a group which developed into Friends of the Earth. Research also suggests that the French arm of the House of Rothschild has been seeking to monopolise nuclear power technology and reprocessing technology in time for the predicted exhaustion of oil and gas supplies. The Rothschilds now control 80% of the world's uranium supplies.

The manipulation has also occurred on an international stage. In the 1980s Pakistan, under Ali Bhutto, proposed independent expansion of its nuclear power programme. Kissinger's threats weren't sufficient to stop Bhutto so a Kissinger-inspired coup removed him from power and the world passively looked on as he was hanged.

Mind Manipulation

Mind control experiments, so-called Nazi science, has been on-going for decades using esoteric knowledge about the human psyche. By ridiculing any spiritual interpretation of life and mobilising the forces of conventional science the Elite have convinced the public of the non-existence of psychic, 'higher' levels so it is easy to keep hidden technology which manipulates these levels.

Mass hypnosis is possible by the repetition of a basic theme until it is accepted as fact by the subconscious and then conscious mind. Such messages can be flashed during t.v. programmes or films and are not perceived by the eyes and conscious mind. Alternatively, the mesmerising and sedating effect of television puts the subconscious mind into an ideal state to receive messages sent to the psyche via carrier t.v./radio waves. It is understood by Elite science how, by broadcasting at certain frequencies, non-physical magnetic levels can be imbalanced to cause physical, emotional and mental illness. Technology also exists whereby thoughts can be induced by stimulating brainwaves.

The most sinister and far-reaching mind control programme is Project MK Ultra, run on behalf of the CIA. During Operation Paperclip, Nazi scientists were moved to the US and given prestigious positions at the leading colleges, universities and NASA after World War II to continue their experiments in which thousands of 'lesser human beings' – prisoners, mental patients, victims of paedophilia and incest etc. – have been forced to participate. Experiments have included removing a person's existing personality by electrotherapy and then compartmentalising and programming new ones by psychic driving. This makes the 'subject' obsessed with certain ideas and is undoubtedly used to 'programme' so-called lone assassins. The CIA openly admit to having used this form of subversive technology for use against America's political enemies but flatly denies that it would ever be used on home territory.

Project Monarch

An integral part of MK-Ultra is Project Monarch – perhaps the most damning episode in the history of mind control – whereby the minds of women and children are brutally taken over in order to provide paedophiles, politicians, criminals and practising Satanists with willing sex slaves who could also double as covert operatives by having their personalities and memories switched on and off at will. (See also Further Examples of Manipulation – Satanists)

The details of this horrific plan by the Elite to take over the planet through mass mind-control have come from the ex-CIA mind-controlled slave, Cathy O'Brien, and are described in harrowing detail in her book Trance Formation Of America. After a lifetime in the clutches of the MK-Ultra Project Monarch mind-control program she became what is known as a 'Presidential Model', a sex slave used specifically by the presidents for perverted abuse. Her abusers include the presidents Gerald Ford, Ronald Reagan and George Bush as well as a host of other key US politicians. These fiends would routinely torture and rape her and later her daughter, Kelly, for personal gratification whilst using drugs and electric shock trauma to further compartmentalise her memory of such events in order to hide their actions. Because of her status and entirely programmable mind Cathy was used in many major political/criminal covert operations and was used to pass on Top Secret information in such affairs as the Iran-Contra deals.

Cathy's life began as the victim of multigenerational paedophilic incest. Her first memory in life is being choked by her father's penis in her throat. This initial trauma began to cause her mind to compartmentalise into separate personalities which could deal with traumatic situations – as a mental survival tool – whilst her 'normal' personality was left to deal with everyday events. Her mind dissociated from the memory of abuse whilst developing another personality which belonged to her father and was triggered on the sight of his arousal. This was the beginning of the creation within Cathy's psyche of a phenomenon known as Multiple Personality Disorder (MPD), now known as Dissociative Identity Disorder (DID).

One side-effect of MPD is the creation of a photographic memory. Since her rescue and de-programming in 1988, Cathy has been able to recall in stunning detail every encounter with her adversaries and their sordid plans for world domination. These were freely revealed to Cathy by leading US politicians and criminals over a number of years whilst presuming that their high-tech programming could never be interfered with and it was therefore safe to do so. Another side-effect of the programming is the development of a visual acuity which is 44 times that of the average person.

Subsequent abuse came daily from her father and uncles who had also been victims of paedophile parents. Separate personalities were created for each situation, whilst Cathy was still little more than a toddler.

Her Uncle Bob, a regular paedophilic abuser, often boasted to her that he was a pilot in Air Force Intelligence and worked for the Vatican. It was Bob who first introduced Cathy to child pornographer and head of the local Michigan Mafia, Gerald Ford (of the Warren Commission who investigated the death of JFK, and later became President of the US after Nixon). Ford had begun recruiting 'Multigenerational incest abused children with MPD for its genetic mind-control studies', a Top Secret Defence Intelligence Agency project. By selling Cathy into this programme, her father gained immunity from prosecution having recently been caught selling pornography which involved Cathy and her pet boxer dog, Buster.

Her father was soon enrolled on a two week course at Harvard where he was taught his role in preparing Cathy for the project. He then returned home to enthusiastically announce that the family would be having more children. Cathy now has two sisters and four brothers; each victims of paedophilic abuse.

Preparation for The Project was based upon continual trauma, food and water deprivation, sensory deprivation and included constantly slave driving Cathy into exhaustion just like Cinderella. She was repeatedly prostituted to local Freemasons, police, a Catholic priest, Satanists and relatives in order that she further dissociated and enforced the realisation that there was no place to run and hide. She was also prostituted to Michigan State Senator, Guy VanderJagt (later US Congressman and chairman of the Republican National Congressional Committee which appointed George Bush as president) who gave her a Rosy Cross necklace and told her that he and her Uncle Bob had been to the Vatican where the secrets of other dimensions of existence were kept. On one occasion, both he and Ford brutally raped her in an horrific threesome backstage at a political parade; they then took the stage in front of the crowd which included all of Cathy's schoolmates to present her with a US flag which only moments previously they had inserted into her rectum.

Despite these daily horrors she excelled at her studies; due mainly to her photographic memory. No one had any idea that any of this was going on.

In 1968, VanderJagt introduced Cathy to the Canadian Prime Minister Pierre Trudeau who then abused her and used her for porn involving a French poodle which he had given her as a pet.

Once Cathy reached adolescence and began to develop breasts, VanderJagt found her less attractive and she was 'given' to US Senator and Ku Klux Klan affiliate, Robert C. Byrd who found pleasure in repeatedly torturing her in Sado-Masochistic sex and porn from which she still bears the scars all over her body.

By now Cathy was unable to tell reality from dreams and vice versa. This was reinforced through an advanced form of mind-control known as 'Satanic reversals' whereby every sensory input was controlled and words and sentences perverted to always have sinister double or triple meanings pertaining to abuse. She was further prepared for Project Monarch when she was taken out of school and relocated at Muskegon Catholic Central High School, with other Monarch 'Chosen Ones' as they were referred to.

The final event which literally drove Cathy out of her mind and destroyed her one remaining 'normal' personality happened in 1974 after a parade in Cedar Springs, Michigan when Ford brutally assaulted her and delivered electric shock treatment in order that she would forget the event. Now every compartment of her mind was associated with abuse.

The programme soon began to involve high-tech military bases for further traumatisation and programming. For this they used centres such as the MacDill Airforce Base at Tampa; Fort Campbell in Kentucky; Fort McKlellen at Anniston, Alabama; Redstone Arsenal and Marshall Space Flight Centre in Huntsville, Alabama; the NASA Kennedy Space Centre, Cape Canaveral in Florida and NASA's Goddard Space Flight Centre near Washington D.C..

Cathy was sold and 'married' to her owner, Byrd in a contract which made her father a millionaire overnight. Although 'owned' by Byrd, Cathy was given 'handlers' to keep an eye on and further traumatise her. One such person was Wayne Cox, a Satanist and serial killer his calling card is to remove one hand of his victims which he calls the 'Hands of Glory') who had gained immunity from prosecution through his involvement in Project Monarch. He was introduced to Cathy whilst playing for a country music band at the Grand Old Opry in Nashville, Tennessee. According to Cathy, no one makes it in this town unless they are slaves or CIA operatives. Names of leading slave handlers and CIA operatives include Kris Kristofferson (described by Cathy as a 'Vatican based Project Monarch slave runner'), Boxcar Willie (who has abused Cathy's daughter, Kelly, in three separate mental institutions) and Merle Haggard – whose song 'Freedom Train' is the code-word for this aspect of the mind-control plan. Project

SUPPRESSED INTELLIGENCE REPORTS

Monarch Slaves include the singer Barbara Mandrell and her sisters, who are also owned by Byrd, and Loretta Lynn who's handler is Neo-Nazi paedophile and CIA operative, Ken Riley.

Cox involved Cathy in drug running and cannibalistic Satanism with his mother. He also caused her to conceive six times in order to use the foetuses in these rituals and became the natural father of Cathy's only daughter, Kelly, who was born in 1980. During one drug run with Cox to Tinker Air Force Base in Ouachita National Forrest near Hot Springs, Arkansas, Cathy met, then Governor of Arkansas, Bill Clinton. She was then cued to reveal to him a secret message from Senator Bennett Johnson of Louisiana and then handed over a particularly fine batch of cocaine (Clinton's drug of choice) for his personal use.

In 1980, Cathy was programmed at Fort Campbell, Kentucky by Lt. Colonel Michael Aquino, a confessed neo-Nazi and founder of the Himmler-inspired Temple of Set (Satan), who holds Top Secret clearance in the DIA's Psychological Warfare Division (he was also once charge with ritual and sexual abuse of children at the Presidio Day Care Centre in San Francisco). He used atrocious trauma techniques using NASA technology on both Cathy and Kelly.

Perversely, Lucifarian religions are constitutionally protected in the USA and Britain!

One sex slave training camp is known as the 'Charm School' in Youngstown, Ohio and is operated by the 'Governor', Dick Thornburgh (Governor of Pennsylvania, US Attorney General and secretary for the UN). Here he worked with Congressman Jim Trafficant using high-tech programming techniques.

A further insight into the New World Order mentality comes from these passages from Trance Formation of America:

(Byrd) often threatened me that I was considered 'disposable' because after all, "The first Presidential Model, Marilyn Monroe, was killed right in front of the public eye and no one knew what happened".'

Furthermore:

…he loved to hear himself talk and would often drone on and on in his famous long-winded recitations, while I was photographically recording every word he said. He detailed the inner operational structure of the world domination effort, including psychological warfare strategies, and explained how he had and would use his 'expert' knowledge of the Constitution to manipulate it and the so called US Justice System, and more.

…Byrd 'justified' mind-control atrocities as a means of thrusting mankind into accelerated evolution, according to the Neo-Nazi principles to which he adhered. He 'justified' manipulating mankind's religion to bring about the prophesied biblical 'world peace' through the 'only means available' – total mind-control in the New World Order. 'After all,' he proclaimed, 'even the Pope and the Mormon Prophet know this is the only way to peace and they co-operate fully with The Project.' (my highlights added)

…He adhered to the belief that 95% of the (world's) people WANT to be led by the 5%, and claimed that this can be proven because the 95% DO NOT WANT TO KNOW what really goes on in government.' Byrd believed that in order for this world to survive, mankind must take a 'giant step in evolution through creating a 'superior race', Byrd believed in the Nazi and KKK principles of 'annihilation of underprivileged races and cultures' through genocide, to alter genetics and breed 'the more gifted – the blondes of this world'.

SUPPRESSED INTELLIGENCE REPORTS

Cathy's first position as a 'Presidential Model' was to Ronald Reagan – known to slaves as 'The Wizard of OZ'. One of his favourite pastimes was perverted porn – especially bestiality. He would instruct his personal pornographer, Larry Flynt (owner of Hustler magazine) to make pictures to his own specifications which became known as 'Uncle Ronnie's Bedtime Stories'. Reagan's personal attaché, Philip Habib's favourite pastime was to sodomise Cathy whilst electrocuting her to create the desired rectal spasm. Habib later introduced her to King Fahd of Saudi Arabia whose tastes were frighteningly similar.

Fahd was to fund the Contras via Panamanian Dictator and CIA operative, Manuel Noriega for Reagan and Cathy was used as the messenger in 'Operation Carrier Pidgeon'.

One of the most brutal of all of Cathy's abusers was Dick Cheney (White House Chief of Staff to Ford, member of the CFR and later Secretary of Defence to Reagan – despite having no military background). He would regularly organise an event known as 'A Most Dangerous Game'. This involved releasing Monarch slaves into the woods and then hunting them down with dogs and guns for sport as a means of further traumatising victims as well as for his own perversity.

One operation, organised by Cheney and Ford was 'Operation Shell Game'. This involved Cathy being used as a 'Carrier Pidgeon':

He (Ford) began talking as though I were a machine and he was dictating a message. 'Take this message to Dick Chaney, Pentagon. The Mob has agreed to transfer the $2.3 million (porn profits) to the Bank of Credit and Commerce International. Let's pool our money now and we'll be swimming in it. This operation has been an enterprising success. Let's keep it that way. Cease agreement with Panama. All Mexican channels are implemented (cocaine and heroin). Hail to the chief'.

As a replacement for Cox, Cathy was given a new handler; paedophile, ventriloquist and hypnotist, Alex Houston. (Cox now breeds goats for Satanic rituals and runs a trade in human body parts for Satanists.) In 1982, Houston dealt cocaine to Bill Clinton whilst Cathy was taken to meet his wife, Hilary Clinton. At the sight of Cathy's vagina (which had previously been mutilated without anaesthetic to resemble a demon's head – the head of Baphomet which is worshipped by the Templars and their offshoots) Hilary Clinton became aroused and performed oral sex upon her.

In 1983, George Bush began sodomising and electrocuting Kelly, now merely three and a half years old. Her rectum usually bled for days after. Furthermore, constant threats were made by Bush on Kelly's life in order to keep Cathy in line. He also claimed to be an ET and could activate a holographic image within Cathy's mind in which he would change into a lizard-like alien creature.

Bohemian Grove in California is an exclusive club where all sexual and satanic perversions are catered for – including necrophilia. Attendees are referred to as 'Grovers'. Reagan's Secretary of Education and later Legal Counsel to Clinton, Bill Bennett and his brother Bob assaulted Kelly here in 1988. Bennett has intimate knowledge of Catholic/Jesuit mind-control techniques and is using them to implement 'Education 2000' which is ,'designed to increase children's learning capacity while destroying the ability to think for themselves'. Bennett, like Bush, also claims to be an alien. Another plan known as World Vision is a Jesuit fund raising operation to implement world peace through mind-control.

SUPPRESSED INTELLIGENCE REPORTS

The Order of the Rose – a Templar derivative – is very prominent among the New World Order brigade. Many slaves have a red rose tattooed on their left wrists. The Canadian Prime Minister, Brian Mulroney is also part of this clique, as is VandrJegt and Madelaine Albright who, according to Bush, '...rose in the UN through me to implement the New World Order'.

Among the Order of the Rose, George Bush is referred to as 'The Rose'.

In 1986, Cathy and Kelly were taken to Mount/Lake Shasta in California under the guise of a music festival run by Merle Haggard. This is the base for a multi-juristictional police force which will be used to enforce the New World Order with an arsenal of black helicopters and an army of mind-controlled military personnel. Here, Bush and Cheney played the 'Most Dangerous Game' with Cathy. As a punishment for being caught, Bush (under the influence of his favourite drug – heroin) sodomised Kelly and burnt Cathy's thighs with a red hot poker.

When Cathy was 29 she became aware that Presidential Models were not allowed to live much beyond the age of 30. Plans were formed and agreed with Reagan that she would meet her end in a Snuff Movie whereby she would be burned alive. At this point Senator Patrick Leahy (Vice Chairman on US Senate Intelligence Committee and close friend of Byrd) 'acquired' her for a time. At his own personal torture lab he abused Cathy which included slowly inserting a wire into her right eye whilst forcing Kelly to watch.

In February 1988, two months after Cathy's thirtieth birthday, both she and Kelly were abducted from Alex Houston by his business partner and former CIA operative Mark Phillips – acknowledged by the US mental health and law enforcement officials as an expert in 'the most secret technology known to man: Trauma-based mind control' which is 'The only form of human control that is absolute'. He managed to smuggle them out of the clutches of their captors to Alaska with the aid of 'insider' assistance in the 'intelligence community' and began an intensive de-programming which has culminated in the recovery of Cathy's sanity as well as the information outlined in Trance Formation Of America.

It was also discovered that Kelly had been 'programmed' by Wayne Cox to die by using a mind-control technique known as 'hypnosleep'. This manifested in chronic and increasingly severe asthma.

According to Phillips the present field of mental health is so backward that:

> In the present climate, referring mind-controlled victims to mental health professionals for treatment would be tantamount to subjecting a patient needing delicate surgery to a surgeon who was blind-folded and hand-cuffed.

The subsequent lives of the threesome has been one filled with trauma, death threats and legal battles. Kelly is now effectively a political prisoner in a mental institution because of her suicidal tendencies and is not allowed to have contact with Phillips – one of the few people who could help her to regain her sanity. All requests for legal investigations into the claims made by them to the legal authorities have been prevented 'For reasons of National Security', despite the mass of verifiable evidence which they have been able to uncover This is due to the loopholes created by the National security Act, 1947 and the 1986 Reagan Amendment, which means that the government can censor and/or cover up anything in the interests of National Security.

The extraordinary bravery of Cathy, Kelly and Mark has seen to it that this abuse and its perpetrators will be held accountable for their actions. Through their mass publicity attempts in the face of death at every turn we now have a pretty clear picture of the mentality of the New World Order Elite operatives. It is now up to all of us to see that such sacrifice has not been in vain.

According to my sources in Britain. The British counterpart to Project Monarch is Project Ultra Green and was initiated by a Nazi scientist named Grunenberg.

One US security agency, the National Security Agency, which wields the power behind the CIA and is heavily involved in the Black Ops and Black Arts has a base in England at a place called Menwith Hill which is near Ilkley Moor in North Yorkshire. Here the Elite operate a covert surveillance operation of Britain which includes a mass phone tapping system (try dropping a few of the code names mentioned in this book into your conversations on the phone and you will hear the 'clicks' in the background as their recording machinery is activated by specific 'buzz words') and high-tech satellite surveillance operation which was developed under the cover of Reagan's 'Star Wars' Programme. Interestingly, George Lucas, the writer and director of the Star Wars movies is named by Cathy O'Brien as a NASA/NSA operative.

Fluoride

The apathy of the public towards their manipulation has also been influenced very deliberately by the addition of chemicals to food and water supplies. For example, this happened when sodium fluoride was introduced into our water supply and the majority of our tooth-pastes, supposedly to prevent dental caries in the under twelve-year-olds. What they did not tell the public was that sodium fluoride is a highly toxic by-product of the aluminium manufacturing process and the refining of phosphate rock (see Further Examples of Manipulation – The BSE Case) which was once used as rat poison and also pollutes the atmosphere and water environment due to overuse of the aerosol propellants Chlorofluorocarbons (CFCs). Fluorine is a major component of most of today's major sedative drugs and even new supposedly less addictive drugs such as Prozac (Fluoxetine) and its derivatives. (Prozac also contains benzene which is, according to the World Health Organisation, 'a known carcinogen with no known safe level'. Prozac is currently the world's most popular anti-depressant despite having documented side-effects such as: suicidal ideation, violent behaviour, nervousness, anxiety, insomnia, anorexia and sexual dysfunction!)

The following statement is extracted from 'Address in Reply to the Government's Speech to Parliament', as recorded in Victorian Hansard of 12 August 1987, by Mr Harley Rivers Dickinson, Liberal Party Member of the Victorian Parliament for South Barwon. Hence the title.

At the end of the Second World War, the United States Government sent Charles Eliot Perkins, a research worker in chemistry, biochemistry, physiology and pathology, to take charge of the vast Farben chemical plants in Germany.

While there he was told by the German chemists of a scheme which had been worked out by them during the war and adopted by the German General Staff.

This was to control the population in any given area through mass medication of drinking water. In this scheme, sodium fluoride occupied a prominent place.

Repeated doses of infinitesimal amounts of fluoride will in time reduce an individual's power to resist domination by slowly poisoning and narcotising a certain area of the brain and will thus make him submissive to the will of those who wish to govern him.

Both the Germans and the Russians added sodium fluoride to the drinking water of prisoners of war to make them stupid and docile.'

After the war, I.G. Farben was dismantled but later emerged in the many guises of the companies with whom they had signed cartel agreements including Procter and Gamble, the company who domesticated the word fluoride with official encouragement in 1958 with the 'Crest' fluoridated toothpaste campaign. Moreover, an adviser to the US Government on hypnotism and psychological behaviour control, Dr. George Estabrooks, later became Chairman, Department of Psychology, Colgate University. Internationally, Colgate was and remains the most ardent producer and advocate for the fluoridation of toothpaste.

Fluoride is active in parts per million and acts as a potentiator for other drugs, i.e. it increases their effect. In 1954, Charles Elliot Perkins, scientist and author stated:

'The real purpose behind water fluoridation is to reduce the resistance of the masses to domination and control and loss of liberty' and, 'I can say this in all earnestness and sincerity as a scientist who has spent nearly twenty years research into the chemistry, bio-chemistry, physiology and pathology of fluorine: any person who drinks artificially fluorinated water for a period of one year or more will never again be the same person, mentally or physically'.

Interestingly, the chemical industry now has a mass market for a once hard to dispose of toxic waste material and the Illuminati have a sedated and more easily controlled population.

A Microchipped Population

In the Elite's misguided judgement the ideal form of control will be via a microchipped population connected to a global computer. Money will be obsolete and all financial transactions will be carried out via a microchip inserted under the skin used in much the same way as a credit or smart card – swipe your wrist over the sensor to pay for your goods. Convenient, easy... and enables the Elite to have complete knowledge about you and your transactions. With no cash alternative if your 'wrist' is refused for some reason you can be prevented from buying anything and effectively ostracised from society. Moves to implement this are already underway and public opinion is being softened up to accept it: in the 1970s Swedish hospital patients were implanted without their knowledge; pets, new-born babies in maternity wards and criminals are being electronically tagged; a need for identity cards is being expressed (to combat crime); supermarkets are experimenting with bar-coded cards to keep a tally of purchases without the need for check-out assistants; the 'pay at the pump' systems recently introduced in some petrol stations; and in 1994 the Intel Corporation was given a five year contract to research into an under the skin microchip for identity/financial transactions.

IBM have already developed an invisible bar coding system of three sets of six numbers which is painless and can be 'installed' on the skin by laser in a fraction of a second without the person being aware of its existence and is currently in use on cattle. Watch out for gradual insistence on personal computerisation and electrical devices which could potentially be used to control us all. Remember, they create problems and then offer solutions.

Dr. Carl W. Sanders is an electronics engineer, inventor, author and consultant with various government organisations as well as IBM and General Electric. He spent thirty two years developing microchip technology for use in medicine which resulted in the chip which he describes as 'the Mark of the Beast'. It is a tiny chip which is recharged by body temperature and whose prime location would, therefore, be in the forehead, just below the hairline, or alternatively on the back of the hand. This chip has been tested as a contraception device in India and as a behaviour modifier in Vietnam veterans, amongst other things. A specific identification chip was developed which contained details of a person's name, picture of their face, security number, finger print, physical description, family history, address, occupation, income tax information and criminal record.

Dr. Sanders admits to attending many 'One World' meetings with Henry Kissinger and people from the CIA where it was discussed, 'How can you control people if you cannot identify them?' and, 'How do you make people aware of the need for something like this chip?' The answer was simple, 'Let's make them aware of lost children etc.' The CIA then came up with the idea of putting pictures of lost children on milk cartons, a procedure which ceased when the microchip became accepted. Bills have been put before Congress in the USA that will allow the government to microchip children at birth, The president of the USA, under the 'Control of Imigration Act of 1986', Section 100, has the authority to deem whatever type of identification is necessary. All of these sinister ploys are merely waiting in the wings to happen, and they have been manipulated into existence with the same problem/solution tactics which have been used for centuries to control the world's population.

Indeed, this interesting passage from the book of Revelation in the Christian Bible does appear to prophesy something similar to the human bar/microchip coding system:

'And he causeth all, both small and great, rich and poor, free and bond, to receive a mark in their right hand or in their foreheads:

And that no man might buy or sell, save he that had the mark, or the name of the beast, or the number of his name. Here is wisdom. Let him that hath understanding count the number of the beast: for it is the number of a man; and his number [is] Six hundred threescore [and]six.'

Revelation 13:16-18

As well as messages from the chip to the computer, messages can also be sent the other way – in much the same way as satellite t.v. receivers can be programmed remotely. As long ago as 1966, a CIA psychologist was talking about brain control through two-way communication between an implanted brain and a computer. Once a chip has been inserted there will be no end to the aspects of our lives which can be controlled – birth control, programmed actions to create more 'problems' demanding 'solutions', etc. A robot society will have been created.

FURTHER EXAMPLES OF MANIPULATION

The abuse of power and exploitation for personal and corporate gain by the visible components of the Elite hierarchy is quite astonishing. In the following cases we have been duped into believing as truth the version of events portrayed by the mass media.

Watergate

In 1972, a Republican surveillance team working for Nixon's re-election committee, subsequently named the 'Plumbers', broke into the Democrat headquarters at the Watergate Buildings in Washington. This was engineered by Kissinger and his protégé George Bush to remove the final pretence of 'democracy' and hand complete control of the US administration to the Elite. As Head of the State Department and the National Security Council, Kissinger effectively ran the Nixon presidency.

The 'Plumbers' were agents working for the White House Special Investigations Unit, created by Nixon (Kissinger) with money from the president of Bush-owned Pennzoil and other business associates of George Bush. At the time the Watergate story broke, Bush had been made chairman of the Republican National Committee yet claimed to have no knowledge of the situation.

After the break-in became public knowledge, Nixon was eventually forced to resign on the release of recordings in which he discussed ways to frustrate the Watergate investigations. The recordings were done by David Young, who worked for the Rockefellers and was appointed by Kissinger, and they were revealed by Butterworth, the White House liaison with the Kissinger-led secret service. In the same recordings, Nixon implicated certain 'Texans' which referred to Bush and his associates, but Nixon was forced out of office before the trial at which this would have been revealed.

Gerald Ford. a 33rd degree freemason and Rockefeller puppet, became president and pardoned Nixon so that the case never came to court. He appointed Nelson Rockefeller to be his vice-president and put him in charge of the Watergate investigations, which, unsurprisingly, discovered nothing of consequence.

Iran-Contra

In 1975, George Bush, who had been a CIA asset since the 1950s, became director of the CIA which, by a series of measures implemented by President Ford (Rockefeller), had increasing power over the US Intelligence services. As his associate deputy director for covert operations Bush named Theodore Shackley who, with Oliver North, had masterminded Operation Phoenix in Vietnam and ran an assassination and drugs operation throughout the 1970s with Donald Gregg and Felix Rodriquez. During the 1979-80 election campaign Shackley became Bush's speech writer (?!) and when Bush became vice-president under Reagan, Gregg, assisted by Rodriquez, was appointed as his main advisor on national security. Oliver North also became an official on the National Security Council. Working out of Bush's office this group co-ordinated the arms-for-drugs racket that has become known as Iran-Contra.

The Sandinista regime in Nicaragua sought to pursue the interests of its own economy and people rather than US corporate interests so the rebel Contras were backed by the CIA. They were supplied with arms in exchange for drugs which were flown on CIA chartered planes into Homestead Airforce Base using a CIA code signal. One trafficker flew weapons to the Contras in return for CIA help in flying cocaine into the US via an airstrip of one of North's CIA associates. Oliver North also co-ordinated the arms-for-hostages deals with Iran. The money was laundered through the Elite's banking headquarters in Switzerland.

One reason for the deals with Iran was to pay back the Khomeini regime for it delaying the release of 51 US hostages to prevent Carter taking the credit. Once he had been replaced by Reagan/Bush the hostages were released as arranged at a meeting in Paris between Iranian officials and Bush, Gregg and John Tower. When the scandal became public Tower led the investigations into the affair which did not prosecute Bush or Reagan and those that were identified as being involved were pardoned by Bush before public trials. Tower was to die in a plane crash just when he was beginning to talk openly about the affair.

SUPPRESSED INTELLIGENCE REPORTS

The Drugs Trade

The trade in hard drugs is very important to the Elite for a number of reasons: it provides a source of income to finance other covert operations; it creates a 'problem' for which the public demands a 'solution' of increased police powers and the erosion of personal freedom in an effort to stop the supply; and, by addicting large numbers of particularly the younger generation to hard drugs, self-respect and the ability to think independently are diminished.

The background to many engineered conflicts is illuminated by analysis of the drug implications. In Vietnam a Pepsi Cola bottling plant was a drug distribution point with CIA helicopters supplying it with drugs from the fields. Drugs were also smuggled back to the US in the body cavities of carefully labelled corpses.

In 1986, Bo Gritz, America's most decorated war hero was sent by the US government into Burma's infamous 'Golden Triangle' to report on missing US prisoners of war. He discovered a man named Khun Sa who is deemed to be the overlord of heroin in the world, sending an ever-increasing excess of 1000 tons of heroin into the 'free' world per year. He also discovered that the whole rescue mission of the prisoners was being prevented by the CIA because these soldiers knew too many details of the operation between Khun Sa and the CIA to traffic these drugs. Later, he was told by Jerry King, head of Intelligence Support Activity (ISA) in the CIA that

'...we've been ordered to put operation Grand Eagle (the rescue mission) on the shelf as if it never existed. There are still too many beurocrats that don't want to see American prisoners of war come back alive.'

The conflict between the US and Panama was a result of Bush turning against Noriega who was a CIA asset while Bush was director and who had been paid to run drugs. However, having seized power in 1984, despite losing the democratic election and yet still being officially recognised by President Reagan, Noriega incurred US wrath by refusing to bow to their pressure for his country to invade Nicaragua. The US suddenly turned against the Panama administration under the pretext of drugs, corruption and a lack of democracy. In 1988, Noriega was indicted on drug charges all bar one of which pre-dated 1984, to a time when he was still on the CIA payroll. In order to arrest one man the US invaded Panama in 1989, killing 3000 civilians. Allegedly the Drug Enforcement Agency (DEA) paid him $4.7 million to keep quiet about CIA involvement and at his trial no CIA documents were allowed to be examined. A new government was installed by the US, headed by a president and vice-president involved with banks known for drug money laundering and under this new administration drug trafficking from Panama has increased.

Nixon and Reagan and George Bush (despite the latter two being regular heroin users), have led public campaigns against drugs which unsurprisingly have achieved little. In association with the major drug cartels, the CIA has arranged small 'busts' to lend credibility to the campaigns but these are usually to remove insignificant players or larger ones who have outlived their usefulness. In 1981, during the Reagan/Bush administration, the CIA convened a meeting of Columbian dealers to form the Medellin Cartel – an infamous group of 200 dealers. There is also evidence to suggest that the Zapata Oil Corporation is a CIA front and that Zapata Offshore is involved in drug smuggling. Both of these companies were set up and are headed by Bush.

SUPPRESSED INTELLIGENCE REPORTS

George Bush was succeeded in the White House by Bill Clinton, a Rhodes Scholar, whose drug credentials are on a par with his predecessor. Whilst Governor of Arkansas he created the Arkansas Development Finance Authority (ADFA) which was to finance drug trafficking. All loan applications were handled by the Rose Law Firm, run by Hilary Clinton, and those which were granted were to Clinton's business associates for use in trafficking. For example, one loan was given to Web Hubbel of Park-O-Meter which manufactured retrofit nose cones for drug shipping. The loans were not paid back, but large donations were given to Clinton's election fund. Web Hubbel became acting US attorney general under Clinton, and some think he still fulfils that role behind Janet Reno.

During the Reagan/Bush anti-drug campaign, whilst Clinton governed Arkansas, the United State's biggest drug trafficking operation was set up in Mena Arkansas by a DEA pilot.

Many people speaking out or investigating Bill Clinton have died in mysterious circumstances, for which the official cause of death is given as 'suicide'. Conveniently, in a law introduced into Arkansas by Clinton just prior to the first suspicious deaths no autopsy needs to be performed in cases of deaths attributed to suicide.

Satanism

One of the most sinister elements to the manipulation of society is the abuse of esoteric knowledge by the world's secret societies both for the purposes of political control and for sick personal pleasure.

In the US each year 400,000 children are reported missing, and in the UK this number is 98,000. Not all are recovered.

All over the world children are hijacked into a life of sexual abuse, psychological and physical torture. They are bought and sold by members of paedophile rings, often by their own parents, who act as 'recruiters' and 'handlers' in the lower echelons of the secret society network. They are systematically abused, tortured and murdered in ritualistic ceremonies by people who occupy places throughout the social hierarchy all the way to the top. Eye witness accounts, such as those given by a friend of mine named Patti who was 'recruited' as a child of three, have implicated members of the aristocracy, doctors, lawyers, members of the clergy, high level businessmen, media stars, members of the world's governments (see Who We Are – Mind Manipulation/Project Monarch).

Sophisticated mind control techniques are used to compartmentalise the memories of the abused to prevent them from revealing the awful truth to the public. Patti has displayed many separate personalities whilst recounting her horrific experiences, displaying the classic symptoms of Multiple Personality Disorder. Often victims are too scared to even mention such things to each other, never mind to strangers. They are brought up in the certain knowledge that they can be easily picked up off the streets or from their beds and drugged for use in abuse at any time. They are fully aware also that their abusers are everywhere, including in the medical professions and police. Victims are ceremonially 'married' to the leaders of the cult and are given their own 'dark companion', a sinister thought-form who will be ever present in order to inform on them if they should ever step out of line. They are often forced to take part in the abuse, murder and disposal of other victims in order to ensure a total attack upon the psyche of the individual concerned and the victim is soon convinced that they have become at least as guilty of these crimes as their assailants. Therefore, they are ever paranoid and terrified of revealing the truth to anyone other that those who have themselves been victims.

Methods of abuse are truly horrendous and include: live burials with the uncertainty of being retrieved, physical mutilation, sexual abuse, the enforced killing of family members and animals which have previously been given as pets, the enforced pregnancy for the purpose of subsequent removal of the child for sacrifice, the enforced drinking of blood, eating of faeces and cannibalism upon bodies of sacrificial victims, general sustained humiliation etc.. The list is as long as the imagination of the perpetrators of such atrocities allows it to be.

Many of the Satanic rituals are performed at the altars of out of the way and redundant churches for the purpose of generating terror and negativity within these sacred sites. The energy is then harnessed for personal power and the perpetuation of the Luciferic force upon the Earth (as well as to further traumatise their slaves for mind-control purposes such as Project Ultra Green/MK-Ultra Project Monarch/Freedom Train). In this way the Earth's energy matrix – the collective unconscious, which is continuous with the human psyche, is kept in a negatively imbalanced state – whilst the sickest members of the human race have an obscene outlet for their perverse fantasies..

The British intelligence agencies and the USA's CIA and NSA are well aware of such organised anathemata including the identities of those involved and the code names used for such operations, such as Ultra Green and Project Monarch. Patti herself has given her details to various agencies including England's Scotland Yard. However, this global underbelly is so deeply entrenched in the System that these people are left entirely untouched by the legal system. Many cult-busting and rescue organisations exist, most working in tandem with the police (who are rife with this problem), but are themselves kept a closely guarded secret, supposedly in order to minimise the problem of infiltration. This is yet another way of maintaining overall secrecy via compart-mentalisation within the pyramidal structure in order to preserve the status quo.

Even today, at the age of thirty seven, Patti is regularly picked up off the streets to be drugged, raped, tortured or made to actually perform in Satanic ceremonies in the role of one of her personalities which is a priestess within the cult. All of which further traumatises her and enforces the compartmentalisation of her personalities. Her assailants also have an intimate knowledge of black magic and are able to summon her remotely to various locations under the control of her various personalities in order to abduct her.

One evening, Patti had paid Shona a visit whilst I was at work and spent the entire night flipping from one personality to another. These personalities ranged from the totally meek, 'Nothing', aged three, through variously aged 'Patricias' to the quite nasty and foul-mouthed 'Cathy'. In the early hours she became obsessed with leaving the house to take part in a ritual which she knew was taking place nearby and expressed an overwhelming desire to drink blood. This began at ten past three – the time which Satanists associate with Satan's greatest moment upon Earth – the time of the Crucifixion of Jesus. A little after five, when the ritual would have been completed, Patti began to normalise but revealed to Shona that she had taken a drugs overdose, though not enough to do any serious harm. This was entirely out of character for her as she has spent her life loving and protecting her three children from her 'Family' as she calls them. This did correspond, however, with threats which had been made to her merely a week earlier by five men who had abducted her during a visit to her home town of Darlington, that if she and we did not 'back off' then they would kill her via an injected overdose and make it look like suicide. They had explained to her that this could be prepared easily through a series of manipulated 'suicide attempts' which would give her the appearance of being in a suicidal state.

The extensive information which Patti has revealed of the names, dates and methods of the British paedophile/Satanic ring are now in the hands of many individuals throughout Britain. If any 'accident' should 'mysteriously' befall Patti or anyone involved in this book and its distribution, these names along with a mass of evidence (including prominent members of the aristocracy, active politicians, a former British Prime Minister, eye witnesses, the ring leaders and 'lackeys' etc.) will be made public. Furthermore, I wish it to be known that both Shona and I are in perfect mental and physical health and are looking forward to being present throughout the transformation of the Earth and on into a glorious future.

The BSE Case

In 1986, in Britain, the first recorded case was recognised of Bovine Spongiform Encephalopathy (BSE), a new disease which was affecting the nervous systems of cattle, causing Parkinsonian/ dementia-like symptoms. The official cause was identified by the Ministry for Agriculture Fisheries and Food (MAFF) as cross-contamination of a previously known sheep disease called Scrapie via cattle feeds which contained meat and bone meal from sheep. By 1996, the numbers of cows said to have been infected with BSE had risen to 27,800 despite the ban on meat feeds for cattle in 1989. The increasing incidence of a similar disease in humans called Creutzfeld-Jacob Disease (CJD), in which the brain becomes mushroom-like and full of holes causing sufferers to become gradually more confused until death, has been blamed upon the consumption of infected beef products. Therefore, a mass slaughter of British cattle was initiated in 1996 in order to resolve the problem. BSE has also infected many other animals such as domestic cats, birds of prey and zoo animals given infected meat.

Despite assurances that BSE was confined to very few cases, the number of cases of CJD has increased in England from 27 in 1985, to 42 in 1994, and 55 in 1995.

Significantly, there are three recognised types of CJD (the types 1 and 2 being similar to Alzheimer's Disease with confusion and memory loss as the main symptoms) whereas the cases of CJD since 1985 have been mainly of a new type-3 (which is indicated by additional loss of muscle co-ordination and balance).

This is essentially the story which has been fed to the mass public via the media and has caused a panic among consumers who have begun to avoid British beef products. It even initiated what was described in the press as a 'trade war' with Europe spearheaded by the British Prime Minister John Major in a typical 'white knight' fashion.

The truth of the situation is far more sinister and has implications for everyone, meat eaters and vegetarians alike. The discovery was made by organic farmer, Mark Purdy. That is, BSE and type-3 CJD is caused not by an entirely new form of infection (called a prion by the investigating scientists) but is caused by poisoning by organo-phosphate fertilisers.

Several inconsistencies have been conveniently overlooked by the 'experts' investigating this case:

1. that no organic farmer (those not using chemicals such as pesticides) has had a case

of BSE despite using the same meat/bone-meal feeds as everyone else, and 2. that despite virtually the whole of Europe using these same feeds, there have been very few cases of BSE on the continent. So it can hardly be the Scrapie-contaminated feed, can it?

During the Second World War, I.G. Farben (the Nazi chemical company responsible for Zyclon B which was allegedly used to gas the Jews in the Holocaust and who used the inmates of Auschwitz as slave labour and as guinea pigs for testing of chemicals) developed a fluorinated nerve gas known as Sarin which was also used by the Iraquis during the Gulf War. This is an organo-phosphate (OP) compound which is very similar to that used by farmers in low concentrations to spray crops and dip sheep to prevent tick infestation, but it is used in much higher concentrations to treat cattle against warble-fly infestation.

In the 1980s, the MAFF began a war against the warble fly and imposed a mode of treatment upon Britain's farmers. This was that twice a year a preparation of OP concentrate be poured over the backs of all cattle. The OP is fat-soluble and is therefore absorbed by cow through the skin for a systemic effect to occur. Subsequently, an imprecise amount of OP is absorbed and the area most exposed to the compound is the spinal column i.e. directly into the central nervous system. The OP kills the warble fly by attacking the nervous system. The reported cases of BSE have been in the areas of warble fly infestation.

It has been established that, in cases of BSE, the prion protein in the brain becomes corrupted and mutates causing the familiar spongy brain situation. It has also been established that OPs bind to prion protein causing brain cells to mutate in a chain reaction. – as has been established in the case of the OP, Thalamide, a constituent of Thalidomide, which caused massive birth deformities in the late 60s and early 70s. Human brains also contain prion proteins!

Cases of BSE have been significantly higher in Switzerland and Northern Ireland. These countries have one other thing in common with mainland Britain, that is: they also use OPs – predominantly the compound Phosmet – in a strength which is four times that of the rest of Europe.

For several years now, many British farmers using OPs have been developing a severely debilitating condition which is not officially recognised despite the many claims and obvious links to OPs. The symptoms which are displayed in this syndrome are: severe malaise and fatigue, chest pain, Parkinson-like tremors and other nervous disorders. However, organic farmers are not affected by this 'mysterious' syndrome.

Up to more than 25 times the allowed amounts of OPs have been found in conventionally grown carrots in England. The investigations by (MAFF) showed that, in 8% of carrots, the contents were higher than the international Maximum Residue Level (MRL) limit. OPs both attack the brain and weaken the immune system and are undoubtedly a major factor in the 20th Century disease process such as the increasing incidence of recurrent infections and the immuno-suppressive diseases such as AIDS.

The most significant lab tests using this theory have been performed, initiated by Purdey's, research by the Government's Medical Research Council in Britain but have shown to be inconclusive. However, the MRC have admitted that they have not been using actual prion proteins for these tests, but have been experimenting on synthetic prion proteins! Could this be because it was the British Government, through MAFF, in the 1980s who made OPs compulsory and therefore caused BSE? If the truth were accepted then there would be grounds for the recovery of huge sums of money in damages claims both from the government and from the petrochemical producers of the OPs themselves, such as Wellcome and ICI.

The Government has clearly been using the BSE crisis in Britain to achieve a political agenda. Meanwhile, the true cause of CJD is kept well hidden.

THE PHARMACEUTICAL RACKET

In the early half of this century the petrochemical giants organised a coup on the medical research establishments, hospitals and universities. The Rockefellers did this by sponsoring research and donating monetary gifts to US universities and medical schools where research was drug based and further extended this policy to foreign medical establishments via their International Education Board. Those who were not drug based were refused funding and were soon dissolved in favour of the more lucrative pharmaceutical-based projects.

In 1939 the 'Drug Trust' alliance was formed by the Rockefeller Empire and I.G. Farben. After the war, I.G. Farben was dismantled but later emerged in the many guises of the companies with whom they had signed cartel agreements. These companies include: Imperial Chemical Industries (ICI), Borden, Carnation, General Mills, M.W. Kellogg Co., Nestle, Pet Milk, Squibb and Sons, Bristol Meyers, Whitehall laboratories, Procter and Gamble, Roche, Hoechst and Beyer and Co. (two extant pharmaceutical companies who initially employed convicted war criminals Friedrich Jaehne and Fritz ter Meer as board chairmen). The Rockefeller Empire – in tandem with the Chase Manhattan Bank now owns over half of the USA's pharmaceutical interests and is the largest drug manufacturing combine in the world. Since the war the drug industry has steadily netted an ever increasing profit from sales of drugs to become the second largest manufacturing industry in the world next to the arms industry (also owned by the self same Elite agencies).

Today, health care is a multi-billion pound industry world-wide with ever increasing expenditure by taxpayers into the system which funnels the majority of this staggering profit into the hands of the drug manufacturers who are, as we have seen, headed by the major Elite manipulators of this century. These companies now control the vast majority of health care and set the standards for the practice of medicine in all developed countries. Doctors are no longer free to choose the most reliable and safe forms of therapy available but are at the mercy of their financial reliance on sponsoring (frequently bribing) drug companies. Once out of drug-company sponsored medical school, doctors embark on a career of increasing workloads and have ever increasing amounts of new pharmaceutical products to use and understand. The sheer volume of literature which a GP will receive from drug sales reps has resulted in the present situation whereby GPs are poorly educated about the chemicals which they are giving to their patients and are essentially gleaning most of their post-graduate training from the salesmen of private business. The moral implications of this are staggering.

The number of available drug preparations is now well in excess of 200,000. In 1980, the World Health organisation advised that a mere 240 drugs are necessary in order to provide good health care in the Third World (which should be more than adequate for First World needs considering we are a significantly healthier proportion of the population) whilst in 1981 the United Nations Industrial Development Organisation stated that a mere 26 of these are considered 'indispensables'. Most of the many drugs which are now available are known as 'me-too' drugs, i.e. recombinations and exact reproductions of drugs already available but which are irresistible to other companies who wish to share in their market. For example, the standard analgesics Paracetamol and Aspirin come in a multitude of forms under a variety of different brand names and yet these products can vary in price to a factor of ten or more times for the exact same formula depending on brand type chosen. Often the consumer erroneously presumes that increased price is equivalent to increased quality in this case and are entirely unaware that the drugs they are buying and those which they are rejecting are identical. Doctors are also often guilty of prescribing drugs by trade name and thus netting greater profits for the favoured company whilst cheaper versions are available to the unwary consumer/patient. Usually, before handing in a prescription it pays to consult the attending pharmacist if there is an equivalent and cheaper drug available. This can save some chronic drug users hundreds of pounds per year.

Pharmaceutical companies rely upon ill health in the population to survive and reap their profits. No drug company has a vested interest in curing disease. They do, however, have a massive vested interest in maintaining ill-health, creating disease and manufacturing chemicals which will promote this under the guise of 'therapy' for the symptoms – rarely ever the cause – of disease. Dr John Braithwaite, now a Trade Practices Commissioner, in his expose, Corporate Crime in the Pharmaceutical Industry, states:

'International bribery and corruption, fraud in the testing of drugs, criminal negligence in the unsafe manufacturing of drugs – the pharmaceutical industry has a worse record of law-breaking than any other industry.'

In the US in 1978 1.5 million people were hospitalised because of medication side-effects alone. In 1991 in the US, 72,000 people were killed due to iatrogenic – that is doctor-induced – causes whilst 24,073 died of victims of firearms shootings, which makes doctors nearly three times more lethal than guns! This has serious implications for other countries including Britain because the US are the foremost pioneers in the health care field and what occurs in health care in the US is usually implemented in Britain a decade later.

The drugs industry has managed to sell to the majority of the world the idea that disease is largely an inevitable part of life, especially during the later years. Through its front-line representatives – the medical system – it has effectively reduced the range of choices of health care to which the public has access. Through funding and educational control it has seen to it that natural forms of treatment are largely ignored and grossly under-researched. Those organisations which do reveal the true causes of disease and promote effective forms of disease prevention, such as nutritional medicine, healing and naturopathy are regularly attacked in the mass media and publicly labelled as quacks by pharmaceutically-sponsored de-bunking organisations such as the Campaign Against Health Fraud, now called Healthwatch.

They have also sold to us the idea that natural remedies and cures which have been successfully employed for centuries are 'alternatives' and to be treated with great scepticism and caution. Frequently, we are told of how one or two people have been injured or killed through the misapplication of a herbal remedy by dubious alternative practitioners but are not told at the same time of the thousands who are damaged by the conventional drugs which are handed out like sweets by our doctors.

During their initiation into the Western medical tradition most of our young doctors are repeatedly informed by their superiors that therapies which are alternative to classic western medicine are fraudulent and quackish. They are told that there is no scientific evidence to support any of the claims of psychic healing, crystal therapy, colour therapy and the like and the whole area is dismissed with a superior grin and a wave of the hand. A mountain of study is then hurled at the junior doctors, on top of an already inhumane workload of practical hours, to be spent absorbing the biased views of their forebears. A junior doctor has not even enough time to explore the realms of stress-free relaxation never mind alternative thought and therapies. Much the same methods are used by certain religious organisations to indoctrinate the minds of their followers into a single belief system. The key tactics, to which most doctors will relate, are: maintenance of sleep deprivation so as to minimise resistance to teachings, isolation from the outside world until one is literally eating, breathing and sleeping the set doctrine of the cult, and maintenance of a fear of failure to conform through almost unachievably high level goal setting; often via frequent examinations.

I believe that western medicine is as much a dogmatic cult as popular Christianity or the Moonies. It breeds its young on dogma to the exclusion of free will and reasoned thought in order to perpetuate itself. It is controlled by instilling into its members the fear of failure and it thrives by exploiting the initial motivation of its members, which is love and a desire to help and heal others.

At the apex of the pyramid of medicine lie the controllers; not doctors, but the multinational pharmaceutical companies who exist, not for the benefit of others, but for the desire for money and power. And behind them lies the sinister organisation of global secret societies headed by the Illuminati.

It is through this subtle mind control that the System maintains itself. Veiled in secrecy and fuelled by fear, the monster machine controls every aspect of our lives. The medical system is an integral part, but nevertheless only one aspect, of the overall design which seeks power and neither cares how this power is achieved, nor how many individuals are destroyed in the process.

As an example of the fraud perpetuated by the pharmaceutical companies, the next section will take a close look at the AIDS scandal, which illuminates how these companies have infiltrated every area of the healthcare system are willing to endanger people, allowing them to be killed, for profit via the industry's tool of corruption and front organisation, our own medical system:

What is AIDS?

AIDS is defined as any one of twenty five unrelated diseases plus a positive test for the presence of antibodies to the Human Immuno-deficiency Virus (HIV). It is said to be transferred through intimate sexual contact via the transfer of bodily fluids such as semen and blood. It is also said to be passed on through intravenous means by needle-sharing drug users and infected blood transfusions.

Nearly five hundred scientists world-wide, including eminent doctors such as leading University of California Professor of Molecular Biology, Peter Duesberg, and Australian biophysicist Eleni Papadopoulous-Eleopoulos, Dr Charles Thomas (former Harvard Professor of Biochemistry), Dr Kary Mullis (1993 Nobel Prize-winner for Chemistry), Dr Hank Loman (Professor of Biophysical Chemistry, Free University of Amsterdam), and Dr Steven Lomas (Professor of Preventative Medicine, State University of New York) are now convinced that AIDS is not caused by HIV.

SUPPRESSED INTELLIGENCE REPORTS

In simple terms, the facts just do not add up. For example, there are many people with AIDS but without HIV and vast numbers of people who are HIV positive are not developing AIDS. The tests for the presence of retrovirus HIV – the Western Blot Test and the ELISA Test – which show up HIV positive status, are so inaccurate that false positive tests can occur due to many diseases such as malnutrition, multiple infections, multiple sclerosis, tuberculosis, leprosy, having once had the 'flu' or measles and the bodies natural response to anal semen.

Once diagnosed as HIV positive, patients are given regular blood tests to monitor their immunological responses, particularly for a drop in T-cell count. T-cells are released in the immune response to disease to attack invading antigens. A significant T-cell drop, in many clinics, is the indicator that active drug therapy should be commenced. However, using T-cell counts as an indicator of disease is entirely useless as the average T-cell count for a healthy person can range from 200 to 2000 over the course of a normal day. Professor Ian Weller, who co-ordinated the British arm of the Concorde AZT trial testing the drug on healthy HIV-positive volunteers, commented:

'The thing we have to remember about CD4 (T-cell) counts is they are very variable. They can vary in an individual over the time of day... lower in the morning and higher in the evening. They can be affected by things that you do such as walking to the clinic, as opposed to riding a bike... the amount of sunshine can affect them. Smoking as well.'

This whole area of inaccurate testing in the area of AIDS and AIDS Related Conditions (ARC) has accounted for many people being incorrectly diagnosed as HIV positive, such as in Africa where there is a supposed epidemic; there is also a massive amount of otherwise unrelated disease there too and it is this factor which is causing the false positives.

Once diagnosed, patients are then initiated onto courses of highly toxic drugs such as AZT, DDI and Septrin, many of the side effects of which are the self same symptoms as those of AIDS.

None of these AIDS defining diseases are new. What is new, however, is the HIV test. All research into this syndrome has been based upon the findings of Robert Gallo, the co-founder and patent holder of the test, which have since been found to be fraudulent. Gallo's partner and co-founder of the HIV theory, Luc Montagnier, declared in 1989:

'HIV is not capable of causing the destruction to the immune system which is seen in people with AIDS'.

One medical doctor who has practised and lectured on medicine world-wide for over thirty five years, Dr. Robert E. Wilner has even publicly demonstrated that HIV does not cause disease by injecting himself with the blood of an HIV positive patient on Spain's most popular television show; yet this never made it to the press outside of Spain! In his book 'Deadly Deception: The Proof That Sex And HIV Absolutely Do Not Cause AIDS', Dr. Wilner cites AZT as one of the major causes of AIDS, he also insists that 'HIV is simply a harmless piece of tissue, not unlike numerous other retroviruses that exist in our body' and that 'AIDS is not transmitted sexually nor is it contagious by any method!'

Dr Duesberg, recognised as one of, if not the foremost retrovirus expert in the world, points out:

'AZT is A Random Killer Of Infected And Non-Infected Cells. AZT cannot discriminate among them. It kills T-cells, B-cells, red cells, it kills all cells. AZT is a chain terminator of DNA synthesis of all cells – no exceptions. It wipes out everything. In the long run it can only lead to death of the organism – and the cemetery. AZT is a certain killer! Who will be responsible for the death of patients (some 200,000 now being treated with AZT and countless thousands who have already died from it in the past decade) that results from AZT therapy – pharmacological homicide?'

And furthermore, that:

'HIV does not cause AIDS... The point that everyone is missing is that all of those original papers, Gallo wrote on HIV have been found fraudulent... The HIV hypothesis was based on those papers.'

It is my opinion that these scientists are correct and that HIV is not the cause of AIDS. AIDS is not a single viral disease but a collection of, in part, unrelated diseases which are caused by disharmonious energies in the fields of the holistic body, brought about by all sorts of reasons. Undoubtedly one of the major causes of death by AIDS-related diseases is the inability of the body to fight off the manifested disease because the body has been weakened by the very drugs given to suppress the disease. Tests have shown that the only effective treatments for AIDS are those which involve the cessation of conventional drugs in favour of unconventional natural therapies such as Essiac, Oxygen/Ozone Therapy and CanCell. However, these natural therapies share a common theme in that they have all been suppressed or withdrawn by governmental agencies and those with vested interests in the pharmaceutical industry.

(To further support the fact that HIV is not transferred sexually, Cathy O'Brien in her book Trance Formation Of America, points out that, despite being prostituted to men in areas supposedly rife with AIDS, none of her political abusers ever wore protection during sex with her.)

Wellcome to Hell

Wellcome (Wellcome Burroughs in the US) began as a pharmaceutical company set up in 1880 by Henry Wellcome and Silas Burroughs. Its links to the Rockefeller Empire were apparent in Henry Wellcome's appointing of John and Allen Dulles of the Sullivan and Cromwell law firm as those responsible for any legal matters relating to the company and his own will. With Henry Wellcome's death in 1936, the Wellcome Trust was set up in conjunction with the company (now the Wellcome Foundation) and this has now become one of the largest funders of medical research in Europe. The Rockefeller connection was also strengthened in the late 50's when Wellcome took over the running of aspects of the Rockefeller funded London University College Hospital Medical School and their joint interests in tropical illness research via the London School of Hygiene and Tropical Medicine.

Over the following decades, Wellcome pursued several aspects of pharmaceutical healthcare with interests in general over-the-counter remedies, anti-virals, animal healthcare, genetic engineering and biotechnology. It strengthened its connections within the government, the media, medical academia and the various committees, societies and associations that were continuously being set up to review, regulate and control all aspects of scientific medical research and education. It did this by making donations to many of these organisations, such as the British Association for the Advancement of Science, the Parliamentary Science and

SUPPRESSED INTELLIGENCE REPORTS

Technology Foundation, the Parliamentary Office of Science and Technology, and the British Medical Association's Foundation for AIDS (to which it gave £144,000 between 1988 and 1992), and by placing its own trustees, researchers and 'experts' in prominent positions within them. For example: Sir Alastair Pilkington one time vice president of the Foundation for Science and Technology was a research scientist for Wellcome; Professor C. Gordon Smith, Dean of the London School of Hygiene and Tropical Medicine was a Wellcome trustee; Lord Swann, Director of the BBC in the 1980's was a Wellcome trustee; Sir Alfred Shepperd, a member of the Advisory Council on Science and Technology(ACST) was Chairman of Burroughs Wellcome and the Wellcome Foundation until 1985; Professor Roy Anderson, Head of Pure and Applied Biology at London Imperial College of Science, Technology and medicine and a member of ACST was also a Wellcome trustee.

In the 1980's however, the company went through some major rationalisations. In 1986 the decision was made to sell shares in the Welcome drug company which had previously been owned in its entirety by the Wellcome Trust. In the following six years it also sold off several areas of business including Cooper Animal Healthcare – a joint venture with ICI producing organo-phosphate sheep dip – and its interests in vaccine production. Production of general cough and cold remedies was also reduced to a mere 14% of sales while it began concentrating its funds in the more profitable areas of genetics, biotechnology and anti-virals.

AZT, marketed by Wellcome as Retrovir, had been developed in the 60s as a drug to treat cancer but it had proved to be highly toxic as well as ineffective as it appeared unable to distinguish between cancerous and healthy cells. However, tests in vitro appeared to show some anti-viral properties which was why, after being shelved in the 60s, AZT was re-tested for use in the treatment of AIDS in the 1980s.

Human clinical drug trials, following extensive (though useless) animal testing, usually take place in two parts. Phase I tests for toxicity; Phase II concentrates on the long-term side-effects and efficacy, all of which can take several years. In the case of AZT the Phase II trials in America were halted after 4 months when only 1 of the AZT users as opposed to 19 of the control group had died and the drug was granted a license despite the fact that the patients in the trial were given regular blood transfusions to alleviate the possible side-effects (this should, under usual circumstances, have negated the results of the trial). This licensing of AZT so quickly was unprecedented and made Wellcome's profits double to £1132 million in the space of 4 years! As if this wasn't enough, subsequent licenses for other AIDS drugs were issued subject to the condition that they would have to be tested against AZT and then only prescribed in conjunction with it.

Incredibly, AZT was licensed in the UK without any clinical trials four weeks before it was licensed in the US. This, perhaps, may have been due to the fact that, of the 25 members of the Medicines Commission who are parliamentary advisers on medicine, 5 had interests in Wellcome; one prominent member being Professor Trevor M. Jones, Director of Research and Development at Wellcome. And of the 21 members of the Committee on the Safety of Medicines who grant the licenses, two had interests in the Welcome Foundation.

Within a short space of time, AZT was licensed in 35 countries around the world and Wellcome were promoting it with media advertising, press releases and all-expenses-paid conferences to which they regularly invited the world's top scientists and physicians, all the while denying any suggestions that it caused harmful side-effects.

SUPPRESSED INTELLIGENCE REPORTS

Wellcome's influence on the media and the government continued with its donation of £10,000 to the All Party Parliamentary Group on AIDS (APOGA) as, with the Medical Research Council, Wellcome began the trials of AZT on asymptomatic HIV positive patients – the Concorde trials – in October 1988. From that point onwards most of the doctors presenting information and writing for APGOA were also involved in these trials. Not content with promoting their own research in the area of AIDS they also began to attack any alternative treatments or anyone who challenged the HIV=AIDS hypothesis.

Wellcome had also cornered the British market in AIDS testing kits. With the help of Dr. Robin Weiss and Angus Dalgleish from the Institute of Cancer Research, a second generation kit was marketed based on the research by Campaign Against Health Fraud (now Healthwatch) member, Professor Vincent Marks, head of the Biochemistry Department of Surrey University – a department which has received over half a million pounds from Wellcome since 1985. In order to ensure that anyone found to be HIV positive was immediately directed towards 'help' from AZT-promoting doctors, GP's were given very limited access to the testing kits. They had no choice but to send their patients to Wellcome-infiltrated teaching hospitals and STD clinics in London while the promotion and sale of home testing kits was banned in the UK (in 1992), thereby ensuring Wellcome's complete monopoly in all aspects of AIDS treatment and diagnosis.

Education about HIV and AIDS could also not be overlooked and Wellcome donated substantial funds to pay for a £150,000 package for GPs, produced by the British Medical Association.

The Concorde trials themselves, instead of being independent, were almost totally under Wellcome's influence. The initial reason for the trials was to prove that AZT would be effective in preventing the development of ARC and AIDS in otherwise healthy HIV+ patients. Going against all established regulations for the independence of such trials, which in the past had the drug companies supplying the drug and paying the hospitals to do the trials, the Concorde trial was set up jointly between Wellcome, the Medical Research Council (MRC) and the Department of Health. The MRC paid for the treatment and the Department of Health granted the use of six London hospitals, NHS staff and facilities. Anyone with an HIV positive test was encouraged to join the trial without discussion of any alternative treatments whilst being promised up to 3 years of free healthcare despite the fact that the AZT drug was to be administered at 1000mg per day – twice the dose recommended by the US Food and Drug Administration – and the recent reports of serious side-effects such as muscle wasting, anaemia and impotence. Wellcome's crowning glory in this deal, though, was to also insist that the contract gave them complete control over the writing of any reports about the trial. The only report which had to be agreed between all parties was the one for general publication, if indeed any published report was even deemed necessary.

Just to make absolutely sure of obtaining the desired outcome, Wellcome had the help of several 'friends' in the MRC who had just as many, if not more, commitments to industry and business matters than they did to the medical establishment or the government. Lord Jellicoe, Chairman of the MRC's AIDS committee, was a director of the Rockefeller company Morgan Crucible as well as the sugar company Tate and Lyle and was later chairman of Booker Tate confectionery; Sir Donald Acheson worked for the Department of Health but left in 1991 to work in the Rockefeller funded School of Hygiene and Tropical Medicine; Sir Austin Bide was Chief Executive of Glaxo (now in partnership with Wellcome) and had been a director of J.

SUPPRESSED INTELLIGENCE REPORTS

Lyons & Co confectionery in the 70's. Sir David Crouch, MP for Canterbury until 1987, was director of Pfizer Ltd., a pharmaceutical company which was the only manufacturer of a synthesised ingredient of AZT at that time and also ran several public relations companies one of which, Kingsway Rowland, handled Wellcome's AZT account; Dr J. W. G. Smith, director of the Public Health Laboratory Service since 1985 used to be a Senior Lecturer at the School of Hygiene and Tropical Medicine before going to work for Wellcome as head of Bacteriology in 1969; Professor D. A. Warrell was a director of the Wellcome Tropical Research Unit and has also done malaria research funded by Wellcome and the Rockefeller Foundation; Professor C. N. Hales is a specialist in diabetes whose research is often funded by pharmaceutical companies including Wellcome.

With the above as the only 8 members of the MRC Committee on AIDS and their Chairman Lord Jellicoe, it is not surprising that a drug once deemed to be too toxic, which has never been properly tested and whose side-effects, according to the British National Formulary, bear s striking resemblance to the symptoms of AIDS itself, has been allowed to become the AIDS drug of the 90's and has kept the profits rolling in for Wellcome to the tune of an estimated £400 million a year.

'I will give no deadly medicine to any one if asked.'

(from the Hippocratic Oath)

Walter's position as a staff nurse at Newcastle General Hospital's Infectious Disease Unit (ward 25), which is affiliated with the London School of Tropical Medicine, has given me an insight into the world of AIDS treatment which is rarely seen and it only serves to corroborate the research of the aforementioned enlightened scientists, whose numbers are ever increasing. The world of AIDS care and treatment at the NGH has some very sinister elements and I have no reason to suspect that it is isolated to this regional unit alone. Here is an outline of some of the information which Walter has provided:

* According to the code of conduct provided by the United Kingdom Central Council for nursing and midwifery, the nurse's role is to be the patient's advocate and is, therefore, entrusted to provide care in the best interest of the patient and to decline from doing anything which is detrimental to their well being. One of the major areas covered by this is in the administration of drugs; the nurse is responsible for ensuring the correct dosage of drug is given and is responsible also for being aware of the effects and possible side effects of the medication.

However, in the NGH unit, nurses are expected to give all drugs prescribed by the doctor whether or not any information on the effects of the drug are available. Frequently the prescribing doctor is unaware of the true nature of the drugs and thus unable to inform the nursing staff of the effects and side effects of the drugs they are using. Many and varied substances appear and disappear periodically from the drugs cupboard, often named only as a series of numbers or letters. When challenged as to the reason why they have prescribed such unknown entities, the doctors usually reply that their consultant has ordered it to be given. The consultant is usually unavailable for comment.

* The side effects of the drugs have been seen to be potentially harmful. For example, one commonly used drug, Foscarnet, which is given directly into the heart or eyes of a patient, when dropped on a nurse's tights dissolved them on contact. Common side effects of

this drug include epilepsy, blindness and dementia. Many patients have entered the unit with minor symptoms such as weight loss and have, in a short space of time, become blind and epileptic through using it. Walter has frequently said to me, 'I'm poisoning people for a living', but if he refused to give the drugs as prescribed he would lose his job and someone would be found who would administer them. The same is true of the junior doctors who are afraid of the vengeance from above if they were to challenge the status quo. No challenge has yet been made, even after I presented the unit with detailed papers outlining the research which has negated the 'HIV equals AIDS' myth.

* Once diagnosed as HIV positive, many patients are then informed that the only chance they have for extended survival is to use the drugs provided. Obviously the majority of patients, many of whom show very few symptoms, are too afraid not to co-operate with the regime. They then suffer terribly and die a lingering and undignified death.

As a response to many challenges Walter has made to the medical staff to justify their drugs regime, he has been branded cynical and defeatist; as not wishing to give the patients a chance for survival. In reply to this he has asked on many occasions for the doctors to give him even just one example of anyone whom they have cured of AIDS or significantly improved the quality of life. Not one of them has been able to give such an example.

Even if we were extending people lives, in doing so we also inflict upon them such diseases as makes for little or no quality of life. What is the point of an extra year of life if that year is spent as a living vegetable? If we do have a prognosis of death, then surely it is better to live that remaining life to the full with our eventual demise being as gentle and as dignified as possible.

* On one occasion, the unit exceeded its drugs budget and feared a crisis in care. At this point Wellcome stepped in and offered its services for free on the condition that they would supply the drugs as long as all research notes were given directly to them in return. It appears that the only figures who were aware of anything like the full picture were the consultants in charge and the research nurse appointed by the company, none of whom were willing to reveal anything of the results of these apparently blind drugs trials.

In effect, this means that the patients on this unit are being treated by the pharmaceutical scientists as human guinea pigs, in order to test the various drugs supplied. How are we to know that these drugs are genuinely safe for the purpose of therapy? Might they simply be poisons or ineffectual chemicals thrown onto the research pot in a vain attempt to happen across some element of cure? Are they even actively seeking a cure, knowing what we do of their motivation?

Some of the drugs which have been identified and are in regular use have long since been discontinued in other areas of medicine because they are ineffective and/or dangerous. For example, A.Z.T. was once considered too toxic to be given to terminally ill cancer patients!

Interestingly, the official patient leaflet, 'HIV and AZT, the choices', as supplied to AIDS departments by Wellcome, gives merely three examples of side effects of the drug, i.e. anaemia, which they say effects up to 40% of users; headaches in 1-10% of users; and sickness in 25% of users which: 'almost always disappear after a few weeks of treatment'. The leaflet also states:

SUPPRESSED INTELLIGENCE REPORTS

Most people do not suffer side effects when they take AZT early. If they do occur, there are ways of coping with them. They may be reversed, if necessary by stopping treatment.

If you thought that you may be facing death through an incurable disease would you stop taking the drug that has been hyped as giving an extension of lifespan, I wonder?

Septrin is a combination of two antibiotics and has been shown to be far less effective and far more liable to dramatic side effects than either of the components when used individually (interestingly, it is also nearly three times more expensive than the more effective and less harmful constituent ingredient Trimethorprim).

Even Thalidomide is now being used on Ward 25 for its anti-emetic properties.

* Many patients diagnosed as terminally ill have drawn up living wills in which they often request a cessation of active treatment in the end stages of disease. These are frequently ignored by the doctors who continue to pump toxins into dying patients and claim to be simply following orders from above. The point of which escapes myself and Walter and quite often the doctors themselves.

* When a patient dies, relatives are officially informed that their loved ones are deemed as dangerous waste and must, therefore, be sealed and cremated for hygiene reasons. No mention is made of autopsy or further experimentation and yet Walter has witnessed conversations amongst doctors regarding autopsy findings on such people who were supposed to have gone to cremation unmolested. Is this further pharmaceutical research?

* One evening, in the absence of an available doctor from the unit, Walter had to call upon a consultant from another area to advise upon a matter. Whilst this covering doctor was attending to the issue Walter made known his concerns about the dangerous amounts of drugs a patient was prescribed. This consultant agreed with Walter that it was excessive and dangerous and complied with his request to discontinue the majority of the drugs. He also admitted to Walter that there was definitely something extraordinary and far reaching going on in this area which was beyond his jurisdiction. Furthermore, if he had his way, the majority of the drugs given on the unit would never have been prescribed in the first place. However, 'see no evil, hear no evil, speak no evil' seemed to be the order of the day and that was the end of the matter.

All of this information is deeply disturbing. As more and more evidence mounts against the HIV theory, it seems that the only way to survive AIDS is to steer clear of the medical profession and its terrible drugs. If it is true of this one syndrome then how true is it of other areas of disease? Just how manipulated are we by these companies? And how much wheeling and dealing is going on behind the scenes between consultants and pharmaceutical companies which directly effects our well-being?

AIDS is a huge money spinner providing millions of pounds of profit per day in drugs sales and its offshoot market of condom sales (Wellcome also has links with the London Rubber Company). It has instilled a fear in the heart of our society of free sexual expression and has given rise to much bigotry from the poorly educated who see AIDS as a judgement from God or a punishment for active homosexuality. It has created a huge charity industry, netting millions of pounds from the world population to fund further research to rid the world of this affliction. And how much misery and negativity has it generated? Further research means

334

more experiments on both animals and humans. And the figures for economic growth just rise and rise.

Truth – A Cure For All Disease

As another example of the medical conspiracy; would it shock you to find out that there are, in use today, several medically proven cures for cancer? One such cure is Essiac and has been in use since at least 1922; it has no known adverse side effects. It is made from four common herbs and elevates the immune system. In 1937 it came within three votes of being legalised as a cancer treatment in Canada and was passed on to the British Cancer Campaign by its founder, Rene Caisse, via the Prince of Wales. And yet today, it is still only available through selected, virtually underground, outlets world-wide. I have many dozens of case studies which testify to the efficacy of this treatment (see Appendix IV).

Furthermore, in the 1930s a man named Royal Raymond Rife developed a very high powered microscope, almost seven times more powerful than those in use at the time, which could detect organisms which cause diseases such as infections and cancers. He did this by illuminating these organisms at their own specific frequency of light and could, therefore, examine them and their effects whilst they remained alive as opposed to killing them first using dye stains or high powered electron microscopy as was the norm. He then discovered that, by altering the frequency of their environment microbes could mutate and change their size and shape to resemble viruses and bacteria alike, thereby enabling the same microbe to cause many diverse diseases. For example, the same germs which cause pus – streptococci – could also become the germs which cause pneumonia – pneumococci – in response to an alteration in their environment. Rife also discovered that by bombarding these organisms with higher frequencies of light, he could destroy them. He demonstrated that it was possible to create and destroy cancers at will and succeeded in curing otherwise terminal patients of this disease, as well as others such as polio and typhus, in almost 100% of cases.

Today, it is conventionally accepted that single specific germs are responsible for single specific forms of infection. This theory was advanced by the French scientist Pasteur but was disputed by his rival Bechamp who was in favour of the mutation theory known as pleomorphism. We are rarely informed in text books that, according to his co-worker, Dr Duclaux, Pasteur himself changed his mind and revoked his 'germ theory' in favour of one closer to that of pleomorphism. However, over 100 years later, Pasteur's original germ theory is still the standard working model for the understanding of the action of microbes in the body.

Many types of bacteria exist in a symbiotic relationship with our bodies all of the time and only become symptomatic once the physical body begins to deteriorate due to an unhealthy lifestyle. Bacteria are then free to scavenge the 'soil' produced in the disease process, i.e. when the tissues degenerate to a similar frequency as the microbes, releasing dead organic matter similar to viruses upon which these microbes feed (remember Wilner's definition of the HIV retrovirus?). They then excrete this dead matter as waste products via the bloodstream, faeces or other exudates such as mucous. The extent to which the bacteria can multiply is limited to the amount of soil upon which they have to feed and could not be capable of invading the body to the extent to which science would have us believe unless there was already an adequate food supply. Furthermore, as has been demonstrated in Rife's vibratory work, it is possible for these microbes to mutate into other forms and even to cancer-causing agents according to their environmental conditions, defined by the degree of concentration of waste products and the vibratory rate. The subsequent systemic and metabolic reaction to these toxic excreted waste products, such as sore throat and high temperature (the body's natural way of eradicating the bacteria), are generally the symptoms of diseases which are given priority in day to day general medical practice, whereupon drugs are usually given to suppress them. In giving antibiotics we often succeed in killing the very microbes which are removing the diseased body's dead matter during the natural healing process. In doing so we also open up our bodies to other forms of disease such as fungal infections which are usually kept at bay by the natural presence of bacteria.

Another effective cure for AIDS and cancer has been successfully employed in clinical practise all over the world for at least fifty years and is a cure for virtually all germ diseases. This is Oxygen/Ozone therapy. The principle behind it is simplicity itself and is the reason why the pharmaceutical companies and drug agencies are so afraid of it that they have conspired to suppress it also. It is conventionally accepted that the majority of germs are anaerobic, which means that they survive without oxygen. Therefore, if one floods the bloodstream with oxygen, these organisms cannot survive. Oxygen is one of the fundamental and most necessary elements to human survival. It exists as air, water and most of our food sources such as carbohydrates. The human race has evolved in levels of oxygen far higher than exist in today's polluted and tree-depleted world and we are all running on less than is desirable for optimum health; especially the city-dwellers. Foods and food supplements which release high levels of oxygen such as in the form of Hydrogen Peroxide are beneficial to our well-being. Indeed, Hydrogen Peroxide itself, when taken in dilute form or applied directly to wounds is one of the most effective antiseptics and healing compounds there is.

I believe disease is the result of disharmonious energy fields which can be caused by both physical and non-physical disharmony. Thus, dis-ease can be eradicated by oxygen therapy because it boosts the immune system by raising our vibratory rate, thereby making our bodies healthy. It is a simple fact that disease cannot exist in a healthy body.

According to the testimonies of international MD's assembled at the May 1983 Sixth World Ozone (a concentrated form of Oxygen Therapy) Conference in Washington, D.C.:

Ozone eliminates... viruses and bacteria from blood, human and stored... Medical ozone is successfully used on AIDS, Herpes, Hepatitis, Mononucleosis, Cirrhosis of the liver, Gangrene, Cardiovascular Disease, Arteriosclerosis, High Cholesterol, Cancerous Tumours, Lymphomas, Leukaemia... Highly effective on Rheumatoid and other Arthritis, Allergies of all types... Improves Multiple Sclerosis, ameliorate Alzheimer's Disease, Senility and Parkinson's... Effective on Proctitis, Colitis, Prostate, Candidiasis, Trichomoniasis, Cystitis; Externally, ozone is effective in treating Acne, burns, leg ulcers, open sores and wounds, Eczema and fungus.

In 1976, the US FDA hindered the progress of this form of therapy by stating: Ozone is a toxic gas with no known medical uses.

And yet, one doctor using ozone in his work with colonic cancer patients, Dr Hans Neiper, from Hanover, despite refusing to divulge the names of his cancer patients, stated in 1987:

'President Reagan is a very nice man.' And, 'You wouldn't believe how many FDA officials or relatives or acquaintances of FDA officials come to see me in Hanover. You wouldn't believe this, or directors of the American Medical Association (AMA), or American Cancer Association, or the residents of orthodox cancer institutes. That's the fact.'

SUPPRESSED INTELLIGENCE REPORTS

Oxygen/Ozone therapy researcher and ambassador, Ed McCabe states:

Let's compare medical ozone therapy with prescription drugs. In 1978 the FDA reported 1.5 million were hospitalised in the USA due to the side-effects of medication. On the other hand, medical ozone has been legally used in clinics world-wide on a daily basis since the forties, and in Germany 644 ozone therapists were surveyed, and they reported 384,775 patients had received 5,579,238 ozone treatments. The side-effect rate was only 0.0007% during 5.5 million dosages! Yet, each year approximately 140,000 people in the US die from prescription drug usage.

To this day researchers maintain that the exact causes of and cures for cancer are unknown whilst many others who claim that they do know are frequently the victims of a conspiracy of suppression by governmental agencies and corporate business interests.

It is vital that we understand the true nature of disease if we are to be effective in its eradication. It is imperative that we use the total sum of our knowledge to combat disease and work together as a multi-disciplinarian society, not in isolated, self-interested units. We must open our eyes to the realities and seek the best of conventional and unconventional medicine. We must concentrate on why we are ill and not simply seek to eradicate symptoms of disorders which we often see as inevitable. Disease is not our natural state, it is not inevitable. It is an outward physical display of disharmony whose cause is far more significant than its symptoms. The responsibility for health lies with all of us, not only with doctors or governments.

How many millions flock to the doctor and expect some treatment for a symptom, caring not for the cause but seeking only the relief of discomfort? And who is to blame them? They are victims of the pharmaceutical conspiracy too. According to these scientists, and medical practitioners who find employment within the System, there is little evidence to give credence to any form of medicine other than their own. Or so they and we are told.

They seem deaf to the testimonies of the healers and the healed who stand before them as living proof of the power of mind over matter, homeopathy and herbalism etc. It is healthy to be sceptical but there is a danger of sceptic thought becoming septic thought if it fails to reason with an open mind and allow for progress. Any doctor who fails to open their mind to the information such as is presented in this book is missing the opportunity to fulfil their true role as healers of the sick. There is without doubt a conspiracy of wilful ignorance amongst the cult of western medicine, as even scientifically verified proof of the healing power of channelled energy has been ignored by the majority of practitioners.

One smoke-screen which is constantly employed by the major drug companies is the regular promise that they are 'currently working on a new form of treatment which could soon revolutionise the treatment of...'. Such stories are picked up by the press and t.v science programmes with great fervour. They are nearly always described in terms of 'miracle cure' and point out that adequate funding is necessary for the fulfilment of the prophecy in another 2 or 3 years time. However, when 2 or 3 years time finally arrives we have all conveniently forgotten about the promised miracle drug whilst anxiously awaiting the fulfilment of yet further promises of drugs which are 'hoped' will one day prove to be the end of yet another terrible disease.

And this is the industry which denigrates the field of natural health for taking advantage of the sick and for so cruelly promising fake cures and providing false hope! The obvious lesson here is that to disguise your own sins you must accuse your enemies of them and to always do it before your enemy has a chance to formulate their defence. Mud usually sticks to the one it first lands upon. This a political trick which has been used to devastating effect by the key manipulators of this century in all areas and has been used to shift public opinion in favour of some of the greatest atrocities ever committed.

The Elite via chemo-pharmaceutical companies and food and water production services penetrate all areas of health care and use it to promote and execute their policies of population control, mind control and 'divide and rule', whilst making vast sums of money into the bargain.

Vivisection – far more than an animal rights issue!

This section is intended to be read in order that the sinister implications of animal experiments upon the whole of mankind are thoroughly understood. I am aware, from personal experience of street campaigning for animal rights issues, that many people who care passionately about animals find it simply too distressing to see or read any form of evidence to this effect. Consequently, I have chosen not to give practical details about individual animal experiments in the coming discourse

Instead I will focus upon the scientific fraud perpetrated by vivisectors and how their warped ethos that vivisection is a valuable scientific tool has corrupted the progress of medicine and upset the delicate balance of the minds of millions world-wide. I seek to show how vivisection is an integral part of the manipulation of society (the vivisectors themselves being amongst the most completely manipulated of all) by the very same consciousness and indeed the very same people I have already discussed.

Nothing is worse than vivisection! No other single factor causes more pain, distress and death to humans and animals.

Nor is there any less scientific or ethical method of research currently being employed in industry or educational establishments anywhere in the world.

Unless you have read the books and seen the video footage which I and thousands of other anti-vivisection campaigners have been required to endure, nothing in your imagination can paint for you anything like the true picture of the hell of animal experiments. In fact, if you can conjure up the most heinous spectacle of abuse within your mind, be assured that this is precisely what is being done today, but probably much worse, around the world in schools, universities and research labs owned by private companies – and then some. It is being done with our money, and in order to provide huge mega-wealthy pharmaceutical companies with staggering profit and as an excuse to provide jobs for vivisectors. It is also perpetuated to ensure that mankind never becomes learned about the true nature, cause and cure of disease.

Two thousand animals per minute die as a result of gruesome experiments; that is 250 million per year; approximately 3.5 million per year in Great Britain alone. Over 75% of these experiments are done without anaesthetics, and when they are, they are often inadequately applied. Most experiments are done with public money. 0.2% of the animals used are for the testing of cosmetics. In Britain there are merely 19 Home Office inspectors to cover 20,000 licensed vivisectors.

The practise of animal experimentation has been the mainstay of medical and biological research since the early 1800s even though it has brought about not one major breakthrough in medical science. And yet, every medical student, in order to pass his or her exam and advance in their chosen career must quote the results of animal experiments.

How can respect for life, compassion and empathy be taught to and nurtured in our doctors through a practise which necessitates the ignorance of pain, suffering, anxiety terror and death, as is the case with the training process of US doctors who regularly dissect live animals as part of their training? The answer is simple: It can't.

The animal experimenters are the cornerstone of the highly corrupt and manipulative pharmaceutical industry. These are a pseudo-scientific fraternity who earn vast amounts of money for their employers by performing unbelievably barbaric experiments which can be used to (falsely) substantiate claims that their drugs are safe for human use. Dr. James D. Gallagher, Director of Research of Lederle Laboratories in the Journal of the American Medical Association, March 14, 1964 stated:

'Animal studies are done for legal reasons and not for scientific reasons. The predictive value for such studies for man is meaningless – which means our research may be meaningless.'

There is no British or European law which states that new drugs, chemicals or cosmetics must be tested on animals. However, animal testing ensures that vivisectors get the results they want in order to sell their dangerous chemicals to an unwary public. In numerous legal trials of drug companies who have caused fatalities and injuries, the most effective defence which has been used time and again is that: 'All of the usual and required testing had been done to establish the safety of the drug in question'. A standpoint which most legal authorities are not qualified to dispute. Indeed, the 'experts' upon whom they call for advice in such matters are invariably members of other drug companies or drug sponsored agencies and therefore the animal testing fraternity.

Animal experiments have been cited in many court battles over drugs damages claims and have been used both to defend the idea that such disasters were unforeseen because adequate testing had been employed, but have also been successfully used, as in the Thalidomide case in December 1970, to admonish the drug company (in this case Chemie Grunenthal) who testified that animal tests could never be conclusive for humans.

The very idea that a test or operation done on an animal will show results which are directly translatable to humans is plainly ridiculous. As has been stated by some of the greatest and most influential physicians in medical history: the anatomy, physiology and psychology of animals is entirely different to our own in many ways, and this difference is further exaggerated in the case of animals bred for and/or housed in laboratories. This can be plainly illustrated in many ways; here are just a few:

* The LD 50 (Lethal Dose 50%) test, which is the standard toxicity technique used to establish how much of a chemical toxin is required to kill half of a number of animals. These animals are specifically bred to be exactly identical in every way, i.e. genetically and physically they are the same size and weight. And yet, an equivalent dose of a toxin, in equal quantity and strength will succeed in killing merely half of the batch whilst leaving half to suffer varying degrees of disablement. These results are then haphazardly translated to give the figure for safe and fatal levels for humans. There are 12 different methods which determine

statistically the safety of chemicals for humans from animal experiments. These may disagree by up to a factor of four. * It is accepted that animal tests are successful in identifying cancer-causing agents in only 37% of cases. This means, in effect, that the results of the tests are more times wrong than right and are significantly statistically worse than tossing a coin. * As stated by Hans Ruesch in The Naked Empress or the Great Medical Fraud:

'Two grams of scopolamine kill a human being, but dogs and cats can stand hundred times higher dosages. A single Aminata phalloides mushroom can wipe out a whole human family, but is health food for the rabbit, one of the favourite laboratory animals. A porcupine can eat one lump without discomfort as much opium as a human addict smokes in two weeks, and wash it down with as much prussic acid to poison a regiment of soldiers. The sheep can swallow enormous quantities of arsenic, once the murderer's favourite poison. Morphine, which calms and anaesthetises man, causes maniacal excitement in cats and mice. On the other hand our sweet almond can kill foxes, our common parsley is poisonous to parrots, and our revered penicillin strikes another favourite laboratory animal dead – the guinea pig.'

It is fortunate for many that penicillin was never tested on guinea pigs at the outset where it would have immediately been discarded as dangerous. And if you want to prove that vitamin C is useless, withhold it from the diet of dogs – which produce vitamin C in the gut. Moreover, the whole discipline of surgery and post surgical recovery was hindered for hundreds of years after the Greek Galen (Second Century AD) showed through animal experimentation that the principle laid down by Hippocrates (Fifth century BC) was incorrect – that hygiene and a good diet (as well as establishing the simple fact that nature heals) was essential to good health and medicine. Galen maintained this standpoint, which seems bizarre by today's standards, because animals did not readily succumb to infections following childbirth and surgical procedures. Galen's animal experiments caused a rejection of Hippocratic values and a reduction in surgical asepsis. This destructive attitude was supported by the Catholic Church and was only substantially reversed in the 1800s following the discovery of the germ and how cleanliness and sterilisation could prevent bacterial infection.

The following is a list of drugs which were passed as safe for human consumption on the back of animal tests and the damage which they subsequently caused:

* Eraldin (for heart disease) – Corneal damage including blindness. * Paracetamol (painkiller) – 1,500 people had to be hospitalised in Great Britain in 1971. * Orabilex – caused kidney damages with fatal outcome. * MEL/29 (anti-hypertensive) – caused cataracts. * Methaqualone (hypnotic) – caused severe psychic disturbances leading to at least 366 deaths, mainly through murder or suicide. * Thalidomide (tranquilliser) – caused 10,000 malformed children. * Isoproterenol (asthma) – caused 3,500 deaths in the sixties. * Stilboestrol (prostate cancer) – caused cancer in young women. * Trilergan (anti-allergic) – caused viral hepatitis. * Flamamil (rheumatism) – caused loss of consciousness. * Phenformin (diabetes) – caused 1,000 deaths annually until withdrawn. * Atromid S (cholesterol) – caused deaths from cancer, liver, gallbladder and intestinal disease. * Valium (tranquilliser) – addictive in moderate doses. * Preludin & Maxiton (diet pills) – caused serious damage to the heart and the nervous system. * Nembutal (insomnia) – caused insomnia. * Pronap & Plaxin (tranquilliser) – killed many babies. * Phenacetin (painkiller) – caused severe damages to kidneys and red blood corpuscles. * Amydopyrine (painkiller) – caused blood disease. * Marzine (nausea) – damaged children. * Reserpine (anti-hypertensive) – increased risks of cancer of the brain, pancreas, uterus, ovaries, skin and women's breasts. * Methotrexate (leukaemia) – caused intestinal

haemorrhage, severe anaemia and rumours. * Urethane (leukaemia) – caused cancer of liver, lungs and bone marrow. * Mitotane (leukaemia) – caused kidney damage. * Cyclophospha-mide (cancer) – caused liver and lung damage. * Isoniazid (tuberculosis) – caused liver destruction. * Kanamycin (tuberculosis) – caused deafness and kidney destruction. * Chloromycetin (typhoid) – caused leukaemia, cardiovascular collapse and death. * Phenol-phthalein (laxative) – caused kidney damage, delirium and death. * Clioquinol (diarrhoea) – caused blindness, paralysis and death. * DES (prevent miscarriage) – caused birth defects and cancer. * Debendox (nausea) – caused birth defects. * Accutane (acne) – caused deaf-ness and kidney destruction.

(Taken from Vivisection: Science or Sham by Dr. Roy Kupsinel, and Naked Empress by Hans Ruesch)

Vivisectors often claim credit for many advances in medicine which have been brought about by non-vivisection methods. Frequently, they will quote animal experiments which show the same results without also disclosing the pioneering previous non-animal discovery. One example of this is the case of vaccinations. Whilst it is certainly true that many diseases which have decimated mankind for centuries, such as polio, smallpox, whooping cough, tuberculo-sis, diphtheria and tetanus have seen a dramatic decline over the last century or so, it is not because of the introduction of vaccinations. Figures show that such diseases were long in decline before the introduction of vaccinations and that the rate of fall was severely impeded once they were introduced. Advances in hygiene, sanitation, nutrition and wealth status are the obvious reasons for the improvement of the world's health overall. Vaccinations are re-sponsible for causing many of the diseases they are supposed to cure as well as compromis-ing the immune systems of the vulnerable, especially babies who are statistically more likely to suffer Sudden Infant Death Syndrome within weeks of having their initial standard vaccina-tions.

The vivisectionists are master manipulators. They invest huge amounts of money in massive PR organisations such as the Research Defence Society in the UK. Furthermore, they have infiltrated many areas of the Anti-Vivisection (AV) movement and have created much confusion in the minds of the public as to the truth behind this barbaric trade in misery. An example of this was highlighted in possibly the greatest expose of vivisection industry ever written, The Slaughter of the Innocent by Hans Ruesch:

An interesting case was the Animal Protection league of Basel. Its president, Dr Rudolph Schenkel, professor of ethology, criticised the revival of antivivisectionist feeling in Switzerland. Thereafter, the establishment press could write that 'even the animal defenders disapprove of the antivivisectionists' views.' A closer look at Schenkel revealed that:

1. His league had received a donation of 200,000 Swiss francs (about $100,000) from Hoffman-La Roche, 'for its animal shelter' – with no questions asked. 2. His own wife was ex-perimenting on animals in the endocrinology department of Ceiba-Geigy.

When my CIVIS organisation brought about these facts, Schenkel dropped all pre-tence of being an animal protectionist: at the next convention of Swiss animal protection groups (SPCAs), he argued that 'since laboratory animals are a product of human enterprise, we can do with them as we please.' (My highlight added.)

(This infiltration tactic is not solely within the realms of the AV movement but is widespread throughout the animal rights movement. This is exemplified at present by the large scale enrolment of blood-sports practitioners [fox and stag hunters etc.] with the RSPCA whereby they are steadily creating a significant policy influencing force by taking advantage of the apathy of many members who do not turn out to vote upon Society matters. The RSPCA also has financial investments in companies that support vivisection.)

The smoke-screen perpetuated by vivisectors that it is preferable to test drugs on animals than on humans, and the emotive stance that 'it's your child or an animal', is probably the most effective way that they ensure public support for their industry. What they always fail to say is that all drugs are tested on humans immediately after the animal trials and often without the patient's knowledge or consent. Those that are informed of the trial are usually reassured to know that 'animal studies have shown the drug to be safe'.

AV supporters are simply people who have come to realise the truth about this situation and have committed themselves to being a part of the process of change and reformation to abolish this massive and system of cruel fraud, both for the sake of the animals and humans. However, they are usually portrayed in the media as extremists; an inevitable side-effect of a necessary evil. Ordinary people who are deemed responsible enough to bear and raise children, minister to the sick, save lives, handle the nation's wealth, run for political seats etc., once they have made an AV stance, are immediately demoted to, at best 'irrational' and 'over-sensitive', or, at worst, 'people-hating terrorists' with no right to express an opinion about such matters. Once branded as such they are given about as much regard as are the animals in the laboratory cages and are made largely impotent on the political scene because MPs do not consider it a wise career move or vote winner to consort with anyone considered to be extremist.

In the case of vivisection, the public is all too willing to accept that it is a necessary part of modern progress and not really cruel at all. One reason for this is because the alternative, i.e. the truth, is almost too great a burden to accept. Such a stance is often taken in defence of one's own sanity as a mental survival technique in order that one does not go mad with the anger, sorrow, frustration and terrible empathy which the idea of vivisection evokes in us. Therefore, the vivisectors have yet another advantage over the masses in the battle to keep them convinced of the verity of their cause, whilst the AV organisations have to face a perpetual uphill struggle against the tide of wealth, mind control, tradition and human apathy which is forever on the side of the manipulators.

As George Bernard Shaw once stated, 'Whoever doesn't hesitate to vivisect will hardly hesitate to lie about it'.

By creating a 'healthcare' (more accurately termed 'ill-healthcare') system which relies upon the misleading results of animal experiments, the manipulators of this century have ensured that, within the system, the true causes and cures for disease will never be revealed. This in turn creates a self-perpetuating industry for the multinationals who, by creating disease via their drugs, can be assured of massive funding in order to discover a) the reason for the drug error, which is guaranteed to involve further animal studies, and b) further drugs to treat the results of the initial drug error. In the, by now, all too familiar pattern: the manipulators perpetuate the problem of a state of global ill health and therefore the need for the solution which is offered in the form of more and more pharmaceutical involvement.

For the sake of your selves, your children and the animals: WAKE UP PEOPLE! Take back your power over your own health and stop supporting these barbaric and sick individuals. Only you can do this. The time to do this is now.

In 1975, a man called Dannion Brinkley was struck by lightning and had a near death experience which he recounts in his book 'Saved by the Light'. During the twenty-eight minutes while he was officially dead he was led by a spirit being through the dark tunnel to a crystal city. He was visited by thirteen beings who are described as light beings similar to classic ETs and angels.

He recalls a total of 117 events showed to him on a screen which pertained to predicted events on Earth between 1975 and 2000. At the time of the release of his book in 1994, 95 of these events had occurred, including Ronald Reagan's presidency, the Gulf War, the Chenobyl disaster and the fall of the Soviet Union. Events which have not yet occurred include American bankruptcy, the development of chemical and biological weaponry to be used against France and mass destruction due to World War III.

One of the final visions he was shown was computer chip technology slowly infiltrating every aspect of our day to day lives. Ultimately the controller/owner of this technology would become corrupt a see the potential for world supremacy. Eventually a computer chip would be inserted under the skin of every member of the Earth's population containing total information of everyone's medical history, social status and credit rating which could be read by a scanner and fed to a mainframe. Governments would use these chips to control the population and could also dissolve the chips to release a lethal virus in order to avoid the costs of an elderly population. Those who refused chips would be outcasts from society, unemployable and untouchable by the System's benefits.

Dannion was informed by the Beings that if mankind did not deter from the projected future then these things would come to pass. If, however, action was taken now then it could all be avoided. They informed him that those who have decided to come to Earth are seen as adventurers and are the heroes and heroines who have come to co-create with God where no other spiritual beings have had the courage so to do. The parting message was that the answer lies in 'treating others the way they themselves want to be treated'.

Dannion Brinkley's experience is not unique by any means. Every day people are becoming aware of our angelic hosts and are being given messages of guidance and hope for the future. I have seen such a being of light myself during astral projection and I know they exist all around us, within the higher vibrationary atmosphere of the Earth. We are being given our final warnings and opportunities to do all we can to emerge from the despair of the old dark order into the new future of light. The only way to achieve this is to recognise the pitfalls of the Luciferic influence and live our spiritual ideals in deed as well as in thought.

Firstly, we have to be aware of the clues to the methods employed by the Brotherhood in their ultimate goal of centralised world control. The tools they use to fight their ultimate wars are ourselves. They program our thoughts, our very conception of who we are, what is right and wrong and we, in turn, give them what they wish in the belief that this is the right, or the only way to live long and prosper. We build the prisons in which to house ourselves and hand the keys to our gaolers who are the Brotherhood elite. The crazy part about all of this is that we do it willingly and because they ask us to.

In order to facilitate the Transformation we must resist the urge to identify those who would seek to control us as hopelessly 'evil'. We must recognise the System for what it is and seek to change it in a loving, positive and balanced way. Even at the highest levels of the Brotherhood elite, the most misguided of the Illuminati, are not immune from the effects of the global reawakening. It is those who are most imbalanced towards negativity who have the greatest positive potential. If just one of these elite Luciferic controlled minds is returned to its natural balanced state then virtually the entire process could be reversed over night. This is a potential, and any potential is possible. It all depends on how much energy we channel into that potential to make it a reality.

Furthermore, it is essential that we take what we are being fed through the media and education with a pinch of salt for not all of it will be truth. Events are engineered on a global scale and then a version of it is transmitted to us in order to perpetuate certain states such as fear and apathy within the mass population. So much of little consequence to us is thrown our way to divert us from free thought and we are bombarded with sex, violence, sport and graphic horror. We are often more concerned with who is being transferred from which football team to another, or what the royal family had for tea than the fact that the planet is being destroyed around us and our neighbours are dying of cold, starvation and despair for the want of a little kindness and love. These are very effective diversionary tactics and manipulative devices.

We must begin look at the world through new eyes if we are to really make a difference and take back the right to autonomy and free will which is ours by Divine law. This is a long term plot against humanity, a war of stealth and attrition; a war which the majority of us are not even aware exists because of its scale and slowly cumulative nature. By viewing all of these things on a large scale and by linking patterns and events which we are traditionally encouraged to see as separate, we can piece together the real agendas behind the Illuminati smoke screens. Nothing in the universe is truly separate from anything else. If we analyse just who it is in the world who benefit from the negativity and manipulation, we see that it is the same people over and over again. They represent a consciousness which is like a black hole and is sucking in our vitality with every passing day. This is the direction of the energy flow and its polarity is towards negativity. Wherever we see this trend and recognise it we can begin to work to reverse the polarity back towards the balance point. This relies on our ability to recognise Truth and be prepared to act on our knowledge. It takes you and me, and it takes love.

These methods which they use to persuade us to imprison ourselves are very basic, yet awesomely effective. They engineer situations within our society up to the point where the public are so outraged that they insist on action from those in power. The powers that be (Brotherhood pawns) offer, as a solution, the very thing it wanted to impose in the first place. The public accept the proffered solution so the Brotherhood's desires are implemented with public support. For example, in order to give the police greater powers of arrest, detention and search-at-will to serve the Brotherhood, they manipulate society into creating more crime and despondency. The people cry out for a solution and the politicians come up with more government legislation to counteract the problem. What better way to gain greater control over a population than persuade its people that, for an improvement in their quality of life, they need a larger network of agencies such as MI5, CIA, FBI and the police, and with greater powers than ever before? We must always be on the alert for the hidden agendas behind legislation and economics before we subscribe to the suggested solution. Remember, these people kill or cause people to be killed for profit, pleasure and power. No one is inexpendable and most of the executors of these hidden agendas are entirely unaware or wilfully ignorant of what they are really being used for.

Where we see terrorism, where we see wars, legislation against minorities to restrict their freedom, anywhere we see more powers given to the establishment and less to the free people we must ask ourselves the true reasons behind these actions.

It has been shown how the bankers financed and helped to manipulate into existence the major wars of this century; how the same banks that were backing Hitler and the Nazi war machine during WWII were also behind the Allies. At the end of the war, with the world in chaos and the people's morale depleted, these same banks and their pawns, the politicians, were able to reassemble the world's economy right on target for the New World Order. The future world army was initiated under the guise of a Peacekeeping force we now know as the United Nations. And the people were so grateful to these powers for ridding the world of such an evil menace that they entirely surrendered themselves, once again, to the policies and propaganda of the people who had created the war in the first place. And so, the process continues to this day.

We must challenge automatic thought patterns and habitual life styles which are the weapons employed against us. We must constantly question and never betray ourselves to the power of thought-forms of the masses. The world is full of fashion victims, not only in the sense of clothing but in life-styles and thought patterns too. These fashions have been provided by, fed, watered and nurtured by the Brotherhood in order to feed their lust for money and power.

Every penny we spend gets back to their banks in the end. Everything we work for and achieve will be theirs if we allow it. Moves are under way now to replace money entirely with credit. Credit cards, debit cards and smart cards are now being developed at such a runaway rate that soon we will all be rated as credit. Technology exists now to use chips in cards both for access to personal details and to transmit messages into the psyche of the carrier to control behaviour. More and more opportunities are being sought to use this micro-technology: as tags for criminals, as pet identi-chips, as surgical implants and as locators for potentially missing children and babies. It is a small step to the 'under-the-skin' control chip.

Efforts are under way to centralise world government powers. Plans for a federal Europe under a single European government have been under way for years now. Step by step, power is taken away from the masses and delivered into the hands of the few.

Watch out for calls for larger armies and greater powers. Have you noticed how the U.N. 'peacekeeping' forces are always too late and in too little numbers to actually be effective? Watch out for a call for a centralised world army on order to provide greater 'peacekeeping' potential, it would really be a double bluff to give more power to the Brotherhood elite.

Watch out too for those situations which the ruling classes and governments vehemently oppose and be careful not to support something just because those whom you oppose are against it. This is one of the oldest, but most effective tricks in the book and it has duped millions time and time again. Don't allow the further decline or the consequences may be disastrous. Always be true to yourself first and foremost and see beneath the veil of deceit.

The coming Transformation to a unified multidimensional Christ consciousness will affect everyone, the Brotherhood included. We can only be controlled if we allow ourselves to be so. Nothing is impossible. We are the vehicles for the Divine Consciousness, we are the creative hands of God. It is up to all of us, and that includes the Brotherhood, to re-evaluate our position, for we cannot escape ourselves and the karma we create.

As Mark Phillips once explained to Cathy O'Brien:

Good always prevails through positive application, whereas the bad guys are hindered and slowed in their criminal endeavours through having to cover-up their negative actions with lies to support lies. This inevitably allows the truth to emerge.

MIND CONTROL

THE SECRET HISTORY

The Secret History of Mind Control

CKLN-FM Mind Control Series

CKLN 88.1 FM

Ryerson Polytechnical University Toronto

Ontario International Connection Mind Control Series Producer/Interviewer: Wayne Morris

Wayne Morris:

Good morning and welcome to International Connection. We are in show #33 in our series on Mind Control, and today we are going to hear a presentation, The Secret History of Mind Control, given by Walter Bowart at the Ritual Trauma Child Abuse and Mind Control Conference in Atlanta in October, 1997. Walter Bowart is an investigative journalist and author of one of the original books about mind control in the late seventies entitled, Operational Mind Control. And now, Walter Bowart:

Introduction by Sylvia Gillotte:

I guess Walter almost needs no introduction because he was really probably the first person to publicly write about mind control and its origins and so forth. His book, Operation Mind Control, is available at his table at the back. Most recently Walter was involved as a consultant in the making of the movie, Conspiracy Theory, and some of you may have seen him actually interviewed for an HBO special promoting the movie. It was the first time I ever got to see what Walter looked like so I could recognize him when he came. He has the Freedom of Thought Foundation, which he will tell you about. He is going to share his information with you, so welcome Walter.

Walter Bowart:

I would like to thank some people. I was going to save it until the end but I want to get it right up front since a couple of them are here. I would like to thank Mike Coyle for what he contributed to this. What you are going to see is a series of out-takes, some are from videos, and a lot of them are still … it's a very rough presentation of what's going to be a documentary. I would like to thank Mike Coyle who is retired from the field. He had the Mindnet Journal which was on the internet, and he did a terrific job of research. He is finding that a lot of the critical things that we are going to talk about as we get toward the end of this show, are actually removed from journals ... pages torn out of academic research journals and things. Somebody doesn't want this information out.

I am going to cover things going back ... Sylvia asked me to do the history of mind control but I'm going to go farther afield ... probably than most of you had heard about. It is so far beyond any technology you are talking about, like electromagnetic spectrum stuff ... we are into post-quantum physics here, and now we are working with physicists.

I would also like to thank Blanche Chavoustie who is here for the long years of friendship and the documentation and research that she has helped us with and Cheryl Welsh, who I think is not here, who also contributed boxes and boxes of research, and Doreen Pratt who is hospitalized and not able to travel ... she is blind, legally blind, and you will see some of her work in this presentation. And I would like to thank all the members of the Freedom of Thought Foundation for their assistance, and friendship and guidance over the 20 years that we have been doing this.

The big key to the thing is that only the small secrets need to be kept. You can find just about anything the government is doing by going into scientific journals and doing research. But the big secrets are kept by public incredulity and your study and your experience is in an area which is not secret. All this has been known for a long time, but people don't want to believe it and there is a great deal of denial.

[Slide] With the evolution of man came the evolution of science, and here's an example of an early treatment by the foremost practitioners of "mental health science". This is an etching from 1745. It shows a ward in Bethlehem Hospital in London. It was pronounced Bethlem, and it became Bedlam, the famous synonym for the nuthouse.

[Slide] A patient of Bethlem, William Norris, was confined there for 12 years, bound by chains a foot long and to an iron rod at the head of his bed. He died in 1815. Another patient at Bethlem, who we do not have a picture of was James Tilley Matthews. He was incarcerated there for 35 years and escaped only by death, and it is a very interesting story. In the late 1700's he had gone to France as a spy for the British Admiralty, posing as an import-export agent. He travelled in the highest circles of French society. Things went wrong for him when he fell into the hands of Franz Anton Mesmer, the father of hypnotism. Mesmer used to play parlour games by having aristocrats stand in tubs of water while he played DC current over their heads, to what purpose we don't know.

[Slide] This may be one of the first perpetrators of mind control ... one of the founders of our country ... Benjamin Franklin. He was the US ambassador to France at the time, and if you remember, he was the discoverer of electricity which was DC electricity. He discovered it when he flew a kite on a wire during an electrical storm, and it was a shocking experience. Franklin may have used that later for the effects we now know DC current gives. It will induce amnesia easily. Franklin was asked by the French government to look into the activities of Mesmer and his claims of miraculous cures with electricity. They hit it off real well, but it's not surprising. They were both the brothers of the same secret society ... the Masons. Franklin filed a lengthy report favourable to Mesmer to the French government. Another brother Mason who frequently visited them in Paris was Adam Weishaupt, the founder of the Illumaniti. These coincidences bring a lot of questions to your mind about what were these guys really doing over there, and what did they find out?

SUPPRESSED INTELLIGENCE REPORTS

Mesmer happened to be, believe it or not, the godfather of Amadeus Mozart. In fact he raised Mozart, and of course Mozart was this incredible genius musician and his biography will show you more than one obvious example of someone who behaves as if he were suffering from Dissociative Identity Disorder. You can conclude that maybe Mesmer played around to enhance the musical abilities of Mozart at the cost of other parts of his personality.

[slide] We are back to James Tilley Matthews and after a few years of influence by Franklin and Mesmer, he beat a path as soon as he could back to England, reported to the Admiralty the French had developed a devastating instrument of war, an "airloom" which could weave thoughts into a man's mind.

[slide] At the top it says "Illustrations of Madness", that's the name of the book written by John Haslam, the apothecary (in modern terms, the resident medical officer) to Bethlem Hospital toward the end of Matthews' stay. In the first decade of the 19th century Haslam wrote this whole volume called "Illustrations of Madness" just singly on the Matthews case. It was published in 1810. It was the first book length case study of a single patient in British psychiatric history. According to Roy Porter who repackaged Haslam's 1810 book "Illustrations of Madness" in 1988 ... that's the only way you are going to find it. There are rare volumes, you have to pay at least $40 for a used copy.

Because of the book, Matthews' fate became a cause celebre everywhere - in Britain and the United States. It was used against Bethlem Hospital in general, and Haslam in particular, ironically, when the institution came under scathing scrutiny by a House of Commons committee investigating madhouses in 1815. A few years before the madhouse era, there were only a few people declared insane, but by the late 1700's and the early 1800's, there were hundreds of thousands of people now in these madhouses, so-called. While Matthews is interesting to us for other reasons, he was the cause celebre that created social reform in the madhouse business.

According to Porter, the significance of his case was way back about two hundred years ago, he was describing experiences that modern victims of mind control are now describing, even using some of the same terms. Today Matthews would be diagnosed as having "delusional disorder", and I think delusional disorder is a misdiagnosis for a whole lot of things. Maybe he would be diagnosed as suffering from schizophrenia or paranoid schizophrenia, which we now know is an extremely rare disease. When I wrote "Operation Mind Control" back in 1978, there were only 25 MPD cases diagnosed, now there are hundreds of thousands. Most of the people I was writing about were called schizophrenic by the doctors ... and they weren't. Of course, they were D.I.D.

A Dr. George Birkeck of London examined Haslem in those days, and testified before the King's Bench that after paying James Tilley Matthews six visits at Bethlem and having attempted "by every mode of examination which he could devise" to discover the real state of his mind, he said Matthews was not insane. Matthews was talking about sudden death squeezing, lobster cracking. He was admitted on January 28, 1797 to Bethlem after he had been behaving oddly for quite a while, about a year, and among his strange behaviour was writing a letter to his benefactor, Lord Liverpool, who was in the Admiralty and was part of this intelligence scam that he was involved in, "I pronounce your Lordship to be in every sense of the word a most diabolical traitor after a long life of political and real iniquity during which your Lordship, by flattering and deceiving and more than anyone contributing to deceive your

SUPPRESSED INTELLIGENCE REPORTS

King who believing your hypocritical professions, has to be the detriment of many of the country's friends, loaded you with honours and emollients. You have made yourself a principal in schemes of treasons founded upon the most extensive intrigues which have not not only long since laid this country at the feet of its most bitter enemies who have assassinated France, to reap further advantages from those who by such wickedness might in such general assassinating scandal mount the throne ..." and so forth, written in the grand prose of that day. And that will get you locked up, even today that would get you locked up ...

But he is talking about thought-making. Haslam, the doctor who treated him, said, "In this situation he continued for many years, sometimes an automaton, moved by the agencies of persons hereafter to be introduced to the notice of the reader." And of course he talked about spies, thugs and assassins who were putting voices in his head and controlling him. Matthews insisted that in some apartment near London Wall there is a "gang of villains, profoundly skilled in pneumatic chemistry who assail him by means of an airloom." Of a variety of tortures he described so colourfully, were "fluid locking, cutting soul from sense, stone making, thigh talking, kiting involving magnetic impregnations ... sudden death squeezing, lobster cracking caused by pressure from the 'magnetic atmosphere surrounding the persons assailed', apoplexy working with a nutmeg grater, lengthening the brain, thought-making while one of these villains is sucking at the brain of the person assailed to distract his existing sentiments, another of the gang will force into his mind a train of ideas very different from the real subject of his thoughts in which is squeezed upon as the desired information by the person sucking." "Laughter-making, poking, pushing up the quicksilver, bladder filling, tying down, bomb bursting, gas plucking (the extraction of magnetic fluid from a person assailed), foot curving, lethargy-making, spark exploding, knee nailing, burning out, eye screwing, sight stopping, roof stringing, vital tearing, fibre ripping brain sayings ..." and other descriptions of physical and psychological tortures caused by some invisible means which Matthews put into the high tech terms of his day.

Now, this is very similar to what people are describing today. This is the way he drew a layout of the way he was assailed and interrogated by these 17th Century assassins and he said that a pneumatic machine [slide] this is a sketch he made of it ... was used, this was the high technology that was doing all this. If you are interested in this, try to find the book, you may have to do a search for it. But the EM targeted victims of today are not sounding much different than that. This guy is pretty colourful and of course the language is very arcane.

Matthews ... he was the first. It was 200 years ago. He is the first single case ever chronicled in the psychiatric literature that we know of. This is nothing new. Could it be that Franklin and those other guys came up with something that they really did use, because that's what Matthews claims. Today we have the category, and I don't like the term but it is used, "Wavies" — those are people who are targets of electromagnetic waves of some kind, or I prefer the term "EM targeted individuals". Some of these people claim to be alien abductees or government mind control victims, or satanic abused people. There is nothing in Matthews' description that these groups of people haven't also described experiencing.

Then you have to ask, doing what I did for 20 years, hearing all these stories, you are gathering probably the largest data base ... using a 27 page questionnaire, I am looking for mind control victims and of course our questionnaire is on mind control - but it kind of gives you an indication of everything else, including the alien abduction scenario which is very peculiar, very unusual. We have the largest data base ... and after you hear this, you say, "could it be that these delusions, if they are delusions - do we as a species lack such imagination as to keep coming up with the same thing over and over for 200 years?" Can't we go beyond this? Shouldn't madness be really 'out there'? But something is happening here. There is a pattern to this, and you hear people who don't know each other, have had no contact with this thing at all, who never read a book on it, saying the same thing. I sit down with some survivors who have experienced trauma abuse and trauma based programming and compare notes, it will be the same. And it runs true.

This is later. This is now the early 19th century [slide] — we've got the Lavery Electric Phrenometer - it was the high tech of its day, intended to accurately measure the bumps on your head and so predict the nature, type and behaviour of individuals who would hold still for it. And it was taken very seriously for a while, until somebody said, "hey, there's no data base for this, you know?"

[slide] Early 20th century - "Mental Poisoning", it was a popular book written by a psychologist in the early days when people were hearing voices, mental poisoning. And then we got more scientific - this is an obsolete version of Colin Ross's book - he made a contribution to the field by doing that research. But here we go in the 1920's or 30's - everybody was hearing voices, everybody, and all you had to do was turn on a radio. There was no need for implanted electrodes to control your behaviour.

[slide] Here's a Nazi rally in pre-war Germany. Students of Marshall McLuhan will tell you how radio created Nazism, the blitzkreig, and mass obedience like nothing before it. As one psychoscientist put it, "the stentorian voices of the mass media are more universally powerful than the indiscriminate persuasions of any mind altering drug." Most of the survivors in this room probably don't watch a lot of television, right? Does anybody want to confess? Okay. (Never owned one? Yes.)

[slide] Now this is the guy - Freedom of Thought Foundation is going to have an award - and all of you will have a chance to vote on who is going to get the first one - it's very expensive to make those little statues but nobody will pick it up so we can just peel off the brass plate every year and use the same one. We have a few candidates. Jolyon West is a candidate, Martin Orne is a candidate, there are two or three others. But they will all be on the ballot. I have been working on this brain which is about this big, and it's gold, and it's fried black and it's broken off and it's got two electrodes on it and it sits on kind of like a beer can - kind of a nice looking thing.

It's called the Mengele Award after Josef Mengele, this guy here. That's Joe, and he was one of the mind control men, you know, from the ubermentsch ... there's nothing like opening a skull and letting your bare fingers run through someone's brain or freezing human beings to near the point of death and then finding out through trial and error that the easiest way to defrost someone is to put them close to another naked human body. And these are just a few of the brutal experiments, though some of that was valuable for hypothermia ... all of the records of what Joe Mengele did in Nazi concentration camps, and all of the records of his research are now on file at the National Archives. We should probably get them all - I think some of them are still classified. But these are the people he is working on - these are his subjects. Of course Mengele was fascinated by genetics. I haven't really addressed genetics and most survivors realize that it is multigenerational, most sons and daughters of Masons realize that is part of the Masonic belief is that if you program or if you train or educate or whatever the word is, a person over two or three generations the knowledge begins to be true ...

We are heading that way and these twins were a part of Mengele's studies and he did a number of things. Twins appear to be telepathic. With NLP you can understand how that works, and our workshops demonstrate what looks like telepathy by mirroring and matching. If you can sit with somebody and match their breathing pattern and establish this incredible rapport, you will experience, if you are sitting there in a state - imagining sitting there on a mountaintop and the wind is blowing or whatever - you will pick up the wind and you will pick up all the sensory experience that they are having. You might not put it together in the right way, you might say "I am driving in my convertible and the wind is in my hair" or something, but twins are known to be - and you can't match any better than twins - they suffered great atrocities at the hand of Mengele and they are here and they have been interviewed, and that's the last picture that was taken of Dr. Josef Mengele who was said to have been in Arizona in 1960, there is a persistent rumour. But of course they say he wasn't, he was in Argentina and he died down there and yet they are not sure that those are his bones ...

It is also one of the persistent rumours that he was brought over in Project Paperclip. We know he worked on a farm in Germany for a few years before the end of WWII. There is the question of the Green programming, and the two proteges he had that were sent to Harvard and all that, and I am sure you have heard of this and more, but there is no proof of it. I keep harping on this - we won't find any documentation or proof until we repeal the National Security Act. As you begin to research in this thing, and I have been smashing my head against the NSA for 20 years. They do whatever they want. Colonel Fletcher Prouty is a friend of mine. He said "they are over there now", he lives nearby, you can look out the window. "See the lights are on. They are xeroxing forged documents." The National Archives are locked up as far as this stuff goes. Anything that is useful, anything that is about mind control, and we'll get back to that ...

There are so many doctors - I guess Colin Ross is writing a book about it -he's following up on some of our research that we did 25 years ago. He's gotten the papers of Dr. Estabrooks and Estabrooks knew Milton Erickson, who I think was a great guy myself, but he did work for the government, and they all knew each other and Ewen Cameron comes in, it was a Who's Who of everybody who worked in the psychiatric mental health profession of that particular generation, my father's generation.

Sociologists as well, it's been going on for fifty years. Guys like Robert J. Lifton who is thought of very highly, worked with Dr. John Mack, the alien guy, the UFO guy. They had a partnership - they worked in a little company that was funded by the CIA MKULTRA project. And in national mental health, all the universities were used - you know the story - and Operation Mind Control gives you a big list on all this stuff. I mean, it's just scratching the surface.

And I hear some of you gasp at some of this stuff. Have you read Lifton's book, "The Nazi Doctors"? That's a pretty interesting study of how - it takes up the obedience to authority kind of thing, how people can be made to do things they wouldn't ordinarily do. Lest you gasp repeatedly throughout this presentation, let me generalize. Virtually every psychologist, psychiatrist, sociologist, cyberneticist, and so on of that generation previous to mine, were funded either wittingly or unwittingly by the CIA. The CIA through a number of cutout organizations co-opted the entire mental health profession and put it to work on mind control. It's a hard thing finding people that aren't part of the game, you know, part of the bad guys.

SUPPRESSED INTELLIGENCE REPORTS

A few years after the end of WWII, about the CIA was being founded, and one of their first concerns in 1947 - the Soviets engineered a show trial against Roman Catholic Cardinal Minzente who appeared before a kangaroo court in a trance and confessed to everything he was accused of which a few years later he couldn't remember. The CIA looked into this and they said "oh they've got something we don't have, and we need this". We'd better look into this. It was a fledgling agency in those days. We're celebrating its 50th anniversary and I got a big kick out of George Bush standing up next to Richard Helms, who went to jail and was convicted of lying to Congress, he was the Director of the CIA, and Nixon was singing this man's praises, saying what a great patriot he was. If you are a patriot, you lie to everybody, you lie to your country. That's how far our morals and ethics have fallen.

[slide] These are some of the things you find on the internet too, you find a lot of very good stuff, very succinct. And that talks about Harris Isabell in 1955, part of MKULTRA Bluebird, the hospital in Lexington, Kentucky and things ... of course Nelson Rockefeller wanted to become president one day and he was standing at the bedside of lady liberty when she gave birth to her bastard child, the freak of nature, part of the invisible Cold War, information - they christened the baby "Information Warfare", they called it. The father nicknamed it "Brainwashing".

Brainwash. A previous speaker used the term. It is very non-specific, and the term "mind control" isn't much better. But "brainwash" was coined by a CIA propaganda specialist, Ed Hunter, and he advised Allen Dulles who gave a speech at the UN and that's how the term "brainwashing" got started. Dulles' brother was John Foster Dulles. He was the Secretary of State, and Allen called himself the "Secretary of State for Unfriendly Governments". He was the Director of the CIA. They talked about the insidious Fu Manchu Communists in Korea and China who had brainwashed our clean-minded American boys and made them confess to crimes that they did not commit. According to Dulles the Chinese had a way of making strong-minded Americans hallucinate that a US Marine wing had flown a mission over North Korean held territory, dropping germ bombs. Colonel Charles Schwabel here took most of the heat. He was one of the men who allowed himself to be filmed to the US use of germ weapons. The cries of "brainwashing" could not drown out the later revelations that the Marine Air wing had indeed dropped germ bombs on the insidious yellow peoples fighting against the U.S. Later it was revealed that the secret labs at Edgewood Arsenal had developed a race-specific encephalitis germ which infected only oriental people.

... Fu Manchu. Which turned out to be nothing more than isolation, deprivation, alienation ... what this guy was talking about. Very standard stuff. Nothing romantic about it. Just the same old take a person, put their hand in a vise, close the vise, say "talk". They'll talk at some point. That's what brainwashing was. It's like our prison and educational systems. Simple things. The Chinese didn't use drugs or anything sophisticated. But they did get these people to confess readily. So guess what happened? Those of us who served in the military service - we all were the beneficiaries of that - The Code of Conduct. You gave your name, rank and serial number and nothing else. But you wait a certain time and then you can tell them anything because the only thing you have to worry about is tactical information which gets obsolete very fast.

I talked to Laird Gunderson and guys that were in Vietnam and they really stood up to torture. It's an interesting thing to see those men come back in the fifties, standing at a strange angle, behaving like these automatons -it's very interesting - just what isolation, deprivation, alienation can do to somebody. I suffer from it myself, being a writer, sitting in front of that computer so many hours. I catch myself in the mirror, staggering around. So the result was The Code of Conduct.

Out of this came the best psychological study ever done - on 3000 men who were POW's in Korea. They studied them all with a finetooth comb. Most interesting, they had three categories: the guys that collaborated outright with the enemy, the guys who resisted the enemy to the death, and the guys that just went along with the enemy. The ones who just went along with the enemy were the same guys that just went along with our military, they were draftees. The guys that collaborated with the enemy outright were the people in our own military who were known as gung-ho. The people that resisted the enemy were the people that resisted our own military and they wanted us all to resist the enemy the same way that those guys did. They studed the "resisters" and they found there was a spectrum of on one hand, there were the criminals, and then at the other end, there were the ones who were highly creative. They began to study more and they saw that criminality is nothing more than misplaced creativity. We have an actual industry in this country of misplaced creativity.

Slide - Brainwashing in Red China. Edward Hunter, the man who coined the term "brainwashing" wrote several books about it. Then came the fictional version of that story by Richard Condon, The Manchurian Candidate. That caught everybody's attention. I knew Richard when he was alive. He was a PR flack who dropped out. He was sixty, and this was his first novel and it was a big hit. It was the story of a guy who was captured - Laurence Harvey played the assassin in the movie. He was programmed. They captured him behind enemy lines, take him up to Manchuria, programmed him, then he came back. He did assassinate the candidate for president who happened to be a guy he didn't like anyway, it was his stepfather, so ... the Queen of Diamonds over the phone triggered the assassination. I asked Condon over the phone - now that he can't defend himself - some guys are writing that Condon knew all about this. He loved my book back in 1974 - I think he saw a rough draft and he wrote great things about it. He said he just read Pavlov and Salter, and invented the rest because it was a pretty basic premise. Frank Sinatra was in the film, he was one of the progrmamed POW's, and he bought a large piece of the film. It's an interesting movie to watch. When Kennedy was assassinated, he pulled the film out of circulation and it remained out of circulation for probably 15 years which I thought was interesting. Maybe he knew something about the assassination of Kennedy that we don't know.

Slide - These are some of the 1940 stills that I found of soldiers under hypnosis being marched around ... demonstrating before others. In 1978 I went all over the world with these slides. It was shocking to people. They didn't know you could be made to do something against your will and without your knowledge. They didn't know you could do mind over matter kinds of things with your body, control blisters, what have you. I learned from Anthony Robbins when I saw 200 people walk over a bed of coals as long as this room - they were trying to do the Guinness Book of Records. It was a mesquite fire, the hottest kind of fire because of the oil which stuck to their feet. 60% got burns, but 40% didn't. Now you explain that to me ... Andy Wile, the new age healer, he's an MD - he wouldn't walk in it. He knew what a hot fire was. We know you can control blisters.

Cathy O'Brien tells an interesting story about being burned between her breasts with nitrous oxide while in a hypnotic state, and having a baphomet appear - a demonic star, goat like figure which was used by Knights Templar and has a whole history - apparently Noriega was very superstitious and she had a message, she claims, from high ranking government (George Bush) to give to Noriega. To get his attention, her handler gave her that cue phrase and that baphomet appears - it would only come out in that state. Things like that can be done, and have been repeated in laboratory experiments. But in 1940 they weren't doing that. I just threw this in as a filler, because what we are talking about is how to divide your mind.

If Daddy hasn't already done it - I don't know what this guy said - he said it happens at an early age - it's got to be emotional - true. But he didn't say it's got to happen before you can speak. Real DID has to happen before you can talk. So that's a very early age, probably a year, if not before. All of us that have had - that know a lot of MPD stories - realize that there are personalities and different identities anchored to various body parts. I have a great video of the most wonderful little lady - she's on our website - Patty - and I have never seen anybody react like this little lady. She herself is the schoolhouse, and she is full of children, trying to burst out. It's almost like her eyeballs move sideways, and one comes out and says "hey, what about me?" - and she can't control this when she gets started. I was trying to do an interview with her, and I said "let me anchor your executive personality". She is a volunteer for certain police things, she has her take-charge personalities, very competent. I wanted to anchor her in that, so I said "let me touch your knee and every time you go off in another personality I will touch your knee and that's your executive, all right?" So I thought I had anchored it pretty good. Well in the middle of the interview here is this little kid again, so I touched her knee, and she says "what do you think you're doing? you're just touching my knee with your finger ... they used a cattle prod". Then she looked at the camera. My girlfriend was the camera operator, Pat - both of them were Pat - they got along great. But she had this great big old studio video camera. And she says, "you know, we did that before, but there was never a woman running the camera ... we were making blue money". I didn't know what blue money was, which is child porn as it turns out.

Slide - The doctor on the right is B.F.Skinner, and this is his daughter, Debbie Skinner. He was at Harvard, he was respectable, this was the apex of respectable scientific research. He used to work with pigeons, chimpanzees -but this is his daughter, Debbie, and the box they said kept Debbie from being disturbed. She would awaken in her sleep and they would carry on with their regular lifestyle and Debbie was protected from traffic outside, it was air conditioned and everything - Debbie looks pretty happy there. Remember that the beginning of - you've heard a lot about Pavlov. And the Russians have always been big fans of the dark side of our science. They love cybernetics. I'll get to Norbert Weiner in a little while.

They loved a guy named J.B. Watson who was the founder of behaviorism. He had an illegitimate child, Little Albert, which I was surprised to learn this was his child, with the nurse who worked for him. Watson finally got defrocked and he went to work for Madison Avenue. He is the father of mind control in advertising. The most interesting thing about Watson ... here's this little baby, Albert, crawling along the floor, and they want to condition Albert and they had a white bunny rabbit and they let the bunny rabbit out of the cage. As soon as the bunny rabbit would emerge Little Albert would say "whoo woo" and go running for the bunny rabbit, he would get to a certain proximity of the bunny rabbit and Daddy would drop this big steel bar, clanging behind Little Albert, make him jump and cry naturally. Watson did this repeatedly until Little Albert was afraid of anything white, anything that moved that way, anything furry, all of his life.

This boy, the son of the founder of behaviorism, and Debby Skinner, the daughter of one of the leading proponents of behaviorism and if you understand behaviorism, you know it works ... it is a science, and it is uncanny. Both of these young people committed suicide in their twenties. What does that say about their parents and their heritage, this kind of approach to the study of human psychology, I guess it's called. So, that's Debby and the box. Skinner was the apex of science, American intellectual establishment, Harvard University.

Slide - This is the nadir of American intellectual establishment — this is William Jennings Bryant III in L.A. - he is the founder and director of the American Institute of Hypnosis. Anybody heard of him? Yeah. He can run three hypnotic subjects at a time with that panel ... program three people. I was trying to get an interview with him, he kept dodging me as has Martin Orne -once I got him on the golf course and almost succeeded but he ran away. Bryant died on the stage in Las Vegas of a heart attack - according to his widow, within hours of his passing - it was like magic - the signal was sent - the CIA showed up at his office and at his private home - and removed every scrap of paper from his library. There is reason to believe that he was, as is alleged, the programmer of perhaps Sirhan Sirhan, the assassin of Robert Kennedy and maybe one of the programmers of Candy Jones who was the number one pin-up girl during WWII. Slide - Candy Jones. Betty Grable was number one, and she was number two, something like that. She wrote her own book called The Control of Candy Jones - some people would now try to deny that was true ... but indeed it runs true. She was programmed to commit suicide at a certain time by jumping off a cliff. She married a guy - I think the only reason she married him was because he started loosening her programming. His name was Long John Neville, he was a talk-show host in New York, and he was an amateur hypnotist. He started working with her - you can reintegrate just like that (snaps fingers) unless you are continuously restimulated, the natural tendency is to pull it all together again and reintegrate. Suddenly she remembered, "gee whiz, I went on all these trips in southeast Asia", she remembered having her hand in a box with scorpions stinging her and all kinds of other things. Being basically a pigeon, a courier for the cryptocracy ... ran out of three letter words ... secret government. Whatever he did shook loose the thing - she didn't jump off the cliff.

Another - somebody should write a book about Marilyn Monroe. She was an abused child. You know how it goes. Daddy is a pedophile, and Daddy is making movies of abusing the kids in the neighbourhood, and he ships them through the mail and the postal inspector finds this and says "ah we're going to arrest these guys" and they give it to some federal branch of law enforcement because it's a federal crime and then somehow it gets bumped over to the department of defence and the department of defence guys - who are probably CIA or NSA or whatever - they show up and say "ah you're going to jail for a 25 years - otherwise you work for us." Then they say "now we'll show you how to program them." So the whole family ends up and the children of those children end up working for Uncle Cryptocracy for the rest of their lives. You will hear that story over and over. I hope you hear Brice Taylor's presentation, that's a story about this. The reason I know she is real is because I met her when she was with the guy that she can't see anymore ... but I know who it was. A movie star who was a handler. That was years before I met her again in a mind control context. But I think she has totally sanitized her book so that she doesn't name any names. But it should. Operation Mind Control names the names because I got permission to use an earlier version and I changed her name of course so you will have to put two and two together if you want the real story.

[Slide] It says "How to Hypnotize" - this was in a comic book in the 40's or 50's. It was a big thing. Everybody was hypnotizing everybody. Little did they know, just accidentally you can really send somebody on a spin and really have some problems. I hope you don't think I meant to use the word "spin" deliberately. [Slide] That's Cathy O'Brien. I am sure many of you know her or heard her story. It's written in the book "Trance Formations in America". She brought the term "Presidential Model" to the fore, and she presents a kind of National Enquirer version of the MKULTRA story, naming names, sexual preferences, perversions, dimensions and identifying marks of the genitalia of the high government officials. That's probably her main defence. She says "okay". Remember Michael Jackson? They had him drop his drawers because some kids had identified him. Well, she says that about some of the major presidents and secretaries of defence and what-have-you which I think is a great thing to do.

[Slide] She calls it Monarch mind control there - that's the picture. It gives the name of her shrink there, and I called up her shrink and said "can you put me in touch with this lady?" and she called me and I used her pseudonym in the book. She then sent me a blow-up of the picture that she didn't even know was there, because it was on her passport, she had given it to the reporter, the reporter spilled coffee on it, but they had a negative of the picture. The reporter blew the picture up and sent it back to her and she was surprised to find these two images on it. One is the famous butterfly connoting that she was a sexual slave, programmed, and the rose is the assassin program. We find in Operation Mind Control there is a pin for evening wear - the butterfly pin or the rose pin. Some on a lower level, they would actually tattoo the women in certain places. Some of the cattle prods 200,000 volts DC will give you melonin, and give you a nice little mole. Some of them are burned with moles in a certain shape on the face, and you meet many survivors that have had every mole taken off their body just for that reason, because they knew this was identifying. Any of the perpetrators that know the programming can access the person, depending on what pin they are wearing or what they know about the programming.

The history of mind control is the history of male chauvinist secret organizations at work preying upon women. But there are some other things. Women are uniquely susceptible to trauma and especially sexual trauma. The reactions - the difference between men and women in the MPD thing - this mind control falls into MPD - it's just a naturally occurring phenomena which would probably happen in nature. If you go up to a victim at car crash, and they are in the state of what we call "shock" - and give them your card and say "you'll send me a thousand bucks tomorrow, come over here and sit down, are you okay?" change the subject - probably that person will give you a thousand bucks the next day because they are in a state of shock. If you give an embedded command in a positive framework - it's just the way people are - we are all that way. Nothing special about it. So that state is used to traumatize small children - naturally occurring state - is accessed by the government. My cousin - he's the reason I got into this - he was traumatized and we didn't know it. He had a drunken father who used to beat him and his mother up, that wasn't a big deal, it was no big deal - but when he joined the service it showed up on the tests - there it was. This was a person with a high tendency to dissociate - we can use him. He was trained as a courier, to carry secret messages locked behind post-hypnotic amnesia blocks. And today he is still having trouble. He can't sleep very well, so many years later, and he has had 13 years of therapy, he was in hypnosis. It's pretty well in there. He remembers the atrocities he had to witness at interrogations, which ended with decapitation and things like that, really hideous stuff, military stuff, which really hit him.

That little lady was used in ... she was a bomber by the time she was age 3. She was like a set up person who would hang out with the assassin and distract somebody while the guy bumped him. Just a little innocent kid coming into a place like this. Oh a little package, you know. Puts it down, later the place blows up, that kind of thing. She has pretty much recovered, doing really well, I am happy to say.

The best literature on mind control and survivors is self-published literature. The publishing companies won't touch this stuff any more. The only reason I got Operation Mind Control published in 1978 was that my agent was an agent. He belonged to Naval Intelligence. He is now one of the biggest agents in New York, and he paid me a whopping advance because they wanted to control it, and then, man they printed a million copies and ate it, and paid me full royalties and you never found it again. In two weeks it was gone. Now they are paying $650 a copy - if you've got a used copy of Operation Mind Control, sell it. Of course now you can get one for free by becoming a member of of the Freedom of Thought Foundation.

[slide] This was one of the early things of the male chauvinist society - it was called The Battle for Men's Minds, a book by William Sargent. Here is Dr. Sidney Gottlieb of the CIA. He was the guy who gave 147 different drugs to people. John Marks in The Search for the Manchurian Candidate or the Church Committee Reports cover him pretty well. He is a scientist, a doctor. And of course we know about Timothy Leary who is a psychologist, he is the producer of the flower generation, the psychedelic sixties and the slogan "turn on, tune in, drop out" - he worked with Henry Luce and the CIA to turn on the generation known as the Baby Boomers. When I asked Leary if he was witting or unwitting when he got his LSD from the CIA, he said, "Who you would work for - the Yankees or the Dodgers? You want me to work for the KGB?"

[slide] This is a blank slide in memory of Dr. Frank Olson who flew, jumped, or otherwise exited from the 16th floor of the Pennsylvania Hotel in New York City back in the 1950's, and Olson's family was paid $750,000 wrongful death - the federal courts claim act keeps you from suing the government for wrongful death - but it turned out, after the autopsy - the family exhumed the body of Olson - his skull was fractured before he was thrown out the window. He was killed before he was thrown out the window. They probably just laced him with LSD. He was an Edgewood Arsenal chemist and he had qualms about dosing people agains their will and without their knowledge at Edgewood. So they killed him and threw him out the window and made it look like a suicide. Now the family is suing under a different law, and maybe they will get some real money out of this - the culprits should be prosecuted, but we can't prosecute anybody until we - what are we going to do? Repeal the National Security Act and then give everybody amnesty? Man, there's a lot of criminals, a lot of murderers.

[slide] This is Harold Blauer I used to make a joke, on his ass before the government put him there forever. He was a tennis pro. He was given an overdose of a mescaline derivative by the CIA. Every minute of his death is chronicled in cold blood descriptions in their classified files. You can find it verbatim in Operation Mind Control. Like Olson's family Blauer's family received a quarter of a million dollars from Uncle Sam, but they are suing again because he was a private citizen. He didn't sign up.

Now you get the idea right? If you sign up for the government, you're going to give your life for the country. The National Security Act suspends all your civil rights, you get it? After you've given your life for the country, since they didn't need you to survive, they're going to use anything you've got - your body parts, your mind, your soul, anything. That's the way the game is played. Most of the victims of mind control are government related. May 2nd or 3rd generation. Our files contain very detailed debriefings, drawings, sketches of high ranking CIA officials' daughters. Now why would they do this to this person who is now a very competent secretary, and who has been harassed and tortured since she was a small child by some incredible technology that is more advanced ... since she is not one of the DID kind. This is really incredible.

But of course Walter Reed is a place where they program people and ... this story. I just got this recently from Blanche I think, "Sing a Song to Jenny", it's the true account of a secret US raid into China. In 1978 I am in San Francisco doing a talk show for KPIX TV - normally they bus in women's clubs and there I was, the bus broke down, and I am left with nothing but the phone lines which was fortuitous because a Commander in the Navy called and said, "I was on the Black Pajama team working behind ... and they sent us to Walter Reed and now we all have cardboard memories." And this is the story of one guy, not the same guy I think that I talked to, but this is probably the same story of mind control soldiers operating behind enemy lines.

The CIA documents ... to create an involuntary assassin. That was in the seventies, and that was published. That's one of the English editions of Operation Mind Control. That one is worth $650 on the used book market. This is The Mind Manipulators by Alan Scheflin, it came out a year later. Journey Into Madness, Gordon Thomas ... he is Irish and to me, kind of thinks like an Irishman, 'why mess up a good story with the truth?' so he takes wild flights of probably untruth ... but he does cover Ewen Cameron's experiments in Canada very well, and it's good for that. Of course, as a result of Ewen Cameron's experiments, they paid off pretty heavy to the families up there. These people weren't in our government, and Cameron was working under the payroll of the CIA for a long time, doing the experiments for the CIA. Cameron was at the same time the President of the American Psychiatric Association and he was the head shrink for the Nuremburg Trial. You can see the connection with psychiatry ... that's probably why psychiatry stopped dead in the water, probably why it doesn't work, what they are trying to do. And of course, it was useless. We just spent fifty years and how many millions and billions of dollars, and we didn't come up with anything.

David Ferrie was a hypnotist, he was a pilot for the CIA and he was probably the guy who was an on the scene handler for Lee Harvey Oswald, who was probably just a patsy. He said he was a patsy. They ran a CSE on his statement and it appeared to be true, and believe it or not, stress free. So he looks like just a patsy. But David Ferrie had false eyebrows, a wig ... strange dude.

This is another victim of mind control, he was programmed. He was a White Russian. George de Mohrenschildt is his name and he was a friend of Lee Harvey Oswald and Marina Oswald. A friend of mine, Eddie Epstein, was interviewing him for Time Magazine and they took a break for lunch and Oswald got a phone call, and simply said "I understand". Then he took a gun and killed himself. Bang. Just like the Manchurian Candidate. His family believes that's what happened.

This is Luis Enjarocasetio (sp) an attempted assassin of Ferdinand Marcos in the Phillipines. He was arrested by the Phillipine National Bureau of Investigation, the equivalent of the FBI. They called in, unlike in the USA where nobody believes this could happen, those guys called in a hypnotist and began to deprogram this guy. They found four different identities when he was in custody. He had 40 hypnotic sessions from April 3 to June 25, 1967. He displayed four distinct personalities. He was put into a trance and given an empty pistol. In the first personality he would follow whoever was talking with the pistol, pulling the trigger over and over. In the second personality he would aim only at the picture of Marcos and pull the trigger over and over. In the third personality he would end up falling off the table to the floor and remain motionless. The report said, in the last state, a "pathetic sight takes place - the subject turns the pistol to his own temple and squeezes the trigger as many times as his name is repeated."

Notice his clothes. He's got this little sweater kind of thing, notice his haircut, general look. When Sirhan was arrested, the same kind of thing. The interesting thing is that they both had diaries, they both left underlinings. They both repeated things and kind of chanted their program. They both predicted before the crime that they were going to do this.

Sirhan is arrowed. The other guy is Spanish, some kind of Hispanic background. They look enough alike to be brothers. Castile believed that a guy that sounds like Allen Dulles was his father. You find this in the programming. These sadistic jokes are played. Sirhan as you know was programmed to kill Robert Kennedy, and did apparently, shot at him, was in the room anyway. When in custody, he was visited by Dr. Bernard Diamond, shown here, who was hired by the defence, and Diamond is an expert in hypnosis and defence. He thought immediately that Sirhan had been programmed by the way he responded to hypnotic command. At one point he put him in deep trance, and he found that he couldn't speak, but he could write answers. Here's the way it went. He showed him a page of his diary and asked, "is this crazy writing?" "Yes, Yes, Yes," Sirhan wrote. "Are you crazy?" Diamond asked. "No, No, No," Sirhan wrote. "Well, why are you writing crazy?" Diamond asked. "Practice, Practice, Practice," Sirhan wrote. "Practice for what?" Diamond asked. "Mind control, Mind control, Mind control," is what Sirhan wrote.

Here's a guy who did a lot of our work, funded by the CIA through the National Institute of Mental Health. The CIA gave the money to NIMH who gave the money to Harvard University who gave the money to Jose Delgado, famous neurologist who back in the 50's and 60's did a lot of amazing work. He went before Congress I think in 1962 or 1963, and it's in the Congressional Record, and he called for a "Psychocivilized Society" in which everybody would have an electrode implanted in their brain and it would be for the benefit of us all. I know a little kid, he's 15 years old, he's a cyberpunk, and he can't wait to have that because he wants to know the baseball scores. He says "why do I have to remember all this?"

There's a stimoceiver transmitter and receiver in the brain of the bull at the right place and the bull didn't even really attack. That's a puny bull if you ask me, and Delgado looks like a real chicken and he's backing up. He has the cape but he doesn't have the sword and he has the radio transmitter and then the bull gets to a certain point and he pushes a button, and the thing goes into reverse. I mean it was unbelievable, and you can get that. I have seen it even on educational television shows ... A&E did this, it was called "The Bad Trip to Edgewood." That's the headquarters at Edgewood Arsenal, Fort Detrick, Maryland. They started out with monkeys of course. They tried everything ... they started out with gas and injections and that led to human experimentation.

See that mouse and the cat ... that's a famous thing from the sixties. Here's a cat on LSD. This cat is afraid of these mice, and it keeps leaping away. It's unbelievable to see that, and it's a famous experiment. They used a lot of LSD. Of course they cornered the market. I think they went to Sandoz Labs and bought every existing dose of LSD.

SUPPRESSED INTELLIGENCE REPORTS

This guy, Bill Jordan, is a medical "volunteer" and he was a Lt-Colonel —he was probably the highest ranking volunteer. They thought they were going to get gas or something, tear gas — they gave him 100x the normal dose of LSD and these guys now 40 years later are still walking around having flashbacks, epileptic seizures. They gave huge doses — 7000 men were given LSD in these huge doses between 1955 and 1975.

This guy is Col. James Ketchum who was the Army psychiatrist who ran it. Ketchum revealed to Bill Kurtis, who was the A&E anchorman, that they had tested BZ which puts the test subject into a 3 day stupor and is followed by memory loss. They were interested in anything to induce amnesia. One of the test subjects did try to sue the government and he got to the Supreme Court and was turned down because of the Federal Torts Claims Act. But the dissenting opinion of the judges compared the Edgewood experiments to the Nazi experiments of WWII. This is on record. Col. Ketchum didn't take it all that seriously. He said "Most of the volunteers thought of it as an interesting adventure. Many volunteered to do it again." While these injections were going on, other things were being done.

In Lexington, Kentucky (Lexington is a federal "drug rehabilitation" - I don't think there is such a thing as rehabilitation in the prison system these days - there is no concept of it. But in those days they still called it a drug rehabilitation project). They would give them rewards of heroin if they would take LSD and other things. Here's a guy in such a stupor, he can't sit down. This guy starts out early on playing solitaire, pretty soon the cards are all over the table, and he is just a mess. This guy I think is counting spiders on the wall that he thinks are there. This guy is breathing some gas that they measure and then they filled the whole room with BZ or psychotoxic gas then they would put the guy in this suit and see if the suit protected him. Of course they started out with animals. This fellow says it made him violent. It changed his personality and he hasn't had a relationship with his family for 30 years because of it.

Of course that's what they wanted to do. BZ and some of these other drugs were known to produce a violent reaction. One of the things they experimented with was PCP, angel dust, which is now "an underground recreational illegal drug". This is a group of soldiers walking through a cloud of BZ and it brings to mind some eerie scenes from a movie I would recommend that you rent from the video store, called "Jacob's Ladder". This is a movie that is really about the Buddhist afterlife, the guy is already dead. He was part of the Army BZ experiments and he is reliving his life which did take place in Vietnam. It looks very much like this, they reproduced in the movie the whole feeling of this kind of monstrous experimentation.

Of course, here is Richard Helms, and here he is lying to the President's Commission on the assassination of President Kennedy which was one of his first big lies that was documented. Then he went on to lie to Congress and that's when he got sentenced to some time for that. Here's something from Defence Intelligence Agency Report Task #T72-01-14: "Parapsychology can be harnessed to create conditions where one can alter and manipulate the minds of others." This is from Hans Ulrich Dresch, he's a PhD who works in an alcohol rehabilitation program today, and he was a victim of mind control. He was actually an American citizen, but he was born over there of military parents and raised there. He was used in some kind of mind control experiments. Since he is a psychologist, he talks about all those things -MPD, hypnosis, drugs, and all the other stuff. This can be found on the internet and it's probably 40-50 pages long.

This is Alan Frey's early research when he was with G.E. and it's the "Human Auditory

System Response to Elctromagnetic Energy" - in other words, "we are going to put voices in your head" by remote control from a distance. And that was in the 60's, and Ross Adey is another guy who did the research - he was at University of California, Riverside, and he did a lot of research on modulating microwaves so you would hear a voice from a distance. There's a guy in New Mexico who is in Operation Mind Control who will sell you a microwave you can keep in a paper bag. It's about the size of a radar gun. You can buy them now over the counter. Q. is that kind of mind control technology used to discredit the individual, or is it actually used for programming. I would say both. I would say the number one thing is programming because if you take all the technology - drugs, hypnosis - all this electronic stuff - if you take it away the human mind is still the human mind and it works the same way. Basically you can explain that by understanding the subconscious. A lot of it happens over a long period of time. I don't know about 20 years, but I know about 10 years.

Here's another one. Spontaneous regression. This was way before the New Age thing of regression, past life regression. The military and the government were researching this thing. This guy Schneck - this was from State University of New York College of Medicine - a CIA project funded it - and they knew damn well what a powerful regression was. Even if it is just a metaphor.

The father of all this stuff - the greatest mind about hypnosis - and a guy who also worked for the government - was Milton Erickson. When I interviewed him he talked very slowly - you could go into trance just listening to him in a warm room. But I liked him a lot, and of course he is the main model for what is now known as neurolinguistic programming. He had polio so he could not interact with people and he watched how they communicated, and out of that came this beautiful science which is used in computers. "The use of hypnosis in intelligence and related military situations" by Seymour Fischer (sp) 1958 - a declassified CIA document. "The use of hypnosis in warfare" by Alec McQuart, unclassified, it's in the open literature. "Experimenting with the possible antisocial uses of hypnosis" by Milton Erickson. He said there is no problem to it, all you have to do basically is to manipulate context and get an individual to do something against their will and without their knowledge. It was done in a laboratory in a government study where a soldier was made to attack his commanding officer. All they had to say was "this is WWII - this guy is a Japanese guy - it is kill or be killed". They didn't know he had a knife in his boot but luckily they had two armed guards standing there.

This is "Assassination in Hypnosis: political influence" by Joseph Berndt in 1968, after the Kennedy assassination. "Rewriting the Soul" by Ian Hacking, Canadian. He's a sociologist so parts of it aren't correct but it's really interesting to read this different point of view, and he tells some anecdotes about Colin Ross that are pretty good. Elaine Pagel's a friend of mine who did the Nag Hammadi texts and anybody who has had satanic ritual abuse should probably read this book and understand the origin of satan and understand how deeply rooted it is in our society, in Judeao Christian Aristotelian philosphy. This is Mikey's paper, "Mind War". You know Mikey? Yeah, Michael Aquino. This is his very own handwriting. It is the headquarters of the Imperial Storm Trooper Force Office of the Chief of Staff, Mind War Center, Hub 4, and it's the final version of an article going to the military review, "Parameters", which is a war course journal psyops community - the head of which is near my home town in Arizona. He was just then a Major, and he talks about John Alexander's military review and psyops and stuff, and what gave me the creeps is #11 - he cites Operation Mind Control as a source. That gave me a chill. Here he is when he was reviewed for a possible adverse - they are going to throw him out of the Army for molesting children at the Presidio - and of course they couldn't prove he did it, but they couldn't prove he didn't do it - they did a weird thing which they can only do in military law. They didn't acquit him, but they didn't convict him. They just said "we are going to gather more evidence" and of course they are still gathering evidence.

So here he is, a satanist, and high ranking guy - he retired from the military. People raised a stink about it, but the Pentagon says no problem, there's a guy buried in Arlington from the Civil War who is a satanist. This is freedom of religion.

And of course, cybernetics, Norbert Weiner, "Control and Communication in the animal and the machine". The father of cyberpunk. And of course the Russians were of course very good at this and they know what obedience to authority means. Let me tell you a little bit about this guy. He's a member of the KGB, head guy, Vladimir Zukov, a KGB parapsychologist. He's an adept at telepathic hypnosis, a psychic who was especially trained to use a variety of instruments to affect other people's minds at a distance, if you can believe it.

This is part of the history. We are coming to the end. The only success story of that kind of psychotronic warfare is this chess match between Karpov and Korchnoy and Karpov was the darling 27 year old chess champion and Korchnoy was the former chess champion that had defected to the West, so they wanted to make sure Korchnoy lost. Korchnoy, after the thing was over, says he tried to get this guy removed and he complained and complained. He said "he forced me to make bluffs I didn't want to make, he forced me not to play strong. It was Zukov and the powers of mind control that led to my loss." And it was a prestigious international victory for Karpov and Soviety parapsychology.

Here's a photo of Dr. Karl Nakaliev at work in a laboratory on a crystal ball - it's a psychotronic device which allegedly focused the mind in what is called biocomm-unication. The Soviets took it seriously and developed it to a reliable degree and of course our controlled remote viewing is the same kind of thing where we put something that has been generalized and non-specific and unscientific and we disciplined it.

Here are psychotronic devices - the mind concentrates and spins that little wheel. It's from a movie and it's available from A&E. Uri Geller did that for the Stanford Research Institute and Ingo Swann. These are psychotronic devices - they are really interesting. They are not a dental tool, not a sculpture tool, not a kitchen tool - they are used like magic wands to focus energy and direct the mind. This guy is the leading Soviet parapsychologist - when he would do stuff like that, they were measuring his brainwaves so they could duplicate his results. Now we did similar things. One of the most interesting studies the USA did was to measure the brainwaves of people with Multiple Personalities, put them into different personalities, and measure their brainwaves. Each personality had a different brainwave pattern. They then recorded these patterns and sent them to another shrink on the west coast. They then sent the subject to that shrink and told the shrink to play these signals back. I don't know if they played them auditorally — I think so. They stimulated the personalities by playing back the brain wave signals.

This is a psychotronic factory where they are making psychotronic weapons in the Soviet Union and the parabolic mirror looks like ... you can become your own CNN. You know they were seriously doing this - it's not just those of you who have experienced some of this stuff. But these are for you who want to tinker and build your own - take a look at this one. Non lethal weapons, being sold, being promoted in this country for law enforcement and it is the most dangerous step we can take. That kind of psychotronic weaponry or any of the other nonlethal weaponry, especially since the military people and the law enforcement people will be the first targets of it. The term nonlethal is a misnomer because they are lethal.

You know this guy - Dr. Becker. Most of the stuff he talks about is obsolete but it's a must read if you are a serious student of this stuff. Here's a picture of the transponder. Everyone is claiming about having implants. Most of the people who claim they have them are claiming they are from extraterrestrial sources. These are terrestrial implants.

This is a 1960's technology. They have different sizes - small, medium, large. They have some for goats, pigs, dogs. You can buy them from your veterinary store. This is a small one. That's the tip of a guy's finger. That is the electronic technology.

This is all obsolete. Nanotechnology is where it's at. Talk about implants -they don't have to do that stuff. If you want to transplant a transponder in somebody it's going to be the size of a molecule and it's going to be run on an energy source that will last more than a human's lifetime. You will be dead, your body will be decayed and that thing will still be sending off the signals. Nanotechnology is where it presently is at ...

They were talking about putting them in teenagers with the idea of tracking them.

This is Dr. Gwen Deans' comparison between thought reform on the left which is Lifton stuff, ritualized abuse in the middle, and abduction on the right. This is one of her earlier things. There is a bigger one I've got in the slides and we are going skip it ... but this gives you the essence of the thing. First, trivial demands are enforced - the middle one says "must learn cult rules". What you are seeing in the phenomena, the experiences of these individuals who talk about government mind control, or thought reform, or ritualized abuse or abductions is the same thing. Hundreds of reports.

Back to the shrinks. Sidney - Francis Crick, Nobel Prize. Says he found the human soul - the guy's an idiot. But this is the problem with our science. This guy won the Nobel Prize, discovered DNA, but he has no right to talk about the human soul. It's a theological question.

Microwave harassment and mind control experimentation by Julianne McKinney. She was involved in the harassment program which is now defunct. Cheryl Welsh and other folks ... that's Ed Light who runs the Mind Control Forum. These people were on CNN, got a hatchet job when they came out, and of course they didn't find any signals ... they came out with all this instrumentation to measure the environment and they found all kinds of pollution in the environment but this is the normal pollution, and of course it had nothing to do with what they were saying. The scientist said we could find nothing - no reason why these people should be complaining - like Ed is complaining here of the sounds, the hurt, the pain, perhaps voices in his head. Try to tell somebody you are hearing voices in your head. Every time you are making love to your husband there's the voice telling you how to do it, how you are doing it wrong - at the most intimate times in your life there's a voice talking to you. When you are sleeping there are voices talking to you, lights shining at you, 24 hrs a day, year after year. You go to a doctor. He looks it up in his manual - and he says "delusional" or "you're a paranoid schizophrenic". There are only four basic things -hearing voices is only in there four times basically. And then they give you a drug and suppress the symptoms. What does that do?

You know about the radiation experiments. A lot of the mind control victims were used in the radiation experiments. Many of them have Graves disease, lost their thyroids and because mind control victims don't talk or they can be stopped from talking. So they were used in that. At the end of the President's thing on radiation, "Trance on Trial" Alan Scheflin's book -they don't believe in hypnosis, you can't be made to do something against your will in the courts of law. They just don't recognize anybody who has ever had hypnosis. They are discredited as witnesses. It's like a bunch of simpletons.

Multiple personality disorder and criminal responsibility. Very important document written by a UCLA law professor - Ellen Saks. You need that. You need to read that. It's a long thing.

Q. DSM IV has a new options book and there is a category called "Spiritual Problems" - it's the first time that the DSM committee acknowledged that there is something called a spiritual problem. They are defining it in four sentences unfortunately. The proposal was 11 pages. It was a miracle that they accepted it. What they are saying is when there are actual spiritual experiences that are going on right now and are not in alignment with our previous religious experience. I would advise somebody if they are going to go see somebody in the medical field, to refer to that.

This is Robert Moodie and his brother, they look like twins. This man is on death row right now. I am his only link to the outside world. He is diagnosed MPD, DID. I worked with him before he could even get that diagnosis because the aliens' voices in his mind told him to do "choo-choo train" on the test so he would do true, true, false - true, true, false -choo-choo train - and they couldn't get any proof. Psychiatrist got up in court and said he is malingering. But a couple of them said you'd better rule out DID, this, that and the other thing. The judge just said "I'm not going to rule it out." They put him in the nut house for six months and they couldn't do anything with him. He came back and he still wasn't competent to stand trial. He was insane at the time of the crime. And the whole thing about DID and the law has to be re-examined and re-structured.

Here's a guy - I began to work with him. There's Mary, there's Bob. See if you can see some of the changes in him. You can do it in the film, you can really see it. That's the killer personality. His name was XE. He was programmed in a Marine Corps - killed two women in Arizona. He is sentenced to die after his four appeals are exhausted. Anybody want to write to him ... This is Dr. Joyce Vesper who thanks to Colin Ross, we finally found a doctor in Arizona - she is the Arizona Director of the ISSD and she came forward, gave him a five hours of tests, looked at 200 hours of sample videotapes we had taken of this guy. He turned into a little kid. When the Miranda warnings were read to Moodie, he was a nine year old, he didn't know his name. The reason they caught him is he turned himself in to this Sheriff's department saying "run my fingerprints, I don't know who I am". He had a picture of a little girl in his pocket. That was his daughter. He didn't know who she was. He was in amnestic fugue. It's not justice - it's got to change. You can get hit on the head, something else can happen to you, and suddenly you are on death row. It's not the way you treat people.

This is a novel by Michael Youssef, "The Voice" and it's about the voice of satan in a christian preacher of some kind.

Dr. Sheldon Deal looked at - Patrick Flanagan created a thing called the neurophone which proves that somebody can be deaf, their cochleas taken out and they can still hear with this thing. Nick Begitch will tell you more about this thing. There are some incredible therapeutic effects with this thing - that's what Dr. Deal did a study - hearing people can hear a conscious sound and then this thing kind of plays it to your bones, I guess, to the other part of your ear. Begitch will explain it to you. I have known this guy for 30 years. He's a naturopath, holistic healing, used to Mr. Arizona and stuff. Wonderful guy, serious researcher.

Voices in the head - a famous Philip K. Dick novel about VALIS - Vast Active Living System. This is Jack Sarfatiks' physics group talking about VALIS and conscious computer space-craft from the future, time travel, and all that kind of thing, which is coming up fairly prominently in quantum physics. Of course there is something now called post-quantum physics and there are sub-atomic particles called beables - and you had better familiarize yourself with that.

In the 1950's it began - the new science - and the University of Arizona was going to be the first university in America with a chair for this new science, called Cognitive Science, the study of consciousness. This year in April there's a conference discussing this - psychologists, psychiatrists, neurologists, linguists, cyberneticists, theologists, philosophers - all getting together to talk on that topic. Heavy on the computer thing, artificial intelligence is very important. But it all started in the fifties.

J.B. Ryan, Duke University, 1950's - CIA project in extrasensory perception. They are the guys who used the Zener cards that you saw in Ghostbusters. Very important studies. Denied by the CIA. They said "we spent so much money and nothing happened". Don't believe it.

Now they admit - remote viewers even - that's pretty far out. Astral projections, out of body experiences - now it's called controlled remote viewing. I like this book a lot - Dave Morehouse - seems like an honest guy - talking about his experience in the remote viewing thing. The CIA finally admitted it, but here it is in 1975 in a press release telling you all about it. So it's been known that far back - but 1996 they admitted to it.

Here's John Mack, thanks to Blanche, a little thing about John Mack at Harvard, talking about UFO's - working with Lifton. And there's John Shirley, talking about hypnosis. There was a serious study about alien aspects done at MIT and one of the papers in here talks about - they found out that the so-called abductee community was highly dissociative. So the same thing you find in ritual abuse, you find in mind control, you find in alien abductees. And of course, for the first time now, people are beginning to say "yeah I do remember there was a government guy standing around with those little grey things". And of course how many survivors have been asked not to talk about their "alien experiences"? About three years ago I asked that question, and just about everyone I could identify as a survivor raised their hand. They have been told not to talk about it, because it discredits their credibility. They are already telling pretty fantastic tales, you know. There is nobody talking about the Lori Lingenfelter story, or even Cathy O'Brien doesn't talk a lot about her NASA training - but Lingenfelter says that she was trained to be a hostage "witness" - a specially hypnotically trained witness on some kind of an alien ship in a swap deal you know. Incredible stories, but it's worth checking out.

Here is Dr. Dean who did the comparison accounts with ritual maltreatments and ritual abduction, and this is the appendix E in Operation Mind Control. It is just amazing to me to find everybody talking about the same thing in slightly different variations.

Of course on the fiftieth anniversary of the so-called Roswell thing comes out and says yeah I was the guy who placed all the high technology into the R&D stream of the defence developers. He talks about the skin of the craft, the propulsion system, night vision goggles. One thing he doesn't talk about and admits they were there - mind control devices on the ship allegedly, but he doesn't talk about it. His movement away from that, his sudden avoidance of that subject, is to me what gives credibility to this account. You wouldn't talk about it if you were using it the way it apparently was being used. They had a headband that blew the graph, and stuff, he says.

If you read the report from Iron Mountain, you realize how to motivate an economy without war can be a very difficult problem, so there is the Green movement, the ecology movement. Space exploratiion - a bottomless pit. You can sink a lot of money into that but the best motivator is to pose an outside threat of alien invasion. How are they doing? Only 55% don't believe in UFO's in a CNN poll in 1997. Are there visitors from space? 60% don't believe it. They are not doing so well in planting that idea.

This is an implant ... I don't know if you can see it ... it comes from UFO community. It is quite a bit different than the one we showed before, that is actually in production.

You have to read about physics so you might as well start with Tim Allen, it's a pretty good book on basic quantum physics.

Michael Persinger, a neuroscientist in Laurentian University in Sudbury, Ontario is blind-folding people and putting an automobile with selanoids and playing magnetic waves over their temporal lobes, and 80% of the women he claims have temporal lobe epileptic experiences automatically, frequently from time to time throughout their lives. This guy was funded by the NSA ... (Q. he is funded by the US Navy ...). Well you know what he's doing? He is saying that UFO's are electrical phenomena from earthquakes and he's demonstrating, beyond question, that your consciousness can be altered and controlled at a distance, without breaking your skin. It is very transparent though, in the research papers and in his conclusions, his conclusions don't match his arguments. It is pretty obvious. But what he is demonstrating is that a person can be influenced by magnetic waves from a distance, remotely. That's amazing, that he is standing out there doing that ... I don't believe a word the guy says.

The physics of immortality - a must read - Frank Tepler. He says you can find God in the codes and stuff like that. And this is a wonderful thing -hard to find - out of print - Elizabeth Rauscher, she worked with Andreja Puharich, for a while. She has done a lot of government contracts. Electromagentic Phenomena in Complex Geometries and Non-Linear Phenomena, Non-Hurtzian Waves and Magnetics Monopoles. The whole layout of the questions that you've got for "can it be?" Yes it can be and it has been, and it is being.

Then there is Rupert Sheldrake - if you talk to physicists they will say don't pay attention to him - he is only a biologist. Physicists say we make the machines for the doctors, and we only put two buttons on them, one is "off" and the other is "on" ... that's all they can handle. They don't consider doctors scientists ... But this is a very interesting idea, if you know about morphogenic fields. These guys are a hoot, and they are on the internet - Jack Zarfatti, Paul and Fred Allen Wolf - all of them write books and stuff. They are talking about supraluminals, faster than light travel. The answers to your questions about "what's happening to me?" including Carl Preberim, he's a neurologist - he talks about DID/MPD on a subatomic level -and that's the only way to address the question. It reads just like NLP, what he's talking about - the way the tunnelling occurs - and it's pretty amazing. So physics is where it's gotta go ... I don't have time - but if you want some real understanding of the mechanics of what is going on and what you are going to face in the future - because this new technology -once you've been targeted as a guinea pig - it's not going to stop until you stop it, or we stop it. PQM means post quantum mechanics.

That's the answer right there - the microtubule - when I first saw it, it was drawn by Dr. Stewart Amiroff in his scribbling way - it was black and white and it looked like yin and yang - and I said, "wow, it's an on and off switch" 1 is 1, 1 is 0. In the cytoskeleton of the DNA which is that structure of your DNA, it's made up of things that look like pomegranate pods represented by the red and the blue. 1 is a +1 and 1 is a 0, just like a computer. They are programmable by a signal but there's a back way, a feedback phenomenon that is occurring. We don't know what the signal is yet, they haven't decided what that is, the signal of consciousness ... but this is where they are at. In this kind of thinking lies the answer to some of the things that people are thinking. Whether or not it is just a metaphorical paradigm shift that we are experiencing and anthropomorphizing and living out ... or in fact ... as I believe ... somebody understands how to use that or they are dabbling with it. Microtubules in the cytoskeleton of DNA.

New World Vistas and the Space Powers - some of you already know about this ... 13 volumes published by the Air Force. They predict that within the next 50 years, and if they are saying this that means they have already done it ... we are going to have a been there, done that learning technology. Did you ever see the movie, Brain Storm? Rent it, see it. That's what they are talking about. They have probably already got it. Whereas you wear a helmet, record your experience on some kind of medium, play it back to the other guy, the other guy has the taste, touch, smell, sound, sight of the other person as it is happening.

So that's the answer to me. That's what we have to do.

High-Tech Slavery

Mind Control Slavery and the New World Order by Uri Dowbenko

New Improved Entertainment Corp.

PO Box 43

Pray, Montana 59065, USA

High-tech slavery is alive and well on planet Earth. Ever since World War II when the United States Government's Project Paperclip sponsored the resettlement of about 2,000 high-level Nazis in the United States, the technology of mind-control programming has advanced rapidly.

"The Germans under the Nazi government began to do serious scientific research into trauma-based mind control," write Fritz Springmeier and Cisco Wheeler in their book, The Illuminati Formula used to create an Undetectable Total Mind Controlled Slave. "Under the auspices of the Kaiser Wilhelm Medical Institute in Berlin, Josef Mengele conducted mind-control research on thousands of twins and thousands of other hapless victims."

Mengele, known as "the Angel of Death", was one of the approximately 900 military scientists and medical researchers secretly exfiltrated into the United States, where he continued his 'research' and trained others in the black arts of mind control. This work in behaviour manipulation was later incorporated into the CIA's projects Bluebird and Artichoke which, in 1953, became the notorious MKULTRA. The CIA claims that these programs were discontinued, but there is no credible evidence that "The Search for the Manchurian Candidate" (the title of the definitive book by John Marks) ever ceased.

In fact, Captain John McCarthy, US Army Special Forces (Ret.), who ran CIA assassination teams out of Saigon during the Vietnam War, told his friend, LAPD whistleblower Mike Ruppert, that "MKULTRA is a CIA acronym that officially stands for 'Manufacturing Killers Utilizing Lethal Tradecraft Requiring Assassinations'". Thus the CIA's official obsession with producing programmed killers through the MKULTRA contained more than 149 sub-programs in fields ranging from biology, pharmacology, psychology to laser physics and ESP.

More recently, new evidence points to the continuous use of so-called trauma-based programming techniques to accomplish the same goal. This includes the deliberate induction of Multiple Personality Disorder (MPD) in involuntary human subjects - in essence, human guinea pigs.

MPD has been reclassified by the American Psychiatric Association as Dissociative Identity Disorder (DID). The psychiatrists' bible, the Diagnostic and Statistical Manual (DSM-IV, p. 487), characterises it by:

A. The presence of two or more distinct personality states;

B. At least two of these identities or personality states recurrently take control of the person's behaviour;

C. Inability to recall important personal information that is too extensive to be explained by ordinary forgetfulness;

D. The disturbance is not due to the direct physiological effects of a substance or a general medical condition.

No matter what name is assigned to the problem, however, to create this condition by conscious intent is an atrocity so depraved that trauma-based mind-control programming remains the de facto Secret Holocaust of the 20th century. Known as the Monarch Project, it has been verified and corroborated by numerous survivors like Cathy O'Brien, author of TranceFormation of America, Brice Taylor, author of Starshine, and K. Sullivan, author of MK. No paper trail has been found which leads from the CIA's MKULTRA program to the Monarch Project - a catchword for mind control which involves US military, CIA, NASA and other government agencies.

The Franklin Cover-up, attorney John W. DeCamp's groundbreaking book about high-level pedophilia, also describes the sordid details of Monarch. "Drugs are not the deepest level of government-sponsored evil," he writes. "I think the lowest level of Hell is reserved for those who conjured up and carried out the 'Monarch Project'. 'Monarch' refers to young people in America who were victims of mind-control experiments run either by US government agencies such as CIA or military intelligence agencies."

DeCamp's client, Monarch abuse survivor Paul Bonacci, has a story which parallels the victimology of O'Brien, Taylor and Sullivan - an extensive cross-corroboration of perpetrators and their methodology. It's simply "the production of a horde of children in whom the soul is crushed, who would spy, whore, kill and commit suicide", in the words of investigative reporter Anton Chaitkin, quoted by DeCamp in his book.

Recovering Monarch victims speak of ongoing trauma through "ritual abuse", also known as "satanic ritual abuse" because of the identifiable iconography of a belief structure associated with Satanism or Luciferianism. By using drugs, hypnosis, torture and electroshock, the Monarch criminal perpetrators have produced new and succeeding generations of victims.

This is not science fiction, but science fact. MPD involves the creation of personality "alters": alternative personalities or personality fragments which can be used for specific tasks - usually for illegal activities like delivering drugs or other black-market activities (mules), messages (couriers) or killings (assassins). These alters, or soul fragments, are segregated and compartmentalised within the victim's mind by the repeated use of stun guns, drugs and hypnosis, which isolates the memories of their experiences.

An alter can be accessed by anyone who knows the "codes" or "triggers". These triggers, which induce an altered or trance state in a programmed victim, can be anything including telephone tones, nursery rhymes, dialogue from certain movies or hand signals.

According to Springmeier and Wheeler, whose 468-page book has become a reference in the field, "...the basis for the success of the Monarch mind-control programming is that different personalities or personality parts called 'alters' can be created who do not know each other, but who can take the body at different times. The amnesia walls that are built by traumas form a protective shield of secrecy that prevents the abusers from being found out and prevents the front personalities who hold the body much of the time to know how their system of alters is being used."

The mind-control programming, however, has not worked according to plan. In fact, the perpetrators, in their arrogance and hubris, never dreamed that their methods could fail. The retrieval of survivors' photographic-like memories of actual abuse incidents, including images, sounds and smells, constitutes a major exposure of human rights abuses. These victims bear witness to the secret atrocities of the so-called New World Order.

MORE ON ILLUMINATI MIND CONTROL

According to John Coleman, author of Conspirators Hierarchy: The Committee of 300: "...the Illuminati is very much alive and well in America... Since the Illuminati is also known as Satanism, it must follow that the CIA was controlled by a Satanist while Dulles had charge of it. The same holds true for George Bush [a member of the Order of Skull and Bones].

"Given the ghastly mind-control experiments constantly being conducted by the CIA, and its past connections to fiendish monsters like Dr Campbell and Dr Sidney Gottlieb, it does not take much to conclude that the CIA follows satanic roads," Coleman concludes in his monograph, "Illuminati in America".

With regards to "the brainwashing capabilities of the Tavistock Institute as well as US Department of Defense projects like the Advanced Research Project Agency", Coleman writes that "...the bottom line of the projects is mind control as predicted by the book, The Technotronic Era, by Zbigniew Brzezinski. The project goes by the name 'Monarch Program' and it is a vast project involving not only the CIA but the Army, Air Force and Navy with all of their skills and vast resources."

SUPPRESSED INTELLIGENCE REPORTS

SULLIVAN'S TRAVELS

The horrific torture and sexual abuse of children, also called "satanic ritual abuse", has been a key component in the creation of mind-controlled slaves.

Mind-control survivor K. Sullivan has written an astounding book called MK, a fictionalised account of her life, which describes the world of multiple personalities. To her credit, Sullivan has been able to reconstruct from her memories the actual mechanics and methodology of going from one alter state to another. A programmed assassin and sex slave, Sullivan says she was abused and raped by Robert Maxwell, Henry Kissinger, George Bush and Billy Graham, among others. One of her controllers was deceased CIA operative James Jesus Angleton, who has been widely regarded as a KGB and Mossad asset.

In a recent interview, Sullivan spoke about her background as a "family-generational slave" to the elite and about her stepfather, now deceased, who was initially her primary programmer. His cover was a church-going, upstanding citizen, a professional mechanical and systems engineer with a curious interest in robotics.

"There were a number of people who trained, conditioned, then broke my will, broke my psyche and programmed me in different altered states," she said in a recent interview. "My father was the one who did me the most. He did it through terror. He did it through torture. He was a very brilliant man, and he seemed to enjoy doing it to me and other children."

Confirming that her father was "horribly abused as a child", Sullivan added: "I know that for certain. His father was a Welsh Druid who had been sold as a child to a ship captain who brought him over to the US. At least that's the mentality in my family, for slavery of children to be okay. I heard this from older family members. They've never denied it. But my grandfather was a covert Druid as well. I'm sure he brought the religion over with him. One of the things he would do is go to the graveyard near his house and dig up bodies, then take them into the basement and take them apart and have fun with them. And he also did rituals out in the woods sometimes at night. He would sacrifice babies. And I was exposed to that. So I'm sure my father was, too, which left him no other alternative but to become like his father."

And how is this behaviour related to Satanism or is it just generational child abuse?

"I think it's both," she answered slowly. "And what it boils down to is these people are doing illegal activities. Criminals tend to find criminals. They tend to gravitate toward each other. It's amazing how they can find each other out. My grandfather developed connections to the Mafia in our area. I understand it was the Colombo family. I don't know what he did exactly, but I do have one memory of riding in a cement truck where he and other drivers with cement trucks were using the cement from the trucks to bury several bodies. So I guess they just did whatever needed to be done. That was in New York and Pennsylvania. My father was an assassin as well as other things, and these people really enjoy killing people. He killed people more for favours than for hire. He got to have as many kids as he wanted to raise."

Her father also had CIA and NASA connections. "The CIA work seems to be rather covert. He worked for Western Electric and later on for AT&T," Sullivan said. "I found out, since then, that Western Electric has had very strong CIA ties. I have been able to go through some of his papers since his death in 1990, and I have found on his desk calendar for that year that he had several contacts with NASA. Since then I have remembered that there were several facilities that he took me to that were NASA facilities. The NASA connections seem to be directly connected to the Paperclip connection. The Nazis were brought into the country and then were integrated into the NASA structure after the war.

"My father, because of his Celtic background, had very low self-esteem," continued Sullivan. "Being exposed to some of these Nazi war criminals seemed to mean a whole lot to him because he had a mother that was German. Between the Celtic background and a German mother, these men built up his self-esteem as far as being Aryan. He very much identified with them, and I think, from what I understand, he got a lot of his training especially from one man I knew as Dr Schwartz. He had slightly wavy black hair and very dark eyes. He was slim. I can't say his height because I was just a child. He had a definite German accent. People called him Herr Doctor or Dr Schwartz, one of the two. Sometimes he was called Dr Black. He was a pedophile for sure and he was a very cold man. He liked to make kids think that they would feel safe with him, but he would do something that would upset the children and then they would be afraid of him after that."

MULTI-MODE PROGRAMMING

Sullivan said that she was used to sexually service both males and females in the Beta mode, and to do assassination, bodyguarding and intrusions in hostage situations in the Delta mode.

And what is Alpha, Beta, Delta and Theta programming?

"Alpha was the basis for all the other programs," she continued. "It seems to be where a lot of information was stored in my memory, in my mind, that was used by programmers to develop the other programs. It's where some of my more generic alter states were also stored. Beta was the sexual servicing part of me. They also sometimes called the alter state 'Barbie'. It was supposed to be named after Klaus Barbie." Like Barbie doll?

Survivors Cathy O'Brien and Brice Taylor were also subjected to Beta, or sex-slave, programming. They, like actress Marilyn Monroe, were called "presidential models", mind-controlled slaves for the use of high-level politicians.

According to Springmeier's book, "...in 1981, the New World Order made training films for their novice programmers. Monarch slave Cathy O'Brien was used to make the film How To Divide a Personality and How To Create a Sex Slave. Two Huntsville porn photographers were used to help NASA create these training films."

Sullivan recalled: "I was used both as a child and as an adult in those alter states, and I had more than one. In those alter states I would not resist. I had no anger. I was an absolute sexual slave and I would do whatever I was told to do."

Delta programming is military-assassin programming that has trickled into popular consciousness through movies like La Femme Nikita, its American remake, Point of No Return, and The Long Kiss Goodnight.

Regarding the Delta programming, Sullivan said: "...it was when I was used to do hits, kills, and also bodyguarding and hostage extraction. I had a great number of alter personalities that had specialised training and had different modes to do different things."

Why was the training kept separate for different alters?

"Part of it was so I wouldn't recall too much at any one time - if I did start to remember," she said. "And also because they hand-pick each part out for a certain type of situation. If you had a part coming out that was very loyal to people that that part was bodyguarding, you don't want that part going off and killing somebody. And you don't want a part that's specifically programmed to kill coming out and feeling sorry for the target. So you have to keep the emotions and the motives separate as well. And so that's why they had to have different parts."

Sullivan's description of Theta programming seems to correlate with the development and use of so-called extrasensory powers and extraphysical abilities.

"Theta was where they used - I don't like the word 'psychic' because I think it's been so misused - thought energy," she said. "I just knew it as magnetic-type energy from the individual to do a number of different things that they were experimenting with, including long-distance mind connection with other people - even in other countries. I guess you would call it 'remote viewing' - where I could see what a person was doing in another state in a room or something like that.

"It was both actual programming and experimentation. Because what they did -they kept it encapsulated in several parts of me, several altered states. It was a lot of training, a lot of experimentation."

Theta programming also implies the use of thought energy to kill someone at a distance.

"A lot of times I ran across other victims with Theta programming," Sullivan said in a recent CKLN radio interview. "One of the movie and book themes they used extensively was Dune, by Frank Herbert. It won't be too hard to figure because what they taught us was that we could cause things to happen to other people. It was to build up rage inside. It would come out in a form of pure energy that would hit them... They had talked about people imploding internally in their digestive organs. I don't know because I can't see what goes on inside another body, but I do know that it does work."

The calculated admixture of doing good and evil seems to be a hallmark of the Illuminati methodology. It's as if they recognise, at a spiritual level, that all the horrible karma they create can be balanced by generous philanthropic gestures; for example, giving a billion dollars to the United Nations, or other feats of extraordinary compassion.

"Also, they tried to use me for hands-on healing because I had a grandmother who was a healer from Sweden," said Sullivan. "So they were trying - that was me and several other survivors I talked to since - to use them in that mode also. And hands-on healing means that you would focus electromagnetic energy into the other person's body."

BRICE TAYLOR'S ORDEAL

Another book, Brice Taylor's Starshine: One Woman's Valiant Escape from Mind Control, corroborates Cathy O'Brien's and K. Sullivan's experiences. Even though it's a fictionalised account, the book clearly indicates that major crimes have been - and are being - committed by the major players of the world's power elites.

Brice Taylor was also a "presidential model", and in a recent interview she went into intimate details of her many experiences with politicians promoting the New World Order.

"What it [being a presidential model] means," she explained, "is that your program is to have sex with presidents; and I did overhear this, that different politicians were encouraged to use CIA escorts for sex, so they wouldn't be in a vulnerable position if they ever disclosed any national security secrets to anyone on the outside, or for blackmail."

And how would she characterise this so-called New World Order?

"It is an attempt to bring in a One World Government in which elite families have things the way they want. Their belief was that the planet was overpopulated and that something had to be done: psychological and biological warfare. They considered mind control as a tool, their ace in the hole, something really different that would act as an invisible weapon."

ADVENTURES WITH HENRY K. AND THE COUNCIL

In her recovery, Brice Taylor also had memories of being used by Henry Kissinger as a mind-controlled courier.

"If you program someone to have a perfect photographic memory and total recall, then you have the capacity to be able to deal with many different tasks and assignments simultaneously," she explains. "Henry Kissinger created a 'mindfile' inside of my head. I would be sent around to all these leaders to keep their data - on some of their projects or whatever their agenda was - sorted. When they'd meet people, I would be programmed by either Kissinger or Nelson Rockefeller. This was in the mid-1960s."

But who's running the 'show'?

"I think there's this other layer that I call 'the Council' in my book," Taylor explained. "I know that this is a group of men that stand head and shoulders above even Kissinger and the Rockefellers. They have been genetically engineered in a way that they have [she hesitated, searching for the right words] different leadership abilities and that they are actually the ones running the plan."

They refer to themselves as "the Council"?

"Yes. When I was telling other people within the intelligence community about it that were involved in it, they said they call themselves the Council. The CIA has all these mind-control operatives that are working for the Government. Then there's the Council, which also understands about the mind-control project. But the Council is not CIA controlled. They could take someone like myself and be able to debrief me to find out what my agenda was."

MORE BAD MEMORIES

And how did Ms Taylor first figure out she was suffering from MPD and that she was a programmed multiple?

"It started in 1985," said Taylor. "I had a very serious car accident in which my head went through the windshield. I began to have memory flashes like a memory bleed-through from one alter to another. I think what occurred was I began having access to both sides of my brain. Before, with all the sophisticated programming, half my brain was shut away from me. Now the neuron pathways had opened up because of the accident. I know of other women who have also had memories come back."

So a blow to the brain had broken up the programming?

"Exactly," she said. "What happened is my memories began coming back. I was in school, working on my Master's degree in psychology, when a flood of memories came back. I have a closet full of journals. I wrote down everything I was remembering. Once I got to a certain level, I had a lot of therapeutic support because, every time I'd start remembering, I'd want to hurt myself or kill myself. I lost control of my body in a car on the freeway in the fast lane one time as I was trying to really understand how programming worked. I was trying to understand from inside; a part of me was trying to explain programming to me, and I was on the freeway in the fast lane and I could not move my body. It was terrifying. These are the kinds of things I had to constantly fight.

"When I deprogrammed I literally spent two years in my bedroom, drinking coffee, just writing everything down," she said. "They programmed me with perfect photographic memory. When memories came back, like the ones with Kissinger, I not only could hear his words and his voice, I could smell his cigar. I could smell his farts. I mean, I could hear and see as I remembered everything in my mind."

THE SATANIC RITUAL MURDER CONNECTION

Missing children, sexual abuse of children and pedophilia around the world all point to the involvement of an organised network of high-level criminals who covertly control the legal system. Former FBI agent and private investigator Ted Gunderson agrees. He claims that "there's a considerable overlap from various groups and organisations, but one of the driving forces is the satanic cult movement today".

In his video, Satanism and the CIA's International Trafficking of Children, Gunderson refers to the notorious black magician Aleister Crowley. "The Satanists have used his writings as a guide," he says, referring to Crowley's Magick in Theory and Practice.

In Chapter XII, "Of the Bloody Sacrifice" (p. 94), Crowley writes: "It would be unwise to condemn as irrational the practice of those savages who tear the heart and liver from an adversary and devour them while yet warm. In any case it was the theory of the ancient Magicians that any living being is a storehouse of energy, varying in quantity according to the size and health of the animal, and in quality according to its mental and moral character. At the death of the animal this energy is liberated suddenly.

"The animal should therefore be killed within the Circle [the satanic circle] or the Triangle, as the case may be, so that its energy cannot escape. An animal should be selected whose nature accords with that of the ceremony - thus by sacrificing a female lamb one would not obtain any appreciate quantity of the fierce energy useful to the Magician who was invoking Mars. In such a case a ram would be more suitable. And this ram should be virgin - the whole potential of its original total energy should not have been diminished in any way. For the highest spiritual working one must accordingly choose that victim which contains that greatest and purest force. A male child of perfect innocence and high intelligence is the most satisfactory and suitable victim."

"We're talking about human sacrifice here," says Gunderson.

More recently the 'tradition' of human sacrifice has been promoted by the late Anton LaVey, founder of the Church of Satan, who wrote in the Satanic Bible (p. 88) that "the only time a Satanist would perform a human sacrifice would be if he were to serve a twofold purpose; that being to release the magickian's [sic] wrath in throwing a curse and, more importantly, to dispose of a totally obnoxious and deserving person".

SUPPRESSED INTELLIGENCE REPORTS

Note the casual reference to murdering someone because he or she 'displeased' the Satanist/black magician. Ding dong, LaVey is dead, but his crimes live on. He's been named by several of his victim-slaves as a mind-control perpetrator. The late 'perp' himself wrote in the Satanic Bible (p. 90) that "the ideal sacrifice may be emotionally insecure, but nonetheless can in the machinations of his insecurity cause severe damage to your tranquility or sound reputation".

The Satanists, after all, follow Crowley's injunction: "Do what thou wilt. That is the the law." In other words, Satanists as gods themselves will decide what to do - bypassing God's laws as well as the laws of men. It sounds like the modus operandi of the Illuminati.

Gunderson makes this further comment in his video: "In my estimation, there are over three million practising Satanists in America today. How did I come up with these figures? I have informants. For instance, in the South Bay area of Los Angeles with a population of 200,000, he told me there are 3,000 practising Satanists. That is where the well-known McMartin Pre-school case took place. I have an informant in Lincoln, Nebraska. In Iowa City, Iowa, a town of 150,000 - 1,500 Satanists. It averages to about 1.5 per cent of the population."

Gunderson asserts that "...50,000 to 60,000 individuals are sacrificed every year. There are about eight satanic holidays."

The sick joke of it all? The FBI keeps a count of stolen or missing cars, but has yet to keep a tab on missing children in America.

CRYPTO-SATANIST IN THE FBI?

You shouldn't be surprised to know that FBI Supervisory Special Agent Kenneth V. Lanning, of the Behavioral Science Unit of the National Center for the Analysis of Violent Crime, denies the existence of satanic ritual abuse in his 1992 Investigator's Guide to Allegations of Ritual Child Abuse. Lanning's intellectual posturing and specious reasoning should be studied as a prime example of serpentine logic. His semantics are brilliant, as he claims that "the words 'satanic', 'occult' and 'ritual' are often used interchangeably" and "it is difficult to define Satanism precisely". Then he frames the discussion of Satanism in non-judgemental terms, that "it is important to realize that for some people any religious belief system other than their own is satanic".

As Pilate asked "What is truth?", Lanning asks "What is Satanism?" He writes that at "...law enforcement training conferences, it is witchcraft, santeria, paganism and the occult that are most often referred to as forms of Satanism. It may be a matter of definition, but these things are not necessarily the same as traditional Satanism." He almost trips over himself de-claiming the impossibility of knowing the definition. Then he dismisses satanic ritual abuse as a simple psychological problem: "Obsessive Compulsive Disorder".

Of course, if he had taken the time to interview true believers, he would know that it's an actual belief system based on the ritual performance of torture and murder in loyalty to Satan and as an exchange for future rewards from the forces of darkness.

Lanning's denial, ignoring the evidence of mind-control atrocities and ritual abuse, is astonishing. Is Lanning a crypto-Satanist? He's publicly denied it, but he didn't have to bother. His "freedom of religion" is protected by the US Constitution.

SUPPRESSED INTELLIGENCE REPORTS

FATAL JUSTICE REVISITED

Private investigator Ted L. Gunderson was dragged kicking and screaming into the netherworld of Satanism, child kidnapping, drug smuggling and other corruption.

Before he retired in 1979, Gunderson was the FBI Special Agent in Charge (SAC) in Los Angeles. He headed the FBI office, where he had 800 people under him and a yearly budget of over US$24 million. Since then, Gunderson's role as a private investigator and security consultant has led him to expose CIA drug dealing, child kidnapping and trafficking, mind control, and satanic murder-for-hire groups. He has also investigated many high-profile cases like the Dr Jeffrey McDonald case, the McMartin Preschool case, Nebraska's Franklin Cover-up case, the Oklahoma City Bombing case, the Inslaw/Octopus case, and many other real-life criminal conspiracies.

"Shortly after my retirement, I was asked to investigate the Jeffrey R. McDonald case as a private investigator," said Gunderson in a recent interview. "He's a doctor who was convicted of murdering his wife and two children at Fort Bragg, North Carolina on February 17, 1970. I put in about 2,000 hours on the case. He had been convicted and sentenced to three consecutive life sentences. Much to my surprise, the evidence that I read, the information I developed...I've established beyond any question of a doubt that this man is absolutely innocent."

Jerry Allen Potter, author of Fatal Justice, a powerful point-by-point refutation of Joe McGinnis's cover-up book, Fatal Vision, agrees. His book exposes McGinnis's best-seller as pure fiction.

Gunderson continued: "I obtained a signed confession from Helena Stokely, the girl in the floppy hat, for those who are familiar with the case. She said Dr McDonald did not commit these crimes. They were committed, she said '...by my satanic cult group. It was my initiation into the cult that night,' she said."

After a while, Gunderson realised that the McDonald case was a classic case of US Government crime and cover-up.

"She gave me detailed information about movements within the house. She told me she attempted to ride a rocking horse in the child's bedroom that night, but she couldn't ride it because the spring was broken. The only way she could have known that was to have been there that night.

"I submitted an 1100-plus page report in March 1981 to Judge William Webster, who was then the head of the FBI, with a personal letter to him and to the US Department of Justice. Much to my surprise, my 19 witnesses including Helena Stokely started calling me and telling me, 'Hey Ted, they're trying to get me to recant.' And I'm telling myself, 'That isn't the responsibility of the FBI. The FBI is supposed to gather information, not destroy it.' And that was my first clue that we had a serious problem in that case and in the other cases I handled. I noticed in each instance that evidence was destroyed, lost, stolen; that there were strong indications of corruption.

"So I asked myself, 'What's going on here?' And over the years I started gathering materials. Up until about two years ago, I kept saying, 'There's a loose-knit network operating in this country, involving drugs, pedophilia, prostitution, corruption, etc. From my research,

SUPPRESSED INTELLIGENCE REPORTS

I'm convinced it's much more serious. It's much more than a loose-knit network. It is a conspiracy. And you know how the media goes after you when you use that 'c'-word. And I'm going to prove it to you. By the way, this conspiracy involves pornography, drugs, pedophilia and organised child kidnapping.

"My 'missing children' lecture documents that the Finders, an organisation in Washington, DC, is a CIA front," said Gunderson. "It's a covert operation involved in international trafficking of children."

He was referring to a US Customs Service report which states that the Finders case is to be closed because it is "an internal CIA matter".

Gunderson added: "These people - the satanic movement in the world - have set up preschools for the purpose of getting their hands on our children. The parents drop them off at nine in the morning and pick them up at night."

Far-fetched? Think again. In The Law Is For All, Aleister Crowley writes: "Moreover, the Beast 666 [Crowley's reference to himself] adviseth that all children shall be accustomed from infancy to witness every type of sexual act, as also the process of birth, lest falsehood fog and mystery stupefy their minds whose error else might thwart and misdirect the growth of their subconscious system of self-symbolism."

SPIRITUAL WARFARE AND SATANIC IMPERIALISM

Sexual abuse of children and horrific mind control technology may be tenets of 'faith' for the Satanist believer as well as the programmer. Or they may be symptomatic of a larger struggle on a cosmic scale. When you peer in the face of Absolute Evil, you cannot remain complacent.

Therapist Dr M. Scott Peck, author of The People of the Lie, writes: "...at one point I defined evil as 'the exercise of political power that is the imposition of one's will upon others by overt or covert coercion in order to avoid...spiritual growth'".

Psychologist Erich Fromm, author of The Heart of Man, defines this struggle between Good and Evil as biophilia (the love of life) vs necrophilia (the love of death). "The necrophilous person is driven by the desire to transform the organic into the inorganic, to approach life mechanically as if all living persons were things," he writes. "The necrophilous person can relate to an object - a flower or a person - only if he possesses it; hence a threat to his possession is a threat to himself... He loves control and in the act of controlling he kills life... 'Law and order' for them are idols..."

In the end, it may be that spiritual warfare - or the clash of the absolutes - is the real reason why ritual abuse and high-tech mind control have been exposed. Satanic imperialism continues unabated, and the battle for planet Earth moves to the next stage.

References:

* Coleman, John, "Illuminati in America", World in Review (2533 N. Carson St, Carson City, NV 89706), USA, monograph, 1992

* Constantine, Alex, Virtual Government: CIA Mind Control Operations in America, Feral House (2532 Lincoln Blvd #359, Venice, CA 90291), USA, 1997 (USD$14.95)

SUPPRESSED INTELLIGENCE REPORTS

* DeCamp, John, The Franklin Cover-up: Child Abuse, Satanism and Murder in Nebraska, AWT, Inc. (PO Box 85461, Lincoln, NE 68501), USA, 1996, 2ed (USD$13.00)

* Gunderson, Ted, "McMartin Scientific Report" (1993); Corruption: The Satanic Drug Cult Network and Missing Children, vols. 1&endash;4; Satanism & the CIA's International Trafficking in Children (video, USD$20.00), Ted Gunderson, PO Box 18000-259, Las Vegas, NV 89109, USA

* Marks, John, The Search for the Manchurian Candidate: The CIA and Mind Control, McGraw-Hill, 1980

* Mind Control Foundation website, www.mk.net/~mcf

* Mind Control series, CKLN-FM, website, www.mk.net/~mcf/ckln

* O'Brien, Cathy (with Mark Phillips), TranceFormation of America: The True Life Story of a CIA Slave, Reality Marketing (PO Box 27740, Las Vegas, NV 89126) USA, 1995 (USD$20.00)

* Potter, Jerry Allen and Fred Bost, Fatal Justice: Reinvestigating the McDonald Murders, W. W. Norton Co., New York, London, 1997

* Springmeier, Fritz, Bloodlines of the Illuminati, Ambassador House (PO Box 1153, Westminster, CO 80030), USA, 1999 2ed (USD$20.00)

* Springmeier, Fritz and Cisco Wheeler, Illuminati Formula used to create an Undetectable Total Mind Controlled Slave, Fritz and Cisco (916 Linn Ave, Oregon City, OR 97045), USA, 1996 (USD$59.00)

* Stratford, Lauren, Satan's Underground, Pelican Publishing (PO Box 3110, Gretna, LA 70054), USA, 1998 (USD$10.95)

* Sullivan, K., MK, K. Sullivan (PO Box 1328, Soddy Daisy, TN 37384), USA, 1998 (USD$18.00)

* Taylor, Brice, Starshine: One Woman's Valiant Escape from Mind Control, 1995 (USD$20.00); Revivification: A Gentle, Alternative Memory Retrieval Process for Trauma Victims (1998, USD$7.50), Brice Taylor Trust, PO Box 655, Landrum, SC 29356, USA

About the Author:

Uri Dowbenko is CEO of New Improved Entertainment Corp. He can be reached by e-mail at: u.dowbenko@mailcity.com

THE CURRENT SITUATION

MIND CONTROL: THE CURRENT SITUATION

By Harry V. Martin and David Caul

Copyright © FreeAmerica and Harry V. Martin, 1995 Copyright © Napa Sentinel, 1991

In July of 1991, two inmates died at the Vacaville Medical Facility. According to prison officials at the time, the two may have died as a result of medical treatment, that treatment was the use of mind control or behavior modification drugs. A deeper study into the deaths of the two inmates has unraveled a mind-boggling tale of horror that has been part of California penal history for a long time, and one that caused national outcries years ago.

In August of 1991, the Sentinel presented a graphic portrait of some of the mind control experiments that have been allowed to continue in the United States. On November 1974 a U.S. Senate Sub-committee on Constitutional Rights investigated federally-funded behavior modification programs, with emphasis on federal involvement in, and the possible threat to individual constitutional rights of behavior modification, especially involving inmates in prisons and mental institutions.

The Senate committee was appalled after reviewing documents from the following sources:

The Neuro-Research Foundation's study entitled "The Medical Epidemiology of Criminals."

The Center for the Study and Reduction of Violence at UCLA.

The Closed Adolescent Treatment Center.

Senate Investigations of the History of US Mind Control (Based on Testimony before the Senate Sub-Commmittee on Constitutional Rights)

A national uproar was created by various articles in 1974, which prompted the Senate investigation. But after all these years, the news that two inmates at Vacaville may have died from these same experiments indicates that though a nation was shocked in 1974, little was done to end the experimentations. In 1977, a Senate subcommittee on Health and Scientific Research, chaired by Senator Ted Kennedy, focussed on the CIA's testing of LSD on unwitting citizens. Only a mere handful of people within the CIA knew about the scope and details of the program.

To understand the full scope of the problem, it is important to study its origins. The Kennedy subcommittee learned about the CIA Operation MK.-Ultra through the testimony of Dr. Sidney Gottlieb. The purpose of the program, according to his testimony, was to "investigate whether and how it was possible to modify an individual's behavior by covert means".

Claiming the protection of the National Security Act, Dr. Gottlieb was unwilling to tell the Senate subcommittee what had been learned or gained by these experiments.

He did state, however, that the program was initially engendered by a concern that the Soviets and other enemies of the United States would get ahead of the U.S. in this field.

MK-ULTRA Past and Present

(From testimony and files obtained under Freedom Of Information Act)

Through the Freedom of Information Act, researchers are now able to obtain documents detailing the M.K.-Ultra program and other CIA behavior modification projects in a special reading room located on the bottom floor of the Hyatt Regency in Rosslyn, VA.

The most daring phase of the M.K.-Ultra program involved slipping unwitting American citizens LSD in real life situations. The idea for the series of experiments originated in November 1941, when William Donovan, founder and director of the Office of Strategic Services (OSS), the forerunner of the CIA during World War Two. At that time the intelligence agency invested $5000 for the "truth drug" program. Experiments with scopolamine and morphine proved both unfruitful and very dangerous. The program tested scores of other drugs, including mescaline, barbituates, benzedrine, cannabis indica, to name a few.

The U.S. was highly concerned over the heavy losses of freighters and other ships in the North Atlantic, all victims of German U-boats. Information about German U-boat strategy was desperately needed and it was believed that the information could be obtained through drug-influenced interrogations of German naval P.O.W.s, in violation of the Geneva Accords.

Tetrahydrocannabinol acetate, a colorless, odorless marijuana extract, was used to lace a cigarette or food substance without detection. Initially, the experiments were done on volunteer U.S. Army and OSS personnel, and testing was also disguised as a remedy for shell shock. The volunteers became known as "Donovan's Dreamers". The experiments were so hush-hush, that only a few top officials knew about them. President Franklin Roosevelt was aware of the experiments. The "truth drug" achieved mixed success.

The experiments were halted when a memo was written: "The drug defies all but the most expert and search analysis, and for all practical purposes can be considered beyond analysis." The OSS did not, however, halt the program. In 1943 field tests of the extract were being conducted, despite the order to halt them. The most celebrated test was conducted by Captain George Hunter White, an OSS agent and ex-law enforcement official, on August Del Grazio, aka Augie Dallas, aka Dell, aka Little Augie, a New York gangster.

Cigarettes laced with the acetate were offered to Augie without his knowledge of the content. Augie, who had served time in prison for assault and murder, had been one of the world's most notorious drug dealers and smugglers. He operated an opium alkaloid factory in Turkey and he was a leader in the Italian underworld on the Lower East Side of New York. Under the influence of the drug,

Augie revealed volumes of information about the underworld operations, including the names of high ranking officials who took bribes from the mob. These experiments led to the encouragement of Donovan. A new memo was issued: "Cigarette experiments indicated that we had a mechanism which offered promise in relaxing prisoners to be interrogated."

When the OSS was disbanded after the war, Captain White continued to administer behavior modifying drugs. In 1947, the CIA replaced the OSS. White's service record indicates that he worked with the OSS, and by 1954 he was a high ranking Federal Narcotics Bureau officer who had been loaned to the CIA on a part-time basis.

White rented an apartment in Greenwich Village equipped with one-way mirrors, surveillance gadgets and disguised himself as a seaman. White drugged his acquaintances with LSD and brought them back to his apartment. In 1955, the operation shifted to San Francisco. In San Francisco, "safe houses" were established under the code name Operation Midnight Climax. Midnight Climax hired prostitute addicts who lured men from bars back to the safehouses after their drinks had been spiked with LSD. White filmed the events in the safehouses. The purpose of these "national security brothels" was to enable the CIA to experiment with the act of lovemaking for extracting information from men.

The safehouse experiments continued until 1963 until CIA Inspector General John Earman criticized Richard Helms, the director of the CIA and father of the M.K.-Ultra project. Earman charged the new director John McCone had not been fully briefed on the M.K.-Ultra

Project when he took office and that "the concepts involved in manipulating human behavior are found by many people within and outside the Agency to be distasteful and unethical." He stated that "the rights and interest of U.S. citizens are placed in jeopardy". The Inspector General stated that LSD had been tested on individuals at all social levels, high and low, native American and foreign."

Earman's criticisms were rebuffed by Helms, who warned, "Positive operation capacity to use drugs is diminishing owing to a lack of realistic testing. Tests were necessary to keep up with the Soviets." But in 1964, Helms had testified before the Warren Commission investigating the assassination of President John Kennedy, that "Soviet research has consistently lagged five years behind Western research".

Upon leaving government service in 1966, Captain White wrote a startling letter to his superior. In the letter to Dr. Gottlieb, Captain White reminisced about his work in the safehouses with LSD. His comments were frightening. "I was a very minor missionary, actually a heretic, but I toiled wholeheartedly in the vineyards because it was fun, fun, fun," White wrote. "Where else could a red-blooded American boy lie, kill, cheat, steal, rape and pillage with the sanction and blessing of the all-highest?"

The CIA and the Mafia

(Testimony before the 1951 Sub-Committee on Organized Crime and other public sources.)

Though the CIA continued to maintain drug experiments in the streets of America after the program was officially canceled, the United States reaped tremendous value from it. With George Hunter White's connection to underworld figure Little Augie, connections were made with Mafia king-pin Lucky Luciano, who was in Dannemore Prison.

Luciano wanted freedom, the Mafia wanted drugs, and the United States wanted Sicily. The date was 1943. Augie was the go-between between Luciano and the United States War Department.

Luciano was transferred to a less harsh prison and began to be visited by representatives of the Office of Naval Intelligence and from underworld figures, such as Meyer Lansky. A strange alliance was formed between the U.S. Intelligence agencies and the Mafia, who controlled the West Side docks in New York. Luciano regained active leadership in organized crime in America.

The U. S. Intelligence community utilized Luciano's underworld connections in Italy. In July of 1943, Allied forces launched their invasion of Sicily, the beginning push into occupied Europe. General George Patton's Seventh Army advanced through hundreds of miles of territory that was fraught with difficulty, booby trapped roads, snipers, confusing mountain topography, all within close range of 60,000 hostile Italian troops. All this was accomplished in four days, a military "miracle" even for Patton.

Senate Estes Kefauver's Senate Sub committee on Organized Crime asked, in 1951, how all this was possible. The answer was that the Mafia had helped to protect roads from Italian snipers, served as guides through treacherous mountain terrain, and provided needed intelligence to Patton's army. The part of Sicily which Patton's forces traversed had at one time been completely controlled by the Sicilian Mafia, until Benito Mussolini smashed it through the use of police repression.

Just prior to the invasion, it was hardly even able to continue shaking down farmers and shepherds for protection money. But the invasion changed all this, and the Mafia went on to play a very prominent and well-documented role in the American military occupation of Italy.

The expedience of war opened the doors to American drug traffic and Mafia domination. This was the beginning of the Mafia-U.S. Intelligence alliance, an alliance that lasts to this day and helped to support the covert operations of the CIA, such as the Iran-Contra operations.

In these covert operations, the CIA would obtain drugs from South America and Southeast Asia, sell them to the Mafia and use the money for the covert purchase of military equipment. These operations accelerated when Congress cut off military funding for the Contras.

One of the Allies' top occupation priorities was to liberate as many of their own soldiers from garrison duties so that they could participate in the military offensive. In order to accomplish this, Don Calogero's Mafia were pressed into service, and in July of 1943, the Civil Affairs Control Office of the U.S. Army appointed him mayor of Villalba and other Mafia officials as mayors of other towns in Sicily.

As the northern Italian offensive continued, Allied intelligence became very concerned over the extent to which the Italian Communists' resistance to Mussolini had driven Italian politics to the left. Community Party membership had doubled between 1943 and 1944, huge leftist strikes had shut down factories and the Italian underground fighting Mussolini had risen to almost 150,000 men. By mid-1944, the situation came to a head and the U.S. Army terminated arms drops to the Italian Resistance, and started appointing Mafia officials to occupation administration posts. Mafia groups broke up leftists rallies and reactivated black market operations throughout southern Italy.

Lucky Luciano was released from prison in 1946 and deported to Italy, where he rebuilt the heroin trade. The court's decision to release him was made possible by the testimony of intelligence agents at his hearing, and a letter written by a naval officer reciting what Luciano had done for the Navy. Luciano was supposed to have served from 30 to 50 years in prison. Over 100 Mafia members were similarly deported within a couple of years.

Luciano set up a syndicate which transported morphine base from the Middle East to Europe, refined it into heroin, and then shipped it into the United States via Cuba. During the 1950's, Marseilles, in Southern France, became a major city for the heroin labs and the Corsican syndicate began to actively cooperate with the Mafia in the heroin trade. Those became popularly known as the French Connection.

In 1948, Captain White visited Luciano and his narcotics associate Nick Gentile in Europe. Gentile was a former American gangster who had worked for the Allied Military Government in Sicily. By this time, the CIA was already subsidizing Corsican and Italian gangsters to oust Communist unions from the Port of Marseilles.

American strategic planners saw Italy and southern France as extremely important for their Naval bases as a counterbalance to the growing naval forces of the Soviet Union. CIO/ AFL organizer Irving Brown testified that by the time the CIA subsidies were terminated in 1953, U.S. support was no longer needed because the profits from the heroin traffic was sufficient to sustain operations.

When Luciano was originally jailed, the U.S. felt it had eliminated the world's most effective underworld leader and the activities of the Mafia were seriously damaged. Mussolini had been waging a war since 1924 to rid the world of the Sicilian Mafia. Thousands of Mafia members were convicted of crimes and forced to leave the cities and hide out in the mountains.

Mussolini's reign of terror had virtually eradicated the international drug syndicates. Combined with the shipping surveillance during the war years, heroin trafficking had become almost nil. Drug use in the United States, before Luciano's release from prison, was on the verge of being entirely wiped out.

Mind Control Experiments Conducted in Our Name

The U.S. government has conducted three types of mind-control experiments: Real life experiences, such as those used on Little Augie and the LSD experiments in the safehouses of San Francisco and Greenwich Village; experiments on prisoners, such as in the California Medical Facility at Vacaville; experiments conducted in both mental hospitals and the Veterans Administration hospitals.

Such experimentation requires money, and the United States government has funneled funds for drug experiments through different agencies, both overtly and covertly.

The Role of the Law Enforcement Assistance Administration

(Reportorial Sources, Including the Washington Post) One of the funding agencies to contribute to the experimentation is the Law Enforcement Assistance Administration (LEAA), a unit of the U.S. Justice Department and one of President Richard Nixon's favorite pet agencies. The Nixon Administration was, at one time, putting together a program for detaining youngsters who showed a tendency toward violence in "concentration" camps.

According to the Washington Post, the plan was authored by Dr. Arnold Hutschnecker. Health, Education and Welfare Secretary Robert Finch was told by John Erlichman, Chief of Staff for the Nixon White House, to implement the program. He proposed the screening of children of six years of age for tendencies toward criminality. Those who failed these tests were to be destined to be sent to the camps. The program was never implemented.

LEAA came into existence in 1968 with a huge budget to assist various U.S. law enforcement agencies. Its effectiveness, however, was not considered too great. After spending $6 billion, the F.B.I. reports general crime rose 31 percent and violent crime rose 50 percent. But little accountability was required of LEAA on how it spent its funds.

LEAA's role in the behavior modification research began at a meeting held in 1970 in Colorado Springs. Attending that meeting were Richard Nixon, Attorney General John Mitchell, John Erlichman, H.R. Haldemann and other White House staffers. They met with Dr. Bertram Brown, director fo the National Institute of Mental Health, and forged a close collaboration between LEAA and the Institute. LEAA was a product of the Justice Department and the Institute was a product of HEW.

LEAA funded 350 projects involving medical procedures, behavior modification and drugs for delinquency control. Money from the Criminal Justice System was being used to fund mental health projects and vice versa. Eventually, the leadership responsibility and control of the Institute began to deteriorate and their scientists began to answer to LEAA alone.

The Role of the National Institute of Mental Health

(Source: Court Records and US Senate Subcommittee on Constitutional Rights)

The National Institute of Mental Health went on to become one of the greatest supporters of behavior modification research. Throughout the 1960's, court calenders became blighted with lawsuits on the part of "human guinea pigs" who had been experimented upon in prisons and mental institutions. It was these lawsuits which triggered the Senate Subcommittee on Constitutional Rights investigation, headed by Senator Sam Erwin. The subcommittee's harrowing report was virtually ignored by the news media.

The Department of Defense

(Source: CIA Documents released under FOIA and Subcommittee Testimony)

Thirteen behavior modification programs were conducted by the Department of Defense. The Department of Labor had also conducted several experiments, as well as the National Science Foundation. The Veterans' Administration was also deeply involved in behavior modification and mind control. Each of these agencies, including LEAA, and the Institute, were named in secret CIA documents as those who provided research cover for the MK-ULTRA program.

Eventually, LEAA was using much of its budget to fund experiments, including aversive techniques and psychosurgery, which involved, in some cases, irreversible brain surgery on normal brain tissue for the purpose of changing or controlling behavior and/or emotions.

Senator Erwin questioned the head of LEAA concerning ethical standards of the behavior modification projects which LEAA had been funding.

Erwin was extremely dubious about the idea of the government spending money on this kind of project without strict guidelines and reasonable research supervision in order to protect the human subjects. After Senator Erwin's denunciation of the funding polices, LEAA announced that it would no longer fund medical research into behavior modification and psychosurgery.

Lobotomies Performed on Black Activists

(Committee Testimony)

Despite the pledge by LEAA's director, Donald E. Santarelli, LEAA ended up funding 537 research projects dealing with behavior modification. There is strong evidence to indicate psychosurgery was still being used in prisons in the 1980's. Immediately after the funding announcement by LEAA, there were 50 psychosurgical operations at Atmore State Prison in Alabama. The inmates became virtual zombies. The operations, according to Dr. Swan of Fisk University, were done on black prisoners who were considered politically active.

Veteran's Administration Practices

(Committee Testimony)

The Veterans' Administration openly admitted that psychosurgery was a standard procedure for treatment and not used just in experiments. The VA Hospitals in Durham, Long Beach, New York, Syracuse and Minneapolis were known to employ these products on a regular basis. VA clients could typically be subject to these behavior alteration procedures against their will. The Erwin subcommittee concluded that the rights of VA clients had been violated.

LEAA also subsidized the research and development of gadgets and techniques useful to behavior modification. Much of the technology, whose perfection LEAA funded, had originally been developed and made operational for use in the Vietnam War.

Private Companies Involved

Companies like Bangor Punta Corporation and Walter Kidde and Co., through its subsidiary Globe Security System, adapted these devices to domestic use in the U.S. ITT was another company that domesticated the warfare technology for potential use on U.S. citizens. Rand Corporation executive Paul Baran warned that the influx back to the United State of the Vietnam War surveillance gadgets alone, not to mention the behavior modification hardware, could bring about "the most effective, oppressive police state ever created".

Some of the Players

One of the fascinating aspects of the scandals that plague the U.S. Government is the fact that so often the same names appear from scandal to scandal. From the origins of Ronald Reagan's political career, as Governor of California, Dr. Earl Brian and Edward Meese played key advisory roles. Dr. Brian's name has been linked to the October Surprise and is a central figure in the government's theft of PROMIS soft ware from INSLAW. Brian's role touches from the Cabazon Indian scandals to United Press International. He is one of those low-profile key figures.

And, alas, his name appears again in the nation's behavior modification and mind control experiments. Dr. Brian was Reagan's Secretary of Health when Reagan was Governor. Dr. Brian was an advocate of state subsidies for a research center for the study of violent behavior. The center was to begin operations by mid-1975, and its research was intended to shed light on why people murder or rape, or hijack aircraft. The center was to be operated by the University of California at Los Angeles, and its primary purpose, ac cording to Dr. Brian, was to unify scattered studies on anti-social violence and possibly even touch on socially tolerated violence, such as football or war. Dr. Brian sought $1.3 million for the center.

It certainly was possible that prison inmates might be used as volunteer subjects at the center to discover the unknowns which triggered their violent behavior. Dr. Brian's quest for the center came at the same time Governor Reagan concluded his plans to phase the state of California out of the mental hospital business by 1982. Reagan's plan is echoed by Governor Pete Wilson today, to place the responsibility of rehabilitating young offenders squarely on the shoulders of local communities. But as the proposal became known more publicly, a swell of controversy surrounded it. It ended in a fiasco. The inspiration for the violence center came from three doctors in 1967, five years before Dr. Brian and Governor Reagan unveiled their plans.

SUPPRESSED INTELLIGENCE REPORTS

The "Scientific" Basis for Psychosurgery

(Publications of the Participants)

Amidst urban rioting and civil protest, Doctors Sweet, Mark and Ervin of Harvard put forward the thesis that individuals who engage in civil disobedience possess defective or damaged brain cells. If this conclusion were applied to the American Revolution or the Women's Rights Movement, a good portion of American society would be labeled as having brain damage.

In a letter to the Journal of the American Medical Association, they stated: "That poverty, unemployment, slum housing, and inadequate education underlie the nation's urban riots is well known, but the obviousness of these causes may have blinded us to the more subtle role of other possible factors, including brain dysfunction in the rioters who engaged in arson, sniping and physical assault.

"There is evidence from several sources that brain dysfunction related to a focal lesion plays a significant role in the violent and assaultive behavior of thoroughly studied patients. Individuals with electroencephalographic abnormalities in the temporal region have been found to have a much greater frequency of behavioral abnormalities (such as poor impulse control, assaultiveness, and psychosis) than is present in people with a normal brain wave pattern."

Soon after the publication in the Journal, Dr. Ervin and Dr. Mark published their book Violence and the Brain, which included the claim that there were as many as 10 million individuals in the United States "who suffer from obvious brain disease". They argued that the data of their book provided a strong reason for starting a program of mass screening of Americans.

"Our greatest danger no longer comes from famine or communicable disease. Our greatest danger lies in ourselves and in our fellow humans...we need to develop an 'early warning test' of limbic brain function to detect those humans who have a low threshold for impulsive violence...Violence is a public health problem, and the major thrust of any program dealing with violence must be toward its prevention," they wrote.

The Law Enforcement Assistance Administration funded the doctors $108,000 and the National Institute of Mental Health kicked in another $500,000, under pressure from Congress. They believed that psychosurgery would inevitably be performed in connection with the program, and that, since it irreversibly impaired people's emotional and intellectual capacities, it could be used as an instrument of repression and social control.

The doctors wanted screening centers established throughout the nation. In California, the publicity associated with the doctors' report, aided in the development of The Center for the study and Reduction of Violence. Both the state and LEAA provided the funding. The center was to serve as a model for future facilities to be set up throughout the United States.

The Director of the Neurophyschiatric Institute and chairman of the Department of Psychiatry at UCLA, Dr. Louis Jolyon West was selected to run the center. Dr. West is alleged to have been a contract agent for the CIA, who, as part of a network of doctors and scientists, gathered intelligence on hallucinogenic drugs, including LSD, for the super-secret MK-ULTRA program. Like Captain White, West conducted LSD experiments for the CIA on unwitting citizens in the safehouses of San Francisco. He achieved notoriety for his injection of a massive dose of LSD into an elephant at the Oklahoma Zoo, the elephant died when West tried to revive it by administering a combination of drugs.

Dr. West was further known as the psychiatrist who was called upon to examine Jack Ruby, Lee Harvey Oswald's assassin. It was on the basis of West's diagnosis that Ruby was compelled to be treated for mental disorders and put on happy pills. The West examination was ordered after Ruby began to say that he was part of a right-wing conspiracy to kill President John Kennedy. Two years after the commencement of treatment for mental disorder, Ruby died of cancer in prison.

(Note: Dr West is now a member of the Board of Directors of the False Memory Syndrome Foundation.)

The Violence Control Center

(Testimony, FOIA documents, Los Angeles Times, San Francisco Bay Guardian)

After January 11, 1973, when Governor Reagan announced plans for the Violence Center, West wrote a letter to the then Director of Health for California, J. M. Stubblebine:

"Dear Stub:

"I am in possession of confidential in formation that the Army is prepared to turn over Nike missile bases to state and local agencies for non-military purposes. They may look with special favor on health-related applications.

"Such a Nike missile base is located in the Santa Monica Mountains, within a half-hour's drive of the Neuropsychiatric Institute. It is accessible, but relatively remote. The site is securely fenced, and includes various buildings and improvements, making it suitable for prompt occupancy.

"If this site were made available to the Neurophyschiatric Institute as a research facility, perhaps initially as an adjunct to the new Center for the Prevention of Violence, we could put it to very good use. Comparative studies could be carried out there, in an isolated but convenient location, of experimental or model programs for the alteration of undesirable behavior.

"Such programs might include control of drug or alcohol abuse, modification of chronic anti-social or impulsive aggressiveness, etc. The site could also accommodate conferences or retreats for instruction of selected groups of mental-health related professionals and of others (e.g., law enforcement personnel, parole officers, special educators) for whom both demonstration and participation would be effective modes of instruction.

"My understanding is that a direct request by the Governor, or other appropriate officers of the State, to the Secretary of Defense (or, of course, the President), could be most likely to produce prompt results."

Some of the planned areas of study for the Center included:

Studies of violent individuals.

Experiments on prisoners from Vacaville and Atascadero, and hyperkinetic children.

Experiments with violence-producing and violent inhibiting drugs.

SUPPRESSED INTELLIGENCE REPORTS

Hormonal aspects of passivity and aggressiveness in boys.

Studies to discover and compare norms of violence among various ethnic groups.

Studies of pre-delinquent children.

It would also encourage law enforcement to keep computer files on pre-delinquent children, which would make possible the treatment of children before they became delinquents.

The purpose of the Violence Center was not just research. The staff was to include sociologists, lawyers, police officers, clergymen and probation officers. With the backing of Governor Reagan and Dr. Brian, West had secured guarantees of prisoner volunteers from several California correctional institutions, including Vacaville. Vacaville and Atascadero were chosen as the primary sources for the human guinea pigs. These institutions had established a reputation, by that time, of committing some of the worst atrocities in West Coast history. Some of the experimentations differed little from what the Nazis did in the death camps.

Dr. Earl Brian, Governor Ronald Reagan's Secretary of Health, was adamant about his support for mind control centers in California. He felt the behavior modification plan of the Violence Control Centers was important in the prevention of crime.

The Violence Control Center was actually the brain child of William Herrmann as part of a pacification plan for California. A counter insurgency expert for Systems Development Corporation and an advisor to Governor Reagan, Herrmann worked with the Stand Research Institute, the RAND Corporation, and the Hoover Center on Violence. Herrman was also a CIA agent who is now serving an eight year prison sentence for his role in a CIA counterfeiting operation. He was also directly linked with the Iran-Contra affair according to government records and Herrmann's own testimony.

In 1970, Herrmann worked with Colston Westbrook as his CIA control officer when Westbrook formed and implemented the Black Cultural Association at the Vacaville Medical Facility, a facility which in July experienced the death of three inmates who were forcibly subjected to behavior modification drugs. The Black Cultural Association was ostensibly an education program designed to instill black pride identity in prisons, the Association was really a cover for an experimental behavior modification pilot project designed to test the feasibility of programming unstable prisoners to become more manageable.

Westbrook worked for the CIA in Vietnam as a psychological warfare expert, and as an advisor to the Korean equivalent of the CIA and for the Lon Nol regime in Cambodia. Between 1966 and 1969, he was an advisor to the Vietnamese Police Special Branch under the cover of working as an employee of Pacific Architects and Engineers.

His "firm" contracted the building of the interrogation/torture centers in every province of South Vietnam as part of the CIA's Phoenix Program. The program was centered around behavior modification experiments to learn how to extract information from prisoners of war, a direct violation of the Geneva Accords.

Westbrook's most prominent client at Vacaville was Donald DeFreeze, who be tween 1967 and 1969, had worked for the Los Angeles Police Department's Public Disorder Intelligence unit and later became the leader of the Symbionese Liberation Army. Many authorities now believe that the Black Cultural Association at Vacaville was the seedling of the SLA.

SUPPRESSED INTELLIGENCE REPORTS

Westbrook even designed the SLA logo, the cobra with seven heads, and gave De Freeze his African name of Cinque. The SLA was responsible for the assassination of Marcus Foster, superintendent of School in Oakland and the kidnapping of Patty Hearst.

As a counterinsurgency consultant for Systems Development Corporation, a security firm, Herrmann told the Los Angeles Times that a good computer intelligence system "would separate out the activist bent on destroying the system" and then develop a master plan "to win the hearts and minds of the people". The San Francisco-based Bay Guardian, recently identified Herrmann as an international arms dealer working with Iran in 1980, and possibly involved in the October Surprise. Herrmann is in an English prison for counterfeiting. He allegedly met with Iranian officials to ascertain whether the Iranians would trade arms for hostages held in Lebanon.

The London Sunday Telegraph confirmed Herrmann's CIA connections, tracing them from 1976 to 1986. He also worked for the FBI. This information was revealed in his London trial.

In the 1970's, Dr. Brian and Herrmann worked together under Governor Reagan on the Center for the Study and Reduction of Violence, and then, a decade later, again worked under Reagan. Both men have been identified as working for Reagan with the Iranians.

The Violence Center, however, died an agonizing death. Despite the Ervin Senate Committee investigation and condemnation of mind control, the experiments continued. But when the Watergate scandal broke in the early 1970's, Washington felt it was too politically risky to continue to push for mind control centers.

Top doctors began to withdraw from the proposal because they felt that there were not enough safeguards. Even the Law Enforcement Assistance Agency, which funded the program, backed out, stating, the proposal showed "little evidence of established research ability of the kind of level necessary for a study of this cope".

Eventually it became known that control of the Violence Center was not going to rest with the University of California, but instead with the Department of Corrections and other law enforcement officials. This information was released publicly by the Committee Opposed to Psychiatric Abuse of Prisoners. The disclosure of the letter resulted in the main backers of the program bowing out and the eventual demise of the center.

Dr. Brian's final public statement on the matter was that the decision to cut off funding represented "a callous disregard for public safety". Though the Center was not built, the mind control experiments continue to this day.

The Victims of MK-ULTRA

(Court Records, Senate Testimony and FOIA Documents)

The Central Intelligence Agency held two major interests in use of LSD. to alter normal behavior patterns. The first interest centered around obtaining information from prisoners of war and enemy agents, in contravention of the Geneva Accords. The second was to deter the effectiveness of drugs used against the enemy on the battlefield.

The MK-ULTRA program was originally run by a small number of people within the CIA known as the Technical Services Staff (TSS). Another CIA department, the Office of Security,

389

also began its own testing program. Friction arose and then infighting broke out when the Office of Security commenced to spy on TSS people after it was learned that LSD was being tested on unwitting Americans.

Not only did the two branches disagree over the issue of testing the drug on the unwitting, they also disagreed over the issue of how the drug was actually to be used by the CIA. The office of Security envisioned the drug as an interrogation weapon. But the TSS group thought the drug could be used to help destabilize another country, it could be slipped into the food or beverage of a public official in order to make him behave foolishly or oddly in public. One CIA document reveals that L.S.D. could be administered right before an official was to make a public speech.

Realizing that gaining information about the drug in real life situations was crucial to exploiting the drug to its fullest, TSS started conducting experiments on its own people. There was an extensive amount of self-experimentation. The Office of Security felt the TSS group was playing with fire, especially when it was learned that TSS was prepared to spike an annual office Christmas party punch with LSD, the Christmas party of the CIA. L.S.D. could produce serious insanity for periods of eight to 18 hours and possibly longer.

One of the "victims" of the punch was agent Frank Olson. Having never had drugs before, L.S.D. took its toll on Olson. He reported that, every automobile that came by was a terrible monster with fantastic eyes, out to get him personally. Each time a car passed he would huddle down against a parapet, terribly frightened. Olson began to behave erratically. The CIA made preparation to treat Olson at Chestnut Lodge, but before they could, Olson checked into a New York hotel and threw himself out from his tenth story room. The CIA was ordered to cease all drug testing.

Mind control drugs and experiments were torturous to the victims. One of three inmates who died in Vacaville Prison in July of 1991 was scheduled to appear in court in an attempt to stop forced administration of a drug, the very drug that may have played a role in his death.

Joseph Cannata believed he was making progress and did not need forced dosages of the drug Haldol. The Solano County Coroner's Office said that Cannata and two other inmates died of hyperthermia, extremely elevated body temperature. Their bodies all had at least 108 degrees temperature when they died. The psychotropic drugs they were being forced to take will elevate body temperature.

Dr. Ewen Cameron, working at McGill University in Montreal, used a variety of experimental techniques, including keeping subjects unconscious for months at a time, administering huge electroshocks and continual doses of L.S.D.

Massive lawsuits developed as a result of this testing, and many of the subjects who suffered trauma had never agreed to participate in the experiments. Such CIA experiments infringed upon the much-honored Nuremberg Code concerning medical ethics. Dr. Camron was one of the members of the Nuremberg Tribunal.

L.S.D. research was also conducted at the Addiction Research Center of the U.S. Public Health Service in Lexington, Kentucky. This institution was one of several used by the CIA. The National Institute of Mental Health and the U.S. Navy funded this operation. Vast supplies of L.S.D. and other hallucinogenic drugs were required to keep the experiments going.

SUPPRESSED INTELLIGENCE REPORTS

Dr. Harris Isbell ran the program. He was a member of the Food and Drug Administration's Advisory Committee on the Abuse of Depressant and Stimulants Drugs. Almost all of the inmates were black. In many cases, L.S.D. dosage was increased daily for 75 days.

Some 1500 U.S. soldiers were also victims of drug experimentation. Some claimed they had agreed to become guinea pigs only through pressure from their superior officers. Many claimed they suffered from severe depression and other psychological stress.

One such soldier was Master Sergeant Jim Stanley. L.S.D. was put in Stanley's drinking water and he freaked out. Stanley's hallucinations continued even after he returned to his regular duties. His service record suffered, his marriage went on the rocks and he ended up beating his wife and children. It wasn't until 17 years later that Stanley was informed by the military that he had been an L.S.D. experiment. He sued the government, but the Supreme Court ruled no soldier could sue the Army for the LSD experiments. Justice William Brennen disagreed with the Court decision. He wrote, "Experimentation with unknowing human subjects is morally and legally unacceptable."

Private James Thornwell was given L.S.D. in a military test in 1961. For the next 23 years he lived in a mental fog, eventually drowning in a Vallejo swimming pool in 1984. Congress had set up a $625,000 trust fund for him. Large scale L.S.D. tests on American soldiers were conducted at Aberdeen Proving Ground in Maryland, Fort Benning, Georgia, Fort Leavenworth, Kansas, Dugway Proving Ground, Utah, and in Europe and the Pacific. The Army conducted a series of L.S.D. tests at Fort Bragg in North Carolina. The purpose of the tests were to ascertain how well soldiers could perform their tasks on the battlefield while under the influence of L.S.D.

At Fort McClellan, Alabama, 200 officers in the Chemical Corps were given L.S.D. in order to familiarize them with the drug's effects. At Edgewood Arsenal, soldiers were given L.S.D. and then confined to sensory deprivation chambers and later exposed to a harsh interrogation sessions by intelligence people. In these sessions, it was discovered that soldiers would cooperate if promised they would be allowed to get off the L.S.D.

In Operation Derby Hat, foreign nationals accused of drug trafficking were given L.S.D. by the Special Purpose Team, with one subject begging to be killed in order to end his ordeal. Such experiments were also conducted in Saigon on Viet Cong POWs.

One of the most potent drugs in the U.S. arsenal is called BZ or quinuclidinyl benzilate. It is a long-lasting drug and brings on a litany of psychotic experiences and almost completely isolates any person from his environment. The main effects of BZ last up to 80 hours compared to eight hours for L.S.D. Negative after-effects may persist for up to six weeks.

Psychological Warfare Drugs

(Court Records, FOIA Documents, General Accounting Office investigations)

The BZ experiments were conducted on soldiers at Edgewood Arsenal for 16 years. Many of the "victims" claim that the drug permanently affected their lives in a negative way. It so disorientated one paratrooper that he was found taking a shower in his uniform and smoking a cigar. BZ was eventually put in hand grenades and a 750 pound cluster bomb. Other configurations were made for mortars, artillery and missiles. The bomb was tested in Vietnam and CIA documents indicate it was prepared for use by the U.S. in the event of large-scale civilian uprisings.

In Vacaville, psychosurgery has long been a policy. In one set of cases, experimental psychosurgery was conducted on three inmates, a black, a Chicano and a white person. This involved the procedure of pushing electrodes deep into the brain in order to determine the position of defective brain cells, and then shooting enough voltage into the suspected area to kill the defective cells. One prisoner, who appeared to be improving after surgery, was released on parole, but ended up back in prison. The second inmate became violent and there is no information on the third inmate.

Vacaville also administered a "terror drug", Anectine, as a way of "suppressing hazardous behavior". In small doses, Anectine serves as a muscle relaxant; in huge does, it produces prolonged seizure of the respiratory system and a sensation "worse than dying". The drug goes to work within 30 to 40 seconds by paralyzing the small muscles of the fingers, toes, and eyes, and then moves into the the intercostal muscles and the diaphragm. The heart rate subsides to 60 beats per minute, respiratory arrest sets in and the patient remains completely conscious throughout the ordeal, which lasts two to five minutes. The experiments were also used at Atascadero.

Several mind altering drugs were originally developed for non-psychoactive purposes. Some of these drugs are Phenothiazine and Thorzine. The side effects of these drugs can be a living hell. The impact includes the feeling of drowsiness, disorientation, shakiness, dry mouth, blurred vision and an inability to concentrate. Drugs like Prolixin are described by users as "sheer torture" and "becoming a zombie".

The Veterans Administration Hospital has been shown by the General Accounting Office to apply heavy dosages of psychotherapeutic drugs. One patient was taking eight different drugs, three antipsychotic, two antianxiety, one antidepressant, one sedative and one anti-Parkinson. Three of these drugs were being given in dosages equal to the maximum recommended.

Another patient was taking seven different drugs. One report tells of a patient who refused to take the drug. "I told them I don't want the drug to start with, they grabbed me and strapped me down and gave me a forced intramuscular shot of Prolixin. They gave me Artane to counteract the Prolixin and they gave me Sinequan, which is a kind of tranquilizer to make me calm down, which over calmed me, so rather than letting up on the medication, they then gave me Ritalin to pep me up."

Prolixin lasts for two weeks. One patient describes how the drug does not calm or sedate nerves, but instead attacks from so deep inside you, you cannot locate the source of the pain. "The drugs turn your nerves in upon yourself. Against your will, your resistance, your resolve, are directed at your own tissues, your own muscles, reflexes, etc.." The patient continues, "The pain grinds into your fiber, your vision is so blurred you cannot read. You ache with restlessness, so that you feel you have to walk, to pace. And then as soon as you start pacing, the opposite occurs to you, you must sit and rest. Back and forth, up and down, you go in pain you cannot locate. In such wretched anxiety you are overwhelmed because you cannot get relief even in breathing."

SUPPRESSED INTELLIGENCE REPORTS

Doctor Jose Delgado: "Man does not have the right to develop his own mind."

(Congressional Record, New York Times)

"We need a program of psychosurgery for political control of our society. The purpose is physical control of the mind. Everyone who deviates from the given norm can be surgically mutilated.

"The individual may think that the most important reality is his own existence, but this is only his personal point of view. This lacks historical perspective.

"Man does not have the right to develop his own mind. This kind of liberal orientation has great appeal. We must electrically control the brain. Some day armies and generals will be controlled by electric stimulation of the brain."

These were the remarks of Dr. Jose Delgado as they appeared in the February 24, 1974 edition of the Congressional Record, No. 262E, Vol. 118.

Despite Dr. Delgado's outlandish statements before Congress, his work was financed by grants from the Office of Naval Research, the Air Force Aero-Medical Research Laboratory, and the Public Health Foundation of Boston.

Dr. Delgado was a pioneer of the technology of Electrical Stimulation of the Brain (ESB). The New York Times ran an article on May 17, 1965 entitled Matador With a Radio Stops Wild Bull. The story details Dr. Delgado's experiments at Yale University School of Medicine and work in the field at Cordova, Spain. The New York Times stated:

"Afternoon sunlight poured over the high wooden barriers into the ring, as the brave bull bore down on the unarmed matador, a scientist who had never faced fighting bull. But the charging animal's horn never reached the man behind the heavy red cape. Moments before that could happen, Dr. Delgado pressed a button on a small radio transmitter in his hand and the bull braked to a halt. Then he pressed another button on the transmitter, and the bull obediently turned to the right and trotted away. The bull was obeying commands in his brain that were being called forth by electrical stimulation by the radio signals to certain regions in which fine wires had been painlessly planted the day before."

According to Dr. Delgado, experiments of this type have also been performed on humans. While giving a lecture on the Brain in 1965, Dr. Delgado said, "Science has developed a new methodology for the study and control of cerebral function in animals and humans."

Russian Experiments in Hypnotism and Radio Control of the Mind

(Scientific papers and books)

The late L.L. Vasiliev, professor of physiology at the University of Leningrad wrote in a paper about hypnotism: "As a control of the subject's condition, when she was outside the laboratory in another set of experiments, a radio set was used. The results obtained indicate that the method of using radio signals substantially enhances the experimental possibilities." The professor continued to write, "I.F. Tomaschevsky (a Russian physiologist) carried out the first experiments with this subject at a distance of one or two rooms, and under conditions that the participant would not know or suspect that she would be experimented with. In other cases, the sender was not in the same house, and someone else observed the subject's behavior. Subsequent experiments at considerable distances were successful. One such experiment was carried out in a park at a distance. Mental suggestions to go to sleep were complied with within a minute."

The Russian experiments in the control of a person's mind through hypnosis and radio waves were conducted in the 1930s, some 30 years before Dr. Delgado's bull experiment. Dr. Vasiliev definitely demonstrated that radio transmission can produce stimulation of the brain. It is not a complex process. In fact, it need not be implanted within the skull or be productive of stimulation of the brain, itself. All that is needed to accomplish the radio control of the brain is a twitching muscle. The subject becomes hypnotized and a muscle stimulant is implanted. The subject, while still under hypnosis, is commanded to respond when the muscle stimulant is activated, in this case by radio transmission.

Lincoln Lawrence wrote a book entitled Were We Controlled? Lawrance wrote, "If the subject is placed under hypnosis and mentally programmed to maintain a determination eventually to perform one specific act, perhaps to shoot someone, it is suggested thereafter, each time a particular muscle twitches in a certain manner, which is then demonstrated by using the transmitter, he will increase this determination even more strongly. As the hypnotic spell is renewed again and again, he makes it his life's purpose to carry out this act until it is finally achieved. Thus are the two complementary aspects of Radio-Hypnotic Intracerebral Control (RHIC) joined to reinforce each other, and perpetuate the control, until such time as the controlled behavior is called for. This is done by a second session with the hypnotist giving final instructions. These might be reinforced with radio stimulation in more frequent cycles. They could even carry over the moments after the act to reassure calm behavior during the escape period, or to assure that one conspirator would not indicate that he was aware of the co-conspirator's role, or that he was even acquainted with him."

US Experiments in Radio Control of the Mind

(Public Statements of the Principals)

RHIC constitutes the joining of two well known tools, the radio part and the hypnotism part. People have found it difficult to accept that an individual can be hypnotized to perform an act which is against his moral principles. Some experiments have been conducted by the U.S. Army which show that this popular perception is untrue.

The chairman of the Department of Psychology at Colgate University, Dr. Estabrooks, has stated, "I can hypnotize a man without his knowledge or consent into committing treason against the United States." Estabrooks was one of the nation's most authoritative sources in the hypnotic field.

The psychologist told officials in Washington that a mere 200 well trained hypnotists could develop an army of mind-controlled sixth columnists in wartime United States. He laid out a scenario of an enemy doctor placing thousands of patients under hypnotic mind control, and eventually programming key military officers to follow his assignment. Through such maneuvers, he said, the entire U.S. Army could be taken over. Large numbers of saboteurs could also be created using hypnotism through the work of a doctor practicing in a neighborhood or foreign born nationals with close cultural ties with an enemy power.

SUPPRESSED INTELLIGENCE REPORTS

Dr. Estabrooks actually conducted experiments on U.S. soldiers to prove his point. Soldiers of low rank and little formal education were placed under hypnotism and their memories tested. Surprisingly, hypnotists were able to control the subjects' ability to retain complicated verbal information. J. G. Watkins followed in Estabrooks steps and induced soldiers of lower rank to commit acts which conflicted not only with their moral code, but also the military code which they had come to accept through their basic training. One of the experiments involved placing a normal, stable army private in a deep trance. Watkins was trying to see if he could get the private to attack a superior officer, a cardinal sin in the military. While the private was in a deep trance, Watkins told him that the officer sitting across from him was an enemy soldier who was going to attempt to kill him. In the private's mind, it was a kill or be killed situation. The private immediately jumped up and grabbed the officer by the throat. The experiment was repeated several times, and in one case the man who was hypnotized and the man who was attacked were very close friends. The results were always the same. In one experiment, the hypnotized subject pulled out a knife and nearly stabbed another person.

Watkins concluded that people could be induced to commit acts contrary to their morality if their reality was distorted by the hypnotism. Similar experiments were conducted by Watkins using WACs exploring the possibility of making military personnel divulge military secrets. A related experiment had to be discontinued because a researcher, who had been one of the subjects, was exposing numerous top-secret projects to his hypnotist, who did not have the proper security clearance for such information. The information was divulged before an audience of 200 military personnel.

Dr. Watson's Experiments on Babies

In man's quest to control the behavior of humans, there was a great breakthrough established by Pavlov, who devised a way to make dogs salivate on cue. He perfected his conditioning response technique by cutting holes in the cheeks of dogs and measured the amount they salivated in response to different stimuli. Pavlov verified that "quality, rate and frequency of the salivation changed depending upon the quality, rate and frequency of the stimuli."

Though Pavlov's work falls far short of human mind control, it did lay the groundwork for future studies in mind and behavior control of humans. John B. Watson conducted experiments in the United States on an 11-month-old infant. After allowing the infant to establish a rapport with a white rat, Watson began to beat on the floor with an iron bar every time the infant came in contact with the rat. After a time, the infant made the association between the appearance of the rat and the frightening sound, and began to cry every time the rat came into view. Eventually, the infant developed a fear of any type of small animal. Watson was the founder of the behaviorist school of psychology.

"Give me the baby, and I'll make it climb and use its hands in constructing buildings or stone or wood. I'll make it a thief, a gunman or a dope fiend. The possibilities of shaping in any direction are almost endless. Even gross differences in anatomical structure limits are far less than you may think. Make him a deaf mute, and I will build you a Helen Keller. Men are built, not born,"

Watson proclaimed. His psychology did not recognize inner feelings and thoughts as legitimate objects of scientific study, he was only interested in overt behavior.

SUPPRESSED INTELLIGENCE REPORTS

Though Watson's work was the beginning of man's attempts to control human actions, the real work was done by B.F. Skinner, the high priest of the behaviorists movement. The key to Skinner's work was the concept of operant conditioning, which relied on the notion of reinforcement, all behavior which is learned is rooted in either a positive or negative response to that action. There are two corollaries of operant conditioning" Aversion therapy and desensitization.

Aversion therapy uses unpleasant reinforcement to a response which is undesirable. This can take the form of electric shock, exposing the subject to fear producing situations, and the infliction of pain in general. It has been used as a way of "curing" homosexuality, alcoholism and stuttering. Desensitization involves forcing the subject to view disturbing images over and over again until they no longer produce any anxiety, then moving on to more extreme images, and repeating the process over again until no anxiety is produced. Eventually, the subject becomes immune to even the most extreme images. This technique is typically used to treat people's phobias. Thus, the violence shown on T.V. could be said to have the unsystematic and unintended effect of desensitization.

Skinnerian behaviorism has been accused of attempting to deprive man of his free will, his dignity and his autonomy. It is said to be intolerant of uncertainty in human behavior, and refuses to recognize the private, the ineffable, and the unpredictable. It sees the individual merely as a medical, chemical and mechanistic entity which has no comprehension of its real interests.

Skinner believed that people are going to be manipulated. "I just want them to be manipulated effectively," he said. He measured his success by the absence of resistance and counter control on the part of the person he was manipulating. He thought that his techniques could be perfected to the point that the subject would not even suspect that he was being manipulated.

Dr. James V. McConnel, head of the Department of Mental Health Research at the University of Michigan, said, "The day has come when we can combine sensory deprivation with the use of drugs, hypnosis, and the astute manipulation of reward and punishment to gain almost absolute control over an individual's behavior. We want to reshape our society drastically."

The Navy's Murderers

(Statements of Lt. Commander Thomas Narut, The London Times)

A U.S. Navy psychologist claims that the Office of Naval Intelligence had taken convicted murderers from military prisons, used behavior modification techniques on them, and then relocated them in American embassies throughout the world. Just prior to that time, the U.S. Senate Intelligence Committee had censured the CIA for its global political assassination plots, including plots against Fidel Castro. The Navy psychologist was Lt. Commander Thomas Narut of the U.S. Regional Medical Center in Naples, Italy. The information was divulged at an Oslo NATO conference of 120 psychologists from the eleven nation alliance.

According to Dr. Narut, the U.S. Navy was an excellent place for a researcher to find "captive personnel" whom they could could use as guinea pigs in experiments. The Navy provided all the funding necessary, according to Narut.

SUPPRESSED INTELLIGENCE REPORTS

Dr. Narut, in a question and answer session with reporters from many nations, revealed how the Navy was secretly programming large numbers of assassins. He said that the men he had worked with for the Navy were being prepared for commando-type operations, as well as covert operations in U.S. embassies worldwide. He described the men who went through his program as "hit men and assassins" who could kill on command.

Careful screening of the subjects was accomplished by Navy psychologists through the military records, and those who actually received assignments where their training could be utilized, were drawn mainly from submarine crews, the paratroops, and many were convicted murderers serving military prison sentences. Several men who had been awarded medals for bravery were drafted into the program.

The assassins were conditioned through "audio-visual desensitization". The process involved the showing of films of people being injured or killed in a variety of ways, starting with very mild depictions, leading up to the more extreme forms of mayhem. Eventually, the subjects would be able to detach their feelings even when viewing the most horrible of films. The conditioning was most successful when applied to "passive-aggressive" types, and most of these ended up being able to kill without any regrets. The prime indicator of violent tendencies was the Minnesota Multiphasic Personality Inventory. Dr. Narut knew of two Navy programming centers, the neuropsychiatric laboratory in San Diego and the U.S. Regional Medical Center in Italy, where he worked.

During the audio-visual desensitization programming, restraints were used to force the subject to view the films. A device was used on the subjects eyelids to prevent him from blinking. Typically, the preliminary film was on an African youth being ritualistically circumcised with a dull knife and without any anesthetic. The second film showed a sawmill scene in which a man accidentally cut off his fingers.

In addition to the desensitization films, the potential assassins underwent programming to create prejudicial attitude in the men, to think of their future enemies, especially the leaders of these countries, as sub-human. Films and lectures were presented demeaning the culture and habits of the people of the countries where it had been decided they would be sent.

After his NATO lecture, Dr. Narut disappeared. He could not be located. Within a week of so after the lecture, the Pentagon issued an emphatic denial that the U.S. Navy had "engaged in psychological training or other types of training of personnel as assassins." They disavowed the programming centers in San Diego and Naples and stated they were unable to locate Narut, but did provide confirmation that he was a staff member of the U.S. Regional Medical Center in Naples.

Dr. Alfred Zitani, an American delegate to the Oslo conference, did verify Narut's remarks and they were published in the Sunday Times.

Sometime later, Dr. Narut surfaced again in London and recanted his remarks, stating that he was "talking in theoretical and not practical terms." Shortly thereafter, the U.S. Naval headquarters in London issued a statement indicating that Dr. Narut's remarks at the NATO conference should be discounted because he had "personal problems". Dr. Narut never made any further public statements about the program.

During the NATO conference in Oslo, Dr. Narut had remarked that the reason he was divulging the information was because he believed that the information was coming out anyway. The doctor was referring to the disclosure by a Congressional subcommittee which were then appearing in the press concerning various CIA assassination plots. However, what Dr. Narut had failed to realize at the time, was that the Navy's assassination plots were not destined to be revealed to the public at that time.

Electromagnetic Control of Human Behavior

(Published scientific papers and press reports)

There were three scientists who pioneered the work of using an electromagnetic field to control human behavior. Their work began 25 years ago. These three were Dr. Jose Delgado, psychology professor at Yale University; Dr. W. Ross Adey, a physiologist at the Brain Research Institute at UCLA; and Dr. Wilder Penfield, a Canadian.

Dr. Penfield's experiments consisted of the implantation of electrodes deep into the cortexes of epilepsy patients who were to undergo surgery; he was able to drastically improve the memories of these patients through electrical stimulation. Dr. Adey implanted transmitters in the brains of cats and chimpanzees that could send signals to a receiver regarding the electrical activity of the brain; additional radio signals were sent back into the brains of the animals which modified their behavior at the direction of the doctor. Dr. Delgado was able to stop and turn a charging bull through the use of an implanted radio receiver.

Other experiments using platinum, gold and stainless steel electrode implants enabled researchers to induce total madness in cats, put monkeys into a stupor, or to set human beings jerking their arms up and down. Much of Delgado's work was financed by the CIA through phony funding conduits masking themselves as charitable organizations.

Following the successes of Delgado's work, the CIA set up their own research program in the field of electromagnetic behavior modification under the code name Sleeping Beauty. With the guidance of Dr. Ivor Browning, a laboratory was set up in New Mexico, specializing in working with the hypothalamus or "sweet spot" of the brain. Here it was found that stimulating this area could produce intense euphoria.

Dr. Browning was able to wire a radio receiver-amplifier into the "sweet spot" of a donkey which picked up a five-micro-amp signal, such that he could create intense happiness in the animal. Using the jolts of happiness as an "electronic carrot", Browning was able to send the donkey up a 2000 foot New Mexico mountain and back to its point of origin. When the donkey was proceeding up the path toward its destination, it was rewarded; when it deviated, the signal stopped. "You've never seen a donkey so eager to keep on course in your whole life," Dr. Browning exclaimed.

The CIA utilized the electronic carrot technique in getting trained pigeons to fly miniature microphone-transmitters to the ledge of a KGB safe house where the devices monitored conversations for months. There was a move within the CIA to conduct further experiments on humans, foreigners and prisoners, but officially the White House vetoed the idea as being unethical.

In May 1989, it was learned by the CIA that the KGB was subjecting people undergoing interrogation to electromagnetic fields, which produced a panic reaction, thereby bringing them closer to breaking down under questioning. The subjects were not told that they were being placed under the influence of these beams. A few years earlier, Dr. Ross Adey released photographs and a fact sheet concerning what he called the Russian Lida machine. This consisted of a small transmitter emitting 10-hertz waves which makes the subject susceptible to hypnotic suggestion. The device utilized the outmoded vacuum-tube design. American POWs in Korea have indicated that similar devices had been used for interrogation purposes in POW camps.

The ELF Connection

The general, long term goal of the CIA was to find out whether or not mind control could be achieved through the use of a precise, external, electromagnetic beam. The electrical activity of the brain operates within the range of 100 hertz frequency. This spectrum is called ELF or Extremely Low Frequency range. ELF waves carry very little ionizing radiation and very low heat, and therefore do not manifest gross, observable physical effects on living organisms. Published Soviet experiments with ELFs reveal that there was a marked increase in psychiatric and central nervous system disorders and symptoms of stress for sailors working close to ELF generators.

In the mid-1970s, American interest in combining EMR techniques with hypnosis was very prominent. Plans were on file to develop these techniques through experiments on human volunteers. The spoken word of the hypnotist could be conveyed by modulated electromagnetic energy directly into the subconscious parts of the human brain without employing any technical devices for receiving or transacting the messages and without the person exposed to such influence having a chance to control the information input consciously.

In California, it was discovered by Dr. Adey that animal brain waves could be altered directly by ELF fields. It was found that monkey brains would fall in phase with ELF waves. These waves could easily pass through the skull, which normally protected the central nervous system from outside influence.

In San Leandro, Dr. Elizabeth Rauscher, director of Technic Research Laboratory, has been doing ELF/brain research with human subjects for some time. One of the frequencies produces nausea for more than an hour. Another frequency, she calls it the marijuana frequency, gets people laughing. "Give me the money and three months," she says, "and I'll be able to affect the behavior of eighty percent of the people in this town without their knowing it."

The Devastating Mental and Physical Effect of Microwaves

(Soviet Research, State Department Admissions, Public Record)

In the past, the Soviet Union has invested large sums of time and money investigating microwaves. In 1952, while the Cold War was showing no signs of thawing, there was a secret meeting at the Sandia Corporation in New Mexico between U.S. and Soviet scientists involving the exchange of information regarding the biological hazards and safety levels of EMR. The Soviets possessed the greater preponderance of information, and the American scientists were unwilling to take it seriously. In subsequent meetings, the Soviet scientists continued to stress the seriousness of the risks, while American scientists downplayed their importance.

Shortly after the last Sandia meeting, the Soviets began directing a microwave beam at the U.S. embassy in Moscow, using embassy workers as guinea pigs for low-level EMR experiments. Washington, D.C. was oddly quiescent, regarding the Moscow embassy bombardment.

Discovered in 1962, the Moscow signal was investigated by the CIA, which hired a consultant, Milton Zaret, and code named the research Project Pandora. According to Zaret, the Moscow signal was composed of several frequencies, and was focused precisely upon the Ambassador's office. The intensity of the bombardment was not made public, but when the State Department finally admitted the existence of the signal, it announced that it was fairly low.

There was consensus among Soviet EMR researchers that a beam such as the Moscow signal was destined to produced blurred vision and loss of mental concentration. The Boston Globe reported that the American ambassador had not only developed a leukemia-like blood disease, but also suffered from bleeding eyes and chronic headaches. Under the CIA's Project Pandora, monkeys were brought into the embassy and exposed to the Moscow signal; they were found to have developed blood composition anomalies and unusual chromosome counts. Embassy personnel were found to have a 40 percent higher than average white blood cell count. While Operation Pandora's data gathering proceeded, embassy personnel continued working in the facility and were not informed of the bombardment until 10 years later. Embassy employees were eventually granted a 20 percent hardship allowance for their service in an unhealthful post. Throughout the period of bombardment, the CIA used the opportunity to gather data on psychological and biological effects of the beam on American personnel.

The U.S. government began to examine the affects of the Moscow signal. The job was turned over to the Defense Advanced Research Projects Agency (DARPA). DARPA is now developing electromagnetic weaponry. The man in charge of the DARPA program, Dr. Jack Verona, is so important and so secretive that he doesn't even return President George Bush's telephone calls.

The American public was never informed that the military had planned to develop electromagnetic weapons until 1982, when the revelation appeared in a technical Air Force magazine.

The magazine article stated, "....specifically generated radio-frequency radiation (RFR) fields may pose powerful and revolutionary anti-personnel military trends." The article indicated that that it would be very easy to use electromagnetic fields to disrupt the human brain because the brain, itself, was an electrically mediated organ. It further indicated that a rapidly scanning RFR system would have a stunning or killing capability over a large area. The system was developable.

Navy Captain Dr. Paul E. Taylor read a paper at the Air University Center for Aerospace Doctrine, Research and Education, at Maxwell Air Force Base, Alabama. Dr. Taylor was responsible for the Navy's Radiation Laboratory and had been studying radiation effects on humans. In his paper, Dr. Taylor stated, "The ability of individuals to function (as soldiers) could be degraded to such a point that would be combat ineffective." The system was so sophisticated that it employed microwaves and millimeter waves and was transportable by a large truck.

Lawrence Livermore National Laboratory in the South Bay, are working on the development of a "brain bomb". A bomb could be dropped in the middle of a battlefield which would produce microwaves, incapacitating the minds of soldiers within a circumscribed area.

SUPPRESSED INTELLIGENCE REPORTS

Applications of microwave technology in espionage were available for over 25 years. In a meeting in Berkeley of the American Association for the Advancement of Science as early as 1965, Professor J. Anthony Deutsch of New York University, provided an important segment of research in the field of memory control. In layman terms, Professor Deutsch indicated that the mind is a transmitter and if too much information is received, like too many vehicles on a crowded freeway, the brain ceases to transmit. The Professor indicated that an excess of acetyl choline in the brain can interfere with the memory process and control. He indicated excess amounts of acetyl choline can be artificially produced, through both the administration of drugs or through the use of radio waves. The process is called Electronic Dissolution of Memory (EDOM). The memory transmission can be stopped for as long as the radio signal continues.

As a result, the awareness of the person skips over those minutes during which he is subjected to the radio signal. Memory is distorted, and time-orientation is destroyed.

According to Lincoln Lawrence, author of Were We Controlled, EDOM is now operational. "There is already in use a small EDOM generator/transmitter which can be concealed on the body of the person.

Contact with this person, a casual handshake or even just a touch, transmits a tiny electronic charge plus an ultra-sonic signal tone which for a short period will disturb the time-orientation of the person affected....it can be a potent weapon for hopelessly confusing evidence in the investigation of a crime "

Microwave Transmission of Voices Direct to the Brain

Thirty years ago, Allen Frey discovered that microwaves of 300 to 3000 megahertz could be "heard" by people, even if they were deaf, if pulsed at a certain rate. Appearing to be originating just in back of the head, the sound boomed, clicked, hissed or buzzed, depending upon the frequency. Later research has shown that the perception of the waves take place just in front of the ears. The microwaves causes pressure waves in the brain tissue, and this phenomenon vibrates the sound receptors in the inner ear through the bone structure. Some microwaves are capable of directly stimulating the nerve cells of the auditory pathways.

This has been confirmed with experiments with rats, in which the sound registers 120 decibels, which is equal to the volume of a nearby jet during takeoff. Aside from having the capability of causing pain and preventing auditory communication, a more subtle effect was demonstrated at the Walter Reed Army Institute of Research by Dr. Joseph C. Sharp. Dr. Sharp, himself, was the subject of an experiment in which pulsed microwave audiograms, or the microwave analog of the sound vibrations of spoken words, were delivered to his brain in such a way that he was able to understand the words that were spoken. Military and undercover uses of such a device might include driving a subject crazy with inner voices in order to discredit him, or conveying undetectable instructions to a programmed assassin.

But the technology has been carried even a step further. It has been demonstrated by Dr. Ross Adey that microwaves can be used to directly bring about changes in the electrical patterns of different parts of the brain. His experiments showed that he could achieve the same mind control over animals as Dr. Delgado did in the bull incident. Dr. Delgado used brain implants in his animals, Dr. Adey used microwave devices without preconditioning. He made animals act and look like electronic toys.

SUPPRESSED INTELLIGENCE REPORTS

Nazi Mind Control Experiments

(Report from the US Naval Technical Mission)

At the conclusion of World War Two, American investigators learned that Nazi doctors at the Dachau concentration camp in Germany had been conducting mind control experiments on inmates. They experimented with hypnosis and with the drug mescaline.

Mescaline is a quasi-synthetic extract of the peyote cactus, and is very similar to LSD in the hallucinations which it produces. Though they did not achieve the degree of success they had desired, the SS interrogators in conjunction with the Dachau doctors were able to extract the most intimate secrets from the prisoners when the inmates were given very high doses of mescaline.

There were fatal mind control experiments conducted at Auschwitz. The experiments there were described by one informant as "brainwashing with chemicals". The informant said the Gestapo wasn't satisfied with extracting information by torture. "So the next question was, why don't we do it like the Russians, who have been able to get confessions of guilt at their show trials?" They tried various barbiturates and morphine derivatives. After prisoners were fed a coffee-like substance, two of them died in the night and others died later.

The Dachau mescaline experiments were written up in a lengthy report issued by the U.S. Naval Technical Mission, whose job it was at the conclusion of the war to scour all of Europe for every shred of industrial and scientific material that had been produced by the Third Reich. It was as a result of this report that the U.S. Navy became interested in mescaline as an interrogation tool. The Navy initiated Project Chatter in 1947, the same year the Central Intelligence Agency was formed. The Chatter format included developing methods for acquiring information from people against their will, but without inflicting harm or pain. At the conclusion of the war, the OSS was designated as the investigative unit for the International Military Tribunal, which was to become known as the Nuremberg Trials. The purpose of Nuremberg was to try the principal Nazi leaders. Some Nazis were on trial for their experiments, and the U.S. was using its own "truth drugs" on these principal Nazi prisoners, namely Goring, Ribbentrop, Speer and eight others. The Justice in charge of the tribunal had given the OSS permission to use the drugs.

The Dachau doctors who performed the mescaline experiments also were involved in aviation medicine. The aviation experiments at Dachau fascinated Heinrich Himmler. Himmler followed the progress of the tests, studied their findings and often suggested improvements. The Germans had a keen interest in several medical problems in the field of flying, they were interested in preventing pilots from slowly becoming unconscious as a result of breathing the thin air of the high altitudes and there was interest in enhancing night vision.

The main research in this area was at the Institute of Aviation in Munich, which had excellent laboratories. The experiments in relationship to the Institute were conducted at Dachau. Inmates had been immersed in tubs of ice water with instruments placed in their orifices in order to monitor their painful deaths. Dr. Hubertus Strughold, who ran the German aviation medicine team, confirmed that he had heard humans were used for the Dachau experiments. Hidden in a cave in Hallein were files recording the Dachau experiments.

SUPPRESSED INTELLIGENCE REPORTS

Nazi Altitude and Cold Endurance Experiments

On May 15, 1941, Dr. Sigmund Rascher wrote a letter to Himmler requesting permission to use the Dachau inmates for experiments on the physiology of high altitudes. Rascher lamented the fact that no such experiments have been done using human subjects. "The experiments are very dangerous and we cannot attract volunteers," he told Himmler. His request was approved.

Dachau was filled with Communists and Social Democrats, Jews, Jehovah's Witnesses, Gypsies, clergymen, homosexuals, and people critical of the Nazi government. Upon entering Dachau, prisoners lost all legal status, their hair was shaved off, all their possessions confiscated, they were poorly fed, and they were used as slaves for both the corporations and the government. The SS guards were brutal and sadistic. The idea to test subjects at Dachau was really the brain child of Erich Hippke, chief surgeon of the Luftwaffe.

Between March and August of 1942 extensive experiments were conducted at Dachau regarding the limits of human endurance at high altitudes. These experiments were conducted for the benefit of the German Air Force. The experiments took place in a low-pressure chamber in which altitudes of up to 68,000 feet could be simulated. The subjects were placed in the chamber and the altitude was raised, many inmates died as a result. The survivors often suffered serious injury. One witness at the Nuremberg trails, Anton Pacholegg, who was sent to Dachau in 1942, gave an eyewitness account of the typical pressure test:

"The Luftwaffe delivered a cabinet constructed of wood and metal. It was possible in the cabinet to either decrease or increase the air pressure. You could observe through a little window the reaction of the subject inside the chamber. The purpose of these experiments was to test human energy and the subject's capacity...to take large amounts of pure oxygen, and then to test his reaction to a gradual decrease in oxygen. I have personally seen through the observation window of the chamber when a prisoner inside would stand a vacuum until his lungs ruptured. Some experiments gave men such pressure in their heads that they would go mad and pull out their hair in an effort to relieve the pressure. They would tear their heads and face with their fingers and nails in an attempt to maim themselves in their madness. They would beat the walls with their hands and head and scream in an effort to relieve pressure in their eardrums. These cases of extreme vacuums generally ended in the death of the subjects."

The former prisoner also testified, "An extreme experiment was so certain to result in death that in many instances the chamber was used for routine execution purposes rather than an experiment." A minimum 200 prisoners were known to have died in these experiments.

The doctors directly involved with the research held very high positions: Karl Brandt was Hitler's personal doctor; Oskar Schroeder was the Chief of the Medical Services of the Luftwaffe; Karl Gebhardt was Chief Surgeon on the Staff of the Reich Physician SS and Police and German Red Cross President; Joachim Mrugowsky was Chief of the Hygienic Institute of the Waffen SS; Helmut Poppendick was a senior colonel in the SS and Chief of the Personal Staff of the Reich Physicians SS and Police; Siegfried Ruff was Director of the Department of Aviation Medicine.

The first human guinea pig was a 37 year old Jew in good health. Himmler invited 40 top

SUPPRESSED INTELLIGENCE REPORTS

Luftwaffe officers to view a movie of an inmate dying in the pressure chamber. After the pressure chamber tests, the cold treatment experiments began. The experiments consisted of immersing inmates in freezing water while their vital signs were monitored. The goal was to discover the cause of death. Heart failure was the answer. An inmate described the procedures:

"The basins were filled with water and ice was added until the water measured 37.4 F and the experimental subjects were either dressed in a flying suit or were placed in the water naked. The temperature was measured rectally and through the stomach. The lowering of the body temperature to 32 degrees was terrible for experimental subjects. At 32 degrees the subject lost consciousness. They were frozen to 25 degrees. The worst experiment was performed on two Russian officer POWs. They were placed in the basin naked. Hour after hour passed, and while usually after a short time, 60 minutes, freezing had set in, these two Russians were still conscious after two hours. After the third hour one Russian told the other, 'Comrade, tell that officer to shoot us.' The other replied, 'Don't expect any mercy from this Fascist dog.' Then they shook hands and said goodbye. The experiment lasted at least five hours until death occurred.

"Dry freezing experiments were also carried out at Dachau. One subject was put outdoors on a stretcher at night when it was extremely cold. While covered with a linen sheet, a bucket of cold water was poured over him every hour. He was kept outdoors under sub-freezing conditions. In subsequent experiments, subjects were simply left outside naked in a court under freezing conditions for hours. Himmler gave permission to move the experiments to Auschwitz, because it was more private and because the subjects of the experiment would howl all night as they froze. The physical pain of freezing was terrible. The subjects died by inches, heartbeat became totally irregular, breathing difficulties and lung endema resulted, hands and feet became frozen white." As the Germans began to lose the war, the aviation doctors began too keep their names from appearing in Himmler's files for fear of future recriminations.

The Nazi doctors who experimented on the inmates of prison camps during World War Two were tried for murder at the Nuremberg Tribunal. The accused were educated, trained physicians, they did not kill in anger or in malice, they were creating a science of death. Ironically, in 1933, the Nazi's passed a law for the protection of animals. The law cited the prevention of cruelty and indifference to animals as one of the highest moral values of a people, animal experimentation was unthinkable, but human experimentations were acceptable. The victims of the crime of these doctors numbered into the thousands.

US Contempt for International Human Experimentation Protocols

In 1953, while the Central Intelligence Agency was still conducting mind control and behavior modification on unwitting humans in this country, the United States signed the Nuremberg Code, a code born out of the ashes of war and human suffering. The document was a solemn promise never to tolerate such human atrocities again. The Code maintains three fundamental principles:

1.The subjects of any experimentation must be volunteers who thoroughly understand the purpose and the dangers of the experiments.

2.They must be free to give consent and the consent must be without pressure and they must be free to quit the experiments at any time.

3.The experiments must be likely to yield knowledge which is valuable to everyone. The knowledge must be such that it could not be gained in any other way.

The experiments must be conducted by only the most competent doctors, and they must exercise extreme care.

The Nazi aviation experiments met none of these conditions. Most inmates at Dachau knew that the experiments in the pressure chamber were fatal. From the very beginning, control of the experiments was largely in the hands of the SS, which was later judged to be a criminal organization by the Nuremberg Tribunal.

Despite our lessons from Nuremberg and the death camps, the CIA, U.S. Navy and the U.S. Army Chemical Corps targeted specific groups of people for experimentation who were not able to resist, prisoners, mental patients, foreigners, ethnic minorities, sex deviants, the terminally ill, children and U.S. military personnel and prisoners of war.

They violated the Nuremberg Code for conducting and subsidizing experiments on unwitting citizens. The CIA began its mind control projects in 1953, the very year that the U.S. signed the Nuremberg Code and pledged with the international community of nations to respect basic human rights and to prohibit experimentation on captive populations without full and free consent.

Dr. Cameron, a CIA operative, was one of the worst offenders against the Code, yet he was a member of the Nuremberg Tribunal, with full knowledge of its testimony. In 1973, a three judge court in Michigan ruled, "experimental psychosurgery, which is irreversible and intrusive, often leads to the blunting of emotions, the deadening of memory, the reduction of affect, and limits the ability to generate new ideas. Its potential for injury to the creativity of the individual is great and can infringe on the right of the individual to be free from interference with his mental process.

"The state's interest in performing psychosurgery and the legal ability of the involuntarily detained mental patient to give consent, must bow to the First Amendment, which protects the generation and free flow of ideas from unwarranted interference with one's mental processes."

Citing the Nuremberg Code, the court found that "the very nature of the subject's incarceration diminishes the capacity to consent to psychosurgery."

In 1973, the Commonwealth of Massachusetts enacted regulations which would require informed written consent from voluntary patients before electroshock treatment could be performed.

Senator Sam Ervin's Committee lashed out bitterly at the mind control and behavior modification experiments and ordered them discontinued, they were not.

The New England Journal of Medicine states, that the consent provisions now in place are "no more than an elaborate ritual." They called it "a device that when the subject is uneducated and uncomprehending, confers no more than a semblance of propriety on human experimentation."

The Nuremberg Tribunal brought to light that some of the most respected figures in the medical profession were involved in the vast crime network of the SS. Only 23 persons were charged with criminal activity in this area, despite the fact that hundreds of medical personnel were involved. The defendants were charged with crimes against humanity. They were found guilty of planning and executing experiments on humans without their consent, in a cruel and brutal manner which involved severe torture, deliberate murder and with the full knowledge of the gravity of their deeds. Only seven of the defendants were sentenced to death and hanged, others received life sentences. Five who were involved in the experiments were not tried. Ernest Grawitz committed suicide, Carl Clauberg was tried in the Soviet Union, Josef Mengele escaped to South America and was later captured by Israeli agents, Horst Schumann disappeared and Siegmund Rascher was executed by Himmler.

US Use of Dachau Data and "Friendly" Nazi Doctors

There were 200 German medical doctors conducting these medical experiments. Most of these doctors were friends of the United States before the war, and despite their inhuman experiments, the U.S. attempted to rebuild a relationship with them after the war. The knowledge the Germans had accumulated at the expense of human life and suffering, was considered a "booty of war", by the Americans and the Russians. The Americans tracked down Dr. Strughold, the aviation doctor who was in charge of the Dachau experiments.

With full knowledge that the experiments were conducted on captive humans, the U.S. recruited the doctors to work for them. General Dwight D. Eisenhower gave his personal approval to exploit the work and research of the Nazi's in the death camps.

Within weeks of Eisenhower's order, many of these notorious doctors were working for the U.S. Army at Heidelberg. Army teams scoured Europe for scientific experimental apparatus such as pressure chambers, compressors, G-force machines, giant centrifuges, and electron microscopes. These doctors were wined and dined by the U.S. Army while most of Germany's post-war citizens virtually starved.

The German doctors were brought to the U.S. and went to work for Project Paperclip. All these doctors had been insulated against war crime charges. The Nuremberg prosecutors were shocked that U.S. authorities were using the German doctors despite their criminal past.

Under the leadership of Strughold, 34 scientists accepted contracts from Project Paperclip, and were moved to Randolph Air Force Base at San Antonio, Texas. The authorization to hire these Nazi scientists came directly for the Joint Chiefs of Staff. The top military brass stated that they wished to exploit these rare minds. Project Paperclip, ironically, would use Nazi doctors to develop methods of interrogating German prisoners of war.

As hostilities began to build after the war between the Americans and the Russians, the U.S. imported as many as 1000 former Nazi scientists.

In 1969, Americans landed on the moon, and two groups of scientist in the control center shared the credit, the rocket team from Peenemunde, Germany, under the leadership of Werner von Braun, these men had perfected the V-2s which were built in the Nordhausen caves where 20,000 slave laborers from prison camp Dora had been worked to death. The second group were the space doctors, lead by 71-year-old Dr. Hubertus Strughold, whose work was pioneered in Experimental Block No. 5 of the Dachau concentration camp and the torture and death of hundreds of inmates. The torture chambers that was used to slowly kill the prisoners of the Nazi's were the test beds for the apparatus that protected Neil Armstrong from harm, from lack of oxygen, and pressure, when he walked on the moon.

BIBLIOGRAPHY: The Napa Sentinel would like to acknowledge the exceptional contribution of radio commentator David Emory and his extensive archives. Other source material included:

Acid Dreams by Martin Lee & Bruce Shlain

From the Belly of the Beast, Jack Henry Abbott

Congressional Record, No. 26, Vol. 118, Feb. 24, 1974: testimony of Jose Delgado

The Glass House Tapes, by Louis Tackwood

The Great Heroin Coup, by Henrik Kruger

"Individual Rights and the Federal Role in Behavior Modification," 93rd Congress, 2nd Session, 1974. Sam Ervin Senate Subcommittee on Constitutional 'Rights

The Last Hero, Wild Bill Donovan, by Anthony Cave Brown

Mind Control, by Peter Schrag

The Mind Stealers, by Samuel Chavkin

"Matador with a radio stops wild bull," New York Times, May 17, 1965

Operation Mind Control, Water Bowart

The Phoenix Program, Douglas Valentine

The Physical Control of the Mind, Jose M. R. Delgado, MD

The Politics of Heroin in Southeast Asia, Alfred McCoy

"Role of Brain Disease in Riots and urban Violence," by Vernon H. Mark, Frank R. Ervin, and William H. Sweet. Journal of the American Medical Association, September 11, 1967.

San Francisco Bay Guardian, August 28, 1991

"Convict Talks of 1984 Arms Talks With Iran," San Francisco Chronicle, December 29, 1986

San Francisco Chronicle, January 13, 1973

Guy Wright Column, San Francisco Chronicle, July 5, 1987 BR>

Sunday Times, July 1975.

Violence and the Brain, by Vernon H. Mark and Frank R. Ervin

War on the Mind: The Military Uses and Abuses of Psychology, by Peter Watson

Were We Controlled? - by Lincoln Lawrence

"Why Was Patricia Hearst Kidnapped?" by Mae Brussell, The Realist

SUPPRESSED INTELLIGENCE REPORTS